TAKING SIDES

Clashing Views in

Criminal Justice

TAKING SIDES

Clashing Views in

Criminal Justice

Selected, Edited, and with Introductions by

Thomas J. Hickey
University of Tampa

This book is dedicated to my wife Nancy; my son, Michael; my daughter, Megan; Tom, Sr.; Norma; Roslyn; Steven; and Rose.

Cover Acknowledgment
Maggie Lytle

Manufactured in the United States of America

First Edition

123456789DOCDOC98765

0-07-282817-X
ISSN: 1557-6361

Printed on Recycled Paper

Preface

This is an exciting time to study the U.S. justice system. Every morning when we pick up the newspaper or turn on the evening news, issues involving the justice system appear in the headlines. Given our society's fascination with the justice system, it should not come as a surprise that a recent *New York Times* article described criminal justice as one of the most rapidly expanding academic majors in the country. As an academic discipline, criminal justice analyzes justice system issues in a scientific manner. It is a dynamic field that focuses on the component elements of the legal system: the police, the courts, and the punishment mechanisms that society has developed in response to criminal behavior.

This edition presents compelling debates about justice system issues that exert a significant impact on the quality of life in the United States. The topics included in this book were selected in an effort to encourage the exchange of different viewpoints. Hopefully, the ideas developed by the authors will generate controversy, analysis, and discussion. Such exchange helps to formulate the basis for the development of critical thinking skills—the mark of a high-quality educational experience and an educated individual.

In developing your positions on the issues considered in this book, it is important as well to consider carefully the opinions of others. To paraphrase nineteenth-century philosopher John Stuart Mill, intellectual opponents are vital for several reasons. First, consider the fact that your viewpoint may be wrong. An exchange of views with someone who disagrees with you may move you toward the truth. Second, your viewpoint may contain only a part of the truth. Discussion of your views may help to improve your position. Third, a lively discussion of your viewpoints may cause you to embrace those positions even more closely. In fact, after your viewpoint has survived a collision with error, you may become convinced that your position is the correct one.

In any event, try to keep an open mind when you discuss the issues presented in this text. Consider the possibility that you may be wrong, or that your viewpoint may be incomplete. The exchange of ideas is an exciting way to learn.

Organization of the book This book considers 20 issues in criminal justice and includes 40 articles presented in a pro and con format. The *Introduction* to each issue presents a synopsis and sets the stage for the *Yes* and *No* debate between the authors. All issues conclude with a *Postscript* that considers some of the more important points in the debate and includes up-to-date suggestions for further reading on the topics. In addition, the *On the Internet* page that accompanies each part provides a list of Internet site addresses (URLs) that should prove informative. At the back of the book is a list of the *contributors to this volume*, which provides a short biographical sketch of each contributing author.

This edition This is a new edition of *Taking Sides*. It continues the tradition of providing a detailed analysis of contemporary social issues. This edition focuses on controversial issues in criminal justice. The topics were selected in an effort to generate debate about the most pressing issues in the field. The book is organized into five parts: systemic issues, legal issues, processional issues, punishment, and social justice issues. Topics include, among other things, the U.S. crime problem, terrorism, sex offenders, gun control laws, the war on drugs, the exclusionary rule of evidence, the *Miranda* rule, "three strikes laws," supermax prisons, and capital punishment for juveniles. Probably the most challenging aspect of developing this edition was the selection of topics. Your suggestions for additional topics, or deletion of existing ones, will be considered carefully and greatly appreciated.

A word to the instructor An *Instructor's Manual With Test Questions* (multiple-choice and essay) is available from the publisher for instructors using *Taking Sides* in their courses. A guidebook, *Using Taking Sides in the Classroom*, which considers methods and techniques for integrating the pro-con format into a classroom setting, is available as well. An online version of *Using Taking Sides in the Classroom* and a correspondence service for adopters can be found at `http://www.mhcls.com/usingts/`.

Acknowledgments I would like to thank several of my friends and colleagues for their help and support: Rolando del Carmen, Sue Titus Reid, John P. Matthews, Jeff Klepfer, Steve Kucera, Richard Ayre, Joe O'Neill, Tony LaRose, Chris Capsambelis, Alisa Smith, Jim Beckman, Bob Kerstein, Wes Johnson, and Steven Hekkanen. My research assistant Christine Carpenter and staff assistant Diane Keffer did a fine job as always.

Thomas J. Hickey
University of Tampa

Contents in Brief

Contents

Preface v
Introduction xvii

PART 1 SYSTEMIC ISSUES 1

Issue 1. Are U.S. Crime Problems a Result of Our Failure to Get Tough on Crime? 2

YES: James Q. Wilson, from *Thinking About Crime* (First Vintage Books Edition, 1985) 4

NO: Jeffrey Reiman, from *The Rich Get Richer and the Poor Get Prison: Ideology, Class, and Criminal Justice,* 7th ed. (Pearson, 2004) 27

Professor and celebrated author James Q. Wilson argues that criminal behavior is a rational choice. Crime rates will decline when society increases the penalties of such behavior and makes the alternatives to crime more attractive. Philosopher Jeffrey Reiman argues that the U.S. criminal justice system is designed to fail because the current system produces substantial benefits for those in power. Moreover, he asserts that the wealthy use ideology to convince people that our present justice system is the best one that people can create and therefore cooperate with an unjust social order.

Issue 2. Does the United States Have a Right to Torture Suspected Terrorists? 52

YES: Andrew A. Moher, from "The Lesser of Two Evils? An Argument for Judicially Sanctioned Torture in a Post–9/11 World," *Thomas Jefferson Law Review* (Spring 2004) 54

NO: Elisa Massimino, from "Leading by Example? U.S. Interrogation of Prisoners in the War on Terror," *Criminal Justice Ethics* (Winter 2004) 67

Attorney Andrew A. Moher argues that judicially sanctioned torture of terrorists is appropriate for the purpose of preventing a greater evil. He further contends a judicially monitored system in the United States would be far superior to the current policy of practicing torture "under the radar screen" in other countries. Elisa Massimino believes that the use of torture is immoral and counterproductive for the United States. She asserts that if the United States wishes to rely on the protections of the Geneva Conventions, then it must comply with its provisions prohibiting the torture of prisoners.

Issue 3. Should Serious Sex Offenders Be Castrated? 75

YES: Lawrence Wright, from "The Case for Castration," *Texas Monthly* (May 1992) 77

NO: Kari A. Vanderzyl, from "Castration as an Alternative to Incarceration: An Impotent Approach to the Punishmnent of Sex Offenders," *The Northern Illinois University Law Review* (Fall 1994) 84

Attorney Lawrence Wright argues that while castration may not be an ideal solution, if we treat it as therapy rather than punishment, as help instead of revenge, and if we view offenders as troubled victims, not monsters, then perhaps castration will become an accepted and humane option for sex offender treatment. Attorney Kari A. Vanderzyl asserts that castration should be rejected as an unacceptable, ineffective, and unconstitutional alternative to imprisonment for sex offenders.

Issue 4. Will Strict Gun Control Laws Reduce the Number of Homicides in the United States? 93

YES: Franklin E. Zimring, from "Firearms, Violence, and the Potential Impact of Firearms Control," *The Journal of Law, Medicine & Ethics* (Spring 2004) 95

NO: Lance K. Stell, from "The Production of Criminal Violence in America: Is Strict Gun Control the Solution?" *The Journal of Law, Medicine & Ethics* (Spring 2004) 102

Professor Franklin E. Zimring argues that there is a strong relationship between gun use and the death rate from violent crime and that handgun use increases the death rate from violence by a factor of three to five. Professor Lance K. Stell asserts that strict gun control institutionalizes the natural predatory advantages of larger, stronger, violence-prone persons and increases the risks of violent victimization for less well-off law-abiding citizens.

PART 2 LEGAL ISSUES 121

Issue 5. Should the United States Abolish the Exclusionary Rule of Evidence in Criminal Cases? 122

YES: Akhil Reed Amar, from "Against Exclusion (Except to Protect Truth or Prevent Privacy Violations)," *Harvard Journal of Law and Public Policy* (Winter 1997) 124

NO: Yale Kamisar, from "In Defense of the Search and Seizure Exclusionary Rule," *Harvard Journal of Law and Public Policy* (Winter 2003) 132

Yale law professor Akhil Reed Amar argues that if reliable evidence is excluded from trials, wrongful acquittals and erroneous convictions will result. Moreover, he believes that the exclusionary rule of evidence hurts innocent defendants while helping the guilty ones. University of Michigan law professor Yale Kamisar contends that the exclusionary rule is the sole effective remedy to secure compliance with the Constitution by the police and that admitting evidence obtained illegally requires courts to condone lawless activities of law enforcement officers.

Issue 6. Is "Black Rage" a Legitimate Defense in Criminal Proceedings? 154

YES: Paul Harris, from *Black Rage Confronts the Law* (NYU Press, 1997) 156

NO: Alan M. Dershowitz, from *The Abuse Excuse: And Other Cop-Outs, Sob Stories, and Evasions of Responsibility* (Little, Brown and Company, 1994) 167

NO: Douglas D. Guidorizzi, from "Should We Really Ban Plea Bargaining? The Core Concerns of Plea Bargaining Critics," *Emory Law Journal* (Spring 1998) 240

Jeff Palmer argues that plea bargaining must be abolished in order to reinstate justice in the United States and restore the public's confidence in the criminal justice system. Attorney Douglas C. Guidorizzi asserts that accepting plea bargaining as a natural feature of the adversarial system allows the criticisms of the practice to be addressed with tailored reforms. Moreover, he believes that the corruption of institutional values associated with plea bargaining can be avoided by eliminating the bargaining aspect of this practice.

Issue 10. Should the United States Abolish the Juvenile Court Systems? 253

YES: Barry C. Feld, from "Abolish the Juvenile Court: Youthfulness, Criminal Responsibility, and Sentencing Policy," *Journal of Criminal Law & Criminology* (Fall 1997) 255

NO: Thomas F. Geraghty, from "Justice for Children: How Do We Get There?" *Journal of Criminal Law & Criminology* (Fall 1997) 266

Law professor Barry C. Feld argues that juvenile courts have become deficient criminal courts in which children receive neither therapeutic treatment nor sufficient due process safeguards. Attorney Thomas F. Geraghty, who frequently represents children in juvenile court, contends that juvenile courts should be retained after being reinvigorated with financial and human resources.

Issue 11. Should Cameras Be Allowed Inside U.S. Courtrooms? 287

YES: Steven Brill, from "Courtroom Cameras," *Notre Dame Law Review* (May 1997) 289

NO: Anonymous, from "Judicial Conference Nixes Cameras in Courtrooms," *Defense Counsel Journal* (September 6, 2000) 298

Steven Brill, the founder of the Courtroom Television Network, asserts that the public lacks confidence in the U.S. legal system because they have not been exposed to the real workings of the system. Brill believes that cameras in the courtrooms may remedy this problem and restore the public's faith in the court system. U.S. Court of Appeals Chief Judge Edward R. Becker contends that camera coverage can do irreparable harm to a citizen's right to a fair trial and create privacy concerns and courtroom security problems.

Issue 12. Do "Three Strikes" Sentencing Laws Help to Reduce Serious Crime? 309

YES: John R. Schafer, from "The Deterrent Effect of Three Strikes Law," *FBI Law Enforcement Bulletin* (April 1999) 311

NO: Michael Vitiello, from "Three Strikes Laws," *Human Rights* (Spring 2002) 316

This approach may increase the safety of staff and inmates at other locations in the system and allow them to operate in a more effective manner. Rodney J. Henningsen, W. Wesley Johnson, and Terry Wells argue, however, that supermax prisons are symbolic of the desperation Americans face in trying to reduce crime using traditional formal social control methods. Moreover, as the cost of incarceration continues to increase, public officials may be forced to consider a more balanced approach to crime control.

Issue 16. Should Private "For Profit" Corporations Be Allowed to Run U.S. Prisons? 382

YES: Wayne H. Calabrese, from "Low Cost, High Quality, Good Fit: Why Not Privatization?" in Gary W. Bowman, Simon Hakim, and Paul Seidenstat, eds., *Privatizing Correctional Institutions* (Transaction Publishers, 1993) 384

NO: Jeff Sinden, from "The Problem of Prison Privatization: The U.S. Experience," in Andrew Coyle, Allison Campbell, and Rodney Newfeld, eds., *Capitalist Punishment: Prison Privatization & Human Rights* (Clarity Press, 2003) 390

Wayne H. Calabrese, vice president of the Wackenhut Corporation, argues that the privatization of U.S. prisons saves money and provides quality services. Jeff Sinden, managing editor of *Human Rights Tribune*, contends that the private prison industry has failed to achieve substantial cost savings and that there have been systemic human rights abuses in for-profit correctional institutions.

PART 5 SOCIAL JUSTICE ISSUES 401

Issue 17. Is the Death Penalty an Unacceptable Punishment for Juveniles? 402

YES: Anthony Kennedy, from Opinion, *Roper v. Simmons,* U.S. Supreme Court (2005) 404

NO: Antonin Scalia, from Dissenting Opinion, *Roper v. Simmons,* U.S. Supreme Court (2005) 412

Associate Justice Anthony Kennedy, writing for the Court, asserts that the death penalty is an unacceptable punishment for juveniles who commit murder because it constitutes cruel and unusual punishment in violation of the Eighth and Fourteenth Amendments. Associate Justice Antonin Scalia, dissenting in the same case, argues that there is no clear social consensus that would favor abolishing the death penalty in these cases and that in doing so the Court's majority is usurping the powers of state legislatures.

Issue 18. Should Law Enforcement Agencies Use Affirmative Action Programs to Increase the Number of Minority Police Officers? 424

YES: Brad Bennett, from "Beyond Affirmative Action, Police Response to a Changing Society," *Journal of California Law Enforcement* (vol. 33, no. 2, 1999) 426

Dr. Brad Bennett, chief of police and fire for South Lake Tahoe, California, asserts that although there has been a recent backlash against affirmative action programs, the acceptance of diversity is essential to modern police organizations. Authors Jan Golab and Erica Walter argue that the Los Angeles Police Department (LAPD) was once regarded as the world's best police department due to its stringent screening of police recruits; however, in an effort to appease racial activists and meet federal court decrees, strict screening and testing measures were dismantled. Golab and Walter believe that this has resulted in the wholesale corruption of this once fine police department.

Author Jeanne McDowell contends that in some important ways, including a cool, calm, and communicative demeanor, female police officers may be more effective than their male counterparts in defusing violent situations. Writer Erica Walter asserts that law enforcement organizations must respect the reality that male and female officers are not interchangeable. Moreover, female officers' limited ability to handle violent encounters with citizens may endanger both the police and the public.

Michael Coyle, a research associate with The Sentencing Project, asserts that crack cocaine sentencing policy is unconscionable in light of its impact on minority group members. Moreover, crack cocaine laws punish poor people more severely because they obtain the more affordable form of the drug, while wealthier people, who are more likely to use powdered cocaine, are punished less stringently. Harvard Law School Professor Randall Kennedy contends, however, that racial disparities in crack cocaine sentencing are not a mark of discrimination by white legislatures against blacks as much as a sensible response to the desires of all law-abiding people for protection against criminals.

Introduction

During a recent conversation, the editor of this project asked an excellent question: What is the difference between the study of criminology and criminal justice? The answer to her question establishes the tone and direction for this edition. Criminology involves an analysis of the etiology of crime–what causes it, how it is distributed throughout society, who commits crime, and who its victims are. Criminal justice, in contrast, focuses on the modern components of the justice system–the study of the police, legal system, and punishment mechanisms that society has developed in response to criminal behavior. Although there is necessarily some overlap between the two areas, they are conceptually distinct fields of study.

Controversial issues in criminal justice are the focus of this edition. Topics include the legitimacy of our justice system, the nature of U.S. criminal law, processional issues impacting the justice process, punishment, and social justice issues. These are fascinating issues that pose intense moral dilemmas and directly impact the quality of life in the United States. Many of the issues considered in this volume are interrelated. For example, the so-called U.S. war on drugs is directly related to the contemporary prevalence of "three strikes" mandatory sentencing laws, which mandate that offenders will receive automatic life prison sentences upon conviction of a third felony. Such laws have swept much of the country and resulted in many of our prisons becoming expensive retirement homes for an aging inmate population.

Social Policies and the Principle of Utility

Criminal justice issues are matters of public policy. Because entire graduate courses are devoted to the issue of social policy analysis, a detailed consideration of this topic is beyond the scope of the present essay; however, one rather easy way to analyze justice system policies is to think about whether they satisfy the principle of social utility. During the eighteenth century, British philosopher and reformer Jeremy Bentham asserted that social policies, which are often embodied in legislation and law, should be assessed according to whether they tend to produce "benefit, advantage, pleasure, good, or happiness or [tend] to prevent the happening of mischief, pain, evil, or unhappiness" to the individual.[1] Stated Bentham: "An action then may be said to be conformable to the principle of utility . . . when the tendency which it has to augment the happiness of the community is greater than any it has to diminish it."[2] In the social policy arena, Bentham believed that happiness was synonymous with benefit or public good.

At first glance, this may appear to be a relatively easy way to assess a social policy: We need only determine if it tends to produce the greatest benefit for the community. As usual, however, a more detailed look at questions of social utility indicate that the actual calculation may be more complex than originally thought. For example, suppose the U.S. Congress passed a law that allowed the use of judicially sanctioned torture for suspected terrorists who may possess information that would save the lives of innocent persons. The knee-jerk answer to the question of whether this new policy would satisfy the principle of utility is an emphatic yes, because it appears to constitute the greatest good for the greatest number; however, the issue is more complex than it may initially appear. To sanction such a policy, additional issues need to be addressed. These may include: What is the definition of a "terrorist?" Is the "terrorist label" something that is reserved for those who threaten to kill other people, or does it include persons who throw red paint on those wearing fur coats in order to discourage the sale of animal skins? What does it mean to be a "suspected" terrorist, and who will make that determination? Is the information we may glean from a suspected terrorist worth losing the "moral high ground" in the war on terrorism? What is the greatest good for the greatest number? Is it finding out the information that a potential terrorist may possess, or maintaining a society that respects individual rights and the rule of law? Do you trust the government to answer these questions in good faith?

Justice System Policies and the Lessons of History

Many of the justice system policy issues debated in this volume have been considered in earlier times. During the late 1700s, Cesare Beccaria, an Italian criminologist considered by many to be one of the foremost legal reformers in modern Western history, proposed that society abolish the death penalty and adopt instead inflexible mandatory imprisonment policies. In fact, the penal innovations established by Beccaria became the model for European legal reform during much of the eighteenth and nineteenth cnturies. For better or worse, they were reconsidered, and many were changed during the late 1800s.

Moreover, a number of the issues considered by Beccaria in the late 1700s remain unresolved today. For example, criminologists remain uncertain about the efficacy of the death penalty. Moreover, stringent mandatory sentencing legislation, such as "three strikes" laws, seems to be losing favor once again, as they did during the late 1800s. Although our politicians' "get tough on crime" rhetoric, which produced three strikes laws, makes for good electioneering and television sound bites, it seems to have little true effect on crime rates and serves only to further strain already tight governmental budgets.

From a social policy perspective, however, a crucial question is whether mandatory sentencing laws satisfy the principle of utility: Do these laws produce the greatest possible benefit for the community? Supporters of three strikes laws would assert that these policies contribute to an overall decline in crime rates and keep serious offenders behind bars. Critics of three strikes laws, however, counter that crime rates for middle-age offenders fall dramatically because criminal behavior decreases significantly with increasing age. In effect, the vast majority of criminals appear to "age out" of crime. Thus, while confining youthful violent offenders may be an effective social policy, keeping them locked up for life after they have reached middle age is often a waste of time and money.

The research available in this area is highly informative and can shed light on the question of the social utility of mandatory sentencing policies. The Bureau of Justice Statistics has found that in 2000, persons 45 years of age or more, who comprise approximately 33 percent of the U.S. population, accounted for less than 10 percent of the serious crime arrests.[3] One study has projected that in 2010, U.S. prisons will house approximately 200,000 elderly inmates, who will require special treatment and advanced medical care.[4] At an average cost of $75,000 for each elderly inmate, that amounts to a price tag of approximately $15 billion annually to confine individuals who, in the aggregate, represent little threat to society. In fact, we could house these individuals in many of our nation's Hilton hotels for far less money than we spend on keeping them locked up in prison. While some serious offenders such as mass murderers and psychotic killers should be confined permanently because they represent a continuing menace to society, the weight of the evidence indicates that diverting elderly inmates into less expensive community-based correctional programs may produce the greatest benefit for society in the long run.

Justice System Policies and the Constitution

In the United States, our laws and justice system policies must conform to the mandates imposed by the U.S. Constitution, which was designed specifically to limit governmental power. For example, suppose that an overly zealous police official working on a drug interdiction task force decides that he or she will search all "suspicious" persons in a particular neighborhood for drugs. Assume further that the officer deems someone to be "suspicious looking" and, upon conducting a search of the suspect's pockets, finds 10 grams of marijuana. In this case, a reviewing court is likely to conclude that the exclusionary rule of evidence will bar the illegally seized marijuana because the police officer lacked probable cause to conduct the search.

Likewise, assume that your state legislature adopts a law providing that "homosexual conduct" is illegal. Moreover, the new law defines the actions that constitute homosexual conduct and classifies the crime as a felony, punishable by up to two years in prison and a $10,000 fine. Such laws were quite common in this country until recently. If the state charges someone with violating this statute, a reviewing court is very likely to hold that it is unconstitutional. In 2003, in *Lawrence v. Texas*, 539 U.S. 558 (2003), the U.S. Supreme Court held:

> [A]dults may choose to enter upon [an intimate] relationship in the confines of their homes and their own private lives and still retain their dignity as free persons. When sexuality finds overt expression in intimate conduct with another person, the conduct can be but one element in a personal bond that is more enduring. The liberty protected by the Constitution allows homosexual persons the right to make this choice.

Thus, states may not regulate intimate conduct between consenting adults in the privacy of their own homes. Laws that attempt to do so are likely to be held unconstitutional.

Additional constitutional restraints impact justice system policy formulation as well. For example, the U.S. Supreme Court has recently considered the use of race-conscious affirmative action programs. *Grutter v. Bollinger,* 539 U.S. 558 (2003), analyzed an affirmative action program used at the University of Michigan School of Law, which had been developed to enhance student body diversity. The Court held that "attainment of a diverse student body" was a compelling state interest that "promotes racial cross-understanding, helps to break down racial stereotypes, and enables students to better understand persons of different races." Because the admissions program used at the law school adopted a multifactor admissions plan, which ensured that each applicant was considered as an individual and not in a way that made his or her race the defining feature of the application, it was sustained. Justice Sandra Day O'Connor, however, appeared to strike the eventual death knell of government-sponsored affirmative action programs stating: "[W]e expect that 25 years from now, the use of racial preferences will no longer be necessary to further the interest approved today."

A second case involving the University of Michigan further helped to clarify the permissible scope of affirmative action policies. *Gratz v. Bollinger,* 539 U.S. 244 (2003), analyzed a different affirmative action program utilized by the university's College of Literature, Science and the Arts. This program, however, which automatically granted 20 points on a 100-point admissions scale to "underrepresented" minority group members was held unconstitutional because it was not narrowly tailored to achieve the university's interest in educational diversity. The Court further held that a university must use an individualized analysis of each applicant if it wishes to use race as a factor in making an admissions decision.

Grutter and *Gratz* have significant implications for justice system agency race-conscious recruitment policies. First, justice system agencies must demonstrate an important reason for developing an affirmative action program, such as a history of discrimination against particular minority groups. Second, in order to survive judicial scrutiny, justice system agencies must develop multifactor recruitment programs that do not use racial quotas. For example, suppose that a municipal police department with a history of discrimination against African-Americans develops an affirmative action program with a stated goal of increasing the number of minority officers. Assume further that the agency adopts a recruitment plan that requires an individual assessment of each applicant and considers numerous relevant factors about each person, including race. If such a program is challenged, it is likely to survive scrutiny by the courts.

The preceding cases indicate that the law impacts all aspects of U.S. justice system policy formulation. As such, justice system agency administrators must remain acutely aware of recent legal developments and develop effective policies and procedures that insure equitable treatment for all persons. Those administrators who fail to do so may expose themselves, their agencies, and their municipalities to substantial legal liability.

Thinking Outside the Box and Justice System Policies

This is an exciting time to study the U.S. justice system. As you read the articles in this edition, try to develop your own alternatives to contemporary justice system policies. For example, Professors Akhi Reed Amar and Yale Kamisar present opposing views of the exclusionary rule of evidence in criminal proceedings in Issue 6. Can you propose an alternative to the positions these authors embrace that would maintain the integrity of our justice system and, at the same time, promote justice in individual cases? Likewise, in Issue 2, author Andrew A. Moher proposes judicially sanctioned torture of suspected terrorists, while Elisa Massimino believes that such practices are universally unacceptable. Can you identify a middle ground between these positions that will comport with principles of human dignity while permitting society to obtain information that may prevent the slaughter of innocent persons?

Issues such as these make the study of the U.S. justice system a truly vital and fascinating enterprise. We can only hope that the application of enlightened policy analysis to study contemporary justice system practices will help practitioners to develop creative solutions to some of the most compelling problems that we face as a society.

References

1. Jeremy Bentham, *The Principles of Morals and Legislation* (originally published in 1789) (Hafner Publishing Co, 1948), p. 2.
2. Ibid.
3. Bureau of Justice Statistics, *Sourcebook of Criminal Justice Statistics 2001* (U.S. Department of Justice, 2002).
4. Herbert J. Hoelter, "Proceedings: Technologies for Successful Aging: Institutional Issues," *Journal of Rehavilitation Research and Development* (vol. 38, no. 1, p. 238, 2001).

On the Internet . . .

Academy of Criminal Justice Sciences

This site is an excellent resource for a wide variety of information about the U.S. justice system. It provides links to a number of resources that consider various aspects of justice system processes, including the police, the courts, punishment, and corrections.

http://www.acjs.org/

American Society of Criminology

An excellent starting point for a study of all aspects of criminology and criminal justice, this page provides links to sites on criminal justice in general, international criminal justice, juvenile justice, the courts, the police, and the government.

http://www.asc41.com/

Findlaw

This database is an excellent place to conduct basic legal research.

http://www.findlaw.com/

National Criminal Justice Reference Service (NCJRS)

This very comprehensive database provides a wealth of information about justice system processes. Topics include corrections, courts, crime prevention, crime rates, drugs, the criminal justice system, juvenile justice, law enforcement, and the victims of crime. It also provides links to NCJRS-sponsored research on virtually every aspect of the criminal justice system.

http://www.ncjrs.org/

National Crime Victims Research and Treatment Center

This site, sponsored by the National Crime Victims Research and Treatment Center of the Medical University of South Carolina, provides excellent links to resources focusing on victimization and various criminological treatment options.

http://www.musc.edu/cvc/

National Institute of Justice (NIJ)

The NIJ sponsors projects and disseminates research about justice system issues. This site provides links to NIJ research, programs, publications, and various other initiatives.

http://www.ojp.usdoj.gov/nij/

PART 1

Systemic Issues

The present state of the U.S. justice system reflects the conscious decisions of social policymakers who are entrusted to maintain our social stability. While some believe that our justice system is failing because we have been too soft on crime and criminals, others assert that the failure of the system to reduce crime is functional. It deflects society's attention away from the truly harmful acts committed by wealthy individuals and corporations. Should society eliminate criminal behavior? Are there limits to how far we as a society should go to suppress criminal behavior? These are important issues for social policymakers as well as those who study the U.S. justice system.

- Are U.S. Crime Problems a Result of Our Failure to Get Tough on Crime?
- Does the United States Have a Right to Torture Suspected Terrorists?
- Should Serious Sex Offenders Be Castrated?
- Will Strict Gun Control Laws Reduce the Number of Homicides in the United States?

ISSUE 1

Are U.S. Crime Problems a Result of Our Failure to Get Tough on Crime?

YES: James Q. Wilson, from *Thinking About Crime,* rev. ed. (First Vintage Books Edition, 1985)

NO: Jeffrey Reiman, from *The Rich Get Richer and the Poor Get Prison: Ideology, Class, and Criminal Justice,* 7th ed. (Pearson, 2004)

ISSUE SUMMARY

YES: Professor and celebrated author James Q. Wilson argues that criminal behavior is a rational choice. Crime rates will decline when society increases the penalties for such behavior and makes the alternatives to crime more attractive.

NO: Professor Jeffrey Reiman contends that the U.S. criminal justice system is designed to fail because the current system produces substantial benefits for those in power. Moreover, he asserts that the wealthy use ideology to convince people that our present justice system is the best one that people can create and therefore cooperate with an unjust social order.

Is our justice system failing to eliminate crime because we have not been tough enough on criminals? Is it true that all we need to do in order to solve the crime problem is to provide more attractive alternatives to criminal behavior and increase the punishments for those who do break the law? Or, conversely, is the U.S. justice system failing to eliminate crime because it works effectively to persuade society that the types of conduct that threaten us are the actions of the poor, thus deflecting attention from the more harmful acts of corporations and wealthy people? Moreover, is it even possible or desirable to eliminate crime? These are compelling questions that defy a simple resolution.

Emile Durkheim, an influential nineteenth-century French sociologist, believed that society would never eliminate crime because it was a "normal" part of social life. In a now-famous passage from *The Rules of Sociological Method*, Durkheim stated:

> Imagine a society of saints, a perfect cloister of exemplary individuals. Crimes, properly so called, will there be unknown; but faults which appear venial to the layman will create there the same scandal that the ordinary offense does in ordinary consciousness. If then, this society has the power to judge and punish, it will define these acts as criminal and will treat them as such.

What, then, is Durkheim saying in this passage? Watching a group of four-year-olds at play can provide a hint. Those of us who have supervised children know well the kinds of offenses that they consider significant: name-calling, pushing, not playing nicely, or the assertion that someone is not being a good boy or good girl. Durkheim's point is that within a society of four-year-olds, offenses such as these, which would be considered only minor transgressions by most adults, generate the "same scandal" in the four-year-olds' minds that serious crimes would cause in the adult world. Crime is essentially relative–if a society were without truly serious offenses, other misconduct would take on the same significance that crime does in contemporary society.

But why does every society appear to "need" crime? Durkheim believed that the criminal "plays a definite role in social life" that is functional for society because crime is "indispensable to the normal evolution of morality and law." Stated Durkheim:

> To make progress, individual originality must be able to express itself. In order that the originality of the idealist whose dreams transcend his century may find expression, it is necessary that the originality of the criminal, who is below the level of his time, shall also be possible. One does not occur without the other.

Durkheim used the condemnation of Socrates, who was a criminal under Athenian law, to illustrate his point: Socrates' crime, the independence of his thought, "served to prepare a new morality and faith" that helped Western civilization to evolve.

Professor James Q. Wilson contends that criminal behavior is a rational choice. Crime rates will decline when society increases the costs of such behavior and makes alternative behaviors more attractive. This approach to punishing criminal behavior has been termed a "logical general deterrence model" of justice system policy. The same approach to punishment was embraced by Cesare Beccaria and Jeremy Bentham during the late 1700s.

Professor Jeffrey Reiman, in contrast, believes that the U.S. justice system is designed to fail because it produces substantial benefits for those in positions of power. Moreover, Reiman asserts that "virtually no student of the crime problem believes we can arrest and imprison our way out of the crime problem." Reiman suggests legalizing the production and sale of "illicit drugs" and dealing with addiction as a medical problem as partial solutions to the U.S. crime problem. Moreover, he believes that "a more just distribution of wealth and income" would "reduce the temptations to crime produced by poverty."

James Q. Wilson

Penalties and Opportunities

The average citizen hardly needs to be persuaded of the view that crime will be more frequently committed if, other things being equal, crime becomes more profitable compared to other ways of spending one's time. Accordingly, the average citizen thinks it obvious that one major reason why crime has gone up is that people have discovered it is easier to get away with it, by the same token, the average citizen thinks a good way to reduce crime is to make the consequences of crime to the would-be offender more costly (by making penalties swifter, more certain, or more severe), or to make the value of alternatives to crime more attractive (by increasing the availability and pay of legitimate jobs), or both. Such opinions spring naturally to mind among persons who notice, as a fact of everyday life, that people take their hands off hot stoves, shop around to find the best buy, smack their children to teach them not to run out into a busy street, and change jobs when the opportunity arises to earn more money for the same amount of effort.

These citizens may be surprised to learn that social scientists who study crime are deeply divided over the correctness of such views. To some scholars, especially economists, the popular view is also the scientifically correct one—becoming a criminal can be explained in much the same way we explain becoming a carpenter or buying a car. To other scholars, especially sociologists, the popular view is wrong—crime rates do not go up because people discover they can get away with it and will not come down just because society decides to get tough on criminals.

The debate over the effect on crime rates of changing the costs and benefits of crime is usually referred to as a debate over deterrence—a debate, that is, over the efficacy (and perhaps even the propriety) of trying to prevent crime by making would-be offenders more fearful of committing crime. But that is something of a misnomer, because the theory of human nature on which is erected the idea of deterrence (the theory that people respond to the penalties associated with crime) is also the theory of human nature that supports the idea that people will take jobs in preference to crime if the jobs are more attractive. In both cases, we are saying that would-be offenders are reasonably rational and respond to their perception of the costs and benefits attached to alternative courses of action. When we use the word "deterrence," we are calling attention only to the cost side of the equation. There is no word in common scientific usage to call attention to the benefit side of the equation; perhaps "inducement" might serve. To a psychologist, deterring persons from committing crimes or inducing persons to engage in noncriminal activities are but special cases of using "reinforcements" (or rewards) to alter behavior.

The reason there is a debate among scholars about deterrence is that the socially imposed consequences of committing a crime, unlike the market consequences of shopping around for the best price, are characterized by delay, uncertainty, and ignorance. In addition, some scholars contend that a large fraction of crime is committed by persons who are so impulsive, irrational, or abnormal that even if there were no delay, uncertainty, or ignorance attached to the consequences of criminality, we would still have a lot of crime.

Imagine a young man walking down the street at night with nothing on his mind but a desire for good times and high living. Suddenly he sees a little old lady standing alone on a dark corner stuffing the proceeds of her recently cashed social security check into her purse. There is nobody else in view. If the boy steals the purse, he gets the money immediately. That is a powerful incentive, and it is available immediately and without doubt. The costs of taking it are uncertain; the odds are at least fourteen to one that the police will not catch a given robber, and even if he is caught the odds are very good that he will not go to prison, unless he has a long record. On the average, no more than three felonies out of one hundred result in the imprisonment of the offender. In addition to this uncertainty, whatever penalty may come his way will come only after a long delay; in some jurisdictions, it might take a year or more to complete the court disposition of the offender, assuming he is caught in the first place. Moreover, this young man may, in his ignorance of how the world works, think the odds in his favor are even greater and that the delay will be even longer.

Compounding the problems of delay and uncertainty is the fact that society cannot feasibly reduce the uncertainty attached to the chances of being arrested by more than a modest amount, . . . and though it can to some degree increase the probability and severity of a prison sentence for those who are caught, it cannot do so drastically by, for example, summarily executing all convicted robbers or even by sending all robbers to twenty-year prison terms. . . . Some scholars add a further complication: the young man may be incapable of assessing the risks of crime. How, they ask, is he to know his chances of being caught and punished? And even if he does know, is he perhaps "driven" by uncontrollable impulses to snatch purses whatever the risks?

As if all this were not bad enough, the principal method by which scholars have attempted to measure the effect on crime of differences in the probability and severity of punishment has involved using data about aggregates of people (entire cities, counties, states, and even nations) rather than about individuals. In a typical study, of which there have been several dozen, the rate at which, say, robbery is committed in each state is "explained" by means of a statistical procedure in which the analyst takes into account both the socioeconomic features of each state that might affect the supply of robbers (for example, the percentage of persons with low incomes, the unemployment rate, or the population density of the big cities) and the operation of the criminal justice system of each state as it attempts to cope with robbery (for example, the probability of being caught and imprisoned for a given robbery and the length of the average prison term for robbery). Most such studies find, after controlling for socioeconomic differences among the states, that the higher the probability of being imprisoned, the lower the robbery rate. Isaac Ehrlich, an economist, produced the best known of such analyses using data on crime in the United States in 1940, 1950, and 1960. To simplify a complex analysis, he found, after controlling for such factors as the income level and age distribution of the population, that the higher the probability of imprisonment for those convicted of robbery, the lower the robbery rate. Thus, differences in the certainty of punishment seem to make a difference in the level of crime. At the same time, Ehrlich did not find that the severity of punishment (the average time served in prison for robbery) had, independently of certainty, an effect on robbery rates in two of the three time periods (1940 and 1960).

But there are some problems associated with studying the effect of sanctions on crime rates using aggregate data of this sort. One is that many of the most important factors are not known with any accuracy. For example, we are dependent on police reports for our measure of the robbery rate, and these undoubtedly vary in accuracy from place to place. If all police departments were inaccurate to the same degree, this would not be important; unfortunately, some departments are probably much less accurate than others, and this variable error can introduce a serious bias into the statistical estimates of the effect of the criminal justice system.

Moreover, if one omits from the equation some factor that affects the crime rate, then the estimated effect of the factors that are in the equation may be in error because some of the causal power belonging to the omitted factor will be falsely attributed to the included factors. For example, suppose we want to find out whether differences in the number of policemen on patrol among American cities are associated with differences in the rate at which robberies take place in those cities. If we fail to include in our equation a measure of the population density of the city, we may wrongly conclude that the more police there are on the streets, the *higher* the robbery rate and thus give support to the absurd policy proposition that the way to reduce robberies is to fire police officers. Since robberies are more likely to occur in larger, densely settled cities (which also tend to have a higher proportion of police), it would be a grave error to omit such measures of population from the equation. Since we are not certain what causes crime, we always run the risk of inadvertently omitting a key factor from our efforts to see if deterrence works.

Even if we manage to overcome these problems, a final difficulty lies in wait. The observed fact (and it has been observed many times) that states in which the probability of going to prison for robbery is low are also states which have high rates of robbery can be interpreted in one of two ways. It can mean *either* that the higher robbery rates are the results of the lower imprisonment rates (and thus evidence that deterrence works) *or* that the lower imprisonment rates are caused by the higher robbery rates. To see how the latter might be true, imagine a state that is experiencing, for some reason, a rapidly rising robbery rate. It arrests, convicts, and imprisons more and more robbers as more and more robberies are committed, but it cannot quite keep up. The robberies are increasing so fast that they "swamp" the criminal justice system; prosecutors and judges respond by letting more robbers off without a prison sentence, or perhaps without even a trial, in order to keep the system from becoming hopelessly clogged. As a result, the proportion of arrested robbers who go to prison goes down while the robbery rate goes up. In this case, we ought to conclude, not that prison deters robbers, but that high robbery rates "deter" prosecutors and judges.

The best analysis of these problems in statistical studies of deterrence is to be found in a report of the Panel on Research on Deterrent and Incapacitative Effects, set up by the National Research Council (an arm of the National Academy of Sciences). That panel, chaired by Alfred Blumstein of Carnegie-Mellon University, concluded that the available statistical evidence (as of 1978) did not warrant reaching any strong conclusions about the deterrent effect of existing differences among states or cities in the probability of punishment. The panel (of which I was a member) noted that "the evidence certainly favors a proposition supporting deterrence more than it favors one asserting that deterrence is absent" but urged "scientific caution" in interpreting this evidence.

Subsequently, other criticisms of deterrence research, generally along the same lines as those of the panel, were published by Colin Loftin and by Stephen S. Brier and Stephen E. Feinberg.

Some commentators believe that these criticisms have proved that "deterrence doesn't work" and thus the decks have now been cleared to get on with the task of investing in those programs, such as job creation and income maintenance, that *will* have an effect on crime. Such a conclusion is, to put it mildly, a bit premature.

Rehabilitating Deterrence

People are governed in their daily lives by rewards and penalties of every sort. We shop for bargain prices, praise our children for good behavior and scold them for bad, expect lower interest rates to stimulate home building and fear that higher ones will depress it, and conduct ourselves in public in ways that lead our friends and neighbors to form good opinions of us. To assert that "deterrence doesn't work" is tantamount to either denying the plainest facts of everyday life or claiming that would-be criminals are utterly different from the rest of us. They may well be different to some degree—they most likely have a weaker conscience, worry less about their reputation in polite society, and find it harder to postpone gratifying their urges—but these differences of degree do not make them indifferent to the risks and gains of crime. If they were truly indifferent, they would scarcely be able to function at all, for their willingness to take risks would be offset by their indifference to loot. Their lives would consist of little more than the erratic display of animal instincts and fleeting impulses.

The question before us is whether feasible changes in the deferred and uncertain penalties of crime (and, as we shall see, in the deferred and uncertain opportunities for employment) will affect crime rates in ways that can be detected by the data and statistical methods at our disposal. Though the unreliability of crime data and the limitations of statistical analysis are real enough and are accurately portrayed by the Panel of the National Research Council, there are remedies and rejoinders that, on balance, strengthen the case for the claim that not only does deterrence work (the panel never denied that), it probably works in ways that can be measured, even in the aggregate.

The errors in official statistics about crime rates have been addressed by employing other measures of crime, in particular reports gathered by Census Bureau interviewers from citizens who have been victims of crime. While these victim surveys have problems of their own (such as the forgetfulness of citizens), they are not the same problems as those that affect police reports of crime. Thus, if we obtain essentially the same findings about the effect of sanctions on crime from studies that use victim data as we do from studies using police data, our confidence in these findings is strengthened. Studies of this sort have been done by Itzhak Goldberg at Stanford and by Barbara Boland and myself, and the results are quite consistent with those from research based on police reports. As sanctions become more likely, crime becomes less common.

There is a danger that important factors will be omitted from any statistical study of crime in ways that bias the results, but this problem is no greater in studies of penalties than it is in studies of unemployment rates, voting behavior, or any of a hundred other socially significant topics. Since we can never know with certainty everything that may affect crime (or unemployment, or voting), we must base our conclusions not on any single piece of research, but on the general thrust of a variety of studies analyzing many different causal factors. The Panel of the National Research Council took exactly this position. While noting that "there is the possibility that as yet unknown and so untested" factors may be affecting crime, "this is not a sufficient basis for dismissing" the common finding that crime goes up as sanctions become less certain because "many of the analyses have included some of the more obvious possible third causes and they still find negative associations between sanctions and crimes."

It is possible that rising crime rates "swamp" the criminal justice system so that a negative statistical association between, say, rates of theft and the chances of going to prison for theft may mean not that a decline in imprisonment is causing theft to increase, but rather that a rise in theft is causing imprisonment to become less likely. This might occur particularly with respect to less serious crimes, such as shoplifting or petty larceny; indeed, the proportion of prisoners who are shoplifters or petty thieves has gone down over the last two decades. But it is hard to imagine that the criminal justice system would respond to an increase in murder or armed robbery by letting some murderers or armed robbers off with no punishment. There is no evidence that convicted murderers are any less likely to go to prison today than they were twenty years ago. Moreover, the apparent deterrent effect of prison on serious crimes, such as murder and robbery, was apparently as great in 1940 or 1950, when these crimes *were* much less common, as it is today, suggesting that swamping has not occurred.

The best studies of deterrence that manage to overcome many of these problems provide evidence that deterrence works. Alfred Blumstein and Daniel Nagin studied the relationship between draft evasion and the penalties imposed for evading the draft. After controlling for the socioeconomic characteristics of the states, they found that the higher the probability of conviction for draft evasion, the lower the evasion rates. This is an especially strong finding because it is largely immune to some of the problems of other research. Draft evasion is more accurately measured than street crime, hence errors arising from poor data are not a problem. And draft evasion cases did not swamp the federal courts in which they were tried, in part because such cases (like murder in state courts) make up only a small fraction of the courts' workload (7 percent in the case of draft evasion) and in part because the attorney general had instructed federal prosecutors to give high priority to these cases. Blumstein and Nagin concluded that draft evasion is deterrable.

Another way of testing whether deterrence works is to look, not at differences among states at one point in time, but at changes in the nation as a whole over a long period of time. Historical data on the criminal justice system in America is so spotty that such research is difficult to do here, but it is not at all difficult in England where the data are excellent. Kenneth I. Wolpin analyzed changes in crime rates and in various parts of the criminal justice system (the chances of being arrested, convicted, and punished) for the period 1894 to 1967, and concluded that changes in the probability of being punished seemed to cause changes in the crime rate. He offers reasons for believing that this causal connection cannot be explained away by the argument that the criminal justice system was being swamped.

Given what we are trying to measure—changes in the behavior of a small number of hard-to-observe persons who are responding to delayed and uncertain penalties—we will never be entirely sure that our statistical manipulations have proved that deterrence works. What is impressive is that so many (but not all) studies using such different methods come to similar conclusions. . . . [We] shall discover that, though the evidence as to whether capital punishment deters crime is quite ambiguous, most of the studies find that the chances of being imprisoned for murder do seem to affect the murder rate. Even after wading through all this, the skeptical reader may remain unconvinced. Given the difficulties of any aggregate statistical analysis, that is understandable. But if unconvinced, the reader cannot conclude that criticisms of the statistical claims for deterrence have by implication enhanced the statistical claims for job-creation. This is one time when, if you throw out the bath water, you will have to throw out the baby as well.

Evaluating Employment

Deterrence and job-creation are not different crime-fighting strategies; they are two sides of the same strategy. The former emphasizes (and tries to increase) the costs of crime; the latter emphasizes (and tries to increase) the benefits of noncrime. Both depend on the assumption that we are dealing with reasonably rational persons who respond to incentives. The principal means used to estimate the effect on crime rates of changes in the benefits of noncrime have been exactly the same as the ones used to evaluate the effect of changes in the costs of crime—the statistical techniques reviewed by the National Research Council Panel.

To make this clear, let us return to our original example. The young man who was trying to decide whether to mug a little old lady is still yearning for the money necessary to enjoy some high living. Let us assume that he considers, as a way of getting money, finding a job. He knows he will have to look for one, and this will take time. Even if he gets a job, he will have to wait to obtain his first paycheck. Moreover, he knows that young men have difficulty finding their first jobs, especially in inner-city neighborhoods such as his, and there is a great deal of uncertainty attached to even the delayed benefits of legitimate employment. Thus, he cannot be certain that the job he might get would provide benefits that exceed the costs. Working forty hours a week as a messenger, a dish-washer, or a busboy might not be worth the sacrifice in time, effort, and reputation on the street corner that it entails. The young man may be wrong about all this, but if he is ignorant of the true risks of crime, he is probably just as ignorant of the true benefits of noncrime.

In addition to the problems of delay, uncertainty, and ignorance is the fact that society cannot make more than modest changes in the employment prospects of young men. Job creation takes a long time when it can be done at all, and many of the jobs created will go to the "wrong" (that is, not criminally inclined) persons; thus, youth unemployment rates will not vary greatly among states and will change only slowly over time. And if we are to detect the effects of existing differences in unemployment rates (or income levels) on crime, we must estimate those effects by exactly the same statistical techniques that are used to estimate the effects of criminal justice sanctions. Indeed, they involve the very same equations (remember, to measure the effects of sanctions, we first had to hold constant the effects of socioeconomic variables; now, to measure the effects of the latter, we must first hold constant the former).

The problem of measurement error arises because we do not know with much accuracy the teenage or youthful unemployment rate by city or state. Much depends on who is looking for work and how hard, how we count students who are looking for only part-time jobs, and whether we can distinguish between people out of work for long periods and those who happen to be between jobs at the moment. Again, since inaccuracies in these data vary from place to place, we will obtain biased results.

The problem of omitted factors is also real, as is evident in a frequently cited study done in 1976 by Harvey Brenner of Johns Hopkins University. He claimed to find that, between 1940 and 1973, increases in the unemployment rate led to increases in the homicide rate. But he omitted from his analysis any measures of changes in the certainty or the severity of sentences for murder, factors that other scholars have found to have a strong effect on homicide.

Finally, there is probably a complex, not a simple, relationship between crime and unemployment (or poverty), just as there may be a complex relationship between imprisonment and crime. For example, suppose in a statistical study that managed to overcome the problems already mentioned, we discover that as unemployment rates go up, crime rates go up. One's natural instinct is to interpret this as meaning that rising unemployment causes rising crime. It is just as possible that rising crime causes rising unemployment. This could be the case if young men examining the world about them concluded that crime pays more than jobs (for instance, that stealing cars is more profitable than washing them). They might then leave their jobs in favor of crime. That this happens is no mere conjecture; it lies at the heart of some unknown but probably large fraction of the growing "underground economy." Some young men find dealing in drugs or other rackets much more attractive than nine-to-five jobs, but technically they are "unemployed." Or it may be the case that both crime and unemployment are the results of some common underlying cause. In 1964, the unemployment rate for black men aged twenty to twenty-four was 10 percent; by 1978 it was 23 percent. During the same period, crime rates, in particular those involving young black men, went up. Among the several possible explanations are the changes that have occurred in the inner parts of large cities where so many young blacks live. . . . [There] has been a movement out of the inner cities of both jobs and the social infrastructure that is manned by adult members of the middle class. The departure of the jobs led to increased unemployment, the departure of the middle class to lessened social control and hence to more crime. If we knew more than we now know, we would probably discover that all three relationships are working simultaneously—for some persons, unemployment leads to crime, for others crime leads to unemployment, and for still others social disintegration or personal inadquacies leads to both crime and unemployment.

That several of these relationships are in fact at work is suggested by the previously mentioned study of Brenner's. Even if the effect of unemployment on homicide persisted after taking into account changes in penalties (which it probably does not), Brenner himself noted that the murder rate also went up with increases in per capita income and (sometimes) inflation as well as with a rise in joblessness. But if the stress of joblessness leads to more murders, what is it about increases in average income (or in inflation) that also lead to more murders? And if society attempts to reduce the murder rate by reducing unemployment, how can it do this without at the same time increasing the murder rate because, as a result of lessened unemployment, it has managed to increase per capita incomes or stimulate inflation?

I do not say this to explain away the studies purporting to show that unemployment or poverty causes crime, for in fact (contrary to what many people assert) there are very few decent pieces of research that in fact show a relationship between economic factors and crime. Robert W. Gillespie reviewed studies available as of 1975 and was able to find three that asserted the existence of a significant relationship between unemployment and crime but seven which did not. Thomas Orsagh and Ann Dryden Witte in 1981 reviewed the studies that had appeared since 1975 and found very little statistically strong or consistent evidence to support the existence of a connection. The evidence linking income (or poverty) and crime is similarly inconclusive, and probably for the same reasons: there are grave methodological problems confronting anyone trying to find the relationship, and the relationship, to the extent it exists, is probably quite complex (some people may turn to crime because they are poor, some people may be poor because they have turned to crime but are not very good at it, and still other persons may have been made both poor and criminal because of some common underlying factor). To quote Orsagh and Witte: "Research using aggregate data provides only weak support for the simple proposition that unemployment causes crime . . . [and] does not provide convincing tests of the relationship between low income and crime."

Back to Square One: Studying Individuals

We seem to be at a dead end. But we are not. Whenever we are trying to discover a relationship between hard-to-measure factors that operate deep inside a complex social structure, we are well advised not to rely on any single method of analysis and particularly well advised not to rely on "statistical studies using aggregate data. We should attack the same problem from a number of angles, using different kinds of data and various methodologies. Above all, we should look at what happens to individuals (rather than to cities or states) and what happens when a new program is tried (rather than measuring the natural variation found in the world as it is).

Ideally, we would like to know how the probability or severity of a possible punishment will affect the behavior of persons who *might* commit a serious crime. Such persons probably constitute only a small fraction of the total population, but they are an important fraction. Most of us would not commit a serious crime because of the operation of internal controls on our behavior, reinforced by the fear of embarrassment should our misconduct be detected. A few of us may commit serious crimes with only small regard to the risks, unless those risks can be made great and immediate. For example, most men would never dream of killing their wives, and a few men might kill them (perhaps in an alcoholic rage) unless a police officer were standing right next to them. But for a certain fraction of men, the idea of doing away with their wives is strongly conditioned by their perception of the risks. Wives, and in particular feminist organizations, concede this when they demand, as they have with increasing vigor, the strict enforcement of laws against wife-abuse. (Not long ago, the New York Police Department was obliged to promise in writing to arrest and prosecute wife-beating men who previously had been handled in a more conciliatory fashion.)

I mention wife-abuse and murder because some people think of such actions as inevitably the result of a deranged or irrational mind, and thus of one insensitive to the risks attendant on such actions. Sometimes this may be so, but more often it is not, as is evident by the fact that the arrival of a police officer usually results in the end of the fight, at least in its physical phase. Even when no officer is there, people pay attention to some costs when engaged in even the most emotional behavior. As my colleague Richard Herrnstein likes to point out, when husbands and wives start throwing dishes at each other, they are more likely to throw the everyday crockery rather than the fine china. I can imagine getting drunk enough or mad enough to challenge somebody in a bar to a fight, but I cannot imagine getting drunk or mad enough to challenge that somebody if his name happens to be Sugar Ray Leonard or Mean Joe Greene.

If the consequences of even emotional and impulsive acts are given some weight by most people, then the consequences of less emotional acts (such as shoplifting, auto theft, robbery, and burglary) are likely to play an even larger role in affecting the willingness of people to engage in them. What we would like to know is how changes in the prospective costs of crime and the prospective benefits of pursuing legitimate alternatives to crime affect, at the margin, the behavior of those individuals who are "at risk."

Persons who are "at risk" are those who lack strong, internalized inhibitions against misconduct, who value highly the excitement and thrills of breaking the law, who have a low stake in conformity, who are willing to take greater chances than the rest of us, and who greatly value quick access to ready cash. Such persons tend, disproportionately, to be young males. As Philip J. Cook has argued, it is not necessary for those would-be offenders to be entirely rational or fully informed for the criminal justice system (or the legitimate labor market) to have an effect on them. It is only necessary that they attach some value to the consequences of their actions (since we know they attach a positive value to the loot, it is reasonable to suppose they also attach some value—a negative one, that is—to the chances of being caught) and that they operate on the basis of at least a crude rule of thumb about how great or small those risks are, a rule of thumb that can be affected by society.

Most of us are probably not very well informed about the true costs of crime; being law-abiding, we probably imagine that the chances of being caught are higher than in fact they are and that the severity of the sentence (measured in years in prison) is greater than it really is. But most of us depend for our information on newspaper stories, detective programs on television, and our own deep fear of being exposed as a disreputable person. But persons at risk (young men hanging around on street corners and thieves who associate with other thieves) have quite different sources of information. These are the accounts of other young men and other thieves who have had a run-in with the police or the courts and who therefore can supply to their colleagues a crudely accurate rule of thumb: "the heat is on" or "the heat is off," Judge Bruce MacDonald* is either "Maximum Mac" or "Turn 'Em Loose Bruce," the prosecutor will let you "cop out" to a burglary charge so that it gets marked down to a misdemeanor larceny or will "throw the book at you" and demand "felony time."

It is the behavior of these persons, thus informed, that we wish to observe. But how? As we have seen, we cannot easily do it with aggregate statistical studies in which the behavior of these persons is often buried in the

*A fictional name

"noise" generated by the behavior of the majority of people who do not commit crimes whatever the advantages. There have in fact been only a few efforts to measure the deterrent effect of the sanctions of the criminal justice system on individuals, as opposed to cities or states. . . . One such effort was made by Ann Witte, who followed for about three years the activities of 641 men released from prison in North Carolina. She gathered information not only about their subsequent brushes with the law (80 percent were rearrested) but also about their experiences with the law before being imprisoned (their prior risk of being arrested, convicted, and imprisoned), the time it took them to find a job after release and the amount it paid in wages, and such aspects of their life style as their involvement with alcohol and drugs.

Witte could not find out directly how these ex-convicts evaluated their chances of being caught if they broke the law in the future, but she could observe how frequently in the past (that is, before being imprisoned the last time) their arrests had led to a conviction and their convictions had led to imprisonment. Her assumption was that these men might be influenced in their future conduct by their past experience with the criminal justice system. The results of her analysis based on this assumption were complex and not entirely consistent, but in general she found that "deterrence works"—the higher the probability of being punished in the past, the lower the number of arrests per month free on the street in the future. She also found that deterrence works differently for different kinds of offenders. For persons who engaged in violent offenses or drug use, the severity of the prior sentence seemed to have the greatest effect, whereas for persons who engaged in less serious property offenses the certainty of imprisonment seemed to be most significant. Deterrence may not work, judging from her data, for thieves who were also drug addicts. The availability of jobs had no consistent effect on subsequent criminality.

There are some obvious limitations to this study. One is that, as Witte notes, it is a study of "losers"—older men (the average age was thirty-two) who had already been in prison, often many times. What we would prefer knowing is whether differences in sanctions or job availability affect the behavior of persons not yet involved in crime or young men involved for the first time. Because her group consisted of older, ex-cons, it is quite possible her findings understate the true effect of either sanctions or jobs.

A comparable study was carried out in Cook County, Illinois, and this was aimed at the young offender. Charles A. Murray and Louis A. Cox, Jr. followed the criminal careers (measured by the number of times they were arrested per month free on the street) of 317 Chicago boys who had been incarcerated for the first time by the Illinois Department of Corrections. Though young (their average age was sixteen), they were scarcely novices at crime: they had been arrested an average of thirteen times each before receiving this, their first prison sentence. Nor were their offenses trivial: as a group, they had been charged with fourteen homicides, twenty-three rapes, over three hundred assaults and a like number of auto thefts, nearly two hundred armed robberies, and over seven hundred burglaries. The patience of the court finally exhausted, they were sent off to a correctional institution, where they served an average sentence of ten months. Murray and Cox followed them for (on the average) seventeen months after their release. During this period, the frequency with which they were arrested (that is, arrests per month per one hundred boys) declined by about two-thirds. To be exact, the members of this group of hard-core delinquents were arrested 6.3 times each during the year before being sent away but only 2.9 times each during the seventeen months on the street after release.

Murray and Cox refer to this as the "suppression effect"; namely, the tendency of the first exposure to prison to suppress the rate at which delinquents are arrested and, presumably, the rate at which they actually were committing crimes. . . . [We] shall consider some additional implications of this study as well as some of the objections that have been raised to it.

The Murray and Cox study, one of the few of its kind that has been carried out, adds some support to the deterrence theory. But it still focuses on persons who have already committed crimes; we remain uncertain about the effect of changes in the criminal justice system on would-be offenders. It is almost impossible to study behavior that does not occur except to ask, as some scholars have done, various persons, often students, whether they would commit or have committed a crime when they perceived the penalties to be of a given severity and a given probability. One such study was done among students at an eastern college, and another among high school students in Arizona. Both found that the students who believed there was a high probability of being punished for a particular criminal act were less likely to report (anonymously) having committed the act than were students who thought there was a low probability of being punished. Both studies are broadly consistent with the view that deterrence works, but both are also difficult to interpret. It is hard to be confident that the number of offenses the students reported bears any relationship to the number they actually committed. More important, the studies raise the possibility that what actually deters these students (very few of whom commit any serious acts with any frequency) is not what they guess to be the chances of being caught, but the moral opprobrium with which such acts are viewed. . . . [For] most people in most circumstances, the moral nature of the act and the internalized inhibitions on misconduct arising out of that moral code are probably the major deterrents to crime. Interviewing students may high-light that fact, but it cannot tell us what happens, at the margin, when society alters the certainty or severity of punishment for a given offense. And for purposes of public policy, that is exactly what we want to know.

*Another study of individual responses to sanctions was carried out among shoplifters caught by store detectives in a large California department store. Of the 371 individuals caught shoplifting during one year, only 3 were caught again during the year in any of the department stores in that region, even though the majority who were caught were not taken to court. The authors interpret this as evidence of the deterrent effect of apprehension, though the lack of any control group (persons shoplifting but not caught) render this conclusion somewhat speculative. Lawrence E. Cohen and Rodney Stark, "Discriminatory Labeling and the Five-Finger Discount: An Empirical Analysis of Differential Shoplifting Dispositions," *Journal of Research in Crime and Delinquency* 11 (1974): 25–39. For a similar conclusion, see also Mary Owen Cameron, *The Booster and the Snitch* (New York: Free Press, 1964), pp. 159–170.

Experimenting with Changing the Costs of Crime

The best way to find out the circumstances under which punishing or helping people will affect the likelihood of such persons committing crimes is to try it. Unfortunately, learning from experience is harder than acquiring experience, because many things that are tried as ways of reducing crime, including both alterations in the penalties for crime and in the opportunities for avoiding crime, are never evaluated in any serious way. As a result, the study of public policy toward crime is cluttered with unsupported assertions and reinvented wheels.

There have been some efforts to make changes under conditions permitting a serious and competent evaluation, and we can report the results. A few were designed from the first as true experiments, . . . others have been "quasi-experiments"—changes in policy that were accompanied by efforts to find out what happened (such as the assignment of more officers to the New York City subways. . . .)

Most experiments in deterrence have involved changes in police behavior rather than changes in the behavior of judges and prosecutors. . . . [The] result of those changes seem to indicate that the more focused and aggressive the police effort, the greater the chance of it making a difference. Changes in the level of random preventive patrol in marked cars seemed to make little difference in crime rates in Kansas City, but changes in the number of officers riding New York subway cars and changes in the aggressiveness with which San Diego police stopped and interrogated persons on the streets did seem to make a difference.* Comparable results come from a study of drunk driving in Great Britain. The police began a program to use a breathalyzer to catch inebriated motorists in hopes of reducing traffic accidents, especially fatal ones. A careful study by H. Laurence Ross clearly indicates that these hopes were born out: "the Road Safety Act caused a reduction in casualties" by as much as two-thirds during weekend evenings when drunk driving is likely to be most common. Unhappily, the police did not like to enforce this law, which could lead to the mandatory revocation of the driving license of a motorist whose blood alcohol level exceeded .08 percent. In time, the authorities made a highly publicized effort to get the police to make random stops and administer breathalyzer tests, and once again accidents declined.

*A study by Barbara Boland and myself involving a complex statistical analysis of the relationship between police behavior and robbery rates in thirty-five large American cities seems to confirm these experimental findings. The number of police officers on the street and the aggressiveness with which they patrolled had, independently, effects on the reported rate of robberies. The study employed methods (estimating simultaneous equations using two-stage least squares) and assumptions designed to eliminate the risk that the finding of a deterrent effect would be spurious owing to the reciprocal relationship between crime and the number and behavior of police officers. In particular, it was designed to overcome the problems mentioned earlier in this chapter and in the report of the National Research Council Panel on Deterrence arising from the fact that the number of robberies may affect the number of police and the rate at which they make arrests just as the number of police and the arrest rate may affect the number of robberies. James Q. Wilson and Barbara Boland, "The Effect of the Police on Crime," *Law and Society Review* 12 (Spring 1978): 367–390, and "The Effects of the Police on Crime: A Rejoinder," *Law and Society Review* 16 (1981–1982): 163–169.

Perhaps the most dramatic evidence of the operation of deterrence—dramatic because it involved a true experiment on individuals in the real world—comes from an effort in Minneapolis to find out how the police can best handle incidents of spouse assault. The conventional wisdom had been that if one or both parties to such an assault were handled by the officer informally—by mediation or referral to a social work agency—the parties would be better off than if the assaulter were arrested. And the police themselves often preferred not to make an arrest because it took time and effort and often led to no prosecution when the victim refused to press charges. With the advice of the Police Foundation, a group of Minneapolis officers began handling their misdemeanor spouse-assault cases by randomly assigning the assaulter to one of three dispositions: arresting him, advising him, or sending him out of the house to cool off. Over 250 cases were treated in this experimental fashion and followed up for six months. The assaulters who were arrested were less likely to be reported to the police for a subsequent assault than were those advised and much less likely than those sent out of the house. And this was true even though the arrested person, in the vast majority of cases, spent no more than a week in jail.

These police experiments and quasi-experiments support the concept of deterrence, but they are not an especially hard test of it. The police are the persons closest to a potential offender, and if they suddenly act in a more conspicuous or aggressive manner, these changes are often quickly noticed by would-be offenders who then alter their behavior accordingly. Moreover, the kinds of offenses most worrisome to citizens are often those, such as burglary, street robbery, and assault, that are difficult for the police to detect or intercept. The deterrent effect of policing is likely to be greatest when the police can act in a visible way in a closed system (such as a subway or in a school building) or when they can take action on their own initiative without first waiting for a report that a crime has occurred (as in stopping motorists and administering breathalyzer tests or questioning suspicious teenagers on a street corner). The deterrent value of the police is likely to be least when the crime to be deterred involves stealth (such as burglary).

A tougher and, for policy purposes, more useful test of deterrence would be to alter the sentences a person gets without altering police conduct. We have surprisingly few careful studies of the results of doing that even though sentences are regularly altered. Many states have passed mandatory minimum sentences for certain offenses and some have tried to eliminate plea bargaining or, at least, to insure that serious offenders cannot have the charges against them reduced simply to induce a guilty plea. Unfortunately, most of these changes were made under circumstances that rendered any serious evaluation of their effect difficult, if not impossible.

The two best-known changes in sentencing practices that have been studied were the so-called Rockefeller drug laws in New York and the Bartley-Fox gun law in Massachusetts. In 1973, New York State revised its criminal statutes relating to drug trafficking in an attempt to make more severe and more certain the penalties for the sale and possession of heroin (the law affecting other drugs was changed as well, but the focus of the effort, and the most severe penalties, were reserved for heroin). The major pushers—those who sold an ounce or more of heroin—would be liable for a minimum prison term of at least fifteen years and the possibility of life imprisonment. There were some loopholes. An ounce dealer could plea bargain the charges against him down, but to no lower a charge than would entail a mandatory one-year minimum prison sentence. Police informants could get probation instead of prison, and persons under the age of sixteen were exempt from the mandatory sentences. Persons ages sixteen to eighteen might be exempted from the law, a provision that was made explicit by amendments passed in 1975. A group was formed to evaluate the effect of this law. Its report, issued in 1977, concluded that there was no evidence the law had reduced either the availability of heroin on the streets of New York City or the kinds of property crime often committed by drug users. Of course, it is almost impossible to measure directly the amount of an illegal drug in circulation or to observe the illicit transactions between dealers and users, but a good deal of circumstantial evidence, gathered by the study group, suggests that no large changes occurred. There were no marked shifts in deaths from narcotics overdoses, in admissions to drug treatment programs, in the incidence of serum hepatitis (a disease frequently contracted by junkies who use dirty needles), or in the price and purity of heroin available for sale on the street (as inferred from undercover buys of heroin made by narcotics agents).

The explanation for this disappointing experience, in the opinion of the study group, was that difficulties in administering the law weakened its deterrent power, with the result that most offenders and would-be offenders did not experience a significantly higher risk of apprehension and punishment. There was no increase (or decrease, for that matter) in the number of arrests, no increase in the number of indictments, and a slight decline in the proportion of indictments resulting in conviction. Offsetting this was a higher probability that a person convicted would go to prison. The net effect of these offsetting trends—fewer indictments but a higher risk of imprisonment if indicted and convicted—was that the probability of imprisonment for arrested drug dealers did not change as a result of the law: it was about one imprisonment per nine arrests before the law, and about one in nine afterward. On the other hand, the sentences received by those who did go to prison became more severe. Before the law was passed, only 3 percent of persons imprisoned for drug offenses received a sentence of three years or more. After the law went into effect, 22 percent received such sentences. Perhaps because sentences became more severe, more accused persons demanded trials instead of pleading guilty and, as a result, the time it took to dispose of the average drug case nearly doubled.

Does the experience under the Rockefeller law disprove the claim that deterrence works? Not at all. If we mean by "deterrence" changing behavior by increasing either the certainty or the swiftness of punishment, then the Rockefeller law, as it was administered, could not have deterred behavior because it made no change in the certainty of punishent and actually reduced the swiftness of it. If, on the other hand, we define "deterrence" as changing behavior by increasing the severity of punishment, then deterrence did not work in this case. What we would like to know is whether heroin trafficking would have been reduced if the penalties associated with it could have been made swifter or more certain.

It is possible that severity is the enemy of certainty and speed. As penalties get tougher, defendants and their lawyers have a greater incentive to slow down the process, and those prosecutors and judges who oppose heavy sentences for drug dealing may use their discretionary powers to decline indictment, accept plea bargains, grant continuances, and modify penalties in ways that reduce the certainty and the celerity of punishment. The group that evaluated the Rockefeller law suggests that reducing severity in favor of certainty might create the only real possibility of testing the deterrent effect of changes in sentences.

The Bartley-Fox gun law in Massachusetts was administered and evaluated in ways that avoided some of the problems of interpreting the results of the Rockefeller drug laws. In 1974, the Massachusetts legislature amended the law that had long required persons carrying a handgun to have a license by stipulating that a violation of this law would now entail a mandatory penalty of one year in prison, which may not be reduced by probation, parole, or judicial finagling. When the law went into effect in April 1975, various efforts were made to evaluate both the compliance of the criminal justice system with it and the law's impact on crimes involving handguns. James A. Beha traced the application of the law for two years and concluded that, despite widespread predictions to the contrary, the police, prosecutors, and judges were not evading the law. As in New York, more persons asked for trials, and delays in disposition apparently increased, but unlike in New York the probability of punishment increased for those arrested. Beha estimated in 1977 (at a time when not all the early arrests had yet worked their way through the system) that prison sentences were being imposed four times more frequently on persons arrested for illegally carrying firearms than had been true before the law was passed. Owing to some combination of the heavy publicity given to the Bartley-Fox law and to the real increase in the risk of imprisonment facing persons arrested while carrying a firearm without a license, the casual carrying of firearms in Massachusetts seems to have decreased. This was the view expressed to interviewers by participants in the system, including persons being held in jail, and it was buttressed by the fact that there was a sharp drop in the proportion of drug dealers arrested by the Boston police who, at the time of their arrest, were found to be carrying firearms.

Three studies were made of the impact of the law on serious crime. They used slightly different methods, but in general came to the same conclusion; namely, that there was a measurable decline in the kinds of crimes that involve the casual use of firearms. More exactly, there appeared to be a decline in the proportion of assaults, robberies, and homicides in which a gun was used even though the total number of assaults and robberies in Boston was going up and the number of murders was constant. Moreover, the proportion of assaults and robberies in which guns were used did not go down in other large cities in the United States during this time. In sum, the Bartley-Fox law, as applied, seems, at least during the years in which its effect was studied, to have increased the risk associated with carrying a gun, reduced the frequency with which guns were casually carried, and thereby reduced the rate at which certain gun-related crimes were committed.

An effort to achieve the same results in Michigan did not work out as well, in large measure because the judges there (in particular the judges in Wayne County, which includes Detroit) refused to apply the law. The Michigan Felony Firearm Law, which went into effect in 1977, required the imposition of a two-year prison sentence for possessing a firearm while committing a felony, and the two-year firearm sentence was to be added on to whatever sentence was imposed for the other felony. There was no general change in either the certainty or the severity of sentences issued to gun-carrying felons. To avoid adding on the two-year term required by the Felony Firearm Law, many judges would reduce the sentence given for the original felony (say, assault or robbery) in order to compensate for the add-on. In other cases, the judge would dismiss the gun count or the defendant would be allowed to plea to a less serious charge. Given this evasion, it is not surprising to learn that there was little effect of the law on the rate at which gun-related crimes were committed.

Several states have recently altered the legal minimum drinking age; because of the effect of teenage drinking on highway fatalities, these changes have been closely studied. Between 1970 and 1973, twenty-five states lowered their legal drinking age. Shortly thereafter, Allan F. Williams and his associates examined the effect of these age reductions on highway accidents and concluded that the changes in the laws had contributed to an increase in fatal motor vehicle accidents. Reacting to the implications of such findings, at least fourteen states, beginning in 1976, raised their minimum drinking ages from eighteen or nineteen to twenty or twenty-one. Williams and associates studied these changes in nine states and concluded that making it illegal for young persons (typically, those eighteen and under) to buy alcoholic beverages led to a reduction in fatal auto accidents occurring at night (when most drink-related accidents take place). Alexander C. Wagenaar looked closely at one state, Michigan, and came to the same conclusion. When the legal drinking age there was lowered to eighteen, the number of persons ages eighteen to twenty involved in accidents who reportedly had been drinking began to when the drinking age was raised to twenty-one, the number of such ns in crashes began to decrease. Comparable conclusions were leached from a study of the consequences of altering the legal drinking gage in Maine. In his evaluation of laws governing drunk driving around the world, H. Laurence Ross concluded that increasing the certainty of punishment reduces the level of drunk driving. By contrast, decriminalizing abortions in Hawaii did not seem to affect the estimated number of abortions performed.

In sum, the evidence from these quasi-experiments is that changes in the probability of being punished can lead to changes in behavior, though this may not happen when the legal changes exist only on paper and not in practice or when the benefits to be had from violating the law are so great as to make would-be perpetrators indifferent to the slight alteration in the risks facing them. For example, when the prospective gains from heroin trafficking or obtaining (and supplying) illegal abortions are very large, these gains can swamp the effect of modest changes in the costs of these actions, especially when (as with the New York drug law and the Michigan firearms law) the criminal justice system does not in practice impose greater risks. When the prospective benefits from violating the law are small (as with teenage drinking or perhaps with carrying an unlicensed gun), small changes in the risks can have significant effects on behavior.

All this means that it is difficult, but not impossible, to achieve increased deterrent effects through changes in the law. To obtain these effects, society must walk a narrow line—the penalties to be imposed must be sufficiently great to offset, at the margin, the benefits of the illegal act but not so great as to generate resistance in the criminal justice system to their prompt imposition.

Experiments with Changing the Benefits of Noncrime

The hope, widespread in the 1960s, that job-creation and job-training programs would solve many social problems, including crime, led to countless efforts both to prevent crime by supplying jobs to crime-prone youth and to reduce crime among convicted offenders by supplying them with better job opportunities after their release from prison. One preventive program was the Neighborhood Youth Corps that gave jobs to poor young persons during the afternoons and evenings and all days during the summer. Gerald D. Robins evaluated the results of such programs among poor blacks in Cincinnati and Detroit. He found no evidence that participation in the Youth Corps had any effect on the proportion of enrollees who came into contact with the police. Essentially the same gloomy conclusion was reached by the authors of a survey of some ninety-six delinquency prevention programs, though there were a few glimmers of hope that certain programs might provide some benefits to some persons. For example, persons who had gone through a Job Corps program that featured intensive remedial education and job training in a residential camp were apparently less likely to be arrested six months after finishing their training than a control group.

Though preventing crime and delinquency by job programs of the sort developed by the "Great Society" seemed a lost hope, there was, initially at least, more success reported from efforts to reduce crime among ex-offenders. Philip Cook followed 325 men who had been released from Massachusetts prisons in 1959 and found that those parolees who were able to find "satisfactory" jobs (not just any job) were less likely to have their parole revoked because they committed a new crime during an eighteen-month follow-up period. This was true even after controlling for the personal attributes of the parolees, such as race, intelligence, marital status, education, prior occupation, and military service.

Findings such as Cook's may have reinforced the belief of policy makers that if only we could reintegrate the ex-offender into the labor market, we could cut crime and at the same time save money through reduced prison populations. By the early 1970s, forty-two states had adopted some variety of "work-release" programs for prisoners by which convicts nearing the end of their prison terms were released into the community in order to work at various jobs during the day, returning to prison at night or on weekends. Gordon P. Waldo and Theodore G. Chiricos evaluated the results of work-release in Florida, and did so on the basis of a particularly sophisticated research design. Eligible inmates were *randomly* assigned to either a work-release or a nonrelease group, to insure that there were no differences between those enrolled in the program and those not enrolled. And many different measures of recidivism were calculated, not just whether the offender was later arrested (. . . this is a common flaw in most experiments on rehabilitation), but also the *rate* of arrests per month free. Waldo and Chiricos found no differences whatsoever in the rearrest rate (or in any measure of recidivism) between persons in work-release and persons not. An equally unpromising result was found by Ann Witte in North Carolina, though there work-release may have led offenders to commit somewhat less serious offenses.

If work-release seems not to reduce crime rates, perhaps it is because it focuses on work rather than wealth. Perhaps if ex-offenders had more money, especially during the crucial few months after their release, they would not need to steal in order to support themselves. Some preliminary evidence gives credence to this view. In Baltimore, about four hundred ex-convicts had been randomly assigned to one of four groups: those receiving nothing, those receiving employment assistance, those receiving financial aid, and those receiving both job placement services and financial aid. After two years, it was clear that getting employment counseling made no difference in the chances of being rearrested but that getting financial aid ($60 a week for thirteen weeks) did make a small difference (about 8 percent). There were a host of problems with this finding, however. For one thing, recidivism was defined as whether or not the person was rearrested, not the *rate* at which he was rearrested (thus possibly obscuring changes in the frequency with which persons committed crimes). Moreover, the study excluded first offenders, alcoholics, heroin users, and persons who had not committed property offenses.

A fuller test of the combined effects of employment and wealth on criminal behavior was made in Georgia and Texas. Called TARP (Transitional Aid Research Program), it involved randomly assigning about two thousand ex-convicts in each state to groups that on release from prison received financial aid, job placement services, or nothing. This experiment was not only much larger than the one in Baltimore, it did not exclude certain categories of offenders, and it used the number of arrests (and not simply whether or not arrested even once) as the measure of the outcome. It also arranged for the financial aid that ex-convicts received to be reduced, dollar for dollar, by any income they received from jobs—a more realistic assumption than operated in Baltimore, where the ex-convicts got to keep their financial aid whether or not they worked.

The ex-convicts receiving financial aid and/or employment counseling had about the same arrest rate after release as did the group not receiving the aid or the counseling. Moreover, individuals receiving TARP financial aid worked less than those who did not, so the money could be said to have discouraged, rather than encouraged, employment. The authors of the evaluation, however, were not discouraged by these findings. A complex statistical analysis led them to claim that *if* the financial aid had not induced the ex-convicts to reduce the amount of time they worked, then the payments might have reduced the ex-cons' tendency to commit crimes. That speculation, weak at best, has been challenged by critics. What is not in dispute is that, as administered, the TARP payments did not reduce crime.

The reader who has followed this far a somewhat confusing array of findings should conclude, I think, something like this: there is some experimental evidence (the Cook study, TARP) that unemployment among ex-convicts tends to contribute to crime, but it is by no means easy to find ways of decreasing that unemployment (the work-release evaluation), and unemployment can be artificially increased by paying people not to work (TARP).

The best and most recent effort to master the link between employment and crime was the "supported work" program of the Manpower Demonstration Research Corporation (MDRC). In ten locations around the country, MDRC randomly assigned four kinds of people with employment problems to special workshops or to control groups. The four kinds of problem persons were long-term welfare (Aid to Families of Dependent Children) recipients, youthful school dropouts, former drug addicts, and ex-convicts. The workshops provided employment in unskilled jobs supplemented by training in job-related personal skills. The unique feature of the program was that all the participants in a given work setting were drawn from the people with problems so as to minimize the usual difficulties experienced by persons with chronic unemployment problems when they find themselves competing with persons who are successful job seekers and job holders. Moreover, the workshops were led by sympathetic supervisors (often themselves ex-addicts or ex-convicts) who gradually increased the level of expected performance until, after a year or so, the trainees were able to go out into the regular job market on their own. This government-subsidized work in a supportive environment, coupled with training in personal skills, was the most ambitious effort of all we have examined to get persons with chronic problems into the labor force. Unlike vocational training in prison, supported work provided real jobs in the civilian world and training directly related to what the recipient was paid to do. Unlike work-release programs, supported work did not leave the ex-convict to sink or swim on his own in the competitive civilian job market.

Welfare recipients and ex-addicts benefited from supported work, but ex-convicts and youthful school dropouts did not. Over a twenty-seven-month observation period, the school dropouts in the project were arrested as frequently as the similar dropouts in the control group, and the ex-offenders in the project actually were arrested more frequently (seventeen more arrests per hundred persons) than the ex-offenders in the control group.

Some individuals did benefit, and they are exactly the ones we would predict would have benefited given what we know about the criminal career. School dropouts who had not been arrested before they joined the program were less likely to be arrested later on than similar dropouts in the control group; on the other hand, youths with a prior arrest record did not benefit at all from the program. . . . [This] is consistent with what we have learned from various efforts at rehabilitation; namely, young persons inexperienced in crime are much easier to change than young persons who have committed several crimes. By the same token, the older (over age thirty-five) ex-convicts seemed to benefit more from the program than the younger ex-offenders. This is consistent with the well-known tendency of many persons to "mature out of crime" in their thirties; the supported work program probably gave these people a little extra push in this direction.

The clear implication, I think, of the supported work project—and of all the studies to which I have referred—is that unemployment and other economic factors may well be connected with criminality, but the connection is not a simple one. If, as some persons often assume, "unemployment causes crime," then simply providing jobs to would-be criminals or to convicted criminals would reduce their crime rates. There is very little evidence that this is true, at least for the kinds of persons helped by MDRC. Whether the crime rate would go down if dropouts and ex-convicts held on to their jobs, we cannot say, because, as the supported work project clearly showed, within a year-and-a-half after entering the program, the dropouts and ex-convicts were no more likely to be employed than those who had never entered the program at all, despite the great and compassionate efforts made on their behalf. There are some persons for whom help, training, and jobs will make a difference—the young and criminally inexperienced dropout, the older "burned-out" ex-addict, the more mature (over age thirty-five) ex-convict. But ex-addicts, middle-aged ex-cons, and inexperienced youths do not commit most of the crimes that worry us. These are committed by the young, chronic offender.

Recall what we learned in chapter 1 from Marvin Wolfgang and his colleagues at the University of Pennsylvania. By following the criminal careers of about ten thousand boys born in Philadelphia in 1945, these scholars found that about one-third of the boys were arrested, but for about half of these, their criminal "careers" stopped with their first arrest. However, once a juvenile had been arrested three times, the chances that he would be arrested again were over 70 percent. These findings are consistent with the view that, for novice offenders (to say nothing of nonoffenders), some combination of informal social control, the deterrent effect of punishment, and the desire for normal entry into the world of work served to restrain the growth of criminality. It is among this group that we should look for evidence of the effects of changes in the probability and severity of punishment and of changes in job availability. At the other end of the scale, 6 percent of the Philadelphia boys committed five or more crimes before they were eighteen, accounting for over half of all the recorded delinquencies of the entire ten thousand boys and about two-thirds of all the violent crimes committed by the entire cohort. The evidence from MDRC is consistent with the view that job programs are not likely to be effective with these repeat offenders. Since we have only a few studies of the effect of deterrence on individuals (as opposed to large aggregates of people), we cannot be confident that increasing the certainty or severity of punishment would affect this group of hard-core, high-rate offenders, but there is some evidence in the Witte and Murray and Cox studies that it may.

Conclusions

The relationship between crime on the one hand and the rewards and penalties at the disposal of society on the other is complicated. It is not complicated, however, in the way some people imagine. It is not the case (except for a tiny handful of pathological personalities) that criminals are so unlike the rest of us as to be indifferent to the costs and benefits of the opportunities open to them. Nor is it the case that criminals have no opportunities. In the TARP study, for example, about half the convicts were employed just prior to being imprisoned. And in the Cook study, it was clear that ex-convicts can find jobs of a sort, though often not very attractive ones.

It is better to think of both people and social controls as arrayed on a continuum. People differ by degrees in the extent to which they are governed by internal restraints on criminal behavior and in the stake they have in conformity; they also differ by degrees in the extent to which they can find, hold, and benefit from a job. Similarly, sanctions and opportunities are changeable only within modest limits. We want to find out to what extent feasible changes in the certainty, swiftness, or severity of penalties will make a difference in the behavior of those "at the margin"—those, that is, who are neither so innocent nor so depraved as to be prepared to ignore small changes (which are, in fact, the only feasible changes) in the prospects of punishment. By the same token, we want to know what feasible (and again, inevitably small) changes in the availability of jobs will affect those at the margin of the labor market—those, that is, who are neither so eager for a good job or so contemptuous of "jerks" who take "straight jobs" as to ignore modest changes in job opportunities. I am aware of no evidence supporting the conventional liberal view that while the number of persons who will be affected by changing penalties is very small, the number who will be affected by increasing jobs is very large; nor am I aware of any evidence supporting the conventional conservative view, which is the opposite of this.

I believe that the weight of the evidence—aggregate statistical analyses, evaluations of experiments and quasi-experiments, and studies of individual behavior—supports the view that the rate of crime is influenced by its costs. This influence is greater—or easier to observe—for some crimes and persons than for others. It is possible to lower the crime rate by increasing the certainty of sanctions, but inducing the criminal justice system to make those changes is difficult, especially if committing the offense confers substantial benefits on the perpetrator, if apprehending and punishing the offender does not provide substantial rewards to members of the criminal justice system, or if the crime itself lacks the strong moral condemnation of society. In theory, the rate of crime should also be sensitive to the benefits of noncrime—for example, the value and availability of jobs—but thus far efforts to show that relationship have led to inconclusive results. Moreover, the nature of the connection between crime and legitimate opportunities is complex: unemployment (and prosperity!) can cause crime, crime can cause unemployment (but probably not prosperity), and both crime and unemployment may be caused by common third factors. Economic factors probably have the greatest influence on the behavior of low-rate, novice offenders and the least on high-rate, experienced ones. Despite the uncertainty that attaches to the connection between the economy and crime, I believe the wisest course of action for society is to try simultaneously to increase both the benefits of noncrime and the costs of crime, all the while bearing in mind that no feasible changes in either part of the equation is likely to produce big changes in crime rates.

Some may grant my argument that it makes sense to continue to try to make those marginal gains that are possible by simultaneously changing in desirable directions both the costs of crime and benefits of noncrime, but they may still feel that it is better to spend more heavily on one side or the other of the cost-benefit equation. I have attended numerous scholarly gatherings where I have heard learned persons subject to the most searching scrutiny any evidence purporting to show the deterrent effect of sanctions but accept with scarcely a blink the theory that crime is caused by a "lack of opportunities." Perhaps what they mean is that since the evidence on both propositions is equivocal, then it does less harm to believe in—and invest in—the "benign" (that is, job-creation) program. If so, they are surely wrong. If we try to make the penalties for crime swifter and more certain, and it should turn out that deterrence does not work, then all we have done is increase the risks facing persons who commit a crime. If we fail to increase the certainty and swiftness of penalties, and it should turn out that deterrence *does* work, then we have needlessly increased the risk of innocent persons being victimized.

There is one objection to this line of analysis with which I do agree. If we try to improve on deterrence by sharply increasing the severity of sentences, and we are wrong, then we may spend a great deal of money and unnecessarily blight the lives of offenders who could safely be punished for much shorter periods of time. Reaching a sound judgment about how severe penalties should be is a much more difficult matter than deciding how certain they should be; indeed, one cannot reach such a judgment at all on purely empirical grounds. The problem of severity is inextricably bound up with the problem of justice. However, we can say some things, on scientific grounds, about what the crime-reduction effect of prison sentences of varying lengths may be, regardless of whether anybody is deterred by the prospect of such a sentence. This is the question of incapacitation. . . .

NO 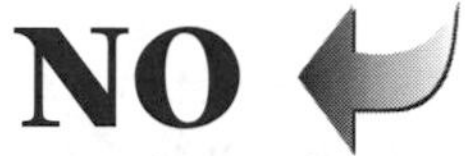

Jeffrey Reiman

To the Vanquished Belong the Spoils: Who Is Winning the Losing War against Crime?

> In every case the laws are made by the ruling party in its own interest; a democracy makes democratic laws, a despot autocratic ones, and so on. By making these laws they define as "just" for their subjects whatever is for their own interest, and they call anyone who breaks them a "wrongdoer" and punish him accordingly.
>
> —Thrasymachus, in Plato's *Republic*

Why Is the Criminal Justice System Failing?

The streams of my argument flow together at this point in a question: *Why is it happening?* I have shown how it is no accident that "the offender at the end of the road in prison is likely to be a member of the lowest social and economic groups in the country." I have shown that this is not an accurate group portrait of who threatens society—it is a picture of whom the criminal justice system *selects* for arrest and imprisonment from among those who threaten society. It is an image distorted by the shape of the criminal justice carnival mirror. This much we have seen and now we want to know why: *Why is the criminal justice system allowed to function in a fashion that neither protects society nor achieves justice? Why is the criminal justice system failing?*

My answer to these questions will require looking at who benefits from this failure and who suffers from it. More particularly, I will argue that the rich and powerful in the United States—those who derive the greatest advantage from the persistence of the social and economic system as it is currently organized—reap benefits from the failure of criminal justice that has been documented in this book. However—as I cautioned early on—this should not lead the reader to think that my explanation for the current shape of the criminal justice system is a "conspiracy theory."

A conspiracy theory would argue that the rich and the powerful, seeing the benefits to be derived from the failure of criminal justice, consciously set out to use their wealth and power to make it fail. There are many problems

From Jeffrey Reiman, THE RICH GET RICHER AND THE POOR GET PRISON: IDEOLOGY, CLASS AND CRIMINAL JUSTICE 5/E. Published by Allyn and Bacon, Boston, MA. Notes omitted.

with such a theory. First, it is virtually impossible to prove. If the conspiracy succeeds, then this is possible only to the extent that it is kept secret. Thus, evidence for a conspiracy would be as difficult to obtain as the conspiracy was successful. Second, conspiracy theories strain credibility precisely because the degree of secrecy they would require seems virtually impossible in a society as open and fractious as our own. If there is a "ruling elite" in the United States that comprises a group as small as the richest *one-thousandth of 1 percent* of the population, it would still be made up of more than 2,000 people. To think that a conspiracy to make the criminal justice system fail in the way it does could be kept secret among this number of people in a country like ours is just unbelievable. Third, conspiracy theories are not plausible because they do not correspond to the way most people act most of the time. Although there is no paucity of conscious mendacity and manipulation in our politics, most people most of the time seem sincerely to believe that what they are doing is right. Whether this is a tribute to human beings' creative capacities to rationalize what they do or just a matter of shortsightedness, it seems a fact. For all these reasons, it is not plausible that so fateful and harmful a policy as the failure of criminal justice could be purposely maintained by the rich and powerful. Rather, we need an explanation that is compatible with believing that policy makers, on the whole, are simply doing what they sincerely believe is right.

To understand how the Pyrrhic defeat theory explains the current shape of our failing criminal justice policy, note that this failure is really *three* failures that work together. First, there is the failure to implement policies that stand a good chance of reducing crime and the harm it causes. . . . Second, there is the failure to identify as crimes the harmful acts of the rich and powerful. . . . Third, there is the failure to eliminate economic bias in the criminal justice system, so that the poor continue to have a substantially greater chance than better-off people of being arrested, charged, convicted, and penalized for committing the acts that are treated as crimes. . . . The effect of the first failure is that there remains a large amount of crime—even if crime rates occasionally dip as a result of factors outside the control of the criminal justice system, such as the decline in unemployment or the routinization of the illicit drug trade. The effect of the second failure is that the acts identified as crimes are those done predominantly by the poor. The effect of the third failure is that the individuals who are arrested and convicted for crimes are predominantly poor people. The effect of the three failures working together is that we are largely unprotected against the harmful acts of the well off, while at the same time we are confronted on the streets and in our homes with a real and large threat of crime and in the courts and prisons with a large and visible population of poor criminals. And lest it be thought that the public does not feel threatened by crime, consider that a recent poll shows that, though crime is down, 41 percent of Americans believe that there is more crime than there was the year before. In short, the effect of current criminal justice policy is at once to narrow the public's conception of what is dangerous to acts of the poor and to present a convincing embodiment of this danger.

The Pyrrhic defeat theory aims to explain the *persistence* of this failing criminal justice policy, rather than its origins. The criminal justice system we have today originated as a result of complex historical factors that have to do with the development of the common law tradition in England, the particular form in which this was transplanted on American soil, and the zigzagging course of reform and reaction that has marked our history since the English colonies were transformed into an independent American nation. The study of these factors would surely require another book longer than this one—but, more important, for our purposes it would be unnecessary because it is not the origin of criminal justice policy and practices that is puzzling. The focus on one-on-one harm reflects the main ways in which people harmed each other in the days before large-scale industrialization; the refusal to implement policies that might reduce crime (such as gun control or legalization of heroin or amelioration of poverty) reflects a defensive and punitive response to crime that is natural and understandable, if not noble and farsighted; and the existence of economic bias in the criminal justice system reflects the real economic and political inequalities that characterize the society in which that system is embedded. What is puzzling, then, is not how these policies came to be what they are, but why they persist in the face of their failure to achieve either security or justice. The explanation I shall offer for this persistence I call "historical inertia."

The historical inertia explanation argues that current criminal justice policy persists because it fails in a way that does not give rise to an effective demand for change, for two reasons. First, this failing system provides benefits for those with the power to make changes, while it imposes costs on those without such power. Second, because the criminal justice system shapes the public's conception of what is dangerous; it creates the impression that the harms it is fighting are *the real threats* to society—thus, even when people see that the system is less than a roaring success, they generally do no more than demand more of the same: more police, more prisons, longer prison sentences, and so on.

Consider first the benefits that the system provides for those with wealth and power. I have argued that the triple failure of criminal justice policy diverts attention from the harmful (noncriminal) acts of the well off and confronts us in our homes and on our streets with a real, substantial threat of crime and in the courts and prisons with a large and visible population of poor criminals. This in turn conveys a vivid image to the American people, namely, that *there is a real threat to our lives and limbs, and it is a threat from the poor.* This image provides benefits to the rich and powerful in America. It carries an *ideological message* that serves to protect their wealth and privilege. Crudely put, the message is this:

- The threat to "law-abiding Middle America" comes from below them on the economic ladder, not above them.
- The poor are morally defective, and thus their poverty is their own fault, not a symptom of social or economic injustice.

The effect of this message is to funnel the discontent of middle Americans into hostility toward, and fear of, the poor. It leads Americans to ignore the ways in which they are injured and robbed by the acts of the affluent . . . and leads them to demand harsher doses of "law and order" aimed mainly at the lower classes. Most important, it nudges middle Americans toward a *conservative* defense of American society with its large disparities of wealth, power, and opportunity—and nudges them away from a progressive demand for equality and an equitable distribution of wealth and power.

On the other hand, but equally important, is that those who are mainly victimized by the "failure" to reduce crime are by and large the poor themselves. The people who are hurt the most by the failure of the criminal justice system are those with the least power to change it. In 1999, households with annual income less than $7,500 were victims of violent crimes at a rate nearly three times that of households earning $75,000 and above. Indeed, as Table 1 shows, rates of victimization by crimes in all categories are substantially higher for the poorest segment of the population, and drop dramatically as we ascend the economic ladder.

The difference in the rates of property crime victimization between rich and poor understates the difference in the harms that result. The poor are far less likely than the affluent to have insurance against theft, and because they have little to start with, what they lose to theft takes a much deeper bite out of their ability to meet their basic needs. Needless to add, the various noncriminal harms . . . (occupational hazards, pollution, poverty, and so on) also fall more harshly on workers and those at the bottom of society than on those at the top.

Table 1

Criminal Victimization by Family Income, 2000 (Estimated rate of personal victimization per 1,000 Persons age 12 and older)

	Family Income			
Type of Victimization	**Less than $7,500**	**$7,500 to 14,999**	**$25,000 to $34,999**	**$75,000 or More**
Crimes of violence	60.3	37.8	29.8	22.3
Robbery with injuryq	2.1*	1.0	1.0*	0.6*
Rape/Sexual Assault	5.2	1.7	1.9	0.2*
Aggravated Assault	14.7	9.5	6.2	4.4
Household Burglary	67.0	44.2	37.1	23.1

Source: *Criminal Victimization in the United States,* Statistical Tables. BJS, Aug. 2002, NCJ 188290. Table 14. (http://www.ojp.usdoj.gov/bjs/pub/pdf/cvus0001.pdf).

*Based on 10 or fewer cases.

To summarize, those who suffer most from the failure to reduce crime (and the failure to treat noncriminal harms as crimes) are not in a position to change criminal justice policy. Those who are in a position to change the policy are not seriously harmed by its failure—indeed, there are actual benefits to them from that failure. Note that I have not said that criminal justice policy is created to achieve this distribution of benefits and burdens. Instead, my claim is that the criminal justice policy that has emerged piecemeal over time and usually with the best of intentions happens to produce this distribution of benefits. And because criminal justice policy happens to produce this distribution, there is no inclination to change the criminal justice system among people with the power to do so. Moreover, because the criminal justice system shapes the public's conception of what is dangerous, it effectively limits the public's conception of how to protect itself to more of the same. Thus, though it fails, it persists.

Before proceeding, a new component of the explanation of the failure of criminal justice now deserves mention: the growing trend toward the privatization of prisons. The rapid and enormous increase in the U.S. prison population over the past 15 years or so has placed strains on state budgets. New policy initiatives, such as the "three strikes and you're out" statutes enacted in numerous states, are likely only to continue the increase and the budgetary strains. This has given states an incentive to hire out their prison facilities to private contractors, who claim to be able to run prisons at 10 to 20 percent less cost than state governments (though this claim has proven to be exaggerated). Already, 25 states plus Puerto Rico and the District of Columbia have passed laws allowing private contractors to run correctional facilities. The result has been a dramatic increase in the number of prisoners under private control. In the ten years from 1985 to 1995, the number of prison beds under private management grew from 935 to 63,595, an increase of nearly 7,000 percent! Though this is still only a small percentage of all prison beds, Charles Thomas, director of the Private Prisons Project at the University of Florida, estimates that there will be some 360,000 privately run prison beds by the year 2004.

Wall Street has not failed to notice this trend, and many stock analysts are urging their clients to invest in the major corporations in the field, such as Corrections Corporation of America (CCC) and Wackenhut Corrections. An article in *The Wall Street Journal* carries the headline: "Shares of Wackenhut Break Out as Prisons Become a Hot Industry." An article on private prisons in *Forbes* is titled: "A Surefire Growth Industry." Writes Paulette Thomas, in a *Wall Street Journal* article titled "Making Crime Pay":

> The gritty work of criminal justice has become the kind of big-ticket commerce to attract the loftiest names in finance. Goldman Sachs & Co., Prudential Insurance Co. of America, Smith Barney Shearson Inc., and Merrill Lynch & Co. Inc. are among those competing to underwrite prison construction with private tax-exempt bonds—no voter approval required.

Ms. Thomas likens the new development to that of the old "military-industrial complex," of which President Eisenhower warned in his farewell address. The comparison is appropriate because many firms in "the defense establishment are cashing in too, sensing a logical new line of business to help them offset military cutbacks."

Eric Schlosser takes up this analogy in an article in the *Atlantic Monthly,* titled "The Prison-Industrial Complex." He writes:

> The prison-industrial complex is not a conspiracy. . . . It is a confluence of interests that has given prison construction in the United States a seemingly unstoppable momentum. It is composed of politicians . . . who have used the fear of crime to gain votes; impoverished rural areas where prisons have become a cornerstone of economic development; [and] private companies that regard the roughly $35 billion spent each year on corrections not as a burden on American taxpayers but as a lucrative market.

What is most troubling about these developments is that, as criminologist Paul Leighton points out, "they create large numbers of people who have a vested financial interest in having a large and increasing incarceration rate. . . . The American Legislative Exchange Council (ALEC), an organization that lobbies state legislators, and that receives substantial contributions from CCC, says proudly that lawmakers on its crime task force have been actively leading in the drive for more incarceration in the states. The National Institute on Money in State Politics reports that "Private prison companies gave more than $1.1 million in campaign contributions to state-level candidates in 14 Southern states during the 2000 elections." In short, thus far in this book I have been pointing out how *the rich get richer* WHILE *the poor get prison,* but the privatization movement points to a new phase in which *the rich get richer* BECAUSE *the poor get prison!*

My argument in the remainder of this chapter takes the following form. In the section titled "The Poverty of Criminals and the Crime of Poverty," I spell out the content of the ideological message broadcast by the failure of the criminal justice system. In the section titled "Ideology, or How to Fool Enough of the People Enough of the Time," I discuss the *nature* of ideology in general and the *need* for it in America. For those who doubt that our legal system could function in such questionable ways, I also present evidence on how the criminal justice system has been used in the past to protect the rich and powerful against those who would challenge their privileges or their policies. These sections, then, flesh out the historical inertia explanation of the failure of criminal justice by showing the ideological benefits that that failure yields and to whom.

Ultimately, the test of the argument in this chapter is whether it provides a plausible explanation of the failure of criminal justice and draws the arguments of the previous chapters together into a coherent theory of contemporary criminal justice policy and practice.

The Poverty of Criminals and the Crime of Poverty

Criminal justice is a very visible part of the American scene. As fact and fiction, countless images of crime and the struggle against it assail our senses daily, even hourly. In every newspaper, in every TV or radio newscast, there is at least one criminal justice story and often more. It is as if we live in an embattled city, besieged by the forces of crime and bravely defended by the forces of the law, and as we go about our daily tasks, we are always conscious of the war raging not very far away. Newspapers bring us daily and newscasts bring us hourly reports from the "front." Between reports, we are vividly reminded of the stakes and the desperateness of the battle by fictionalized portrayals of the struggle between the forces of the law and the breakers of the law. There is scarcely an hour on television without some dramatization of the struggle against crime. ("Before the average American child leaves elementary school, researchers estimate that he or she will have witnessed more than 8,000 murders on television." Although a few of these are killed by science fiction monsters, the figure still suggests that the extent of the impact of the televised portrayal of crime and the struggle against it on the imaginations of Americans is nothing short of astounding—particularly on children. And, in a joint statement on the impact of entertainment violence on children, issued on July 26, 2000, the American Academy of Pediatrics, American Medical Association, American Academy of Child and Adolescent Psychiatry, and the American Psychological Association, stated that "the average American child spends as much as 28 hours a week watching television," and "well over 1000 studies—including reports from the Surgeon General's office, the National Institute of Mental Health, and numerous studies conducted by leading figures within our medical and public health organizations—our own members—point overwhelmingly to a causal connection between media violence and aggressive behavior in some children.") In the mid-1980s, it was estimated that "detective, police, and other criminal justice-related programs accounted for some eighty percent of prime-time TV viewing." A quick look at the television section of the newspaper suggests that, if anything, this has only increased in recent years. If we add to this the news accounts, the panel discussions, the movies, the novels, the comic books, and the TV cartoon shows that imitate the comics, as well as the political speeches about crime, there can be no doubt that as fact or fantasy or both, criminal justice is vividly present in the imaginations of most Americans.

This is no accident. Everyone can relate to criminal justice in personal and emotional terms. Everyone has some fear of crime, and . . . just about everyone has committed some. Everyone knows the primitive satisfaction of seeing justice done and the evildoers served up their just deserts. Furthermore, in reality or in fiction, criminal justice is naturally dramatic. It contains the acts of courage and cunning, the high risks and high stakes, and the life-and-death struggle between good and evil missing from the routine lives so many of us lead. To identify with the struggle against crime is to expand one's experience vicariously to include the danger, the suspense, the triumphs, the meaningfulness—in a word, the drama—often missing in ordinary life. How else can we explain the seemingly bottomless appetite Americans have for the endless repetition, in only slightly altered form, of the same theme: the struggle of the forces of law against the forces of crime? Criminal justice has a firm grip on the imaginations of Americans and is thus in a unique position to convey a message to Americans and to convey it with drama and with conviction.

Let us now look at this message in detail. Our task falls naturally into two parts. There is an ideological message supportive of the status quo, built into *any* criminal justice system by its very nature. Even if the criminal justice system were not failing, even if it were not biased against the poor, it would still—by its very nature—broadcast a message supportive of established institutions. This is the *implicit ideology of criminal justice.* Beyond this, there is an additional ideological message conveyed by the *failure* of the system and by its *biased* concentration on the poor. I call this the *bonus of bias.*

The Implicit Ideology of Criminal Justice

Any criminal justice system like ours conveys a subtle yet powerful message in support of established institutions. It does this for two interconnected reasons. First, it concentrates on *individual* wrongdoers. This means that *it diverts our attention away from our institutions, away from consideration of whether our institutions themselves are wrong or unjust or indeed "criminal."*

Second, the criminal law is put forth as the *minimum neutral ground rules* for any social living. We are taught that no society can exist without rules against theft and violence, and thus the criminal law seems to be politically neutral, the minimum requirements for *any* society, the minimum obligations that any individual owes his or her fellows to make social life of any decent sort possible. Thus, it not only diverts our attention away from the possible injustice of our social institutions, the criminal law bestows upon those institutions the mantle of its own neutrality.

Because the criminal law protects the established institutions (the prevailing economic arrangements are protected by laws against theft, and so on), attacks on those established institutions become equivalent to violations of the minimum requirements for any social life at all. In effect, the criminal law enshrines the established institutions as equivalent to the minimum requirements for *any* decent social existence—and it brands the individual who attacks those institutions as one who has declared war on *all* organized society and who must therefore be met with the weapons of war.

This is the powerful magic of criminal justice. By virtue of its focus on *individual* criminals, it diverts us from the evils of the social order. By virtue of its presumed neutrality, it transforms the established social (and economic) order from being merely *one* form of society open to critical comparison with others into *the* conditions of *any* social order and thus immune from criticism. Let us look more closely at this process.

What is the effect of focusing on individual guilt? Not only does this divert our attention from the possible evils in our institutions, it puts forth half the problem of justice as if it were the *whole* problem. To focus on individual guilt is to ask whether the individual citizen has fulfilled his or her obligations to his or her fellow citizens. *It is to look away from the issue of whether the fellow citizens have fulfilled their obligations to him or her.* To look only at individual responsibility is to look away from social responsibility. Writing about her stint as a "story analyst" for a prime-time TV "real crime" show based on videotapes of actual police busts, Debra Seagal describes the way focus on individual criminals deflects attention away from the social context of crime and how television reproduces this effect in millions of homes daily:

> By the time our 9 million viewers flip on their tubes, we've reduced fifty or sixty hours of mundane and compromising video into short, action-packed segments of tantalizing, crack-filled, dope-dealing, junkie-busting cop culture. How easily we downplay the pathos of the suspect; how cleverly we breeze past the complexities that cast doubt on the very system that has produced the criminal activity in the first place.

Seagal's description illustrates as well how a television program that shows nothing but videos of actual events, that uses no reenactments whatsoever, can distort reality by selecting and recombining pieces of real events.

A study of 69 TV law and crime dramas finds that fictional presentations of homicide focus on individual motivations and ignore social conditions:

> Television crime dramas portray these events as specific psychological episodes in the characters' lives and little, if any, effort is made to connect them to basic social institutions or the nature of society within which they occur.

To look only at individual criminality is to close one's eyes to social injustice and to close one's ears to the question of whether our social institutions have exploited or violated the individual. *Justice is a two-way street—but criminal justice is a one-way street.* Individuals owe obligations to their fellow citizens because their fellow citizens owe obligations to them. Criminal justice focuses on the first and looks away from the second. *Thus, by focusing on individual responsibility for crime, the criminal justice system effectively acquits the existing social order of any charge of injustice!*

This is an extremely important bit of ideological alchemy. It stems from the fact that the same act can be criminal or not, unjust or just, depending on the circumstances in which it takes place. Killing someone is ordinarily a crime, but if it is in self-defense or to stop a deadly crime, it is not. Taking property by force is usually a crime, but if the taking is retrieving what has been stolen, then no crime has been committed. Acts of violence are ordinarily crimes, but if the violence is provoked by the threat of violence or by oppressive conditions, then, like the Boston Tea Party, what might ordinarily be called criminal is celebrated as just. This means that when we call an act a crime, *we are also making an implicit judgment about the conditions in response to which it takes place.* When we call an act a crime, we are saying that the conditions in which it occurs are not themselves criminal or deadly or oppressive or so unjust as to make an extreme response reasonable or justified or non-criminal. This means that when the system holds an individual responsible for a crime, *it implicitly conveys the message that the social conditions in which the crime occurred are not responsible for the crime,* that they are not so unjust as to make a violent response to them excusable.

Judges are prone to hold that an individual's responsibility for a violent crime is diminished if it was provoked by something that might lead a "reasonable man" to respond violently and that criminal responsibility is eliminated if the act was in response to conditions so intolerable that any "reasonable man" would have been likely to respond in the same way. In this vein, the law acquits those who kill or injure in self-defense and treats leniently those who commit a crime when confronted with extreme provocation. The law treats understandingly the man who kills his wife's lover and the woman who kills her brutal husband, even when neither has acted directly in self-defense. By this logic, when we hold an individual completely responsible for a crime, we are saying that the conditions in which it occurred are such that a "reasonable man" should find them tolerable. In other words, by focusing on individual responsibility for crimes, *the criminal justice system broadcasts the message that the social order itself is reasonable and not intolerably unjust.*

Thus, the criminal justice system focuses moral condemnation on individuals and deflects it away from the social order that may have either violated the individual's rights or dignity or literally pushed him or her to the brink of the crime. This not only serves to carry the message that our social institutions are not in need of fundamental questioning, it further suggests that the justice of our institutions is obvious, not to be doubted. Indeed, because it is deviations from these institutions that are crimes, the established institutions become the implicit standard of justice from which criminal deviations are measured.

This leads to the second way in which a criminal justice system always conveys an implicit ideology. It arises from the presumption that the criminal law is nothing but the politically neutral minimum requirements of any decent social life. What is the consequence of this? As already suggested, this presumption transforms the prevailing social order into justice incarnate and all violations of the prevailing order into injustice incarnate. This process is so obvious that it may be easily missed.

Consider, for example, the law against theft. It does seem to be one of the minimum requirements of social living. As long as there is scarcity, any society—capitalist or socialist—will need rules to deter individuals from taking what does not belong to them. The law against theft, however, is more: It is a law against stealing what individuals *presently own.* Such a law has the effect of making present property relations a part of the criminal law.

Because stealing is a violation of the law, this means that present property relations become the implicit standard of justice against which criminal deviations are measured. Because criminal law is thought of as the minimum requirements of *any* social life, this means that present property relations become the equivalent of the minimum requirements of *any* social life. The criminal who would alter the present property relations becomes someone who is declaring war on all organized society. The question of whether this "war" is provoked by the injustice or brutality of the society is swept aside. Indeed, this suggests yet another way in which the criminal justice system conveys an ideological message in support of the established society.

Not only does the criminal justice system acquit the social order of any charge of injustice; it specifically cloaks the society's own crime-producing tendencies. I have already observed that by blaming the individual for a crime, the society is acquitted of the charge of injustice. I would like to go further now and argue that by blaming the individual for a crime, the society is acquitted of the charge of *complicity* in that crime. This is a point worth developing, because many observers have maintained that modern competitive societies such as our own have structural features that tend to generate crime. Thus, holding the individual responsible for his or her crime serves the function of taking the rest of society off the hook for their role in sustaining and benefiting from social arrangements that produce crime. Let us take a brief detour to look more closely at this process.

Cloward and Ohlin argued in their book, *Delinquency and Opportunity,* that much crime is the result of the discrepancy between social goals and the legitimate opportunities available for achieving them. Simply put, in our society every-one is encouraged to be a success, but the avenues to success are open only to some. The conventional wisdom of our free-enterprise democracy is that anyone can be a success if he or she has the talent and the ambition. Thus, if one is not a success, it is because of one's own shortcomings: laziness or lack of ability or both. On the other hand, opportunities to achieve success are not equally open to all. Access to the best schools and the best jobs is effectively closed to all but a few of the poor and becomes more available only as one goes up the economic ladder. The result is that many are called but few are chosen. Many who have taken the bait and accepted the belief in the importance of success and the belief that achieving success is a result of individual ability must cope with feelings of frustration and failure that result when they find the avenues to success closed. Cloward and Ohlin argue that one method of coping with these stresses is to develop alternative avenues to success. Crime is such an alternative avenue.

Crime is a means by which people who believe in the American dream pursue it when they find the traditional routes barred. Indeed, it is plain to see that the goals pursued by most criminals are as American as apple pie. I suspect one of the reasons that American moviegoers enjoy gangster films—movies in which gangsters such as Al Capone, Bonnie and Clyde, or Butch Cassidy and the Sundance Kid are the heroes, as distinct from police and detective films whose heroes are defenders of the law—is that even when we deplore the hero's methods, we identify with his or her notion of success, because it is ours as well, and we admire the courage and cunning displayed in achieving that success.

It is important to note that the discrepancy between success goals and legitimate opportunities in America is not an aberration. It is a structural feature of modern competitive industrialized society, a feature from which many benefits flow. Cloward and Ohlin write that

> . . . a crucial problem in the industrial world is to locate and train the most talented persons in every generation, irrespective of the vicissitudes of birth, to occupy technical work roles. Since we cannot know in advance who can best fulfill the requirements of the various occupational roles, the matter is presumably settled through the process of competition. But how can men throughout the social order be motivated to participate in this competition?
>
> One of the ways in which the industrial society attempts to solve this problem is by defining success-goals as potentially accessible to all, regardless of race, creed, or socioeconomic position.

Because these universal goals are urged to encourage a competition to select the best, there are necessarily fewer openings than seekers. Also, because those who achieve success are in a particularly good position to exploit their success to make access for their own children easier, the competition is rigged to work in favor of the middle and upper classes. As a result, "many lower-class persons are the victims of a contradiction between the goals toward which they have been led to orient themselves and socially structured means of striving for these goals."

> [The poor] experience desperation born of the certainty that their position in the economic structure is relatively fixed and immutable—a desperation made all the more poignant by their exposure to a cultural ideology in which failure to orient oneself upward is regarded as a moral defect and failure to become mobile as a proof of it.

The outcome is predictable. "Under these conditions, there is an acute pressure to depart from institutional norms and to adopt illegitimate alternatives."

This means that the very way in which our society is structured to draw out the talents and energies that go into producing our high standard of living has a costly side effect: It produces crime. By holding individuals responsible for this crime, those who enjoy that high standard of living can have their cake and eat it too. They can reap the benefits of the competition for success and escape the responsibility of paying for the costs of the competition. By holding the poor crook legally and morally guilty, the rest of society not only passes the costs of competition on to the poor, they effectively deny that they (the affluent) are the beneficiaries of an economic system that exacts such a high toll in frustration and suffering.

William Bonger, the Dutch Marxist criminologist, maintained that competitive capitalism produces egotistic motives and undermines compassion for the misfortunes of others and thus makes human beings literally *more capable of crime*—more capable of preying on their fellows without moral inhibition or remorse—than earlier cultures that emphasized cooperation rather than competition. Here again, the criminal justice system relieves those who benefit from the American economic system of the costs of that system. By holding criminals morally and individually responsible for their crimes, we can forget that the motives that lead to crime—the drive for success at any cost, linked with the beliefs that success means outdoing others and that violence is an acceptable way of achieving one's goals—are the *same motives* that powered that drive across the American continent and that continue to fuel the engine of America's prosperity.

David Gordon, a contemporary political economist, maintains "that nearly all crimes in capitalist societies represent perfectly *rational* responses to the structure of institutions upon which capitalist societies are based." Like Bonger, Gordon believes that capitalism tends to provoke crime in all economic strata. This is so because most crime is motivated by a desire for property or money and is an understandable way of coping with the pressures of inequality, competition, and insecurity, all of which are essential ingredients of capitalism. Capitalism depends, Gordon writes,

> . . . on basically competitive forms of social and economic interaction and upon substantial inequalities in the allocation of social resources. Without inequalities, it would be much more difficult to induce workers to work in alienating environments. Without competition and a competitive ideology, workers might not be inclined to struggle to improve their relative income and status in society by working harder. Finally, although rights of property are protected, capitalist societies do not guarantee economic security to most of their individual members. Individuals must fend for themselves, finding the best available opportunities to provide for themselves and their families. Driven by the fear of economic insecurity and by a competitive desire to gain some o the goods unequally distributed throughout the society, many individuals will eventually become "criminals."

To the extent that a society makes crime a reasonable alternative for a large number of its members from all classes, that society is itself not very reasonably or humanely organized and bears some degree of responsibility for the crime it encourages. Because the criminal law is put forth as the minimum requirements that can be expected of any "reasonable man," its enforcement amounts to a denial of the real nature of the social order to which Gordon and the others point. Here again, by blaming the individual criminal, the criminal justice system serves implicitly but dramatically to acquit the society of its criminality.

The Bonus of Bias

We now consider the additional ideological bonus derived from the criminal justice system's bias against the poor. This bonus is a product of the association of crime and poverty in the popular mind. This association, the merging of the "criminal classes" and the "lower classes" into the "dangerous classes," was not invented in America. The word *villain is* derived from the Latin *villanus,* which means a farm servant. The term *villein* was used in feudal England to refer to a serf who farmed the land of a great lord and who was wholly subject to that lord. In this respect, our present criminal justice system is heir to a long tradition.

The value of this association was already seen when we explored the average citizen's concept of the Typical Criminal and the Typical Crime. It is quite obvious that throughout the great mass of Middle America, far more fear and hostility are directed toward the predatory acts of the poor than toward the acts of the rich. Compare the fate of politicians in recent history who call for tax reform, income redistribution, prosecution of corporate crime, and any sort of regulation of business that would make it better serve American social goals with that of politicians who erect their platform on a call for "law and order," more police, fewer limits on police power, and stiffer prison sentences for criminals—and consider this in light of what we have already seen about the real dangers posed by corporate crime and "business as usual."

It seems clear that Americans have been effectively deceived as to what are the greatest dangers to their lives, limbs, and possessions. The very persistence with which the system functions to apprehend and punish poor crooks and ignore or slap on the wrist equally or more dangerous individuals is testimony to the sticking power of this deception. That Americans continue to tolerate the comparatively gentle treatment meted out to white-collar criminals, corporate price fixers, industrial polluters, and political-influence peddlers while voting in droves to lock up more poor people faster and for longer indicates the degree to which they harbor illusions as to who most threatens them. It is perhaps also part of the explanation for the continued dismal failure of class-based politics in America. American workers rarely seem able to forget their differences and unite to defend their shared interests against the rich whose wealth they produce. Ethnic divisions serve this divisive function well, but undoubtedly the vivid portrayal of the poor—and, of course, blacks—as hovering birds of prey waiting for the opportunity to snatch away the worker's meager gains serves also to deflect opposition away from the upper classes. A politician who promises to keep working-class communities free of blacks and the prisons full of them can get votes even if the major portion of his or her policies amount to continuation of the favored treatment of the rich at their expense. The sensationalistic use, in the 1988 presidential election, of photos of Willie Horton (a convicted black criminal who committed a brutal rape while out of prison on a furlough) suggests that such tactics are effective politics.

The most important "bonus" derived from the identification of crime and poverty is that it paints the picture that the threat to decent middle Americans comes from those below them on the economic ladder, not from those above. For this to happen the system must not only identify crime and poverty, *it must also fail to reduce crime so that it remains a real threat.* By doing this, it deflects the fear and discontent of middle Americans, and their possible opposition, away from the wealthy.

There are other bonuses as well. For instance, if the criminal justice system sends out a message that bestows legitimacy on present property relations, the dramatic impact is greatly enhanced if the violator of the present arrangements is without property. In other words, the crimes of the well-to-do "redistribute" property among the haves. In that sense, they do not pose a symbolic challenge to the larger system in which some have much and many have little or nothing. If the criminal threat can be portrayed as coming from the poor, then the punishment of the poor criminal becomes a morality play in which the sanctity and legitimacy of the system in which some have plenty and others have little or nothing is dramatically affirmed. It matters little whom the poor criminals really victimize. What counts is that middle Americans come to fear that those poor criminals are out to steal what they own.

There is yet another bonus for the powerful in America, produced by the identification of crime and poverty. It might be thought that the identification of crime and poverty would produce sympathy for the criminals. My suspicion is that it produces or at least reinforces the reverse: *hostility toward the poor.*

There is little evidence that Americans are very sympathetic to poor criminals. Very few Americans believe poverty to be a cause of crime (6 percent of those questioned in a 1981 survey, although 21 percent thought unemployment was a cause—in keeping with our general blindness to class, these questions are not even to be found in recent surveys). Other surveys find that most Americans believe that the police should be tougher than they are now in dealing with crime (83 percent of those questioned in a 1972 survey); that courts do not deal harshly enough with criminals (68 percent of those questioned in 2000); that a majority of Americans would vote for the death penalty for convicted murderers (73 percent of those questioned in 1996); and that most would be more likely to vote for a candidate who advocated tougher sentences for lawbreakers (83 percent of those questioned in a 1972 survey).

Indeed, the experience with white collar crime . . . suggests that sympathy for criminals begins to flower only when we approach the higher reaches of the ladder of wealth and power. For some poor ghetto youth who robs a liquor store, five years in a penitentiary is our idea of tempering justice with mercy. When corporate crooks rob millions, incarceration is rare. A fine is usually thought sufficient punishment.

My view is that, because the criminal justice system, in fact and fiction, deals with *individual legal and moral guilt,* the association of crime with poverty does not mitigate the image of individual moral responsibility for crime, the image that crime is the result of an individual's poor character. It does the reverse: It generates the association of poverty and individual moral failing and thus *the belief that poverty itself is a sign of poor or weak character.* The clearest evidence that Americans hold this belief is to be found in the fact that attempts to aid the poor are regarded as acts of charity rather than as acts of justice. Our welfare system has all the demeaning attributes of an institution designed to give handouts to the undeserving and none of the dignity of an institution designed to make good on our responsibilities to our fellow human beings. If we acknowledged the degree to which our economic and social institutions themselves breed poverty, we would have to recognize our own responsibilities toward the poor. If we can convince ourselves that the poor are poor because of their own shortcomings, particularly moral shortcomings such as incontinence and indolence, then we need acknowledge no such responsibility to the poor. Indeed, we can go further and pat ourselves on the back for our generosity in handing out the little that we do, and, of course, we can make our recipients go through all the indignities that mark them as the undeserving objects of our benevolence. By and large, this has been the way in which Americans have dealt with their poor. It is a way that enables us to avoid asking the question of why the richest nation in the world continues to produce massive poverty. It is my view that this conception of the poor is subtly conveyed by how our criminal justice system functions.

Obviously, no ideological message could be more supportive of the present social and economic order than this. It suggests that poverty is a sign of individual failing, not a symptom of social or economic injustice. It tells us loud and clear that massive poverty in the midst of abundance is not a sign pointing toward the need for fundamental changes in our social and economic institutions. It suggests that the poor are poor because they deserve to be poor or at least because they lack the strength of character to overcome poverty. When the poor are seen to be poor in character, then economic poverty coincides with moral poverty and the economic order coincides with the moral order. As if a divine hand guided its workings, capitalism leads to everyone getting what he or she morally deserves!

If this association takes root, then when the poor individual is found guilty of a crime, the criminal justice system acquits the society of its responsibility not only for crime *but for poverty as well.*

With this, the ideological message of criminal justice is complete. The poor rather than the rich are seen as the enemies of the majority of decent middle Americans. Our social and economic institutions are held to be responsible for neither crime nor poverty and thus are in need of no fundamental questioning or reform. The poor are poor because they are poor of character. The economic order and the moral order are one. To the extent that this message sinks in, the wealthy can rest easily—even if they cannot sleep the sleep of the just.

We can understand why the criminal justice system is allowed to create the image of crime as the work of the poor and fails to reduce it so that the threat of crime remains real and credible. The result is ideological alchemy of the highest order. The poor are seen as the real threat to decent society. The ultimate sanctions of criminal justice dramatically sanctify the present social and economic order, and *the poverty of criminals makes poverty itself an individual moral crime!*

Such are the ideological fruits of a losing war against crime whose distorted image is reflected in the criminal justice carnival mirror and widely broadcast to reach the minds and imaginations of America.

Ideology, or How to Fool Enough of the People Enough of the Time

What Is Ideology?

The view that the laws of a state or nation are made to serve the interests of those with power, rather than to promote the well-being of the whole society, is not a new discovery made in the wake of Watergate. It is a doctrine with a pedigree even older than Christianity. Writing during the fourth century B.C., virtually at the dawn of Western thought, Plato expressed this view through the lips of Thrasymachus. A more contemporary and more systematic formulation of the idea is found in the works of Karl Marx, written during the nineteenth century, not long after the dawn of Western industrialism. Marx wrote in *The Communist Manifesto* that the bourgeoisie—the class of owners of businesses and factories, the class of capitalists—has

> . . . conquered for itself, in the modern representative State, exclusive political sway. The executive of the modern tile is but a committee for managing the common affairs of the whole bourgeoisie.

Anyone who thinks this is a ridiculous idea ought to look at the backgrounds of our political leaders. The vast majority of the president's cabinet, the administrators of the federal regulatory agencies, and the members of the two houses of Congress come from the ranks of business or are lawyers who serve business. Many still maintain their business ties or law practices, with no sense of a conflict of interest with their political role. Even those who start from humble beginnings are usually quite rich by the time they finally make it into office. If either Thrasymachus or Marx is right, there *is* no conflict with their political role because that role is to protect and promote the interests of business.

It is clear that the most powerful criminal justice policy makers come from the have-plenties, not from the have-littles. It is no surprise that legislators and judges—those who make the laws that define criminality and those who interpret those laws—are predominantly members of the upper classes, if not at birth then surely by the time they take office. One study of justices appointed to the U.S. Supreme Court between 1933 and 1957 found that 81 percent were sons of fathers with high-social-status occupations and that 61 percent had been educated in schools of high standing. Richard Quinney compiled background data on key members of criminal justice policy-making and policy-advising committees and agencies, such as the President's Commission on Law Enforcement and Administration of Justice, the National Advisory Commission on Civil Disorders, the National Commission on the Causes and Prevention of Violence, the Senate Judiciary Committee's Subcommittee on Criminal Laws and Procedures (the subcommittee had a strong hand in shaping the Omnibus Crime Control and Safe Streets Act of 1968), the

Law Enforcement Assistance Administration, the Federal Bureau of Investigation, and, last but not least, the U.S. Department of Justice. With few exceptions, Quinney's report reads like *a Who's Who* of the business, legal, and political elite. For instance, 63 percent of the members of the President's Crime Commission had business and corporate connections.

Further, there is considerable evidence that the American criminal justice system has been used throughout its history in rather unsubtle ways to protect the interests of the powerful against the lower classes and political dissenters. The use of the FBI and local police forces to repress dissent by discrediting, harassing, and undermining dissident individuals and groups has been recently revealed. The FBI, often with active cooperation or tacit consent of local police, has engaged in literally hundreds of illegal burglaries of the offices of law-abiding left-wing political parties, and in political sabotage against the Black Panthers (e.g., "a Catholic priest, the Rev. Frank Curran, became the target of FBI operations because he permitted the Black Panthers to use his church for serving breakfasts to ghetto children"). It conducted a campaign to discredit the late Martin Luther King, Jr. ("the FBI secretly categorized King as a 'Communist' months before it ever started investigating him"). Directors of the FBI have said that the bureau is "truly sorry" for these past abuses and that they are over. Later reports indicate that abuses continue.

These acts of repression are only the latest in a long tradition. The first organized uniformed police force in the English-speaking world was established in London in 1829. They came to be called "bobbies" because of the role played by Sir Robert Peel in securing passage of the London Metropolitan Police Act, which established the force. The first full-time uniformed police force in the United States was set up in New York City in 1845. It was also in the period from the 1820s to the 1840s that the movement to build penitentiaries to house and reform criminals began in New York and Pennsylvania and spread rapidly through the states of the young nation. That these are also the years that saw the beginnings of a large industrial working class in the cities of England and America is a coincidence too striking to ignore.

The police were repeatedly used to break strikes and harass strikers. The penitentiaries were used mainly to house the laborers and foreigners (often one and the same) whom the middle and upper classes perceived as a threat. Throughout the formative years of the American labor movement, public police forces, private police such as the Pinkertons, regular army troops, and the National Guard were used repeatedly to protect the interests of capital against the attempts of labor to organize in defense of its interests. The result was that "the United States has had the bloodiest and most violent labor history of any industrialized nation in the world"—with most of the casualties on the side of labor.

Marx, of course, went further. Not only are the laws of a society made to protect the interests of the most powerful economic class, but also, Marx argued, the prevailing ways of thinking about the world—from economic theory to religion to conventional moral ideas about good and evil, guilt and responsibility—are shaped in ways that promote the belief that the existing society is the best of all possible worlds. Marx wrote that

> . . . the ideas of the ruling class are in every epoch the ruling ideas: i.e. the class which is the ruling material force of society, is at the same time its ruling intellectual force. The class which has the means of material production at its disposal, has control at the same time over the means of mental production.

Because those who have economic power own the newspapers, endow the universities, finance the publication of books and journals, and (in our own time) control the television and radio industries, they have a prevailing say in what is heard, thought, and believed by the millions who get their ideas—their picture of reality—from these sources. This does not mean that the controllers of the "means of mental production" consciously deceive or manipulate those who receive their message. What it means is that the picture of reality held by these controllers—believed by them, no doubt sincerely, to be an accurate representation of reality—will be largely the picture of reality that fills the heads of the readers and viewers of the mass media. Recognizing this involves no disrespect of the so-called common person. It is simply a matter of facing reality. The average man or woman is almost wholly occupied with the personal tasks of earning a living, piloting a family, and the like. He or she lacks the time (and usually the training) necessary to seek out and evaluate alternative sources of information. Most people are lucky when they have the time to catch a bit of news on television or in the papers. Moreover, except when there is division of opinion among those who control the media, the average person is so surrounded by unbroken "consensus" that he or she takes it simply as the way things are, with no particular reason even to consider the possibility that there are other sides of the issue to be considered, much less to seek these out. Then, even if people do come up with alternative sources of information, there are no general forums available for the sharing of views among members of the public. What we call mass communication is communication to the masses, not among them.

Consequently, the vast majority of people will accept, as a true picture of reality, the picture held by those who control the media. This is likely to be a distorted picture, even if those who create it act with the best of intentions and sincerity. The point is that, for a wide variety of reasons, people will tend to view the world in ways that make their own role in it (particularly the advantages and privileges they have in it) seem morally just, indeed, part of the best of all possible worlds. Thus, without any intention to deceive at all, those who control the content of the mass media are virtually certain to convey a picture of reality that supports the existing social order.

As a result, even in a society such as ours, where freedom of expression has reached a level probably unparalleled in history, there is almost never any fundamental questioning of our political-economic institutions in the mass media, that is, television and radio, the major newspapers, or the news weeklies such as *Time* or *Newsweek.* There is much criticism of individuals and of individual policies. How often, though, does one find the mass media questioning whether the free-enterprise system is really the best choice for America, or whether our political and legal arrangements systematically promote the domination of society by the owners of big business? These issues are rarely, if ever, raised. Instead, it is taken for granted that, although they need some reform tinkering from time to time, our economic institutions are the most productive, our political institutions the freest, and our legal institutions the most just that *there can be.*

In other words, even in a society as free as ours, the ideas that fill the heads of most Americans and shape their picture of reality either explicitly or implicitly convey the message that our leaders are pursuing the common good (with only occasional lapses into personal venality—note how we congratulate ourselves on how "the system is working" when we expose these "aberrations" and then return to business as usual). Thus, we are told that the interests of the powerful coincide with the common interests of us all—that "what's good for General Motors is good for the country." Where this picture of reality shows up some blemishes, they will always be portrayed as localized problems that can be remedied without fundamental overhaul of the entire social order, aberrations in an otherwise well-functioning social system. Indeed, the very willingness to publicize these blemishes "proves" there is nothing fundamentally wrong with the social system, because if the media are free, willing, and able to portray the blemishes, they would surely portray fundamental problems with the social system if there were any—and because they do not, there must not be any! When ideas, however unintentionally, distort reality in a way that justifies the prevailing distribution of power and wealth, hides society's injustices, and thus secures uncritical allegiance to the existing social order, we have what Marx called *ideology.*

Ideology is not conscious deception. People may spout ideology simply because it is all they know or all they have been taught or because they do not see beyond the "conventional wisdom" that surrounds them. This can be just as true of scholars who fail to see beyond the conventional assumptions of their disciplines as it is of laypersons who fail to see beyond the oversimplifications of what is commonly called "common sense." Such individuals do not mouth an ideology out of a willful desire to deceive and manipulate their fellows, but rather because their own view of reality is distorted by untruths and half-truths—and criminal justice is one source of such distortion. One way in which this works without conscious lying is that we have become so used to the criminal justice carnival mirror . . . that we don't notice its curves. It looks flat, and thus we take it as an accurate picture of who threatens us in society.

It should be noted in passing that not everyone uses the term *ideology* as I have, to point to what is necessarily deceptive. Some writers speak of ideology as if it meant any individual or group's "belief system" or "value system" or *Weltanschauung,* that is, "world view." I do not intend to quibble about semantics. However, such a moral neutralization of the concept of "ideology" strikes me as dulling an instrument that thinkers such as Marx and others have sharpened into an effective tool for cutting through the illusions that dog our political life. Such tools are few and hard to find. Once found, they should be carefully preserved, especially when concepts such as "belief system" and "world view" are available to perform the more neutral function.

The Need for Ideology

A simple and persuasive argument can be made for the claim that the rich and powerful in America have an interest in conveying an ideological message to the rest of the nation. The have-nots and have-littles far outnumber the have-plenties. This means, to put it rather crudely, that the have-nots and the have-littles could have more if they decided to take it from the have-plenties. This, in turn, means that the have-plenties need the cooperation of the have-nots and the have-littles. Because the have-plenties are such a small minority that they could never *force* this cooperation on the have-nots and have-littles, this cooperation must be voluntary. For the cooperation to be voluntary, the have-nots and the have-littles must believe it would not be right or reasonable to take away what the have-plenties have. In other words, they must believe that for all its problems, the present social, political, and economic order, with its disparities of wealth and power and privilege, is about the best that human beings can create. More specifically, the have-nots and have-littles must believe that they are not being exploited by the have-plenties. Now this seems to me to add up to an extremely plausible argument that ours is a social system that requires for its continued operation a set of beliefs necessary to secure the allegiance of the less-well-off majority. These beliefs must be in some considerable degree false, because the distribution of wealth and power in the United States is so evidently arbitrary and unjust. Ergo, the need for ideology.

A disquisition on the inequitable distribution of wealth and income in the United States is beyond the scope and purpose of this book. This subject, as well as the existence of a "dominant" or "ruling" class in America, has been documented extensively by others. I will make only two points here. First, there are indeed wide disparities in the distribution of wealth and income in the United States. Second, these disparities are so obviously unjust that it is reasonable to assume that the vast majority of people who must struggle to make ends meet put up with them only because they have been sold a bill of goods, that is, an ideology.

In 1999, the richest 20 percent of American families were expected to receive 50.4 percent of the after-tax income received by all families, whereas the poorest 60 percent of American families will receive 28.6 percent of the total income. In crude terms, this means that while the wealthiest 53 million Americans will have more than half the money pie to themselves, the least wealthy 159 million Americans will share less than a third of that pie among them. At the outer edges the figures are more extreme: The richest 1 percent of families are expected to receive 12.9 percent of total after-tax income, about the same as the poorest 40 percent of families, who will receive 13.9 percent. This means that the richest 1 percent—maybe 13 million people—have more money to divide among themselves than the 106 million persons who make up the bottom 40 percent.

The distribution of *wealth* (property such as stocks and land that generate income and tend to give one a say in major economic decisions) is even worse than the distribution of income. In 1995, it was estimated that the top one-fifth of households own 84 percent of the nation's wealth, and the remaining four-fifths own 16 percent. recent study of long-term trends in wealth inequality shows that the top one-fifth of households has owned three-quarters of the nation's wealth at least over the period from 1962 to 1989. The author writes: "If anything, wealth concentration increased during the 1980s. It is estimated that the top 1 percent of households in 1989 owned 33 percent of household wealth, compared to 30 percent in 1986 and 28 percent in 1983." Looking back over the whole period from colonial times to the present, the author concludes, "at no time has the majority of the U.S. adult population or households managed to gain title to any more than about 10 percent of the nation's wealth." And, she adds, "the governmental policies of the past two decades have been hostile to progressive tax rates and economic measures benefiting workers. Real per capita income began declining in the early 1970s, benefits eroded in the 1980s. . . . This situation suggests that the lower four quintiles' share of total wealth may well shrink in future years." A recent report by the Federal Reserve confirms this prediction. According to *The Washington Post* for January 23, 2003: "The rising economic tide of the late 1990s lifted the boats of almost all American families but also sharply increased the wealth gap between the rich and the rest of society, according to a survey released yesterday by the Federal Reserve."

I offer no complicated philosophical argument to prove that these disparities are unjust, although such arguments abound for those who are interested. It is a scandal that, in a nation as rich as ours, some 32.3 million people (somewhat less when reckoned with the most generous valuation of in-kind benefits) live below what the government conservatively defines as the poverty level and that many millions more must scramble to make ends meet. It is shameful that more than a third of the individuals below the poverty line are children! It is tragic that in our wealthy nation so many millions cannot afford a proper diet, a college education, a decent place to live, and good health care. We know too much about the causes of wealth and poverty to believe that the rich become rich simply because of their talent or contribution to society or that the poor are poor because they are lazy or incapable. Because we are nowhere near offering all Americans a good education and an equal opportunity to get ahead, we have no right to think that the distribution of income reflects what people have truly earned. The distribution of income in America is so fundamentally shaped by factors such as race, educational opportunity, and the economic class of one's parents that few people who are well off can honestly claim they deserve *all* that they have. Those who think they do should ask themselves where they would be today if they had been born to migrant laborers in California or to a poor black family in the Harlem ghetto.

Enough said. I take it, then, as established that the disparities of wealth and income in America are wide and unjustified. For the vast majority, the many millions struggling hard to satisfy basic needs, to acquiesce to the vast wealth of a small minority, it is necessary that the majority come to believe that these disparities are justified, that the present order is the best that human beings can accomplish, and that they are not being exploited by the have-plenties. In other words, the system requires an effective ideology to fool enough of the people enough of the time.

This account of the nature and need for ideology, coupled with the historical inertia explanation of the persistence of criminal justice in its current form and the analysis of the ideological benefits produced by the criminal justice system, adds up to an explanation of the continued failure of criminal justice in the United States.

Summary

This chapter has resented the "historical inertia" explanation of the triple failure of criminal justice in the United States (1) to institute policies likely to reduce the incidence of crime, (2) to treat as crime the dangerous acts of the well off, and (3) to eliminate the bias against the poor in the treatment of those acts labeled crimes. It was argued that these failures harm most those who lack the power to change things and benefit those who have that power. They benefit the latter by broadcasting the message that the threat to Americans' well-being comes from below them on the economic ladder, not from above them, and that poverty results not from social causes but from the moral depravity of the poor. It was also argued that, aside from these "bonuses of bias," there is an implicit ideological message of any criminal justice system, insofar as such systems, by focusing on individual guilt, implicitly broadcast the message that the social system itself is a just one.

POSTSCRIPT

Are U.S. Crime Problems a Result of Our Failure to Get Tough on Crime?

Have you ever listened to a conversation among friends about crime? If so, you may well have been exposed to common theories that emphasize stringent punishments. At the beginning of my criminology class last year, one student observed: "My relatives all know how to reduce crime—lock them all up and throw away the key." Such sentiments, which may be termed a logical general deterrence model of punishment, are highly popular. But, does the logical general deterrence model of punishment really work? Does increasing the likelihood of being arrested or punished have a significant impact on crime? The best evidence suggests that there is little relationship between these factors.

James Q. Wilson asserts that criminal behavior is a product of a rational choice by offenders. If we increase the costs of crime and make the alternatives to criminal behavior more attractive, crime rates will decrease. Wilson's theory has a great deal of intuitive appeal. It is based on the idea that people have free will and control their own destinies. There is also some evidence to suggest that Wilson's theory may work when the authorities are able to increase the likelihood of being caught for committing a particular offense.

Jeffrey Reiman, however, believes that the U.S. justice system itself is designed to fail and this failure serves a purpose—deflecting attention away from the actions of wealthy individuals, which represent the true threat to society, toward the acts of poor people, who are much more likely to commit street crimes.

It seems likely that the definitive answer to the question of adopting tougher crime-control policies is likely to be found somewhere toward the middle of these two approaches: While increasing the severity of punishment for some "rationally motivated" offenses may reduce some types of crime, it is also clear that a number of our current justice system policies must be examined critically and revised.

Fortunately, there are a number of outstanding resources that shed additional light on the issues presented in this section. An excellent article that considers the relationship between the probability of being arrested and crime rates is by Robert Bursik, Harold Grasmick, and Mitchell Chamlin, "The Effect of Longitudinal Arrest Patterns on the Development of Robbery Trends at the Neighborhood Level," *Criminology* (vol. 28, 1990); see in addition, Daniel Nagin and Greg Pogarsky, "Integrating Celerity, Impulsivity, and Extralegal Sanction Threats into a Model of General Deterrence," *Criminology* (vol. 39, 2001). Additional resources that present a critical analysis of the U.S. justice system include: Barbara Sims, "Crime, Punishment, and the American

Dream: Toward a Marxist Integration," *Journal of Research in Crime and Delinquency* (vol. 34, 1997); Anthony Platt, "Criminology in the 1980s, Progressive Alternatives to 'Law and Order,' " *Crime and Social Justice* (vols. 21-22, 1985); Matthew Petrocelli, Alex Piquero, and Michael Smith, "Conflict Theory and Racial Profiling: An Empirical Analysis of Police Traffic Stop Data," *Journal of Criminal Justice* (vol. 31, 2003); and David Greenberg and Valerie West, "State Prison Populations and their Growth, 1971-1991," *Criminology* (vol. 39, 2001).

Additional resources include: Ian Taylor, Paul Walton, and Jock Young, *The New Criminology: For a Social Theory of Deviance* (Routledge, 1973); Willem Bonger, *Criminality and Economic Conditions* (Indiana University Press, 1969); David Greenberg, ed., *Crime and Capitalism* (Mayfield, 1981); Richard Quinney, *The Social Reality of Crime* (Little, Brown, 1970); George B. Vold, Thomas J. Bernard, and Jeffrey Snipes, *Theoretical Criminology,* 4th ed. (Oxford University Press, 1998); Ronald L. Akers, *Criminological Theories: Introduction, Evaluation, and Application,* 3rd ed. (Roxbury, 2000); Sue Titus Reid, *Crime and Criminology,* 11th ed. (McGraw Hill, 2005); and Frank P. Williams III and Marilyn McShane, *Criminological Theory* (Prentice Hall, 2004).

ISSUE 2

Does the United States Have a Right to Torture Suspected Terrorists?

YES: Andrew A. Moher, from "The Lesser of Two Evils? An Argument for Judicially Sanctioned Torture in a Post–9/11 World," *Thomas Jefferson Law Review* (Spring 2004)

NO: Elisa Massimino, from "Leading by Example? U.S. Interrogation of Prisoners in the War on Terror," *Criminal Justice Ethics* (Winter 2004)

ISSUE SUMMARY

Yes: Attorney Andrew A. Moher argues that judicially sanctioned torture of terrorists is appropriate for the purpose of preventing a greater evil. He further contends a judicially monitored system in the United States would be far superior to the current policy of practicing torture "under the radar screen" in other countries.

No: Elisa Massimino believes that the use of torture is immoral and counterproductive for the United States. She asserts that if the United States wishes to rely on the protections of the Geneva Conventions, then it must comply with its provisions prohibiting the torture of prisoners.

Consider the following hypothetical situation: A suspected terrorist has planted a nuclear bomb somewhere in a large U.S. city of 2 million people. Based on information from an informant, who has proven to be completely reliable on many past occasions, government authorities have reason to believe that the nuclear bomb is set to explode in three hours. It would be impossible to evacuate the city within this time frame. Moreover, the informant has given the authorities the name and description of the suspected terrorist, and he is taken into custody. If the suspect refuses to talk, is torture justified?

The Introduction to this work discussed the doctrine of utilitarianism, which asserts that a social policy should be assessed according to whether it produces the greatest benefit or public good. In our hypothetical situation, the greatest public benefit would be served by locating the bomb and defusing it. Do you believe that the greatest public good would be served by using whatever means were necessary to extract the information from the suspect? This situation illustrates a potential deficiency in the doctrine of utilitarianism—perhaps there are absolute principles that should never be compromised, regardless of whether an action will serve the greatest public good. The use of torture to extract information *may* be one of these principles.

U.S. courts have consistently condemned the use of torture by government authorities to gain information from criminal suspects because it violates due process of law, a "principle of justice so rooted in the traditions and conscience of our people as to be ranked as fundamental." For example, in *Brown v. Mississippi,* 297 U.S. 278 (1936), sheriff's deputies obtained the confessions of three African-American suspects in a murder case by whipping and hanging them. Approximately five days later, a Mississippi court convicted the men of murder, and they were sentenced to death. When one of the deputies who administered the torture was asked during the trial about whether the whipping he had administered to gain the confessions was too severe, he stated: "[It was] not too much for a negro; not as much as I would have done if it were left to me."

Rather than trying to use torture as an interrogation method in the war on terrorism inside the United States, news reports indicate that the government has used the practice of "rendition." Under this practice, suspected terrorists are taken for interrogation to nations that do not forbid the use of torture. Do you believe that rendition is consistent with "the fundamental principles of liberty and justice which lie at the base of all our civil and political institutions?"

The authors of the articles in this section have different viewpoints on the use of torture to extract information from suspected terrorists. Andrew Moher argues that judicially sanctioned torture of terrorists is appropriate for the purpose of preventing a greater evil. He further contends a judicially monitored system in the United States would be far superior to the current policy of practicing torture "under the radar screen" in other countries. Moher's position is fundamentally a statement of a utilitarian approach to the use of torture to extract information from terrorists.

Elisa Massimino, in contrast, believes that the use of torture is immoral and counterproductive for the United States. She asserts that if the United States wishes to rely on the protections of the Geneva Conventions, then it must comply with its provisions regarding torture of prisoners. Massimino's position is consistent with an absolutist position regarding the use of torture—it is contrary to human dignity and always wrong.

What is your position regarding the use of torture to extract information from suspected terrorists? Are your views influenced by the bombing of the World Trade Center in New York City on 9/11/2001? As you read the articles in this section, try to develop a sense of whether you support the utilitarian or absolutist positions regarding the use of torture.

Andrew A. Moher

The Lesser of Two Evils? An Argument for Judicially Sanctioned Torture in a Post–9/11 World

I. Introduction

Torture is illegal under both United States and international law. It is considered among the most heinous practices in human history, and its use is publicly condemned by nearly every government in existence today. However, it is also considered an effective method of gathering information, and to that end it is habitually employed "under the radar screen" in desperate situations by these same governments. Since the catastrophic attacks of September 11, 2001, several noted scholars and politicians have advocated the use of torture in extreme scenarios, while others have expressed fear that legitimizing torture would spawn a dangerous slippery-slope of morally reprehensible state actions. Specifically, the use of torture to extract information from terrorists with knowledge of impending attacks has been the subject of intense debate.

Before surveying the landscape of state sponsored torture, it is essential to distinguish between two categories of torture. The more notorious form of torture is punishment-based. It is inextricably intertwined with medieval images of diabolical torture devices found in movies and museums around the world. Such methods have historically been used in violent tyrannies and dictatorships, and exist in "rogue" states today. This type of torture is morally indefensible and is not at issue here. Rather, this discussion deals with torture for the purpose of preventing a greater evil, as part of the interrogation process. Such methods have been used in the past, with some success.

An interesting dialogue might be fashioned on whether the United States should adhere to international restrictions on torture under the shadow of post- 9/11 threats of terrorism. After all, many potential subjects of torture are "part of the conspiracy [to destroy] . . . innocent Americans." Conversely, there is a danger that condoning torture of suspects might harm innocents unnecessarily, or that American captives would be subjected to inhumane treatment in response to United States policy. These contentions are largely beyond the scope of this discussion, and serve as background to the present debate.

From *Thomas Jefferson Law Review*, vol. 26, issue, 2, Spring 2004, pp. 469-289.

This Note will argue that judicially sanctioned torture is appropriate, but only under certain, well-defined circumstances. Part II will discuss the current status of domestic and international law as it applies to torture. Part III will analyze the pattern of United States noncompliance with these laws, and the general ineffectiveness of the current policy on torture. Finally, Part IV will illustrate why a balanced approach allowing judicially sanctioned torture would be a more effective and humane alternative to the current practice of using torture "under the radar screen."

II. The Legality of Torture Under Current United States Law

The United States is compelled by both domestic and international law not to practice torture. Torture is banned by several amendments to the Constitution, and implicitly barred by the sentiment of the Constitution itself. Furthermore, the practice of torture conflicts with United States obligations under international law, including signed and ratified treaties. Over the years, the prohibition against torture has become a fixture of international law, and has been routinely condemned by the vast plurality of nations. Today, the torturer is considered "hostis humani generis," an enemy of all mankind.

A. Constitutional Prohibitions on Torture

The practice of torture runs directly counter to the Fifth, Eighth and Fourteenth Amendments of the Constitution. Some advocates of legalizing torture have argued that loopholes exist in each of these amendments, and suggest torture could be rationalized under existing law. Upon closer examination, it is clear the use of torture is wholly incompatible with the Constitution. This contention is further borne out by important court decisions emphasizing the protections of personal liberty from governmental intrusion.

The Eighth Amendment bans all cruel and unusual punishment. This prohibition would ostensibly include torture, as the drafters of the amendment were "primarily concerned . . . with proscribing 'tortures' and other barbarous forms of punishment." On the other hand, the Eighth Amendment has been construed by the Supreme Court to protect only those convicted of crimes. Thus, it stands to reason that although convicted criminals are protected under the Eighth Amendment, others (such as prisoners of war, or so-called "enemy combatants") are not protected. Through this loophole created under the guise of the Supreme Court's interpretation, the Eighth Amendment would most likely be deemed ineffectual in cases involving suspected terrorists that have not yet been convicted in the criminal justice system.

Even if the practice of torture were to effectively circumvent the Eighth Amendment, it would almost certainly be found unconstitutional under the due process protections of the Fifth and Fourteenth Amendments. These protections grant all persons the substantive rights not to be deprived of life, liberty, and property, without due process of law. Although substantive due process is admittedly a very subjective and malleable standard, it has been utilized in the past to overturn practices less odious than torture. In recent years, the Supreme Court has adopted the rationale that state conduct that "shocks the conscience" will violate due process protections.

In *Brown v. Mississippi,* the police severely whipped a subject while hanging him from a tree to coerce a confession. The Supreme Court of the United States declared, "[I]t would be difficult to conceive of methods more revolting to the sense of justice than those taken to procure [these] confessions." The Court later lowered the bar when it found less violent conduct to meet the "shock the conscience" benchmark. In *Rochin v. United States,* the Supreme Court found a violation of due process when authorities pumped the stomach of a man suspected of swallowing morphine capsules. Speaking for the court in *Rochin,* Justice Frankfurter defined the objective of substantive due process as "respect for those personal immunities which . . . are 'so rooted in the traditions and conscience of our people as to be ranked as fundamental.' "

Brown and its progeny illustrate the scope of substantive due process, and its incompatibility with the practice of torture. Indeed, the atrocious whipping in *Brown* could easily be analogized to torture, and that conduct was found to violate due process. The broader standard put forth in *Rochin* further strengthens the case against torture. If the right to be free from torture was not egregious enough to meet justice Frankfurter's standard of fundamental rights, it would be hard to imagine what conduct would be. Based on these cases, and the Court's obvious desire to protect bodily integrity, the intentional infliction of pain by torture would sufficiently "shock the conscience" to violate due process.

B. International Prohibitions Against Torture

The United States is further bound by several international treaties that prohibit the practice of torture. International treaties have authority so long as they do not offend the Constitution. The United States is obligated to provide humane treatment to prisoners of war under the 1949 incarnation of the Geneva Convention. The United States is also bound by the International Covenant on Civil and Political Rights, or ICCPR, which contains express prohibitions against torture. Article 7 of the ICCPR states, inter alia, "No one shall be subjected to torture or to cruel, inhuman, or degrading treatment or punishment." Under the Convention, the right to be protected from torture is nonderogable, meaning that it applies at all times, including wartime. The ICCPR, like the Geneva Convention, bars torture under any and all circumstances.

The United States is also party to the Convention against Torture (CAT), a subsidiary to the ICCPR that was ratified by the United States in 1994. Under UUU Article 4, the CAT demands that "each state party . . . ensure that all acts of torture are offences under its criminal law," and that the offences are "punishable by appropriate penalties which take into account their grave nature." The State Department recently confirmed the full implementation of the CAT into United States law, averring, "every act constituting torture under the [CAT] constitutes a criminal offense under the law of the United States."

Finally, the United States must adhere to jus cogens. According to the Vienna Convention on the Law of Treaties, jus cogens are international legal standards that are "accepted and recognized by the international community of States as a whole as a norm from which no derogation is permitted and which can be modified only by a subsequent norm of general international law having the same character." In other words, universally abhorred practices such as genocide, slavery, and summary executions qualify as jus cogens and are illegal at all times and all places, regardless of existing laws. Torture has long been considered an immutable violation of jus cogens, and declared as such in Federal court. The United States is therefore bound by jus cogens not to practice torture under any conceivable scenario.

III. The Reality of Torture Under Current United States Law

Few writers would be naive enough to suggest torture has been completely eradicated from all societies today. Yet many would underestimate its prevalence as a tool of interrogation, particularly in "civilized" countries such as the United States. There has been a plethora of evidence since the September 11 attacks suggesting United States complicity in interrogational torture and yet no tangible ramifications have been encountered to date. Often, a nation can avoid responsibility by exploiting the amorphous definition of torture under various laws. It has become evident that the implementation mechanisms of the international system are not compatible with the security concerns of the post 9/11 world.

A. United States Evasion of International Law

As arguably the world's lone remaining superpower, the United States is in a unique position with regards to its participation in international law, most notably in its ability to avoid repercussions for its legal offenses. International law has long been criticized as ineffective because of its weak enforcement mechanisms. For example, Iraq has been a party to the ICCPR since before the United States' ratification, yet has managed to avoid responsibility for its government's blatantly illegal mass murder of the Kurds in the north of the country. Indeed, the most damaging punishment for a nation's violation of international law is often the so-called "mobilization of shame," whereby the publication of the offending nation's transgressions can damage its perception among the other nations of the world. The sheer power and influence of the United States at the present time renders it all but immune from this attempt at deterrence, and in this light the consequences of offending the international law system appear obsolete.

To that end, the United States has acted evasively in carrying out its obligations under international treaties. For example, the United States recently rebuffed claims that it was in violation of the Geneva Convention regarding its treatment of suspected former Taliban fighters at Camp X-Ray in Guantanamo Bay, Cuba. The United States government escaped liability under the provisions of the Convention by refusing to label the captives 'prisoners of war.' By repudiating any classification of the Guantanamo inmates, the government was successful in employing an obvious labeling loophole in the Geneva Convention, thereby allowing the United States to interrogate the prisoners in a manner unrestricted by the Convention. The United States Supreme Court will decide this year whether the Guantanamo inmates can appeal their detentions to the Government, or whether they will continue to be held in a prison that operates entirely outside of the law. In the interim, the United States and similarly situated nations continue to exploit the inefficacies of the international law system.

B. Torture Under a Different Name

The Convention Against Torture (CAT) defines torture as:

> [A]ny act by which severe pain or suffering, whether physical or mental, is intentionally inflicted on a person for such purposes as obtaining from him or a third person information or a confession, punishing him for an act he or a third person has committed or is suspected of having committed, or for any reason based on discrimination of any kind, when such pain or suffering is inflicted by or at the instigation of, or with the consent or acquiescence of a public official or other person acting in an official capacity.

This definition, while not dispositive, is certainly illustrative of the general conception of torture and its legal boundaries. Many nations, however, sidestep admissions of the practice of torture simply by redefining the word. Recently, academics and politicians have analyzed the distinction between "torture" and "torture lite." The latter, it is reasoned, is tantamount to aggressive but legal interrogation and is distinguishable from the traditional concept of torture in several important ways.

Torture is intended, it would seem, to encompass activities that bring about severe pain and suffering. Understandably, the question of what is severe has never been definitively resolved. Traditional methods of torture, such as mutilation, amputation, mock executions, rape, and stoning are presumably intended to cause severe pain. By contrast, torture lite is commonly understood as referring to interrogation methods such as sleep deprivation, exposure to extreme temperatures, mild physical abuse, use of drugs to cause confusion, or psychological coercion. Arguably, these types of methods do not cause severe pain, and are therefore beyond the dominion of torture, at least as defined by the CAT.

The result of this exercise in semantics is increased confusion about what exactly is allowed under international law and what is prohibited. The Geneva Convention, for instance, bans all mistreatment of prisoners during wartime, which probably prohibits both torture and torture lite. In contrast, the International Covenant on Civil and Political Rights may leave the door open to torture lite practices with its subjective "cruel, inhuman, or degrading standard." Under this paradigm, a nation acting from purely selfish interests would likely argue that practices such as mind games and sleep deprivation do not meet the threshold of cruel, inhuman, or degrading punishment. Similarly, the CAT definition of torture presents the aforementioned uncertainty of what is severe. A ruling by the United Nations High Commissioner for Human Rights under the CAT underscores the ambiguity of the law: "[W]hen employed for the purpose of breaking a prisoner's will, sleep deprivation may in some cases constitute torture." Such deviation in the definition of torture leads to a classic slippery slope scenario, where the lines may be loosely drawn to serve the interests of the interrogating nation.

Not surprisingly, there remains a lack of consensus among international courts regarding the point at which interrogation becomes torture. In 1976, the European Commission of Human Rights found that a British combination of five tactics used against Northern Irish prisoners collectively constituted torture under the European Convention of Human Rights. The tactics used included subjecting the prisoners to hooding, extended wall standing in painful postures, loud noises, sleep deprivation, and deprivation of food and drink. Two years later, the European Court for Human Rights reversed this ruling, declaring the conduct had risen to the level of "inhuman and degrading treatment," but not torture. This TT decision influenced one official inquiry by the state of Israel, defining moderate physical pressure against a suspected Palestinian terrorist as compatible with international laws on interrogation. The Israeli High Court of justice later declared this treatment illegal. These inconsistent interpretations of the law allow countries to practice torture under a different name, which cannot be an acceptable solution to the problem of torture.

C. Evidence of United States Practice of Torture

Whether the United States uses torture as a method of interrogation is an open question, subject to both the interpretation of testimony and the definition of torture itself. It would not be inaccurate to conclude the questioning methods of the United States often transcend the lines of humane interrogation. Representatives of the United States have repeatedly implied that torture-like methods are utilized to prevent future terrorist attacks. Cofer Black, then-head of the CIA Counterterrorist Center joint hearing of the House and Senate Intelligence Committees, acknowledged, "[T]here was a before 9/11, and there was an after 9/11. After 9/11 the gloves come off." An unnamed official, interviewed by the *Washington Post,* added: "[I]f you don't violate someone's human rights some of the time, you probably aren't doing your job."

Third party accounts by respected non-governmental organizations also tend to support the notion that the United States uses torturous techniques in its interrogations. Amnesty International reported that prisoners under United States control at the Bagram Air Base in Afghanistan were deprived of sleep with a 24-hour bombardment of lights, held in awkward, painful positions, and constantly subjected to stress and duress techniques. Indeed, many prisoners have attempted suicide at Camp X-Ray in Guantanamo Bay. Human Rights Watch added in their report that prisoners were "subjected to electric shocks . . . and beaten throughout the night." In an open letter to President

George W. Bush, Human Rights Watch Executive Director Kenneth Roth relayed his concern that the United States might be "in violation of some of the most fundamental prohibitions of international human rights law."

The Central Intelligence Agency ("CIA"), though understandably reluctant to admit such practices, is fully cognizant of the effectiveness of torture in investigation. CIA officials sometimes refer to the Kubark Manual, a journal of interrogative techniques, which includes physical and psychological tactics that could easily be classified as torture. A representative from the CIA described the questioning methods used against a typical high-level terrorist suspect:

> He would most likely have been locked naked in a cell with no trace of daylight. The space would be filled day and night with light and noise, and would be so small that he would be unable to stand upright, to sit comfortably, or to recline fully. He would be kept awake, cold, and probably wet. If he managed to doze, he would be roughly awakened. He would be fed infrequently and irregularly, and then only with thin, tasteless meals . . . . On occasion he might be given a drug to elevate his mood prior to interrogation; marijuana, heroin, and sodium pentothal have been shown to overcome a reluctance to speak, and methamphetamine can unleash a torrent of talk in even the most stubborn subjects.

It is interesting to note that all of these techniques, individually, might be classified as torture lite. Taken together, however, they seem to epitomize a routine of torture so devious that it cannot reasonably be described any other way. It becomes impractical to make legal exceptions for torture lite practices when they will add up to extreme torture in the aggregate.

D. The Question of Rendition

The most obvious example of United States complicity in torture is the practice of irregular rendition. Rendition, a system of sending captives to other countries with less progressive human rights standards in order to interrogate them more aggressively, often results in torture. Since September 11, the United States has sent prisoners to Pakistan, Saudi Arabia, Egypt, Morocco, and Uzbekistan, as well as other countries with documented histories of torturing suspects. Through this process, the United States can gain valuable information with impunity, while claiming that they have "no direct knowledge" of the host country's interrogation methods. Fred Hitz, the former CIA Inspector General, commented on the practice of rendition: "We don't do torture, and we can't countenance torture in terms of we can't know of it. But if a country offers information gleaned from interrogations, we can use the fruits of it."

There is no accountability in rendition, and some nations have accused the United States of rendering suspects for immoral or political reasons. The case of Maher Arar is illustrative. Arar, a longtime Canadian citizen, was captured by United States authorities and rendered to Syria. He was tortured at the hands of Syrian and Jordanian authorities, which ceased the treatment only when he "confessed" to being associated with another Canadian citizen who had been arrested. The rendition of Mr. Arar has sparked criticism from various human rights groups.

Renditions are also considered dangerous because the interrogation methods of the receiving countries are often ghastly in nature. The case of Abdul Hakim Murad sheds light on the procedures used during some renditions. Murad was rendered to the Philippines in 1995. According to the *Washington Post,* Philippine authority agents beat Murad, "with a chair and a long piece of wood [breaking most of his ribs], forced water into his mouth, and crushed lighted cigarettes into his private parts." After 63 days of this "tactical interrogation," Murad disclosed a plan to assassinate the pope, and to crash eleven commercial airliners carrying approximately four thousand passengers into the Pacific Ocean, as well as to fly a private plane packed with explosives into CIA headquarters. Although the veracity of Murad's confessions has recently come into dispute, his experience remains an informative example of the techniques utilized during rendition.

The consequence of rendition is the manipulation of the international law system, as well as the circumnavigation of domestic law prohibitions against torture. Again, mobilization of shame appears the most effective international remedy against nations suspected of irregular rendition, and again, some nations are influenced far more than others. Human Rights Watch utilized a mobilization of shame tactic when they publicly announced: "The United States . . . has a duty to refrain from sending persons to countries with a history of torture without explicit, verifiable guarantees that they will not be tortured or otherwise mistreated." The United States' response was evasive, insisting that the renditions occur for the purpose of cultural affinities, as opposed to illegal interrogations. Although this might conceivably be a factor in the renditions, the totality of the evidence yields the conclusion that torture has become a frequent by-product of these renditions.

E. The Two Choices

The stark reality that torture is practiced today leaves a responsible society with two choices. The first is the implementation of an effective international body to regulate torture. In order to address the many problems of today's system, the body would first need a controlling definition of torture. This would effectively limit a nation's ability to practice torture under the guise of torture lite. An effective body would also have implementation powers beyond that of the current mobilization of shame. Without such "teeth," the system would not be effective against powerful nations. Finally, the body would have to make rendition explicitly illegal, and punish countries accordingly. Unfortunately, without drastic and unprecedented cooperation among the myriad nations of the world, this model is not realistic under today's international system.

The other choice is to legalize torture.

IV. Should Torture Be Legalized?

In his farewell address from the presidency, Ronald Reagan spoke of America as a "shining city upon the hill." Reagan's Utopian vision included a principled commitment to human rights and freedoms, similar to that espoused by the current United States administration. In the 2002 State of the Union Address, President George W. Bush proclaimed, "America will always stand firm for the non-negotiable rights of human dignity." This self-imposed higher standard of morality may prove to be both a blessing and a curse. On one hand, this approach has traditionally given the United States a powerful and respected voice in the world community. On the other, the legalization of torture might be considered irreconcilable with President Reagan's "shining city." Although it may be difficult to conceive of a moral society practicing torture, there is an argument to be made that legalizing torture would actually enhance the moral stature of the United States when juxtaposed against the current policy of underground torture.

A. History of State-Sponsored Torture

The concept of state-sponsored torture is not without precedent. The English overtly incorporated torture into their legal system in the seventeenth century. The English employed torture warrants against people that were thought to have information necessary to prevent attacks on the state. The torture warrant served several beneficial purposes, such as making the practice more visible and thus "more subject to public accountability." However, the English torture policy was conducted at a time quite different than our own, and by a government structured quite different than our own.

Perhaps a more germane comparison to this debate is the Israeli experience. Few, if any, countries in the history of the world have been under the constant shadow of terrorism as much as modern-day Israel. The Israelis face threats from both hostile neighboring countries and international terrorist organizations such as Hamas, Hizbollah, and Islamic Jihad. In order to cope with the threat of homicide bombings, the Israelis have traditionally employed torture lite tactics. In 1987, a commission led by former Israeli Supreme Court President Moshe Landau investigated the interrogation practices of the Israeli General security Service. The commission found that, under the rule of necessity, the use of force in interrogation was authorized if the interrogator reasonably believed the lesser evil of force was necessary to get information that would prevent the greater evil of loss of innocent lives. This ruling temporarily established the foundation for legalized torture in Israel.

Predictably, there were both significant benefits and significant problems associated with the Israeli legalization of torture. Like the English model, the use of torture was publicized and became more visible. However, witnesses claim that Israeli interrogators were loathe to stop at the proscribed limits of questioning. In fact, some authors suggest that up to 85% of Palestinian inmates were tortured by Israeli authorities. Moreover, at least 10 Palestinians died as a result of torture prior to 1994. The publication of these abuses alarmed the United Nations, and their involvement led to a landmark 1999 decision in which the High Court of justice in Israel found the use of moderate physical pressure in interrogation to "[infringe] on both the suspect's dignity and his privacy." The Israeli government subsequently scaled back physical force during interrogations, although some suggest the ruling merely moved the torture movement underground.

B. The Dershowitz Torture Warrant

In his book *Why Terrorism Works: Understanding the Threat, Responding to the Challenge,* Professor Alan Dershowitz analyzes the applicability of judicially sanctioned torture to modernday American jurisprudence. Specifically, Professor Dershowitz addresses the problem of the ticking-bomb terrorist, who possesses crucial information of an imminent disastrous attack, but refuses to give information to his captors. In this situation, one writer emphasizes, society "pay[s] for his silence in blood."

To obtain this critical information, Professor Dershowitz introduces the concept of a torture warrant: a process whereby a neutral magistrate would decide whether there was sufficient evidence to compel a suspect to be subjected to torture. Unlike the current policy, the torture would be medically supervised and designed not to cause any permanent physical damage. One possibility anticipated in the book is the insertion of a long needle under the fingernail, intended to cause excruciating pain but no lasting damage. Professor Dershowitz's proposal is largely based on a cost-benefit framework, reminiscent of philosopher Jeremy Bentham's moral calculus of utility. In the end, Professor Dershowitz theorizes, "absolute opposition to torture—even nonlethal torture in the ticking bomb case—may rest more on historical and aesthetic considerations than on moral or logical ones."

Professor Dershowitz's support of torture is not without its critics. Theorists have unleashed a parade of horribles that could result from the legalization of torture. Foremost among these events are the violation of human dignity, the potential for abusing the law, and the fear of instigating a domino effect and creating a world of legalized torture. Although these arguments are meritorious in their own respects, they are all easily answered from Professor Dershowitz's perspective. With regards to human dignity, the legalization of torture would promote respect for human dignity, insofar as torture would be changed from an inhumane tool of oppression to a last-resort tool for saving lives. The potential for abusing the law is another legitimate concern, but this can be addressed by instituting the necessary and appropriate safeguards. Finally, worldwide legalization of torture is not a negative event in Professor Dershowitz's eyes, if it can be regulated effectively. The legalization of torture is not a perfect solution, and it doubtless would have its downfalls. As Professor Dershowitz observes, "[S]uch is the nature of tragic choices in a complex world."

C. "Degrees" of Torture and the Balancing Test

When weighing the benefits of legalizing torture against preserving the status quo, it is essential to understand the difference in "degrees" of torture. Torture in a legalized system would consist of a nonpermanent act meant to maximize the possibility of gaining crucial information, while minimizing necessary pain. By contrast, torture in rendition might utilize the mind-numbing tactics used against Abdul Hakim Murad in the Philippines, if not worse. The torturers in these situations are not accountable to any authority, and seemingly would not hesitate to take the lives of uncooperative subjects. The degree of torture used in the legalization proposal is, therefore, inherently more humane than the degree of torture practiced today.

Courts often use balancing tests to influence the direction of the law. For instance, in a classic decision on due process, the Supreme Court explained that whether an individual's constitutional rights have been violated "must be determined by balancing [the individual's] liberty interest against the relevant state interests." Here, this logic would probably support the use of torture in a dire situation. Assume, for example, that a known terrorist announced the presence of a nuclear bomb in a major U.S. city that would kill thousands of people. The terrorist further stated that he knew the location and time assigned for the detonation of the bomb, but refused to disclose these crucial details. The terrorist's liberty interest in not being tortured is, no doubt, significant. However, the state interest in saving thousands of lives is far more compelling. Applying Constitutional due process analysis, the use of torture would seemingly be upheld.

There are additional benefits that may be gained from the system without resorting to torture. According to the Kubark Manual, "the threat of coercion usually weakens or destroys resistance more effectively than coercion itself." For example, it is an effective practice to stage mock executions in neighboring cells while a prisoner is interrogated. The CIA's finding that the threat of coercion often leads to compliance, without the actual use of coercion (i.e. torture), is promising. If such a system were implemented, it is possible that important information might be gleaned from a suspect without having to ever resort to torture. Similarly, a transparent regulation of torture practice would encourage dialogue among prisoners such as Maher Arar, without fear of deportation or forced confessions. Both of these factors weigh heavily in favor of a regulated torture system.

There are negative factors that must be considered as well. Legalizing torture would set a dangerous precedent for other countries who might abuse their newfound ability to practice torture. United States officials might abuse their discretion in validating torture warrants. The truth of the statements made under duress of torture might be questioned. Furthermore, some writers have made the argument that legalizing torture would do little to curb the existence of underground torture. For instance, writer Jean Maria Arrigo hypothesized, "[A] regulated program cannot eliminate use of rogue torture interrogation services, because they still serve to circumvent moral and procedural constraints on the official program." Although there is undoubtedly some truth in this theory, there is still hope that a regulated system would curb underground torture to a very significant degree.

Furthermore, these dangers pale in comparison to the dangers in today's system. Currently, the United States participates in underground rendition, which leads to undocumented torture and manipulation. This practice involves a more severe and brutal form of torture, and likely contributes to many undocumented fatalities. Moreover, the information gained from this process is probably less reliable than information extrapolated from a judicially monitored system. The documentation of rendition activities is sparse, and the penalties for offending international laws on torture are virtually nonexistent. On balance, there is much more to lose by embracing the status quo. The balancing test in this analysis yields the conclusion that legalizing torture provides an overall benefit for humankind.

D. Towards a More Humane System

Assuming the requisite support in principle for legalizing torture, the creation and implementation of the torture policy would be both complicated and controversial. Every ambit of these new laws would be duly scrutinized on such an unstable world stage. Who would make the decision of granting or denying the torture warrant? Would there be an adequate appeals system? How would the safety of the torture subjects be ensured? How could the United States condone a policy that offends its Constitution and flagrantly violates the peremptory norms of international law?

Many of these questions are directed towards the intricacies of the torture system itself, and are thus beyond the scope of this Note. However, there are some policy concerns worth discussing. Time constraints would likely pose the biggest roadblock to an effective policy. If a terrorist threatens a bomb strike within hours, it becomes a formidable task to employ a traditional appeals process before initiating torture. The protocol would necessarily be more elaborate than the search warrant process, which demands only an objectively reasonable action by a police officer to obtain a search warrant. The former Israeli standard (reasonable belief that force is necessary to prevent a greater evil) is probably not exacting enough to justify torture. Perhaps the standard should mirror that of the public necessity defense under American tort law, which is limited to actions necessary to avert an impending public disaster. Whatever the solution, it is of the utmost importance that torture be used as a last resort in only the most desperate of scenarios.

An interesting blueprint for a torture warrant procedure might be drawn from the Foreign Intelligence Surveillance Act (FISA) and its implementation." FISA was created by the United States government as a corollary to the public legal system in order to discreetly process search warrants against suspected terrorists and spies. As initially enacted, FISA allowed specially designated judges to authorize surveillance to acquire foreign intelligence information under certain circumstances, on a court known as the Foreign Intelligence Surveillance Committee (FISC). The seven-judge FISC court was expanded to eleven judges under the 2001 USA Patriot Act. This model is adaptable to the torture warrant proposal, insofar as an eleven-judge panel might be effective at quickly expediting decisions on torture warrants, and making tough decisions regarding ticking-bomb terrorists.

Unfortunately, the FISC model (as amended by the Patriot Act and other legislation) has also proved an embodiment of the critics' worst fears. The records and files of cases involving FISC search warrants are sealed and may only be revealed to an extremely limited degree. Furthermore, the annual reports to Congress for the calendar year 2002 showed that 1,226 of 1,228 applications for search warrants had been approved by the FISC. The remaining two were approved by the supplementary appeals council to the FISC, the FISCR. A system that always approves torture warrant applications would bluntly defeat the purpose of the system. Moreover, the sealing of the documents would defeat the goals of transparency and accountability. Only an arrangement that accounted for these inherent flaws in government-run judgment panels would be able to legitimize torture and bring an appropriate warrant system to fruition.

V. Conclusion

It is incumbent upon us to engage in an open and truthful debate about the state of torture in the world today. Even if there is no perfect solution, the creation of a transparent and judicially monitored system on torture would mark a dramatic improvement over the current policy of ignorance. The dangers for abuse in the current system are truly boundless, and the practice of rendition often leaves the fate of suspects in the dangerous hands of acknowledged torturers. The practice of torture should not be denied simply because it is concealed and hidden half a world away. Legalizing torture certainly presents imposing obstacles, both in its challenging implementation and in its visceral dissonance. Compared to the current policy of practicing torture "under the radar screen," however, it may indeed be the lesser of two evils.

NO 

Elisa Massimino

Leading by Example? U.S. Interrogation of Prisoners in the War on Terror

When "trophy photos" taken by soldiers involved in the abuse of Iraqi prisoners at Abu Ghraib prison—one of the most notorious under Saddam Hussein's regime—were made public in late April 2004, the Pentagon had already completed two investigations into allegations of abuse at the prison. The graphic and disturbing photographs, some aired on prime-time American television, show naked Iraqi prisoners in humiliating poses, many with smiling uniformed soldiers looking on and pointing or giving a "thumbs up" sign. In one of the photographs, two naked prisoners are posed to make it look as though one is performing oral sex on another. Another shows a hooded prisoner standing on a box with wires attached to his wrists; the army says the prisoner was told that if he fell off the box, he would be electrocuted. Two pictures show dead prisoners—one with a battered and bruised face, the other whose bloodied body was wrapped in cellophane and packed in ice. One shows an empty room, splattered with blood. Reportedly, there is video as well.

These gruesome photographs were splashed across the front pages of newspapers in the Middle East and around the world, the headlines screaming "TORTURE." But the abuse was not news to the Pentagon. According to news accounts, a scathing 53-page report by Major General Antonio M. Taguba, completed in February, concluded that there was ongoing systematic and criminal abuse of detainees at the Abu Ghraib prison. As Seymour Hersh reported in the *New Yorker* magazine in May, General Taguba's report confirmed that abuses were taking place at the prison, including: threatening male detainees with rape, sodomizing a male detainee with a broomstick or chemical light, threatening detainees with dogs, and pouring chemicals from broken light bulbs onto detainees. As a result of this investigation, six soldiers are facing court-martial on charges that include cruelty toward prisoners, dereliction of duty, and indecent acts.

Are the soldiers who engaged in these acts just "sick bastards," as their commanding officer recently said, or is there something more profoundly disturbing going on here? Why did the soldiers feel free to document their crimes on camera? Some answers to these questions will likely emerge in the prosecu-

From *Criminal Justice Ethics*, vol. 23, issue 1, Winter 2004, pp. 2-5. Notes omitted.

tion of the soldiers involved. But it appears from the information already available that this was abuse with a particular purpose—to "create conditions favorable for successful interrogation"—that is, to break down a prisoner's will.

The Descent to Lawlessness

As shocking as these abuses are, to anyone who has followed closely the Bush Administration's descent into lawlessness in its prosecution of the "war on terrorism," they are not surprising. Three factors contribute to an environment in which such torture and cruelty can proliferate.

First is the Administration's persistent degradation of the Geneva Conventions and other international standards governing its conduct toward prisoners. Beginning with the initial transfer of prisoners from Afghanistan to Guantanamo, White House officials argued that the Geneva Conventions were not relevant to the war on terrorism. Later, under pressure from secretary of State Colin Powell and other current and former military officers who revere the Geneva Conventions as a source of protection in case of capture, the Administration announced that it "believes in the principles" of the Geneva Conventions, but neither Taliban fighters nor al Qaeda suspects were eligible for their protections. Thus, as we continue to learn from Guantanamo, Bagram, and now Abu Ghraib, believing in the principles of the Geneva Conventions and actually complying with them are two different things—and there is no in-between. Complying with the Geneva Conventions requires that all of the detainees on Guantanamo and elsewhere have a recognized legal status. This, the Administration has steadfastly refused to do. But if the United States wants to be able to rely on the protections in the Geneva Conventions, then it must comply with them—not just in word, but in deed. Failing to do so not only places U.S. soldiers at greater risk, but contributes to a situation in which the details and importance of the Geneva Conventions are completely unrecognized by soldiers, like those at Abu Ghraib, charged with guarding and interrogating prisoners.

Second is the way in which the United States has played fast and loose with the prohibition on torture and cruel, inhuman, or degrading treatment. For example, one government official described the interrogation of an alleged high-ranking al Qaeda operative as "not quite torture, but about as close as you can get." Various administration officials—as well as some detainees who have been released—report that prisoners in U.S. custody have been beaten; thrown into walls; subjected to loud noises and extreme heat and cold; deprived of sleep, light, food, and water; bound or forced to stand in painful positions for long periods of time; kept naked; hooded; and shackled to the ceiling. Euphemistically called "stress and duress" techniques, U.S. officials who admit to these practices seem to think they are permissible so long as they don't cross the line into "outright torture." They are mistaken. When President Bush's father pushed the Convention Against Torture through the Senate, he committed to interpret the phrase "cruel, inhuman or degrading treatment or punishment" in ways consistent with the Eighth Amendment's prohibition on cruel and unusual punishment. To put these "stress and duress" techniques into constitutional context, the U.S. Supreme Court ruled in 2002 that handcuffing a prisoner to a hitching post in a painful position for eight hours clearly violated the protection against cruel and unusual punishment. While there are certainly some interrogation methods that are unpleasant but not illegal, "stress and duress" interrogation techniques are clearly illegal. Pentagon General Counsel William J. Haynes III asserts that U.S. policy is "to treat all detainees and conduct all interrogations wherever they may occur, in a manner consistent with" the prohibition on cruel treatment. But because many detainees are interrogated without the presence of lawyers or even the confidentiality-bound International Committee of the Red Cross (ICRC), it is difficult to know if that policy is known to interrogators, let alone whether they comply with it.

The third factor contributing to the kinds of interrogation abuses that are now coming to light is the Administration's focus on using interrogation almost exclusively for the purpose of obtaining information, rather than to obtain a confession or other evidence admissible in court. When the goal of interrogation is prosecution, the rules are familiar: Miranda, lawyers, a day in court. But what are the rules when there is no day in court in a detainee's future? Almost immediately after September 11, 2001, Attorney General Ashcroft and other senior officials at the Justice Department began talking about a fundamental shift in approach when dealing with terrorist suspects, from prosecution to prevention. Facilitated by an "enemy combatant" policy that so far has allowed the government to keep even U.S. citizens in incommunicado detention for prolonged periods, the Administration argues that detainees have no rights—to counsel, to appear before a judge, to speak to anyone at all—that might interfere with the sense of dependency and lack of control designed to make a detainee "lose hope."

Justifying Torture

Most discussions of interrogation and torture begin with the so-called "ticking time bomb" scenario, which posits a situation in which a detainee has information that, if revealed, could spare those about to be slaughtered. Is torture permissible if it would save those lives? People who focus on this hypothetical often do so in order to expose as "soft" those wide-eyed moralists unwilling to "do what is necessary" for the greater good. Since September 11, some lawyers and even judges have argued that if the taboo against torture has not already been broken, it should be now. Harvard law professor Alan Dershowitz proposed "torture warrants" for the ticking time bomb scenario, so that the abuses could be undertaken with judicial and societal sanction. Federal Judge Richard Posner has said that anyone who doubts torture is permissible when the stakes are high enough should not be in a position of responsibility. The end—saving innocent lives—justifies the means.

This is tough talk. But those who advocate for torture in these circumstances are the ones who are out of touch with reality. Many experienced interrogators have pointed out that the "ticking time bomb" scenario, with its factual (if not moral) clarity, is a fantasy, a situation that simply never presents itself in the real world. Abu Ghraib prison, on the other hand, is reality, and it is a reality where the means—torture and humiliation—quite likely will help to undermine the ends that the U.S. government is pursuing—Iraqi acceptance of a US military presence in a free and democratic Iraq.

Outlawing Torture

Just before the beating deaths of two Afghan prisoners who died under interrogation at Bagram Air Force Base were made public, I told a friend of mine—a senior military officer at the Pentagon—how disturbed I was by the fact that so many Americans with whom I talked casually believed, without distress or the slightest bit of cognitive dissonance, that the United States was torturing suspects for information. I asked my friend whether he believed that prisoners being held by the United States were being tortured. "I can't believe that," he said. "I could never be involved in a mission that relied on torture and abuse. It's a betrayal of everything we stand for."

Not only that, it's also illegal. When the U.S. Senate gave its advice and consent to ratification of the United Nations Convention Against Torture and Other Cruel, Inhuman or Degrading Treatment or Punishment, it recognized that ratification would have to await the passage and implementation of legislation, required by the treaty, making torture a crime. Congress did so in 1994. Title 18, Section 2340 of the United States Code defines torture as "an act committed by a person acting under the color of law specifically intended to inflict severe physical or mental pain or suffering (other than pain or suffering incidental to lawful sanctions) upon another person within his custody or physical control." Section 2340A makes torture, attempted torture, and conspiracy to commit torture a federal crime, punishable by up to 20 years in prison; if the victim dies as a result of torture, the punishment could be death. The law applies only to torture committed outside the United States, but includes acts by U.S. citizens. While the conduct of U.S. soldiers is governed by the Uniform Code of Military Justice (hence the charges of "cruelty" and "indecent acts" in the Abu Ghraib prison abuse case), it appears that other U.S. personnel—private contractors and intelligence officials—may also have been involved in the abuse. In the 10 years that the anti-torture law has been on the books, not a single person has been charged under its provisions. That may now change.

No Exceptions

Regardless of the words used to prohibit it, the ban on the use of torture is absolute. Unlike other provisions of international human rights law—such as the right to be free from arbitrary arrest or detention—that can be suspended during a declared emergency that "threatens the life of the nation," no exigency can justify torture.

This prohibition applies to the outsourcing option as well. International law prohibits the United States, as a signatory of the Convention Against Torture, from sending a person to a country where there is a substantial likelihood that he will be tortured. Congress reiterated this obligation in legislation in 1998, requiring regulations from all relevant executive agencies detailing how this obligation would be implemented. The Departments of Justice and State both issued regulations; the Pentagon and the CIA never complied. Over the last 18 months, a number of Administration officials have confirmed that the United States is handing some al Qaeda suspects in military or CIA custody over to other governments for interrogation. These transfers are known as "extraordinary rendition"—a highly legalistic term for a completely extralegal arrangement. Some of the countries where the detainees are sent—Egypt, Syria, Morocco—are places where, according to the State Department's annual country reports on human rights practices, torture and other prisoner abuse is routine. Some detainees have been transferred with a list of questions that their American interrogators want answered; in other cases, U.S. officials maintain more of a distance, simply receiving the fruits of the interrogation. It is unclear whether U.S. officials are ever present at these sessions. But even if they are not, it is a fiction that "extraordinary rendition" allows the United States to preserve clean hands, despite one U.S. official's claim that "We don't kick the [expletive] out of them. We send them to other countries so they can kick the [expletive] out of them." Interestingly, when those countries comply, they may get a free pass from the State Department. In 2002, new instructions were issued to U.S. embassy personnel who draft the human rights reports: "Actions by governments taken at the request of the United States or with the expressed support of the United States should not be included in the report."

When pressed to explain how its policy of "extraordinary rendition" to countries known to practice torture comports with its obligations under both the Convention Against Torture and domestic law, the Administration's response is either disingenuous or rather naïve. In a letter to Senator Patrick Leahy responding to just this question, Pentagon General Counsel Haynes said that when it transfers a detainee to a third country, U.S. policy is "to obtain specific assurances from the receiving country that it will not torture the individual being transferred to that country." In other words, we just take Syria's word for it. As Senator Leahy responded, "mere assurances from countries that are known to practice torture systematically are not sufficient." Though Haynes has said that the United States will follow up on any evidence that these "diplomatic assurances" were not being honored, it seems that it would be awfully rare that such evidence would ever emerge, since the detention is likely to be incommunicado.

However, though rare, such evidence is not impossible. In September of 2002, U.S. officials arrested Maher Arar, a dual citizen of Canada and Syria, as he was changing planes at JFK airport in New York, en route home to Canada. Although he was traveling on his Canadian passport, U.S. officials—apparently CIA and Justice Department working together—secretly transferred Arar first to Jordan then to Syria, a move that evoked strong protest in Canada. Arar arrived in Syria after being interrogated for 11 days at a CIA interrogation center in Jordan. He then spent 10 months in a Syrian jail, during which time he alleges he was repeatedly tortured. Under increasing public pressure from

Canadians and human rights groups, Syria finally released Arar, claiming they never had any interest in him anyway, but had only jailed and interrogated him to curry favor with the United States. This case provides an opportunity to test whether the United States is serious about the safeguards it says it employs when it transfers detainees to the custody of other governments. Did the United States government seek "diplomatic assurances" from Syria before handing Arar over? It hasn't said. If it did, has it complained to Syria that its treatment of Arar violates those assurances? It appears not. Perhaps that is because, as Arar alleges, the transfer to Syria was for the purpose of interrogation under torture. While in Syrian custody, Arar confessed to being a terrorist and having trained in an al Qaeda camp, all of which he now denies. With the Syrian government's later dismissal of Arar's importance, it appears even the Syrians did not believe his confessions.

Credibility

If another country is willing to torture a prisoner in whom it has no independent interest just to appease the United States, imagine what effect we are having on repressive governments anxious to legitimize their own abusive conduct towards political dissidents and others they wish to silence. As the world stares in horror at pictures of grinning American soldiers engaging in war crimes, it is becoming increasingly deaf to the President's proclamation that "America will always stand firm for the non-negotiable demands of human dignity." Last summer, the President issued a clear and forceful statement reaffirming the "inalienable human right" to be free from torture. "The United States is committed to the world-wide elimination of torture and we are leading this fight by example," President Bush said in a statement commemorating the U.N. International Day in Support of Victims of Torture. Now, nearly a year later, the world has good reason to doubt the integrity of the President's pledge.

POSTSCRIPT

Does the United States Have a Right to Torture Suspected Terrorists?

U.S. Supreme Court Associate Justice Hugo Black once stated that in times of social crisis "the fog of public excitement obscures the ancient landmarks set up in our Bill of Rights. Yet then, of all times, should this Court adhere more closely to the course they mark." The Bill of Rights, the first ten amendments to the U.S. Constitution, establishes the framework for protection of basic liberties by our government. The rights provided therein include some of the most fundamental values of American society: freedom of the press, speech, and religion, the right to be free from unreasonable searches and seizures, the right to be free from double jeopardy, the privilege against self-incrimination, the right to counsel, the right to a trial by jury, the right not to be subjected to cruel and unusual punishment, and the right to due process of law.

Do you agree with Justice Black's statement that at times of social crisis, public sentiment may tempt us to compromise our most important social values? What are the implications of Justice Black's position for the development of laws in the wake of the war on terrorism?

In the articles presented in this section, attorney Andrew A. Moher argues for laws permitting judicially sanctioned torture of terrorists when it is necessary to prevent a greater evil. Moreover, Moher asserts that a judicially monitored system in the United States is far preferable to the Bush administration's current policy of practicing torture "under the radar screen." Elisa Massimino, in contrast, believes that the use of torture is immoral and counterproductive. She asserts that if the United States wishes to rely on the protections of the Geneva Conventions, then it must comply with its provisions prohibiting the torture of prisoners.

After reading the articles in this section and considering Justice Black's statement, what is your position of the use of torture of suspected terrorists? Is there any middle ground in this debate?

There is a good deal of compelling and recent literature relevant to the issue considered in this section. For an excellent analysis of the philosophical problems associated with using torture, see David Sussman, "What's Wrong with Torture?" *Philosophy and Public Affairs* (Winter 2005). Anthony Lewis, the author of *Gideon's Trumpet,* has also written a very interesting article discussing the state of civil liberties in the aftermath of the war on terrorism, "One Liberty at a Time," *Mother Jones* (May/June 2004); see also, Harvey Silverglate, "Civil Liberties and Enemy Combatants," *Reason* (January 2005); Mark Bowden, "The Dark Art of Interrogation," *The Atlantic Monthly* (October 2003); Christopher Tindale, "The Logic of Torture: A Critical Examination," *Social Theory and Practice* (Fall 1996); George J. Annas, "Unspeakably Cruel—Torture, Medical Ethics, and the Law," *The New England Journal of Medicine* (May 19, 2005); Stuart Taylor, "The Perils of Torturing Suspected Terrorists," *National Journal* (May 8, 2004); and Laura M. Kelly, "Big Brother Inc: Surveillance, Security and the U.S. Citizen," *Analog Science Fiction & Fact* (May 2005).

ISSUE 3

Should Serious Sex Offenders Be Castrated?

YES: Lawrence Wright, from "The Case for Castration," *Texas Monthly* (May 1992)

NO: Kari A. Vanderzyl, from "Castration as an Alternative to Incarceration: An Impotent Approach to the Punishment of Sex Offenders," *The Northern Illinois University Law Review* (Fall 1994)

ISSUE SUMMARY

YES: Attorney Lawrence Wright argues that while castration may not be an ideal solution, if we treat it as therapy rather than punishment, as help instead of revenge, and if we view offenders as troubled victims, not monsters, then perhaps castration will become an accepted and humane option for sex offender treatment.

YES: Attorney Kari A. Vanderzyl asserts that castration should be rejected as an unacceptable, ineffective, and unconstitutional alternative to imprisonment for sex offenders.

Castration of sex offenders is a frightening issue that for some will conjure images of Joseph Mengele, the Nazi physician who performed horrible experiments on human subjects in concentration camps during World War II. Is it possible to view castration, however, as a voluntary and humane therapeutic solution for serious sex offenders? Moreover, does castration work? If serious offenders are castrated, will they cease committing sex offenses? The articles in this section demonstrate that at least three different issues must be examined before considering castration as a routine form of treatment for sex offenders: the empirical evidence, its constitutionality, and the moral propriety of castrating sex offenders.

The available evidence on castrating sex offenders is interesting indeed. A German study conducted between 1970 and 1980 analyzed 104 individuals who had undergone voluntary castration as a form of treatment. Seventy percent of these individuals were categorized as pedophiles, 25 percent were aggressive sex offenders, 3 percent were exhibitionists, and 2 percent were classified as homosexuals. The control group consisted of individuals who had applied for castration during the same period but did not have the surgery. The researchers found that sexual interest, sex drive, erection, and ejaculation had generally decreased in 75 percent of the cases within six months of the operation. Moreover, the postoperative recidivism rate for sex crimes was 3 percent at most, compared to 46 percent for non-castrated subjects. The authors of the study also concluded that the social adjustment of the castrated subjects appeared to be more favorable than that of the non-castrated individuals. Among the castrated subjects, 70 percent were satisfied with the treatment, 20 percent were ambivalent, and 10 percent were not satisfied.

The U.S. Supreme Court has not expressly considered the issue of the constitutionality of castration as a form of treatment for sex offenders. In *Buck v. Bell,* 274 U.S. 200 (1927), however, a Virginia law was upheld that provided for the involuntary sterilization of persons confined to a state mental institution who were found to be afflicted with a hereditary form of insanity or imbecility. Justice Oliver Wendell Holmes, widely regarded as one of the greatest Supreme Court justices in U.S. history, stated: "It is better for all the world, if instead of waiting to execute degenerate offspring for crime, or to let them starve for their imbecility, society can prevent those who are manifestly unfit from continuing their kind. . . . Three generations of imbeciles is enough."

Fifteen years later, in *Skinner v. Oklahoma,* 316 U.S. 535 (1942), the Court considered a related issue—the constitutionality of an Oklahoma law that provided for the forced sterilization of habitual criminals for committing a third felony involving "moral turpitude." Stated Justice William O. Douglas:

> We are dealing here with legislation which involves one of the basic civil rights of man. Marriage and procreations are fundamental to the very existence and survival of the race. The power to sterilize, if exercised, may have subtle, far-reaching and devastating effects. In evil or reckless hands it can cause races or types which are inimical to the dominant group to wither and disappear. (541).

So, where are we regarding the Supreme Court's likely handling of mandatory sex offender castration laws? Although *Buck v. Bell* has been strongly criticized, more recent state court decisions have upheld compulsory sterilization laws in the context of mentally incompetent individuals. In addition, four states, including Texas, Florida, California, and Montana, have enacted laws to require involuntary chemical or surgical castration of certain convicted sex offenders. It will be very interesting to see whether U.S. courts will uphold *mandatory* castration laws.

What are your views on the issue of castrating serious sex offenders? Should it become a routine form of treatment for all those who cannot control their sexual urges? Or, should it be reserved for particular types of egregious sex offenders, such as pedophiles and serial rapists? Moreover, how should society draw the line between the types of sex offenders who are castrated and those who receive other forms of "treatment"? Is there a moral principle that should limit the use of this form of treatment, regardless of its utility?

Lawrence Wright

The Case for Castration

Everybody from Jesse Jackson to feminist leaders told child molester Steve Butler he shouldn't be able to trade his manhood for his freedom. Everybody was wrong.

There is a lesson in every disaster. Now that the hysteria has quieted in Houston, we can survey the ruins left by the Great Castration Fiasco. When a young black man named Steve Allen Butler offered to place his testicles on the scales of justice, he began a debate that spread through Texas and soon across the entire country, illuminating the divisions between classes, races, and genders. Concerns were raised about the Constitution and medical ethics. Charges were hurled and mud was slung. The image of the state of Texas was damaged by the sneering of the national press. And yet the question that no one in this broad argument seemed willing to address was exactly what we should do with our sex offenders.

If one thing is clear in this whole messy episode, it's that what we're doing now is a failure. Again and again, critics have said that castration is not an effective answer to sexual offense. So far no one has asked, "Compared with what?" Today there are nearly eight thousand sex offenders in Texas prisons. Their crimes include indecent exposure, sex with minors, incest, aggravated sexual assault, and rape. Yet only two hundred are receiving counseling—an indication of how little faith we place in therapeutic solutions. Given the turnover in our prisons, most of those offenders will be out on the streets after serving a small portion of their sentences. More than half will be arrested for another sex crime in fewer than three years.

We may despise the people who commit such acts, but we should realize that most of them are victims themselves, not just of childhood sexual abuse but of their own overwhelming sexual impulses. As was evident in the Butler case, some of the offenders are crying out for another form of treatment. They want to be castrated. Until we find a better solution, perhaps voluntary castration of sex offenders is a good idea.

From *Texas Monthly,* vol. 20, issue 5, May 1992, pp. 108–122.

The debate began last fall at a dinner party in Tanglewood. "Like every gathering I've been to in Houston recently, the subject of crime captured the whole conversation," recalls state district judge Michael Mc Spadden. . . .

It was at that dinner party that Dr. Louis J. Girard mentioned his then-unpublished paper on castration. . . . Being a scientist, Girard decided to examine what factors influence criminal behavior. "A lot of crime is based on high levels of testosterone," he concluded. This powerful hormone determines a man's body shape, his hair patterns, the pitch of his voice. "It also produces aggressiveness in the males," Girard told the judge. "It is the reason that stallions are high-strung and impossible to train, the reason male dogs become vicious and start to bite people. It's why boys take chances and chase girls, why they drive too fast and deliberately start fights. In violent criminals, these tendencies are exaggerated and carried to extremes." In Girard's opinion, castration would reduce and possibly eliminate such aggressive impulses. The castrated criminal would be more docile and have a better opportunity to be rehabilitated, educated, and to become a worthwhile citizen," Girard contended.

Girard's idea rang a bell with McSpadden. If there was a painless, inexpensive procedure that would reduce the overflowing prison population, allow criminals to gain control over their violent natures, make them more susceptible to rehabilitation, and also act as a powerful deterrent to other offenders, what could be wrong with that? . . .

The controversy might have died out soon after that except for 27-year-old Steve Butler, who read about it in the paper in October. At the time, Butler was sitting on the fifth floor of the Harris County jail, accused of having had sex with a 13-year-old girl. Butler was already on probation in McSpadden's court for fondling a 7-year-old girl in 1989. The new charge could result in a lengthy prison term. Butler might get life, plus 10 years for violating his probation. He had already rejected the plea bargain offered by the assistant district attorney handling the case, Bill Hawkins, in which Butler would plead guilty to aggravated sexual assault and receive 35 years. Because it was an aggravated charge (meaning that the victim was under 14), Butler would have to serve at least one fourth of his time before he would be eligible for parole. He would spend the next 8 years and 9 months in prison as a convicted child molester, the lowest rung on the criminal hierarchy. . . .

Butler's problem, as he later admitted to psychologists who examined him, was that he had no control over his sexual impulses. Dr. Michael Cox, a well-respected therapist at Baylor College of Medicine who counsels sex offenders, examined Butler at Judge McSpadden's request. After administering a battery of standard psychological tests, Cox found Butler to be mildly depressed but otherwise sane and competent. Butler "didn't look any different from the garden-variety child molesters I see in the program," says Cox. "He had been abused when he was young. He seemed to be more of a situational offender—in other words, his sexual preference is for adult women. But he does have a drinking problem, and if there is a female child available and he's been drinking, one thing can lead to another." . . .

As for Butler, his motives were varied. "I just think it would help me a whole lot," he admits. "I could be a better person. I could go on with my life and take care of my family." He is also frightened by the idea of going to prison, especially as a child molester. "I've heard stories about it," he says in a near whisper. "Some say it's hard. You have to fight."

"Frankly, I think the judge is titillated by the idea of cutting the balls off a black man," says the Reverend Jew Don Boney, the chairman of the Houston chapter of the Black United Front. "This is McSpadden playing God. It's unprecedented; it's outside of normal legal bounds; and it introduces a whole new level of inhumanity into the criminal justice system." . . .

Castration is a profound symbol of the historic oppression of black men. In 1855 the Territory of Kansas introduced judicial castration of Negroes and mulattoes who raped or attempted to rape white women. In the South, blacks were sometimes castrated before being lynched. "It's a reminder of what I read about in the days of slavery and in the late eighteen-hundreds and early nineteen-hundreds," says Burns. "If this is the best we can come up with in terms of punishing or trying to deal with people guilty of that type of crime, then I'm wondering what changes we have made between 1892 and 1992." "It's just too close to an ugly part of our history," says Robert Newberry. "You would have to have gone through that type of history to really feel the emotional impact of how our forefathers were treated." Newberry recalls seeing a photo of a lynched black man with a bloody gash where his sex organs had been. "This castration issue brings it all back. It stirs up the pain."

For many black people, the contrast between the white judge—maverick Republican who plays tennis at the Houston Racquet Club—and the shine man sitting in the jailhouse seemed to characterize the imbalance of power between the races. One had privilege and the respect of society; the other was a high school dropout with no prospects, the sort of castoff that society notices only when he becomes a statistic in the criminal justice system. What was there left to take away from Steve Butler—except his manliness?

That Butler himself sought castration was rarely commented upon, except to say that he was a victim of judicial coercion. In fact, McSpadden had been elaborately cautious in making sure that Butler's choice was free and informed. He instructed Butler to talk to four psychiatrists and therapists, including Michael Cox, who was outspokenly opposed to the castration option. No one was able to change Butler's mind. He still preferred castration to prison, a choice denounced as "a very dangerous precedent" by Frank Burns. And yet when I asked Burns what he would do if he were in Butler's place, having to choose between a lengthy spell in prison or castration, he said he "may very well" make the same choice: castration and freedom. . . .

"People hear the word 'castration' and it scares them," McSpadden told me one afternoon in his chambers. "They don't realize it is a simple surgical procedure that can be done on an outpatient basis. It's not cutting off the penis. It's far less intrusive than a hysterectomy. What's more, the crime we see in Texas is a direct result of the failure of present punishments to serve their intended purposes of retribution, rehabilitation, and deterrence. If castration does work, then we not only let that person live a normal life because of a simple medical treatment, but we also protect society from that same person for years to come." . . .

It was clear from the hundreds of calls and letters that the castration issue strikes a deep chord of fear and anger and a longing for revenge. That is exactly what worries Cassandra Thomas, the director of the rape program at the Houston Area Women's Center. "I don't think castration should be used as punishment," she says. "It only buys into the myth that sexual assault is about sex, and so therefore if you get rid of sexual desires you get rid of rape. The reality is that sexual assault is about violence; it's about a need for power and control. It has nothing to do with the genital organs." Castration, she says, is "an empty symbolic gesture." . . .

Many women see rape as a political act, evidence of the male need to control the female. Viewed through that lens, treating the problem by removing the sex organs will only frustrate men and make them, as Thomas argues, "more likely to use violence as a way of dealing with their issues of inadequacy and powerlessness and helplessness that perpetuate sexual assaults in the first place." . . .

Nearly everyone involved in the Butler case—like nearly everyone in Texas—has had some experience with castrated animals. The district attorney of Harris County, Johnny Holmes, keeps a herd of Longhorns, and he has personally castrated many of them. "My experience is that they get a lot bigger and a lot gentler," says Holmes. Girard castrated bulls when he was young; he also played polo at the Bayou Club. "Believe me, there's a tremendous difference in the amount of control you have between a gelding and a stallion." Recently one of his German shepherds became cantankerous and nipped Girard's daughter and his niece. "So I just castrated him, and he stopped." Michael Cox, the Baylor sex therapist, had his cat castrated. "He doesn't get into fights about female cats, but he still fights over territory.". . .

Voluntary castration became legally permissible in Denmark through the Access to Sterilization law of 1929, which permitted the operation on a "person whose sexual drive is abnormal in power or tendency, thus making him liable to commit crimes." Although the Danish law did permit forced castrations, that provision was never put into practice and was subsequently eliminated. Other European countries implemented similar voluntary programs. In this country, Oklahoma allowed forced castration of repeated felons convicted of crimes involving "moral turpitude"—a larger category than sex offenses—until the U.S. Supreme Court declared its law unconstitutional in 1942. Recently bills were knocked down in Washington, Alabama, and Indiana that would have permitted sex offenders to be castrated in exchange for a reduction in their sentences. The historical associations make it difficult to talk about castration without the specter of government-imposed sterilization becoming a part of the argument. Unfortunately, that is exactly the way Girard and McSpadden have framed their proposal.

Dr. John Bradford of the Royal Ottawa Hospital in Canada says that as a rule, the recidivism rate of sex offenders (that is, their likelihood to offend again) averages 80 percent before castration, dropping to less than 5 percent afterwards. In Europe, many studies on the consequences of therapeutic castration show essentially the same thing—that it is profoundly effective in lowering the rates of repeated sex offenses. A 1973 Swiss study of 121 castrated offenders found that their recidivism rate dropped to 4.3 percent, compared with 76.8 percent for the control group. In Germany, a similar report showed a post-operative recidivism rate of 2.3 percent for sex offenses, compared with 84 percent for non-castrates. Various Danish studies have followed as many as 900 castrated sex offenders for several decades; they show that recidivism rates drop to 2.2 percent. What is also important is that 90 percent of the castrated men reported that they themselves are satisfied with the outcome. "The main conclusion to be derived from all this material on castrated men," wrote Dr. Georg K. Sturup, chief psychiatrist of Denmark's Herstedvester Detention Center, in 1968, "is that a person who has suffered acutely as a result of his sexual drive will, after castration, feel a great sense of relief at being freed from these urges." . . .

Many people who oppose castration believe that the main problem sex offenders have is psychological, not physical. Therefore, they assume, diligent treatment involving therapy and the latest behavior modification techniques should make a difference. In fact, when counseling succeeds, it is only with a very limited group. It's an inside joke among sex counselors that if you want to have a successful program, you fill it with incest perpetrators, whose reoffense rate is about 3 percent, and keep out all the difficult cases, especially the rapists. . . .

No doubt there is progress in the field of sex offender treatment. No doubt some offenders are susceptible to treatment and others are not. But the stark fact is that none of these programs compares in effectiveness with castration.

The cost of our failure to treat sex offenders can't be known or measured, only guessed at. The tendency to sexually offend is usually lifelong. The chances of ever being arrested for a sex crime are very small—2 percent by some measures. "I went twelve years without being arrested, but I never went more than three days without acting out," an exhibitionist told me. The sheer number of offenses buried in the term "recidivate" can be imagined by a ten-year study of 550 sex offenders (many of whom had never been arrested), which asked each perpetrator how many victims he could specifically identify. The tally was 190,000 victims. . . .

The pressure was building on Steve Butler. The Reverend Jesse Jackson came to Houston and was allowed to see Butler, even against Butler's request not to see any visitors. Butler still wouldn't talk about his case. "This is not just a Houston matter, just as Selma was not just for Alabama," Jackson proclaimed outside the jailhouse, thus putting the matter of Butler's voluntary castration on a par with the civil rights movement. "We shall make a broad public appeal here and around the country, because such a precedent would be an ugly and dangerous precedent. Rape is sickness. Castration is sickness. The judge's complicity is sickness. We must break this cycle of sickness." . . .

Meanwhile, in Dallas, a man accused of sexually assaulting two girls seven months after being released from prison, said he would prefer castration to prison. "If you cut off man's desire to have sex whatsoever, that should solve the problem," Andrew Jackson, a 52-year-old white man, told a reporter. The prosecutor refused his offer, but it is clear that the castration issue in Texas isn't going to go away with the Butler case. It is also dear that Butler himself is not going to be castrated, despite his own wishes. The surgeon who had volunteered to perform the operation backed out when the publicity became too intense. Another doctor called the judge's office and left word that he'd be happy to perform the procedure for free, but on investigation the man turned out to be a dentist.

It was, finally, the lack of a surgeon that caused McSpadden to resign from the case. The weekend before he did so, he agreed to meet with Butler's five sisters and their attorney. "I told them step by step what had happened, but they were convinced it was a white conspiracy to railroad their younger brother," says McSpadden. The sisters were demanding that Butler be granted probation, which the prosecution had no interest in offering.

Now Butler's case will go to another court. If the victim's mother agrees to let her testify, Butler may be convicted and sent to prison for a long time. He may decide to reconsider the state's offer of 35 years and expect to be out in about a decade. If the victim doesn't testify, Butler will be a free man—free, but probably unchanged. The likelihood that he will reoffend is high even if he does join the eight thousand sex offenders we are currently incarcerating. Because eventually Butler will be back in society, as will the rest of them. Nothing that we are doing with the offender population has made any real difference in their lives; on the other hand, what sex offenders are doing to us, the rest of society, is seen every day in the courts and hospitals and rape crisis centers and child treatment programs—the circle of tragedy touches us all, somehow, if only in the financial burden of caring for the victims and jailing the perpetrators. We do a sorry job even of that.

Now that the Butler case is out of the news, perhaps it's time to think about whether voluntary castration has a place in the treatment of sex offenders. It is a mistake to make castration a punishment, as Girard and McSpadden have proposed; the Supreme Court would probably rule it unconstitutional, and in any case it is simply too offensive to too many people. Moreover, it should be limited to sex offenders. Castration does lower testosterone, which influences aggressive and violent behavior, but taking away the sex drive won't make a bad man good. It should be reserved for those men with uncontrollable sexual urges. In the case of pedophiles, when they exercise their sexuality they violate the law, not to mention the damage they do to the children. What good is their sexuality to them? If they want to be relieved of it, why can't they be?

Most sex offenders are white; this is a crime where blacks are not overly represented in the prison system. There is no reason for this to be a race issue or even a class issue, since sex offenses cut across economic lines as well. "If I saw some semblance of evidence that this would work, I'd be for it," Robert Newberry admitted after the Butler case cooled off, "but let it start with a white man." Given the history of castration in this country, that may be a fair request.

Finally, it is a foolish consistency to castrate women for sexual or other crimes. There can be a change in behavior after such an operation, but so far it has never been correlated with sex crimes. That said, the fact is that women can have their Fallopian tubes tied as a contraceptive measure or their entire uterus removed as treatment for premenstrual syndrome, while men who rape or molest children or expose themselves up to thirty times a day can't be castrated because that would be barbarous.

"Why can't it be like abortion, available on demand?" one offender asks. That seems a reasonable question. As it stands now, the only way Butler could be castrated is if he gets a sex-change operation. Society poses no objection to that.

We should acknowledge that men who seek castration are making a sacrifice. The way we can do so is by reducing their prison time and giving them adequate adjustment counseling. The critics may be right that some men may reoffend, but everything we know about the subjects suggests that castration works better than any other approach. Why can't we honor the plea of Steve Butler and many other men and give them the help they are begging for? Castration may not be an ideal solution, but if we treat it as therapy rather than punishment, as help instead of revenge, and if we view offenders as troubled victims, not monsters, then perhaps the castration option will be seen as evidence of our wisdom and humanity, not of our backwardness and cruelty.

NO 

Kari A. Vanderzyl

Castration as an Alternative to Incarceration: An Impotent Approach to the Punishment of Sex Offenders

The use of castration as a punitive measure, practiced for centuries by other cultures, has enjoyed newfound prominence in this country's criminal justice system as a potential remedy for the proliferation of sex offenses. Not surprisingly, the implementation of castration as an alternative to incarceration has generated considerable debate, including questions regarding its constitutionality and desirability from a public policy standpoint. Fueling the controversy, several recently convicted sex offenders have requested that they be castrated rather than receive lengthy prison sentences.

In March of 1992, Steven Allen Butler, a convicted rapist, stood before Texas District Court Judge Michael McSpadden and requested that the judge order surgical castration rather than sentencing him to prison. Judge McSpadden initially assented to the request, but ultimately withdrew approval in the wake of national publicity and protests by civil libertarians. Physicians in the area refused to perform the operation, and even Butler found himself reconsidering his unusual request.

In Great Britain, a man with a forty-year history of child sex abuse privately arranged for his own surgical castration after prison authorities ignored his repeated pleas for the operation. The subject, a sixty year old former coal miner, has served numerous prison terms for sex offenses against children and has threatened suicide, gone on hunger strikes and even attempted to castrate himself. Although officials at a psychiatric hospital offered to administer chemical castration, the offender refused such treatment, considering chemical castration a temporary, and therefore inadequate, solution to his deviant behavior.

Sharing this desire for sterilization, a thirty-eight year old convicted rapist sentenced in McLean County, Illinois, expressed a preference for castration rather than a prison sentence. Despite the offender's request for sterilization, the sentencing judge concluded that castration was not a viable alternative to incarceration and sentenced the repeat offender to a thirty-seven year term of imprisonment.

From *Northern Illinois University Law Review,* 15 N. Ill University Law Review 107 (Fall 1994). All notes and citations in the original have been omitted. Ellipses in the article reflect material that has been omitted from the original text.

This [article] addresses the legal implications of castration as a punitive measure, tracing the development of compulsory sterilization from its origins in the eugenics movement in the early twentieth century to its present status as an alternative to imprisonment. In particular, the first section explores the rise of eugenics legislation in the United States, the Supreme Court's legitimization of compulsory sterilization and the current practice among the courts of upholding sterilization legislation for the mentally retarded. Within the second section, the use of castration as a punitive measure both in the United States and abroad is discussed. In addition, the second section describes methods of male sterilization, including surgical castration, vasectomy and the non-surgical alternative, chemical castration. The third section analyzes common constitutional challenges to compulsory castration and asserts that the use of castration as an alternative to incarceration violates the rights of privacy and procreation, and may also violate the Eighth Amendment protection against cruel and unusual punishment. In the fourth section, the reasonable relationship test is applied to castration as a term of probation, yielding mixed results. The informed consent objection presented in the fifth section suggests that castration as an alternative to a prison sentence violates the voluntariness requirement of the informed consent doctrine. Finally, section six explores the economic and social policy considerations implicated by sterilization in the punitive context, focusing on the financial burdens to society and the failure of castration to address the uncontrollable hostility manifesting itself in acts of sexual violence. The article concludes by asserting that castration in any form constitutes an ineffective, unconstitutional alternative to incarceration.

Background

Historical Framework: Eugenics and the Socially Unfit

Compulsory sterilization is not a novel concept. The controversy over a court's or state agency's authority to destroy an individual's ability to procreate has persisted for over a century, since the notion of involuntary sterilization originated with the eugenics movement. Defined by its creator, Sir Francis Galton, as "the science which deals with all influences that improve the unborn qualities of the race . . . [and] develop them to the utmost advantage," eugenics seeks to achieve the elimination of social ills through biological reformation. American eugenicists relied upon Darwin's theory of evolution and Mendel's genetics experimentation to provide scientific support for their movement. Borrowing from the research of Darwin and Mendel, eugenicists theorized that feeble-mindedness and other negative qualities resulted from inferior genes. Operating on this premise, proponents of eugenics linked every existing social problem to heredity and concluded that the solution to the country's social ills required control over human reproduction. Through lecture tours and written propaganda, positive eugenics encouraged individuals with superior genes to select mates from within their own ranks and to maximize family size. Negative eugenics utilized a different approach, calling for the implementation of a program of sterilization to eliminate procreation of the unfit. Before 1900, compulsory sterilization of the unfit enjoyed limited popular support. Surgical castration, that era's prevailing method of sterilization, produced hormonal imbalance and psychological and physiological effects. With the emergence of two less severe methods, vasectomy and salpingectomy, compulsory eugenics sterilization grew in popularity.

Compulsory Sterilization Legislation

Inspired by the eugenics rationale that played on the pervasive fear of a growing mentally retarded citizenry, in the early 1900's, a number of states enacted compulsory sterilization legislation. State laws mandated sterilization for punitive and therapeutic purposes, with surgical procedures such as castration, vasectomies and salpingectomies performed to punish convicted felons and rehabilitate mentally retarded individuals in state institutions. State officials invoked the doctrine of *parens patriae* to justify the involuntary sterilization of the mentally retarded, claiming to act in the best interests of the institutionalized individuals. Under the doctrine of *parens patriae,* the state bears the responsibility of caring for citizens incapable of protecting their own interests. Despite legislators' efforts to legitimize the practice of involuntary sterilization through reliance on the *parens patriae* justification, the courts nevertheless established a pattern of invalidating compulsory sterilization laws as violations of equal protection or due process.

"Three Generations of Imbeciles. . .": *Buck V. Bell* and the Aftermath

At the height of the United States eugenics movement, proponents found an unlikely ally in the nation's highest court. In the now famous case of an institutionalized sixteen year old girl facing compulsory sterilization pursuant to a Virginia statute, the Court upheld the legislation as a valid exercise of the state's police power. Writing for the majority, Justice Holmes reasoned that it would be "better for all the world, if instead of waiting to execute degenerate offspring for crime, or to let them starve for their imbecility, society can prevent those who are manifestly unfit from continuing their kind. . . . Three generations of imbeciles are enough." . . .

Castration as a Punitive Measure

While the involuntary sterilization of mentally retarded persons remains a prominent issue, the greatest and most recent controversy regarding procreative rights has arisen in the punitive context. As an alternative to imprisonment, male sex offenders may elect to undergo castration as punishment for their crimes, raising a number of legal, social and moral issues. . . .

Constitutional Challenges to Sterilization in the Punitive Context

The sterilization of individuals for punitive purposes raises a number of constitutional issues. Government interference with an individual's ability to reproduce implicates constitutional rights to privacy and procreation and the guarantee against cruel and unusual punishment. To achieve recognition as a legitimate, viable alternative to incarceration, male sterilization must pass constitutional muster in each of the areas implicated. . . .

Castration and the Right to Privacy

Although the Constitution contains no explicit mention of a privacy right, the Supreme Court has acknowledged an implied right to privacy under the Fourteenth Amendment protecting an individual's autonomy in making decisions concerning childbearing and contraception. In *Griswold v. Connecticut,* the Court held that a state statute barring married persons' use of contraceptives violated the Fourteenth Amendment's Due Process Clause, reasoning that the penumbras of the Bill of Rights' enumerated protections created a "zone of privacy." The Court in *Griswold* characterized an individual's privacy interest as a fundamental right upon which the state cannot intrude in the absence of a compelling governmental interest. The Supreme Court further articulated the protected realm of privacy in *Eisenstadt v. Baird,* concluding that to have any meaning at all, the right of privacy must include the "right of any individual, married or single, to be free from unwarranted governmental intrusion" into his or her decision of whether or not to have children. . . .

An interference with an individual's ability to reproduce, whether permanent or temporary, clearly implicates the constitutional right of privacy. By offering castration to convicted sex offenders as an alternative to imprisonment, legislatures and courts intrude upon an offender's decision whether or not to have children, a decision the (U.S. Supreme) Court . . . deemed protected from unwarranted governmental invasion under the Fourteenth Amendment. Just as a state may not prohibit married and single persons from using contraception, so it should not be allowed to compel individuals to practice contraception. Proponents of the use of castration as a form of punishment for sex offenders may argue that because the offender has the opportunity to reject sterilization and choose incarceration instead, no intrusion of protected privacy rights occurs. However, the inherently coercive nature of the choice between freedom through castration and an extended prison sentence renders voluntary consent to sterilization an impossibility. The privacy right primarily implicated by castration in the punitive context is the fundamental right of procreation, a privacy interest meriting a separate discussion that includes analysis under the strict scrutiny standard.

The Fundamental Right of Procreation

Castration as an alternative to incarceration, whether surgical or chemical, violates the right of procreative freedom. To render a convicted sex offender sterile is to deprive him of his right to procreate, a right characterized by Justice Douglas in *Skinner [v. Oklahoma]* as "one of the basic civil rights of man." Castration, like a vasectomy, eliminates the offender's capacity for procreation. However, castration by surgery or injections represents a more intrusive procedure than the vasectomy at issue in *Skinner* because it results in the cessation of the sexual drive. . . .

Castration as Cruel and Unusual Punishment

Another objection to male sterilization as an alternative to incarceration may be premised on the prohibition against cruel and unusual punishment provided by the Eighth Amendment. An Eighth Amendment analysis of castration as punishment for convicted sex offenders requires an examination of . . . whether the procedure constitutes cruel and unusual punishment. . . .

While the Eighth Amendment may have been originally intended to protect against punishment deemed inhuman and barbarous, the Supreme Court has construed the provision more broadly. In *Weems v. United States,* for example, the Court focused on the disproportionality between the penalty and offense to determine whether the defendant's sentence constituted cruel and unusual punishment. Not merely a static concept, the Eighth Amendment "must draw its meaning from the evolving standards of decency that mark the progress of a maturing society." Despite its seeming reluctance to explicitly define the limits of the provision prohibiting cruel and unusual punishment, the Court has established some guidelines for determining Eighth Amendment violations. The Court has incorporated three interrelated tests to identify cruel and unusual punishment: (1) whether the punishment is inherently cruel; (2) whether the punishment is disproportionate to the offense; and (3) whether the punishment exceeds the extent necessary to achieve the legitimate governmental objectives. . . .

[T]he Supreme Court of South Carolina voided the suspended sentence of a sex offender where the suspension and probation were conditioned on the offender's submission to surgical castration. According to the court in *State v. Brown,* because castration constitutes physical mutilation, it satisfies the cruelty requirement of the prohibition against cruel and unusual punishment. While the *Brown* decision seems to focus on the physical suffering associated with castration, "mutilation" as used by the court also suggests an element of degradation, consistent with earlier courts' analysis of cruelty. . . .

The preceding analysis of constitutional objections to castration demonstrates that sex offenders possess the fundamental right to be free from unwarranted governmental intrusion into their decision-making concerning procreation. Because castration is not the least restrictive means available to effectuate the governmental interest of protecting society, sterilization as a punitive measure violates offenders' Fourteenth Amendment privacy rights. Additionally, offenders enjoy a constitutionally protected liberty interest to refuse unwanted medical treatment in the form of surgical or pharmacological castration, or vasectomy. Finally, castration implicates the Eighth Amendment prohibition against cruel and unusual punishment. Failing to qualify as treatment, when subjected to scrutiny under any of the established tests, castration would most likely be found to constitute cruel and unusual punishment violative of the Eighth Amendment. . . .

Policy Considerations

In addition to its constitutional and common law implications, castration raises several significant policy considerations. Most important to a determination of its viability as an alternative to incarceration is its effectiveness as a punitive measure. According to recent studies, approximately forty percent of rapists and pedophiles will repeat their crimes. A primary criticism of castration as a form of punishment for sex offenders is that it fails to address the anger and hatred motivating sex offenses against women and children. To take away an offender's ability to procreate is merely to eliminate one channel of aggression. While advocates of chemical castration hail its five percent recidivism rate as evidence of the program's success, that statistic may be misleading. A high percentage of sex crimes go unreported, and further, most treatment programs track participants' progress for only a short time after the termination of treatment, when the risk of relapse is the lowest.

Critics also attack castration as a sanctioning alternative for its seeming lenience. Instead of serving thirty years in prison, a convicted sex offender may elect to undergo surgical castration, vasectomy, or chemical castration and retain his freedom. Victims of serious sex offenses would most likely not be reassured knowing that the violent offender who injured them will escape incarceration upon completion of a sterilization procedure. Moreover, castration merely validates the offender's distorted self-portrait, that he is a victim who cannot help himself. The source of the violence, the uncontrollable anger and hostility, will remain long after the scalpel or injection removes the offender's capability to procreate.

Finally, the cost to society of practicing compulsory castration may also undermine its viability. Admittedly, the state would incur minimal expense in surgically castrating sex offenders in relation to the money spent keeping those same offenders in prison. However, castrated offenders may very well vent their aggression in other criminal ways and therefore ultimately require incarceration. Similarly, those offenders undergoing chemical castration and counseling present a financial burden. Not only must the state cover the cost of the drug for those offenders unable to pay for their own treatment, but financial resources must also be used to provide counseling services. A counseling staff must be funded in order to treat and monitor the progress of chemically castrated offenders. Such a program requires a great deal of both time and money to operate effectively. Viewed in terms of the above social and economic considerations, sterilization does not appear to be a viable alternative to incarceration.

Conclusion

Castration should be rejected as an unacceptable, ineffective and unconstitutional alternative to imprisonment. A lingering spectre from the American eugenics movement at the turn of the century, the sterilization of criminals has enjoyed limited legislative and judicial support in contemporary society. However, relatively recent technological developments resulting in the marketing of hormone suppressers has added a new dimension to the issue of sterilization of sex offenders and has received support for its non-surgical method of temporarily reducing the sexual drives of paraphiliac offenders. Despite the procedural differences, however, chemical castration and its surgical equivalents share constitutional flaws which render them inappropriate substitutes for incarceration.

The prevailing forms of male sterilization interfere with an offender's ability to produce offspring, and, as a consequence, violate the offender's constitutionally protected privacy rights, including the fundamental right of procreation. Moreover, the offender maintains a liberty interest in exercising his right to refuse unwanted medical treatment. A state is therefore precluded from forcing an offender to undergo sterilization unless it demonstrates a legitimate interest overriding the offender's right of self-determination. Subjected to Eighth Amendment analysis, castration in any form fails to qualify as treatment and instead constitutes cruel and unusual punishment. . . .

Finally, policy considerations mandate the elimination of punitive sterilization practices for sex offenders. The seemingly low recidivism rate hailed by proponents as evidence of chemical castration's success fails to reflect the high number of sex crimes that go unreported each year. Proponents additionally ignore the substantial administrative costs associated with implementing a treatment program of chemical castration for criminals who cannot pay for it themselves and who may likely have to continue treatment for long periods of time. Not only does this procedure drain valuable public resources, but at the same time, it subjects the offenders to potentially dangerous side effects, the full extent of which remains unknown. In a society besieged by crime and the fear it begets, where prison overcrowding has grown to massive proportions and society is desperate for a cure, castration may seem to be the definitive remedy. Nevertheless, a remedy which necessitates the deprivation of fundamental rights and personal liberties and which fails to address the source of the problem must be rejected as an unacceptable solution.

POSTSCRIPT

Should Serious Sex Offenders Be Castrated?

At first glance, castrating serious sex offenders seems to be a radical and somewhat Orwellian solution to a difficult social problem. But, what if it works? If we can significantly reduce serious sex offender recidivism by castrating them and eliminating their sexual urges, is it a good social policy?

Kari A. Vanderzyl asserts that a primary criticism of castration is that it fails to address the anger and hatred motivating sex offenses against women and children. Thus, castration merely eliminates one channel of an offender's aggression. Vanderzyl asserts that the source of the violence, anger, and hostility will remain. She believes as well that the low recidivism rates reported in castration studies may be misleading. A high number of sex offenses go unreported, and most treatment programs track offender progress for only a short time. Moreover, Vanderzyl believes that castration as a form of treatment conjures an image of eugenics movements and is a deprivation of fundamental rights and personal liberties.

Lawrence Wright argues, however, that even though castrating sex offenders is not an ideal solution, it works better than any other approach. In addition, it may be a more humane form of sex offender treatment because it will help offenders control their behavior and reduce prison time.

Castration as a form of sex offender treatment does appear to be gaining some momentum in the United States. It will be interesting to see whether the public and the courts are receptive to this form of treatment, or if it will be rejected as an approach that is barbaric and unacceptable in society.

There are a number of additional resources that may shed light on the issues discussed in this section. See, for example, J. Michael Bailey and Aaron S. Greenberg, "The Science and Ethics of Castration: Lessons from the *Morse* Case," *Northwestern University Law Review* (Summer 1998); William Winslade, "Castrating Pedophiles Convicted of Sex Offenses Against Children: New Treatment or Old Punishment?" *Southern Methodist University Law Review* (1998, vol. 51, p. 349); Douglas J. Besharov and Andrew Fachhs, "Sex Offenders: Is Castration an Acceptable Punishment?" *American Bar Association Journal* (July 1992); Nickolaus Heim and Carolyn J. Hursch, "Castration for Sex Offenders: Treatment or Punishment? A Review of Recent European Literature," *Archives of Sexual Behavior* (1979, vol. 8); and Christopher Meisenkothen, "Chemical Castration–Breaking the Cycle of Paraphiliac Recidivism," *Social Justice* (Spring 1999).

Additional resources include: Reinhard Wille and Klaus M. Beier, "Castration in Germany," *Annals of Sex Research* (1989, vol. 2, pp. 103–133), which examined the results of a treatment program for a sample of 104 men who underwent voluntary castration over a 10-year period. This study found a postoperative recidivism rate of approximately 3 percent. Other resources are Marjorie A. Fonza, "A Review of Sex Offender Treatment Programs," *ABNF Journal* (Mar/Apr 2001); Catherine A. Gallagher, David B. Wilson, Paul Hirshfield, Mark B. Coggeshall, and Doris L. MacKenzie, "A Quantitative Review of the Effects of Sex Offender Treatment on Sexual Reoffending," *Corrections Management Quarterly* (Fall 1999); Craig Turk, "Kinder Cut," *The New Republic* (Aug. 25, 1997); and J. Paul Federoff and Beverly Moran, "Myths and Misconceptions About Sex Offenders," *The Canadian Journal of Human Sexuality* (1997, vol. 6, issue 4).

ISSUE 4

Will Strict Gun Control Laws Reduce the Number of Homicides in the United States?

YES: Franklin E. Zimring, from "Firearms, Violence, and the Potential Impact of Firearms Control," *The Journal of Law, Medicine & Ethics* (Spring 2004)

NO: Lance K. Stell, from "The Production of Criminal Violence in America: Is Strict Gun Control the Solution?" *The Journal of Law, Medicine & Ethics* (Spring 2004)

ISSUE SUMMARY

YES: Professor Franklin E. Zimring argues that there is a strong relationship between gun use and the death rate from violent crime and that handgun use increases the death rate from violence by a factor of three to five.

NO: Professor Lance K. Stell asserts that strict gun control institutionalizes the natural predatory advantages of larger, stronger, violence-prone persons and increases the risks of violent victimization for less well-off law-abiding citizens.

Do strict gun control laws help to reduce violent crime? Or, do gun control laws fail to stem violent behavior and help social predators to victimize law-abiding citizens? Does the Second Amendment to the U.S. Constitution give people an absolute right to bear arms? These are interesting questions that have important implications for violence control in U.S. society.

Because the issue of a constitutional right to bear arms has been so controversial, perhaps it is best to begin our analysis here. The Second Amendment states: "A well regulated Militia being necessary to the security of a free State, the right of the people to keep and bear Arms shall not be infringed." While the U.S. Supreme Court has held that most of the protections in the U.S. Constitution's Bill of Rights—"fundamental rights"—apply to state proceedings, it has never held that the Second Amendment's "right to bear arms" is fundamental. The Supreme Court's main decision interpreting the Second

Amendment, *United States v. Miller,* 307 U.S. 174 (1939), upheld the National Firearms Act of 1934, which required the registration of sawed-off shotguns. The Court stated:

> [Without] any evidence tending to show that possession or use of a shotgun having a barrel of less than 18 inches in length at this time has some reasonable relationship to the preservation or efficiency of a well regulated militia, we cannot say that the Second Amendment guarantees the right to keep and bear such an instrument.

As *Miller* illustrates, the Supreme Court and most lower courts have tied the right to bear arms to the maintenance of a "well regulated militia." They have not construed the Second Amendment to convey a more generalized right of the citizenry to own all types of firearms.

A number of lower court decisions over the years have indicated that states and other governmental subdivisions, such as cities or counties, are free to impose reasonable restrictions on firearms ownership. For example, in 1981, the Village of Morton Grove, Illinois, adopted the following ordinance: "No person shall possess, in the Village of Morton Grove the following: C. Any handgun, unless the same has been rendered permanently inoperative." It further provided that a person violating this law is guilty of a petty offense and "shall be fined no less than fifty dollars ($50.00) nor more than five hundred dollars ($500.00) or incarcerated for up to six months for each offense." Shortly after it was passed, the ordinance was challenged in federal court.

In *Quilici v. Village of Morton Grove,* 695 F. 2d 261 (7th Cir. 1982), the U.S. Court of Appeals held that "the right to bear arms is inextricably connected to the preservation of a militia." Moreover, because it has never been held by the Supreme Court to be a fundamental right, the right to bear arms is not binding on state proceedings and therefore Morton Grove's ordinance does not violate the Second Amendment. The U.S. Supreme Court later refused a request to review the case and the decision of the lower court was left in force. Thus, the current legal status of state and local gun control laws is clear.

Professor Lance K. Stell contends, however, that strict gun control laws institutionalize the natural predatory advantages of larger, stronger, violence-prone persons and increase the risks of violent victimization for less well-off law-abiding citizens. In response to the arguments posed by Dr. Zimring, Professor Snell states: "[P]ursuing any gun control measure designed to impose (hand)gun scarcity on the general population is both needless and useless."

What is your position regarding the ownership of firearms? Should the right to own a firearm be a fundamental right of citizenship in the United States? Should states and their municipal subdivisions have the authority to regulate gun ownership? Would taking guns from the population effectively reduce homicide rates in the United States? These are important questions that directly impact our quality of life. As you read the articles in this section try to develop a sense of whether gun ownership should be freely permitted, restricted, or banned altogether.

Franklin E. Zimring

Firearms, Violence, and the Potential Impact of Firearms Control

This paper organizes the question of gun controls as violence policy under two quite different headings. The first issue to be discussed is the relationship between gun use and the death rate from violent crime. The second question is whether and how firearms control strategies might reduce the death rate from violence. When we review the evidence on the relationship between guns and violence, it seems clear that gun use, usually handgun use, increases the death rate from violence by a factor of three to five. Nobody in mainstream social science or criminology argues against such weapon effects these days, although some are more skeptical of the magnitude estimated than others (one example is Lance Stell).[1] Thus the problem is both genuine and important. When we review the extent to which particular approaches to controlling firearms might reduce the death rate from violence, the evidence for modern attempts at gun control saving lives is much weaker than the evidence that gun use causes death. So gun control is a potential life-saving tool but only if the use of guns in attack can be reduced, and achieving that in our city streets will neither be easy or cheap.

Gun Use and Violence

It is not true that guns are used in most criminal events, nor can we say that guns are employed in most violent crimes. . . .

Guns are only used in 4% of all crimes, and only 20% of all violent crimes, but about 70% of all criminal killings. This tells us immediately what the special problem of gun use is in violent crime—an increase in the death rate per 100 violent attacks. If the problem you worry about is crime, guns are involved in 4% of the acts. If the problem is lethal violence, the market share for firearms is 70%. Guns alone account for twice as many criminal deaths as all other means of killing combined. Why is that?

Most criminal homicides result from violent assaults without any other criminal motive such as robbery or rape. Gun assaults are seven times as likely to kill as all other kinds of criminal assault,[2] and about five times as likely to kill as are knives, the next most deadly weapon that is frequently used in criminal attacks. Firearms robbery is about four times as likely to produce a victim death as a non-firearms robbery.

From *Journal of Law, Medicine and Ethics*, vol. 32, issue 1, Spring 2004, pp. 34-37.

In this section, I discuss what elements of gun use might increase the lethality of gun assaults and then briefly discuss the situation with gun versus non-gun robbery.

The Causes of Differential Lethality

Guns may cause increases in the death rate from assault in a variety of different ways. The use of guns as opposed to other weapons in assault may be associated with both mechanical and social changes in violent assault that can increase its death rate. Among the mechanical or instrumentality aspects of gun use that can increase death rates are: the greater injurious impact of bullets; the longer range of firearms; and the greater capacity of firearms for executing multiple attacks. Among the features in social setting related to gun use are: the need to use more lethal instruments of assault in situations where an attacker fears that his adversary may have a gun, the need to sustain or intensify a deadly assault because an opponent possesses or is using firearms, and the increased willingness to use guns and other lethal weapons in personal conflict because such weapons are used generally. All of these aspects may increase the lethality of assaults committed with guns, but by no means to the same degree. There are also two social impacts of gun possession and use that can lower death rates: the deterrence of assaults because of fear of gun-owning victims and the prevention of attempted assaults by an armed victim.

In this paper, I will stress the most important of the mechanisms that increase death rates when guns are used, so-called instrumentality effects. For a summary of all these other potential causes and their assessment, see Zimring and Hawkins.[3]

Instrumentality Effects

Of all the possible ways that gun use increases the deadliness of attacks, the theory that gunshot wounds inflict more damage than other methods of personal attacks is considered the most important and has been the subject of the most research. The early debate about the dangerousness of guns on deaths from assault involved different theories of the types of intention that produced assaults that lead to death. Marvin Wolfgang in his study of homicide doubted that the weapon used in an attack made much difference in the chance that a death would result since so many different weapons could produce death if an attacker tried hard enough.[4] I responded to this assertion with a study of knife and gun assaults in Chicago.[5]

My data suggested that many homicides were the result of attacks apparently conducted with less than a single-minded intent to kill. Unlike the Wolfgang study where only fatal attacks were examined, the Zimring studies compared fatal and nonfatal gun and knife assaults in Chicago over four police periods in 1968 and gun assaults in 1972. The studies found that 70 percent of all gun killings in Chicago were the result of attacks that resulted in only one wound to the victim,[6] and that most attacks with guns or knives that killed a victim looked quite similar to the knife and gun attacks that did not kill.[7] From this data, I argued that most homicides were the result of ambiguously motivated assaults, so that the offender would risk his victim's death, but usually did not press on until death was assured.

Under such circumstances, the capacity of a weapon to inflict life-threatening injury would have an important influence on the death rate from assault. The 1908 Chicago study found that gun attacks were about five times as likely to kill as knife attacks, and this ratio held when the comparison was controlled for the number of wounds inflicted and the specific location of the most serious wound.[8] Since knives were the next most deadly frequently used method of inflicting injury in attacks, the large difference in death rate suggested that substituting knives or other less dangerous instruments for guns would reduce the death rate from assault.

This weapon dangerousness comparison was first reported for Chicago in 1908 and has been replicated in other sites.[9] The follow-up study demonstrated that a difference in weapon as subtle as firearm caliber can double the death rate from gun assaults.[10] The summary conclusion from this line of research can be simply stated: the objective dangerousness of a weapon used in violent assaults appears to be a major influence on the number of victims who will die from attacks. This "instrumentality effect" is the major documented influence of guns on death rate.[11]

The use of guns in robbery is different from their use in woundings since the weapon is not necessarily used to inflict harm. Because robberies with guns frighten their victims into complying with the robbers' demands more often than other robberies, a smaller number of gun robberies result in woundings than personal force robberies and robberies with knives. Still, the greater dangerousness of guns when they are fired more than compensates for the lower number of wounds. For street robberies and those that take place in commercial establishments, the death rate for every 1,000 gun robberies is about three times that generated by robberies at knife point, and about ten times the death rate from robberies involving personal force.[12]

Firearms as a Contributing Cause of Lethal Violence

The use of firearms in assault and robbery is the single environmental feature of American society that is most clearly linked to the extraordinary death rate from interpersonal violence in the United States. But the strength of this relationship does not mean that firearms ownership and use has a simple, invariable, or independent influence on homicide rates. In this section, I consider the question of the causal connection between gun use and lethality. I do this not only because it is an important issue in relation to firearms and lethal violence, but also because reflecting on the questions of causation that arise in connection with firearms teaches us an important lesson about the role of many other environmental influences on the incidence of lethal violence.

The American debate about guns has produced one of the few causal critiques ever to appear on a bumper sticker: the famous slogan "Guns don't kill people, people kill people." Behind the strong sentiment that inspired this and a multitude of related appeals lies an important logical point. Firearms ownership and use is neither a necessary nor a sufficient cause of violent death in the United States. Firearms are not a necessary cause of killings because of the wide army of alternative methods of killing that are available ranging from the strangler's hands to car bombs. Even in the United States at the turn of the 21st century, nearly 30 percent of all killings did not involve guns. Moreover, the widespread availability of firearms is not a sufficient condition for intentional homicide by a wide margin. Almost one-half of all American households own some kind of guns and it is estimated that one-quarter of all households own a handgun—the weapon used in more than three-quarters of all gun homicides. Yet only a small fraction of all gun owners become gun attackers. The logical point here is that guns do not become dangerous instruments of attack if they are not used in an attack.

If gun use is neither a necessary nor a sufficient cause of violent death, what is the proper descriptive label for the role gun use plays in deaths due to intentional injury? The most accurate label for the role of firearms in those cases of death and injury from intentional attacks in which they are used is contributing cause. Even where the availability of a gun plays no important role in the decision to commit an assault, the use of a gun can be an important contributing cause in the death and injury that results for gun attacks. When guns are used in a high proportion of such attacks, the death rate from violent attack will be high. Current evidence suggests that a combination of the ready availability of guns and the willingness to use maximum force in interpersonal conflict is the most important single contribution to the high U.S. death rate from violence. Our rate of assault is not exceptional; our death rate from assault is exceptional.[13]

The role of gun use as a contributing cause means that the net effect of firearms on violence will depend on the interaction of gun availability with other factors which influence the rate of violent assaults in a society and the willingness of people to use guns in such assaults. So the precise contribution of firearms to the death toll from violence is contingent on many other factors that may influence the number and character of violent attacks.

Some implications of this contingency deserve emphasis. Introducing 10,000 loaded handguns into a social environment where violent assault is a rare occurrence will not produce a large number of additional homicide deaths unless it also increases the rate of assault. The percentage increase in homicide might be considerable if guns become substitutes for less lethal weapons. But the additional number of killings would be small because of the low rate of attack. Introducing 10,000 handguns into an environment where rates of attack and willingness to use handguns in attack are both high is a change that would produce many more additional deaths. The net effect of guns depends on how they are likely to be used.

One corollary of viewing guns as an interactive and contributing cause to intentional homicide is that societies with low rates of violent assault will pay a lower price if they allow guns to be widely available than will societies with higher rates of violence. The sanguine sound bite encountered in American debates about guns is: "An armed society is a polite society."[14] As stated on the bumper sticker, this does not seem particularly plausible, but it does seem likely that only a very polite society can be heavily armed without paying a high price.

The United States of 2004 is far from that polite society, although things are better now than they were as recently as 1994. Our considerable propensity for violent conflict would be a serious societal problem even if gun availability and use were low. But the very fact that the United States is a high-violence environment makes the contribution of gun use to the death toll from violence very much greater. When viewed in the light of the concept of contributing causation, the United States has both a violence problem and a gun problem, and each makes the other more deadly.

Varieties of Firearms Control

The objective of almost all forms of firearms control is to reduce the use of loaded guns in attacks and robberies and thus to reduce the death rate from crime. There turns out to be several different strategies of control, many different intensities of gun regulation, and many different contexts in which controls can be attempted. One common strategy is to prohibit dangerous uses of guns—so that hundreds if not thousands of statutes prohibit concealed handguns from being carried at all, and from being taken into airports, churches, schools, and courthouses. Other "time, place and manner laws" prohibit shooting in city streets. The idea is that some settings are so dangerous that otherwise allowable weapons and uses should be prohibited.

One dispute about a "time, place and manner" regulation generated its own considerable literature in the late 1990s. John Lott provided an econometric study which argued that expanding the criteria for concealed weapons permits was associated with lower crime rates.[15] Several published criticisms have undermined Lott's findings either by criticizing the quality of his multivariate regression evidence[16] or by counter-demonstrations using similar methodology.[17] Because the impact of such laws on citizen gun carrying behavior and the use of guns in self defense has not been measured, the evidence that "shall issue" permit-to-carry laws has impact on crime rates is thin.

A second class of controls attempt to restrict dangerous users from obtaining and using guns. In federal law, convicted felons, youth, and certain diagnosed and previously institutionalized persons with emotional illnesses are excluded from being eligible to obtain weapons. This is the primary type of firearms control strategy in federal law and in most states.

A third approach is to try to exclude from general ownership particular types of guns that are too easily misused. Federal law has all but banned automatic weapons and sawed-off shotguns since 1934, and the Federal Gun Control Act of 1908 added "destructive devices" such as bazookas and hand grenades to the list of classes of weapon thought too dangerous for general ownership.[18] In the late 1980s, a controversy arose over semi-automatic weapons with large ammunition magazines—so-called assault weapons—which have been restricted in a variety of ways under different laws with different definitions.[19] And special restrictions also exist in a few states and cities for handguns.

A "dangerous uses" approach tries to govern the use of guns without reference to the people who can possess them or the kind of guns that can be owned. A "dangerous user" strategy tries to segregate higher risk users without making any guns unavailable for the rest of the population. A "dangerous guns" strategy tries to restrict the general availability of certain types of guns. Every state and city has a mix of different laws—there are no examples in the United States of jurisdictions that rely on only one general approach and not any I know of with only one set of regulations.

Can Gun Control Work?

The answer to this general question is a highly qualified "yes, but." If and to the extent that regulation reduces the use of loaded guns in crimes it will save American lives. But reducing the share of violence with guns is not an easy task to achieve in urban environments with large inventories of available handguns. Most gun control efforts do not make measurable impacts on gun use, particularly low budget symbolic legislation. If Congress when creating what it called a "gun-free school zone" by legislation did reduce firearms violence, the result would be on a par with that of the miracle of loaves and the fishes. But New York City's effort to tightly enforce one of the nation's most restrictive handgun laws did apparently have a substantial payoff in reduced shootings that saved many lives.[20]

What I would emphasize here is the fallacy of categorical generalizations. We have no business asking whether broad classes of laws—criminal prohibitions, anti-theft statutes or gun control strategies—work or don't. That is an aggregation error as long as guns are a contributing cause to the death rate from violent crime in the United States. The serious work is in identifying the specific strategies and contexts in which regulation can reduce the use of firearms in violent assault and attempting to achieve these results at tolerable public and personal cost.

References

1. J. B. Jacobs, *Can Gun Control Work?* (New York: Oxford University Press, 2002).
2. F. E. Zimring and G. Hawkins, *Crime Is Not the Problem: Lethal Violence in America* (New York: Oxford University Press, 1997): at 108.
3. See Zimring and Hawkins, supra note 2: 113-122.
4. M. Wolfgang, *Patterns in Criminal Homicide* (Philadelphia: University of Pennsylvania Press, 1958).
5. F. E. Zimring, "Is Gun Control Likely to Reduce Violent Killings?" *University of Chicago Law Review* 35 (1968):721-737.
6. F. E. Zimring, "The Medium is the Message: Firearms Caliber as a Determinant of the Death Rate from Assault," *Journal of Legal Studies* 1 (1972): 97-123.

7. See Zimring, supra note 5.
8. Zimring, supra note 5.
9. T. Vinson, "Gun and Knife Attacks," *Australian Journal of Forensic Sciences* 7 (1974): 76; R. Sarvesvaran and C.H.S. Jayewarclene, "The Role of the Weapon in the Homicide Drama," *Medicine and Law* 4 (1985): 315-326.
10. Zimring, supra note 6.
11. P. J. Cook, "The Technology of Personal Violence," in M. Tonry, ed., *Crime and Justice: A Review of Research* (Chicago: Chicago University Press, 1991).
12. F. E. Zimring and J. Zuehl, "Victim Injury and Death in Urban Robbery: A Chicago Study," *Journal of Legal Studies* 15 (1986):1-40; Cook supra note 11: 17.
13. Zimring and Hawkins, supra note 2: 34-50.
14. Handgun Control Inc., *Carrying Concealed Weapons: Questions and Answers* (Washington, D.C.: Handgun Control Inc., 1995).
15. J. R. Lott, *More Guns, Less Crime* (second edition) (Chicago: University of Chicago Press, 2000).
16. D. Black and D. Nagin, "Do 'Right-to-Carry' Laws Deter Violent Crime?" *Journal of Legal Studies* 27 (1998): 209-219; F. E. Zimring and G. Hawkins, "Concealed Handguns: The Counterfeit Deterrent," *The Responsive Community* 1 (1997): 46-60.
17. J. Donohue and I. Ayers, "Shooting Down the More Guns, Less Crime Hypothesis," National Bureau of Economic Research (working paper no. w9336, 2002); J. Donohue and I. Ayers, "The Latest Misfires in Support of the More Guns, Less Crime Hypothesis," *Stanford Law Review* 55 (2003): 1371-1398.
18. F. E. Zimring, "Firearms and Federal Law: The Gun Control Act of 1968," *Journal of Legal Studies* 4 (1975): 133-198.
19. F. E. Zimring, "The Problem of Assault Firearms," *Crime and Delinquency* 35 (1989): 538-545.
20. J. Fagan, F. E. Zimring, and J. Kim, "Declining Homicide in New York City: A Tale of Two Trends," *Journal of Criminal Law and Criminology* 88 (1998): 1277-1323.

Lance K. Stell

The Production of Criminal Violence in America: Is Strict Gun Control the Solution?

"Strict gun control" (SGC) has no clear meaning, so it is necessary to clarify it. I define SGC as an array of legally sanctioned restrictions designed to impose firearm scarcity on the general population. SGC's public policy goal, gun scarcity, commonly rests on the predicates that "dangerous criminal control" is not the central problem for reducing the problem of criminal gun violence but rather that it is the social prevalence of the distinctively-lethal instruments (guns) by which both supposedly "good citizens" as well as violent criminals inflict a staggeringly high percentage of injury and death.

Professor Zimring is one SGC's most distinguished, prolific and comprehensive theorists. He has advocated for handgun scarcity among the general population since at least 1969.[1] Recognizing that Americans have had a long love affair with their guns and are loathe to give them up, Zimring has been candid that stigmatizing guns must be a component of a violence-reduction strategy that seeks ultimately to impose gun scarcity on the general population.[2] He has been candid too in acknowledging that none of this will be accomplished quickly, easily, or cheaply. Thus, in 1989, he predicted a grim, culture-rending and violent future for America over the near term, even if the policies he favors were enacted. He wrote "The most marked reduction in firearms violence cannot be expected until well past the introduction of legislation designed to achieve handgun scarcity and long after the period of most intense social and political detriment or cost."[3]

Professor Zimring argues that even the most cursory review of American gun-homicide data show that reducing guns' "market share" of homicide must be a key ingredient of an enlightened firearms policy. This supposedly follows from the fact that gun assaults are 5–7 times more likely to result in death than non-gun assaults and from the fact that 70% of American homicides are committed with guns. Other countries with assault rates similar to America's but with lower gun prevalence and with a commensurately lower percentage of homicide committed with guns enjoy homicide rates 50%+ lower than America. He concludes that it only stands to reason that were a

From *Journal of Law, Medicine and Ethics*, vol. 32, issue 1, Spring 2004, pp. 38-46.

smaller percentage of America's assaults committed with guns, its homicide rate must marginally decline, if the overall assault rate stayed the same.

Points of Convergence

Professor Zimring and I agree that carefully-crafted, well-enforced firearms control policies can contribute to marginal reductions in criminal violence. We agree that what matters from the standpoint of enlightened gun policy making is the question of who has guns, how they use their guns and the incentive effects that gun policy can have on both "who" and "how" at the margin. I also agree with Professor Zimring's speculative hypothetical claim that putting an additional 10,000 guns on the street will not automatically result in a proportional increase in the homicide rate. Finally, we agree that while no firearms policy by itself can usher in a Utopian, violence-free social order, even marginal reductions in criminal violence are worth pursing when the benefits exceed the costs and the method pursued is cost-effective. Changes in gun policy that reasonably hold out such promise deserve thoughtful consideration.[4]

Overview

In this paper, I will demonstrate the speciousness of Professor Zimring's argument that reducing the percentage of homicides committed with guns is the key to reducing America's homicide rate. I will further argue that pursuing any gun control measure designed to impose (hand)gun scarcity on the general population is both needless and useless. Whether it is ethically enlightened to fuel America's culture wars by encouraging gun-stigmatization and blatant displays of intolerance directed at private gun ownership per se is a topic for another day.[5]

Zimring's Argument for Changing Course with America's Firearm Policy

Professor Zimring thinks that gun control laws can marginally reduce the homicide rate by making guns progressively scarcer in the social environment. How large a marginal reduction might such policies win over time? Zimring has relied on a single FBI statistic to tell the tale.[6] Guns are used in approximately 70% of all criminal killings. He writes "this tells us immediately what the special problem of gun use is in violent crime—an increase in the death rate . . ." Because he subscribes to (and can fairly claim to be have originated) the "instrumentality hypothesis," according to which the (supposed) greater inherent lethality of guns makes assaults committed with them 5–7 times more deadly, independent of perpetrator-factors, Professor Zimring intimates that the potential marginal reduction in the homicide rate resulting from supply-side restrictions might be quite large.

Professor Zimring claims that all mainstream criminologists now recognize that guns are an independent "contributing cause" to society's homicide rate and that the terms of their intramural debates now concern how large a homicide rate reduction might result were guns' "market share" of assaults reduced.

Although suicide is not a crime and so, by definition, does not qualify as a criminal assault, it is common to count a suicide as a violent death. If so, Zimring's "instrumentality hypothesis" should also extend to a lethality reduction analysis of "self-assaults" (suicide attempts). America's suicide rate is approximately twice as high as its current homicide rate (roughly 11 versus roughly 6). More than 30,000 Americans commit suicide each year, putting suicide in the top ten causes of death. Guns' "market share" in suicide is 50%—not as large as their market share in homicide, percentage-wise, but the body count is nearly twice as high.

Assuming that guns are 5–7 times inherently more lethal than other mechanisms of injury, and with guns' market share of suicide at 50%, the instrumentality thesis says that America's suicide rate should fall if fewer self-assaults were committed with guns, if the overall number of self-assaults (suicide attempts) were to remain the same. And the instrumentality hypothesis predicts finding lower suicide rates in countries where comparative gun scarcity results in a smaller percentage of suicides committed with guns.

Unfortunately, the hypothesis generated by the suicide corollary of the instrumentality thesis is false. Countries known for having very restrictive gun policies and for having much lower gun prevalence than the United States (for examples, Hungary, Denmark, Austria, Norway, and France) nevertheless have persistently higher suicide rates, notwithstanding that a comparatively low percentage are committed with guns.[7]

The Seventy Percent Solution?

The statistic that Zimring finds so telling in favor of his instrumentality thesis does not tell the tale he thinks it does. America's estimated homicide rate fluctuated by an order of magnitude—from a reported low of 1.1 per 100,000 in 1903 to a high of 10.7 in 1980.[8]

In summary:

- At the beginning of the century, there were 1.2 homicides per 100,000 population.
- Rates rose significantly after 1904 reaching a peak of 9.7 in 1933.
- From 1934 to 1944 (encompassing the years of the Great Depression) rates fell to 5.0 in 1944.
- After a slight increase from 1945 and 1946 when rates reached 6.1, rates declined, falling to 4.5 in 1955.
- After 1955 rates increased slightly each year until the mid 1960s when there was a steep increase reaching a peak of 10.1 in 1974.
- Rates fell slightly in 1975 and 1976 but began rising thereafter, reaching an all time high of 10.7 in 1980.
- From 1981 to 1984, rates declined, falling to 8.4 in 1984.

- After 1985, rates increased again peaking in 1991 at 10.5.
- After 1991 rates declined slightly but remained at around 10 through 1993.
- Starting in 1994, rates declined each year, reaching 6.1 in 2000, the lowest rate since 1967.

However, unlike the nation's homicide rate, a random sampling indicates that the percentage of homicides committed with firearms remained comparatively constant. For example, in the period 1920–26, 71% of homicides were by gun.[9] According to the FBI, the percentage of homicides committed with guns dropped to 62% in 1989[10] but was back up to 70% in 1993, as Professor Zimring has noted. Most recently, the FBI estimated that, of the 16,204 homicides committed in 2002, 67% were committed with firearms.[11]

Since the homicide rate varied remarkably over the last 100 years but the percentage of homicides committed with guns did not, the latter figure cannot provide an explanation for the former. Instead of giving us insight, a century's worth of data say that America's homicide rate is virtually independent of the percentage of homicides committed with guns.

This is not a subtle point, so I reiterate its importance for Professor Zimring's argument. The data do not support that America's homicide rate is strongly and independently determined by the percentage of homicides committed with guns. Therefore, we should not infer "immediately" that reducing guns' 70% "market share" of criminal killings must be sine qua non in a comprehensive strategy to reduce the nation's homicide rate.[12]

Professor Zimring may be correct to say that the debate amongst mainstream contemporary criminologists has shifted from perpetrator-focused theories to their arguing the magnitude of the instrumentality effect on the homicide rate, but the data support only those criminologists who estimate its effect as very small or negligible.[13]

It is not clear what might explain a shift Zimring claims to have occurred amongst "mainstream" criminologists. Kleck's comprehensive review of the data and of the criminological literature found no empirical basis for it.[14] For example, Kleck notes that in 1972 Zimring acknowledged "differential intention or personality may play some role in gross intercaliber differences in death rates."

Kleck further notes that in 1982 Philip Cook, another strong proponent of SGC, seemed to share Zimring's view that perpetrator factors cannot be ignored when he postulated that "the task determines the tool." And again in 1987, Cook opined that "the choice of weapon may also be associated with . . . the assailant's intent. If the robber plans to kill the victim, then presumably he will try to equip himself with the most appropriate tool for the task." However, by 1991, both Cook and Zimring apparently had abandoned acknowledging that perpetrator factors (such as his intent and his ability to sustain murderous motivation during the few seconds it takes to inflict lethal injuries) are important lethality-enhancers that make a difference in both weapon selection and use. If we infer the comparative importance a criminologist attributes to various lethality-enhancing factors in the production of criminal violence from the emphasis he gives it, it seems that Zimring now discounts a perpetrator's lethality-enhancing factors in favor of the instrumentality effect. Thus he says, "fatality seem[s] to be an almost accidental outcome of a large number of assaults committed with guns or knives."[15] And in his article, he says his data "suggested that many homicides were the result of attacks apparently conducted with less than a single-minded intent to kill."

Zimring does not further define "large number," or "many," nor does he say how one might reliably discern whether a killer was single-minded or ambivalent or acting inadvertently during the seconds or minutes it took him/her to inflict a mortal wound on a victim. Why does it matter that we have such clarifications and accounts? Because we should demand, at a minimum, clear and convincing evidence to rebut our presumptions that competent adults, including perpetrators of criminal gun assaults, intend the reasonably foreseeable consequences of what they do and that they perform acts intentionally (such as, carry a loaded gun rather than a pack of chewing gum in anticipation of their criminal encounters, pull the trigger while the gun is pointed at the victim, or thrust the blade when the victim's abdomen is within arm's length) precisely because they intend to produce or are willing to risk producing the reasonably expectable results. Absent a compelling account for comparatively neglecting perpetrator-factors, Zimring seems to be claiming that in "a large number of assaults," the killer is as much a victim of circumstance as the person he kills—just luckier, because of where the gun was pointed when the trigger pulled his finger.

Inherent Lethality?

On cursory review, this graph might seem to confirm Professor Zimring's "market share" hypothesis about homicide. Beginning approximately in 1993, there commenced a remarkable decline in firearm use in crime. Associated with the declining use of guns in crime was a 40% decline in the homicide rate. So far so good for the market-share corollary of the instrumentality thesis.

However, the 40% decline in the homicide rate was not associated with a remarkable reduction in the percentage of homicides committed with guns (which at 67% in 2002, remained close to the 70% level found in 1993). And, it should not be necessary to add that the homicide rate decline was not associated with any documented, progressive gun-scarcity among the general population nor among criminals.

In 2002, incidents involving a firearm constituted 7% of the 4.9 million violent crimes of rape, sexual assault, robbery, and aggravated and simple assault. Over the period 1993–2002, the non-fatal, firearm-related violent victimization rate fell to the lowest level ever recorded.

So what do these data tell us about the truth of the instrumentality thesis?

- Firearms have not become scarce among the general population.
- As far as we know, the percentage of criminals who own guns has not declined.

- There has been a dramatic decline in criminal gun use.
- The rate of non-fatal firearm assaults has declined to the lowest level ever recorded.
- The homicide rate has declined to a level last seen in the mid-1960s.
- Yet, the percentage of homicides committed with firearms remains within a narrow range that has held constant for 100 years.

These data suggest that the instrumentality thesis is almost certainly false.

Perpetrators and Their Tools

It is a truism that gun assaults are perpetrated by gun-armed perpetrators. But in this case, the truism is not too true to be good. The data on fatal outcome frequency do not permit our distinguishing a weapon's inherent lethal properties from the closely related effects of a perpetrator's dangerousness.

It is obvious and unarguable that some killings occur that wouldn't have occurred had the perpetrator possessed some other weapon type or none at all. However, we must not be too hasty to map gun/non-gun onto this point. Substituting some other gun, different from the one actually used to kill, one unfamiliar to the perpetrator, heavier, more awkward, and with a very stiff grip safety (as some 1911s have) might have made the outcome non-fatal. The perpetrator may not have been able to make the imaginary-substitute firearm fire at all, or while fiddling with it, trying it to figure out why it wouldn't fire, the victim might have taken the opportunity to escape, or frustration resulting from an inability to make the gun fire might have cooled our would-be killer's murderous motivation. But there is no free lunch. A clunky, hard-to-use firearm may interfere with an otherwise comparatively helpless person's lawful use of deadly force in self-defense such that she dies in the assault she might otherwise have forestalled.

That injuries inflicted with firearms are 5–7 times more likely to result in death does not prove that guns are inherently "more lethal" mechanisms for inflicting injury than others, such as bombs, bludgeons or butcher knives. The lethality of a suicide bomber, for example, importantly involves "personality factors," appearance factors, facts about his/her intent and willingness to "push the button" when the time comes, not merely the contents of the belt s/he wears, concealed from view. (Would suicide bombers become more lethal by substituting firearms for their explosive under-garments? Palestinian terrorists used to use firearms in their attacks, but the scope of their planned carnage was too often truncated by armed victim/bystander intervention.)

The limitations of our criminological data notwithstanding, the trauma literature enables a clearer focus on comparative inherent lethality by mechanism of injury. However, this evidence source seems not to support that gunshot wounds, as a class, are remarkably more life-threatening than wounds inflicted by other mechanisms, such as butcher knives or ice-picks. For example, a study published in the Annals of Surgery investigated the mortality associated with 430 cases involving penetrating wounds to the abdomen. In 266 cases the mechanism of injury was known. Shotguns proved the most lethal with a mortality of 20.4%. Pistol-inflicted abdominal wounds had a mortality of 16.8%. Ice picks wounds and butcher knife wounds ranked next with 14.3% and 13.3% mortality respectively. These findings support that gun shot wounds (GSWs) to the abdomen are somewhat more life-threatening than penetrating wounds inflicted with other weapons, but not 5–7 times more life-threatening.[16]

It is plausible to suppose that perpetrators of assault who are generally more willing to inflict lethal injuries and who desire to be thus perceived by others (and who, unlike suicide-bombers, want to survive the assault themselves), are also more likely to choose guns rather than other mechanisms. Whether guns have 5–7 times greater intimidation value than other weapons in a criminal assault is unknown, but in so far as guns have marginally greater intimidation value than some other weapons, it is partially because of the estimated increased seriousness of purpose that gun possession tends to convey to others.

Behavior modification theory also suggests that a criminal may index his own intimidation level to the weapon he carries. Thus he may select a gun type widely regarded among fellow gang members as more intimidating and he may actually become more intimidating when he has it in his possession. ("I must be a pretty tough guy, after all I'm carrying a .45 caliber model 1911 just like the toughest of my drug-dealer buddies, not some wussy, nickel-plated .25 caliber 'pimp gun'.")

It is well-appreciated that gun-underwritten intimidation deters victim resistance and increases victim compliance and submission. That gun-armed robbers are less likely to inflict injury on their victims than unarmed robbers or robbers armed with other weapons is consistent with their preferring submission to inflicting injury. The type of victim on whom the perpetrator typically preys will also play a role in his choice of weapon. Robbing children of their lunch money requires a different calculus of intimidation than robbing convenience stores, banks or fellow drug dealers. Robbing drug dealers is risky because they enjoy a reputation for violence and will almost certainly be armed. But bank robber Willie Sutton's principle still recommends considering them because drug dealers are known to carry large amounts of unmarked cash and will likely not report victimization to the police. (Sutton was once asked "Why do you rob banks?" He replied, "Because, that's where the money is.")

A preference for victim submission does not rule out a criminal's contingent willingness to inflict injury, nor does it exclude his having a comparatively high susceptibility to preference inversions regarding violence that may be triggered by seemingly trivial situational factors such as his victim's having an "attitude" (or even having a contemptible lack of it). The criminological dynamics of labile preferences amongst opportunistic criminals has been well described by James Q. Wilson and Richard J. Herrnstein.[17]

Who Shoots People, Who Gets Shot?

The romantic stereotype of gun-shot-wound-inflicting-criminal perpetrators as ordinary folk, like you and me, who just happen to have a gun ready when momentarily provoked to anger by friends or family members does not square with the facts. In so far as the data permits stereotyping, neither killers nor their victims are just plain folks.[18] It has long been appreciated that killers are significantly more likely than the general population to suffer from below-average cognitive ability, brain dysfunction, brain injury or mental illness, alcoholism or other substance abuse or all or several of these in combination. Violent offenders also tend to have histories of personal violence from childhood, initially as a victim and eventually as victimizers of other children, siblings and non-human animals.[19] Data gathered from 1960 to date indicate that most homicide perpetrators are male, younger than 30, 70–80% have criminal records and average four arrests for major felonies. By contrast, 85% of the general population has never once been arrested. None of these statistics permit inferring that any individual captured by this demographic profile who has not yet murdered anyone, to a high degree of certainty, will do so eventually. Most will not.

The demographic profile of homicide victims tends to mirror that of their killers. A study of GSWs reported to the police in Charlotte, NC, found that 71% of adult victims had criminal records. The Bureau of Justice Statistics reports that young African American males are 6 times more likely to murder someone and 6 times more likely to be a murder victim than their white counterparts. As Professor Zimring documents in *Crime Is Not The Problem,* America's lethal violence problem is overwhelmingly and disproportionately a problem among its young, poor, African American population. Blacks are more than seven times as likely as whites to be arrested for violent offenses and more than eight times as likely to be arrested for homicide. Assaults by black offenders are more than twice as likely to result in a death than assaults committed by white offenders. Zimring notes that the concentration of serious violence among blacks is so much greater than the concentration of other criminal offenses that if robbery and homicide were not so concentrated among black offenders, the United States would be a much safer country,[20] and most especially for African-Americans.[21] But again, these relative-risk statistics must be balanced by the facts that most young African-American males whether poor or not poor, do not commit robbery or homicide and that homicide statistics have improved for African-Americans just as they have for every other demographic category.

10,000 Guns

Professor Zimring claims that introducing 10,000 guns into an environment where violent assault is rare will not produce a large number of additional deaths unless doing so somehow were to increase the assault rate. On the other hand, were 10,000 guns added to an environment where rates of criminal attack are already high the contribution made to the expectable increase in the death toll from violence must be high.

This thought experiment (taken from his book Crime Is Not the Problem) captures Zimring's sociological theory of lethal violence in a nutshell. Note that, in the hypotheticals he considers, Zimring limits speculating to whether a bolus of 10,000 (of not further specified types of) guns added to an imaginary society would result in a small or large number of additional deaths. He does not even consider that adding 10,000 guns to a social environment might have no net-effect on the number of deaths. Nor does he consider that an additional 10,000 guns might actually be associated with an overall decline in the violent death total or rate. That adding 10,000 guns might have net-positive social effects is not even among the remote possibilities.

But we needn't limit ourselves to subjectively speculating along with Professor Zimring about the more or less likely consequences of adding 10,000 guns in a simulated social experiment. Instead we can analyze data from a real-world experiment that enables less speculative answers. We have Bureau for Alcohol, Tobacco and Firearms (BATF) firearms production/import/export data that enables an objective estimate of how large a bolus of guns America has actually received over the past 20 years. We also have the perspective provided by a century's worth of year-by-year homicide data. And we have a huge, county-by-county data-set from the entire United States that enables a judgment whether the nation's 34 CCW states' putting approximately 3+ million non-police carriers of concealed handguns on the streets has transformed them into the bloodiest jurisdictions.

According to BATF's data,[22] from 1982-2001 American gun manufacturers produced 77,361,013 firearms, including 34,484,470 handguns. All were sold in the American retail market except for 64,813 handguns and 96,861 long guns (rifles and shotguns) that were exported. What was happening in the homicide market over that period?

. . . The number of homicides committed with "other guns" (which would include shotguns that the trauma data say are inherently more lethal than handguns), knives, blunt objects and "other methods" held remarkably constant. By contrast, the number of homicides committed with handguns is much higher and more highly variable.

In 1980, when America's homicide rate hit its all time high (10.7), there were 23,040 homicides, with slightly fewer than 50% committed with handguns. By 1992, the homicide rate was 9.3 but the homicide total hit an all-time high, 24,700. In 1993, while the number of homicides committed with handguns soared to more than 14,000 (with homicide from all mechanisms totaling 24,530), the homicide rate actually had declined (albeit not much) from its 1980 all-time high to 9.5.

Beginning in 1993, the homicide rate began a steep decline to its current level of 6/100,000, the lowest since the mid 1960s. Handgun homicides also declined sharply. However, the handgun infusion continued, albeit also declining from a peak of 2.6 million in 1993 to 943,213 in 2001. Handgun killings declined, handgun production declined and the homicide rate declined. But I reiterate, the percentage of killings committed with firearms, to which Professor Zimring's lethality hypothesis attaches such great importance, did not change remarkably (namely, 67% in 2002) from what it had been in 1993 (namely, 70%).

Beginning in Florida in 1987 and now including 34 CCW-issuing states, more than 3 million so-called "shall issue" licenses to carry a concealed handgun have been obtained by qualified persons. Typically, these laws prohibit the carrying of concealed handguns to anyone who has not satisfied statutory requirements but mandate issuing a permit to every person who satisfies them. Requirements include age restrictions; a personal history free of felony convictions or arrests for violence and a medical history free from documented mental illness as verified by an applicant-authorized investigation of his/her medical records; enrollment in a state-approved course on gun safety, legally permissible gun use in personal protection, and demonstrated minimum proficiency in actual gun use, finger-printing and FBI background check. Associated application fees, course-tuition fees, etc vary the costs associated with obtaining a (renewable) license from $150-$500.

The most important and rigorous work on the criminological consequences of CCW laws has been done by John Lott who claims to have found a substantial reduction in criminal violence in CCW-issuing jurisdictions, with the apparent deterrent effects being proportionally greater in counties that issue licenses in proportionally greater numbers.[23] Lott has freely shared his data set with anyone who requests it. Several scholars have replicated Lott's findings, others have been highly critical on methodological grounds and many harshly so, on political grounds.

Irrespective the details of the Lott-related controversy, it is unarguable that jurisdictions that have adopted CCW laws have not paid a heavy price in blood and gore, as was first predicted for Florida in 1987 and predicted again and again in every subsequent political battle over their adoption elsewhere. Criminological theories rarely enjoy such a direct verifying/falsifying reality check. Some theories have been rescued from refutation by contrary appearances by making the logically-available claim that CCW laws did not did not change social reality, they only made legal what was widely done when illegal. This might make all Lott's "discoveries" investigation-relative artifacts, absorbed into nothingness by properly-done regressions. If so, logic provides a refuge for proponents of Zimring's instrumentality thesis and the nation's experience with CCW does not necessarily "slam dunk" over the theoretical obstacle interposed by it after all.

Why Zimring Ignores the Apparent Benefits of Armed Self-Defense

Professor Zimring has always opposed the use of force in self-defense. Initially, his arguments against resisting criminal attack were pragmatic. Early analysis of the data on victim-resistance showed that victims who were criminally attacked and resisted were also more likely to be injured or killed than victims who put up no resistance at all. However, the early analysis only found a statistically significant association between victims who did worse and victims who resisted. The data were not recorded in such a way as to permit inferring that resisters did worse because their resistance provoked an injury-causing attack that might have not have occurred otherwise. And the early analysis did not distinguish between gun-backed resistance and non-gun resistance.

However, further analysis of the data did distinguish between types of resistance. It was found that victims who used a gun to resist criminal attack not only did better than victims who resisted by other means, they also did better than victims who offered no resistance whatsoever. Where once we had no data on the efficacy and frequency of defensive gun use (DGU), we now have at least 15 such studies. The most statistically sophisticated of these supports that DGU occurs more frequently than criminal gun-assaults, probably not significantly less than 2.5 million times per year and perhaps more frequently.[24]

These findings have apparently prompted Zimring to shift his ground. With apparent benefit and frequency of civilian defensive gun use now established, Zimring now denies that there is a valid difference between criminal lethal violence and lawful use force in self-defense. He lumps these together under the general rubric "lethal violence." Indeed, Zimring thinks that the American tradition that attaches ethical importance to the distinction between criminal violence and lawful use of force in self-defense contributes to perpetuating America's violence-problem. This explains why Professor Zimring thinks that America's "violence problem" is not merely criminological, but comprehensively societal.

Since Zimring regards all uses of deadly force as malignant, irrespective whether it is perpetrated by criminals or used by (allegedly) "good citizens" in self-defense, his social calculus refuses to count as beneficial any use of deadly force by private citizens. Theoretically, this makes the now-substantial literature on defensive gun use irrelevant to an ethical inquiry whether the net-effect of firearms violence is beneficial, or malignant. It's all malignant per se.

It is also noteworthy that Zimring ignores lethal violence perpetrated by government officials, irrespective whether clearly lawful, e.g., when a law enforcement officer justifiably shoots a violent felon in the line of duty or outrageously violates individual rights under the color of law, e.g., as when the attorney general of the United States authorized use of tanks, incendiaries and automatic weapons to kill indiscriminately men, women and 19 children, as she did in Waco, Texas in 1994.

Conclusion

The fundamental ethical problem posed by imposing gun scarcity on the general population has nothing to do with the comparatively trivial "sporting interests" of the public. Nor does gun control implicate merely idiosyncratic, outmoded notions of personal liberty. On the contrary, the fundamental ethical problems posed for proponents of SGC arise when they subscribe simultaneously to the following propositions:

1. An ethically legitimate state must recognize and respect equally the fundamental, individual right to bodily integrity, which includes a fundamental, serious right to self-defense, and;
2. the state has no general duty to provide minimally adequate protection from criminal violence to any individual, nor does it incur a special obligation to anyone by expressly promising an individual that it will provide her a reasonable, minimum of protection from criminal violence, and;
3. the State's inherent police powers include the authority to threaten competent, non-felon adults with criminal penalties for having arms for self-preservation and defense.[25]
4. A state whose laws seriously impairs the right of a competent, trustworthy citizen to defend herself from violence, owes her compensating protection from bodily injury.

Affirming 1-3 is incoherent. 2 & 3 rule out 1.[26] Prohibitory gun laws directly implicate the state's duty to respect equally each person's interest in bodily integrity. If the state bans civilian possession of "equalizers" by invoking a monopoly power under prospect 3, it forbids those who are, as a result, made vulnerable to offset the criminological effects of natural inequalities (of being frailer, smaller and weaker). Machiavelli put it crisply: "There simply is no equality between a man who is armed and one who is not."[27]

Strict gun control, by effect if not intent, institutionalizes the natural predatory advantages of larger, stronger, violence-prone persons or gangs of such persons, and yet its proponents incur no liability to offset resulting risks unless they renounce proposition 2 above.

Prohibiting competent, adult, non-felons to possess "equalizers" also has distributional wealth effects not only between criminals and the law-abiding, but also among the law-abiding. Strict gun control disproportionately increases the risks of violent victimization for less well-off law-abiding citizens who cannot take advantage of the privileged connections to officials that wealthier citizens take for granted. Less well-off citizens cannot afford the services of professional body guards who guard our social elites. They cannot afford alarm systems or the enhanced physical security that comes with living in exclusive, gated communities. Strict gun control institutionalizes unequal respect for each citizen's fundamental interest in bodily integrity.

Similarly, banning "cheap" so-called Saturday Night Specials effectively discounts the equal bodily integrity interests of poorer citizens, and not merely the interests of predatory criminals, who tend generally to be poorer than average. Outlawing "cheap" guns threatens to transform poor but law-abiding citizens into lawbreakers solely for choosing a product on the basis of its affordability. Too, eliminating a class of "cheap" guns necessarily demotes what were formerly "marginally non-cheap" guns to "cheap" gun status, eligible for banning as "cheap guns," step by step.

Since supply-side restricting gun control laws that target the general population mitigate the citizen's fundamental interest in bodily integrity and as well as his/her interest in being a political equal, while also materially affect the balance of advantage between criminals and the law-abiding in favor of criminals, and have distributional wealth effects among the law-abiding, effectively pricing lives differentially, every rational, liberal-minded person has reason to get the data necessary for responsible reflection on supply-side restrictive gun control.

We should also consider the associated administrative and enforcement costs secondary to enacting gun laws aimed at the general population and predicate all discussions about the costs/benefits of gun control on an assumption of imperfect compliance. Prohibiting murder has not eliminated it; nor has punishing its perpetrators with death. Banning handguns cannot make them disappear, nor even make them scarce. Despite decades prosecuting our socially and economically ruinous "war on drugs," cocaine, crack and other banned substances remain readily available.

Finally, we should never forget that officially authorized violence, whether inflicted in war against aliens or inflicted in genocidal, domestic exterminations perpetrated under the color of law, has a grim, stubbornly enduring history. When compared with the officially-sanctioned killing fields in Cambodia or Rwanda or Kosovo or Iraq, or Hitler's massive extermination apparatus, or Stalin's mass killings, or Mao's various "Campaigns" against "Bad Elements," private violence, mere criminality, pales in comparison.[28] Enthusiasm for a state monopoly over firearms must be tempered by these memories.

References

1. See F.E. Zimring, "Is Gun Control Likely to Reduce Violent Killings?" *University of Chicago Law Review* 35 (1968):721-37.
2. See F.E. Zimring and G. Hawkins, *Crime Is Not The Problem: Lethal Violence in America* (New York: Oxford University Press, 1997). "Putting social stigma on the instruments of lethal violence [irrespective who uses them, is key because] The rhetorical high ground in violence prevention may leave little room for distinguishing between types of violence," p. 208. By "distinguishing between types of violence," Zimring means the currently-made distinction between unlawful offensive violence and lawful defensive violence.
3. See F.E. Zimring and G. Hawkins, *The Citizen's Guide to Gun Control* (New York: Macmillan Press, 1989): 205.
4. Urging "thoughtful consideration" of gun policy changes may be as oxymoronic politically as commending "thoughtful consideration" of changes in abortion policy.
5. A "back of the envelope," county-based calculation indicates that, in the 2000 Presidential Election, counties going for Al Gore had a homicide rate of 13.2, while counties going for Bush had a homicide rate of 1.2. Our current fascination with red v. blue states and or counties underwrites effective political strategy but is potentially very harmful to the country as a whole.
6. In *Crime Is Not the Problem,* he additionally supports it by noting that the homicide rates in the G7 countries are markedly lower than that in the United States despite their having assault rates similar to the United States'. See especially Chapter 7, 106–110.
7. See D.H. Kates, H.E. Schaffer J.K. Lattimer G.H. Murray and E.H. Cassem, "Guns and Public Health: Epidemic of Violence or Pandemic of Propaganda?"

Tennessee Law Review 62 (1995): 513-596 at 563. The problem of differential suicide-attempt rates remains. Since many developed countries have suicide rates higher than the United States', it would seem that their attempt-rates must be higher too, since every suicide presupposes a (successful) attempt. The number of failed attempts is largely unknowable, for a host of obvious reasons.

8. The graph of the nation's homicide rate is available at the Bureau of Justice Statistics Website. It should be noted that at the beginning of the 20th Century, several states known or suspected of having comparatively high homicide rates did not report their homicide data to the federal government. This suggests that the nation's homicide rate must have been higher than the reported national estimate during those years.

    Professor Kleck has pointed out to me in a personal communication that "The data for 1903–1932 are not actually national data, but rather merely cover the changing subsets of the U.S. that were included in the 'Death Registration Area' (DRA), which consisted of those states that have achieved relatively complete coverage of deaths in their vital statistics systems. Most the apparently enormous increase in homicide rates from 1903–1920, and part of the 1921–1933 increase, is a statistical mirage, attributable to new, mostly high homicide, states being added to the DRA. Only a minority of the U.S. was covered by the 1903 DRA, predominantly low-homicide Northeast states, while all of it was covered by 1933. Unfortunately, there was a systematic pattern to which states got added to the DRA latest—generally the states that were the last to get their statistical systems up to speed and join the DRA also tended to be the homicide states, mostly from the South and Southwest. E.g., the very last state to join was Texas, a huge contributor to the national homicide rate both because of its high rate and its large population. In reality, the increase in the U.S. homicide rate was much milder than your chart indicates, up until Prohibition went into effect in 1920, at which point homicide really did jump up, though not as much as the DRA-based data seems to indicate."

9. See Brearley, cited in G. Kleck, *Point Blank: Guns and Violence in America* (New York: Aldine deGruyter,1991): 20.

10. FBI data cited in Kleck, supra note 9:20.

11. Firearms and Crime Statistics, at http://www.ojp.usdoj.gov/bjs/guns.htm (last checked February 29, 2004).

12. Supra note 2:199-202.

13. For a further, critical discussion of the comparative merits of perpetrator theories and instrumentality theories, see D.D. Palsy and D.B. Kats, "American Homicide Exceptionalism," *University of Colorado Law Review* 69, no. 4 (1998): 969-1008.

14. See G. Kleck, *Targeting Guns: Firearms and Their Control* (New York: Aldine de Gruyter,1997): 227-230.

15. F.E. Zimring, "Firearms, Violence and Public Policy," *Scientific American* 265 (1991): 48-58, at 49.

16. See H. Wilson and R. Shaman, "Civilian Penetrating Wounds of the Abdomen," *Annals of Surgery* 153, no. 5 (1961): 639-649.

17. See J.Q. Wilson and R.J. Herrnstein, *Crime and Human Nature: The Definitive Study of the Causes of Crime* (New York: Simon & Schuster,1985), especially chapter 2.

18. Supra note 13, esp. 992-999.

19. See L.H. Athens, *The Creation of Dangerous Violent Criminals* (Urbana and Chicago: University of Illinois Press, 1992). Also See R. Rhodes, Why They Kill:

The Discoveries of a Maverick Criminologist.(New York: Knopf Publishers, 1999).

20. See, esp. Supra note 2: 75ff.

21. By federal law, every firearm produced by American gun manufacturers must bear a serial number. Each firearm imported must also bear a serial number. Domestic production totals, imports and exports must be reported annually to the Bureau of Alcohol, Firearms and Tobacco. The trade publication *Shooting Industry* also publishes annually, based on BATF-provided data, the number of firearms produced over a running 20 year period. These data include BATF totals by handgun type (revolvers and pistols) and by caliber. They enable an objective basis for evaluating market trends and for estimating and updating the number of civilian-owned guns.

    Using BATF figures to establish a 1945 baseline, Gary Kleck has developed a production-based model that cumulates annual domestic production, adds imports and subtracts exports. From 1945–1994, the American civilian gun total rose from an estimated 46,909,183 guns to an estimated 235,604,001 guns, an increase of 502.25%. Over that period, the number of privately-owned handguns increased from an estimated 12,657,618 to an estimated 84,665,690, a gain of 668.9%. From 1945-1994, Americans bought handguns at a higher rate than they bought long guns. The whole-period handgun growth rate was 151% of the whole period long gun growth rate (a total handgun increase of 668.9% vs. a total long gun increase of 440.7%).

    Between 1993–1999 the industry produced approximately 28.6 million firearms, including 12.5 million handguns. Allowing for imports and subtracting for exports, we may reasonably estimate that the current gun total approximates the size of the U.S. population, including approximately 95-100 million handguns. Figured on a per capita basis, American civilians probably own guns at a rate between 969 and 1016 per 1,000 adults, including a rate between 365 and 388 handguns per 1000 adults.

22. See J.R. Lott, *More Guns, Less Crime: Understanding Crime and Gun Control Laws* (2d Edition) (Chicago: University of Chicago Press, 2000).

23. See supra note 14, ch.5 for a comprehensive review.

24. See H. Lafollette, "Gun Control," *Ethics* 266 (2000): 110 for an otherwise sophisticated discussion that ignores the ethical implications of the "public service" doctrine of State immunity.

25. See S. Wheeler, "Self-Defense and Coerced Risk-Acceptance," *Public Affairs Quarterly* 11 (1997): 431.

26. N. Machiavelli, *The Prince* (New York: Penguin Books, 1981): 88.

27. See, S. Wheeler, "Arms as Insurance," *Public Affairs Quarterly* 13 (1999): 111.

POSTSCRIPT

Will Strict Gun Control Laws Reduce the Number of Homicides in the United States?

Violent crime is an unfortunate fact of life in the United States. According to a "Family Violence Statistics" study published in June 2005 by the U.S. Bureau of Justice Statistics (BJS), 16,204 murders were committed in the United States in 2002. The study also included information about the types of weapons used in these crimes. For all murders in 2002 in which the type of weapon used was known, 64 percent were committed with firearms. Interestingly, 51.7 percent of the murders were committed with handguns, 4.3 percent rifles, 4.3 percent shotguns, and 3.6 percent were not specified. Moreover, knives were used in 16.5 percent of the cases, and blunt objects were used 5.7 percent of the time.

Similar patterns were observed in family violence cases. In the 1,958 murder cases involving family members, 50.1 percent used firearms: 36.8 percent involved handguns, 4.4 percent used rifles, 6.1 percent used shotguns, and 2.9 percent were not specified.

What then, do these statistics tell us about murder in the United States? First, a majority of murders are committed with firearms. Moreover, a large percentage of all murder cases involved handguns. In 2002, murder cases involving family members were somewhat less likely to involve firearms; however, a large number of these murders involved guns as well.

Based on these findings, do you believe that states should pass laws to remove firearms from the population? The authors of the articles in this section would be likely to answer this question in very different ways. Professor Franklin E. Zimring would be likely to assert that the number of murders committed with firearms would support gun ownership restrictions. Conversely, Professor Lance K. Stell would contend that restricting gun ownership would harm law-abiding citizens.

After reading the articles in this section, are you more or less likely to support restrictions on firearms ownership in the United States? Is there a middle ground in this debate that you would support, such as a ban on assault weapons, or handguns?

In any case, gun control is an issue that generates heated debate. Fortunately, there are many compelling resources that shed additional light on this topic. For example, see Robert J. Sptizer, *The Politics of Gun Control* (Chatham House, 1995); Lisa D. Brush, "Blown Away: American Women and Guns," *Violence Against Women* (September 2005); Linda A. Teplin, Gary M. McClelland, Karen M. Abram, and Darinka Miluesnic, "Early Violent Death Among

Delinquent Youth: A Prospective Longitudinal Study," *Pediatrics* (June 2005); Jeffrey B. Bingenheimer, Robert T. Brennan, and Felton J. Earls, "Firearm Violence Exposure and Serious Violent Behavior," *Science* (May 27, 2005); Janice Hopkins Tanne, "U.S. Workers Who Carry Guns Are More Likely to Be Killed on the Job," *British Medical Journal* (International Edition) (May 7, 2005); Amie L. Neilsen, Ramiro Martinez, Jr., and Richard Rosenfeld, "Firearm Use, Injury, and Lethality in Assaultive Violence: An Examination of Ethnic Differences," *Homicide Studies* (May, 2005).

See, as well, Abigail A. Kohn, Don B. Kates, Wendy Faminer, and Michael I. Krauss, "Straight Shooting on Gun Control," *Reason* (May 2005); Ik-Whan G. Kwon and Daniel W. Baack, "The Effectiveness of Legislation Controlling Gun Usage: A Holistic Measure of Gun Control Legislation," *The American Journal of Economics and Sociology* (April 2005); James O. E. Norell, "The Great Debate," *American Rifleman* (January 2005); Linda L. Dahlberg, Robin M. Ikeda, and Marcie-jo Kresnow, "Guns in the Home and Risk of a Violent Death in the Home: Findings from a National Study," *American Journal of Epidemiology* (November 15, 2004); and John Casteen, "Ditching the Rubric on Gun Control: Notes from an American Moderate," *The Virginia Quarterly Review* (Fall 2004).

On the Internet . . .

Findlaw

This database is an excellent place to conduct basic legal research.

http://www.findlaw.com/

LexisNexis

LexisNexis provides legal, news, public records information, including tax and regulatory publications in online ROM formats.

http://www.lexisnexis.com

National Criminal Justice Reference Service (NCJRS)

This very comprehensive database provides a wealth of information about justice system processes. Topics include corrections, courts, crime prevention, crime rates, drugs, the criminal justice system, juvenile justice, law enforcement, and the victims of crime. It also provides links to NCJRS-sponsored research on virtually every aspect of the criminal justice system.

http://www.ncjrs.org/

National Crime Victims Research and Treatment Center

This site, sponsored by the National Crime Victims Research and Treatment Center of the Medical University of South Carolina, provides excellent links to resources focusing on victimization and various criminological treatment options.

http://www.musc.edu/cvc/

National Institute of Justice (NIJ)

The NIJ sponsors projects and disseminates research about justice system issues. This site provides links to NIJ research, programs, publications, and various other initiatives.

http://www.ojp.usdoj.gov/nij/

PART 2

Legal Issues

Legal issues influence virtually every facet of the U.S. justice system. From the moment a suspect is arrested until he or she is tried, convicted, sentenced, and punished, the requirements of due process of law inform all aspects of the case. The U.S. Constitution, which was intentionally designed by the founding fathers to limit governmental authority, provides an accused with procedural safeguards that justice system personnel must carefully administer. In addition, federal and state statutes and court rules provide additional detailed protections for the accused. In the U.S. justice system, the essential question is not whether an accused is factually guilty. Rather, our system requires the government to abide by the rule of law and prove an individual's guilt beyond a reasonable doubt. Such issues are explored in this section.

- Should the United States Abolish the Exclusionary Rule of Evidence in Criminal Cases?
- Is "Black Rage" a Legitimate Defense in Criminal Proceedings?
- Should U.S. Courts Abandon the *Miranda* Rule?
- Should a Judge Be Permitted to Admit Evidence About an Alleged Rape Victim's History as a Prostitute?

ISSUE 5

Should the United States Abolish the Exclusionary Rule of Evidence in Criminal Cases?

YES: Akhil Reed Amar, from "Against Exclusion (Except to Protect Truth or Prevent Privacy Violations)," *Harvard Journal of Law and Public Policy* (Winter 1997)

NO: Yale Kamisar, from "In Defense of the Search and Seizure Exclusionary Rule," *Harvard Journal of Law and Public Policy* (Winter 2003)

ISSUE SUMMARY

YES: Yale law professor Akhil Reed Amar argues that if reliable evidence is excluded from trials, wrongful acquittals and erroneous convictions will result. Moreover, he believes that the exclusionary rule of evidence hurts innocent defendants while helping the guilty ones.

NO: University of Michigan law professor Yale Kamisar contends that the exclusionary rule is the sole effective remedy to secure compliance with the Constitution by the police and that admitting evidence obtained illegally requires courts to condone lawless activities of law enforcement officers.

The exclusionary rule of evidence is a prophylactic device that has been developed by U.S. courts to insure that police officers comply with the requirements of the Constitution. It provides that evidence obtained unlawfully may not be used in a criminal proceeding as evidence of guilt. Exclusionary rule issues may arise from violations of a suspect's Fourth Amendment rights by virtue of an illegal search and seizure, Fifth Amendment rights due to a violation of the suspect's privilege against self-incrimination, or Sixth Amendment protections because of a violation of an individual's right to counsel.

Questions about whether we should use an exclusionary rule of evidence have been debated in the U.S. justice system for many years. In *People v. DeFore*, 150 N.E. 585 (1926), a case decided by the New York Court of Appeals, Benjamin Cardozo, who later became one of the greatest U.S. Supreme Court justices in U.S. history, posed the exclusionary dilemma as follows: Is the criminal to go free because the constable has blundered? Years later, in *Mapp v. Ohio*, 367 U.S. 643 (1961), Justice Tom C. Clark provided an answer to Justice Cardozo's earlier question, stating: "The criminal goes free, if he must, but it is the law that sets him free. Nothing can destroy a government more quickly than its failure to observe its own laws, or worse, its disregard of the charter of its own existence."

For a number of years prior to *Mapp v. Ohio*, the Supreme Court had appeared reluctant to impose the exclusionary rule on state criminal proceedings. For example, in *Wolf v. Colorado*, 338 U.S. 25 (1949), the Court applied the Fourth Amendment right to be free from unreasonable searches and seizures to the states through the Fourteenth Amendment's due process clause; however, it declined to extend the exclusionary rule to the states at that time because it believed that a vigilant press and public opinion could deter the police from conducting illegal searches and seizures. Three years later, in *Rochin v. California*, 342 U.S. 165 (1952), the Court extended the exclusionary rule protection to state proceedings when the conduct of law enforcement officers "shocks the conscience." Finally, in *Mapp v. Ohio*, a majority of the Court concluded that it was necessary to make the exclusionary rule mandatory in state criminal trials as part of the due process guarantee of the Fourteenth Amendment.

In general, proponents of the exclusionary rule believe that it needed to insure the integrity of our justice system. Exclusionary rule opponents assert that it deprives society of the opportunity to convict guilty people who have violated its laws. But, what is the true impact of the exclusionary rule of evidence on society? Are legions of factually guilty defendants being released on legal technicalities and allowed to prey on society?

Based on the available evidence, should the United States abolish the exclusionary rule? The authors of the articles in this section provide very different answers to this question. Yale law professor Akhil Reed Amar argues that if reliable evidence is excluded from trials, wrongful acquittals and erroneous convictions will result. Moreover, he believes that the exclusionary rule hurts innocent defendants while helping the guilty ones.

Based on your personal experiences or on what you have read in the newspapers and seen on television, do you believe that without the exclusionary rule, police officers would commit illegal acts in order to enforce the law?

As you read the articles in this section, think about whether there are any reasonable alternatives to the exclusionary rule. Is there a middle ground between the positions adopted by Professors Amar and Kamisar?

Akhil Reed Amar

Against Exclusion (Except to Protect Truth or Prevent Privacy Violations)

The title of this Panel is a question: "What Belongs in a Criminal Trial?" Now if my mother, who is not a lawyer, asked me what belongs in a criminal trial, I would look her in the eye and say, "Mom, the truth." And if my brother, who is a lawyer, asked me what belongs in a criminal trial, I would say, "Vik, reliable evidence subject to true privacy privileges"—a more elaborate answer, but the same basic idea.

There should be two principles guiding the exclusion of evidence in a criminal trial.[1] First, if the introduction of X where X is testimony or physical evidence, words or things would itself tend to risk a distinctively inaccurate verdict in some very substantial way, then X should be excluded.[2] This is especially true when X creates an unacceptably high risk that an innocent defendant will be erroneously convicted, for our system is, quite properly, particularly concerned with erroneous convictions.[3] When prejudice truly outweighs probative value, there is an argument for exclusion: the evidence is just so unreliable or misleading that the decisionmaker simply cannot assess it fairly. This principle may not apply to a great many situations, but it has normative appeal.

The second principle is that true privacy privileges may constrain the search for truth. Now, in the Anglo-American tradition, we—rightly—believe that trials are public events,[4] and yet we also—rightly—believe that some matters are best kept altogether private. When these beliefs bump up against each other, one can make a good argument that certain things simply should not come into the public trial at all, and thus should remain private. These exclusions prevent private facts from ever becoming public. They do not remedy an out-of-court privacy violation, they prevent an in-court privacy violation. These exclusions exist in order to protect some valuable social relationships such as the spousal relationship, or the priest-penitent, lawyer-client, and doctor-patient relationships. These relationships implicate true privacy privileges.

Now, one might ask, what is a true privacy privilege? One test is that a true privacy privilege is one that applies to all witnesses, not merely defendants, and in all actions, not just criminal cases.[5] On this account, the Fifth

From *Harvard Journal of Law & Public Policy*, vol. 20, issue 2, Winter 1997, pp. 457-266.

Amendment[6] privilege against self-incrimination is not a true privacy privilege, because it can be overcome by immunity. Furthermore, it applies only in criminal, but not civil, cases. So, for instance, Oliver North has no Fifth Amendment privacy privilege. If we want his "private" story badly enough, we can force him to give it. All we have to do is grant him a certain kind of criminal immunity. The key question is, then, what kind of immunity do we have to give him? The question of immunity does not even arise in priest-penitent or doctor-patient or spousal or attorney-client relationships, because these implicate true privacy privileges: one has an absolute right to keep these conversations private, and so the privacy violation is the compelled statement itself. The test of universal applicability also explains why the Fourth Amendment exclusionary rule is not a true privacy privilege: if introduction of illegally found evidence were itself a privacy violation, exclusion would be required in all civil as well as criminal cases, and yet this has never been the law. A true privacy privilege is one where courtroom exclusion prevents the privacy violation—exposure in court—from ever occurring, rather than "remedying" an antecedent breach of privacy that has already occurred, out of court.[7]

Let me now try to elaborate on my general vision of what does belong in a criminal trial by going through the Fourth[8], Fifth, and Sixth[9] Amendments. Remember, the subtitle of our Panel is "The Role of Exclusionary Rules"—a plural word—and exclusionary rules derive not just from the Fourth but also from the Fifth and Sixth Amendments. These Amendments have been misunderstood in their purpose and effect.

Let us start with the Fourth. The Fourth Amendment generally does not require, does not call for, does not even invite, the exclusion of evidence as a remedy for an unconstitutional search or seizure. Nowhere does the text say such a thing. Indeed, the text never distinguishes between civil and criminal cases, yet exclusionary rule doctrine always has. When we do exclude, we exclude in criminal cases but never, as a general matter, in civil cases. So, the text obviously does not support the current exclusionary rule.

What about history? The history emphatically rejects any idea of exclusion.[10] The English common law cases underlying the Fourth Amendment never recognized exclusion. England still does not recognize exclusion. Canada, until the 1980s, resisted the temptation. None of the Founders ever linked the Fourth Amendment to exclusion. In the first century after Independence, no federal court ever recognized exclusion. No state court—and remember, virtually every State's constitution had a counterpart to the Fourth Amendment—ever excluded evidence in this first century.

When the most thoughtful judges of the era were presented with the case for exclusion—and it came up rarely, because it was so outlandish—they dismissed it out of hand. Joseph Story, who was no slouch as a scholar, confronted the argument for exclusion, and said that he had never heard of a case in the Anglo-American world excluding evidence on the ground that it was illegally obtained.[11] The Massachusetts Supreme Judicial Court reached the same conclusion a generation later, in a case presided over by its great Chief Justice Lemuel Shaw.[12]

So much for text. So much for history. How about structure? The structure of our Constitution generally, and of our criminal procedure provisions in particular, corresponds to my principles. The structure of the Constitution basically advocates truthseeking procedures constrained by privacy privileges, and so Fourth Amendment exclusion derives no support from a proper understanding of the Fourth, Fifth, and Sixth Amendments.

One obvious question is, then, where did this exclusion doctrine come from? It did not develop, as is taught in law schools, as a deterrence-based remedy for an antecedent Fourth Amendment violation. Rather, in about twenty United States Supreme Court cases—landmark cases beginning with Boyd in 1886[13] and continuing to the 1960s—judicial proponents of exclusion put forth an argument combining the Fourth Amendment and the Fifth Amendment privilege against self-incrimination.[14] This combination swayed the Court. It drives Justice Hugo Black's fifth vote in Mapp[15] and appears no less than six times, if one reads carefully, in Justice Clark's majority opinion in Mapp.[16] It goes as follows.

Consider a diary. (Most of these early cases involved personal papers.) When the government illegally grabs your most personal papers and your diaries, and then seeks to introduce all this stuff in a criminal proceeding, the introduction of that diary is itself a new Fifth Amendment-like constitutional violation (the argument goes). In effect, you are being made an involuntary witness against yourself when your personal papers testify against you. That was the theory, anyway.

So, exclusion was not designed to remedy an antecedent violation, but to prevent a new one from occurring in the courtroom itself, a violation rooted in Fifth Amendment self-incrimination concerns. This explains: (1) where the exclusionary rule came from; (2) why it has always applied in criminal cases but never in civil cases[17] (because the Fifth Amendment applies only in criminal cases); (3) why illegally obtained evidence could always be used against any defendant other than the searchee[18] (because your papers, as an extension of your person, your voice, your testimony, could not be made to testify against you—but, just as you could be forced to testify against someone else, so could your papers); and finally, (4) why the courts have always treated illegal seizures of persons differently from illegal searches and seizures of objects (because the Fifth Amendment self-incrimination idea did not apply to the body of the defendant and we never exclude the body of the defendant from the trial).[19]

Now, this doctrine of Fourth-Fifth fusion, which is the only principled—if incorrect—constitutional basis for exclusion, has been plainly repudiated by the recent Supreme Court. The Court repudiated it in both the Fisher and Leon cases,[20] leaving us only with three more modern arguments for exclusion. First, some claim that the exclusionary rule preserves judicial integrity. This argument is hard to take seriously, because the rule does not apply to civil cases. Furthermore, other countries with judicial systems characterized by integrity do not exclude evidence. In fact, integrity is also threatened when we exclude true evidence, and thereby deprive the trial and the world of relevant facts.

Second, there is the non-profit principle—the idea that government should not profit from its own wrong. This is incorrect as a constitutional rule, both factually and normatively. Factually, it simply is not true that the government is always actually and clearly better off because, and only because, it violated the Fourth Amendment. In many cases, even though the Constitution was violated, the violation was not the but-for cause of the government's later possession of the evidence. Often, it could have gotten the evidence utterly lawfully. Suppose, for example, that law-enforcement officers had probable cause but did not obtain a warrant before conducting a search for a bloody knife. If they found the knife, under current exclusionary rules, judges would still suppress it as the fruit of an illegal search. This result is disturbing because the police (by hypothesis) easily could have gotten a warrant. Frank Easterbrook has written thoughtfully on just this problem in a Seventh Circuit opinion.[21] So, the standard of inevitable discovery discussed by Carol Steiker[22] actually is not overbroad, but rather is radically underinclusive. After all, there are many situations with a seventy-percent likelihood that the government would have found the evidence. But unless that likelihood is ninety-nine percent, judges tend to say that the government can never use that evidence. The criminal, therefore, is the one affirmatively better off, because once the government initially acquires something illegal, it rarely can be used against the defendant. In short, there is a huge causation gap.

But there is also a normative problem, because the government always has been able, in some sense, to profit from its wrongs. It does not have to give stolen goods back to a thief. It does not have to give drugs back to a drug dealer or contraband back to a smuggler. This is basically because the thief is not entitled, morally or legally speaking, to the stolen goods, nor is the drug dealer to the drugs, nor the smuggler to the contraband. Similarly, they are not entitled to the evidence of their crimes. The law is entitled to every person's evidence; so, normatively, the government should be able to use the evidence just as it is able to keep the stolen goods.

Finally, there is the third modern argument for the exclusionary rule—deterrence. Here I disagree with Bill Stuntz.[23] Every scheme of deterrence will prevent some inappropriate searches and seizures. But not every deterrence scheme is sensible. The Founders knew about deterrence and talked about it a great deal. They never talked about exclusion, though. Instead, they talked about punitive damages and civil tort suits. Those schemes of deterrence have huge advantages over the exclusionary rule. They focus on the scope of the violation, which occurs when the search and seizure takes place, rather than when it happens to come up with otherwise admissible evidence.[24] If the police bop me on the nose, their action is not really related to whether or not they find evidence. Bopping me on the nose is, however, an independent constitutional wrong.

Tort law and deterrence remedies can focus on that independent wrong. We could enforce punitive damages. If there is too little or too much deterrence, we could raise the punitive damages or lower them as needed. Such remedies would also change the distribution of the benefits of deterrence. Right now, the benefits of deterrence go to the guilty more than the innocent. If the police know you are innocent and just want to hassle you because of your race, your sex, your politics, and the search—predictably—finds no evidence, the exclusionary rule is no deterrent whatsoever. It is no help for you at all. In Stanley Surrey's phrase, the distribution of benefits under the exclusionary rule is "upside down," helping the guilty, not the innocent.[25] This is why many countries around the world do not have our exclusionary scheme. The Founders did not intend to enact our scheme, and, with all due respect, they understood deterrence better than Bill Stuntz does. I should say that Bill Stuntz has written very thoughtfully about all of this. I just disagree with his judgment about what is the most functionally desirable system. But even if I am wrong about that, there remain these small matters of text, history, and structure to contend with.

Now let us turn to the Fifth Amendment. This Amendment is a rule requiring exclusion, but only of words, of testimony, of witnessing. The Amendment applies in criminal, and only criminal, cases. It can be overcome by immunity. And it does not apply to objects. (Schmerber[26] tells us that we can force people to give up a sample of their own blood, even if it might hang them.)

What is the reason for the Fifth Amendment rule of exclusion, then? The reason is reliability. One basic concern is that when words are coerced from suspects—especially in a preGideon[27] world—the suspects might not have the advice of a lawyer. If suspects were forced to take the stand, clever prosecutors could make them look guilty even if they are not. The cruelty is in forcing the innocent to take the stand, twisting their own words against them, making them look guilty, and thus making them effectively hang themselves. If that is the account, it is easy to understand why the privilege applies to criminal, rather than civil, cases. After all, we are far more concerned about erroneous convictions in criminal contexts. Moreover, it is clear why immunity overcomes the privilege, because immunity insures that your words will never be introduced against you in a criminal trial. Finally, it explains why the Self-Incrimination Clause does not apply to objects, because physical evidence such as blood is far more reliable than words.

Using this analysis, we can actually compel Oliver North to testify before Congress—that is not a criminal case—and so long as his words are never introduced in a criminal case in which he is a defendant, no Fifth Amendment violation will ever have occurred. Simply put, he will never have been made a witness against himself in a criminal trial. Similarly, outside the trial of a criminal defendant, we can actually force the defendant to disclose where the body is buried or where the bloody knife is hidden, and the defendant must tell us, under penalty of perjury. The lawyer is there to provide advice, just as in civil discovery, and the actual words will never be introduced at trial. So long as only the fruit of this discovery is introduced—the body and the bloody knife, with defendant's fingerprints all over them—there will never be any Fifth Amendment violation.

The Fourth Amendment is about things—houses, papers, effects, stuff—but it is not about exclusion. The Fifth Amendment is about exclusion in criminal cases—but only about excluding words, because they can be unreliable.

I am not going to be able to go into Sixth Amendment doctrine in detail here, but there are rules of exclusion there too, based both on the attorney-client privilege and the speedy trial ideal. As I have explained elsewhere, [28] Sixth Amendment exclusion doctrine is defensible only to the extent it prevents unreliable adjudication or preserves legitimate privacy.

The current rules, which exclude much too much reliable physical evidence on Fourth Amendment, Fifth Amendment, and Sixth Amendment speedy trial grounds—are upside down in two ways. And here I do agree with Bill Stuntz's biggest point: [29] these rules do have the unfortunate effect of letting guilty people go free, but more significantly, they also often make innocent people affirmatively worse off.

The exclusionary rule often leads judges to constrict what counts as a Fourth Amendment violation, and that hurts innocent people. Similarly, because we have such overbroad principles of exclusion under the Fifth Amendment Self-Incrimination Clause, innocent defendants actually suffer because they cannot compel the production of witnesses in their favor. Even if I as an innocent defendant actually know who did it, I cannot currently put that person on the stand if that person takes the Fifth. Under a proper reading of the Fifth Amendment, that would change.[30]

When truth is excluded from trials, there will be two types of systemic errors: wrongful, erroneous convictions and erroneous acquittals. The rules hurt innocent defendants while helping the guilty ones. And I have a hard time explaining to my mother or my brother why that makes sense.

Notes

1. My remarks summarize themes developed in much greater detail in AKHIL REED AMAR, THE CONSTITUTION AND CRIMINAL PROCEDURE: FIRST PRINCIPLES (1997). Instead of cluttering my summary presentation here with excessive footnotes, I have tried to steer the interested reader to the relevant passages of this book, which contains much more elaboration and documentation.
2. In many situations, properly instructed juries might be able to assess and properly discount partially unreliable evidence. See AMAR, supra note 1, at 131. Cf. id. at 203-04 n. 21 (suggesting that properly crafted instructions may not always work).
3. See, e.g., id. at 90-92, 154-55, 191 n.124, 214 n.1g1.
4. See id. at 117-19 (describing the concept of the public trial).
5. See id. at 65-66, 69-70 (critiquing a privacy rationale for the Self-Incrimination Clause).
6. U.S. CONST. amend. V ("... [N]or shall [any person] be compelled in any criminal case to be a witness against himself. . . .").
7. See AMAR, supra note 1, at 137-38 (further discussing privacy privileges).

8. U.S. CONST. amend. IV ("The right of the people to be secure in their persons, houses, papers, and effects, against unreasonable searches and seizures, shall not be violated. . . .").
9. U.S. CONST. amend. VI ("In all criminal prosecutions, the accused shall enjoy the right to a speedy and public trial . . . and to have the Assistance of Counsel for his defense.").
10. See generally id. at 20-25, 191 n.132 (discussing historical attitudes toward the exclusionary rule, both in the U.S. and abroad).
11. *United States v. La Jeune Eugenie*, 26 F. Cas. 832, 84344 (C.C.D. Mass. 1822) (No. 15,551) (stating that "the right of using evidence does not depend, nor, as far as I have any recollection, has ever been supposed to depend, upon the lawfulness or unlawfulness of the mode, by which it is obtained").
12. *Commonwealth v. Dana*, 43 Mass. (2 Met.) 329, 337-38 (1841) ("When papers are offered in evidence, the court can take no notice how they were obtained, whether lawfully or unlawfully; nor would they form a collateral issue to determine that question.") The opinion was actually written by Justice Wilde, see id. at 333, but Chief Justice Shaw then overruled the defendant's motion to arrest the judgment. See id. at 343.
13. See *Boyd v. United States*, 116 U.S. 616, 630, 633-36 (1886) (holding that compulsory production of private papers for use against their owner is prohibited both by the Fourth Amendment privilege against unreasonable search and seizure and by the Fifth Amendment privilege against self-incrimination). The case is discussed in AMAR, supra note 1, at 22-25.
14. These cases are listed in AMAR, supra note 1, at 250 n.28.
15. See *Mapp v. Ohio*, 367 U.S. 643, 661-66 (1961) (Black, J., concurring) (incorporating the exclusionary rules against the States).
16. See id. at 646-47, 646 n.5, 655-57 (opinion of the Court). For a list of the six passages, see AMAR, supra note 1, at 251 n.33.
17. See generally *United States v. Janis*, 428 U.S. 433, 447 (1976) ("In the complex and turbulent history of the [exclusionary] rule, the Court has never applied it to exclude evidence from a civil proceeding, federal or state.").
18. See *Agnello v. United States*, 269 U.S. 20, 35 (1925) (refusing to grant a new trial to co-defendants of a person against whom an unlawful search had been made, even though their convictions depended in part on the unlawfully-found evidence, because the constitutional rights of the co-defendants had not been violated); *Alderman v. United States*, 394 U.S. 165, 171-76 (1969) (restricting exclusionary rule standing to those whose rights were violated by the search itself).
19. See, e.g., *Holt v. United States*, 218 U.S. 245, 252-53 (1910) (holding that requiring a defendant to put on a shirt, in order to prove that it fit him, was not prohibited by the Fifth Amendment, because "the prohibition of compelling a man in a criminal court to be witness against himself is a prohibition of the use of physical or moral compulsion to extort communications from him, not an exclusion of his body as evidence when it may be material"); *Schmerber v. California*, 384 U.S. 757, 760-72 (1966) (holding that the Constitution does

not prohibit the use of involuntarily-given blood samples from a criminal defendant). These cases are discussed in AMAR, supra note 1, at 23, 62-63. If the government kidnapped you utterly illegally, a court would never "exclude" your body and hold that the government had to dismiss the charges, let you go, close its eyes, count to 20, and then try to catch you again. See id. at 108, 236-37 n.84 (citing and discussing cases).

20. See *Fisher v. United States,* 425 U.S. 391, 40708 (1976) (repudiating Boyd); *United States v. Leon,* 468 U.S. 897, 905-06 (1984) (same).
21. See *United States v. Brown,* 64 F.3d 1083, 1084-86 (7th Cir. 1995) (permitting use of evidence discovered, though not seized, in a warrantless search of a defendant's home, because the police had believed the apartment did not belong to the defendant and had conducted the search for safety reasons).
22. See Carol S. Steiker, Counter-Revolution in Constitutional Criminal Procedure?, 20 HARV. J.L. & PUB. POL'Y 435 (1997).
23. See William J. Stuntz, The Virtues and Vices of the Exclusionary Rule, 20 HARV. J.L. & PUB. POL'Y 443 (1997).
24. For more analysis on this point, see AMAR at supra note 1, at 15658.
25. See generally STANLEY S. SURREY, PATHWAYS TO TAX REFORM: THE CONCEPT OF TAX EXPENDITURES (1973).
26. See *Schmerber v. California,* 384 U.S. 757 (1966).
27. See *Gideon v. Wainwright,* 372 U.S. 335 (1963) (instituting the right to state-paid counsel for indigent defendants in all criminal felony trials, federal and state).
28. See AMAR, supra note 1, at 96-116, 136-38.
29. See Stuntz, supra note 23, at 454.
30. See AMAR, supra note 1, at 49-51, 71-73, 134-36 (explaining how narrower Fifth Amendment immunity would lead to broader rights of defendants to compel other witnesses to testify against themselves).

NO 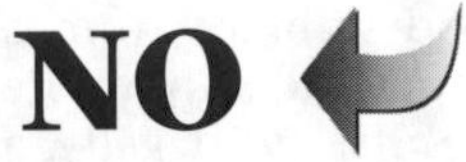

Yale Kamisar

In Defense of the Search and Seizure Exclusionary Rule

Introduction[1]

About a quarter-century ago, after my co-authors and I had published the fourth edition of our criminal procedure casebook,[2] I attended a conference with A. Kenneth Pye, then the Dean of the Duke Law School. During a break in the conference proceedings, Dean Pye, a strong admirer of the Warren Court,[3] took me aside to give me some advice about casebook writing. This is a fairly accurate recollection of what Dean Pye said:

> On thumbing through the new edition of your casebook, I couldn't help noticing that you have eliminated a number of the pre-Warren Court cases you had in the earlier editions. I realize you were responding to the need to add a good deal of new material to the book without letting an already big book get any larger. But taking out the old cases has serious costs. In the years ahead, as more and more interesting new cases are handed down, you will feel much pressure to take out still more older cases. But this is a process you must resist.
>
> Otherwise, by the time you and your co-authors publish your eighth or tenth edition, the confessions chapter will begin with Miranda[4] and the search and seizure chapter with Mapp.[5] This would be calamitous. For many law students (and a few young criminal procedure professors) won't appreciate Mapp and Miranda—won't really understand why the Court felt the need to take the big steps it did—unless casebooks like yours contain material that enables readers of the books to get some idea of how unsatisfactory the prevailing rules and doctrines were before the Warren Court arrived on the scene.

I think Dean Pye's advice about casebook writing was sound, [6] and what he had to say also applies to discussions and debates about such issues as the search and seizure exclusionary rule. We cannot (at least we should not) begin with *Mapp v. Ohio*. We need a prelude.

From *Harvard Journal of Law & Public Policy*, vol. 26, issue 1, Winter 2003, pp. 119.

The Pre-Mapp Era

Perhaps we should begin with *People v. Cahan*,[7] the pre-Mapp case in which California adopted the exclusionary rule on its own initiative.[8] At first, Justice Roger Traynor, who wrote the majority opinion, had not been a proponent of the exclusionary rule. Indeed, thirteen years earlier, he had written the opinion of the California Supreme Court reaffirming the admissibility of illegally seized evidence.[9] By 1955, he and a majority of his colleagues felt compelled to overrule state precedents and adopt the exclusionary rule. Why? The Cahan majority explained:

> [O]ther remedies have completely failed to secure compliance with the constitutional provisions on the part of police officers with the attendant result that the courts under the old rule [of admissibility] have been constantly required to participate in, and in effect condone, the lawless activities of law enforcement officers.[10]

Justice Traynor and his colleagues seemed astounded by how casually and routinely illegally seized evidence was being offered and admitted in the California courts. After noting that Los Angeles police had candidly admitted that they had illegally installed listening devices in the defendants' homes and had described, with equal candor, how they had forcibly entered buildings without bothering to obtain warrants by breaking windows and kicking in doors,[11] Justice Traynor observed:

> [W]ithout fear of criminal punishment or other discipline, law enforcement officers . . . frankly admit their deliberate, flagrant [unconstitutional] acts. . . . It is clearly apparent from their testimony that [Los Angeles police officers] casually regard [their illegal acts] as nothing, more than the performance of their ordinary duties for which the City employs and pays them.[12]

Perhaps we should go back in time still further, three-quarters of a century, to *People v. Defore*,[13] the occasion for Judge (later Justice) Cardozo's famous opinion explaining why New York would not adopt the federal exclusionary rule. Cardozo maintained, as have most critics of the exclusionary rule ever since, that excluding the illegally seized evidence was not the only effective way to enforce the Fourth Amendment (or its state constitutional counterpart): "The [offending] officer might have been resisted, or sued for damages, or even prosecuted for oppression. He was subject to removal or other discipline at the hands of his superiors.[14]

Two decades later, in *Wolf v. Colorado*,[15] when the Supreme Court declined to impose the federal exclusionary rule on the states as a matter of Fourteenth Amendment Due Process, the Wolf majority, per Justice Frankfurter, made a similar argument. Indeed, the Court relied partly on what it called Cardozo's "[w]eighty testimony" about the availability of various alternatives to the exclusionary rule.[16]

The states that had rejected the federal exclusionary rule, Justice Frankfurter assured us, had "not left the right to privacy without other means of protection."[17] It could not, therefore, be regard[ed] as a departure from basic standards to remand [victims of unlawful searches and seizures] to the remedies of private action and such protection as the internal discipline of the police, under the eyes of an alert public opinion, may afford."[18]

A majority of the Court took a very different view of the various alternatives (perhaps one should say, theoretical alternatives) to the exclusionary rule a dozen years later when it handed down *Mapp v. Ohio*,[19] overruling *Wolf*. This time the Court dismissed alternatives to the exclusionary rule, noting that "[t]he experience of California that such other remedies have been worthless and futile is buttressed by the experience of other States."[20] But the Court had nothing specific to say about the experience in any state other than California nor did it rely on empirical studies. Instead, the Court relied on comments by Justice Traynor in Cahan.

Asserting that the various alternatives to the exclusionary rule are worthless (or quoting statements by the California Supreme Court to the same effect) does not necessarily make them so—just as asserting (or assuming) that alternative remedies are meaningful (as both Cardozo and Frankfurter did) does not make that so. Fortunately, impressive evidence of the ineffectiveness of the so-called alternatives to the exclusionary rule does exist. But it is not to be found in the *Mapp* opinion itself. It is to be found rather in the reaction of law enforcement officials to the *Mapp* decision. To borrow a phrase, this reaction is the "weighty testimony"[21] that (despite the claims of Cardozo, Frankfurter, and others) reliance on tort remedies, criminal prosecutions, and the internal discipline of the police indeed left "the right to privacy without other means of protection."[22]

The Law Enforcement Community's Reaction to Mapp

Although Michael Murphy, the police commissioner of New York City at the time, did not say so in so many words, he left no doubt that because New York courts (relying on the *Defore* case) had permitted the prosecution to use illegally seized evidence up to the time of *Mapp*, neither the commissioner nor the thousands of officers who worked for him had been taking the law of search and seizure at all seriously. As the commissioner recalled some time later:

> I can think of no decision in recent times in the field of law enforcement which had such a dramatic and traumatic effect as [*Mapp*]. As the then commissioner of the largest police force in this country I was immediately caught up in the entire problem of reevaluating our procedures, which had followed the *Defore* rule, and . . . creating new policies and new instructions for the implementation of *Mapp* . . . . [Decisions such as *Mapp*] create tidal waves and earthquakes which require rebuilding of our institutions sometimes from their very foundations upward. Retraining sessions had to be held from the very top administrators down to each of the thou-

sands of foot patrolmen and detectives engaged in the daily basic enforcement function.[23]

Why was *Mapp's* effect so "dramatic and traumatic"? Why did it create "tidal waves and earthquakes"? Why did it require "retraining" from top to bottom? Had there been any search and seizure training before *Mapp*?

What did the commissioner mean when he told us that prior to *Mapp* his police department's procedures "had followed the *Defore* case"? *Defore* did not set forth any procedures or permit the police to establish any procedures other than those that complied with the Fourth Amendment. It did allow New York prosecutors to use illegally seized evidence, but it did not (as the commissioner seemed to think) allow New York police to commit illegal searches and seizures. Is there any better evidence of the inadequacies of the existing alternatives to the exclusionary rule than the police reaction to the imposition of the rule?[24]

It appears that, prior to *Mapp*, New York prosecutors were also unfamiliar with and uninterested in the law of search and seizure. Professor Richard Uviller, a New York prosecuting attorney at the time *Mapp* was handed down, recalled that he "cranked out a crude summary" of federal search and seizure law just in time for the next state convention of district attorneys and that summary turned out to be "an instant runaway best seller. It was as though we had made a belated discovery that the fourth amendment applied in the State of New York . . . ".[25] That, I think, says it all.

The response of New York law enforcement officials to the imposition of the search and seizure rule is hardly unique. Six years earlier, when the California Supreme Court adopted the exclusionary rule on its own initiative in *People v. Cahan*,[26] the reaction of the Los Angeles Chief of Police, William Parker, had been quite similar to the one his New York City counterpart displayed when *Mapp* was decided.[27]

In Pennsylvania—another state whose courts had admitted illegally seized evidence prior to *Mapp*—a young Philadelphia assistant district attorney (and a future U.S. Senator), Arlen Specter, left little doubt that in this state, too, the so-called alternative remedies to the exclusionary rule had had virtually no effect. Commissioner Murphy had likened *Mapp* to a "tidal wave" and an "earthquake"; Mr. Specter compared it to a revolution:

> Police practices and prosecution procedures were revolutionized in many states by the holding in . . . *Mapp v. Ohio* that evidence obtained from an illegal search and seizure cannot be used in a criminal proceeding . . . . [There are indications] that the imposition of the exclusionary rule upon the states is the most significant event in criminal law since the adoption of the fourteenth amendment . . . . *Mapp* has rewritten the criminal law treatise for states which had admitted evidence regardless of how it was obtained.[28]
>
> Mr. Specter, like Commissioner Murphy, seemed to equate the relevance of the law of search and seizure with the presence or absence of the exclusionary rule, a remedy for the violation of a body of law the police were supposed to be obeying all along: [T]he *Mapp* decision has significantly impaired the ability of the police to secure evidence to convict the

> guilty . . . . The law abiding citizen who must walk on some Philadelphia streets at two o'clock in the morning would doubtless prefer to be subjected to a search, without any cause, and have the police do the same to the man standing idly at a comer; but that cannot be done under *Mapp*.[29]

Has the Exclusionary Rule Inhibited the Development of Alternative Remedies?

One can hear the critics of the exclusionary rule now. *Mapp v. Ohio*, some say, removed both the incentive and the opportunity to develop effective alternative means of enforcing the Fourth Amendment. Indeed, Chief Justice Warren Burger once said that "the continued existence of [the exclusionary rule] inhibits the development of rational alternatives."[30] However, it is hard to take this argument seriously.

First of all, as opponents of the exclusionary rule never tire of telling us, large portions of police activity relating to the seizing of criminal property do not produce (and may not even have been designed to produce) incriminating evidence, and thus do not result in criminal prosecutions.[31] Whatever the reason for the failure to impose direct sanctions on the offending officers in these instances, it cannot be the existence of the exclusionary rule. The issue need not, and should not, be framed in terms of whether we should enforce the Fourth Amendment by an exclusionary rule or tort remedies against the offending officers or departmental sanctions. Nothing prevents the use of "internal sanctions" against the police "simultaneously with the use of the exclusionary rule."[32] After all, "[n]o proponent of the exclusionary rule has suggested that it should act in isolation."[33]

Moreover, blaming the failure to develop any effective "direct sanctions" against offending police officers on the exclusionary rule itself, to borrow a phrase from Carol Steiker, "ignores history."[34] For many decades a large number of states had no exclusionary rule, yet none of them produced any meaningful alternatives to the rule. Almost half a century passed between the time the federal courts adopted the exclusionary rule[35] and the time the Court finally imposed the rule on the states. But in all that time, not one of the twenty-four states that still admitted illegally seized evidence on the eve of *Mapp* had developed an effective alternative to the rule.[36] Thus, five decades of post-Weeks "freedom" from the inhibiting effect of the federal exclusionary rule failed to produce any meaningful alternative to the exclusionary rule in any jurisdiction.

One can hear the critics of the exclusionary rule again. Some of them are telling us that times have changed. Have they?

Are Today's Politicians More Likely to Impose Effective "Direct Sanctions" Against the Police Than the Politicians of Yesteryear?

Is there any reason to believe that today's or tomorrow's politicians are, or will be, any less fearful of appearing "soft on crime" or any more interested in protecting people under investigation by the police than the politicians of any other era? Is there any reason to think that the lawmakers of our day are any more willing than their predecessors to invigorate tort remedies (or any other "direct sanction") against police officers who act overzealously in the pursuit of "criminals"?

"If anything," observes Carol Steiker, "the escalating public hysteria over violent crime from the 1960s through the present makes it is [sic] even more 'politically suicidal' today to support restrictions on police behavior than it was before 1961."[37] Consider, too, the disheartening comments of Donald Dripps:

> American legislatures consistently have failed to address defects in the criminal process, even when they rise to crisis-level proportions. For example, when the Miranda Court invited Congress and the states to experiment with alternatives to traditional backroom police interrogation, Congress responded by adopting Title II [of the Omnibus Crime Control and Safe Streets Act of 1968], which stubbornly insisted on the traditional practice. To this day only two American jurisdictions, Alaska and Minnesota, require taping interrogations. In both instances the state courts, rather than the state legislature, were the source of reform.
>
> Legislatures across the United States have found billions of dollars for prisons, but the support for indigent defense is shamefully inadequate.[38] No legislature has adopted reforms of police identification procedures, even though we have known since the 1930s that mistaken identification is the leading cause of false convictions.[39] Legislatures . . . have not adopted statutory requirements for judicial warrants, or the preservation of exculpatory evidence, or plugged holes in the exclusionary rule, let alone delivered the effective tort remedy exclusionary rule critics have advocated for decades.
>
> The record is not an accident, but the product of rational political incentives. Almost everyone has an interest in controlling crime. Only young men, disproportionately black, are at significant risk of erroneous prosecution for garden-variety felonies. Abuses of police search and seizure or interrogation powers rarely fall upon middle-aged, middle-class citizens . . . . [S]o long as the vast bulk of police and prosecutorial power targets the relatively powerless (and when will that ever be otherwise?), criminal procedure rules that limit public power will come from the courts or they will come from nowhere.[40]

A new book by Welsh White relates an incident that illustrates the formidable political power possessed by the law enforcement community.[41] As the result of a lawsuit brought by an alleged victim of abusive police interrogation practices, a police investigator looked into charges against a Chicago police commander and those working for him. He concluded that for a period of more than ten years the commander and his men had been torturing suspects into confessing. In 1993, the commander was dismissed from the police force.[42] But allegations of police misconduct continued to fill the air. For example, ten Illinois prisoners on death row maintained that the Chicago commander and his men had extracted confessions from them by torture.[43]

In the wake of the controversy surrounding these alleged police torture cases, the Illinois legislature at one point seemed prepared to enact a law requiring the police to video or audiotape their interrogation practices. But the law enforcement community expressed its strong opposition to the bill, claiming that it would create new obstacles and expand the rights of the accused "at the expense of crime victims, public safety and law enforcement."[44] The bill died in committee.[45]

As Justice Traynor noted long ago in Cahan, "even when it becomes generally known that the police conduct illegal searches and seizures, public opinion is not aroused as it is in the case of other violations of constitutional rights" because illegal arrests and unlawful searches "lack the obvious brutality of coerced confessions and the third degree and do not so clearly strike at the very basis of our civil liberties as do unfair trials . . . ."[46] Moreover, unlike the Chicago torture cases, illegal searches and seizures do not raise doubts as to a defendant's innocence. If the police and their allies can crush legislative reform efforts in the confessions area as decisively as they did in the wake of the Chicago police scandal—despite serious questions about the guilt of a number of people on death row—how much difficulty will they have defeating legislative proposals to impose direct sanctions on them for committing Fourth Amendment violations?

One half of Judge Guido Calabresi's proposed alternative to the exclusionary rule is to impose a system of "direct punishment" on the offending police officer.[47] Perhaps Judge Calabresi has in mind the imposition of substantial fines, suspensions without pay, or dismissal from the force, depending on the seriousness of the officer's Fourth Amendment violation. One fails to see, however, why this part of his proposal will fare any better in the political arena than many other "direct sanction" proposals that have failed over the years.

Police Perjury and Judicial "Winking"

As other critics of the exclusionary rule have done,[48] Judge Calabresi notes that the police frequently lie in court to evade the exclusionary rule.[49] Still worse, there is good reason to believe that in a significant number of cases, judges "knowingly accept police perjury as truthful."[50] There are at least two responses to this criticism of the exclusionary rule.

First, Myron Orfield's interviews with approximately forty Chicago criminal division judges, prosecutors, and public defenders left no doubt that police perjury and judicial toleration of it were widespread, but he concluded:

> Although recognizing the [exclusionary] rule's imperfections, respondents believe it is the only mechanism that injects any restraint in the system, or any respect for rights. Though often evaded, the respondents believe that by creating a possibility of suppression, the rule makes the Fourth Amendment a factor in police and judicial thinking. . . .[51]

Critics might also argue that pervasive perjury is a cost of the exclusionary rule, and as such, outweighs any incremental benefit gained by the rule's uneven deterrent effect. Respondents . . . nevertheless believe that the exclusionary rule has dramatically improved police behavior and should be retained . . . . Today, while police often perjure themselves, they also, because of the exclusionary rule, often obey the Fourth Amendment. By any measure, this is an improvement [over pre-*Mapp* days].[52]

Second, as Laurie Levenson recently observed, there is no evidence and no reason to believe "that a police officer will be any less motivated to lie in an administrative hearing, where [his] reputation and job position are at risk, than in a criminal proceeding where the court threatens to exclude evidence."[53] "[I]t is important to realize," admonishes Orfield, in the course of concluding his study of Chicago narcotics officers, "that any remedial scheme that imposes a personal sanction on an officer is likely to encourage perjury."[54]

The Costs of the Exclusionary Rule

[Many critics of the exclusionary role have assumed][55] that the criminal defendant who benefits from the application of the search and seizure exclusionary rule will often be a murderer or rapist.[56] However, an empirical study by Thomas Davies, called "[t]he most careful and balanced assessment conducted to date of all available empirical data,"[57] reveals that the exclusion of evidence in murder, rape, and other violent cases is exceedingly rare.[58] "The most striking feature of the data," reports Davies, "is the concentration of illegal searches in drug arrests (and possibly weapons possession arrests) and the extremely small effects in arrests for other offenses, including violent crimes."[59]

It may be that search and seizure problems arise much less frequently in murder, forcible rape, and other violent crime cases than they do in drug and weapons possession cases. Myron Orfield furnishes two other explanations, one encouraging, the other not.

The first explanation is that the more serious the crime, the greater the officer's desire to see the perpetrator convicted and, because the police care more about convictions in these cases, the more potent the exclusionary rule's deterrent effects.[60] Moreover, "big cases" are more likely to involve officers in specialized units "who are more likely to take the time and care necessary to comply with the Fourth Amendment."[61]

The second explanation is that in "heater" cases (i.e., big cases that have "the potential to arouse public ire" if the defendant "goes free" because the police violated the Fourth Amendment), [62] many judges will feel tremendous pressure to admit the illegally seized evidence and will often find a way to do so.[63] It is almost as if many judges, at least those who have to run for re-election, have informally adopted one law professor's proposal to make an exception to the exclusionary rule in prosecutions for treason, espionage, murder, armed robbery, and kidnapping.[64] I find this an unfortunate and dispiriting development, [65] but it is only one of a number of ways in which the courts have accommodated the needs of law enforcement in the exclusionary rule era.

The Warren Court has been disbanded for more than thirty years. Since then, with only a few exceptions,[66] the Burger and Rehnquist Courts have waged a kind of "guerilla warfare" against the law of search and seizure.[67] As a result, Judge Cardozo's oft-quoted criticism of the exclusionary rule—"[t]he criminal is to go free because the constable has blundered"[68]—is out of date. The Court has taken a grudging view of what amounts to a "search" or "seizure" within the meaning of the Fourth Amendment and has taken a relaxed view of what constitutes consent to an otherwise illegal search or seizure; it has so softened the "probable cause" requirement, so increased the occasions on which the police may act on the basis of "reasonable suspicion" or in the absence of any reasonable suspicion, and so narrowed the thrust of the exclusionary rule that nowadays the criminal only "goes free" if and when the constable has blundered badly.[69]

Judge Calabresi argues that the downsizing of the Fourth Amendment and the protections to privacy it provides, because of the pressure the exclusionary rule puts on courts to avoid freeing a guilty defendant, should make liberals hate the exclusionary rule.[70] I think not.

A meaningful tort remedy or administrative sanction or any other effective alternative to the exclusionary rule would also exert strong pressure on courts to make the rules governing search and seizure more "police-friendly." As Monrad Paulsen noted on the eve of the Mapp case: "Whenever the rules are enforced by meaningful sanctions, our attention is drawn to their content. The comfort of Freedom's words spoken in the abstract is always disturbed by their application to a contested instance. Any rule of police regulation enforced in fact will generate pressures to weaken the rule."[71]

There is no denying that one of the effects of the exclusionary rule has been to diminish the protection provided by the Fourth Amendment. But this is probably the price we would have had to pay for any means of enforcing the Amendment that had a bite—one that actually worked.

The only time the Amendment would not impose the societal costs that critics of the exclusionary rule complain about—and the only time it would not put pressure on the courts to water down the rules governing search and seizure—would be if it were "an unenforced honor code that the police may follow in their discretion."[72]

Judge Calabresi's Proposal

As Tracey Maclin has reminded us,[73] ever since the 1930s,[74] commentators have deplored the inadequacies of existing tort remedies against offending police officers and proposed various ways to invigorate these remedies (although nothing seems to have come of it). Therefore, I find quite noteworthy Judge Calabresi's view that, in the ordinary unlawful arrest or illegal search case, tort remedies will not work.[75] I agree with him that, although jurors often identify with the plaintiff in a tort action, they are unlikely to do so when the plaintiff is a criminal or a suspected criminal.[76] However, I find the alternative to the exclusionary rule that Judge Calabresi proposes disappointing.

Judge Calabresi's proposal has two parts: First, after the person has been convicted, a hearing would take place to determine whether the police had obtained evidence illegally and, if so, whether the officer(s) had done so inadvertently, negligently, willfully, or wantonly. Based on the flagrancy of the police misconduct, the defendant would then be given a reduction of two, three, or four points on the sentencing guidelines.[77] Second, the officer or officers who were found to have violated the Fourth Amendment would then be subjected to a separate system of direct punishment which would vary, depending upon the flagrancy of the misconduct.[78] I assume that one or more of the officer's superiors would determine what the punishment should be.

A reduction of the prison sentence, based on the degree to which the police violated the defendant's rights, is an unusual aspect of Judge Calabresi's proposal. He assures us that this feature would provide the defendant with a significant incentive to bring up the fact that the evidence introduced by the state was obtained illegally. Perhaps so,[79] but the more relevant question is how, if at all, this part of the judge's proposal would influence the police. Would it constitute a disincentive—a means of eliminating, or at least reducing, significant police incentives to illegal searches where the police contemplate prosecution and conviction?[80] I think not. This feature of Judge Calabresi's proposal would likely have no impact on the police at all.

Chief Justice Burger once argued that the exclusionary rule does not affect police officers' behavior.[81] However, Myron Orfield's Chicago study strongly indicates otherwise.[82] Every judge, prosecutor, and public defender he interviewed expressed the belief that "officers care about convictions and experience adverse personal reactions when they lose evidence."[83]

Under Judge Calabresi's proposal, however, the victim of the police misconduct could be, and would be, convicted on the basis of evidence the police obtained in violation of the Fourth Amendment, even when the violation was gross or willful. I am convinced that the police do care whether the evidence they obtained leads to a conviction or whether such evidence is thrown out by the court. But a conviction is one thing; the length of the sentence is something else. I find it hard to believe that the police care one whit whether the person convicted on the basis of their unlawful acquisition of evidence is sentenced to four years or five, ten months or twelve. From the perspective of the police, the important thing—perhaps the only thing—is that their actions resulted in the conviction of a criminal and a substantial stretch of prison time for him. In other words, their illegal actions "paid off."

Therefore, the efficacy of Judge Calabresi's proposed alternative to the exclusionary rule must turn on the other half of his proposal—what he calls a separate system of direct punishment of the individual officer after a post-trial determination that the officer committed a search and seizure violation.[84]

We can be fairly certain that if the police believed Judge Calabresi's system of direct punishment for Fourth Amendment violations would really work, they would resist its adoption for the same reasons they would be unhappy about other systems of "direct sanctions" against them (such as tort remedies) that really worked. They would argue forcefully, and with some plausibility, that if six-month suspensions without pay and/or substantial fines were imposed on them for search and seizure violations (presumably the kind of "direct punishments" Judge Calabresi contemplates), they "would be afraid to conduct the searches they should make."[85]

Orfield's study of Chicago narcotics officers discloses that they clearly preferred the exclusionary rule to a system of "direct sanctions" against them. [86] This finding may be somewhat misleading. Few police are enamored of the exclusionary rule. If they had their druthers, most would prefer the pre-*Mapp* days, when, in many states, no viable means of enforcing the protection against unreasonable search and seizure existed.[87] However, the police would rather live with an "indirect" sanction, like the exclusionary rule, than a direct one. Moreover, the exclusionary rule is not something the police can fight and defeat in the political arena—it is a remedy that judges control and can apply "without being dependent upon the actions of other branches of government."[88]

The police can, however, have a large effect on the alternatives to the exclusionary rule, because other actors such as legislators, prosecutors, and police brass control these.[89] For one thing, the police can invoke their formidable political clout [90] to prevent a plan like Judge Calabresi's from ever being adopted. Moreover, even if such a plan were adopted, the police could prevent it from being applied in appropriate cases.

Judge Calabresi's proposed system would probably not overcome the resulting police resistance. But the greater danger is that a plan like the judge's might be adopted, displacing the exclusionary rule, yet rarely be enforced. It might turn out to exist only on paper.

One cannot help thinking of *INS v. Lopez-Mendoza*,[91] a case that declined to apply the exclusionary rule to civil deportation proceedings. One reason the Court gave for the conclusion it reached was that the Immigration and Naturalization Services ("INS") "has its own comprehensive scheme for deterring Fourth Amendment violations by its officers"[92]—a system of rules and regulations restricting INS agents' conduct in dealing with aliens, a program for giving new officers "instruction and examination in Fourth Amendment law," and "a procedure for investigating and punishing immigration officers who commit Fourth Amendment violations."[93] These programs and procedures, the Court assured us, "reduce the likely deterrent value of the exclusionary rule."[94]

The trouble was, as dissenting Justice White was quick to point out, that the *Lopez-Mendoza* majority failed to cite "a single instance" in which the INS procedures had been invoked.[95] Moreover, other portions of the majority opinion were likely to shake one's confidence in the vaunted procedures the INS was supposed to have in place for deterring, investigating, and punishing Fourth Amendment violations. Even an "occasional invocation of the exclusionary rule might significantly change and complicate the character of [deportation] proceedings," the Court told us, because "[n]either the hearing officers nor the attorneys participating in those hearings are likely to be well versed in the intricacies of Fourth Amendment law."[96] The Court also indicated that application of the exclusionary rule to deportation proceedings "might well result in the suppression of large amounts of information that had been obtained entirely lawfully," because "INS arrests occur in crowded and confused circumstances."[97] Moreover, the Court told us that requiring INS agents to keep "a precise account of exactly what happened in each particular arrest" would be impractical, considering the "massed numbers of ascertainably illegal aliens. . . ."[98]

To avoid a replay of the paper procedures for deterring Fourth Amendment violations in place at the INS, I suggest that we proceed slowly and cautiously with [proposals to change the exclusionary rule]. As noted earlier, many unlawful arrests and searches do not turn up any incriminating evidence or result in any criminal prosecutions.[99] In the unlikely event that Judge Calabresi's scheme of directly punishing the offending officer is put in place, a better plan is to keep the exclusionary rule in the first three to five years for instances of police misconduct that result in criminal prosecutions and to use the new administrative sanctions against those officers whose misconduct failed to produce any incriminating evidence. In the unlikely event that an appraisal of the situation three or five years later demonstrates that the judge's system of direct punishment really works—that police officers are regularly punished for "the frequent infringements [of the Fourth Amendment] motivated by commendable zeal" as well as for "the grossest of violations"[100]—there will be time enough to abolish the exclusionary rule.

Notes

1. There is a vast literature on this subject. For a good sampling, see WAYNE R. LAFAVE, SEARCH AND SEIZURE: A TREATISE ON THE FOURTH AMENDMENT 1-373 (3d ed. 1996); Francis A. Allen, Federalism and the Fourth Amendment: A Requiem for Wolf, 1961 SUP. CT. REV. 1; Akhil Reed Amar, Fourth Amendment First Principles, 107 HARV. L. REV. 757 (1994); Anthony G. Amsterdam, Perspectives on the Fourth Amendment, 58 MINN. L. REV. 349 (1974); Edward L. Barrett, Jr., Exclusion of Evidence Obtained by Illegal Searches—A Comment on People vs. Cahan, 43 CAL. L. REV. 565 (1955); Yale Kamisar, Does (Did) (Should) the Exclusionary Rule Rest on a "Principled Basis" Rather than an "Empirical Proposition"?, 16 CREIGHTON L. REV. 565 (1983); Tracey Maclin, When the Cure for the Fourth Amendment is Worse than the Disease, 68 S. CAL. L. REV. 1 (1994); Dallin H. Oaks, Studying the Exclusionary Rule in Search and Seizure, 37 U. CHI. L. REV. 665 (1970); Monrad G. Paulsen, The Exclusionary Rule and Misconduct by the Police, 52 J. CRIM. L.C. & P.S. 255 (1961); Christopher Slobogin, Why Liberals Should Chuck the Exclusionary Rule, 1999 U. ILL. L. REV. 363; Carol S. Steiker, Second Thoughts About First Principles, 107 HARV. L. REV. 820 (1994); Potter Stewart, The Road to Mapp v. Ohio and Beyond: The Origins, Development and Future of the Exclusionary Rule in Search-and-Seizure Cases, 83 COLUM. L. REV. 1365 (1983); John Barker Waite, Judges and the Crime Burden, 54 MICH. L. REV. 169 (1955); Silas Wasserstrom & William J. Mertens, The Exclusionary Rule on the Scaffold: But Was It a Fair Trial?, 22 AM. GRIM. L. REV. 85 (1984); John H. Wigmore, Using Evidence Obtained by Illegal Search and Seizure, 8 A.B.A. J. 479 (1922). It is very hard to select the best long article ever written on the exclusionary rule, but it is relatively easy to pick the best short one—William J. Stuntz, The Virtues and Vices of the Exclusionary Rule, 20 HARV. J.L. & PUB. POL'Y 443 (1997).

2. YALE KAMISAR ET AL., MODERN CRIMINAL PROCEDURE (4th ed. 1974).
3. See, e.g., A. Kenneth Pye, The Warren Court and Criminal Procedure, 67 MICH. L. REV. 249 (1968). At the time he gave me advice about writing criminal procedure casebooks, Pye was one of the nation's leading criminal procedure commentators, but in later years Pye's administrative obligations as law school dean, university chancellor and university president diverted his efforts from legal scholarship. See generally Francis A. Allen, The Scholarship of Kenneth Pye, 49 SMU L. REV. 439 (1996).
4. Miranda v. Arizona, 384 U.S. 436 (1966).
5. Mapp v. Ohio, 367 U.S. 643 (1961).
6. Our casebook is now in its tenth edition. See YALE KAMISAR ET AL., MODERN CRIMINAL PROCEDURE (10th ed. 2002). The chapter on search and seizure still does not begin with Mapp; the chapter on confessions still does not begin with Miranda.
7. 282 P.2d 905 (Cal. 1955).
8. Prior to Mapp, state courts were free to admit or to exclude illegally seized evidence. In 1949, thirty-one states declined to exclude such evidence. A decade later, on the eve of Mapp, twenty-four states still rejected the exclusionary rule. See Yale Kamisar, The Exclusionary Rule in Historical Perspective: The Struggle to Make the Fourth Amendment More than "an Empty Blessing", 62 JUDICATURE 337, 346 (1979).
9. See People v. Gonzales, 124 P.2d 44 (Cal. 1942). What is even more ironic is that in 1942 Earl Warren was the California Attorney General who successfully urged Justice Traynor and his colleagues to reaffirm the rule permitting the use of illegally seized evidence. See id.
10. Cahan, 282 P.2d at 911-12.
11. See id. at 906 (citation omitted).
12. Id. at 907. See also Roger Traynor, Mapp v. Ohio at Large in the Fifty States, 1962 DUKE L. J. 319 (1962): My misgivings about [the admissibility of illegally seized evidence] grew as I observed that time after time it was being offered and admitted as routine procedure. It became impossible to ignore the corollary that illegal searches and seizures were also a routine procedure subject to no effective deterrent; else how could illegally obtained evidence come into court with such regularity? Id. At 321-22.
13. 150 N.E. 585 (NY App. Ct. 1926).
14. Id. at 586-87.
15. 338 U.S. 25 (1949).
16. Id. at 31. The Court quoted from Judge Cardozo's Defore opinion at considerable length. See id. at 31-32 n.2.
17. Id. at 30.
18. Id. at 31.
19. 367 U.S. 643 (1961).
20. Id. at 652.
21. Wolf, 338 U.S. at 31.
22. Id. at 30.

23. Michael Murphy, Judicial Review of Police Methods in Law Enforcement: The Problem of Compliance by Police Departments, 44 TEX. L. REV. 939, 941 (1966) (citation omitted) (emphasis added).
24. If any police official's post-Mapp comments are more revealing than Commissioner Murphy's, it may be those of New York City Deputy Police Commissioner Leonard Reisman. Reisman told a large group of police officers why they had to learn the law of seizure at such a late date in their careers: "[In the past] nobody bothered to take out search warrants. . . . [T]he Supreme Court had ruled that evidence obtained without a warrant—illegally if you will—was admissible in state courts. So the feeling was, why bother?" Sidney E. Zion, Detectives Get a Course in Law, N.Y. TIMES, Apr. 28, 1965, at A50.
25. H. Richard Uviller, The Acquisition of Evidence for Criminal Prosecution: Some Constitutional Premises and Practices in Transition, 35 VAND. L. REV. 501, 502 (1982).
26. 282 P.2d 905 (Cal. 1955); see supra note 7 and accompanying text.
27. Chief Parker told the public that the commission of a serious crime would no longer "justify affirmative police action until such time as the police have armed themselves with sufficient information to constitute 'probable cause.'" WILLIAM H. PARKER, POLICE 117 (Wilson ed., 1957), quoted in Yale Kamisar, Wolf and Lustig Ten Years Later: Illegal State Evidence in State and Federal Courts, 43 MINN. L. REV. 1083, 1153-54 (1959). He also pledged that he and his officers would work "within the framework of limitations" imposed by the law of search and seizure "[a]s long as the Exclusionary Rule is the law of California." Id. at 131. For substantial extracts from Chief Parker's responses to the Cahan decision and for comments on his reaction, see Kamisar, supra, at 1153-54.
28. Arlen Specter, Mapp v. Ohio: Pandora's Problems for the Prosecutor, 111 U. PA. L. REV. 4(1962).
29. Id. at 42.
30. Stone v. Powell, 428 U.S. 465,500 (1976) (Burger, C.J., concurring).
31. See, e.g., Akhil Reed Amar, Against Exclusion (Except to Protect Truth or Prevent Privacy Violations), 20 HARV. J.L. & PUB. POL'Y 457, 463-64 (1997) (describing alternate benefits of illegal evidence seizure).
32. Cf. A. Kenneth Pye, Charles Fahy and the Criminal Law, 54 GEO. L.J. 1055, 1072 (1966) (explaining that exclusionary rule is invoked because of failure of "internal sanctions" above).
33. Id.
34. Steiker, supra note 1, at 849; see also Kamisar, supra note 8, at 346, 350 (describing lack of initiative on part of states to develop alternatives between adoption of federal exclusionary rule and decisions of Mapp, 367 U.S. 643 (1961) and Wolf, 338 U.S. 25 (1949)).
35. See Weeks v. United States, 232 U.S. 383 (1914).
36. See Elkins v. United States, 364 U.S. 206, 224-25 (1960).
37. Steiker, supra note 1, at 850 (citation omitted); see also Amsterdam, supra note 1, at 379 ("[T]here will remain more than enough crime and fear of it in American society to keep our legislatures from the politically suicidal undertaking of police control.").

38. See, e.g., Note, Gideon's Promise Unfulfilled: The Need for Litigated Reform of Indigent Defense, 113 HARV. L. REV. 2062, 2067 (2000) (alluding to congressional and local jurisdictional decreases in resources devoted to indigent defense).
39. See also Francis A. Allen, The Judicial Quest for Penal Justice: The Warren Court and the Criminal Cases, 1975 U. ILL. L.F. 518, 542 (1975) (deploring the fact that Congress simply attempted to repeal the 1967 Supreme Court cases extending right to counsel to police lineups without offering anything in their place).
40. Donald A. Dripps, Constitutional Theory for Criminal Procedure: Dickerson, Miranda, and the Continuing Quest for Broad-But-Shallow, 43 WM. & MARY L. REV. 1, 45-46 (2001) (citations omitted).
41. See WELSH S. WHITE, MIRANDA'S WANING PROTECTIONS 128-36 (2001).
42. See id. at 130.
43. See id. at 130-31.
44. Id. at 136.
45. See id.
46. 282 P.2d 905, 913 (Cal. 1955).
47. Guido Calabresi, The Exclusionary Rule, 26 HARV. J.L. & PUB. POL'Y 111, 116 (2002).
48. See, e.g., L. Timothy Perrin, et al., If It's Broken, Fix It: Moving Beyond the Exclusionary Rule, 83 IOWA L. REV. 669, 677 (1998).
49. See Calabresi, supra note 47, at 113.
50. Myron W. Orfield, Jr., Deterrence, Perjury, and the Heater Factor: An Exclusionary Rule in the Chicago Criminal Courts, 63 U. COLO. L. REV. 75, 83 (1992). The study was based on interviews with thirteen judges, eleven prosecutors, and fourteen public defenders in the Chicago criminal court system. See id. at 81.
51. Id. at 123.
52. Id. at 132.
53. Laurie L. Levenson, Administrative Replacements: How Much Can They Do?, 26 PEPP. L. REV. 879, 881 (1999).
54. Myron W. Orfield, Jr., Comment, The Exclusionary Rule and Deterrence: An Empirical Study of Chicago Narcotics Officers, 54 U. CHI. L. REV. 1016, 1055 (1987). This study, based on interviews with twenty-six narcotics officers in the Chicago Police Department, was conducted while Orfield was still a law student. Seven years later when Orfield published his second empirical study, he reported that "many" of the judges, prosecutors and public defenders interviewed expressed the view "that to the extent a tort remedy would actually impose damages on police officers, it would cause the police to perjure themselves even more frequently [than they do now to thwart the impact of the exclusionary rule]." Orfield, supra note 50, at 126.

    It strikes me that what Orfield has to say about tort actions applies to administrative sanctions as well. An officer is likely to be just as fearful about being dismissed or suspended (without pay) from the police force, or forced to pay a substantial fine, as he is about having to pay tort damages.
55. See California v. Minjares, 443 U.S. 916, 927 (1979) (Rehnquist, J., dissenting from denial of stay); Stone v. Powell, 428 U.S 465, 501

(1976)(Burger, C.J., concurring); Bivens v. Six Unknown Named Agents, 403 U.S. 388, 413 (1971) (Burger, C.J., dissenting); Amar, supra note 1, at 793-98; Stephen J. Markman, Six Observations on the Exclusionary Rule, 20 HARV. J.L. & PUB. POL'Y 425, 432-33 (1997).

56. See Calabresi, supra note 47, at 115.
57. LAFAVE, supra note 1, at 58.
58. See Thomas Y. Davies, A Hard Look at What We Know (and Still Need to Learn) About the "Costs" of the Exclusionary Rule: The NIJ Study and Other Studies of "Lost" Arrests, 1983 AM. B. FOUND. RES. J. 611, 640, 645. According to a five-year study of California data, illegal search and seizure problems were given as the reason for the rejection of only thirteen of more than 14,000 forcible rape arrests (0.09%) and only eight of approximately 12,000 homicide arrests (0.06%). See id. Another study, a three-state (Illinois, Michigan and Pennsylvania) study by Peter Nardulli involving some 7,500 cases, disclosed that none of the successful motions to exclude illegally seized evidence "involved exceptionally serious cases such as murder, rape, armed robbery, or even unarmed robbery." Peter F. Nardulli, The Societal Cost of the Exclusionary Rule: An Empirical Assessment, 1983 AM. B. FOUND. RES. J. 585, 596 n.47.
59. Davies, supra note 58, at 680. The California data reveals that less than 0.3% (fewer than three in 1,000) of arrests for all non-drug offenses are rejected by prosecutors because of illegal searches. Id. at 619. Davies estimates that "the cumulative loss of drug arrests at all stages of felony processing in California is around 7.1%." Id. at 681. In United States v. Leon, the Court, per Justice White, estimated that "the cumulative loss due to nonprosecution or nonconviction of individuals arrested on felony drug charges is probably in the range of 2.8% to 7.1%." 468 U.S. 897, 907 n.6 (1984). One may argue, as the Court did in Leon, that the small percentages of cases lost because of the exclusionary rule "mask a large absolute number." Id. at 907 n.6. As Davies has pointed out, however, "raw numbers are not as useful for policy evaluation as percentages. In a system as large as the American criminal justice system . . . almost any nationwide measurement or estimate will look large if expressed in raw numbers." Davies, supra note 58, at 670.
60. See Orfield, supra note 50, at 82, 85, 115.
61. Id. at 115.
62. Id. at 116.
63. See id. at 115-23.
64. See John Kaplan, The Limits of the Exclusionary Rule, 26 STAN. L. REV. 1027, 1046-49 (1974).
65. For extensive criticism of Professor Kaplan's proposal to limit the impact of the exclusionary rule see Yale Kamisar, "Comparative Reprehensibility" and the Fourth Amendment Exclusionary Rule, 86 MICH. L. REV. 1 (1987). But see Stuntz, supra note 1, at 447 ("[T]he visibility of the criminal who walks away [because of the exclusionary rule] . . . makes courts see the consequences of [their rulings and may be] . . . a way of limiting counter-majoritarian excess.").
66. See, e.g., Kyllo v. United States, 533 U.S. 27, 34 (2001) (holding that the use of a thermal imager or, more generally, any "sense-enhanc-

ing" technology to obtain "any information regarding the interior of the home that could not otherwise have been obtained without physical 'intrusion into a constitutionally protected area' constitutes a search—at least where (as here) the technology in question is not in general use") (citation omitted).

67. Albert W. Alschuler, Failed Pragmatism: Reflections on the Burger Court, 100 HARV. L. REV. 1436, 1442 (1987).
68. People v. Defore, 150 N.E. 585, 587 (N.Y. 1926).
69. A dozen cases should suffice. See, e.g., Pa. Bd. of Prob. & Parole v. Scott, 524 U.S. 357 (1998) (concluding that exclusionary rule does not apply to parole revocation hearings even when officer who conducted illegal search was aware of person's parole status); Whren v. United States, 517 U.S. 806 (1996) (ruling that police may stop a motorist where there are adequate grounds to believe that some traffic violation has occurred, even though the stop is pretextual); Illinois v. Rodriguez, 497 U.S. 177 (1990) (ruling that police may search dwelling house on "apparent authority" of a third party who lacks actual authority to consent); Mich. Dep't of State Police v. Sitz, 496 U.S. 444 (1990) (holding that in order to combat drunk driving, police may stop all motorists at sobriety check points absent any individualized suspicion); Alabama v. White, 496 U.S. 325 (1990) (illustrating how little is needed to constitute "reasonable suspicion" to stop suspect's car and to question her); California v. Greenwood, 486 U.S. 35 (1988) (finding that police examination, for evidence of crime, of contents of opaque sealed plastic trash bags left for collection not a "search"); California v. Ciraolo, 476 U.S. 207 (1986) (holding that police aerial surveillance of a fenced-in backyard not a "search"); Illinois v. LaFayette, 462 U.S. 640 (1983) (finding that police may search through shoulder bag at stationhouse inventory of arrestee's effects, even though all the inventory objectives could be achieved "in a less intrusive manner"); Illinois v. Gates, 462 U.S. 213 (1983) (replacing existing probable cause structure with "totality-of-circumstances" test and stressing that probable cause is a "fluid concept" and that it requires only a "substantial chance of criminal activity"); Florida v. Royer, 460 U.S. 491 (1983) (stating in passing that certain police-citizen "encounters" or "contacts," such as asking a person at an airport to show her driver's license and airline ticket, were not a "seizure"); New York v. Belton, 453 U.S. 454 (1981) (finding that even though police lack any reason to believe that a car contains evidence of crime, if they have adequate grounds to make a custodial arrest of driver, they may search the entire interior of the car, including closed containers found in that area, even after the driver has been removed from the car and handcuffed); Schneckloth v. Bustamonte, 412 U.S. 218 (1973) (holding that suspect may effectively consent to an otherwise unlawful search even though he was never informed, and no evidence existed that he was ever aware, of his right to refuse officer' s request).
70. See Calabresi, supra note 47, at 112. See also Slobogin, supra note 1 (arguing that the exclusionary rule is systemically harmful to Fourth Amendment values).
71. Paulsen, supra note 1, at 256.

72. U.S. v. Leon, 468 U.S. 897, 978 (1984)(Stevens, J., dissenting).
73. See Maclin, supra note 1, at 60 n.289.
74. See Jerome Hall, The Law of Arrest in Relation to Contemporary Social Problems, 3 U. CHI. L. REV. 345 (1936); William T. Plumb, Jr., Illegal Enforcement of the Law, 24 CORNELL L.Q. 337 (1939).
75. See Calabresi, supra note 47, at 114.
76. See id.
77. See id. at 116.
78. See id. at 116-17.
79. Judge Calabresi assures us that since, under his proposal, the legality of the police conduct would not be examined until the trial was over and the defendant convicted, the prosecutor would lack any incentive to charge more. See id. at 116. But every conscientious prosecutor would know at the outset, long before a post-trial hearing took place, whether or not the police acted illegally in the case, or, at the very least, whether or not there was a serious possibility that, at a post-trial hearing, one or more officers might be found to have acted illegally.
80. See generally Amsterdam, supra note 1, at 431-32; Phillip Johnson, New Approaches to Enforcing the Fourth Amendment 4 (Working Papers, Sept. 1978) (on file in the University of Michigan Law Library), quoted in YALE KAMISAR ET AL., MODERN CRIMINAL PROCEDURE 229-30 (5th ed. 1980) and cited in United States v. Leon, 468 U.S. 897, 916 n.14 (1984).
81. See Bivens v. Six Unknown Named Agents, 403 U.S. 388, 416-17 (Burger, C.J., dissenting).
82. See Orfield, supra note 50 and accompanying text.
83. Id. at 82. Those interviewed also believed that "police change their behavior in response to the suppression of evidence" and that the operation of the exclusionary rule "effectively educates officers in the law of search and seizure and that the law is not too complicated for police officers to do their jobs effectively." Id.

    For an earlier study by the same author of Chicago narcotics officers see the discussion in note 54, revealing that officers experience "personal disappointment at the loss of a potential conviction" and that "[t]he significant amount of time spent on these investigations, together with their danger and uncertainty, create a strong emotional commitment to conviction." Orfield, supra note 54, at 1042.
84. See Calabresi, supra note 47, at 116.
85. For an example of this line of thought, see Orfield, supra note 54, at 1053. See also Stuntz, supra note 1: [O]verdeterrence is a danger because the police have no strong incentive to undertake the marginal (legal) search or arrest. The result is that the usual legal tool--damages, fines, criminal punishment—are likely to cause more harm than good if they are widely used. If an officer faces serious loss whenever he makes a bad arrest, he will make fewer bad arrests, but also many fewer good ones. Id. at 445.
86. See Orfield, supra note 54, at 1051-54.
87. See supra notes 10-29. But see Milton A. Loewenthal, Evaluating the Exclusionary Rule in Search and Seizure, 49 UMKC L. REV. 24 (1980). This is, so far as I know, the most comprehensive study of

police attitudes toward the exclusionary rule. Loewenthal, who taught police officer students at John Jay College of the City University of New York at the time, conducted many interviews with police commanders on all levels, as well as with the police officer students. He was also a participant-observer on forty tours of duty concerning various phases of police work. Professor Loewenthal found "strong evidence that, regardless of the effectiveness of direct sanctions, police officers could neither understand nor respect a Court which purported to impose constitutional standards on the police without excluding evidence obtained in violation of those standards." Id. at 29. He also found that the police "have great difficulty believing that standards can have any real meaning if the government can profit from violating them," id. at 39, and that regardless of what substitute remedies may be provided, the police "are bound to view the elimination of the exclusionary rule as an indication that the fourth amendment is not a serious matter, if indeed it applies to them at all." Id. at 30. See also Orfield, supra note 50, at 128 ("None of the narcotics officers previously interviewed believed that the exclusionary rule should be abolished. Several officers said they appreciated the rule because it gave them a reason, within their peer group, to act properly. Some thought a 'good faith exception' would be appropriate."); Orfield, supra note 54, at 1051-52 (same).

88. Morgan Cloud, Judicial Review and the Exclusionary Rule, 26 PEPP. L. REV. 835, 838 (1999).
89. See id.
90. See supra notes 37-46 and accompanying text.
91. 468 U.S. 1032 (1984).
92. Id. at 1044.
93. Id. at 1044-45.
94. Id. at 1045.
95. Id. at 1054 (White, J., dissenting). Nor did the INS claim that any of the eleven officers terminated and any of the nine officers suspended in recent years for misconduct toward aliens had been disciplined for Fourth Amendment violations, and it appears that all the officers terminated "were terminated for rape or assault." Id. at 1055 n.2.

    One of the exclusionary rule's virtues is that "[c]laims are inexpensive to raise, and the facts on which they rest usually do not involve much independent digging by defense counsel." Stuntz, supra note 1, at 453. Moreover, the fact that the exclusionary rule is tied to criminal prosecutions "ensures that lots of claims are raised, which in turn allows courts to serve as reasonably good watchdogs for certain kinds of police misbehavior." Id. at 455.
96. Lopez-Mendoza, 468 U.S. at 1048.
97. Id. at 1049.
98. Id. at 1049-50. This led dissenting Justice White to say: Rather than constituting a rejection of the application of the exclusionary rule in civil deportation proceedings, however, [the majority's] argument amounts to a rejection of the application of the Fourth Amendment to the activities of INS agents. If the pandemonium attending immigration arrests is so great that violations of the

Fourth Amendment cannot be ascertained for the purpose of applying the exclusionary rule, there is no reason to think that such violations can be ascertained for purposes of civil suits or internal disciplinary proceedings, both of which are proceedings that the majority suggests provide adequate deterrence against Fourth Amendment violations. Id. at 1059 (White, J., dissenting).

99. See supra note31.

100. I have borrowed language from the lectures on search and seizure delivered by Justice Potter Stewart shortly after he stepped down from the Supreme Court. Stewart, supra note 1: "Taken together, the currently available alternatives to the exclusionary rule . . . punish and perhaps deter the grossest of violations . . . . But they do little, if anything, to reduce the likelihood of the vast majority of fourth amendment violations—the frequent infringements motivated by commendable zeal, not condemnable malice." Id. at 1388-89. See also Cloud, supra note 88: "Remedies aimed directly at officers who break the law . . . are rational methods for pursuing the goal of deterring misconduct. Undoubtedly, they are more likely to get the attention of individual officers than is the suppression of evidence in criminal prosecutions. The problem, of course, is that no one seriously expects that those remedies will be rigorously enforced in any but the most egregious cases. This is true, in part, because enforcing those remedies is a task for other government actors, including police departments and prosecutors. It is not a task for judges . . . ." Id. at 853.

POSTSCRIPT

Should the United States Abolish the Exclusionary Rule of Evidence in Criminal Cases?

The potential abolition of the exclusionary rule of evidence has been a controversial issue in the U.S. justice system. On one hand, the exclusionary rule prevents a judge or jury from considering highly credible evidence of a defendant's guilt. Proponents of the exclusionary rule in its present form believe, however, that it is needed to guarantee the legitimacy of the justice system itself. From this perspective, it is never acceptable for the police to break the law in order to enforce it.

The introduction to this issue asked you to think about a possible middle ground between the positions advocated by Professors Amar and Kamisar. Over the years, scholars and justice system practitioners have proposed a variety of alternatives to the exclusionary rule in its present form.

One such alternative has been described as "the Former British Model." Under this system, illegally obtained evidence could be used at trial. However, the police officers who obtained the illegal evidence were subject to internal departmental discipline. More recently, British law has been changed to give judges the discretion to refuse to admit illegally obtained evidence.

A second alternative to the exclusionary rule is civil tort lawsuits against the police. In theory, a person who is victimized by an illegal search and seizure could sue the police officer for monetary damages. Most experienced attorneys would reject this alternative, however, because in practice it is very difficult to successfully sue police officers.

A third alternative that has been suggested is the use of civilian review panels composed of citizens who examine alleged instances of police misconduct. Such panels have proved unpopular with police agencies, however, because many officers believe that panel members have unrealistic expectations for the police.

Do you believe that any of the alternatives considered above would constitute a reasonable alternative to the exclusionary rule of evidence? Can you think of another alternative? Do you agree with Professor Amar or Professor Kamisar's position on these issues?

Since the Supreme Court decided *Mapp v. Ohio* in 1961, a number of more recent cases have restricted the scope of the rule's protections for criminal defendants. In the final analysis, the Court may have settled on the best approach of all—maintain the rule in its present form, but restrict its application in cases when the police are acting in good faith.

Fortunately, there are a large number of excellent resources that can shed additional light on these issues. See Rolando V. del Carmen, *Criminal Procedure,* 6th ed. (Wadsworth, 2004); Yale Kamisar, Wayne R. LaFave, Jerold H. Israel, and Nancy J. King, *Modern Criminal Procedure,* 11th ed. (West, 2005); Thomas J. Hickey, *Criminal Procedure* (McGraw Hill, 2001); and George F. Cole and Christopher E. Smith, *Introduction to Criminal Justice,* 10th ed. (Wadsworth, 2004).

See, as well, the following articles: Raymond A. Atkins and Paul H. Rubin, "Effects of Criminal Procedure on Crime Rates: Mapping out the Consequences of the Exclusionary Rule," *Journal of Law and Economics* (vol. 46 no.1, 2003); American Bar Association Special Committee on Criminal Justice in a Free Society, "Criminal Justice in Crisis," 21 (vol. 21, no. 844, 1988); Donald Dripps, "The Case for the Contingent Exclusionary Rule," *The American Criminal Law Review* (vol. 38, no. 1, 2001); Jeffrey Standen, "The Exclusionary Rule and Damages: An Economic Comparison of Private Remedies for Unconstitutional Police Conduct," *Brigham Young University Law Review* (vol. 2000, no. 4, 2000); L. Timothy Perrin, H. Mitchell Caldwell, and Carol A. Chase, "If It's Broken, Fix It: Moving Beyond the Exclusionary Rule," *Search & Seizure Law Report* (vol. 26, no. 7, 1999); Evan Osborne, "Is the Exclusionary Rule Worthwhile?" *Contemporary Economic Policy* (vol. 17, no. 3, 1999); Stephen J. Markman, "Six Observations on the Exclusionary Rule," *Harvard Journal of Law and Public Policy* (vol. 20, no. 2, 1997); Heather A. Jackson, "Arizona v. Evans: Expanding Exclusionary Rule Exceptions and Contracting Fourth Amendment Protection," *Journal of Criminal Law & Criminology* (vol. 86, no. 4, 1996); James J. Fyfe, "Stops, Frisks, Searches, and the Constitution," *Criminology & Public Policy* (vol. 3, no. 3, 2004); Zack Bray, "Appellate Review and the Exclusionary Rule," *The Yale Law Journal* (vol. 113, no. 5, 2004); and Marvin Zalman and Elsa Shartsis, "A Roadblock too Far? Justice O'Connor's Left Turn on the Fourth," *Journal of Contemporary Criminal Justice* (vol. 19, no. 2, 2003).

ISSUE 6

Is "Black Rage" a Legitimate Defense in Criminal Proceedings?

YES: Paul Harris, from *Black Rage Confronts the Law* (NYU Press, 1997)

NO: Alan M. Dershowitz, from *The Abuse Excuse and Other Cop-Outs, Sob Stories, and Evasions of Responsibility* (Little, Brown and Company, 1994)

ISSUE SUMMARY

YES: Attorney and law professor Paul Harris argues that black rage, which contends that a defendant's crimes are a product of social racism, is a legitimate defense in criminal cases. Harris maintains that this type of defense brings the racial reality of America into court by presenting "social context" evidence.

NO: Harvard Law School professor Alan M. Dershowitz, in contrast, asserts that a history of racial victimization is not a license to commit crimes. Moreover, he believes that the black rage defense is an abuse of legitimate criminal defenses that is leading to a backlash in society.

The U.S. legal system recognizes that legitimate excuses may influence someone's behavior and mitigate their degree of criminal responsibility. Basically, a legal excuse asserts that a defendant should not be held to be fully blameworthy for a criminal act because he or she did not foster full criminal intent, or "mens rea." The types of traditional excuses recognized in our legal system include infancy, insanity, duress, involuntary intoxication, duress, and entrapment.

For example, a child who is less than 7 years of age is presumed to be incapable of committing a crime in many states. Although the laws vary from state to state, children aged 7 to 14 years are also *presumed* to be incapable of having full criminal intent, although the state may be allowed to present evidence to show that a particular child is sufficiently mature to understand the consequences of his or her actions. In many places, a child 15 to18 years old may be "certified" to stand trial as an adult in serious cases if the state can show that the individual was mature enough to understand his or her actions. This occurs most often in cases involving a serious violent crime, such as when a child intentionally kills a playmate. Remember that a legal excuse asserts only that an accused is less culpable, not that the act was righteous conduct under the circumstances.

A legal justification, in contrast, argues that a defendant's conduct was proper in the circumstances of the case because it was necessary to prevent a greater harm. For example, suppose that your friend was bleeding profusely from a cut sustained in an accident and that while driving him to the hospital you violated the posted speed limit. If you were charged with speeding, the law would likely recognize the justification for your offense as a legitimate one. Another example of a type of legal justification defense that has been tried without success on many different occasions has involved defendants who have attempted to block entrances to abortion clinics or nuclear power plants. Basically, these defendants argue that because the harm they are attempting to prevent is so substantial, they are justified in preventing access to these facilities. Such justifications are rarely successful, however. Because a legal justification is a complete defense that seeks to absolve a defendant from all criminal responsibility, it is less likely to be used successfully in a criminal trial than an excuse, which seeks only to mitigate blame.

The preceding discussion considered the types of excuses for criminal behavior that have been traditionally recognized in our legal system. A black rage defense asserts that because a defendant's crimes are the result of society's racism, he or she should not be held criminally responsible. This defense was not found among the traditional criminal excuses. Thus, by advocating for the legitimacy of a black rage defense, attorney and law professor Paul Harris is trying to expand the boundaries of criminal law. This is a novel idea, and its implications are highly controversial.

Professor Alan M. Dershowitz, in contrast, argues that a history of racial victimization is not a license to commit crimes. Moreover, he believes that the black rage defense is an example of an abuse of legitimate criminal defenses that is leading to a backlash in society. The title of Dershowitz's book (*The Abuse Excuse and Other Cop-Outs, Sob Stories, and Evasions of Responsibility*) clearly demonstrates his attitude about expanding the boundaries of the criminal law to include new defenses such as black rage.

What is your opinion of defenses that seek to mitigate a defendant's criminal responsibility? Could it be possible that a criminal defendant has become so hardened by society's racism that he or she would not be able to foster full criminal intent and should therefore be held less blameworthy than a normal person? As you read the articles in this section, think about social policy implications of expanding criminal defenses such as black rage.

Paul Harris

Black Rage Confronts the Law

. . . The black rage defense is *a legal strategy* used in criminal cases. It is not a simplistic environmental defense. The overwhelming majority of African Americans who never commit crimes and who lead productive lives against overwhelming odds prove that poverty and racial oppression do not necessarily cause an individual to resort to theft, drugs, and violence. But it cannot be denied that there is a causal connection between environment and crime. A black rage defense explores that connection in the context of an individual defendant on trial.

There has always been a strain in American jurisprudence which argued that the social and economic system must bear part of the responsibility for crime. Even the dominant legal philosophy, which perpetuates the myth that each person is free to act as he or she wishes, acknowledges that environmental conditions may lead to criminal behavior. Criminal law is based on the doctrine that the individual must be held responsible for his or her acts. But it has also reluctantly recognized that in cases where environmental factors do contribute to the crime, lawyers must be free to argue factors such as poverty and racism in defense of the charges or in mitigation of the penalties.

In a country divided by color and class, racial oppression and poverty have always been causal agents of theft and violence. However, lawyers have had difficulty translating these consequences of racism into the language of the criminal courtroom. The law does not allow the simple fact of racial discrimination as a defense to murder. Long-term unemployment is not accepted as a defense to bank robbery. French novelist Anatole France's famous ironic quote about the law is an accurate explanation of the inequality of the American legal system: "The law, in its majestic equality, forbids the rich as well as the poor to sleep under bridges, to beg in the streets, and to steal bread." Although legal doctrine has maintained a claim of class neutrality and a facade of colorblindness, in some cases lawyers have been able to break through the criminal law's resistance to allowing social reality into the courtroom. In 1846 William Henry Seward, one of the foremost lawyers and politicians of the time, defended twenty-one-year-old-William Freeman by arguing that the consequences of slavery and the continued oppression of black people had driven his client mad and caused him to commit murder. Seward thrust the awful conditions suffered by black people into the crucible of the trial. Unfortunately, this ground-breaking defense has basically been lost to the modern generation.

In 1925 Clarence Darrow, the most famous criminal lawyer in American history, again confronted the criminal law with the reality of discrimination and hatred against blacks. He defended Dr. Ossian Sweet, his wife Gladys, his brother Henry, and seven other blacks who were tried for murder when one of them shot into a mob of white people attempting to force the Sweets out of their home in a previously all-white neighborhood in Detroit.

The Freeman and Sweet cases were not described at the time as black rage defenses. But they were stunning examples of lawyers articulating how white supremacy had led to murder charges against blacks. They also were examples of confronting white juries, white judges, and a white legal system with the rage, pride, and strength of black people.

Between the 1930s and the 1970S the best-known black rage case was a fictional one. Richard Wright, in *Native Son,* created the classic case of a lawyer arguing that the system of white supremacy had produced his client's crimes. Although *Native Son* was published in 1940, Wright depicted the anguish and bottled-up fury experienced by many of today's black youth. In the opening scene Bigger Thomas, a young black man, kills a huge rat that has attacked him in his family's ghetto apartment. As his sister comforts their mother, Bigger tries to shut the crying out of his mind.

> He hated his family because he knew that they were suffering and that he was powerless to help them. He knew that the moment he allowed himself to feel to its fulness how they lived, the shame and misery of their lives, he would be swept out of himself with fear and despair. So he held toward them an attitude of iron reserve; he lived with them, but behind a wall, a curtain. And toward himself he was even more exacting. He knew that the moment he allowed what his life meant to enter fully into his consciousness, he would either kill himself or someone else. So he denied himself and acted tough. . . .

> Too many people are suffering
> Too many people are sad
> Too little people got everything while
> Too many people got nothing.
> Remake the world . . .
> Be you black, Be you white.
>
> —Jimmy Cliff, "Remake the World"

"Remake the World"

What is the future of the black rage defense in America's courtrooms? To answer that question we must first look at the social construction of crime.

Second, we need to look at how the cataclysmic economic changes taking place today will affect African Americans. We can then look at two areas where the black rage defense is expanding and suggest situations in which such a defense is most appropriate and useful.

Crime is real. However, the depiction of crime in America is often fictitious. The media's drive for profits results in the overreporting and sensationalizing of murder and assault. Stories are considered newsworthy if they sell newspapers or grab the attention of fidgety remote control–wielding television viewers. The Center for Media and Public Affairs reported that the three network television news shows broadcast four times as many crime stories in 1995 as in 1991, even though FBI statistics show that serious crimes actually decreased during that period.

There is a social construct to crime. The way in which antisocial behavior is characterized, classified, and punished molds the way people think and feel about crime. The savings-and-loan rip-off, fraudulent corporate cost overruns, and white-collar crimes cost the taxpayer far more than street crime. Corporate violations of health and safety laws result in thousands of worker injuries and deaths. Corporate crimes against the environment pose a larger threat to the future of society than car theft and robbery. These costly crimes are committed almost completely by white males, yet the social perception of the criminal is that he is a black male.

A telling example of the institutional racism that infects our concept of crime is the controversy around the different punishments for possession of powdered cocaine versus crack cocaine. In federal court possession of five grams of crack draws *a mandatory* five-year minimum while possession of five grams of powdered cocaine has no mandatory minimum and first-time offenders usually receive probation. One has to possess a hundred times more powdered cocaine than crack to be sentenced to five years. This, plus law enforcement's admitted choice to target the crack world over the cocaine world, has resulted in large numbers of poor African American men and women going to federal prison instead of middle-class white men and women.

Sentencing disparity is not limited to the crack–powdered cocaine distinction. In 1995 an official study of all eighty thousand federal convictions over two years showed that African Americans receive sentences that are on average 10 percent longer than those of whites for similar crimes.

Combining state and federal jurisdictions, almost one third (32 percent) of African American men 20–29 years old are incarcerated, on parole, or on probation. This represents an increase of 10 percent over the last five years. Men are not the only ones who are being entangled in the criminal law web. Since 1989, African American women have experienced the greatest increase in involvement with the criminal justice system—a 78 percent jump.

Institutional racism is prevalent in every area of criminal law. A 1996 study in California showed that once arrested, whites have their charges reduced more often than African Americans and Latinos, and that white offenders received community-based rehabilitation placements at twice the rate of African Americans.

In 1995 Paul Butler, a professor at George Washington University Law School, shocked the legal community by advocating that African American jurors in nonviolent cases such as theft and drugs engage in jury nullification by refusing to convict black defendants. Butler was not shooting from the hip; he is a former federal prosecutor and had written a well-documented piece. He argued that a system of white supremacy "creates and sustains the criminal breeding ground, which produces the black criminal." He correctly asserted that rehabilitation is no longer a goal of the criminal law system and concluded that the consequence of the racism in the criminal justice system is that the black community is losing valuable human resources. He suggested that jurors engage in a social cost-benefit analysis and use their power to refuse to be part of the assembly line that sends black men and women to jail.

Although the social construct of crime is based on fiction and tainted by racism, crime itself is real and frightening. In a 1994 *National Law Journal* poll 62 percent of people said they were "truly desperate" about personal safety. That was an almost too percent increase since 1989. Thirty-eight percent of African Americans said they have been victims of crimes involving violence or the threat of violence, a substantial increase since 1989. In order to understand the reality of crime, I try to put myself in the jury box. At the inception of a trial jurors are always asked the following question: "Have you or anyone in your family been a victim of a crime?" If I were a juror, this would be my answer: "My sixty-year-old mother was knocked unconscious during a mugging in Hollywood. A few years later her friend was murdered during a street robbery in front of her apartment house in Venice, California. My father had his head split open in Chicago when he helped an older man being harassed by four young men. Years later, as he was walking home he was smashed in the face by a teenager for no discernible reason. He and other passengers were robbed at gunpoint at the subway station. His home was burglarized numerous times. His car was stolen and burned. One of my brothers had a random bullet come through his second-story window. One of my other brothers, while working at a retail store, was thrown to the floor by robbers, who stepped on his neck and held a gun to his head. Another time a gun was pulled on him at the basketball court. A gang of teenagers attacked him, hitting him with chairs and locks, which resulted in thirteen stitches in his head. My stepfather, while in his sixties, was slugged in the face and robbed by two men. My sons have been mugged. Our cars have been stolen and stripped beyond repair. My youngest son has had two friends murdered. My wife was robbed at gunpoint. Another brother had a gun put to the side of his head in a robbery. As he raised his hand in a reflex to push the revolver away he touched its cold steel and froze, knowing he was an instant away from death."

Is crime real? Is the threat of crime terrifying? Of course. But putting more and more people in prison will not change this reality. If California were a country, it would have the world's eighth-largest economy. Prisons are its third leading industry. Investment counselors are actually advising their clients to put money into prison construction as a safe, profitable venture. Nationally, criminal law repression is the growth industry of the nineties. But three-strikes laws and more punitive measures do not change the fact that 95 percent of people in jail will return to the community. Most will return uneducated, brutalized, and filled with rage.

Will crime go away? Given the predicted future of the economy, the only thing that will go away are jobs for what once was a productive, hard-working, semiskilled and unskilled working class. It is noteworthy that the U.S. secretary of labor, a cutting-edge Marxist magazine, and one of the giants of American sociology all concur on much of the economic reality of the 1990s. Robert Reich has likened the conflict between the new technologies and old industrialism to "tectonic plates colliding," destroying the old mass-production system and causing the "economic earth to crack open." *Cy. Rev,* a socialist magazine that analyzes the cybernetic revolution, explains that the new economic changes are being driven by a fundamental shift in how wealth is produced. Information technology is the new means of production. One of *cy. Rev's* founders, himself a former steelworker, gives a poignant example of the change from physical to intellectual labor. He worked at U.S. Steel in Chicago, eventually moving from unskilled labor at the blast furnace to a five-year program learning to be a machinist. As a machinist in the mass-production economy he would have been ensured a good salary and work almost anywhere in the country. But information technology took what he had learned, imprinted it on a chip, and inserted the chip directly into the lathe. Now the chip runs the machine, and his job was reduced from complex and stimulating work to simply pushing buttons at the beginning of the shift to input that day's production program. One worker could monitor four machines, so three workers lost their jobs. Soon the giant U.S. Steel mill was employing only a fraction of its previous workforce, and a few years it later closed altogether. A study of former steelworkers from this plant showed an increase in divorce, sickness, and failed mortgages and significant feelings of anger and violence.

Reich and *cy. Rev* agree that corporations, driven to compete and maximize profits, are changing workers' relationships to their jobs, creating a new group of people who fall outside the economy. Now that layoffs are permanent, Reich suggests that we should use a new word to describe these workers—"castoffs." These castoffs will have little or no productive role in society.

Many people have warned of the negative impact of the technological revolution on minority communities. As far back as 1970, Sidney Willhelm in *Who Needs the Negro* forecasted that the destruction of the mass-production economy would change the situation of African Americans from "exploitation to uselessness."

Alvin and Heidi Toffler, the "Third Wave" economic theorists admired by both Al Gore and Newt Gingrich, pointed out that just one day before the Rodney King riots began the *Los Angeles Times* published a list of the top one hundred U.S. companies. Missing from the list were the mass-production manufacturers of autos, steel, textiles, tires, and cement that previously had provided stable, decent-paying jobs for a black proletariat. The

Tofflers warn against the writing off of entire minority communities such as South-Central Los Angeles.

In the midst of a torrent of statistics on increasing poverty at the low end of the scale and articles analyzing the death of the industrial age, Harvard sociologist William Julius Wilson has written a detailed and profound study of the consequences of these changes, entitled *When Work Disappears* (1996). Wilson's thesis is that a poor but working community is "entirely different" from a poor and unemployed community. In a concrete study of three neighborhoods in Chicago, he shows that long-term joblessness rends the social fabric of the community. Ninety-five percent of these neighborhoods have been and still are African American. In 1950, 70 percent of black males in those neighborhoods were working. In 1990, only 37 percent were working. Williams argues persuasively that this concentration of joblessness robs people of what they need to grow and prosper. The structure provided by getting up and going to a full-time job every day translates into discipline and a sense of responsibility, which form a productive personality. Chronic unemployment causes a chronic illness of spirit. When young men and women have nothing to look forward to, they develop despair, cynicism, and a fatalistic attitude toward their lives.

Williams shows how the decline of the mass-production system has meant the end of work, which in turn has caused a severe disruption of support networks. The church, the family, and civic organizations—all of which played a positive role in counterbalancing poverty and racism—have been damaged by years of persistent unemployment. With the supportive culture of their communities wrecked by forces beyond their control, the citizens of these neighborhoods have been left isolated and hurting. Is it any wonder that crime takes root and thrives amid devastation?

When African Americans such as Butler look at the appalling numbers of their community members in prisons, they see the detrimental consequences of a white supremacy construction of crime. They cry out, "You cannot put every young black man in prison!" When the average white person looks at the same statistics, he believes that they are the natural result of blacks being more criminally inclined than other races. *The black rage defense is a tool to expose the fallacy of such racist thinking.* When shown how racial and economic oppression shape a defendant's actions, other people begin to realize that African Americans are not inherently criminal. The jurors who acquitted Steven Robinson, James Johnson, and Henry Sweet had to confront their own stereotypes and make a connection between societal racism and criminal behavior.

The previous chapters have emphasized psychiatric and self-defense cases. There is another area of law in which the black rage defense is growing and where its capability of overcoming racial stereotyping will be severely tested. This field of criminal law is death penalty mitigation. If a person is convicted of a capital crime, he is entitled to a separate hearing. At that "penalty phase," a minitrial takes place in which the prosecutor introduces "aggravation" evidence. This is evidence that portrays the defendant as an evil person whose crime is not a result of social forces but rather of a "malignant heart."

The defense is allowed to introduce "mitigation" evidence. The courts have held that a defense lawyer has a legal responsibility to bring all evidence to the jury's attention that "humanizes" the defendant. This duty grows out of the nature of the sentencing hearing, which is "defense counsel's chance to show the jury that the defendant, despite the crime, is worth saving as a human being." The courts have ruled that evidence of one's cultural background is admissible. In one case, the Ninth Circuit Court of Appeals determined that it was ineffective aid of counsel to fail to produce evidence of the defendant's Thai culture, "including Thai concepts of remorse and shame which might well have bridged a cultural gap between the jury and the accused." These rulings afford precedent for admitting evidence of black culture and the effects of racial and economic discrimination.

The few lawyers who specialize in death penalty cases are well versed in preparing a social history of their clients. The challenge for all lawyers doing such work is to integrate the fundamentals of the black rage defense into their presentations at both the trial and the appellate levels.

The black rage defense is a strategy used primarily in criminal cases. However, there are times when criminal and civil law intersect. In such situations the basics of the black rage defense may be used in both areas. An example discussed in earlier chapters was the James Johnson cases. The racism practiced by Chrysler Corporation contributed to Johnson's mental illness, providing an insanity defense in the criminal trial and creating a basis for disability in the workers' compensation hearing. This is not an isolated example. There is great potential for black rage–type legal actions, if only lawyers would not be frightened by age-old and narrow interpretations of the rules of evidence. The cases analyzed in this book are part of a legal history that is constantly being shaped by innovative pleadings, new conceptual arguments, and fearless advocacy. What is permissible in court is determined by struggle. In 1996 a case unfolded in Brooklyn that epitomizes the power of such creative legal action.

The Noble Drew Ali Plaza housing project is located in the Brownsville section of Brooklyn. Three hundred seventy-five African American families and eight Hispanic families reside there. The project was owned by three white men (Linden Realty), who hired an all-white group of onsite managers. The project was subsidized by the federal government, and rents were set by the government at fair market rates of $650 per month for a one-bedroom to $950 for a four-bedroom apartment. Each family paid 30 percent of its adjusted gross income, and the rest was paid by the federal subsidy.

During the seven years in which this virtually all-black project was run by an all-white group, conditions deteriorated to the point where living there became an environmental nightmare. Tenant Charlene Burwell and her six children were forced to spend three days with raw sewage, including human excrement, overflowing from the toilets, sinks, and bathtub. Yvette Dozier constantly complained about the rotting bedroom floor, fearing for the safety of her two little children. No repair was made, and one day

Dozier actually fell through the floor to the apartment below and herniated a disc. Barbara Kelley had an eleven-year-old daughter who was seriously disabled with cerebral palsy and respiratory illness. They lived on the sixth floor and elevators were always broken. When her daughter Rachel needed emergency medical care, the medical workers could not take her down the stairs on a stretcher. As the terrified girl gasped for air, they had to carry her to the roof, cross over to the adjoining building, carry her down to that building's elevator, and finally rush her to the hospital. During one year Rachel needed emergency medical treatment six times—and each time the elevators were broken. Serena Audain lived with her two children, three and six years old. In just one week she caught eight rats in her apartment as they crawled in through holes in walls and cupboards, which the management had not fixed. Rats roamed unchecked in all the buildings.

All the tenants suffered freezing cold in winter, sewage backup with a persistent nauseating stench invading their homes, water leaks, inadequate security, broken fixtures, and management indifference. As Burwell would state in her affidavit, "If we were criminals and lived in a penitentiary, the way we live would be considered cruel and unusual punishment."

Linden Realty was not the sole cause of this despicable situation. The federal government disregarded its own legal responsibility to ensure "safe, decent, and sanitary" housing to the tenants. The Department of Housing and Urban Development (HUD) paid the owners over $15 million in subsidies during a seven-year period. One of the tenants put her finger on the problem: "Even when we pay white people's rents, they still give us black people's services, which is no services at all."

Brooklyn Legal Services attorney Richard Wagner filed a complicated federal lawsuit against Linden Realty on behalf of the Tenants' Association. Wagner has a reputation as a brilliant legal thinker who has demonstrated an unswerving commitment to racial justice. Within six months the case was won. Title was taken away from the owners, and HUD agreed to do almost $5 million in repairs and renovations, after which ownership would be transferred to the Tenants' Association.

Wagner was not content with this victory. He wanted the previous owners to pay for the damage they had done to the lives of the tenants. Barred from suing for damages by constraints placed on Legal Services by a conservative Congress, Wagner took the case to private attorneys. He described in powerful terms the human consequences resulting from seven years of living in deplorable, dehumanizing conditions.

> Any child, whether white or black, would find life at a Noble Drew Ali Plaza physically miserable. Any child would find it difficult if not impossible to perform well at school. Any child would feel embarrassed and humiliated at the way they are forced to live.
>
> But I submit that NOT any child would blame herself for these conditions. Not any child would associate her environment with "the way black people live," and think of the very concept of decent living conditions as being white and slumlike conditions as being black.

> The fatalism, nihilism, loss of self-esteem and individual ambition, and, ultimately, destruction of the future human potential that is experienced by the *black* children is more a function of racism than physical environment. IT IS BLACK RAGE TURNED INWARD AND THE EMOTIONAL, SCHOLASTIC AND ECONOMIC DAMAGE IT DOES TO ITS VICTIMS LASTS A LIFETIME.

Wagner was dismayed by the attitudes of most attorneys he approached. Instead of being excited about developing a strategy to translate black rage into legal damages, they muttered about how future scholastic and economic damage would be difficult to prove. They viewed the situation only through the prism of profit-loss, afraid that the task of pushing the courts forward in recognizing the potential economic and psychological damages caused by racism would be outweighed by the time, energy, and risk of losing that the case entailed. Fortunately, a few lawyers around the country think otherwise. One of them is Mercedes Marquez in Los Angeles. For ten years Marquez has accepted the challenge of proving the harm done to people of color by slumlords and an uncaring government, winning a $600,000 jury award among others, and recently settling a case for $2.5 million. As more tenants organize against life-crippling housing conditions, we need lawyers who will expand the black rage defense to civil actions and educate opposing lawyers, judges, and juries to the destructive effects of present-day racism.

One cannot read about rats biting children at Noble Drew without thinking about Bigger Thomas in Richard Wright's novel *Native Son.* The book opens with Bigger trying to protect his mother, sister, and little brother from a large rat. "A huge black rat squealed and leaped at Bigger's trouser-leg and snagged it in his teeth. . . . Bigger took a shoe and pounded the rat's head, crushing it, cursing hysterically. . . . His mother sank to her knees and buried her face in the quilts and sobbed." Bigger Thomas turned his rage outward, eventually killing two people. As Rick Wagner interacted with his clients, he saw children and teenagers who also turned their fury outward, becoming violent and predatory. He argued that "these children are as much the victims of black rage as those who turn it inward, except that they find ways to share their pain with society in a way that society does not like but for which it refuses to accept any responsibility."

The Noble Drew housing project is an example of existing racism. Unfortunately, as much of the public is unable to understand black poverty and crime as the result of past discrimination, it is therefore incumbent on lawyers defending children who have grown up in slum housing to expose the present-day racism. A black rage defense would show the intersection of greedy private landlords and an indifferent government that fails to enforce the tenants' right to decent, safe housing. Whenever the government prosecutes a young person who has grown up in a place like Noble Drew, the government itself should be put on trial for its willful acceptance of the dehumanizing practices of slumlords. We can and must show how present-day racism warps these defendants just as racism in the 1940s deformed Bigger Thomas.

Since the black rage defense is by definition a discussion of race set in an intensely emotional context, it is necessary for lawyers, legal workers, and defense committees to think through the social and philosophical ramifications of each case.

The different black rage cases analyzed in this book allow us to draw some conclusions about when the defense is appropriate and what elements give it the best chance of winning. The potential for the jury to empathize with the defendant should be an overriding concern, informing all tactical decisions. The strategic questions to be considered are as follows:

1. What is the nature of the crime? A property crime is qualitatively different from a homicide.
2. Who or what is the target of the crime? A robbery of a bank that has refused a loan to a burned-down black church is more understandable than a robbery for personal gain. An attack on a person who has racially humiliated and abused a defendant is quite different from a random assault on a passing motorist.
3. Is there a concrete connection between the crime and the defendant's personal history of racial oppression?
4. Has the defendant suffered serious economic hardship?
5. Does the personal history of the defendant tie into the motivation for the crime in a sympathetic manner?
6. What is the attitude of the defendant? Does she see herself as a victim, blaming everyone else for her problems? Or does she present herself as a proud person struggling in a hostile environment?
7. Are there elements of the defendant's culture, either positive or negative, which can be explained to a judge or jury as contributing causes of the crime?
8. Is the defendant capable of taking the stand and, with proper preparation, making a good impression?

The weight one gives to each element will differ depending on the type of case—self-defense, riot situation, duress, diminished capacity, insanity, or mitigation. The presentation will differ depending on whether one is trying to persuade a jury to acquit, a district attorney to reduce charges, or a judge to lower a sentence. In a civil case there will be other elements to consider. But one must always analyze the interplay between a system of white supremacy and the client's personal history and culture.

Peter Kim, a Korean American student at the University of California at Berkeley and a member of the rap group San Francisco Street Music, has written that "the Black Panthers were more than black." He means that the Panthers' messages of pride and empowerment and their programs of breakfast for children, health care, senior citizen security, and food distribution were relevant to all poor communities regardless of race. Similarly, the black rage defense is not limited to African Americans. The main thrust of the defense is to tie together individual behavior and societal conditions. That is why a black rage–type defense was used successfully in a self-defense case for

Native American Patrick Hooty Croy and in an insanity case for white ex-convict John Zimmerman.

The black rage defense refutes the idea that there is a lower class of people who are inherently criminal and can be written off by society. It tries to educate people about the oppressive structures and behaviors in society that produce and increase criminality. It has been said that ignoring race is a privilege that only white people have. This defense forces whites, for a critical moment in time, to give up that privilege and think about the consequences of a system of white supremacy. The black rage defense is not based on race hatred. Rather, it is an antiracist defense, and those who use it should shape their strategies to embrace all people and to teach that society must share the responsibility for crime. This is certainly not a new concept. Indeed, the essence of the black rage defense may have been best stated by the Arabic philosopher, artist, and poet Kahlil Gibran more than seventy years ago:

> The righteous is not innocent of the deeds
> of the wicked,
> And the white-handed is not clean in the
> doings of the felon.
> Yea, the guilty is often times the victim of the injured,
> And still more often the condemned is the
> burden bearer for the guiltless and unblamed.
> You cannot separate the just from the unjust
> and the good from the wicked;
> For they stand together before the face of
> the sun even as the black thread and the white are woven together.

NO 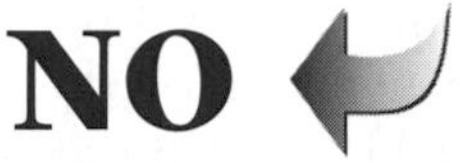

Alan M. Dershowitz

The Abuse Excuse: and Other Cop-outs, Sob Stories, and Evasions of Responsibility

THE "ABUSE EXCUSE"—the legal tactic by which criminal defendants claim a history of abuse as an excuse for violent retaliation—is quickly becoming a license to kill and maim. More and more defense lawyers are employing this tactic and more and more jurors are buying it. It is a dangerous trend, with serious and widespread implications for the safety and liberty of every American.

Among the recent excuses that have been accepted by at least some jurors have been "battered woman syndrome," "abused child syndrome," "rape trauma syndrome," and "urban survival syndrome." This has encouraged lawyers to try other abuse excuses, such as "black rage." For example, the defense lawyer for Colin Ferguson—the black man accused of killing white commuters on the Long Island Railroad—has acknowledged that his black rage variation on the insanity defense "is similar to the utilization of the battered woman's syndrome, the posttraumatic stress syndrome and the child abuse syndrome in other cases to negate criminal accountability."

On the surface, the abuse excuse affects only the few handfuls of defendants who raise it, and those who are most immediately impacted by an acquittal or reduced charge. But at a deeper level, the abuse excuse is a symptom of a general abdication of responsibility by individuals, families, groups, and even nations. Its widespread acceptance is dangerous to the very tenets of democracy, which presuppose personal accountability for choices and actions.[1] It also endangers our collective safety by legitimating a sense of vigilantism that reflects our frustration over the apparent inability of law enforcement to reduce the rampant violence that engulfs us.

At a time of ever-hardening attitudes toward crime and punishment, it may seem anomalous that so many jurors—indeed, so many Americans—appear to be sympathetic to the abuse excuse. But it is not anomalous at all, since the abuse excuse is a modern-day form of vigilantism—a recognition that since official law enforcement does not seem able to prevent or punish abuse, the victim should be entitled to take the law into his or her own hands.

In philosophical terms, the claim is that society has broken its "social contract" with the abused victim by not according him or her adequate protection. Because it has broken that social contract, the victim has been returned to a "state of nature" in which "might makes right" and the victim is entitled to invoke the law of the jungle—"kill or be killed." Indeed, these very terms were used in a recent Texas case in which one black youth killed two other blacks in a dangerous urban neighborhood. The result was a hung jury.

But vigilantism—whether it takes the old-fashioned form of the lynch mob or the new-fashioned form of the abuse victim's killing her sleeping husband—threatens the very fabric of our democracy and sows the seeds of anarchy and autocracy. The abuse excuse is dangerous, therefore, both in its narrow manifestation as a legal defense and in its broader manifestation as an abrogation of societal responsibility.

The other characteristic shared by these defenses is that they are often "politically correct," thus reflecting current trends toward employing different criteria of culpability when judging disadvantaged groups. In effect, these abuse excuse defenses, by emphasizing historical discrimination suffered by particular groups, seek to introduce some degree of affirmative action into our criminal-justice system.

These abuse-excuse defenses are the daily fare of the proliferating menu of TV and radio talk shows. It is virtually impossible to flip the TV channels during the daytime hours without seeing a bevy of sobbing women and men justifying their failed lives by reference to some past abuse, real or imagined. Personal responsibility does not sell soap as well as sob stories. Jurors who watch this stuff begin to believe it, despite its status as junk science. The very fact that Sally Jessy and Montel repeat it as if it were gospel tends to legitimate it in the minds of some jurors. They are thus receptive to it in the courtroom, especially when the defendant is portrayed as sympathetic, and his dead victim is unsympathetic. William Kunstler is quick to point to recent public-opinion polls that show that "two-thirds of blacks and almost half the whites surveyed recognize the validity of our [black rage] theory of Mr. Ferguson's defense."

But neither public opinion polls nor TV talk shows establish the empirical or normative validity of such abuse-excuse defenses. The basic fallacy underlying each of them is that the vast majority of people who have experienced abuses—whether it be sexual, racial, or anything else—do not commit violent crimes. Thus the abuse excuse neither explains nor justifies the violence. A history of abuse is not a psychological or a legal license to kill. It may, in some instances, be relevant at sentencing, but certainly not always.

Lest it be thought that the abuse excuse is credited only by radical defense lawyers, lay jurors, and talk-show-watching stay-at-homes, a quotation from the attorney general of the United States illustrates how pervasive this sort of thinking is becoming. In April 1993, Janet Reno was quoted as commenting on urban riots as follows: "An angry young man who lashes out in violence because he never had a childhood might do the right thing," and when the "right thing" is in contradiction with the law, "you try to get the law changed." I wonder if the angry young man's innocent victim agrees that the violence directed against his shop was the "right thing" and that the law protecting his property should be "changed."

The worst consequence of these abuse excuses is that they stigmatize all abuse victims with the violence of the very few who have used their victimization as a justification to kill or maim. The vast majority of abuse victims are neither prone to violence nor to making excuses. Moreover, abuse excuses legitimate a cycle of abuse and further abuse, since most abusers have themselves been victims of abuse. Thus, by taking the abuse excuse to its logical conclusion, virtually no abusers would ever be culpable. . . .

Black Rage Defense

IT WAS ONLY A MATTER of time before the abuse excuse was taken to its illogical conclusion and extended to cover an entire race of "abused" people. Radical lawyer William Kunstler recently announced that he would defend a black client accused of murdering six passengers on a Long Island train on the ground that he was insane as the result of "black rage."

Kunstler said that Colin Ferguson's shooting spree was caused by the anger that many black Americans feel as the result of centuries of unjust treatment. "If you treat people as second-class citizens, they're going to snap," declared Kunstler's law partner. Though the lawyers conceded that racial injustice alone might not justify an acquittal, they claimed that it was the "catalyst" that pushed Mr. Ferguson over the edge into insanity

Kunstler has used racial defenses previously. Several years ago, he defended a black man named Larry Davis, who had participated in a shootout with several policemen during an arrest and was charged with attempted murder. Kunstler claimed that Davis was acting in self-defense. Some blacks rallied to Davis's defense, seeing him as an "avenging angel" and a "folk hero." Kunstler played this race card and persuaded a largely minority jury that Davis was protecting himself from a police conspiracy to kill him. Kunstler is preparing to play the race card once again by raising the "black rage" defense before what he hopes will be a racially sympathetic jury.

It is unlikely that this racial gambit will succeed, regardless of the composition of the jurors, since the "black rage" variation on the abuse-excuse defense is an insult to millions of law-abiding black Americans. The vast majority of African Americans who never break the law have not used the mistreatment they have suffered as an excuse to mistreat others. Crime is not a function of group characteristics: It is an individual phenomenon that must be treated on an individual basis.

Indeed, it is the essence of racism to make the kind of group "rage" and group "abuse" arguments that Kunstler is now raising. It will reaffirm racist fears among too many Americans that violent crime is a "black problem." If black rage produces violent crime, or even if it is a "catalyst" for it, then racists will be quick to justify their fear of blacks as a group.

Moreover, if blacks as a group have more "rage" than others, and are thus more inclined toward violence, some racists will argue for longer sentences for black recidivists, earlier and harsher police intrusion against black suspects, and other forms of "preventive" intervention in black neighborhoods. This is especially troubling since Kunstler points to centuries of past abuse as the precipitator of crime, and nothing can be done to change history. The black rage argument that Kunstler plans to use is a dangerous invitation to the kind of stereotyping that has long characterized such groups as the Ku Klux Klan and the Nation of Islam. It has no place in the courtrooms of America.

In addition to being a racist defense, it is also without any basis in fact. There is no evidence to support the notion that groups that have been victimized by injustice turn to rage and violence. That has not been true of Holocaust survivors, of Cambodian refugees, of Soviet dissidents, or of a majority of black Americans. According to Kunstler's "social science," what explains the absence of criminality among so many who have been subjected to so much injustice? The search for the particular causes of Colin Ferguson's rage must begin by looking at him, at his own life experiences as a person, and at his prior history. But even if this search were to produce an explanation for Ferguson's murderous actions, no explanation—regardless of how convincing—necessarily requires exculpation. "To understand is not to forgive," says an old and wise proverb. The black rage defense neither explains nor excuses the cold-blooded murder of six innocent train commuters. A history of racial victimization is not a license to kill at random.

It is precisely this kind of abuse of legitimate defenses that is leading to a backlash. Last week, the Supreme Court let stand a ruling permitting the states to abolish the insanity defense, as three have now done. Insanity and other traditional defenses serve an important function in our system of law enforcement, by distinguishing between culpable and nonculpable harmdoers. When these defenses are abused, as they recently have been by the expansion of the abuse excuse to include political defenses, the pendulum will swing in the opposite direction. Neither extreme will serve the interests of justice.

April 1994

Notes

1. "I see this trend as very disturbing. It brought down the Greek democratic experiment, it's that dangerous." Roger L. Conant, director of the American Alliance for Rights and Responsibilities, quoted in *American Bar Association Journal,* June 1994, p. 41.

POSTSCRIPT

Is "Black Rage" a Legitimate Defense in Criminal Proceedings?

Benjamin Cardozo, considered by many to be one of the great justices in U.S. Supreme Court history, once described "the tendency of a principle to expand itself to the limit of its logic." Justice Cardozo was describing what happens to a legal doctrine once it is accepted by the courts and enshrined in law. The principle takes on a life of its own and continues to expand. In a compelling dissenting opinion in *Korematsu v. United States*, 323 U.S. 214 (1944), a case that many consider to be one of the darkest moments in U.S. Supreme Court history, Justice Robert H. Jackson used Cardozo's famous passage to argue against the forced internment of Japanese Americans in prison camps during World War II. Stated Jackson:

> Now the principle of racial discrimination is pushed from support of mild measures to very harsh ones, and from temporary deprivations to indeterminate ones. . . . Because we said that these citizens could be made to stay in their homes during the hours of dark, it is said we must require them to leave home entirely; and if that, we are told they may also be taken into custody for deportation; and if that, it is argued they may also be held for undetermined time in detention camps. How far the principle of this case would be extended before plausible reasons would play out, I do not know.

Consider for a moment Justice Cardozo's aphorism in the context of the black rage defense. If U.S. courts were to accept the principle that a defendant's crimes are a product of social racism and that therefore his or her degree of criminal responsibility is lessened, to paraphrase Justice Jackson, how far would the principle be extended before plausible reasons would play out? Should the rage defense be extended to people from broken homes? What about to people who grew up in conditions of poverty? What about extending the rage defense to people from religious groups who may have experienced—discrimination in the past? It may be difficult to place a principled limitation on this type of defense.

It is essential to carefully consider both sides of this debate. Paul Harris argues compellingly that the black rage defense brings the racial reality of America into court. Alan Dershowitz argues with equal conviction that a history of racial victimization should not be regarded as a license to commit crimes. Who has made the better case? Perhaps the best course is the one that is currently in use—permit judges and juries to consider an individual's circumstances within the context of a particular case, without formally recognizing a new criminal defense.

There are a number of excellent resources that may shed additional light on the issues considered in this section. For a discussion of criminal law defenses in the U.S. legal system, see Wayne R. LaFave and Austin W. Scott, Jr., *Criminal Law,* 2nd ed. (West, 1986). Additional resources include Michael Tigar, "Lawyers, Jails, and the Law's Fake Bargains," *Monthly Review* (vol. 53, no. 3, 2001); Fran Quigley, Jacqueline Ayers, and Elizabeth Stull, "Does Racism Infect the Criminal Justice System?" *Recorder* (April 1, 2005); Graham Boyd, "The Drug War Is the New Jim Crow," *NACLA Report on the Americas* (July/August 2001); and John C. McAdams, "Racial Disparity and the Death Penalty," *Law and Contemporary Problems* (Autumn 1998).

ISSUE 7

Should U.S. Courts Abandon the *Miranda* Rule?

YES: Paul G. Cassell, from "Miranda's 'Negligible' Effect on Law Enforcement: Some Skeptical Observations," *Harvard Journal of Law and Public Policy* (Winter 1997)

NO: Stephen J. Schulhofer, from "Bashing Miranda Is Unjustified—and Harmful," *Harvard Journal of Law and Public Policy* (Winter 1997)

ISSUE SUMMARY

YES: U.S. District Court Judge Paul G. Cassell argues that Miranda's social costs are significant and that this cornerstone of the Warren Court's criminal procedure jurisprudence places unprecedented shackles on the police.

NO: Professor Stephen J. Schulhofer, in contrast, argues that the Miranda protections are required by the U.S. Constitution and that the potential damage to effective law enforcement is not a sufficient reason to disregard a constitutional requirement.

Miranda v. Arizona, 384 U.S. 486 (1966) is one of the most famous criminal cases the U.S. Supreme Court has ever decided. Almost everyone who has ever watched a television show about the police is familiar with the *Miranda* warnings: "You have the right to remain silent; anything you say can be used against you in a court of law; you have the right to the presence of an attorney; if you cannot afford an attorney, one will be appointed for you at no charge." The warnings are often followed with an inquiry by the officer about whether a suspect understands his or her rights and a request for a signed rights waiver.

Before the Supreme Court decided *Miranda,* there was one main requirement for using a confession in a criminal case: It must have been made voluntarily. The voluntariness test uses a totality of circumstances approach for evaluating a confession—a court will consider factors including a defendant's education, understanding of the English language, emotional stability, and where and when the police interrogation occurred. The voluntariness test continues to be relevant in post-*Miranda* cases, because even if a suspect is given the warnings, the confession must still be voluntary. For example, suppose that police officers have probable cause to believe that someone has murdered a child. After the suspect is arrested and taken to the police station, officers advise him of his rights, and he declines to speak. Due to the heinous nature of the crime, however, the officers insist on interrogating him and beat him with a rubber hose until he confesses. A confession extracted in this manner is inadmissible at trial, even though the suspect was provided with the *Miranda* warnings, because it was involuntary.

You should understand that the police are not required to give every suspect the *Miranda* warnings. They are only required to do so when the suspect is in custody and is being interrogated and when they wish to try to use what the suspect says at trial. It is probably a good police practice to give all suspects the *Miranda* warnings, however. That way, if the suspect is riding in the police car on the way to jail and the officer asks about the crime and receives a confession, it can be used as evidence at trial.

Think about what would happen if you were a suspect in a criminal case. Would you talk to the police about the alleged crime? Suppose further that you were arrested and taken to the police station for questioning and you called a lawyer. One of the first things that an experienced criminal lawyer will tell you is "don't speak with the police." This is because if you speak with the police, even though you don't confess to the crime, you may say something that is incriminating. For example, you may admit to being present near the scene of the crime, or that you "hated" the victim. Such statements could later be used against you as evidence at trial.

Does providing a suspect with the *Miranda* warnings make a difference in terms of the probability of whether he or she will confess? In the interests of the administration of justice, should the United States abolish the *Miranda* rule? The authors of the articles in this section provide very different answers to this question.

U.S. District Court Judge Paul G. Cassell argues that *Miranda*'s social costs are significant and that this cornerstone of the Warren Court's criminal procedure jurisprudence places unprecedented shackles on the police. Professor Stephen J. Schulhofer, in contrast, believes that the *Miranda* warnings are required by the U.S. Constitution and that the potential damage to law enforcement interests is not a sufficient reason to disregard a constitutional mandate.

Do you agree with Judge Cassell that we should abandon the *Miranda* protections in order to enhance law enforcement interests? Or, are you more closely aligned with Professor Schulhofer's assertion that the *Miranda* protections are required by the Constitution and symbolize our society's commitment to due process of law? Is there a middle ground between these proposals that you would propose?

Paul G. Cassell

Miranda's "Negligible" Effect on Law Enforcement: Some Skeptical Observations

"Miranda[1] has no effect on law enforcement." This is the story told, and retold, by many of the nation's leading criminal procedure academics.[2] Warming to the task, some even go so far as to maintain that the Miranda requirements[3]"actually facilitate law enforcement efforts."[4] Yet, consider for a moment the striking incongruity of the tale. To a degree unparalleled in our nation's history, Miranda restricts police interrogation of criminal suspects—the "nerve center of crime detection."[5] It requires every criminal suspect to be encouraged, before custodial questioning, to keep quiet. It allows suspects to prevent any police questioning by the simple expedients of declining to waive their rights or asking for a lawyer. Such constraints make no difference at all!?

This Article raises some skeptical notes about this conventional wisdom.[6] The myth of Miranda's benign effects is unsupported and unsupportable in the available empirical data. To the contrary, there is every reason to believe our intuitions have it right in suggesting—indeed, crying out—that Miranda has impeded law enforcement. We owe it to those who suffer from unsolved crimes and unconvicted criminals to pay more careful attention to Miranda's costs.

Before turning specifically to Miranda's harms, let me note in passing that this Article will not develop at any length another promising line of attack against Miranda: that nothing in the Fifth Amendment authorized the Court to create such a codelike set of rules. That sort of conclusion seems almost preordained. It is hard to argue that Miranda follows from the constitutional history and traditions of this country. Professor Grano's thorough book *Confessions, Truth and the Law*[7]explicates this point brilliantly. Indeed, one of the other participants in this Panel, Professor Stephen Schulhofer, recently acknowledged that the Miranda holding was "a radical departure . . . from the assumption of the times" and that the Fifth Amendment approach to regulating police interrogation "seemed so contrary to the weight of then-prevailing precedent that Miranda's lawyers decided not even to argue the Fifth Amendment claim."[8] The characterization that the moderator of this Panel,

Professor Ely, has given to Roe v. Wade seems equally applicable to Miranda. The decision, he wrote, is bad "because it is not constitutional law and gives almost no sense of an obligation to try to be."[9]

In its recent cases, the Court has frankly confessed that the Miranda requirements are not themselves constitutional rights but rather are merely something called "prophylactic rights" designed to safeguard the real Fifth Amendment right against compelled self-incrimination.[10] Having gone beyond the boundaries of the Fifth Amendment, the Court tells us that its writ runs as far as the cost-benefit analysis will take it. Today the Court solemnly claims that the Miranda decision embodies a "carefully crafted balance designed to fully protect both the defendant's and society's interests."[11] Academic acolytes of Miranda likewise justify the decision through instrumental calculation. Professor Yale Kamisar, one of Miranda's leading defenders, reports that striking a balance "is the way Miranda's defenders—not its critics—have talked about the case for the past twenty years."[12]

The starting point for the cost-benefit justification of Miranda is the decision's putative failure to harm law enforcement. But the empirical props for that position are collapsing. Miranda's defenders most often cite the 1966 New Haven study, which claimed that the number of confessions there declined only slightly after the Miranda decision was made.[13] Recently, I reanalyzed the study's underlying data and found that, while the number of confessions fell only slightly, the number of admissible confessions fell sharply. That summer, the New Haven police obtained many confessions by violating Miranda's requirement to stop questioning when asked to do so by the suspect. Excluding these inadmissible confessions reveals that the admissible confession rate (the rate that counts in criminal prosecutions) actually dropped sixteen percentage points after Miranda.[14]

Other real-world data is unkind to the hypothesis of nugatory effects from Miranda. My review of the before-and-after studies conducted around the time of Miranda was the first attempt to quantify how many criminals go free as a result of Miranda. Averaging data from eight reliable studies around the country, I concluded that the rate at which suspects confessed dropped by about sixteen percentage points after Miranda (i.e., if the confession rate was 60% before the decision, it fell to around 44% after).[15] This drop in the confession rate results in the nonprosecution of many dangerous criminals, a substantial social cost.[16]

Responding to my article, Professor Stephen Schulhofer read the same studies as suggesting that the confession rate fell 9.7 percentage points.[17] The implications of Schulhofer's response have not, I think, been widely appreciated. Here is one of the most ardent defenders of Miranda apparently agreeing that the before-and-after studies suggest that Miranda weakened about one in every ten criminal cases. Professor Schulhofer then made further technical adjustments to argue that the true overall social cost of Miranda is "vanishingly small."[18] In turn, I replied to Schulhofer's arguments and explained why they appeared, to me, to be unavailing.[19] That full debate requires extensive discussion of individual before-and-after studies that we will not repeat at length here. Since the publication of those articles, however, one important piece of information supporting my position has become available.

The quantitatively most significant difference between my position on confession rates, and that of Professor Schulhofer, is whether to include a figure from the Los Angeles District Attorney's Office. The Office reported that the confession rate rose ten percentage points within three weeks after Miranda allegedly from 40% before the decision to 50% after. I exclude the Los Angeles figure as unreliable, pointing out that it is far-fetched to believe that confessions increased within three weeks of the decision. This result is attributable not to some sudden rise in the loquaciousness of criminal suspects, but rather to a problem with the survey instruments. The Los Angeles prosecutors received an "after questionnaire" that had been redesigned, with the result that it swept in more statements (including non-incriminating statements) than did the "before questionnaire."[20] In response, Schulhofer characterizes the Los Angeles figures as "a careful study"[21] and claims that my disparagement rests only on the "'summary sheet' used by the law clerk who subsequently tabulated these questionnaires," not the actual questionnaires themselves.[22] Schulhofer further argues that there is no indication that the law clerk recorded different things in the before and after surveys or even that the forms were redesigned.[23] Schulhofer concludes that the Los Angeles number "is one of the least vulnerable" of those available.[24]

To help resolve the difference between the interpretations Professor Schulhofer and I give to the Los Angeles figures, I spoke to the law clerk who actually tabulated the data—now United States Court of Appeals Judge Stephen S. Trott.[25] He reports that the collection of the data—both the before data and the after data—was "extremely haphazard" with little, if any, attention paid to insuring representative samples or consistent survey instruments.[26] The forms were completed and collected under "chaotic" conditions and "ended up measuring apples and oranges." No controls were maintained over who was given the forms and who completed them; many deputies simply ignored them. Those who completed the forms received no adequate instructions on how to do so. Judge Trott states that he reported these problems to his supervisors at the time, suggesting that the whole process was badly flawed. His supervisors replied that, because nothing else was available, the data collected would have to be used. Judge Trott now concludes that the Los Angeles figures "prove nothing" and that researchers should "not draw any conclusions" about Miranda's effects from them.

The more reasonable approach to determining *Miranda's* effect, at least to my mind, is to exclude the Los Angeles figure from consideration.[27] But ultimately, regardless of how the before-and-after data from Los Angeles and other cities is interpreted, our debate about these studies might be regarded as inconclusive. The studies report confession rates in 1966 and 1967, immediately after Miranda was handed down. As a result, defenders of Miranda can argue that, even if these studies show law enforcement impairment, police have since adjusted their questioning methods to eliminate Miranda's harmful effects.[28] A competing possibility, of course, is that the before-and-after studies understate Miranda's harms, because the police had not yet complied with all of its requirements[29] or suspects had not yet realized how to take advantage of them.[30]

To sort through these possibilities, we need data not just from the year following Miranda, but from the decades following the decision. Unfortunately, no direct data on the number of confessions is available from law enforcement reports. Fortunately, an indirect measure is available. The FBI collects data on crime "clearance" rates, that is, the rates at which police solve crimes. A lower confession rate presumably leads to fewer cleared crimes. Indeed, the clearance rate is an extremely conservative measure of Miranda's effect; some lost confessions might be unnecessary to "clear" a crime but nonetheless necessary to successfully prosecute the criminal.[31]

A 1987 article by Professor Schulhofer maintained that within "a year or two" after Miranda, clearance rates "were thought to be returning to pre-Miranda levels."[32] His article epitomizes the conventional academic wisdom, having been cited dozens of times for the proposition that Miranda did not hinder the police. For example, Professor Yale Kamisar has concluded that the article "effectively refutes this contention [that Miranda has harmed law enforcement]."[33]

Yet Professor Schulhofer did not actually collect data on clearance rates but, as the quotation above reveals, simply reported the conventional opinion about such rates. Skeptical of the received wisdom, I collected the FBI's actual data on crime clearance rates, focusing on violent crimes where Miranda might be expected to have much of its effect. . . . [O]n the streets of America violent crime clearance rates fell precipitously immediately after Miranda and never recovered.

In 1965, the violent crime clearance rate had been stable for the previous three years and stood at nearly 60%. Then, as police and suspects adjusted to the new rules in the next three years—1966, 1967, and 1968—the clearance rate plunged below 47%, a drop of more than twelve percentage points. Clearance rates have remained roughly stable ever since. What was it that caused this sudden three-year fall? My hypothesis is the commonsensical one—that Miranda was, at least in part, responsible.

Professor Schulhofer now concedes that violent crime clearance rates fell dramatically immediately after Miranda. Rather than acknowledge that this is evidence of Miranda's harmful effects, as his previous article suggested,[34] he now searches for a new theory to account for what appears to be strong evidence of Miranda's harmful effects. Instead of Miranda, Professor Schulhofer singles out rising crime rates during the 1960s as solely responsible for the dramatic decline in clearance rates. He argues that rising crime rates stretched police agencies thinner and that this overload reduced their ability to solve crimes. He concludes that "there is no reason—none—to blame Miranda, rather than precipitously shrinking resources, for the decline in clearance rates during the late 1960s"[35] and that "soaring rates of violent crime and stagnant levels of police resources easily explain the observed clearance rate trends."[36]

While rising crime rates may well have had some dampening effect on clearance rates, it seems unnecessarily extreme to argue Miranda had no effect whatsoever. Among other things, the no-effect claim appears to conflict with

Schulhofer's own earlier reading of the before-and-after studies, which concluded that confession rates fell more than 9% after Miranda.[37] Schulhofer's claim also requires us to assume that Miranda itself made no contribution to overloading the police. Yet Miranda may itself have increased the crime rate.[38] Moreover, by reducing confessions, Miranda forces police to do more legwork to build prosecutable cases against suspects,[39] leaving less time available for other investigative activities.

The basis for Professor Schulhofer's aggressive position turns out to be several charts plotting clearance rates against what he styles the "clearance capacity" of the criminal justice system—essentially, the number of police officers per known violent crime and the number of real dollars spent on law enforcement per known violent crime.[40] Noting that the clearance capacity declined during the 1960s, Schulhofer points an accusing finger at—and only at—declining clearance capacities, arguing that the system became overloaded precisely when Miranda was decided.

A careful inspection of his charts, however, reveals a few disconcerting points for one staking out so strong a claim. To begin with, clearance capacity as measured both by available officers and dollars fell noticeably from 1962 to 1965 while clearance rates rose slightly during these years.[41] Why didn't the declining capacity hinder police then? Moreover, Professor Schulhofer's charts end in 1974.[42] Yet, it turns out that clearance rates remained roughly stable over the next two decades while the clearance capacity continued to fall significantly.[43] Schulhofer's overload effect thus operates rather erratically both before Miranda and after. In large measure, it is a convenient will-o'-the-wisp, apparently materializing with Chief Justice Warren's opinion in Miranda, and then floating away in the decades after. Schulhofer has company in his failure to document this effect convincingly. Other criminal justice researchers searching for confirming proof of overload have generally met with little success.[44] System overload may be part of the story for declining clearance rates. But to think that it explains all of the decline seems far-fetched.

Professor Schulhofer also deploys another new argument to deflect blame away from Miranda. Shifting ground from examining clearance rates to clearance totals,[45] he notes that police cleared more violent crimes in the years following Miranda.[46] Why, he wonders, isn't Miranda's harmful effect visible in this data?

The answer is straightforward. The depressing effect is found not by looking at the number of cleared crimes, but rather at the number of uncleared crimes. Uncleared crimes accelerated immediately following Miranda. . . . [P]olice consistently cleared the majority of violent crimes from 1950 to 1965. Then, in 1966 the gap narrowed, in 1967 the gap essentially disappeared, and in 1968, for the first time, police failed to clear most violent crimes. Since then, the gap has persisted.[47]

. . . [W]e cannot determine police effectiveness by looking solely at the number of cleared crimes. By this measure, the Chicago Police Department is undoubtedly several times more effective than the Salt Lake City Police Department; each year, the number of cleared crimes in Chicago is most assuredly many times the number of cleared crimes in Salt Lake City simply because there are many more crimes in Chicago. But police effectiveness is never appraised in such terms. Instead, the longstanding measure is clearance rates, a police "batting average" that considers both cleared and uncleared crimes.[48] This practice is so universal that I have been unable to locate even a single scholarly article on either police effectiveness or Miranda focusing on clearance totals rather than clearance rates. This problem permeates Schulhofer's reliance on rising numbers of clearances after 1966. In each of those years, police had more opportunities to clear crimes because of rising crime rates—more "at bats," if you will. A certain number of crimes will be cleared almost as soon as they are committed, either because of their nature (e.g., barroom brawls, domestic violence)[49] or because of the stupidity of their perpetrators.[50] To look solely at clearance totals is akin to discussing the number of hits of a batter without reporting his strikeouts at the plate. To tout a rising number of clearances as proof of rising police effectiveness misses this critical point. By that measure, police were much more "effective" in 1970 than in 1960. Clearance rates paint a different—and more accurate—picture. Police performance declined sharply from 1966 to 1968.

Of course, to resolve conclusively what caused declining clearance rates in this period requires more than simply eyeballing charts. The standard statistical technique for answering such questions is multiple regression analysis. Along with Professor Richard Fowles of the University of Utah's Department of Economics, I have run multiple regression analysis on violent crime clearance rates from 1950 to 1994. Much of the post-Miranda drop is explained by assuming the ability of police to clear crimes shifted in the middle of 1966, immediately after Miranda was decided. . . . [A] basic model of violent crime clearance rates, controlling for relevant criminal justice, demographic, and economic factors, indicates that clearance rates shifted downward at the time of Miranda, a result that is significant at a high confidence level.

Responding to a preliminary version of this regression analysis, Professor Schulhofer claimed that it was flawed in failing to consider interactions among the criminal justice variables. Schulhofer wrote: "Cassell's model tests for the effect of officer and expenditure levels alone, with crime rates held constant. . . . A well-specified clearance capacity variable must take into acount the changing ratio of available resources to needs . . ."[52] To see whether this made any important difference to the conclusion, Professor Fowles and I ran a second equation that included variables measuring the ratio of resource levels to crimes. Even after adding these variables, the parameter associated with the Miranda variable is -7.3, a result that is highly statistically significant. The parameter means that a structural shift centered on July 1966 is associated with a 7.3% reduction in the clearance rate. In other words, if the clearance rate was 60% before July 1, 1966, it fell to below 53% after. As is expected, the inclusion of more explanatory variables in the second equation reduced the value of the parameter slightly, to 7.3% from 8.7%. It should be noted that the second equation may give slightly exaggerated treatment to Schulhofer's theory because it contains five variables that should capture, directly or indirectly, Schulhofer's resource effects: Crime Rate, Police Officers, Police Dollars, Officer Capacity, and Dollar Capacity.[53]

The regression equations are limited. They only tell us that, even after controlling for other relevant variables, a structural shift in the ability of police to clear crimes appears to have taken place in the middle of 1966. The equations, however, do not answer the question of what caused the shift. We must identify a reasonable cause. Having controlled for the criminal justice resource variables identified by Professor Schulhofer and for other economic and demographic factors, Miranda becomes the obvious remaining candidate. At the doctrinal level, Miranda seems to have been the most significant legal change affecting the ability of police to clear crimes in the 1966 to 1968 period.[54]

Practical confirmation of this conclusion comes from asking people who would know: law enforcement officers who adjusted their questioning practices to conform to Miranda's requirements. The surveys of police in the years immediately following Miranda uniformly reported harmful effects. Perhaps the best interviews were done by Otis Stephens and his colleagues, who found virtually all of the officers surveyed in Georgia in 1969 and 1970 believed that Supreme Court decisions had adversely affected their work; most attributed this negative influence first and foremost to Miranda.[55] Other surveys at the time noted similar concern about Miranda. In New Haven in 1966, Yale law students interviewed detectives, who "continually told us that the decision would hurt their clearance rate and that they would therefore look inefficient."[56] Law student Gary L. Wolfstone sent letters in 1970 to police chiefs and prosecutors in each State and the District of Columbia. Most agreed that Miranda raised obstacles to law enforcement.[57] In pseudonymous "Seaside City," James Witt interviewed forty-three police detectives sometime before 1973.[58] He reported that the detectives "were in almost complete agreement over the effect that the Miranda warnings were having on the outputs of formal interrogation. Most believed that they were getting many fewer confessions, admissions and statements."[59]

These consistent police reports pose a substantial problem for academic defenders of Miranda. While the academicians recount a "no effects" story, the officers on the streets saw things quite differently.[60] Their first-hand descriptions confirm our intuition that Miranda hindered police effectiveness after June 1966.

Other data support these police reports. For example, in 1994 Bret Hayman and I collected data on the confession rate in Salt Lake County. We found that 16.3% of suspects given their Miranda rights invoked them to prevent any police questioning.[61] We also found that only 42.2% of the suspects questioned and 33.3% of the suspects in the overall sample gave a confession or incriminating statement.[62] These success rates for police questioning in Salt Lake County in 1994 were considerably below those reported in many other cities before Miranda.[63]

Data from Britain and Canada allow a cross-national comparison that provides further confirmation of declining confession rates after Miranda. Until recently, British police told suspects they had the right to remain silent, but did not follow the other particularly onerous features of the Miranda system, such as the waiver and questioning cutoff rules. Under this regime, British police obtained confessions in 61% to 85% of their cases, a rate that is at least 20% higher than the prevailing American confession rate after Miranda.[64] One observes the same result in Canada, where it appears that the police obtain confessions around 70% of the time.[65] These high foreign confession rates are not attributable to police overbearing; some of the data comes from studies of videotaped or independently observed interrogations.[66]

The British experience not only lets us assess confession rates without the Miranda rules, but also allows us to review what happens as a country moves to a Miranda-style regime. In 1986, Britain adopted a heavily regulated structure for police interrogations that tracks Miranda in many respects. Since then, British confession rates have declined towards American levels. Because of law enforcement protests, Parliament recently modified the warnings given to suspects and made other changes to facilitate police questioning.[67]

What is striking about all of these different methodologies—before-and-after studies, clearance rate trends over time, firsthand police reports, recent confession rate data, cross-national comparisons—is that they all point in the same direction: Miranda hampered law enforcement. The important bottom line is that our initial skepticism about Miranda's supposedly benign effects is borne out in the available empirical evidence.

Naturally, there is a danger in relying solely on empirical evidence to capture the harm of Miranda. Statistics tell us little about the horrors of crimes that go unsolved and criminals that go unpunished. How does one quantify, for example, Miranda's effects in *State v. Oldham*?[68] After arrest, Oldham declined to make a statement and was taken to a jail cell. A new shift then arrived, and a new policewoman went to read him his rights again. Oldham said he knew his rights, had talked to a lawyer, but wanted to confess. He then gave a full and free confession to having horribly abused his two-year-old stepdaughter, acts requiring hospitalization and surgery. The Missouri courts, following Miranda doctrine,[69] held that this confession had to be suppressed.[70] Miranda's real-world effect was to send the defendant home to live again with the stepdaughter he had abused.

The evidence collected here strongly suggests that Oldham is far from the only case in which criminals have avoided capture or conviction because of the Miranda rules. Each of these cases has a tale to tell—of victims denied justice or left to cope with debilitating fear.[71] The pattern of cases itself tells a story of Miranda's disproportionate impact on the poor and racial minorities, who bear the brunt of the burden from unsolved crimes.[72] While Miranda's supporters should be troubled by these costs, they appear to pay scant attention. As Professor Caplan has noted, "[a] striking characteristic of the academic literature on Miranda (and criminal procedure generally) is the absence of anxiety about the decision's impact on public safety and the community's sense of well-being."[73]

While Miranda's social costs are significant in themselves, what makes them an undeniable tragedy is that they are in large measure avoidable. Miranda is but one approach among many to regulating police interrogation consistently with the historical understanding of the Fifth Amendment. Before Miranda, a wide range of options were under consideration, such as taking arrested suspects to magistrates for questioning or tape recording police interrogations, as the American Law Institute proposed around the time of Miranda.[74] The longstanding, pre-Miranda "voluntariness test" must also be regarded as a constitutionally viable, less-costly approach to regulating police questioning.[75] All these alternatives would lead to many more confessions, and thus more convictions, of dangerous criminal suspects. Some of them, such as videotaping, would undoubtedly provide better protection for innocent suspects.[76] Yet Miranda's supporters seem uninterested in finding the least restrictive constitutional means of regulating society's agents of law and order. Instead, Miranda seems to have petrified the discussion about how to regulate police questioning.

It is time for a new Miranda narrative—not the myth that it is costless to indulge this Warren Court invention, but an accurate account of real-world consequences from unprecedented shackles on the police. So far, legal academics (or the Court itself, for that matter) have failed to offer a convincing explanation of why we should ignore the human suffering Miranda inflicts. Perhaps these human costs seem unworthy of much attention from the vantage of the ivory tower. But Miranda's countless victims would doubtless tell a different story.

Notes

1. Miranda v. Arizona, 384 U.S. 436 (1966) (instituting the Miranda warning).
2. See Richard A. Leo, The Impact of Miranda Revisited, 86 J. CRIM. L. & CRIMINOLOGY 621, 645 (1996) (concluding that the view that Miranda has had a negligible effect on law enforcement "has become the conventional wisdom").
3. Miranda requires police to give suspects in custody warnings of certain rights and to obtain an affirmative "waiver" of those rights before questioning. Moreover, if the suspect asks for a lawyer at any time, the questioning must stop.
4. The Jury and the Search for Truth: Hearings on S. 3 Before the Senate Comm. on the Judiciary, 104th Cong., 1st Sess. (1995) (testimony of Professor Carol Steiker) (on file with author).
5. Miranda, 384 U.S. at 501 (1966) (Clark, J., dissenting).
6. Because of space limitations, I can sketch my argument here with only broad strokes. For more detailed treatment, see my articles cited in the footnotes. For a reply to the specific criticisms Professor Schulhofer makes in this journal, see Paul G. Cassell, Reply to Schulhofer's Bashing Miranda is Unjustified (working title), 20 HARV. J.L. & PUB. POL'Y (forthcoming 1997).
7. JOSEPH D. GRANO, CONFESSIONS, TRUTH AND THE LAW (1993).
8. Stephen J. Schulhofer, *Miranda's* Practical Effect: Substantial Benefits and Vanishingly Small Social Costs, 90 Nw. U. L. REV. 500, 552 n.214 (1996) [hereinafter Schulhofer, *Miranda's* Practical Effect]. Perhaps attempting to seize the home court advantage in front of the

Federalist Society, in his reply in this journal Schulhofer claims to be "one of those old-fashioned people who think that we should take seriously the intentions of the Framers." Stephen J. Schulhofer, Bashing Miranda Is Unjustified—And Harmful, 20 HARV. J.L. & PUB. POL'Y 347, 348 (1997) [hereinafter Schulhofer, Bashing Miranda], Observant Federalist Society members will note, however, that Schulhofer fails to provide any reference to James Madison reciting the Miranda warnings or to show that anyone—Framer or otherwise—had even heard of the Miranda warnings before the Warren Court revolution of the 1960s.

9. John H. Ely, The Wages of Crying Wolf: A Comment on Roe v. Wade, 82 YALE L.J. 920, 947 (1973).
10. See, e.g., Michigan v. Tucker, 417 U.S. 433, 443-44 (1974).
11. Moran v. Burbine, 475 U.S. 412, 434 n.4 (1986) (emphasis added).
12. Yale Kamisar, The "Police Practice" Phases of the Criminal Process Revolution and the Three Phases of the Burger Court: Rights and Wrongs in the Supreme Court, 1969-86, in THE BURGER YEARS 143, 150 (Herman Schwarz ed., 1987).
13. See, e.g., 1 WAYNE R. LAFAVE & JEROLD H. ISRAEL, CRIMINAL PROCEDURE section 6.5, at 484 (1984 & 1991 Supp.) (citing Project, Interrogations in New Haven: The Impact of Miranda, 76 YALE L.J. 1519 (1967).
14. See Paul G. Cassell, *Miranda's* Social Costs: An Empirical Reassessment, 90 Nw. U. L. REV. 387, 408-09 (1996), analyzing Project, supra note 13; see also Schulhofer, *Miranda's* Practical Effect, supra note 8, at 530 (agreeing that these suspects' confessions would be excluded and concluding that the New Haven study shows a confession rate decline of 12.3%).
15. See Cassell, supra note 14, at 418.
16. See id. at 437-40, 483-86.
17. See Schulhofer, *Miranda's* Practical Effect, supra note 8, at 538 (concluding that "reanalysis . . . modifies the average before-after change from a 16.1% drop (Professor *Cassell's* figure) to a confesssion-rate drop of only 9.7% in comparison to the 1960s voltuntariness test"); see also id. at 539 (conceding that 9.7% figure may rest on studies that are "perhaps slightly low"). Cf. George C. Thomas, III, Is Miranda A Real-World Failure ? A Plea for More (and Better) Empirical Evidence, 43 UCLA L. REV. 821,826-31 (1996) (reviewing studies and concluding that we cannot reject the null hypothesis of no effect from Miranda); George C. Thomas, III, Plain Talk About the Miranda Empirical Debate: A "Steady-State" Theory of Confessions, 43 UCLA L. REV. 933, 939-44 (1996) (emphasizing the importance of a "conservative approach" to Miranda warnings and their effects).
18. See Schulhofer, *Miranda's* Practical Effect, supra note 8, at 544-47.
19. See Paul G. Cassell, All Benefits, No Costs: The Grand Illusion of *Miranda's* Defenders, 90 NW. U. L. REV. 1084 (1996).
20. Id. at 1097-1101.
21. Stephen J. Schulhofer, Pointing in the Wrong Direction, LEGAL. TIMES, Aug. 12, 1996, at 21.
22. Schulhofer, *Miranda's* Practical Effect, supra note 8, at 535.
23. See id.

24. Id. at 538.
25. See Controlling Crime Through More Effective Law Enforcement: Hearings Before the Subcomm. on Criminal Laws and Procedures of the Senate Comm. on the Judiciary, 90th Cong., 1st Sess. 349 (1967) (alluding to Trott's involvement).
26. Telephone Interview with Judge Stephen S. Trott, U.S. Court of Appeals for the Ninth Circuit (Aug. 20, 1996). All information and quotations in this paragraph are based on the interview with Judge Trott.
27. Accord Thomas, supra note 17, Plain Talk About the Miranda Empirical Debate, at 942 (rejecting "out of hand" the Los Angeles figure for purposes of determining *Miranda's* effects).
28. See, e.g., Schulhofer, *Miranda's* Practical Effect, supra note 8, at 507-10.
29. See *Cassell*, supra note 19, at 1087-88 (collecting evidence on this point).
30. Cf. 1 LAFAVE & ISRAEL, supra note 13, at section 6.5(c), p. 484 (wondering whether effects of Miranda have increased over time "now that . . . the fights declared therein are more widely perceived by the public at large").
31. See *Cassell*, supra note 14, at 398-99.
32. Stephen J. Schulhofer, Reconsidering Miranda, 54 U. CHI. L. REV. 435, 456 (1987); see also Stephen J. Schulhofer, The Fifth Amendment at Justice: A Reply, 54 U. CHI. L. REV. 950, 954 n.17 (1987) (arguing that clearance rates coupled with other evidence refute the notion that Miranda harmed law enforcement).
33. Yale Kamisar, Remembering the "Old World" of Criminal Procedure. A Reply to Professor Grano, 23 U. MICH. J.L. REFORM 537, 586 n.164 (1990).
34. In his 1987 article, Reconsidering Miranda, see supra note 32, Schulhofer argued that the putative return of clearance rates to their pre-Miranda levels is evidence of *Miranda's* lack of harm. If that assertion meant anything—in other words, if it was falsifiable—the converse should also have been true: that the persistence of clearance rates below their pre-Miranda levels is evidence of *Miranda's* harm.
35. Schulhofer, supra note 21, at 24.
36. Stephen J. Schulhofer, Miranda and Clearance Rates, 91 Nw. U. L. Rev. 278 (1996) 278, 280; accord id. (stating "we need only turn to levels of crime and police resources during the period" to understand the clearance rate decline); id. at 285 ("Police efforts to fight violent crime were indeed severely handicapped in the late 1960s—not by *Miranda's* relatively subtle change in interrogation procedure, but by the stark reality that in the brief period between 1960 and 1990, the number of officers available, relative to the level of violent crime, fell by 61 percent.") (emphasis deleted).
37. See supra note 17 and accompanying text.
38. Cf Raymond Atkins & Paul H. Rubin, The Impact of Changing Criminal Procedure on Crime Rates (Oct. 28, 1995) (finding that the creation of the exclusionary rule had an effect on crime rates starting in 1961) (working paper on file with author).

39. See Richard A. Leo, Police Interrogation and Social Control, 3 SOC. & LEG. STUD. 93, 99 (1994) (reporting that a detective believes "[i]f he gets a confession (or even good admissions) he doesn't have to spend hours tracking down witnesses, running fingerprints, putting together line-ups, etc.").
40. See Schulhofer, Bashing Miranda, supra note 8, at 358-61 & figs.2-3; Schulhofer, supra note 36, at 283.
41. See Schulhofer, Bashing Miranda, supra note 8, at 357 fig.1 (clearance capacity in dollars drops from 1962-65 while clearance rate rises slightly); id. at 361 fig.3 (same in officers).
42. Schulhofer relies on a compilation of FBI data that ends in 1974. See Schulhofer, Bashing Miranda, supra note 8, at 356 n.30 (relying on JAMES ALAN FOX, FORECASTING CRIME DATA: AN ECONOMETRIC ANALYSIS 81-86 (1978)).
43. Compare Schulhofer, supra note 21, at 24 (reporting that 51 officers per violent crime were available in 1968 while today there are only 28 officers per violent crime) with Schulhofer, Bashing Miranda supra note 8, at 357 fig. 1 (showing that the violent crime clearance rate from 1968 to 1974 remained roughly stable); see also *Paul G. Cassell*, The Costs of the Miranda Mandate: A Lesson in the Danger of Inflexible, "Prophylactic" Supreme Court Inventions, 28 ARIZ. ST. L.J. 299, 308 (1996) (charting crime rates vs. clearance rates for violent crimes and noting that the patterns do not track each other).
44. See PEGGY S. SULLIVAN, DETERMINANTS OF CRIME AND CLEARANCE RATES FOR SEVEN INDEX CRIMES 171 (1985) (unpublished Ph.D. dissertation, Vanderbilt Univ.) (finding that police officers and law enforcement dollars do not significantly influence violent crime clearance rates but do influence property crime clearance rates); Richard R. Bennett, The Effect of Police Personnel Levels on Crime Clearance Rates: A Cross-National Analysis, 6 INT'L J. COMP. & APPLIED CRIM. JUST. 177, 186 (1982) (finding that a previous increase in the number of crimes increases police ability to solve them in cross-national study); Dale O. Cloninger & Lester C. Sartorius, Crime Rates, Clearance Rates and Enforcement Effort: The Case of Houston, Texas, 38 AM.J. ECON. & SOC. 389 (1979) (finding that clearance rates did not respond to small changes in police expenditures but did respond to large changes in police efforts); Michael Geerkin & Walter R. Gove, Deterrence, Overload, and Incapacitation: An Empirical Evaluation, 56 SOC. FORCES 424, 439 (1977) (concluding that system overload operates primarily not on arrest rates but on imprisonment rates); David F. Greenberg & Ronald C. Kessler, The Effect of Arrests on Crime: A Multivariate Panel Analysis, 60 SOC. FORCES 771, 782 (1982) (finding no consistent evidence on relationship between crime rates and clearance rates); see also David F. Greenberg, Ronald C. Kessler, and Charles H. Logan, A Panel Model of Crime Rates and Arrest Rates, 44 AM. SOC. REV. 843, 849 (1979) (finding no consistent, statistically significant relation between either instantaneous or lagged effect of crime rates on arrest rates); Eric Rasmussen, Stigma and Self-Fulfilling Expectations of Criminality, 39 J.L. & ECON. 519, 522 (1996) (concluding that "the overload theory . . . cannot explain the U.S. pattern of crime").

In his reply, Professor Schulhofer seeks to justify the shift from clearance rates to clearance totals by suggesting that I was "the first to bring clearance totals into the debate." Schulhofer, Bashing Miranda, supra note 8, at 358. But he cites a passage in my earlier article that actually discusses a chart depicting clearance rate data. See Cassell, supra note 19, at 1090 (arguing that "looking just to the clearance rate data . . . one would conclude that about one out of every four violent crimes that was 'cleared' before Miranda was not cleared after") (discussing "Figure 1—Violent Crimes Clearance Rates") (emphasis rearranged).

45. The clearance total is simply the total number of crimes police clear. The clearance rate is this total number of cleared crimes divided by the number of crimes reported to the police.
46. See Schulhofer, Clearance Rates, supra note 36, at 286 & fig. 4.
47. For clarity of presentation, the chart stops (as does Schulhofer's) with 1975. From 1976-1994, the gap persists and grows slightly as the total number of crimes increases from year to year.
48. See, e.g., FED. BUREAU OF INVESTIGATION, U.S. DEP'T OF JUSTICE, CRIME IN THE UNITED STATES 1994, at 206-15 chart 3.1 & tbls.25-28 (1995) (reporting crime clearance rates but not clearance totals). See generally JOHN I. GRIFFIN, STATISTICS ESSENTIAL FOR POLICE EFFICIENCY 69 (2d ed. 1958) ("The most important measure of [police] efficiency is the proportion of offenses cleared by arrest.").
49. See generally Wesley G. Skogan & George E. Antunes, Information, Apprehension, and Deterrence: Exploring the Limits of Police Productivity, 7 J. CRIM. JUST. 217 (1979) (discussing the role of information in solving crimes).
50. Humorous illustrations of dumb crooks are collected weekly in "News of the Weird," a column that appears in many newspapers. See, e.g., Chuck Shephard, News of the Weird, ATLANTA JoURN. & CONST., Jan. 28, 1997 (describing a convenience store robber captured because he had forgotten to pull down his face mask before robbing the store and was consequently filmed from the store's surveillance camera).
51. See Schulhofer, supra note 36, at 291 (emphasis in original).
52. Although Professor Schulhofer claims that our capacity variables are flawed because they are based on crime rates rather than total crimes, see Schulhofer, supra note 21, at 24, our Table 1 divides Police Officers by Crime Rate to produce the Officer Capacity variable. Arithmetically, officers/population divided by crimes/population produces officers/crimes—a figure based on total crimes and not crime rates.
53. For further discussion of this and other such issues, see *Paul G. Cassell* & Richard Fowles, Handcuffing the Cops?: A Thirty Year Perspective on *Miranda's* Harmful Effects (manuscript in progress) (copies available upon request to *Cassell*). In this forthcoming article, Professor Fowles and the author of this Article will present a more detailed rebuttal of Professor Schulhofer's assertions than is here possible. In addition, we plan to conduct a more refined analysis of the clearance rates by individual crime categories and review more

extensively other competing hypotheses to the Miranda effect, such as those now proffered by Professor Schulhofer.

54. Some of the other leading Warren Court decisions were decided well before 1966, e.g., Mapp v. Ohio, 367 U.S. 643 (1961), or affected the prosecution of crimes only after they were cleared by police, e.g., Gideon v. Wainwright, 372 U.S. 335 (1963). In any event, if the regression equations are read as suggesting that other Warren Court decisions combined with Miranda to reduce clearance rates, that finding would still have considerable significance. Legal academics have frequently denied any such connection. See, e.g., Robert Weisberg, Criminal Procedure Doctrine: Some Versions of the Skeptical, 76 J. CRIM. L. & CRIMINOLOGY 832 (1985).
55. See Otis H. Stephens, Jr, Robert L. Flanders, & J. Lewis Cannon, Law Enforcement and the Supreme Court: Police Perceptions of the Miranda Requirements, 39 TENN. L. REV. 407 (1972); see also OTIS H. STEPHENS, JR., THE SUPREME COURT AND CONFESSIONS OF GUILT (1973).
56. Project, supra note 13, at 1612 n.265.
57. See Gary L. Wolfstone, Miranda—A Survey of Its Impact, 7 THE PROSECUTOR 26, 27 (1971).
58. See James W. Witt, Non-Coercive Interrogation and the Administration of Criminal Justice: The Impact of Miranda on Police Effectuality, 64 J. CRIM. L. & CRIMINOLOGY 320 (1973).
59. Id. at 325.
60. These surveys are the most informative on the question of Miranda's effect during the 1960s, because they were done contemporaneously with the decision when officers had experience questioning both with and without the Miranda rules. Today, few officers have personal experience with pre-Miranda interviewing techniques. The two surveys of current police attitudes on Miranda are subject to varying interpretations. Compare *Cassell*, supra note 19, at 1108-10 (discussing Police Executive Research Forum and ABA surveys on police attitudes in 1980s) with Schulhofer, Miranda's Practical Effect, supra note 8, at 507-08 (same).
61. See Paul G. Cassell & Bret S. Hayman, Police Interrogation in the 1990s: An Empirical Study of the Effects of Miranda, 43 UCLA L. REV. 839, 860 & tbl.3 (1996).
62. See id. at 869 tbl.4.
63. See id. at 871-75 (collecting all available pre-Miranda confesssion data). The limited other data on post-Miranda confession rates supports our conclusions. See id. at 875-76. But see Thomas, Plain Talk About the Miranda Empricial Debate, supra note 17, at 939-44 (reviewing Cassell-Hayman study and disputing this claim); Thomas, Is Miranda A Real-World Failure?, supra note 17, at 833-37 (concluding we need more information about *Miranda's* effects); Richard A. Leo, Inside the Interrogation Room, 86 J. CRIM. L. & CRIMINOLOGY 266, 280-81 (1996) (presenting California data and arguing that police have become increasingly successful in gaining confessions).
64. See Cassell, supra note 14, at 419-21.
65. See id. at 421-22.

66. See id. at 478.
67. See id. at 420.
68. See State v. Oldham, 618 S.W.2d 647 (Mo. 1981); 136 CONG. REC. S9027 (June 28, 1990) (statement of Senator Hatch).
69. See Edwards v. Arizona, 451 U.S. 477 (1981).
70. See Oldham, 618 S.W.2d at 649 (holding that trial court erred in not supressing the confession, and overturning the conviction).
71. Cf. Paul G. Cassell, Balancing the Scales of Justice: The Case for and Effects of Utah's Victim's Rights Amendment, 1994 UTAH L. REV. 1373 (discussing victims' perspectives on crime).
72. Cf. CHARLES MURRAY, LOSING GROUND: AMERICAN SOCIAL POLICY; 1950-1980, 117 (1984) (analyzing crime statistics and concluding: "Put simply, it was much more dangerous to be black in 1972 than it was in 1965, whereas it was not much more dangerous to be white.").
73. Gerald M. Caplan, Questioning Miranda, 38 VAND. L. REV. 1417, 1425 n.47 (1985).
74. See Paul G. Kauper, Judicial Examination of the Accused–A Remedy for the Third Degree, 30 MICH. L. REV. 1224, 1239); Akhil Reed Amat & Renee B. Lettow, Fifth Amendment First Principles: The Self-Incrimination Clause, 93 MICH. L. REV. 857, 898-99, 908–09 (1995); A.L.I., A MODEL CODE OF PRE-ARRAIGNMENT PROCEDURE section 130.4 (1975). See generally Cassell, supra note 43, at 310-13 (collecting proposed alternatives).
75. See generally GRANO, supra note 7, at 199-222; OFFICE OF LEGAL POLICY, U.S. DEP'T OF JUSTICE, REPORT TO THE ATTORNEY GENERAL ON THE LAW OF PRETRIAL INTERROGATION, REP. No. 1 (1986), reprinted in 22 U. MICH. J.L. REFORM 437 (1989); HAROLD J. ROTHWAX, GUILTY: THE COLLAPSE OF CRIMINAL JUSTICE 66–87 (1996).
76. See Cassell, supra note 14, at 479-83, 488-89; Leo, supra note 2, at 689-92.
77. Further information on the construction of the variables can be found in Cassell & Fowles, supra note 53.

NO 

Stephen J. Schulhofer

Bashing Miranda Is Unjustified—and Harmful

Readers of this Symposium have seen my views discussed at such length in Professor Paul Cassell's Article that many will feel little need to know more on that subject. And since Professor Cassell has characterized my position as "aggressive," "farfetched" and "extreme,"[1] readers can hardly be blamed for concluding that it is a waste of their time to read further.

In this Article I seek only to make three simple points, all very conventional. I invite readers to compare my actual argument to the caricature that emerges from Professor Cassell's loose paraphrasing of things I have said, and above all to remember that the issue here is, or should be, Miranda,[2] not me.

Three points about Miranda should remain in focus. First, the Miranda protections are required by the Fifth Amendment. Second, law-enforcement damage cannot be a reason to disregard a constitutional requirement; therefore the claim of law-enforcement damage, though emotionally charged, is constitutionally irrelevant. Because that claim is emotionally charged, however, I do not want to leave the impression that I am ducking it. As my third point, I will address that claim head on. I will show why the great majority of academics and police officials are correct in believing that Miranda does not burden our law enforcement effort at all.

My third point—that Miranda does not damage law enforcement—has a subsidiary implication that is worth stressing at the outset. Academics thrive on challenging conventional wisdom, and so the conventional view about Miranda's negligible impact should not be immune from academic scrutiny. But the day is short, human energies are limited, there are victims of crime almost without number, and our law enforcement and crime prevention systems have glaring deficiencies that cry out for discussion and thoughtful repair. When die-hard efforts to blame Miranda for our ills distract attention from other, more serious concerns, even to the point of disparaging the importance of criminal justice resources and the number of police officers on the street,[3] then the victims of crime—present and future—are served very poorly indeed. Scapegoating Miranda is no idle academic exercise; it can become a dangerous diversion from the issues that truly make a difference for the safety of our streets and the quality of our civilization.

From *Harvard Journal of Law & Public Policy*, vol. 20, issue 2, Winter 1997, pp. 347-373.

I. Law Enforcement Need as an Exception to the Bill of Rights?

I will take my second point first. I am one of those old-fashioned people who think that we should take seriously the intentions of the Framers.

In a Federalist Society symposium devoted to constitutional interpretation, it is surprising to find the potential impact on crime victims invoked, over and over, as the most important guide to interpreting what the Bill of Rights means. It is perhaps unfortunate, but nonetheless true, that interpreting the Constitution and protecting victims are not identical goals. In fact, we must acknowledge, however reluctantly, that sometimes these are antithetical goals.

What we have to ask ourselves is this: did the Framers think that the Fifth Amendment would not make law enforcement more difficult? Of course not. The Framers knew perfectly well that sometimes the Fifth Amendment would hinder law enforcement.

To be honest with ourselves, we must put the point even more strongly than that. The Fifth Amendment was intended—obviously intended—to make law enforcement more difficult. The Framers were suspicious of organized government power, for very good reasons. The Framers wanted to limit government's power to question suspects. They intended, in Professor Cassell's phrase, to put "shackles"[4] on questioning. So, if we are committed to respecting the intentions of the Framers, we have to respect the Fifth Amendment, even when it hinders law enforcement.

II. Miranda and the Fifth Amendment

The Fifth Amendment provides that no person may be "compelled" to be a witness against himself in a criminal case. Miranda's critics want to permit relatively free-wheeling police interrogation, and therefore they must insist that such interrogation is not "compelling." What, they wonder, is so compelling about a policeman's asking a single question, "Did you kill your wife?"

In thinking about this issue, we have to remember that Miranda leaves police entirely free in questioning suspects prior to arrest. The Miranda limits apply only when officers want to question a suspect who is held in police custody under arrest. What Miranda's critics really claim not to understand, to put their question in a real-world context, is this: what, they wonder, is so compelling about arresting a suspect, surrounding him with three or four officers, isolating him in an interrogation room, and then asking him, over and over: "Why did you do it? Why did you kill your wife?"

To understand Miranda's link to the Fifth Amendment, all we have to do is to stop for a moment and imagine what it would feel like to be an arrested suspect in this kind of situation. No sweat?

Hardly. The compelling pressure to respond, whether you want to or not, is enormous. You might prefer to take a deep breath, go home and get some sleep. You might prefer to talk over your situation with your Dad, or your priest, or (God forbid!) your lawyer. Too bad. Remember–you are under arrest. You are staying right in that room, under those lights, in front of those four angry and impatient officers, until you answer–whether you want to or not.

There is nothing obscure about why this kind of situation puts a suspect under compelling pressure. What remains obscure (and completely formalistic) is the view, held tenaciously by Miranda's critics, that custodial interrogation–without warnings and without any right to terminate the questioning–does not put the suspect under compelling pressure.

Under the Fifth Amendment, when Congress wanted to question Oliver North, when it wanted to do so in full view of the press, before millions of viewers on national television, he still had an attorney at his side, not just a potted plant, and he was told that he did not have to answer. When a criminal defendant comes into open court with an attorney right at his side, he still cannot be questioned at all unless he agrees.

So, when a suspect is under arrest and isolated in the interrogation room, it takes a lot to explain why he should not at least be told he does not have to answer.

Professor Cassell agrees that the suspect should get a warning. That much of Miranda he accepts. But what if the suspect then says he doesn't want to answer? Professor Cassell would let the police keep questioning him anyway. Professor Cassell's view, what he calls the "common sense" view, is that "these suspects would not be compelled to answer police questions; they would only be compelled to listen."[5]

No one ever thinks of reading the Fifth Amendment that way when the issue is what Congress can do if it wants to question Oliver North. No one ever thinks of reading the Fifth Amendment that way when the issue is what a trial judge can do to a criminal defendant in the courtroom. Unless we are willing to resort to pure sophistry, the Fifth Amendment cannot mean that an isolated suspect in custody can be compelled to undergo questioning–compelled to "listen" to demands for information–after he clearly and specifically asks to be left alone.

The Supreme Court has understood this problem perfectly well, not only in Miranda but ever since.[6] Writing for the Court in 1984, Justice Byron White, initially a bitter critic of Miranda, noted that coercion was "inherent" in custodial interrogation because the suspect "is painfully aware that he literally cannot escape a persistent custodial interrogator."[7] Similarly, in 1993, Justice David Sourer, writing for the Court in *Withrow v. Williams*,[8] acknowledged that "' [p]rophylactic' though it may be, in protecting a defendant's Fifth Amendment privilege against self-incrimination Miranda safeguards a fundamental trial right."[9]

In short, respect for our Constitution, respect for judicial restraint, and respect for principled adjudication all require that we respect the Fifth Amendment. We should expect the Court to apply the Fifth Amendment conscientiously, even if that means some inconvenience and even if Miranda does put some constraints on law enforcement, because the Fifth Amendment was intended to put constraints on law enforcement.

III. Miranda's Effect

The two preceding points conclude my discussion of the most important issues, but I do not want readers to think I concede Professor Cassell's claim about Miranda's terrible effects. Professor Cassell has portrayed Miranda as "an undeniable tragedy."[10] I reject not only the obvious exaggeration of that position but also the split-the-difference logic that observers of this debate could be tempted to adopt. Some might think that even if Professor Cassell's claims are only half true, there is still a serious problem to worry about. But his claims are not even half true. So far as the available evidence indicates, there is no reason to believe that Miranda has burdened the law enforcement effort at all.

In mentioning the need for evidence, I do not disparage the importance of common sense, nor do I imply that legal conclusions must always have rigorous statistical support. But Miranda's impact in the real world is not the kind of fact that can be determined on the basis of faith, a priori logic or pure intuition. Severe restrictions on police interrogation presumably would reduce the flow of confessions. But porous or largely nominal restrictions might have little or no effect. An illusion among suspects that police are severely restricted might lead suspects to lower their guard, and as a result the flow of confessions could actually increase. We need to know not only whether the facts bear out these logical possibilities, but also whether Miranda is a regime of the first, second or third types. To the extent that Miranda, as actually implemented, has elements of all three regimes, its effects are doubly or triply indeterminate on the basis of logic or "common sense" alone.

Alarmists who see Miranda as a severely restrictive regime may feel little need for empirical evidence to confirm what "common sense" tells them about its impact. But that picture of Miranda is itself an assumption, no better or worse than the cynic's assumption that the Miranda regime is an empty illusion.[11] To shed light on the empirical issues, we cannot tip the scales from the outset by assuming, as Professor Cassell sometimes seems to do, that one answer is more logical or commonsensical than the other. We must look to the evidence. And when we do, we consistently find that evidence of Miranda's supposed harmful effects fails to materialize.

In so far as we are willing to base our conclusions on the available facts, therefore, the only tenable assessment is that the Miranda rules do not hinder law enforcement. The evidence consistently shows that the rules are porous, and that police are quite good at getting waivers. That evidence does not imply that Miranda is meaningless, or that it does nothing whatever to further the Fifth Amendment. There is a big difference between getting suspects to talk by fear and intimidation, and getting them to talk as police now do, by exploiting their misplaced confidence in their ability to talk their way out of trouble.[12] What the evidence does mean is that, so far as we can tell, Miranda does not hamper law enforcement—not at all.

This conclusion about Miranda's lack of any harmful effect is the prevailing view among academics, but it is not the view of academics alone. Most police professionals in the field have come to the same conclusion. Most police professionals say the same thing, openly and emphatically.[13]

Professor Cassell's Article places great stress on the anti-Miranda reactions of some police officials in the late 1960s.[14] In that era, many officers familiar with the old way of doing business had not yet adapted to the new regime, and many others overestimated Miranda's likely impact.[15] By the early 1970s, such views were seldom heard any more. For the past twenty years, the great majority of police officials have consistently expressed the opposite view—that Miranda does not burden law enforcement.[16]

Professor Cassell's response to the current police view is to ask dismissively, "How would they know?"[17] Is it so naive to assume that police do know what makes their work easier or more difficult? Police officers (like everyone else) sometimes complain unnecessarily; sometimes they unjustifiably try to pass blame to politicians or to the courts. So police complaints about Miranda could sometimes be overstated. But if Miranda poses a problem for the police, wouldn't we expect them to notice it? And if they noticed it, why on earth would they be keeping so quiet about it for the past twenty years?

A. Data on Confession Rates

Professor Cassell's claim of damage to law enforcement rests heavily on his reading of the available data on confession rates. But when you look closely, each item of his evidence melts away. In a previous article, I discussed each of these pieces of evidence in detail.[18] In the brief space available here, I will try to touch quickly on the main issues.

The first item is Professor Cassell's reanalysis of before-and-after studies that are now almost thirty years old. Professor Cassell says these studies show that, because of Miranda, convictions are lost in 3.8 percent of all arrests.[19] But there are major problems buried in virtually every step of that analysis.

First of all, Cassell's crucial figure—the alleged loss of 3.8% of the cases—is based on 1967 and 1968 data, so it makes no allowance for all the adjustments that police have made in the last twenty-five years. Yet police repeatedly tell us that, whatever the initial problems, they have now learned how to live with Miranda.[20]

Another problem is that in order to build up the case attrition rate to the 3.8% level, Professor Cassell has to exclude one major city, Los Angeles, where more confessions were obtained after Miranda than before. Professor Cassell argues that there might have been a difference between the ways the data were collected in Los Angeles in the "before-Miranda" and in the "after-Miranda" phases. But when he has studies showing a drop in the confession rate, then differences in methodology usually do not concern him.

For example, in Philadelphia and Brooklyn, elected district attorneys who were publicly attacking Miranda—this was back in 1966—conducted studies of Miranda's impact in the following way: they counted the number of confessions after Miranda and then compared that figure to their own seat-of-the-pants guess about the number of confessions before Miranda. They said, oh, the confessions rate before Miranda was much higher, probably about 45%.[21]

We must remember that small differences matter a lot here. We are talking about a net loss of 3.8%. How can you possibly derive a reliable and sufficiently precise number from a ballpark estimate by an advocate in a highly partisan public debate? You simply can't. But in Professor Cassell's analysis, the Philadelphia and Brooklyn estimates stay in. The Los Angeles study was an actual count before and after, and it was a count by a district attorney who happened to be opposed to Miranda. Yet the Los Angeles study gets excluded.

Another study featured in Professor Cassell's presentation is his own 1994 research in Salt Lake County. He reports that "only" 42% of the suspects questioned gave a confession or incriminating statement.[22] But Professor Cassell neglects to mention his own research showing that confession rates commonly reported before Miranda were in the range of 40–45% or even lower, in such cities as Philadelphia, Kings County (Brooklyn, N.Y.), the District of Columbia, New Orleans, Los Angeles, and Baltimore.[23] In addition, Professor Cassell's 42% figure for Salt Lake County excludes two important categories of statements—confessions that he deemed "volunteered" and incriminating "denials with explanation" (such as the statement of an assault suspect who admitted striking the victim but claimed self-defense). When these incriminating statements are added back into the count, as any valid comparison with pre-Miranda figures requires, the success rate in Salt Lake County's custodial interrogations, on Professor Cassell's own data, rises to at least 54%, a total that easily equals or exceeds pre-Miranda results.[24]

In sum, a careful look at the sources from which Professor Cassell has selectively culled his data shows that there is no empirical support for the argument that Miranda measurably reduced confession rates.[25]

I must add a comment here, just for the record, about Professor Cassell's claim that I "agree"[26] that Miranda caused a 9.7% drop in the confession rate. I do not agree and have never said otherwise.[27]

B. Clearance Rates

The other major point stressed in Professor Cassell's Article is the trend in clearance rates, that is, the percentage of known crimes that police are able to solve. Those rates plunged after Miranda and then stabilized a few years later. But does it make sense to say that Miranda caused this development?

In an earlier article,[28] Professor Cassell claimed to have ruled out the most plausible alternative explanations for the clearance-rate trend and wrote that "the challenge for those who cling to the notion that [Miranda] did not harm law enforcement is to provide an alternative 'X factor' that explains the change."[29] In response to Professor Cassell's invitation, I pointed out an important law-enforcement variable, omitted from his analysis that provides a highly plausible candidate for his "X factor"—that is, the development that might explain a sudden drop in clearance rates in 1966. This variable is clearance capacity, measured by the number of dollars and officers available to investigate each reported offense. My suggestion is that there is simply no mystery: clearance rates declined precipitously just at the time that clearance capacity plunged. There is no reason to assume that interrogation rules, rather than disasterously shrinking resources, were responsible for the trend that Professor Cassell so dramatically blamed on Miranda. . . .[30]

I have presented elsewhere a more complete discussion of the clearance rate story,[31] but a few comments here are necessary to dispel some misconceptions that might arise from the way Professor Cassell has tried to paraphrase my argument. First, to clear the ground, I summarize my claim and indicate how it differs from the caricature that Professor Cassell attacks in his Article. I will then bring the merits back into focus and explain why, after allowing for clearance capacity changes, a residual "Miranda" effect cannot be inferred from the evidence.

1. Misconceptions and Distractions

My argument, in a nutshell, is that clearance capacity collapsed in the late 1960s, and that this dramatic change provides the most likely explanation for the sudden decline in clearance rates that occurred at the same time.

Clearance capacity obviously is not the only factor that affects clearance rate trends; the complexity of the forces impacting on law enforcement is a point I have repeatedly stressed.[32] Readers may therefore wonder whether Professor Cassell is being helpful in repeatedly attributing to me the absurd view that clearance capacity was the "sole" reason for the clearance rate decline.[33] Many forces contributed to clearance rate trends; as I will explain, however, there is no reason to think that one particular factor—Miranda—was among the factors playing a causal role.

A similar caveat is necessary regarding the data on crime clearance totals that will become a part of my inquiry. It is hard to understand why Professor Cassell thinks I am arguing that such totals are decisive in themselves, or why he accuses me of ignoring the capacity of a large police department to generate higher clearance totals than a smaller one.[34] Crime clearance totals alone cannot prove anything. They are, however, one place to look for evidence of Miranda's impact, especially if one focuses, as I do, on the number of crimes cleared per officer and per dollar of police expenditure.

Professor Cassell himself was the first to bring clearance totals into the debate, claiming (incorrectly) that "about one out of four violent crimes that was cleared before Miranda was not cleared after!"[35] In fact, as we shall see, the number of violent crimes cleared after Miranda did not decline at all. That fact may not be the most revealing item of all time, but I wonder why it should be considered inappropriate to mention it when Miranda critics like Professor Cassell write as if the opposite were true.

In an era of rapidly rising crime rates, crimes become easier to solve, and one would not necessarily expect clearance totals to decline.[36] But if Miranda hindered law enforcement, the decision might produce a temporary dip, or at least slow the rate of increase in the number of crimes cleared per officer and per dollar. That no effect of this sort is observable is one more reason to be skeptical of claims that Miranda "handcuffed" (or even incrementally burdened) the police.

2. Why clearance capacity?

In his effort to account for the late 1960s drop in clearance rates, Professor Cassell initially dismissed the trends in crime rates and resource levels because neither factor alone fit the pattern of clearance rate changes. Using multiple regression analysis, he tested the effect of each of these variables with the other held constant. Rising crime rates did not seem to explain the change, because clearance rates stabilized around 1970, when crime was still rising. Similarly, resource levels did not seem to explain the clearance rate drop, because resource levels rose steadily throughout the period . . .

[A] structural change did occur precisely at the time when clearance rates plummeted. Violent crime soared in the mid-1960s, but police resources increased much more slowly. The spread between crime and resources widened dramatically after 1965, just when clearance rates dropped. By 1969, the spread stopped growing, just when clearance rates stabilized.

Why might this change in the relationship between crime and resources be important? My hypothesis is that when there is a decline in the number of officers and dollars available to investigate each reported crime, it is plausible to expect the percentage of those crimes that police can solve to decline also. Each officer will have to divide his time over more and more cases. More crime reports will have to be ignored, just for lack of time to investigate them. These trends would tend to drive down clearance rates even if the legal rules governing police work did not change at all.

To test that hypothesis, we need to compare two patterns. One is the pattern of changes in clearance rates, and the other is the pattern of changes in police capacity to clear crime, measured by the ratio of police expenditure or personnel to the number of reported crimes. . . . The pattern of changes in the ratio of police personnel to the number of crimes is virtually identical. . . .

[Police] capacity to clear crimes declined precipitously in the mid-1960s, and then it stabilized by 1970. The clearance rates follow a virtually identical pattern.

. . . But once we know what was happening to police investigative capacity, we can see that there is no reason to blame Miranda, rather than drastically shrinking resources, for the clearance rate trend.[37]

3. Crime Clearance Totals

A possible question raised by these trends is whether, because clearance rates are affected by the level of crime, Miranda's impact is masked by data on clearance rates. One way to avoid that problem is to shift our focus from the percentage of crimes cleared to the total number of crimes cleared. If Miranda hurt the police in solving crimes, we would expect to see some impact, around 1966, in trends in the number of crimes police were able to clear. . . .

[To] anybody who believes, with Professor Cassell, that "law enforcement never recovered from the blow that Miranda inflicted,"[38] . . . the number of crimes cleared did not drop at all. Clearance totals were rising before Miranda, partly because crime rates were rising, so there were more crimes that were easy to solve. But after 1965, after Miranda, the number of crimes cleared continued to rise. There was no dip, not even a temporary dip. There was not even a pause in the rate of increase. If Miranda did hinder law enforcement, there is no hint of that impact here.

The increase . . . in the number of crimes cleared could result from the fact that there were more officers available to do the investigations. Thus, to see whether Miranda had an impact, we have to know the number of crimes cleared per officer and per dollar of law enforcement expenditure. If Miranda hurt the crime-control effort, we should detect some impact, around 1966, in the number of crimes each officer was able to clear. . . .

The data show that before Miranda, police effectiveness in clearing crimes was rising; presumably, once again, because crime rates were rising, so there were more crimes that were easy to solve. But police effectiveness in clearing crimes continued to rise after 1965. Again, there was no dip, and there was no pause in the rate of increase. There is simply no hint in this data that Miranda in any way hurt police efforts to solve crime. So whether we look at clearance rates or clearance totals, there is no evidence—none—that Miranda hindered law enforcement.

C. Regression Evidence?

Professor Cassell now appears to concede that a substantial structural shift in clearance capacity was at least partly responsible for the 1966 clearance rate drop. But he argues—relying on a regression analysis he is in the process of conducting—that the collapse of police clearance capacity in the late 1960s did not account for all of the clearance rate drop. The regression analysis shows, Cassell suggests, that some other development centered in 1966 (presumably Miranda) must be the explanation for the remainder of the decline in clearance rates.

In essence, Professor Cassell's entire argument for a Miranda effect on clearance rates now turns on his regression analysis, a study that is as yet unpublished and is described only in sketchy terms. The simplest point to make, therefore, is that the supposed Miranda effect remains unknown until the regression analysis is fully presented and explained, a task that Professor Cassell has not yet attempted.

Even from Professor Cassell's sketchy description, however, one can see, on close reading, that his regression model is artificial and misleading. In a previous article, I explained in detail seven serious defects in his model, any of which is sufficient to render the model useless as a guide to Miranda's effect.[39] Without retracing all of that ground here, I will focus on three especially critical flaws. First, Professor Cassell still fails to take the collapse of clearance capacity fully into account. Second, he continues to exclude other structural changes that were occurring in the late 1960s, and as a result, his regression model attributes the cumulative effect of the excluded factors to the 1966 event he misleadingly labels "Miranda." The third problem is more technical, but critically important; Professor Cassell's analysis relies on aggregate national data, and it therefore involves a methodologically crude, error-prone model that professional social scientists have long discredited.

1. Clearance capacity. The most striking problem is Professor Cassell's continued failure to take adequate account of clearance capacity, which eroded precipitously with the sudden decline in the ratio of dollars and resources to the number of crimes to be solved. Despite my stress on this point in previously published criticism of Professor Cassell's claim,[40] he has made only an incomplete adjustment, by including a new variable for the ratio of police resources to the crime rate. But officers do not solve crime rates; they need to solve crimes. When the population is rising, a steady crime rate implies a rising number of crimes to be solved. A steady ratio of officers to the crime rate will obscure a decline in clearance capacity, because the increase in population necessarily means that the number of crimes to be investigated by each officer is increasing, even though the ratio of officers to the crime rate remains unchanged. By defining clearance capacity relative to the crime rate, Professor Cassell systematically understates the actual erosion of police clearance capacity.
2. Other omitted variables. Readers unfamiliar with regression analysis must understand that in a model like Professor Cassell's, spanning a forty-four-year period, the before-after dummy variable centered on the year 1966—the variable he chooses to call "Miranda"—does not measure only the impact of causal factors that changed in that year alone. When important factors that affect clearance rates are omitted in such a model, and when the average value of such factors over the period before the pivotal year is different from their average value over the period after the pivotal year, the impact of all such factors inevitably gets included in the dummy variable that carries the "Miranda" label.[41] Numerous causally important variables, all ignored in Professor Cassell's model, made well-known or probable contributions to the clearance rate decline that the dummy variable identifies. It is conceivable, of course, that Miranda also contributed to that clearance rate drop. But labeling the dummy variable "Miranda" does not establish the extent—if any—to which Miranda effects were present. To do that, we must first take account of the factors that had a known or probable effect, and see whether there remains an impact we cannot otherwise explain. Thus, until we allow for other factors that we know to be important, we have no reason to assume that Miranda was responsible for any part of the clearance rate drop that Professor Cassell assigns to the so-called "Miranda" variable. Among the many factors that could, or clearly did, contribute to clearance rate trends, the following are especially relevant:

    a. Urbanization. Clearance rates are consistently lower in the larger cities. For example, in 1954 the clearance rate for violent crimes stood at 71% in cities with less than 250,000 inhabitants, but it was only 60% in cities larger than that size.[42] By 1969 these clearance rates had fallen substantially in cities of all sizes, but the smaller cities still enjoyed a significant advantage—a violent crime clearance rate of 54%, compared with a rate of only 42% for the cities with population over 250,000.[43]

Because of this small-city advantage, a shift in the distribution of crime between large and small cities will alter aggregate clearance rates for the nation as a whole, even if police in each city maintain exactly the same clearance rate year after year. For example, if clearance rates in every individual city remain constant, but if the larger cities get a greater share of the nation's violent crimes, aggregate national clearance rates will drop. The importance of allowing for urbanization in studies of crime rates, clearances and arrests is well known, and stressed in the FBI's Uniform Crime Reports.[44] Yet Professor Cassell's model takes no account of this easily quantifiable factor.

In order to see whether Professor Cassell's omission of urbanization data could cause his results to be biased, we need to examine the distribution of violent crime between large and small cities. When we calculate—for the total violent crime reported in all cities—the portion of the total that was reported in cities with less than 250,000 residents, we find no clear trend in the data. The percentage of total city crime that was located in the smaller cities fluctuates frequently, and that percentage is roughly the same in 1974 (39.4%) as it was in 1950 (41.6%).[45]

But if we compare the trends in small-city share to the trends in the aggregate national clearance rates over the same period, some striking patterns emerge. . . .

[C]learance rates held roughly steady from 1962 to 1965 and again from 1969 to 1974, even though clearance capacity was dropping somewhat during both of these periods. The trend in small-city shares shows one of the many factors that could in part account for this result: the small city share rose sharply during both periods, helping to offset the negative effect of declining clearance capacity and thus to sustain aggregate national clearance rates.

Precisely the opposite trend prevails in the 1965–1969 period that is crucial to Professor Cassell's claim about Miranda's supposed impact. From 1965 to 1969, there is a brief, sudden turnaround, and for four years, the small-city share drops. Downward trends in both clearance capacity and small-city share converge, right after 1965, to reinforce one another in pulling clearance rates sharply lower.

To underscore the obvious, I do not claim that small-city shares are the only explanation for clearance-rate trends. The small-city trends may even be a relatively small part of the overall story. But the distribution of crime between large and small cites is one factor that clearly must be taken into account before we can assume that Miranda must have caused the clearance-rate drop after 1965.

b. Professionalization. Careless and unprofessional recordkeeping procedures were endemic in American police departments in the 1950s and early 1960s. Jerome Skolnick's famous 1966 study devoted a full chapter to the arbitrary and inflated character of the clearance-rate reports of that period.[46] Matters began to change in the late 1960s. The report of the President's Crime Commission, published in 1967, focused on the need to upgrade police personnel and procedures.[47] Greater attention to accurate record keeping was a part of the overall movement for greater professionalism that occurred, coincidentally or not, almost exactly at the time of Miranda.[48] If clearance rates are now lower, all else being equal, than they were in the period from 1950 to 1965, part of the explanation almost certainly is that the clearance-rate figures of that earlier era were to some degree artificially inflated.

c. Greater reporting. Clearance rates reflect the percentage of reported crimes that police solve, but reported crime is a fraction of total crime, and reporting rates vary substantially from crime to crime, from year to year, and from decade to decade. Although there are no accurate estimates of reporting rates for the 1950s and 1960s, the recent trends suggest that reporting rates have been increasing, and it is plausible to infer that a lower percentage of all crime was reported in the pre-1966 era than since.

   Reporting rates are important because a higher rate of reporting will tend to bring into the system cases involving relatively less severe harms that have a weaker claim on police time and attention. If all else remained equal, including the crime rate, but if the proportion of less serious cases was higher, then the clearance rate could well have declined simply because the mix of cases, and the priority police placed on investigating them, had shifted.

d. Other legal changes. Apart from all the social and structural changes that accompanied the upheavals of the late 1960s, there were numerous legal changes—other than Miranda—that could easily affect a police clearance rate. None of these changes occurred precisely on July 1, 1966. But the before-after dummy variable compares the average effect of legal restrictions operative in the 1950-65 period to the average effect of such restrictions during the 1967-94 period. As a result, Miranda is not the only legal change of the Warren era that could have contributed to the effect that is picked up by the dummy variable in Professor Cassell's regression model. Other potentially important decisions include Mapp v. Ohio,[49] creating an exclusionary remedy for illegal search and seizure (1961); Rogers v. Richmond (1961)[50] and Haynes v. Washington (1963),[51] tightening the due process limits on interrogation; United States v. Wade[52] and Stovall v. Denno,[53] imposing Sixth Amendment and due process limits on police line-ups (1967); and Terry v. Ohio,[54] imposing limits on police stops and frisks (1968).

Needless to say, if legal rules such as these did contribute to clearance-rate trends, it does not necessarily follow that these rules should be abandoned. Clearance-rate impact is not a test for constitutionality. Professor Cassell appears to endorse one of the major 1960s innovations (the more sensitive due-process voluntariness test), and others (such as the due-process limits on suggestive line-ups) are ones he should find hard to criticize.

The impact on clearance rates of accepted doctrinal changes other than Miranda is not known with any precision, of course. But it is indefensibly speculative (and implausible) to ignore such cases as Haynes, Mapp, Stovall and Terry, and to assume that clearance-rate changes must have been due to Miranda instead. Unless Professor Cassell can offer some basis for determining what part of the clearance rate drop is due to legal innovations he supports, like Haynes, and separating those effects from the impact of legal innovations he opposes, the claim that law enforcement has suffered because of Miranda will continue to rest on faith, not on evidence.

3. Methodology. The last point is the most technical, but it is crucial. Although Professor Cassell claims to be using "[t]he standard statistical technique for answering [causal] questions,"[55] few professional social scientists would agree. Most econometricians recognize that regression analysis is at best a crude tool. Its use requires many caveats, and even at its best, it is often unsuited to teasing out subtle questions of causation when several social and legal variables are dramatically changing in close proximity.[56]

   Apart from this standard concern, there is a more specific problem; the kind of regression analysis Professor Cassell uses—an analysis of aggregate data for the nation as a whole—is not the "standard statistical technique." Even those economists most sanguine about the value of regression analysis stress the flaws of using aggregate national data: That approach masks effects and distorts relationships because crime variables are subject to prevasive measurement errors, and because trends in one State frequently offset or reinforce unrelated trends occurring simultaneously in other States.[57] The standard procedure for minimizing these effects is cross-sectional time-series analysis, in which data for resource levels, crime rates and all other variables are recorded separately for each affected jurisdiction. Econometric studies of the impact of legal rules on the criminal justice system almost invariably rely on cross-sectional analysis,[58] and almost twenty years ago, the National Academy of

Sciences panel on research methodology in this area stressed the need for using the cross-sectional approach.[59]

4. Summary. The preceding discussion touches on many of the important flaws in Professor Cassell's regression model; I have discussed others elsewhere.[60] The points I have covered here should be sufficient, nonetheless, to indicate why that model, in its present form, is not even suggestive of a possible Miranda effect on clearance rates. The effect identified by the 1966 dummy variable could easily be a spurious artifact of a substandard model, and if the effect identified is real, we have no reason—none—to attribute that effect to Miranda rather than to the many other social, structural and legal circumstances omitted from the model that were changing dramatically at the same time.

IV. In Conclusion

There is one final point to be made. . . .

[I]t is easy to see why people feel nostalgic for the good old 1950s. Clearance rates were well over 60% for most of this period and were as high as 64% or 65% for many of these years. Those who want to restore that world sometimes think they can bring back the days of effective law enforcement by bringing back the law of those days, especially by overruling Miranda. Lawyers and legal scholars are especially prone to think in these "law-centric" terms.

The fallacy in that view is that in 1955, when we had a clearance rate of 64%, we also had 121 police officers for every 100 violent crimes.[61] By 1970, the police personnel figure had fallen from 121 to 45, and today we have only 28 police officers for every 100 violent offenses, less than one-fourth the personnel we deployed in the 1950s.[62] Does anyone really think it makes no difference whether you have 121 officers on hand, or only 28 officers, to handle a workload of 100 reported offenses? Can anyone really think it's because of Miranda that today's police are unable to solve more crimes?

The yearning for the 1950s is understandable, but it is a fantasy to assume that overruling Miranda will move us toward the law enforcement results that police forces of that era were able to achieve. To restore law enforcement to where it was in the 1950s, we have to start making serious improvements in police resources.

All the talk about "terrible Miranda" is therefore worse than just wrong. That kind of talk amounts to picking on a convenient scapegoat and distracting our attention from the real problem.

Obviously, it is smarter politics to blame Miranda and the Warren Court for all our ills than it is to whisper even a single word about raising taxes. But we should not kid ourselves. If we care about victims, and if we care about the quality of our civilization, we have to stop playing games with public fear. We have to insist that criminal justice discussions focus on the issues that can make a difference. Miranda isn't one of them.

Notes

1. Paul G. Cassell, Miranda's Negligible Effect on Law Enforcer: Some Skeptical Observations, 20 HARV. J.L. PUB. POL'Y 327, 334-36 (1997).
2. Miranda v. Arizona, 384 U.S. 436 (1966) (instituting the Miranda warnings).
3. See Cassell, supra note 1, at 336 & n.44.
4. See id. at 345.
5. Paul G. Cassell, All Benefits, No Costs: The Grand Illusion of Miranda's Defenders, 90 Nw. U. L. REV. 1084, 1123 (1996) (emphasis added).
6. See, e.g., Edwards v. Arizona, 451 U.S. 477 (1981) (decided unanimously).
7. Minnesota v. Murphy, 465 U.S. 420 (1984).
8. 113 S. Ct. 1745 (1993).
9. Id. at 1752 (emphasis in original).
10. See Cassell, supra note 1, at 344.
11. The cynics on this subject appear to be far more numerous than the alarmists. See, e.g., GERALD N. ROSENBERG, THE HOLLOW HOPE: CAN COURTS BRING ABOUT SOCIAL CHANGE 326-29 (1991); DAVID SIMON, HOMICIDE: A YEAR ON THE KILLING STREETS 199 (1991).
12. See Stephen J. Schulhofer, Miranda, Practical Effect: Substantial Benefits and Vanishingly Small Social Costs, 90 Nw. U. L. REV. 500, 561-62 (1996).
13. See id., at 501 nn.3-4, 504 nn.9-13, 507 n.23, 559-60 nn.250-252 (1996).
14. See Cassell, supra note 1, at 341-42 & nn.55-60.
15. For example, James Witt's study of an unnamed California city begins with the finding, which Professor Cassell emphasizes, see Cassell, supra note 1, 341-42, that detectives there "were in almost complete agreement . . . that they were getting many fewer confessions." But Witt goes on to report that an empirical study designed to test the accuracy of these impressions found that in fact there was no significant change in the confession rate. See James W. Witt, Non-Coercive Interrogation and the Administration of Criminal Justice: The Impact of Miranda on Police Effectuality, 64 J. CRIM. L. & CRIMINOLOGY 320, 325 (1973); Schulhofer, supra note 12, at 528-30.
16. See Schulhofer, supra note 12.
17. Cassell, supra note 5, at 1109.
18. For a detailed discussion, see Schulhofer, supra note 12, and Stephen J. Schulhofer, Miranda and Clearance Rates, 91 NW. U. L. REV. 278 (1996).
19. See Paul G. Cassell, Miranda's Social Costs: An Empirical Reassessment, 90 NW. U. L. REV. 387, 438 (1996).
20. See Schulhofer, supra note 12, at 507-10.
21. See id., at 524-28; 532-33.
22. See Cassell, supra note 1, at 342 n.61.
23. See Cassell, supra note 19, at 459 & 459 tbl.3.

24. See Schulhofer, supra note 12, at 509 n.28.
25. See Schulhofer, supra note 12.
26. See Cassell, supra note 1, at 330 & nn.17-18.
27. In a critique of Professor Cassell's earlier work, I do note that in five cities the confession rate drop, in comparison to a regime with no warnings at all, was 9.7%, but I stress throughout my article numerous factors that render this figure an unduly inflated estimate of Miranda's causal impact, and I emphasize that "with all necessary qualifications in mind, we find that the properly adjusted attrition rate [due to Miranda] is . . . at most only 0.78%." Schulhofer, supra note 12, at 502 (emphasis in original).
28. Cassell, supra note 5.
29. Id. at 1090-91 n.33.
30. Except as otherwise noted, the data in Figure 1 and in the other Figures presented here are drawn from JAMES ALAN FOX, FORECASTING CRIME DATA: AN ECONOMETRIC ANALYSIS 81-86 (1978). I focus on the period 1950-74 because data for this period are conveniently available in Fox's book, see id., and because developments after 1974 have no bearing on the arguments that Professor Cassell makes about the 1965-69 period. For further discussion of the data underlying the Figures I include here, see Schulhofer, Miranda and Clearance Rates, supra note 18.
31. See Schulhofer, Miranda and Clearance Rates, supra note 18.
32. See Schulhofer, supra note 12; Schulhofer, Miranda and Clearance Rates, supra note 18.
33. See Cassell, supra note 1, at 334 ("Professor Schulhofer singles out rising crime rates during the 1960s as solely responsible for the dramatic decline in clearance rates"); id. at 335 ("Schulhofer points an accusing finger at—and only at—declining clearance capacities.").
34. Id. at 337-38 & fig.2.
35. Cassell, supra note 5, at 1090 (emphasis in original).
36. See Schulhofer, Miranda and Clearance Rates, supra note 18, at 287 & n.19 (noting the "obvious caveat" that "rising crime levels . . . made high clearance totals easier to achieve").
37. Professor Cassell makes much of the point that the match between clearance-rate changes and clearance-capacity changes is not perfect. For example, clearance capacity fell slightly in 1963 and then started falling sharply the year after, but clearance rates rose in 1963 and then declined only slightly for the next two years before starting their precipitous decline in 1966. See Cassell, supra note 1, at 335. Professor Cassell appears to believe that such a discrepancy proves that declining clearance capacity did not hinder police efforts. See id. ("Why didn't the declining capacity hinder police then?"). But it seems at least equally plausible to attribute such lack of perfect congruence to a lag effect, see Schulhofer, Miranda and Clearance Rates, supra note 18, at 292-93, or to the impact of the many other factors that also play a causal role. For example, the sharp rise from 1963 to 1965 in the proportion of violent crime located in smaller cities (where clearance rates are higher) could be part of the reason why clearance rates resisted the decline in clearance capacity during the 1963-65 period. See infra text accompanying notes 42-46.

38. Cassell, supra note 5, at 1091.
39. The problems, in a nutshell, include: Professor Cassell's omission of key variables; failure to disaggregate data where necessary; use of misspecified resource variables; use of a misspecified Miranda variable; use of an inappropriate time period; and failure to consider lag effects and tipping points. For a full discussion and explanation of how these flaws undermine the reliability of the model, see Schulhofer, Miranda and Clearance Rates, supra note 18, at 291-94.
40. See id. at 283-85.
41. It is essential here for readers to understand how a dummy variable works. The dummy variable acts as a catch-all. It puts aside factors that were included separately (like crime rates and unemployment); it then takes all remaining social, structural and legal factors whatsoever, as they stood on average during the period 1950-65, and compares their impact to the impact that such factors had on average during in the period 1967-94. In a time series analysis spanning the period 1950-94, the dummy variable does not simply compare 1965 to 1967; it compares the average state of the world over the entire before-1966 period to the average state of the world over the entire after-1966 period. In a rough way, it amounts to comparing the year 1958 (the approximate midpoint of the 1950-65 period) to the year 1980 (the approximate midpoint of the 1950-65 period). The time trend variable included in Professor Cassell's model will capture the effect of any omitted variables that are changing in a simple linear fashion over the period in question, but non-linear trends could be picked up in the before-after dummy variable instead.
42. Percentages were calculated from FEDERAL BUREAU OF INVESTIGATION, UNIFORM CRIME REPORTS 1954, at 48 tbl.15 (Semiannual Bulletin, vol. 26, no. 1, 1955).
43. Percentages were calculated from FEDERAL BUREAU OF INVESTIGATION, UNIFORM CRIME REPORTS 1969, at 98-99 tbl.12 (1970).
44. See, e.g, id. at vi (stressing population density, community size and numerous other factors essential to interpretation of crime data).
45. See infra Figure 6.
46. Jerome H. Skolnick, JUSTICE WITHOUT TRIAL: LAW ENFORCEMENT IN DEMOCRATIC SOCIETY 164-81 (1966). Skolnick describes one case in which a burglary suspect provided the police with more than 400 "fake" clearances. See id. at 178.
47. See U.S. PRESIDENT'S COMM'N ON LAW ENFORCEMENT AND ADMIN. OF JUSTICE, THE CHALLENGE OF GRIME IN A FREE SOCIETY 106-115 (1967).
48. See id. at 109 (recommending higher standards of education for all police personnel); 114 (recommending that all medium- and large-sized police departments employ a full-time legal advisor); 114-15 (recommending centralized control); 266-69 (noting unreliability of current data and recommending improved record-keeping and information systems).
49. 367 U.S. 643 (1961).
50. 365 U.S. 534 (1961).
51. 373 U.S. 503 (1963).

52. 388 U.S. 218 (1967).
53. 388 U.S. 293 (1967).
54. 392 U.S. 1 (1968).
55. Cassell, supra note 1, at 338.
56. See NATIONAL ACADEMY OF SCIENCES, PANEL ON RESEARCH ON DETERRENT AND INCAPACITATIVE EFFECTS, DETERRENCE AND INCAPACITATION: ESTIMATING THE EFFECTS OF CRIMINAL SANCTIONS ON CRIME RATES 22-50 (1978).
57. See John R. Lott, Jr. & David B. Mustard, Crime, Deterrence, and Right-to-Carry Concealed Handguns, 26 J. LEGAL STUDIES (forthcoming Jan. 1997) (noting a similar problem of heterogeneity even within States); Schulhofer, Miranda and Clearance Rates, supra note 18, at 291.
58. E.g., Lott & Mustard, supra note 58; Isaac Ehrlich, The Deterrent Effect of Capital Punishment: A Question of Life and Death, 65 AM. ECON. REV. (No. 3) 397 (1975); Raymond Atkins & Paul H. Rubin, The Impact of Changing Criminal Procedure on Crime Rates (Oct. 28, 1995) (working paper cited in Cassell, supra note 1, at 335 n.38).
59. NATIONAL ACADEMY OF SCIENCES, supra note 57, at 49.
60. See Schulhofer, Miranda and Clerance Rates, supra note 18, at 291-94.
61. See Schulhofer, Miranda and Clearance Rates, supra note 18, at 288. 64. rd

POSTSCRIPT

Should U.S. Courts Abandon the *Miranda* Rule?

Miranda v. Arizona was a watershed case in U.S. criminal law. First, it was a cornerstone of the Warren Court's "due process revolution." This means that during Earl Warren's tenure as chief justice of the Supreme Court, many of the provisions in the Bill of Rights pertaining to the criminal process were held to be "fundamental" and made binding on state proceedings through the Fourteenth Amendment's due process clause. Second, while some law enforcement officials have maintained that *Miranda* effectively "handcuffed the cops," others assert that it led to increased professionalism among law enforcement officers. States Leonard W. Levy, a prominent Fifth Amendment scholar:

> *Miranda* led to the elimination of police inquisitions and of the third degree; it led too to a better educated and trained police force that relies on the best evidence that can be found to support accusations of crime. Fewer convictions are reversed, and we are all freer because of *Miranda*. . . *Miranda*'s purpose was to eliminate the inherently coercive and inquisitorial atmosphere of the interrogation room and to ensure that any incriminating admissions are made voluntarily. That purpose was the historical heart of the Fifth [Amendment], the basis of its policy.

The question remains, then, should U.S. courts abandon the *Miranda* rule? U.S. District Court Judge Paul M. Cassell argues that *Miranda*'s social costs are significant that this decision places unprecedented shackles on the police. Some of the empirical research on the issue appears to support his position—providing a suspect with the *Miranda* warnings does seem to decrease the likelihood that he or she will make incriminating statements to the police and makes prosecution a more difficult task.

Professor Stephen J. Schulhofer contends, however, that the *Miranda* protections are required by the U.S. Constitution and that the potential damage to prosecution interests is not a sufficient reason to disregard this important constitutional safeguard. Moreover, *Miranda*'s symbolic value is hard to underestimate. It signifies our society's commitment to the spirit of due process and basic fairness in criminal cases.

In the final analysis, the U.S. Supreme Court may have already adopted an effective approach to the issue of whether courts should abandon the *Miranda* rule: maintain the rule in its present form, but recognize certain limited exceptions to the doctrine when a particular case would justify it. This approach may balance society's interest in prosecuting those who have violated its laws with individual due process rights.

Many outstanding resources are available to provide additional information about these topics. See Leonard W. Levy, *Origins of the Fifth Amendment* (Macmillan, 1986); Laurence H. Tribe, *American Constitutional Law*, 2d. ed. (Foundation Press, 1988); and Yale Kamisar, Wayne R. LaFave, Jerold H. Israel, and Nancy J. King, *Modern Criminal Procedure,* 11th ed. (Thomson West, 2005).

Articles discussing the impact of *Miranda v. Arizona* include Daniel S. Nooter, "Is *Missouri v. Seibert* Practicable? Supreme Court Dances the "Two-Step" Around Miranda," *The American Criminal Law Review* (vol. 42, no. 3, 2005); Kimberly A. Crawford, "Civil Liability for Violations of Miranda: The Impact of *Chavez v. Martinez,*" *F.B.I. Law Enforcement Bulletin* (vol. 72, no. 9, 2003); Richard A. Leo, "Questioning the Relevance of Miranda in the Twenty-First Century," *Michigan Law Review* (vol. 99, no 5, 2001); Steven Penney, "Theories of Confession Admissibility: A Historical View," *American Journal of Criminal Law* (vol. 25, no. 2, 1998); Paul G. Cassell and Richard Fowles, "Handcuffing the Cops? A Thirty-Year Perspective on Miranda's Harmful Effects on Law Enforcement," *Stanford Law Review* (vol. 50, no. 4, 1998); George C. Thomas III, "Is Miranda a Real-World Failure? A Plea for More (and Better) Empirical Evidence," *UCLA Law Review* (vol. 43, no. 3, 1996); George C. Thomas III, "Plain Talk about the Miranda Empirical Debate: A 'Steady-State' Theory of Confessions," *UCLA Law Review* (vol. 43, no. 3, 1996); and Paul G. Cassell and Bret S. Hayman, "Police Interrogation in the 1990s: An Empirical Study of the Effects of Miranda," *UCLA Law Review* (vol. 43, no. 3, 1996).

ISSUE 8

Should a Judge Be Permitted to Admit Evidence about an Alleged Rape Victim's History as a Prostitute?

YES: Martha B. Sosman, from Opinion, *Commonwealth v. Richard Harris*, Supreme Judicial Court of Massachusetts (March 24, 2005)

NO: Margaret H. Marshall, from Dissenting Opinion, *Commonwealth v. Richard Harris*, Supreme Judicial Court of Massachusetts (March 24, 2005)

ISSUE SUMMARY

YES: Associate Justice Martha B. Sosman, writing for the Supreme Judicial Court of Massachusetts, asserts that trial judges should have the discretion to admit into evidence an alleged rape victim's past conviction of a crime involving sexual conduct solely for the purpose of impeaching her credibility.

NO: Chief Justice Margaret H. Marshall, in a dissenting opinion, contends that giving trial judges the discretion to admit evidence of a past conviction of a crime involving sexual conduct is contrary to the intent and spirit of the state's rape shield law.

Rape is one of the most heinous crimes imaginable. To paraphrase a recent conversation with a female colleague who has counseled the victims of rape: "Rape is a violation of your innermost person, a crime against your personhood. If there is anything in this world that you should have a right to keep completely private, it is your own body; if that right to self-determination is violated the world becomes a place of confusion and inner turmoil; it's difficult to ever return to a place of personal safety and security."

Only relatively recently did the U.S. legal system truly begin to recognize the traumatic nature of the crime of rape and the impact it has on its victims. In fact, until the advent of rape-shield laws, the victims of rape were effectively put on trial themselves—sometimes callous defense attorneys would call into question the victim's moral character and reputation. In practice, although the victim's sexual intercourse with persons other than the defendant was inadmissible, this type of questioning was designed to show that the victim had engaged in past promiscuous behavior and that this fact somehow made it more likely that she had lied about the incident in the case at hand.

Rape shield laws, however, were developed in the 1970s to address these problems. In fact, a number of states have broadened the coverage of their rape shield laws to include other types of crimes as well. For example, the Massachusetts Rape Shield statute, which was at issue in *Commonwealth v. Harris*, applies to cases charging rape or aggravated rape, assault with intent to rape, indecent assault and battery, rape of a child, rape of a child by force, assault with intent to rape a child, indecent assault and battery on a child, and indecent assault and battery on a mentally retarded person.

Rape shield laws provide generally that evidence of a victim's "reputation for unchastity," which was previously admissible and viewed as relevant to the issue of consent, is now irrelevant. Most states have based their rules of evidence on the Federal Rules. The rape shield law used in the federal courts, FRE 412, provides in relevant part:

> (a) **Evidence generally inadmissible.**
> The following evidence is not admissible in any civil or criminal proceeding involving alleged sexual misconduct except as provided in subdivisions (b) and (c):
> (1) Evidence offered to prove that any alleged victim engaged in other sexual behavior.
> (2) Evidence offered to prove any alleged victim's sexual predisposition.
>
> **(b) Exceptions.**
> (1) In a criminal case, the following evidence is admissible, if otherwise admissible under these rules:
> a. evidence of specific instances of sexual behavior by the alleged victim offered to prove that a person other than the accused was the source of semen, injury, or other physical evidence;
> b. evidence of specific instances of sexual behavior by the alleged victim with respect to the person accused of the sexual misconduct offered by the accused to prove consent or by the prosecution; and
> c. evidence the exclusion of which would violate the constitutional rights of the defendant.

After reading this statute, do you think it is fair? Justice Sosman, writing the majority opinion for the Court, asserts that trial judges should have the discretion to admit into evidence an alleged rape victim's past conviction of a crime involving sexual conduct solely for the purpose of impeaching her credibility. Chief Justice Marshall, however, contends that giving trial judges the discretion to admit such evidence is contrary to the intent and spirit of the state's rape shield law.

Martha B. Sosman

Opinion, *Commonwealth v. Richard Harris*

The defendant was convicted of aggravated rape (two indictments), kidnapping, intimidation of a witness, assault and battery, assault and battery on a public employee, and resisting arrest. On appeal, he contends that the judge erred in ruling that he had no discretion to admit impeachment evidence that the complaining witness had been convicted as a common nightwalker. The defendant thus asks us to revisit whether the rape-shield statute precludes introduction of convictions of the complaining witness under . . . if the convictions are for sex-related offenses, a question addressed but left unresolved by an equally divided court in Commonwealth v. Houston. We conclude that it is within the judge's discretion to admit evidence of such convictions pursuant to G.L., but that the exercise of that discretion must take into consideration the objectives of the rape-shield statute. As such, the judge below erred in failing to exercise discretion when ruling on the defendant's request to introduce the complainant's conviction as a common nightwalker.

The defendant also alleges error in the prosecutor's closing argument. Knowing that the rape-shield statute had precluded the defendant from introducing any evidence of the complaining witness's history of prostitution, the prosecutor attacked the defendant's theory of consensual sexual intercourse with a prostitute by arguing that there was no evidence that the complaining witness was a prostitute. We agree with the defendant that the prosecutor's argument was improper, and that it created a substantial risk of a miscarriage of justice. We therefore vacate the convictions of aggravated rape, kidnapping, intimidation of a witness, and assault and battery, and remand those indictments for a new trial.

1. Facts. The evidence at trial was as follows. At approximately 11 P.M. on January 22, 2002, the complainant's boy friend left her by herself at a bar in Lowell. The complainant was a regular customer at that establishment. The defendant, whom she did not know, was already in the bar when she arrived. The defendant approached the complainant and spoke to her briefly, but she ignored him. At approximately 12:30 A.M., the complainant called her boy friend to pick her up, waited inside the bar for a few minutes, and then went outside to wait for her ride.

Opinion of the Supreme Judicial Court of Massachusetts: Commonwealth vs. Richard Harris, October 5, 2004. Court case citations and notes omitted.

The defendant followed her out of the bar, grabbed her by the arm, and pulled her across the street. He made a remark that he was "loaded," which she took to mean that he had a gun. Once across the street, the defendant forced her down a stairwell, grabbed the back of her head, and pushed her against the wall. He proceeded to rape her twice, penetrating her both vaginally and anally. At some point during the encounter, he forced her to her knees. The defendant warned her not to "rat" on him, and threatened to kill her if she did. Some noise distracted the defendant momentarily, and the complainant was able to break free. Crying, she ran up the stairs and back toward the bar, with the defendant in pursuit. A witness nearby telephoned the police, reporting that a woman was screaming and running down the street, with a man chasing and trying to strike her.

The complainant entered the bar, in a distraught state, followed by the defendant, who acted "nonchalant[]." The complainant told the bartender that she had been raped. Overhearing the complainant's accusation of rape, the defendant said that he "didn't do nothing." He then went over to the pool tables and resumed apparently normal conversation with other patrons. The police arrived in response to the 911 call. The complainant told one of the officers that the defendant had raped her, and pointed the defendant out to him. When the officer asked the defendant to come outside, the defendant replied that he "didn't do nothing wrong" and refused to accompany the officer. While being placed under arrest, the defendant struggled, biting one of the officers. He was eventually subdued with some form of pepper spray.

The complainant was taken to a hospital. She showed the nurse bruises on her knees and a clump of hair (which she said the defendant had pulled from her head). Subsequent testing of the rape kit evidence yielded deoxyribonucleic acid (DNA) samples consistent with the defendant's DNA.

The defendant's version of events was that the complainant was a prostitute who had falsely accused him of rape when he had been unable to pay her the agreed price for consensual intercourse. He testified that he had arrived at the bar around 9:30 P.M. At some point, he had gone over to the complainant and offered to buy her a drink. She declined, as she already had a beer but asked him if he "wanted a date," which he understood to be an offer of sex in exchange for money. She told him that she would be leaving after she finished her beer and that they would meet outside. Later on, when the complainant headed to the door to leave, she turned and winked at him, which he understood as the signal to follow her. After a brief discussion about where they could go, they proceeded across the street and down the stairwell. He inquired about price, and the complainant told him that her price depended on "what [he] wanted." He indicated that he wanted oral sex, and she got down on her knees and began to perform oral sex on him. However, when he changed his mind and wanted intercourse, she told him that the price would be higher. He agreed, and they proceeded to engage in vaginal and anal intercourse, with the complainant on her hands and knees. Afterward, when the complainant demanded payment, the defendant gave her the small amount of money he had left in his pocket and told her that he would have to owe her the rest. A loud argument ensued, and the complainant headed back toward the bar, with the defendant following her, both of them yelling and screaming. Back in the bar, when he heard the complainant saying that she had been raped, he told the bartender that he had not raped her and that she was just angry because she had not been paid. He admitted struggling with the officers (and that he had bitten one of them) when they later arrested him. He also claimed that, when the arresting officer told him he was being arrested for rape, he had explained again that the complainant was just angry because she had not been paid.

2. Discussion. a. Impeachment of the complainant by prior conviction as a common nightwalker. Prior to trial, the Commonwealth filed a motion, seeking to exclude the complainant's "sexual history," including the fact that she had "been convicted of prostitution in the past." The defendant opposed the motion, arguing that he should be allowed to introduce the complainant's prior convictions for the purpose of impeaching her. On May 24, 2002, the complainant had been convicted of being a common nightwalker, for which a fine of one hundred dollars had been imposed. She also had two earlier convictions of common nightwalking in 1999 and 2001, and had been placed on probation for both of those offenses. The judge allowed the Commonwealth's motion with respect to the common nightwalker convictions, on the ground that they were precluded by the rape-shield statute. He also noted that, irrespective of the rape-shield statute, only one of the common nightwalking convictions (the 2002 conviction that resulted in a fine) would satisfy the prerequisites for introduction. He later articulated the view that in light of the rape-shield statute, he was required to exclude that conviction, and that he had exercised no discretion in deciding to exclude it. He did allow the defendant to impeach the complainant with a prior conviction of a nonsexual offense, specifically, a 1997 conviction of larceny of property over $250.

On appeal, the defendant contends that a judge should have discretion to admit evidence of a complaining witness's conviction of a prior sexual offense for purposes of impeaching that witness, notwithstanding the rape-shield statute's prohibition against admitting evidence of a sexual assault victim's "sexual conduct." The court identified the potential conflict between these two statutes in Commonwealth v. Joyce, but declined to decide the question. The court confronted the issue directly in Houston, but were equally divided as to how the competing requirements of the two statutes should be resolved.

The parties have briefed extensively their respective interpretations of Houston, with varying views as to how the procedural history and status of that case should have caused the judge to follow one or the other of the concurring opinions. We need not resolve the arguments about how Houston itself should have been applied, as we are prepared to decide the issue that divided the court in Houston. We agree with the reasoning of the concurring opinions of Justice Lynch and Justice Cowin, and hold that a judge has discretion to allow impeachment of a sexual assault complainant by prior convictions of sexual offenses, but that in exercising that discretion, the purposes of the rape-shield statute should be considered.

We begin with a brief overview of the two statutes involved. A witness's prior criminal conviction "may be shown to affect [the witness's] credibility." The theory is that a witness's "earlier disregard for the law may suggest to the fact finder similar disregard for the courtroom oath. "One who has been convicted of crime is presumed to be less worthy of belief than one who has not been so convicted." Thus, while we do not allow a witness to be impeached by evidence of prior bad acts, if those bad acts have resulted in a conviction, the conviction itself may be admissible under § 21.

In order to be admissible for impeachment purposes, the convictions in question must meet specific requirements based on the degree of the offense (felony or misdemeanor), the nature of the disposition, and the timing and sequence of the convictions. Even where a particular conviction meets those requirements, a judge has discretion to exclude evidence of the conviction. In the exercise of that discretion, the judge is to consider whether the "danger of unfair prejudice outweighs the probative value of the evidence of a prior conviction for the purposes of impeachment." Where the judge decides to allow introduction of a prior conviction under § 21, the potential prejudice may be ameliorated by an appropriate limiting instruction.

The rape-shield statute is applicable to proceedings involving certain sexual offenses. The statute precludes admission of evidence of a victim's "reputation" with respect to "sexual conduct," as well as "evidence of specific instances of a victim's sexual conduct . . . ." The statute creates two exceptions to that prohibition, allowing "evidence of the victim's sexual conduct with the defendant or evidence of recent conduct of the victim alleged to be the cause of any physical feature, characteristic, or condition of the victim." In order for a defendant to introduce such evidence pursuant to either of those exceptions, the judge must first hold a hearing on the defendant's motion and offer of proof, and make a finding that "the weight and relevancy of said evidence is sufficient to outweigh its prejudicial effect to the victim." In addition to the exceptions set forth in the statute, we have ruled that a defendant may introduce evidence of the complaining witness's sexual conduct where that conduct is relevant to the complainant's bias or motive to fabricate. However, even when offered to show bias or motive to lie, the judge should exercise discretion with respect to the introduction of such evidence, bearing in mind "the important policies underlying the rape-shield statute."

The rape-shield statute comports with the common-law rule that a complainant's sexual intercourse with persons other than the defendant is inadmissible. The innovation in the rape-shield statute was not its prohibition of evidence pertaining to "specific instances" of a complainant's sexual conduct, as that evidence was already precluded at common law. Rather, what the statute added was the prohibition of evidence of the complainant's "reputation" in such matters. A complainant's "reputation for unchastity" had been admissible at common law and had been viewed as probative of the complainant's consent. The common-law rule, which prohibits evidence of specific instances of sexual conduct while allowing "reputation" evidence on the same subject, was the product of a strong common-law tradition that allowed proof of character to be introduced solely by means of "reputation" evidence. Under that approach, a rape complainant's "unchaste character" was relevant and could be shown by evidence of her reputation, but that character could not be shown by introducing evidence of, for example, a specific adulterous affair. The rape-shield statute operates to exclude all such evidence, whether in the form of "specific instances" of sexual conduct or in the form of "reputation" evidence.

The common-law rule excluding evidence of the complainant's specific sexual conduct with others, and the rape-shield statute that later codified that aspect of the common-law rule, was premised on the fact that "such evidence has little probative value on the issue of consent." The rape-shield statute also prevents an array of adverse effects on the complaining witness and the process of the trial. Introduction of evidence concerning the complainant's sexual past "would prolong the trial and divert the attention of the trier of fact from the alleged criminal acts of the defendant." In addition, "inquiries into the sexual history of the rape complainant chills her willingness to testify." "Rape-shield statutes are 'aimed at eliminating a common defense strategy of trying the complaining witness rather than the defendant. The result of this strategy was harassment and further humiliation of the victim as well as discouraging victims of rape from reporting the crimes to law enforcement authorities.'"

We now confront the issue of how to harmonize these two statutes when the prior conviction that the defendant seeks to introduce for impeachment purposes under § 21 is for a sexual offense, and thus overlaps with the § 21B prohibition against introduction of the complaining witness's "sexual conduct."

As we attempt to harmonize these statutes, it is not for us to determine which of them is more weighty or worthwhile and to allow that statute to dominate. Instead, we must seek to apply them in a manner that, to the greatest extent possible, serves the policies underlying both. Resort to the sound exercise of the trial judge's discretion, which is already a prerequisite to any introduction of prior convictions as impeachment evidence under § 21, allows for consideration of the purposes of both statutes. This approach reconciles the competing interests of the two statutes by carving out an extremely narrow exception to § 21B, an exception that will be allowed only where the sexual conduct in question has led to a criminal conviction, the conviction in turn meets all the technical requirements of § 21, and the judge is satisfied that the probative value of the conviction for purposes of impeaching the complainant outweighs the prejudice to the Commonwealth and the complainant. The alternative, a complete prohibition on the impeachment use of convictions of any sex-related offense (a prohibition that would not be limited to convictions involving prostitution), would constitute a much larger and totally inflexible exception to § 21. We have neither "express words" nor a "clear implication" suggesting that § 21B was intended to supersede § 21 in that complete fashion.

When the prior conviction is of a sexual offense and is being offered to impeach the complaining witness in a sexual assault case, the judge's consideration of the "prejudicial effect" of introducing the conviction should take into account important policies underlying the rape-shield statute.[1] The judge should thus consider the potential that the jury may misuse the conviction of a sexual offense as indicative of the complaining witness's consent, and the risk that the complaining witness may be subjected to needless humiliation.[2] Under today's ruling, the rape-shield statute remains as an important protection for rape victims, including those who happen to be prostitutes—neither the facts surrounding their sexual conduct nor their reputation in such matters is admissible, and, even if a complainant's prior conviction of prostitution satisfies all the technical prerequisites of § 21, the judge must consider the policies to be promoted by the rape-shield statute and may exclude the conviction due to those policy considerations. We see no reason to fear that trial judges will be insensitive to these concerns, that they will exercise their discretion in ways that will "eviscerate[]" the rape-shield statute, or that they will be heedless of the particular prejudice at issue where the complainant's prior conviction is related to prostitution.

The judge below thus erred in declining to exercise any discretion when ruling on the Commonwealth's motion in limine. That the exercise of discretion could, had it been undertaken, permissibly have resulted in the same decision to exclude the conviction does not necessarily insulate the error from reversal. The Commonwealth argues, with considerable force, that the error here was harmless, as the defendant was allowed to introduce the complainant's conviction of a nonsexual offense (her 1997 conviction of larceny of property over $250), thereby permitting him this method of impeachment without trenching on the concerns underlying the rape-shield statute. While a jury's improper use of the complainant's common nightwalker conviction might have been beneficial to the defendant, there is little if any reason to believe that its proper impeachment value alone would have had any effect on the jury's verdict. The defendant argues, however, that the common nightwalker conviction from 2002 was recent, whereas the 1997 larceny conviction was six years old by the time of trial, and that the impeachment power of two convictions combined would be greater than the power of a single, and somewhat old, offense. We need not resolve the parties' arguments with respect to whether this error alone would require reversal, as, for the reasons discussed below, there was also error in the prosecutor's closing argument raising a substantial risk of a miscarriage of justice and necessitating a new trial.

b. Prosecutor's closing argument. During closing argument, the prosecutor refuted the defense theory of the case by pointing out that there was no evidence that the complaining witness was a prostitute. She further suggested that the complainant was not a prostitute because a prostitute would have known enough to insist on payment in advance and would have had more than a single customer on the night in question. Leading into this argument, the prosecutor also suggested that the complainant's demeanor on the stand (which had been alluded to during the defense closing) was the product of being falsely accused of being a prostitute. There was no objection. On appeal, the defendant contends that the prosecutor's improper exploitation of the exclusion of evidence under the rape-shield statute gave rise to a substantial risk of a miscarriage of justice. We agree.

Under the rape-shield statute, the defendant was precluded from introducing any evidence of the complainant's history of prostitution. The Commonwealth erroneously suggests that the only evidence that had been excluded under the rape-shield statute was the 2002 common nightwalker conviction that the defendant sought to introduce as impeachment evidence. While that was the sole evidence the defendant sought to introduce, it was not the entirety of the evidence that would have been available to the defendant, but for the prohibition codified in the rape-shield statute. At a minimum, the three Lowell District Court convictions of common nightwalking (the most recent of which stemmed from an arrest just two weeks after the alleged rape) would have given defense counsel a good faith basis to ask the complainant about her experience as a prostitute in the area. Fully cognizant of the limitations imposed by the rape-shield statute (as indicated by the prior proceedings on the motion in limine), defense counsel had appropriately refrained from introducing evidence of or alluding to the complainant's history of prostitution.

It was improper for the prosecutor to suggest to the jury that the absence of any evidence that the complainant engaged in prostitution meant that she was not a prostitute. The Commonwealth contends that all the prosecutor was referring to was the absence of any evidence that the complainant was engaged in prostitution "on the night in question." While some of the argument did include references to the complainant's behavior "this night," the context, as reasonably understood by the jury, went beyond the confines of that specific night. At the outset, the prosecutor sought to explain the complainant's demeanor on the stand by invoking a sense of righteous indignation that she would be called a prostitute, suggesting to the jury that what they had seen was an emotional reaction to the ostensible falsity of that offensive label. At the time she made that argument, the prosecutor knew that the label was in fact accurate, and that prosecutors in her own office had proved its accuracy on three separate occasions. Immediately thereafter, the prosecutor asked the jury "what evidence" they had before them that would indicate that the complainant was a prostitute, thereby offering an open invitation to consider the absence of evidence on the entire subject. The prosecutor's next line of argument, the implausibility that a prostitute would fail to ask for payment in advance, was legitimately linked to the specific events of that night, but was phrased in a way that, following on the heels of the previous improper argument, suggested to the jury that the complainant could not have been a prostitute because no experienced prostitute would conduct business that way. Similarly, the references to the complainant's remaining at the bar (without having been seen going in and out) would properly relate to the night in question, but that proper argument would take on further meaning from the prior improper argument—it was but one example of the lack of any evidence to show that the complainant engaged in prostitution at all. The over-all message to the jury from this entire line of argument was that the defendant's testimony concerning the incident was the only evidence they had of the complainant's prostitution and that, in the absence of any other evidence to corroborate his claim that she was a prostitute, the defense theory was not worthy of belief.

Counsel may not, in closing, "exploit[] the absence of evidence that had been excluded at his request." Such exploitation of absent, excluded evidence is "fundamentally unfair" and "reprehensible." As illustrated by the Commonwealth's motion, the Commonwealth objected to introduction of any evidence that would link the complainant to prior acts of prostitution. Having succeeded in excluding all such evidence, the prosecutor could not then ask the jury to infer that the absence of such evidence meant that the complainant could not be a prostitute. The argument was improper. . . .

3. Conclusion. For the foregoing reasons, the convictions of assault and battery on a public employee and resisting arrest are affirmed. The remaining convictions are reversed, the verdicts set aside, and the matter is remanded for a new trial. On retrial, if the defendant seeks to impeach the complainant with evidence of a prior conviction of a sex-related offense, the judge should exercise discretion with respect to the admission or exclusion of that impeachment evidence under G. L. c. 233, § 21, and that exercise of discretion should include consideration of the purposes underlying the rape-shield statute, G. L. c. 233, § 21B.

Notes

1. We note that certain policies underlying the rape-shield statute are not at issue in the admission of prior convictions under § 21. With respect to evidence of prior convictions, there is no potential that such evidence will "prolong the trial" by a diversion into the prior incidents, nor that the witness will be required to relate any embarrassing details of those incidents. When a conviction is introduced under § 21, all that is introduced is the fact of the conviction—neither side may seek to introduce the particulars of how the offense was committed or the circumstances surrounding it. Instead, the evidence of prior convictions is extremely brief and is introduced in almost clinical fashion, usually just a single question asking the witness to acknowledge the date, the court, and the technical term for the offense committed. Allowing defense counsel to introduce a complainant's prior conviction of a sex-related offense does not create an effective opportunity to divert the jury's attention or to make the complainant run an embarrassing gauntlet of questions about her sex life.

   Nor does the introduction of a witness's conviction of a sexual offense constitute an "invasion[] of privacy." Ordinarily, delving into "specific instances" of a witness's sexual conduct would unquestionably intrude on intimate aspects of the witness's private life, but if that sexual conduct is itself a violation of the criminal laws and has resulted in a criminal conviction, it is no longer a "private" matter. The conviction, resting on an accusation that has been made publicly and either proved or admitted in open court, is instead a matter of public record.

2. The judge should also consider whether the defendant has available other impeachment evidence, in particular, whether there are other convictions of nonsexual offenses that may be used to impeach the complainant. And, as is customary, if the prior conviction is admitted in evidence under § 21, an appropriate limiting instruction should be given. Id. We reject the argument that a limiting instruction will be ineffective. We have long held that a testifying defendant may be impeached with prior convictions, including convictions of offenses similar to the offense being tried, and we rely on limiting instructions to cure the otherwise obvious prejudice in such situations. If we rely on limiting instructions to guarantee a defendant a fair trial despite the jury's awareness of the defendant's criminal past, we can rely on them to guarantee the Commonwealth and the complainant a fair trial despite the jury's awareness of the complainant's criminal past.

NO 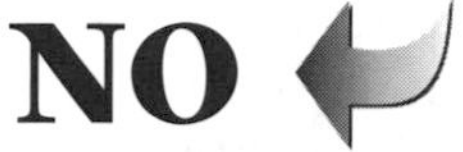

Margaret H. Marshall

Dissenting Opinion, Commonwealth v. Richard Harris

I concur with the court's conclusion that the defendant is entitled to a new trial because the prosecutor's closing argument was improper. I respectfully dissent from so much of the court's opinion as gives a trial judge discretion to admit in evidence a rape complainant's past conviction of a crime involving sexual conduct solely for the purpose of impeaching her credibility.

In Commonwealth v. Houston, I noted that "the Commonwealth's legitimate interest in protecting rape victims sets an important limit on a judge's discretionary authority to admit prior convictions submitted generally to impeach a complainant witness." It has always done so, both before and after the enactment of the general impeachment statute, G. L. c. 233, § 21, and its predecessor statutes.

Today, the court concludes that juries will be permitted to infer that an alleged rape victim is more likely to be fabricating an accusation of rape because she has been convicted of a crime involving sexual conduct, such as being a "common nightwalker." The court reasons that the Legislature, in enacting the rape-shield statute, gave no "clear implication" that it intended to prohibit such use of an alleged rape victim's past conviction. I disagree. The legislative intent to that effect could not be more clear. Moreover, the rape-shield statute is a specific statute, adopted later in time than the impeachment statute, and with a clear purpose. To the extent that any provision of the 1977 rape-shield statute conflicts with the Nineteenth Century general impeachment statute, well-settled principles of statutory construction require that the more recent statute be given full effect.

As to legislative history, when the rape-shield statute was under consideration in 1977, the Legislature affirmatively chose not to permit impeachment of alleged rape victims by evidence of sexual conduct convictions. For more than one century it had been the established law of this Commonwealth that the credibility of an alleged rape victim may not be challenged simply because she had previously engaged in specific acts of sexual intercourse. The explanation for our rule was straightforward: "the victim's consent to [sexual] intercourse with one man does not imply her consent in the case of another." The common law had been reaffirmed by this court just four months before enact-

Opinion of the Supreme Judicial Court of Massachusetts: Commonwealth vs. Richard Harris, October 5, 2004. Court case citations and notes omitted.

ment of the rape-shield statute, so there was no question as to its continued vitality. When the common-law evidentiary rule prohibiting the introduction of "evidence of instances of prior [sexual] intercourse with other persons," was codified by the Legislature in the 1977 rape-shield statute, the Legislature included within that prohibition all "specific instances" of sexual conduct. It did not create any exception for those "instances" of sexual conduct evidenced by a rape victim's conviction. To the contrary, the Legislature considered, but rejected, several bills that would have permitted a rape complainant to be impeached by a conviction of prostitution or other criminal sexual conduct.

Specifically, in early 1977, the Senate referred to its Committee on the Judiciary four "rape-shield" bills. Three of the bills had originated in the House; all three contained an exception to the rape-shield provisions that would have permitted impeachment of a rape complainant by her prior convictions. The fourth bill, which had originated in the Senate, contained no such exception. The subsequently enacted statute did not include the exceptions contained in each of the three House bills that would have permitted rape complainants to be impeached by their prior convictions.

The Legislature's decision not to enact the proposed House bills is convincing, if not conclusive, evidence of legislative intent. Contrary to the court's reasoning, ante at, the "signal on the subject" from the Legislature is indeed clear: it had before it three bills that would permit impeachment of a complaining witness with a prior conviction of sexual conduct. It rejected all three in favor of a statute that does not permit impeachment by a criminal sexual conduct conviction. The court disregards this clear legislative choice. It creates an exception to the scope of rape-shield statute that the Legislature rejected, substituting its judgment for that of the Legislature on an important matter of social policy. This it may not do. The rape-shield statute should be enforced to exclude the evidence, as the Legislature intended.

The Legislature's 1977 decision not to permit impeachment of an alleged rape victim by a prostitution conviction, for example, was entirely reasonable. In the years leading up to the enactment of the rape-shield statute, reports had described the difficulty of obtaining convictions in rape cases because of court room prejudice against alleged rape victims. Prejudice or disbelief occurs with particular intensity when the complainant is a prostitute, and courts have long sought means to minimize jury bias against prostitutes. Prostitutes are frequent victims of rape. Yet societal beliefs persist that prostitutes cannot be raped, or that they are not harmed by rape, or that they somehow deserve to be raped. In enacting the rape-shield statute, the Legislature could well have recognized that these prejudices outweighed the little—or nonexistent—probative value of a sexual conduct conviction in determining a rape complainant's credibility. The likelihood of a jury impermissibly using such evidence would outweigh almost inevitably any modicum of impeachment value such a conviction might have. The Legislature considered but decided not to reject the "long held view" that prostitution (or evidence of other sexual conduct) simply is not relevant to credibility.

General Laws c. 233, § 21, permits the use of a prior conviction solely "to affect [the witness's] credibility." In a case such as this, where the witness is a rape complainant who claims lack of consent, the issue of her credibility mirrors precisely the issue of her consent. The law is settled that a rape complainant's prior instances of sexual conduct are not admissible to prove consent to sexual intercourse. But if a judge may now permit evidence of an alleged rape victim's prior conviction of criminal sexual conduct to be introduced to impeach her credibility, i.e., to show that she is fabricating her testimony to the effect that she did not consent to sexual intercourse, that evidentiary rule is vitiated. And, while in any particular case the evidence of a prior conviction of prostitution or some other sexual offense may be "extremely brief," I cannot regard introduction of that evidence as "almost clinical." Courts have long recognized the difficulty in persuading juries that prostitutes are the victims of rape. Any evidence that reinforces juror prejudice may be decisive.

Established canons of statutory construction reinforce this conclusion. Application of those principles here is not "problematic," as the court suggests, ante at, nor would application be merely "mechanical[]." When a new provision conflicts with a prior statute, the new provision, as the last expression of the Legislature, controls." The evidence at issue in this case—conviction of being a common nightwalker—is an "instance[] of a victim's sexual conduct" inadmissible under the precise terms of the rape-shield statute. But the general impeachment statute, G. L. c. 233, § 21, would permit a judge to admit the conviction in evidence to impeach the complainant. The rape-shield statute, as the more recent expression of the Legislature's intent, must control so as to exclude the evidence. Moreover, when the provisions of two statutes are in conflict, "the more specific provision, particularly where it has been enacted subsequent to a more general rule, applies over the general rule."

There is no need to create artificial constraints —discussing the need to harmonize and alluding to possible implied repeal, to arrive at the result. The rape-shield statute requires that the evidence be excluded. The court's contrary conclusion eviscerates the statute, subverts the Legislature's intent to protect rape victims, and leaves the most vulnerable of victims, almost always women, subject to being put on trial themselves for conduct the Legislature and this court has deemed irrelevant to a jury's consideration. I respectfully dissent.

POSTSCRIPT

Should a Judge Be Permitted to Admit Evidence about an Alleged Rape Victim's History as a Prostitute?

Do you recall the Kobe Bryant rape scandal? In the circumstances of that case, the trial judge ruled admissible evidence indicating that the victim had sexual intercourse with another individual the day after she was allegedly raped by Kobe Bryant. The victim had sustained bruises to her pelvic area that she alleged to have been caused by Bryant. Please recall that rape shield laws prohibit evidence to prove that an alleged victim engaged in other sexual behavior or to prove her sexual predisposition *except* to prove that a person other than the accused was the source of injury. Once the trial judge had made the decision to admit the evidence that the alleged victim had sexual intercourse with someone else the day after she was allegedly raped by Bryant, would you agree that the case was essentially finished? Would there have been any way that the prosecution could have obtained a guilty verdict, regardless of whether Bryant had actually committed the offense? Or, regardless of the judge's instructions that this evidence should be used only to decide the issue of who caused the victim's injuries, would a juror have been tempted to think: "What woman would have had sexual intercourse with another man the day after she was raped?" "These accusations must be false." Is this fair to the victims of rape?

After reading *Commonwealth v. Harris,* how do you feel about rape shield laws? Should a trial judge be able to admit evidence of an alleged rape victim's history as a prostitute? Suppose you were sitting on a jury in a rape case and the defense presented evidence that the accuser had formerly worked as a prostitute. Assume further that the theory of the case put forth by the defense is that the reason the victim has brought rape charges is that the accused refused to pay for the services he received. Would these facts by themselves raise a reasonable doubt in your mind as to the defendant's guilt? If so, would this effectively mean that rapists could victimize former prostitutes with virtual impunity? These are difficult questions. Do you believe that allowing the defense in a rape trial to admit this type of evidence is fair to the victims of this heinous crime?

Fortunately, there are excellent additional resources that can shed light on the issues debated in this section. See Susan Estrich, *Real Rape: How the Legal System Victimizes Women Who Say No* (Harvard University Press, 1987); Christopher B. Mueller and Laird C. Kirkpatrick, *Evidence Under the Rules: Text, Cases, and Problems* (Little, Brown and Company, 1988); Corey Rayburn, "Better Dean Than R(ap)ed? The Patriarchal Rhetoric Driving Capital Rape

Statutes," *St. John's Law Review* (vol. 78, no. 4, 2004); Michelle J. Anderson, "Time to Reform Rape Shield Laws," *Criminal Justice* (vol.19, no. 2, 2004); Cathy Young, "Kobe's Rights," *Reason* (vol. 35, no. 8, 2004); Jane H. Aiken, "Protecting Plaintiff's Sexual Pasts: Coping with Preconceptions Through Discretion," *Emory Law Journal* (vol. 51, no. 2, 2002); J.R. Spencer, "'Rape Shields' and the Right to a Fair Trial," *Cambridge Law Journal* (vol. 60, no. 3, 2001); Cassia Spohn and David Holleran, "Prosecuting Sexual Assault: A Comparison of Charging Decisions in Sexual Assault Cases involving Strangers, Acquaintances, and Intimate Partners," *Justice Quarterly* (vol. 18, no. 3, 2001); Ian Ayres and Katharine K. Baker, "A Separate Crime of Reckless Sex," *The University of Chicago Law Review* (vol. 72, no. 2, 2005); Kathryn M. Carney, "Rape: The Paradigmatic Hate Crime," *St. John's Law Review* (vol. 75, no. 2, 2001); George E. Panichas, "Rape, Autonomy, and Consent," *Law & Society Review* (vol. 35, no. 1, 2001); and Elizabeth J. Kramer, "When Men Are Victims: Applying Rape Shield Laws to Male Same-Sex Rape," *New York University Law Review,* (vol. 73, no. 1, 1998).

On the Internet . . .

Academy of Criminal Justice Sciences

This site is an excellent resource for a wide variety of information about the U.S. justice system. It provides links to a number of resources that consider various aspects of justice system processes, including the police, the courts, punishment, and corrections.

http://www.acjs.org/

American Society of Criminology

An excellent starting point for a study of all aspects of criminology and criminal justice, this page provides links to sites on criminal justice in general, international criminal justice, juvenile justice, the courts, the police, and the government.

http://www.asc41.com/

National Criminal Justice Reference Service (NCJRS)

This very comprehensive database provides a wealth of information about justice system processes. Topics include corrections, courts, crime prevention, crime rates, drugs, the criminal justice system, juvenile justice, law enforcement, and the victims of crime. It also provides links to NCJRS-sponsored research on virtually every aspect of the criminal justice system.

http://www.ncjrs.org/

National Crime Victims Research and Treatment Center

This site, sponsored by the National Crime Victims Research and Treatment Center of the Medical University of South Carolina, provides excellent links to resources focusing on victimization and various criminological treatment options.

http://www.musc.edu/cvc/

PART 3

Processional Issues

Every facet of the U.S. justice system is influenced by process and procedures, which have a tremendous influence on the outcomes of criminal cases and the public's confidence in the legal system. They also have a tremendous impact on the individuals participating in the legal process: defendants, victims, witnesses, police officers, judges, prosecutors, defense attorneys, and the public. This section focuses on justice system issues that implicate process and procedure and influence the quality of justice in our legal system.

ISSUE 9

Should the United States Abolish Plea Bargaining in Criminal Cases?

YES: Jeff Palmer, from "Abolishing Plea Bargaining: An End to the Same Old Song and Dance," *American Journal of Criminal Law* (Summer 1999)

NO: Douglas D. Guidorizzi, from "Should We Really 'Ban' Plea Bargaining? The Core Concerns of Plea Bargaining Critics," *Emory Law Journal* (Spring 1998)

ISSUE SUMMARY

YES: Jeff Palmer argues that plea bargaining must be abolished in order to reinstate justice in the United States and restore the public's confidence in the criminal justice system.

NO: Attorney Douglas D. Guidorizzi asserts that accepting plea bargaining as a natural feature of the adversarial system allows the criticisms of the practice to be addressed with tailored reforms. Moreover, he believes that the corruption of institutional values associated with plea bargaining can be avoided by eliminating the bargaining aspect of this practice.

Those of you who grew up during the 1970s and 1980s may remember a television show titled "Let's Make a Deal." Selected contestants would exchange various gag trinkets with the show's host, Monty Hall, for valuable prizes.

Plea bargaining is a justice system practice that also involves an exchange of benefits. Defendants agree to plead guilty to criminal charges in exchange for some favorable action by the state. For example, the prosecution may agree to reduce a defendant's charges, recommend a particular sentence, or to forego additional opportunities for prosecution.

A plea bargain is essentially a contract between the prosecution and the defendant that must be honored by both parties. If a defendant breaches a plea agreement, the prosecution is free to bring any charges it is able to sustain, including more serious charges than those discussed during plea negotiations. If the prosecution breaches a plea agreement, a defendant is free to withdraw the guilty plea and proceed to trial.

Prosecutors have great discretion in the plea bargaining process. They will often threaten to file more serious criminal charges against a defendant if he or she does not plead guilty. The Supreme Court has upheld such tactics, provided that the threatened charges are supported by probable cause.

Normally, a trial judge will comply with a plea agreement between a defendant and the prosecution. Sometimes, however, a judge will reject a plea bargain agreement. When this occurs, a defendant is free to withdraw his or her plea and proceed to trial. This does not happen often, however, because it is in everyone's interest to keep cases moving through the justice system.

The vast majority of criminal convictions in the United States are obtained as a result of guilty pleas, and approximately 90 percent of these emerge from plea bargains. Consequently, plea bargaining is considered by many to be the "grease that keeps the wheels of the justice system turning."

Plea bargaining is a controversial practice, however. Those who support it suggest that it is a necessary evil—without it, U.S. courts would be unable to handle the huge volume of criminal cases. Opponents assert that it often results in inappropriate sentences for hardened criminals and that the public does not support the practice. Perhaps the most significant criticism is that it may sometimes influence defendants who have not committed an offense to plead guilty in order to avoid the uncertainty of a trial. Moreover, when a defendant pleads guilty, a court does not have the opportunity to scrutinize the police investigation in the case to insure that it conformed to the law.

Should we abolish plea bargaining or modify the present system to conform more closely to justice system ideals? The authors of the articles in this section have very different views on this issue. Jeff Palmer argues that plea bargaining must be abolished in order to reinstate justice in the United States and restore the public's confidence in the criminal justice system. Douglas D. Guidorizzi, in contrast, believes that accepting plea bargaining as a natural feature of the adversarial system allows the criticisms of the practice to be addressed with tailored reforms.

So, which of our contributors is correct? Should we abolish plea bargaining altogether, or modify the practice to restrict prosecutorial discretion? Is there really an alternative to plea bargaining in an already crowded U.S. justice system? Is there a viable middle ground between these positions that could permit plea bargaining in some cases, but not in others? If so, what line would you draw?

Jeff Palmer

YES

Abolishing Plea Bargaining: An End to the Same Old Song and Dance

Introduction

The idea that plea bargaining should be abolished is not a novel one.

However, many legal commentators and participants view plea bargaining as inevitable. Both supporters and opponents of plea bargaining have used various means to support their positions, including economic analysis, courtroom group theory, agency costs, legal studies, and statistics. Now, supporters of abolishing plea bargaining have a new argument raised by the Supreme Court decision in *Bailey v. United States.*

Title 18, United States Code, section 924(c) (1), allows for the enhanced punishment of a defendant who commits a violent crime or drug trafficking offense and uses or carries a firearm during or in relation to either offense. The Court's decision in Bailey changed the interpretation of "use" under this statute to a bright-line test of proximity and accessibility. The Court's decision was enforced retroactively, which brought numerous habeas corpus petitions under 28 U.S.C. (sec) 2255, from prisoners arguing that their sentences were contrary to the United States law. Many of these prisoners were sentenced pursuant to plea bargains, which often dropped serious offenses in return for guilty pleas to lesser included offenses and firearm charges under section 924(c) (1). The on-going problem facing the courts is what effect the plea agreement should be given? Some courts allow reindictment of the prisoner subsequent to a successful collateral attack of the plea agreement, "while other courts have upheld the plea agreement as a contract." This uncertainty about dealing with plea agreements under Bailey gives more support to the general notion of abolishing plea bargaining. Abolishing plea bargaining would eliminate the ability of the now innocent prisoner to be released from jail without serving his debt to society. . . .

History of Plea Bargaining

Plea bargaining has emerged and gained acceptance in the legal community only in recent decades. However, plea bargaining existed before the Civil War.

From *American Journal of Criminal Law,* vol. 26, issue 3, Summer 1999, pp. 505-506. Notes omitted.

One of the earliest indications of plea bargaining was a 1485 English statute, which authorized prosecutions for unlawful hunting before the Justice of the Peace. The statute provided that if a defendant confessed his crime then he was convicted of a summary offense, but if the defendant denied his guilt then he was prosecuted as a felon. Court reporters from appellate courts do not have cases where plea bargaining is involved until after the Civil War. However, many of the courts disapproved of the practice of plea bargaining because of its secrecy and infringement on the defendant's rights. The Louisiana Supreme Court was especially concerned about the implications of plea bargaining on innocent defendants, stating:

> In the instant case the accused accepted the certainty of conviction of what he took to be a minor offense not importing infamy, in order to avoid the risk of conviction of a graver offense importing infamy. Not only was there room for error, but the thing was, what an innocent man might do who found that appearances were against him, and that he might be convicted notwithstanding his innocence.

During this time, the United States Supreme Court was reluctant to permit bargained waivers of procedural rights, suggesting that they would not approve of plea bargaining.

The dominance of plea bargaining was not actually realized until the 1920s, when a number of states and cities conducted surveys of their criminal justice system. Alschuler reported this survey: "In Chicago, 85 percent of all felony convictions were by guilty plea; in Detroit, 78; in Denver, 76; in Minneapolis, 90; in Los Angeles, 81; in Pittsburgh, 74; and in St. Louis, 84." Following the 1920s, the issue of plea bargaining did not reemerge until the 1960s. The re-emergence of plea bargaining was due to a couple of factors: (1) the "crime wave" of the 1960s produced by the World War II baby boom and the increased proportion of young people in society, and (2) the increase in drug usage (especially marijuana) and other cases of victimless crime. In 1967, both the American Bar Association and the President's Commission on Law Enforcement and Administration of Justice noted their approval of plea bargaining. In 1971, the United States Supreme Court specifically accepted plea bargaining as part of the criminal justice system.

"Public disenchantment with the practice of plea bargaining probably reached its peak in the fall of 1973 when Vice President Spiro Agnew, accused of accepting bribes, avoided a possible prison term by being allowed to enter a noto contendere plea to a lesser charge." Two years following the United States Supreme Court's acceptance of plea bargaining, the National Advisory Commission on Criminal Justice Standards and Goals recommended the abolition of all forms of plea bargaining stating, "As soon as possible, but in no event later than 1978, negotiations between prosecutors and defendants—either personally or through their attorneys—concerning concessions to be made in return for guilty pleas should be prohibited. While the Commission's goal of abolishing plea bargaining was never reached, there have been several attempts to abolish plea bargaining."

Nonetheless, plea bargaining remains a part of today's criminal justice system, although the Supreme Court and Federal Rules of Criminal Procedure have placed several limitations on the process. Advocates for each side of the plea bargaining debate continue to assert justifications for their point of view. However, balancing the advantages and disadvantages of plea bargaining makes a convincing case for its abolishment.

The Debate on Plea Bargaining

"The academic literature has consisted largely of attempts to provide a theoretical justification for plea bargaining and, conversely, of calls for the system's abolition." However, "in the past decade, the notion that plea bargaining is a permanent component of our criminal justice system has gained near unanimous acceptance among the system's defenders and critics alike." So the question becomes, why are people still questioning the legitimacy of plea bargaining and calling for its abolishment? The best answer to this question comes from Albert W. Alschuler—one of the leading advocates for abolishing plea bargaining—who said:

Nevertheless, the plea bargaining debate involves fundamental issues of sentencing policy, of the propriety of compromising questions of criminal guilt, and of the use of governmental inducements to secure waivers of constitutional rights. For these reasons, the debate seems likely to continue as long as the practice of plea bargaining persists.

Justifications For Plea Bargaining

Advocates supporting plea bargaining insist that there are no other alternatives and the legal system will collapse without plea bargaining. Chief Justice Burger pointed out the possible devastating effects of abolishing plea bargaining stating:

> The consequence of what might seem on its face a small percentage change in the rate of guilty pleas can be tremendous. A reduction from 90 per cent to 80 per cent in guilty pleas requires the assignment of twice the judicial manpower and facilities—judges, court reporters, bailiffs, clerks, jurors and courtrooms. A reduction to 70 per cent trebles this demand.

Justice Burger points out one of the primary justifications for plea bargaining, allowing the judicial system to handle the ever-increasing case load. Other advantages of plea bargaining are: (1) it allows for the best allocation of resources to reach a mutual end result, (2) it allows for greater flexibility in the system, (3) it allows the defendant to acknowledge guilt and manifest a willingness to assume responsibility for his actions, and (4) it allows victims to be shielded from a trial.

Advocates for plea bargaining argue that plea negotiation is necessary in order to handle the criminal caseload. Plea bargaining advocates point to the fact that "criminal caseloads commonly doubled from one decade to the next, while judicial resources increased only slightly." They also point out that the majority of cases are disposed of by guilty pleas. They contend that abolishing plea bargaining will lead to more defendants wanting their day in court, which in turn will result in the overburdening of the entire criminal justice system.

There is no doubt that guilty pleas do account for the majority of felony convictions. However, there is no reason to believe that abolishing plea bargaining will cause defendants to stop pleading guilty. Defendants may still plead guilty to avoid longer sentences, avoid the "process costs" of a trial, because of lack of defenses, or due to remorse. Likewise, even if abolishing plea bargaining leads to more defendants going to trial, is this really a problem? Chief Justice Burger once said: "An affluent society ought not be miserly in support of justice, for economy is not an objective of the system." There is also skepticism over whether or not caseload pressure can really be justified by plea bargaining since "guilty pleas are often as high in rural and small-city jurisdictions and in jurisdictions with relatively small caseloads as in the most overburdened urban areas." Some attribute plea bargaining as "simply a way to reduce the work."

Another justification of plea bargaining is that it allows for the most efficient allocation of resources. "The bargain is recognized explicitly as a transaction in which unrelated objectives of the defendant and the state are served. The defendant wants to minimize his punishment, wholly without regard to its possible benefit to society or himself. The state wants to avoid a trial." However, abolishing plea bargaining may in fact decrease case disposition time. There is also a question about whether or not the defendant can really minimize his punishment in light of concurrent sentencing, the broad range of sentencing alternatives, and the fact that the judge's presentence report will contain details of the crime. Plea bargaining may just be a windfall for the State.

Plea bargaining also allows for greater flexibility in the criminal justice system. The flexibility of plea bargaining benefits the defendant because he may avoid pre-trial detention, conviction for a felony, and conviction for a crime which has a stigma attached to it. This same flexibility allows the prosecutor to grant concessions to the defendant in return for cooperation, to tailor punishment to the crime without being subject to mandatory sentencing for a crime, and to ensure that the defendant still gets convicted even if evidence is lacking. The prosecutor can take into account various factors related to the individual case, such as the strength of the evidence and the seriousness of the crime. However flexibility is an advantage that all lawless systems exhibit in comparison with systems administering justice by rules. The utility of discretion must be balanced against the utility of pre-ordained rules, which can limit the importance of subjective judgments, promote equality, control corruption, and provide a basis for planning, both before and after controversies arise.

Advocates also argue that plea bargaining allows the defendant to acknowledge guilt and manifest a willingness to assume responsibility for his actions. The American Bar Association has said:

> the defendant by his plea has aided in ensuring the prompt and certain application of correctional measures to him [and] that the concessions will

> make possible alternative correctional measures which are better adapted to achieving rehabilitative, protective, deterrent or other purposes of correctional treatment, or will prevent undue harm to the defendant from the form of conviction.

Further, the Federal Sentencing Guidelines provide for a two-level reduction for "acceptance of responsibility." The argument of assumption of responsibility also goes along with the notion that the defendant is able to actively participate in his own punishment, which will increase his sense of dignity and self-worth and possibly respect for the law and the criminal justice system. However, the "reliance on a bargain for the crucial determination of guilt undermines fundamentally the notion of criminal justice." There is also some debate on whether defendants actually participate in plea bargaining or even whether they should participate. Some opponents of plea bargaining argue that the defendant is not acknowledging guilt or accepting responsibility, but rather just looking for the most lenient sentence.

A final justification for plea bargaining is that it allows victims to be shielded from the emotional stress and sensationalism of trial. "Victims may benefit by avoiding the rigors of a trial and by not having to relive the horrors of their victimization in the presence of the defendant and the public." However, critics of plea bargaining argue that "victims have a tremendous emotional stake in seeing that perpetrators of crime against them receive appropriate punishment," and plea bargaining may only provide a lenient sentence.

Justifications Against Plea Bargaining

Critics of plea bargaining refuse to acknowledge its inevitability and instead argue its many disadvantages. One of the most central arguments against plea bargaining is that it is detrimental to the innocent defendant. An innocent defendant may plead guilty "if convinced that the lighter treatment from a guilty plea is preferable to the possible risk of a harsher sentence following a formal trial." Other disadvantages of plea bargaining are: (1) the problem concerning the interests and motivations of the actors in the system, (2) constitutional issues raised by allowing plea bargaining, (3) legal issues raised by plea bargaining, (4) leniency of sentencing, (5) distorts the public image, and (6) undermines the adversarial process.

Critics of plea bargaining emphasize the possibility of a defendant pleading guilty despite the fact that he is really innocent. The Supreme Court has stated:

> It is critical that the moral force of the criminal law not be diluted by a standard of proof [or a procedure for conviction] that leaves people in doubt whether innocent people are being condemned. It is also important in our free society that every individual going about his ordinary affairs have confidence that his government cannot adjudge him guilty of a criminal offense without convincing a proper factfinder of his guilt with utmost certainty.

The problem of convicting an innocent person is further aggravated by the coercive elements involved in plea bargaining, such as pretrial confinement, overcharging, and differential in sentencing between pleas and trial. Some advocates of plea bargaining contend that the innocence problem does not exist because of the extensive screening of cases prior to charging the defendant with a crime. They argue that most defendants are in fact factually guilty. Other advocates argue that the innocence problem is actually lessened by plea bargaining because the innocent defendant does not have to risk a harsher punishment by going to trial. They contend that "plea bargaining merely reflects the risks of improper conviction that already exist at trial."

Another problem with plea bargaining is the conflicting interests and motivations of the actors in the system. "Because of the pressure of numbers, there is often a unanimity among defense counsel, trial judge, and prosecutor in pushing criminal defendants through the system as quickly as possible." The prosecutor is motivated to plea bargain because "a plea bargain represents the certainty of conviction without the risks of trial." The prosecutor wants "to maximize his own welfare, which is defined by some combination of career advancement, job satisfaction, and leisure." Plea bargaining helps the prosecutor manage his case load while still maintaining a high conviction rate, which will please the district attorney—an elected official and the prosecutor's boss, who wants the public to have the perception that he is tough on crime. The prosecutor has the ultimate power in plea bargaining because he can decide "when cases are brought, which cases are dismissed or pushed and how cases are ultimately settled. The defense attorney also has incentives to avoid trial and plea bargain because he faces financial pressure to minimize time spent on cases, due to the fact that most defense attorneys work for a flat fee paid in advance. Likewise, the appointed attorney works for a flat fee or a low hourly rate, so he has a strong incentive to plea bargain in order to avoid spending time preparing and going to trial without the possibility of adequate compensation." Although the public defender has no financial incentives to avoid trial, he is still motivated to plea bargain in order to manage his case load. The judge is also motivated to plea bargain because of overflowing court dockets, as well as political pressures.

Plea bargaining advocates insist that although each of the actors in the plea bargaining system may have conflicting interests, they all are dedicated to what is in the best interests of justice. They argue that the prosecutor is not motivated by plea bargaining because he can decide whether or not to take the case in the first place and after screening the case, the prosecutor takes the case because he believes the defendant is guilty. Further, one of the primary considerations of a prosecutor in plea bargaining is the strength of the defendant's case, indicating that the only thing motivating the prosecutor is the interests of justice in seeing the defendant convicted. Advocates of plea bargaining emphasize that the defense attorney has an ethical obligation to zealously represent his client, and the only motivation to plea bargain would be to secure a lower sentence. There are also many reasons why the defense attorney may want to delay and go to trial—such as the evidence may be lost, witnesses may become unavailable, and the defense attorney will have more time to file motions to suppress evidence. The appointed attorney also has a duty to zealously represent his client and if he consistently plea bargains good cases, then the judge will presumably stop appointing him cases. The public defender not only has a duty to zealously represent his client but the inherent nature of the job suggests that the attorney has a strong faith in the adversarial nature of the criminal justice system.

Advocates of plea bargaining also argue that the judge has a limited role in plea bargaining in most state courts and in federal court the judge is prohibited from participating in the plea bargaining process. Finally, advocates point out that regardless of the actors' motivations and interests, the decision on whether or not to accept a plea bargain ultimately rests with the defendant.

Plea bargaining also raises many constitutional issues. Critics stress that plea bargaining circumvents the standards of proof and due process imposed in trials. The defendant is encouraged to waive his constitutional right to trial in lieu of receiving a harsher sentence at trial. The defendant also waives his privilege against self-incrimination and the right to confront adverse witnesses.

The indiscriminate manipulation of the powers entrusted to public officials to coerce defendants into yielding important constitutional rights is anathema to those who claim that "steadfast adherence to strict procedural safeguards is our main assurance that there will be equal justice under law." The very possibility of such manipulations breeds contempt and resentment—instead of remorse and resolve—on the part of the defendant and undermines the justice system's credibility and legitimacy in the eyes of the public.

Advocates for plea bargaining argue that "safeguards and guidelines have been developed in many jurisdictions to prevent violations of due process and to insure that innocent defendants not plead guilty under coercion." They also argue that the Supreme Court has explicitly recognized plea bargaining as constitutional despite the waiver of certain constitutional rights. Lastly, they argue that "for most defendants, the punishment is much more important than due process since their guilt is obvious and they have no legal basis for challenging their arrest and later treatment."

Critics of plea bargaining are also concerned about the numerous legal issues raised by plea bargaining. "Plea bargaining has undercut the goals of legal doctrines as diverse as the fourth amendment exclusionary rule, the insanity defense, the right to confrontation, the defendant's right to attend criminal proceedings, and the recently announced right of the press and the public to observe the administration of criminal justice." The prosecutor may secure convictions that could not otherwise be obtained because he may bluff the defendant with inadmissible evidence, such as evidence gained by an unlawful search or hearsay statements. Critics also argue that plea bargaining is determined by systemic factors, none of which are directly related to the notion of justice. Plea bargaining advocates argue that "defendants accept bargains because the threat of much harsher penalties after trial; they are thus forced to give up the protections that the trial system's many formalities provide."

Plea bargaining also results in leniency of sentencing because "many defendants are aware that the deal generated in a plea bargain averages about one half the sentence they would likely receive if they did go to trial and were found guilty." Critics argue that plea bargaining not only results in less severe sentences but also greater sentencing disparity, which tends to undermine the entire criminal system. Critics insist that plea bargaining and the resulting leniency allows the criminal to escape full punishment. "Advocates of plea bargaining argue that leniency is necessary to ensure convictions and that plea bargaining merely represents the risks that would exist at trial." The American Bar Association has also stated:

> The court should not impose upon a defendant any sentence in excess of that which would be justified by any of the rehabilitative, protective, deterrent or other purposes of the criminal law because the defendant has chosen to require the prosecution to prove his guilt at trial rather than to enter a plea of guilty.

Advocates of plea bargaining, pointing to the ABA policy, argue that defendants receive the same sentences whether or not they plea guilty or go to trial.

Critics of plea bargaining also argue that plea bargaining undermines the public image of the criminal justice system.

Plea bargaining is usually presented in one of two ways: it is seen as coercing defendants into entering guilty pleas with a promise of a sentence substantially below the maximum out of fear of receiving a much more severe penalty, or it is seen as allowing guilty defendants to obtain unwarranted reductions in charges and/or sentences by threatening an overworked system with requiring a time-consuming and pointless trial. The first image represents the current system as one that sacrifices the adversarial search for truth in favor of efficiency; the latter represents it as sacrificing the proper punishment of criminals in the name of efficiency.

Since details of plea agreements are not disclosed, the public only sees what in its eyes is a criminal receiving a lenient sentence, rather than the possibility that the only way to convict the criminal was through the use of plea bargaining. The public perceives plea bargaining as a form of modern day shopping, where the defendant shops for sentences, or even less appealing, as a form of gambling where the defendant plea bargains for the gamble of a more lenient sentence.

Another criticism of plea bargaining is that "it erodes the cornerstones of the adversary system: the presumption of innocence and the right to trial. Under the adversarial model the accused is more likely to be presumed innocent; the state carries the heavy burden of convincing a judge and jury that the defendant is guilty beyond a reasonable doubt." Critics argue that "plea bargaining does not resolve uniformly the details and ambiguities on which an accurate determination of guilt and desert to be punished depend." Plea bargaining also results in sentencing concessions, which undermines the court's responsibility to sentence the defendant. Further, "plea bargaining makes a substantial part of an offender's sentence depend, not upon what he did or his personal characteristics, but upon a tactical decision irrelevant to any proper objective of criminal proceedings." Advocates for plea bargaining insist that the adversarial nature of trial still exists but now it is in the form of negotiation of plea bargains. They also argue that the adversarial system is not undermined because the defendant can always assert his right to trial. . . .

Possible Reforms to the Criminal Justice System

There are really two possible approaches to the plea bargaining problem. One approach is to specifically address the problems and defects inherent with plea bargaining and the resulting agreements. The other approach is to reform the entire criminal justice system to cure any problems plea bargaining may present. Both of these approaches however fail to guarantee a solution to the plea bargaining problem, which can be readily attained through abolishment.

The most practical solution to plea bargaining . . . is to require express provisions regarding the effect of a collateral attack. However, some courts have already suggested that express provisions are unnecessary. More importantly, an express provision would mean that the defendant is essentially surrendering one more of his legal rights—the right to collateral attack—and the plea bargain begins to resemble anything but a bargain.

Another possible reform of plea bargaining is to control the charging decision. In 1974, New Orleans District Attorney—Harry Connick—implemented a case screening procedure where an assistant DA reviewed all the cases and made decisions on whether to charge or dismiss. If he decided to dismiss then he needed to explain his decision in writing. The new screening technique resulted in a reduction in cases of twenty percent and the elimination of prosecutors bargaining with the defendant for charges. Other reforms include increasing judicial involvement and requiring a formal pretrial conference, establishing guidelines and standards for plea bargaining, and bail reforms. However, these reforms, like the screening procedure. . . . may just serve to further complicate and lengthen the plea bargaining process.

There are several reforms which could be made to the entire criminal justice system to facilitate plea bargaining. Two possible reforms are expanding pretrial discovery in criminal trials and allowing indigent defendants to select their own attorneys with vouchers. Presumably, pretrial discovery would eliminate the concern of innocent defendants plea bargaining for less severe sentences, but this reform would also consume more judicial resources—time and money. Allowing indigent defendants to select their own attorneys may allow them to receive better representation and decrease the attorney's conflict of interests, but this reform would never be able to eliminate all of the agency costs associated with plea bargaining. There are also reforms which can be made to conserve judicial resources but the conservation of resources will still not resolve all the inherent problems of plea bargaining. Albert W. Alschuler has suggested more severe reforms to the system: (1) eliminate the right to jury trial in misdemeanor cases, (2) eliminate the right to jury trial in all cases, (3) require judges to control the order of proof at trial and to conduct the initial examination of witnesses and (4) require the defendant to testify and allow an adverse inference if he fails to do so. All of these reforms go against embedded constitutional rights—the right to a jury trial and the right against self-incrimination—so they are unlikely to be embraced by the courts much less the public.

The one reform which will undoubtedly resolve the plea bargaining problem is abolishment. Critics argue that abolishing plea bargaining will increase the number of trials, increase the error rate of trials, decrease the number of convictions, and increase sentence disparity. However, when Alaska banned plea bargaining in 1975, while there was an increase in jury trials—from 6.7 to 9.6 percent—case disposition time was cut in half. Likewise, when El Paso abolished plea bargaining, trials increased and guilty pleas decreased as predicted, however there was also an increase in the conviction rate. "Moreover, according to recent studies of jurisdictions where plea bargaining has been banned, guilty plea rates failed to plummet despite the limitations on charge concessions or sentence bargaining." While abolishing plea bargaining does raise concerns of sentence disparity, "when the Coast Guard effectively eliminated plea bargains in special courts-martial, there was no increase in sentence severity." No one claims to know exactly what the results of abolishing plea bargaining will be "but we ought not to accept easily the conclusion that the only reliable method of determining guilt [trial] is so far beyond our resources that we need immediately to find ways to avoid using it very much even if that means punishing some persons excessively."

Conclusion

Plea bargaining must be abolished. "Few practices in the system of criminal justice create a greater sense of unease and suspicion than the negotiated plea of guilty." The justifications for plea bargaining are outweighed by the justifications for its abolishment, especially in light . . . the inconsistent treatment of plea agreements.

So long as the negotiation of pleas is permitted, it will continue, in actual effect, to deprive great numbers of persons of their right to trial, to hide corruption of public officials by wealthy and powerful kingpins of organized crime, and to serve as an escape hatch for the affluent or politically powerful violators of our criminal laws.

Rather than being faced with the predicament of letting criminals circumvent the justice system or being coerced to enforce the contract laws of this nation to its detriment, we must return to a system in the not so distant past, where plea bargaining did not exist.

NO 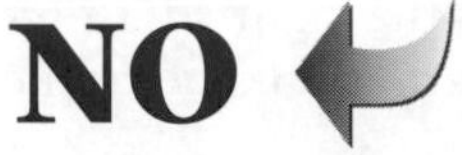

Douglas D. Guidorizzi

Should We Really "Ban" Plea Bargaining? The Core Concerns of Plea Bargaining Critics

Introduction

Although the media exalts the jury trial as the culmination of a criminal investigation, guilty pleas actually account for an overwhelming amount of criminal convictions in this country. A 1992 survey of the seventy-five most populous counties found that guilty pleas accounted for ninety-two percent of all convictions in state courts. While guilty pleas should be distinguished from plea bargaining, the extraordinarily high plea rate clearly suggests that plea bargaining pervades our criminal justice system. Despite its extensive use, scholars as well as policymakers still debate the propriety of plea bargaining. Scholars have argued for years that the system of plea bargaining is inherently flawed and unfair to defendants. On the other hand, policymakers have attempted to "ban" plea bargaining in response to the public's loss of faith in a system that allows "criminals" to receive "bargains." Despite these criticisms, plea bargaining remains the primary method of disposing of criminal cases. This [article] attempts to focus the debate about plea bargaining to reveal the core concerns of the critics and suggest tailored reforms for those jurisdictions that are trying to "ban" plea bargaining . . .

What Is Plea Bargaining?

Definition of Plea Bargaining

No standard definition of plea bargaining exists among practitioners. The definition of "plea bargaining" varies depending on the jurisdiction and on the context of its use. However, to identify the core problems of plea bargaining, we must first settle on a definition that encompasses the broad range of practices that may be considered plea bargaining. Black's Law Dictionary provides a general definition that serves as a useful starting point to highlight the common misunderstandings of what constitutes plea bargaining. Black's defines plea bargaining as:

> the process whereby the accused and the prosecutor in a criminal case work out a mutually satisfactory disposition of the case subject to court approval. It usually involves the defendant's pleading guilty to a lesser offense or to only one or some of the counts of a multi-count indictment in return for a lighter sentence than that possible for the graver charge.

The first part of the definition suggests that plea bargains are "mutually satisfactory dispositions." While it is true that the bargain struck must be agreed upon by both sides and the guilty plea must be made intelligently and voluntarily, this does not guarantee a mutually satisfactory result. The prosecutor may be forced to present a highly favorable offer to a defendant as a result of errors in procedure that may cause evidentiary problems at trial. On the other hand, the strength of the prosecutor's bargaining power may present the defendant with almost equally unfavorable choices. For example, the prosecutor's offer may involve merely not taking advantage of broad powers granted by the legislature such as not overcharging the defendant, not charging him as a multiple offender, or grouping several convictions for the same incident into a single sentence. In either scenario, the description "mutually satisfactory disposition" belies the true nature of the situation.

Also, the phrase "subject to court approval" suggests some sort of judicial review of the plea bargaining agreement prior to acceptance by the judge. However, the true nature of plea bargaining includes situations where judicial review is nonexistent. Implicit plea bargaining, by definition, is never officially subject to court approval. Implicit plea bargaining involves situations where defendants do not negotiate for certain concessions but instead are presented with the fact that if they go to trial they will be punished more severely. Despite the lack of formal agreement for this bargain, this type of plea bargaining is often made quite explicit to the defendant but not subject to court approval. Additionally, prosecutors can independently drop charges against the defendant in exchange for a guilty plea. Moreover, judges seldom reject plea bargaining agreements involving sentencing recommendations by the prosecutor. Therefore, the phrase "subject to court approval" obscures the reality of plea bargaining and inappropriately limits the definition of plea bargaining.

Finally, the suggestion that plea bargaining "usually involves the defendant's pleading guilty to a lesser offense in return for a lighter sentence" also distorts the reality of plea bargaining by ignoring the vast array of concessions that may be offered to a defendant in exchange for his guilty plea. The variety of concessions the state offers defendants extends to the limits of the prosecutor's or judge's imagination. These concessions generally can be divided into two categories: charge bargaining concessions and sentence bargaining concessions. Charge bargaining involves offering a reduction of the charges or the dismissal of one or more of the charges in exchange for the guilty plea. Sentence bargaining, on the other hand, includes a wide range of offers that extends beyond merely an offer for a lighter sentence in return for a guilty plea. Therefore, Black's characterization of the exchange involved in plea bargaining understates the diversity of concessions offered by the state in exchange for the defendant's guilty plea.

To really consider the **core concerns of plea bargaining** critics, the definition of plea bargaining must encompass the broad range of practices that constitute plea bargaining today. A comprehensive definition defines plea bargaining as "the defendant's agreement to plead guilty to a criminal charge with the reasonable expectation of receiving some consideration from the state." This definition encompasses both explicit plea bargaining and implicit plea bargaining. Although some practitioners refuse to acknowledge implicit bargaining as part of the practice, its use as a method of negotiating a guilty plea qualifies it as part of the process of plea bargaining. In considering whether jurisdictions should ban or severely restrict plea bargaining, the comprehensive definition should be used to avoid confusion . . .

Why the Rise of Plea Bargaining?

The transformation of the criminal justice system over the course of the nineteenth century provides a forceful explanation for the emergence of plea bargaining. At common law, the "jury trial was a summary proceeding," conducted by private individuals or sheriffs. Although most states had established a system of public prosecution by 1789, the public prosecutor was primarily considered to be acting as a part of the judicial process. The framers of the Constitution laid the foundations of an adversarial justice system in the new republic, but the operation of that system differed significantly from today's system. "Not much is known about the day-to-day work of the courtroom in . . . 1800"; however, the absence of certain features in the system can be deduced from the adoption of those features through statute or case law. During the early part of the nineteenth century, many criminal prosecutions occurred without lawyers for the defendant, the prosecution, or both. As the American legal profession grew, and more trials involved lawyers, the length of the jury trial also increased. Correspondingly, guilty plea rates increased. Therefore, plea bargaining should be viewed as a natural outgrowth of a progressively adversarial criminal justice system.

However, despite its prevalence, many criticized the displacement of jury trials with plea bargaining as the primary method of criminal case disposition. Observers criticized plea bargaining both as an "incompetent, inefficient, and lazy method of administering justice" and as a compromise of a defendant's right to a jury trial. The response has produced various justifications for the use of plea bargaining that are evident in the Supreme Court's jurisprudence on the subject. These justifications include the benefits provided by plea bargaining to both the state and the defendant, its potential for encouraging rehabilitation, its efficiency, a presumption of equal bargaining power between parties and the characterization of the process as merely a choice between unpleasant alternatives that does not drive defendants to false self-condemnation.

The Supreme Court did not address the constitutionality of plea bargaining until after its establishment as a part of the criminal justice system. Initially, the Court questioned the validity of the plea bargaining process as burdening the defendant's right to a jury trial. In *United States v. Jackson*, the Court invalidated a statute that allowed the imposition of the death penalty only after a jury trial. The Court found that the statute put "an impermissible burden upon the exercise of a constitutional right." In strident language, the majority opinion declared that any provisions the purposes or effects of which are "to chill the assertion of constitutional rights by penalizing those who choose to exercise them, . . . [are] patently unconstitutional." In writing for the majority, Justice Stewart noted that the problem with the statute was not that it coerced guilty pleas and jury waivers, but that "it needlessly encouraged them."

Two years later, the Court changed its tune and limited the holding of Jackson in Brady v. United States. In Brady, the Court pointed out the positive aspects of plea bargaining, emphasizing that the practice benefits both sides in the adversary system. Additionally, the Court justified the practice of plea bargaining by noting that a guilty plea suggests some "hope for success in rehabilitation." The Court upheld a guilty plea where demanding a jury trial could have resulted in a death sentence for the defendant. Noting that not every plea made for fear of the death penalty was invalid, the Court stated that Jackson merely required that guilty pleas be intelligent and voluntary. Yet later that same year, in North Carolina v. Alford, the Court abandoned this rehabilitation rationale for plea bargaining. In upholding the guilty plea the Alford Court emphasized the facts that the defendant had made an intelligent and voluntary choice and that there was strong evidence of guilt in the record.

The Court proffered an additional justification for the constitutionality of plea bargaining the following year in Santobello v. New York. In holding that a court can require specific performance of a plea agreement if the prosecution does not fulfill its end of the bargain, the Court stated that plea bargaining is "an essential component of the administration of justice." It emphasized the state's interest in the quick and efficient disposition of criminal cases, specifically stating that plea bargaining costs less and is faster than full-scale jury trials. In fact, primarily for the same efficiency reasons, the Court added that "[as long as it is] properly administered, [plea bargaining] is to be encouraged." Finally, the Court added that plea bargaining "is not only an essential part of the process but a highly desirable part."

Repelling another attack on the constitutionality of plea bargaining, the Supreme Court addressed a claim of prosecutorial vindictiveness in Bordenkircher v. Hayes. The Court rejected a due process violation claim and found a presumption of equal bargaining power between prosecutors and defendants. In discussing this additional justification, the Court stressed the advantage to both sides in the process, asserting that both sides "arguably possess relatively equal bargaining power." It found that defendants who are advised by competent counsel are "presumptively capable of intelligent choice in response to prosecutorial persuasion, and unlikely to be driven to false self-condemnation" given the procedural safeguards surrounding the plea. Although it noted that "there are undoubtedly constitutional limits" on a prosecutor's discretion in plea bargaining, the Court reaffirmed the prosecutor's broad discretion in presenting a defendant with "the unpleasant alternatives of forgoing trial or facing charges on which he was plainly subject to prosecution." . . .

These justifications, and particularly the Supreme Court's blessing, have created a significant debate that has centered on the constitutionality and propriety of plea bargaining in our justice system. Instead of calling for a complete abolition of plea bargaining, critics should accept plea bargaining as a natural, although not necessarily inevitable, component of our adversary system. Additionally, the justifications for plea bargaining do not consist solely of the need for an efficient administration of justice. Problems associated with plea bargaining may exist as a result of flaws in the assumptions of the different justifications. Therefore, the debate should be shifted to concentrate on addressing these flaws and attempting to remedy the problems of plea bargaining. . . .

General Justifications for Plea Bargaining

Plea bargaining's resiliency and popularity derives from the fact that it provides at least some benefits to all players in the criminal justice system: district attorneys, defense attorneys, defendants, judges and, to a certain extent, victims. These benefits provide strong incentives for participants to engage in plea bargaining and should be acknowledged when presenting possible reforms of plea bargaining.

Plea bargaining provides district attorneys with greater flexibility in disposing of the criminal caseload. District attorneys often operate with limited resources and plea bargaining provides a quick, efficient method of handling a large caseload. For example, in response to a surge in the criminal caseload, the district attorney may increase the attractiveness of plea offers to more efficiently allocate prosecutorial resources. The district attorney also will be able to concentrate the prosecution's efforts on the more serious and high profile cases that will be of greater concern to the public. In addition, individual assistant district attorneys benefit from plea bargaining by being able to quickly dispose of their cases, lighten their caseload and eliminate the pressures involved in going to trial. Plea bargaining may also satisfy what some scholars argue is "an irrepressible tendency toward cooperation among members of the courtroom work group." It allows this "courtroom work group" to satisfy their "mutual interest in avoiding conflict, reducing uncertainty and maintaining group cohesion."

Defense attorneys benefit similarly from plea bargaining. Public defender offices have the same problem as district attorneys in allocating scarce resources. The quick disposition of cases allows public defenders to give more time and effort to the cases they consider more trial-worthy. Attorneys who are not associated with a public defender office but are representing indigent clients may also find it in their direct financial interests to dispose of cases quickly. Many states impose caps on the amount of money allocated to the representation of indigent clients; these amounts do not provide adequate compensation for the time and expense of bringing a case to trial. Plea bargaining provides an easy compromise for an attorney to adequately represent her client and still make a living. In addition, some states assign counsel to represent indigent clients pro bono. Plea bargaining provides an attractive, accepted method for these attorneys to fulfill their obligation while minimizing their costs. In any case, plea bargaining provides a much easier and less time consuming way to dispose of these cases.

Defendants benefit from plea bargaining in the most obvious way. In exchange for pleading guilty and avoiding trial, defendants can receive sentence-related concessions from the prosecutor or the dismissal of some of the charges in their indictment. Although they lose the chance of an acquittal, defendants escape the maximum penalties provided by statute while at the same time "avoiding the anxieties and uncertainties of a trial."

The judiciary also gains from plea bargaining. The quick disposition of cases through plea bargaining may conserve judicial resources inasmuch as the amount of time for a guilty plea is less than a trial. A large number of plea bargains alleviate congested caseloads and reduce the expense of providing jury trials.

Finally, victims may also benefit from the plea bargaining process. Plea bargains allow the victim to gain an immediate sense of closure along with the knowledge that the defendant will not go unpunished for the crime. Additionally, the victim may wish to avoid the rigors of testifying at trial and the possibility of the prosecution not getting a conviction.

Criticisms of Plea Bargaining

Plea bargaining does provide direct benefits to the different players in the judicial system (see infra), but the costs involved may be substantially more indirect. Since the crime commissions of the 1920s brought it to the public's attention, plea bargaining has been subject to a variety of criticisms. The most consistent criticism of plea bargaining centers on the idea that plea bargaining undermines the integrity of the criminal justice system. This criticism still exists today, but the increased number of criminal cases flooding the courts have forced critics to downplay this concern in light of the apparent necessity of plea bargaining in handling the increased number of cases. Instead, critics now emphasize the loss of the virtues inherent in public trials. Additionally, many criticize plea bargaining based on the fact that criminals benefit from bargaining with the state and avoid what may be seen as the appropriate sanction for their crime. Finally, critics assert that the state's bargaining power is so great that it can coerce innocent defendants to plead guilty. These three criticisms have fueled the most forceful arguments in favor of complete abolition of plea bargaining. The concerns behind these criticisms may be addressed through enactment of more specific reforms that address the problems, rather than abolish the practice. However, to address these problems we must first understand the concerns underlying these criticisms.

The primary criticism of plea bargaining lies in the idea that it subverts many of the values of the criminal justice system. Critics argue that the Constitution and the Supreme Court's interpretation of it provide detailed and explicit rules for the determination of guilt and the establishment of punishment. Plea bargaining circumvents these "rigorous standards of due process and proof imposed during trials." Critics contend that in certain cases, a defendant's guilt is decided without a full investigation, presentation of testimony or evidence or any impartial fact finding. The determination of the defendant's culpability and required punishment becomes an administrative determination by the prosecutor. Prosecutors determine their offer by discounting their chance of success at hearings and trial, considerations some argue are irrelevant to any proper objective of criminal justice. Additionally, the purposes served by the rules of evidence and procedure become secondary to the prosecutor's own calculation of the defendant's degree of culpability measured against the ability of the prosecutor to prove it at trial.

Although this criticism has a certain degree of merit to it, the degree to which the plea bargaining subverts the values of the criminal justice system may be exaggerated. The "rigorous standards of due process and proof imposed during trials" do not become irrelevant with plea bargaining but, in fact, influence the nature of the bargain reached. In calculating the plea offer, the prosecutor considers the chance of conviction, including his ability to win pre-trial hearings that may exclude certain evidence. Furthermore, the chance of success at trial is not the only consideration involved in calculating the plea offer. The primary factors influencing the prosecutor's offer in most plea bargains are "the circumstances of the offense and the characteristics of the offender." Additionally, the prosecutor's duty exceeds that of the role of an adversary and includes operating in the interests of justice as well. An administrative determination of the defendant's guilt does not conflict with the prosecutor's role.

This criticism highlights the corruption of institutional values that results from the apparent hypocrisy of criminal procedure. The Constitution provides extensive constitutional safeguards for defendants who proceed to trial, but ninety percent of felony convictions occur without trial. The judiciary articulates great principles that govern the determination of guilt at trial, but then the executive branch, with the approval of the judiciary, bargains with criminals to purchase these procedural entitlements. One critic of plea bargaining suggests that "the plea bargain convinces criminals that the majesty of the law is a fraud, that the law is like a Turkish bazaar." Pervasive bargaining, without specific guidelines, perpetuates the image that justice is for sale. "Just as there is no moral difference between buyers and sellers, there is no moral difference between the criminal and his attorney, the prosecutor, the judge, and the probation officers."

Another criticism of plea bargaining is that it allows criminals to "get away" with lenient sentences. The fact that the prosecutor serves the dual role of an adversary and administrator of justice supports this idea. The prosecutor's consideration of the "interests of justice" and his chances of success at trial undermine his negotiating position. The defense counsel, on the other hand, maintains the singular role of an "adversarial negotiator" which produces more effective results. Statistics support the idea of a defense bias in plea bargaining by disclosing considerable sentencing differentials between guilty pleas and convictions at trial. Therefore, if the sentence imposed at a trial is the appropriate sentence for the defendant's crime, then plea bargaining allows criminals to escape with less than appropriate sentences.

Proponents of plea bargaining respond to this criticism by claiming that the lighter sentences are necessary for securing convictions. The benefits of the certainty of conviction and the efficiency of process outweigh the cost for securing a conviction. Many cases involve ambiguous legal elements, such as intent or recklessness that may be difficult to prove at trial. Therefore, the public interest is served by offering these concessions to obtain convictions.

The concern underlying this criticism, however, is that plea bargaining undermines the deterrent effect of criminal sanctions. Defendants who receive plea bargains often view this as a way to beat the system. Sentencing concessions can vary tremendously among plea bargains for similar crimes. Moreover, the existence of significant sentencing differentials between guilty pleas and jury trials supports the idea that the defendant "got away" with something. Therefore, securing concessions from the prosecutor perpetuates the image that criminals can evade the law provided they are willing to bargain.

The most serious concern with plea bargaining pertains to the possible coercion of innocent defendants to plead guilty. . . . The unilateral power of the state to determine the sanctions for different offenses can provide a broad range of options for prosecutors to overcharge or threaten to pursue the most severe penalty if the defendant goes to trial. The harsh penalties associated with conviction at trial provide the prosecutor with significant leverage to persuade defendants to plead guilty. In some cases, this may result in innocent defendants being faced with a choice where the cost of pleading guilty outweighs the risks of going to trial. Risk-averse defendants will accept the state's offer and plead guilty. The incentives inherent in plea bargaining, therefore, create an increased risk of innocent defendants receiving punishment.

Proponents of plea bargaining stress that the myriad of protections afforded the accused within the criminal justice system keeps this risk negligible. Moreover, the prosecutor's and defense attorney's assessment of their chances of success at trial vectors these risks of litigation. Plea bargaining merely reflects the risks of improper conviction that would already exist at trial. Furthermore, any increased risk of improper conviction is offset by the lighter sentences imposed on these defendants.

The problems associated with plea bargaining are not so great that abolition is the only remedy. Concerns of the corruption of institutional values, the decreased effectiveness of criminal sanctions, and the increased chance of improper convictions can be addressed through specific remedies. Since most critics argue the best solution would be to abolish plea bargaining, this Comment will next review the results of attempts to curtail plea bargaining and evaluate their effectiveness.

Attempts to Curtail Plea Bargaining

In recent years many jurisdictions have made different attempts to curtail plea bargaining. District attorneys and attorneys general have instituted plea . . . bans on plea bargaining after a felony indictment, total bans on plea bargaining, as well as replacing plea bargaining with the jury waiver or the "slow plea." These policies have engendered numerous criticisms as well as some dire predictions of the collapse of the entire criminal justice system if they are enacted. The restrictions on plea bargaining have not caused the collapse of any system, but the question of the proper use of plea bargaining has not been answered by these attempts. The effects of these "bans" do provide certain insights regarding how to remedy the negative effects of plea bargaining . . .

The Plea Ban

Plea bargaining bans have taken two forms: a complete ban on all forms of plea bargaining and a ban on plea bargaining after a felony indictment . . .

Alaska accomplished the most successful documented attempt to abolish plea bargaining when the state Attorney General banned plea bargaining in the entire state in 1975. The policy prohibited both charge bargaining and sentence-related bargaining. After inheriting a system of prosecution with pervasive plea bargaining and low conviction rates, the Attorney General decided to ban plea bargaining to restore public confidence in the justice system. Additionally, he intended the ban to clarify the roles of each agency in the justice system and improve conviction rates by improving the trial skills of his prosecutorial staff.

Many critics of the Attorney General's policy predicted disastrous consequences for Alaska's criminal justice system. The common concerns associated with banning plea bargaining, such as significant backlogs caused by an increase in cases going to trial or the emergence of underground plea bargaining contrary to official policy, did not occur in Alaska. Although the number of trials increased thirty-seven percent the year after the ban, the actual proportion of cases receiving trials increased only 2.9 percent. The dismissal rate remained constant after the ban, but the dismissals occurred earlier in the process, resulting in a more efficient use of prosecutorial resources. Court disposition time, the time from when the case was first filed to the final disposition, continued to decline as it had before the ban.

The elimination of explicit plea bargaining from the official policy in Alaska apparently did not drive the practice underground. The Alaska Judicial Council's study failed to discover evidence that prosecutors engaged in overcharging to solicit guilty pleas. Moreover, interviews with prosecutors during the ban found that they generally approved of the new policy and had no reason to evade it. Additionally, the Supreme Court of Alaska prohibited judges from engaging in negotiated plea bargaining, thereby strengthening the elimination of explicit plea bargaining.

The successful implementation of the plea bargaining ban required the Attorney General to restructure the operations of the prosecutors' offices somewhat. The Attorney General shifted the charging decisions from the police to the prosecutor's office and more carefully screened cases. He required prosecutors to "charge what you can prove and then do not deviate from it unless subsequent facts convince you that you were erroneous in your initial conclusion." This policy prevented defendants from being overcharged and eliminated the use of charge bargaining to obtain guilty pleas. The ban also attempted to eliminate sentence negotiation. The Alaska Judicial Council's study on the ban found that:

> Plea bargaining as an institution was clearly curtailed. The routine expectation of a negotiated settlement was removed; for most practitioners justifiable reliance on negotiation to settle criminal cases greatly diminished in importance. There is less face-to-face discussion between adversaries, and when meetings do occur, they are not usually as productive as they used to be.

. . . Alaska's experience demonstrates the difficulty in maintaining a complete, long-term ban on plea bargaining. The strict screening process for initial charges that characterized the first part of the ban appears to be a significant factor in a jurisdiction's ability to sustain a complete prohibition on plea bargaining. In their re-evaluation of Alaska's plea bargaining ban, Teresa White Carns and John A. Kruse identified two conditions they felt were necessary to maintain the policy: a committed policy maker and public support. In the absence of a committed policy maker, prosecutors began to plea bargain "out of habit." However, public disapproval of sentence bargaining was sufficient to keep prosecutors from making sentence recommendations in exchange for guilty pleas. Alaska's difficulty in committing to a complete prohibition of plea bargaining suggests that the policy may be too broad to solve the concerns of plea bargaining critics . . .

Conclusion

Accepting plea bargaining as a natural feature of the adversarial system allows the concerns of its critics to be addressed with tailored reforms. The concerns of plea bargaining critics—the corruption of institutional values, the decreased effectiveness of criminal sanctions, and the increased chance of improper convictions—can be remedied through regulation of the plea bargaining process. In order to meet the constitutional requirements of due process, a defendant must be represented by counsel during the plea proceeding and the judge must make a finding that the defendant plead guilty knowingly and voluntarily. However, these minimum requirements of due process do not address the negative externalities generated by plea bargaining. Jurisdictions should regulate plea bargaining by establishing predetermined sentencing discounts for guilty pleas and jury waivers, screen cases more effectively to eliminate charge bargaining, and increase the use of jury waivers.

Despite the fact that a significant majority of felony cases are plea bargained, plea bargaining maintains an image of an irregular process of selling justice. The corruption of institutional values resulting from this image can be avoided by eliminating the bargaining element of plea bargaining. The establishment of a set of written sentencing discounts that limits the concessions the prosecutor can offer for a guilty plea will eliminate the perception of prosecutors wheeling and dealing for guilty pleas. The concessions offered will be predetermined and may vary according to the circumstances of the individual case. Of course, allowance for exceptions in extraordinary cases will be required, but the written guidelines will provide all parties with limits to negotiation and will reduce the length of the negotiations themselves. Moreover, fidelity to the guidelines will further equalize treatment of defendants and yield more rational sentencing patterns.

Additionally, a strict adherence to written guidelines by prosecutors will strengthen the deterrent effect of criminal sanctions. The sentencing discount should be limited to a range of ten to twenty percent of the trial sentence to obtain the requisite number of desired pleas. The limited sentencing differential will increase the legitimacy of criminal sanctions and eliminate the perception that the defendant can "work" the system. If the sentencing discount takes the form of sentencing recommendations by the prosecutor, then corresponding judicial sentencing guidelines will be necessary to prevent judges from engaging in implicit plea bargaining by disregarding the prosecutor's recommendation. However, the sentencing discount may be achieved through the predetermined charging concessions offered solely by the prosecutor for guilty pleas.

The concern of improper convictions can be addressed by either an increased use of jury waiver bargaining or strengthening the screening process to prevent weak cases from entering the system. Although jury waiver bargaining may result in some "slow pleas of guilty," the prosecution still must make a presentation of the evidence on the record. Appellate review of the record benefits not only the individual defendant, but the community as well. The opportunity for an acquittal from a bench trial and appellate review of the record decreases the chance of improper conviction. Additionally, a tighter screening process will prevent the overcharging that creates significant leverage for the prosecution in negotiations. Alaska's experience demonstrates the impact charging policies have on the existence of plea bargaining. The elimination of this potential coercive power of the prosecutor will decrease the chance of improper convictions of innocent defendants.

These tailored reforms provide more sensible alternatives to perhaps futile attempts at banning plea bargaining. Moreover, these reforms do not require a complete overhaul of existing systems but instead accept the existing system as legitimate. Most importantly, however, is to move the debate away from the polar extremes of complete abolition of plea bargaining and the encouragement of plea bargaining-based efficiency. Scholars and policymakers should recognize the benefits of alternative methods of reform and attempt to work within the system to change it. The problems of plea bargaining are not so great that major reforms are necessary. Tailored reforms to address the specific problems can achieve the same result.

POSTSCRIPT

Should the United States Abolish Plea Bargaining in Criminal Cases?

Plea bargaining is a controversial practice in the U.S. justice system. While some see it as a necessary evil to keep the present system functioning, others believe that it contravenes the principle of just desserts.

Despite its various shortcomings, U.S. courts have generally sanctioned the practice of plea bargaining. In *Blackledge v. Allison*, 431 U.S. 63 (1977), Justice Potter Stewart stated:

> Whatever might be the situation in the real world, the fact is that the guilty plea and the often concomitant plea bargain are important components of this country's criminal justice system. Properly administered, they can benefit all concerned. The defendant avoids extended pretrial incarceration and the anxieties and uncertainties of a trial; he gains a speedy disposition of his case, the chance to acknowledge his guilt, and a prompt start in realizing whatever potential there may be for rehabilitation. Judges and prosecutors conserve vital and scarce resources. The public is protected from the risks posed by those charged with criminal offenses who are at large on bail while awaiting completion of criminal proceedings. [Footnote omitted.]

Thus, the U.S. Supreme Court appears to believe that plea bargaining is a good deal for everyone involved in the process: Defendants avoid trial and pretrial incarceration, and they receive a speedy trial, the chance to acknowledge their guilt, and a quick start on the road to rehabilitation. Judges and prosecutors conserve time and money, and the public safety is enhanced by keeping potentially dangerous defendants confined.

Attorney Douglas D. Guidorizzi would agree with Justice Stewart's assessment of plea bargaining's benefits. He would further suggest, however, that abuses in the present system should be addressed by developing administrative guidelines to regulate the practice.

Jeff Palmer, however, feels that plea bargaining should be discontinued in the U.S. justice system. He believes that the only way to restore "justice" to our legal system is to end this unsavory form of deal making.

In the final analysis, perhaps the best approach is to once again find a middle ground. Perhaps abolishing plea bargaining for certain types of serious offenses like murder, robbery, rape, and sexual abuse of a minor may lend additional credibility to our justice system. In less serious cases, however, administrative guidelines designed to restrict prosecutorial discretion in the plea bargaining process is an idea whose time has finally come.

Fortunately, there are numerous additional resources that will shed additional light on these topics. See George Fisher, *Plea Bargaining's Triumph: A History of Plea Bargaining in America* (Stanford University Press, 2003); Robert E. Scott and William J. Stuntz, "Plea Bargaining as Contract," *Yale Law Journal* (vol. 101, no. 2, 1992); Michael Gorr, "The Morality of Plea Bargaining," *Social Theory and Practice* (vol. 26, no. 1, 2000); Richard Adelstein and Thomas J. Micell, "Toward a Comparative Economics of Plea Bargaining," *European Journal of Law and Economics* (vol. 11, no. 1, 2001); Thomas J. Bernard and Robin Shepard Engel, "Conceptualizing Criminal Justice Theory," *Justice Quarterly* (vol. 18, no. 1, 2001); Stephanos Bibas, "The Real-World Shift in Criminal Procedure," *Journal of Criminal Law & Criminology* (vol. 93, no. 2/3, 2003); Stephanos Bibas, "Pleas' Progress," *Michigan Law Review* (vol. 102, no. 6, 2004); Chester L. Mirsky and Gabriel Kahn, "No Bargain," *The American Prospect* (vol. 32, 1997); Malcolm D. Holmes, William A. Taggert, and Howard C. Daudistel, "Plea Bargaining Policy and State District Court Caseloads: An Interrupted Time Series Analysis," *Law & Society* (vol. 26, no. 1, 1992); Sergio Herzog, "Plea Bargaining Practices: Less Covert, More Public Support," *Crime & Delinquency* (vol. 50, no. 4, 2004); Nathaniel J. Pallone, "Without Plea-Bargaining, Megan Kanka Would Be Alive Today," *Criminology & Public Policy* (vol. 3, no. 1, 2003); and Teresa White Carns and John A. Kruse, "Alaska's Ban on Plea Bargaining Reevaluated," *Judicature* (vol. 75, no. 6, 1992).

ISSUE 10

Should the United States Abolish the Juvenile Court Systems?

YES: Barry C. Feld, from "Abolish the Juvenile Court: Youthfulness, Criminal Responsibility, and Sentencing Policy," *Journal of Criminal Law & Criminology* (Fall 1997)

NO: Thomas F. Geraghty, from "Justice for Children: How Do We Get There?" *Journal of Criminal Law & Criminology* (Fall 1997)

ISSUE SUMMARY

YES: Law professor Barry C. Feld argues that juvenile courts have become deficient criminal courts in which children receive neither therapeutic treatment nor sufficient due process safeguards.

NO: Attorney Thomas F. Geraghty, who frequently represents children in juvenile court, contends that juvenile courts should be retained after being reinvigorated with financial and human services.

Are U.S. juvenile courts places of refuge and understanding for children who have broken the law? Are they courts of law that provide juveniles suspected of committing crimes with stringent due process safeguards? Or, could it be that they are the worst of both worlds, by failing to provide counseling and understanding for juvenile offenders, or sufficient due process safeguards?

In general, U.S. courts have attempted to strike a balance between the "social service" and "due process" models of the juvenile justice system. The social service model implies that juvenile courts are governmental agencies designed to promote child welfare. In theory, this model asserts that the juvenile courts should strive to serve the best interests of a child. Therefore, the strict utilization of due process safeguards, such as the rules of evidence, which characterize adult criminal proceedings, are of secondary concern. The due process model, in contrast, asserts that procedural safeguards are required for juveniles to receive fair treatment in the U.S. justice system. A seminal case in juvenile law, *In re Gault,* 387 U.S. 1 (1967), illustrates the reasons why.

Gerald Gault, a 15-year-old boy who was on six months' probation for being in the company of another boy who had stolen a wallet, was taken into custody for making a lewd telephone call to a neighbor. At the time the boy was taken into custody, his mother and father were both at work. No notice that Gerald was taken into custody was left at the home. No other steps were taken to advise the parents that their son had been arrested and that he was taken to the children's detention home by a probation officer.

The probation officer filed a petition with the court the next day, but it was not served on Gault's parents. A hearing was held before the juvenile court judge in chambers. Gerald's mother and two probation officers attended. The complaining witness was not present, and no sworn evidence was presented. In addition, no transcript or recording of the proceedings was made. Gerald was questioned by the judge at the hearing about the alleged lewd telephone call. Gerald said only that he had dialed the woman's telephone number and handed the phone to another juvenile. The probation officer and judge later testified that Gault had admitted making the lewd remarks.

At a delinquency hearing before the same juvenile court judge six days later, over Mrs. Gault's objections, the judge asserted that the complaining witness "did not have to be present at the hearing." At the conclusion of the hearing, the judge committed Gerald Gault as a juvenile delinquent to the state industrial school until he reached age 21. The court stated: "[A]fter a full hearing and due deliberation the Court finds that said minor is a delinquent child, and that said minor is of the age of 15 years." No appeal was permitted by Arizona law in juvenile cases. The U.S. Supreme Court granted review and held that Gerald Gault should have been provided with the following due process safeguards before he could be committed to a juvenile detention facility for six years:

1. Notice of the charges;
2. Right to counsel;
3. Right to confrontation and cross-examination;
4. Privilege against self-incrimination;
5. Right to a transcript of the proceeding;
6. Right to appellate review.

In re Gault established the basic due process standards for juvenile delinquency proceedings. What is your opinion on this issue? Should juveniles be treated as adults with full due process safeguards? Or, should they receive therapeutic treatment in a less-adversarial forum? These are interesting issues that have generated a spirited debate in the U.S. legal system.

Barry C. Feld

Abolish the Juvenile Court: Youthfulness, Criminal Responsibility, and Sentencing Policy

Introduction

Within the past three decades, judicial decisions, legislative amendments, and administrative changes have transformed the juvenile court from a nominally rehabilitative social welfare agency into a scaled-down, second-class criminal court for young people. These reforms have converted the historical ideal of the juvenile court as a social welfare institution into a penal system that provides young offenders with neither therapy nor justice. The substantive and procedural convergence between juvenile and criminal courts eliminates virtually all of the conceptual and operational differences in strategies of criminal social control for youths and adults. No compelling reasons exist to maintain separate from an adult criminal court, a punitive juvenile court whose only remaining distinctions are its persisting procedural deficiencies. Rather, states should abolish juvenile courts' delinquency jurisdiction and formally recognize youthfulness as a mitigating factor in the sentencing of younger criminal offenders. Such a policy would provide younger offenders with substantive protections comparable to those afforded by juvenile courts, assure greater procedural regularity in the determination of guilt, and avoid the disjunctions in social control caused by maintaining two duplicative and inconsistent criminal justice systems. . . .

Transformed but Unreformed: The Recent History of the Juvenile Court

The Juvenile Court

Many analysts have examined the social history of the juvenile court. Ideological changes in cultural conceptions of children and in strategies of social control during the nineteenth century led to the creation of the juvenile court in 1899. The juvenile court reform movement removed children from the

From *Journal of Criminal Law & Criminology*, vol. 88, issue 1, Fall 1997.

adult criminal justice and corrections systems, provided them with individualized treatment in a separate system, and substituted a scientific and preventative alternative to the criminal law's punitive policies. By separating children from adults and providing a rehabilitative alternative to punishment, juvenile courts rejected both the criminal law's jurisprudence and its procedural safeguards such as juries and lawyers. Judges conducted confidential and private hearings, limited public access to court proceedings and court records, employed a euphemistic vocabulary to minimize stigma, and adjudicated youths to be delinquent rather than convicted them of crimes. Under the guise of parens patriae, the juvenile court emphasized treatment, supervision, and control rather than punishment. The juvenile court's "rehabilitative ideal" envisioned a specialized judge trained in social science and child development whose empathic qualities and insight would enable her to make individualized therapeutic dispositions in the "best interests" of the child. Reformers pursued benevolent goals, individualized their solicitude, and maximized discretion to provide flexibility in diagnosis and treatment of the "whole child." They regarded a child's crimes primarily as a symptom of her "real needs," and consequently the nature of the offense affected neither the degree nor the duration of intervention. Rather, juvenile court judges imposed indeterminate and non-proportional sentences that potentially continued for the duration of minority. Progressives used a variety of state agencies to "Americanize" immigrants and the poor; from its inception, juvenile courts provided a coercive mechanism to discriminate between "our" children and "other peoples' children"—those from other ethnic backgrounds, cultures, and classes. . . .

The Constitutional Domestication of the Juvenile Court

In In re Gault, the Supreme Court began to transform the juvenile court into a very different institution than the Progressives contemplated. In Gault, the Supreme Court engrafted some formal procedures at trial onto the juvenile court's individualized treatment sentencing schema. Although the Court did not intend its decisions to alter juvenile courts' therapeutic mission, in the aftermath of Gault, judicial, legislative, and administrative changes have fostered a procedural and substantive convergence with adult criminal courts. Several subsequent Supreme Court decisions furthered the "criminalizing" of the juvenile court. In In re Winship, the Court required states to prove juvenile delinquency by the criminal law's standard of proof "beyond a reasonable doubt." In Breed v. Jones, the Court applied the constitutional ban on double jeopardy and posited a functional equivalence between criminal trials and delinquency proceedings.

Gault and Winship unintentionally, but inevitably, transformed the juvenile court system from its original Progressive conception as a social welfare agency into a wholly-owned subsidiary of the criminal justice system. By emphasizing criminal procedural regularity in the determination of delinquency, the Court shifted the focus of juvenile courts from paternalistic assessments of a youth's "real needs" to proof of commission of a crime. By formalizing the connection between criminal conduct and coercive intervention, the Court made explicit a relationship previously implicit, unacknowledged, and deliberately obscured. And, ironically, Gault and Winship's insistence on greater criminal procedural safeguards in juvenile courts may have legitimated more punitive dispositions for young offenders.

In McKeiver v. Pennsylvania, however, the Court denied to juveniles the constitutional right to jury trials in delinquency proceedings and halted the extension of full procedural parity with adult criminal prosecutions. Without elaborating upon or analyzing the distinctions, McKeiver relied upon the rhetorical differences between juvenile courts' treatment rationale and criminal courts' punitive purposes to justify the procedural disparities between the two settings. Because McKeiver endorsed a treatment justification for its decision, the right to a jury trial provides the crucial legal condition precedent to punish youths explicitly in juvenile courts. Several recent juvenile justice legislative reforms provide some youths with a statutory right to a jury in order to expand the punitive sentencing options available to juvenile court judges.

The Transformation of the Juvenile Court

In the decades since Gault, legislative, judicial, and administrative changes have modified juvenile courts' jurisdiction, purpose, and procedures and fostered their convergence with criminal courts. These inter-related developments—increased procedural formality, removal of status offenders from juvenile court jurisdiction, waiver of serious offenders to the adult system, and an increased emphasis on punishment in sentencing delinquents—constitute a form of criminological "triage," crucial components of the criminalizing of the juvenile court, and elements of the erosion of the theoretical and practical differences between the two systems. This "triage" strategy removes many middle-class, white, and female non-criminal status offenders from the juvenile court, simultaneously transfers persistent, violent, and disproportion ally minority youths to criminal court for prosecution as adults, and imposes increasingly punitive sanctions on those middle-range delinquent criminal offenders who remain under the jurisdiction of the juvenile court. As a result of these implicit triage policies, juvenile courts increasingly function similarly to adult criminal courts.

Status Offenses

Legislative recognition that juvenile courts often failed to realize their benevolent purposes has led to a strategic retrenchment of juvenile courts' jurisdiction over non-criminal misconduct such as truancy or incorrigibility, behavior that would not be a crime if committed by an adult. In the 1970s, critics objected that juvenile courts' status jurisdiction treated non-criminal offenders indiscriminately like criminal delinquents, disabled families and other sources of referral through one-sided intervention, and posed insuperable legal issues for the court. Judicial and legislative disillusionment with juvenile courts' responses to noncriminal youths led to diversion, deinstitutionalization, and decriminalization reforms that have removed much of the "soft" end of juvenile court clientele. These legislative and judicial reforms represent a strategic withdrawal from "child saving," an acknowledgment of the limited utility of coercive intervention to provide for child welfare, a reduced role in enforcing normative concepts of childhood, and a diminished prevention mission.

Waiver of Juvenile Offenders to Adult Criminal Court

A second jurisdictional change entails the criminalizing of serious juvenile offenders as courts and legislatures increasingly transfer chronic and violent youths from juvenile to criminal courts for prosecution as adults. Transfer laws simultaneously attempt to resolve both fundamental crime control issues and the ambivalence embedded in our cultural construction of youth. The jurisprudential conflicts reflect many of the current sentencing policy debates: the tensions between rehabilitation or incapacitation and retribution, between basing decisions on characteristics of the individual offender or the seriousness of the offense, between discretion and rules, and between indeterminacy and determinacy. Waiver laws attempt to reconcile the contradictions posed when the child is a criminal and the criminal is a child. What legal processes, crime control policies, and substantive criteria best enable decision-makers to select from among the competing cultural images of youths as responsible and culpable offenders and as immature and salvageable children? . . .

In response to the rise in youth homicide and gun violence in the late-1980s, almost every state has amended its waiver statutes and other provisions of their juvenile codes in a frantic effort to "get tough" and to stem the tide. These recent changes signal a fundamental inversion in juvenile court jurisprudence from treatment to punishment, from rehabilitation to retribution, from immature child to responsible criminal. Legislatures increasingly use age and offense criteria to redefine the boundaries of adulthood, coordinate juvenile transfer and adult sentencing practices, and reduce the "punishment gap." The common over-arching legislative strategy reflects a jurisprudential shift from the principle of individualized justice to the principle of offense, from rehabilitation to retribution, and an emphasis on the seriousness of the offense rather than judges' clinical assessments of offenders' "amenability to treatment." State legislative amendments use offense criteria either as dispositional guidelines to structure and limit judicial discretion, to guide prosecutorial charging decisions, or automatically to exclude certain youths from juvenile court jurisdiction.

Regardless of the details of these legislative strategies, the efforts to "crack down" and to "get tough" repudiate rehabilitation and judicial discretion, narrow juvenile courts' jurisdiction, base youths' "adult" status increasingly on the offense charged, and reflect a shift toward more retributive sentencing policies. Whether the legislature makes the forum decision by excluding offenses, or the prosecutor does so on a discretionary basis via concurrent jurisdiction, these laws reduce or remove both discretionary judicial authority and juvenile courts' clientele. Offense exclusion rejects juvenile courts' philosophical premise that they can aid youth and denies them the opportunity to try without regard to the "real needs" of the offending youth.

Finally, the legal shift to punish more young offenders as adults exposes at least some youths to the possibility of capital punishment for the crimes they committed as juveniles.

Although legislatures and courts transfer youths to criminal court so that they may receive longer sentences as adults than they could in the juvenile system, chronic property offenders constitute the bulk of juveniles judicially waived in most states, and they often receive shorter sentences as adults than do property offenders retained in juvenile court. By contrast, youths convicted of violent offenses in criminal courts appear to receive substantially longer sentences than do their retained juvenile counterparts. For youths and adults convicted of comparable crimes, both types of disparities—shorter sentences for waived youths than for retained juveniles adjudicated for property offenses, and dramatically longer sentences for waived youths than for retained juveniles convicted for violent crimes raise issues of sentencing policy fairness and justice. No coherent policy rationales justify either type of disparities. Rather, some youths experience dramatically different consequences than do other offenders simply because of the disjunction between two separate criminal justice systems. The transition to adulthood also occurs during the peak of youths' criminal careers. Thus, jurisdictional bifurcation undermines the ability of the adult justice system to respond adequately to either persistent or violent young offenders. Without an integrated record system that merges juvenile with adult criminal histories, some chronic offenders may "slip through the cracks" and receive inappropriately lenient sentences as adults.

Sentencing Delinquent Offenders

The same jurisprudential shifts from offender to the offense and from treatment to punishment that inspire changes in waiver policies increasingly affect the sentences that juvenile court judges impose on serious delinquent offenders as well. Progressive reformers envisioned a broader and more encompassing social welfare system for youths and did not circumscribe state power narrowly. Juvenile courts' parens patriae ideology combined social welfare with penal social control in one institution, minimized procedural safeguards, and maximized discretion to provide flexibility in diagnosis and treatment. They focused primary attention on youths' social circumstances and accorded secondary significance either to procedural safeguards or to proof of guilt or the specific offense.

The same public impetus and political pressures to waive the most serious young offenders to criminal courts also impel juvenile courts to "get tough" and punish more severely the remaining criminal delinquents, the residual "less bad of the worst." Several indicators reveal whether a juvenile court judge's disposition punishes a youth for his past offense or treats him for his future welfare. Increasingly, juvenile court legislative purpose clauses and court opinions explicitly endorse punishment as an appropriate component of juvenile sanctions. Currently, nearly half of the states use determinate or mandatory minimum sentencing provisions that base a youth's disposition on the offense she committed rather than her "real needs" to regulate at least some aspects of sentence duration, institutional commitment, or release. Empirical evaluations of juvenile courts' sentencing practices indicate that the present offense and prior record account for most of the explained variance in judges' dispositions of delinquents, and reinforce the criminal orientation of juvenile courts. Despite their penal focus, however, the individualized discretion inherent in juvenile courts' treatment ideology is often synonymous with racial discrimination. Finally, evaluations of conditions of confinement and treatment effectiveness, believe any therapeutic "alternative purpose" to juvenile incarceration. In short, all of these indicators consistently reveal that treating juveniles closely resembles punishing adults. A strong, nationwide policy shift both in theory and in practice away from therapeutic dispositions toward punishment or incapacitation of young offenders characterizes sentencing practice in the contemporary juvenile court. . . .

The Inherent Contradiction of the Juvenile Court

The foregoing jurisdictional, jurisprudential, and procedural changes have transformed the juvenile court from its original model as a social service agency into a deficient second-rate criminal court that provides young people with neither positive treatment nor criminal procedural justice. It effectively punishes young offenders, but uses procedures under which no adult would consent to be tried if she faced the prospect of confinement in a secure facility. The changes in procedures, jurisdiction, and sentencing policies reflect the contradictory roles of juvenile courts and ambivalence about the social control of young offenders. The Progressives sited the juvenile court on a number of unstable cultural and criminological fault lines that exacerbate the conflicted impulses engendered when a child is a criminal and a criminal is a child. In this section, I contend that juvenile courts' social welfare mission cannot and should not be rehabilitated. In the next section, I advocate abolishing the juvenile court and trying all offenders in one integrated criminal court with modifications for the youthfulness of some defendants. . . .

Failure of Implementation versus Conception

The fundamental shortcoming of the juvenile court's welfare idea reflects a failure of conception rather than simply a failure of implementation. The juvenile court's creators envisioned a social service agency in a judicial setting, and attempted to fuse its welfare mission with the power of state coercion. The juvenile court idea that judicial-clinicians successfully can combine social welfare and penal social control in one agency represents an inherent conceptual flaw and an innate contradiction. Combining social welfare and penal social control functions in one agency assures that the court does both badly. Providing for child welfare is a societal responsibility rather than a judicial one. Juvenile courts lack control over the resources necessary to meet child welfare needs exactly because of the social class and racial characteristics of their clients. In practice, juvenile courts subordinate welfare concerns to crime control considerations.

The conflicted impulses engendered between concern for child welfare and punitive responses to criminal violations form the root of the ambivalence embedded in the juvenile court. The hostile reactions that people experience toward other peoples' children, whom they regard as a threat to themselves and their own children, undermine benevolent aspirations and elevate concerns for their control. Juvenile justice personnel simultaneously profess child-saving aspirations but more often function as agents of criminal social control.

The juvenile court inevitably subordinates social welfare to criminal social control because of its built-in penal focus. Legislatures do not define juvenile courts' social welfare jurisdiction on the basis of characteristics of children for which they are not responsible and for which effective intervention could improve their lives. For example, juvenile court law does not define eligibility for services or create an enforceable right or entitlement based upon young peoples' lack of access to decent education, lack of adequate housing or nutrition, unmet health needs, or impoverished families—none of which are their fault. In all of these instances, children bear the social burdens of their parents' circumstances literally as innocent bystanders. If states defined juvenile courts' jurisdiction on the basis of young people's needs for social welfare, then they would declare a broad category of at-risk children who are eligible for public assistance. Such a policy would require a substantial commitment of social resources and public will to children's welfare. . . .

Youthfulness, Criminal Responsibility, and Sentencing Policy: Young Offenders in Criminal Courts

Once we uncouple social welfare from penal social control, then no need remains for a separate juvenile court for young offenders. We can try all offenders in criminal court with certain modifications of substantive and procedural criminal law to accommodate younger defendants. Some proponents of juvenile courts properly object that criminal courts suffer from profound deficiencies: crushing caseloads; ineffective attorneys; insufficient sentencing alternatives; coercive plea bargains; and assembly-line justice. Unfortunately, these shortcomings equally characterize juvenile courts as well. Others argue that because no social or political will exists to reform or provide resources for criminal courts, then juvenile court abolitionists must demonstrate conclusively their irremediable bankruptcy before remitting youths to the criminal courts that inspired their creation. In short, few juvenile court proponents even attempt any longer to defend the institution on its own merits, but only to justify it by comparison with criminal courts, which they contend are worse. In this article, I do not propose simultaneously to completely reform the criminal justice system, but rather only to identify the sentencing policy issues raised when the criminal is a child. Because legislatures, prosecutors, and juvenile court judges already transfer increasing numbers and younger offenders to criminal courts for prosecution as adults, formulating a youth sentencing policy has considerable contemporary salience whether or not states abolish juvenile courts in their entirety.

If the child is a criminal and the "real" reason for formal intervention is criminal social control, then states should abolish juvenile courts' delinquency jurisdiction and try young offenders in criminal courts alongside their adult counterparts. But, if the criminal is a child, then states must modify their criminal justice system to accommodate the youthfulness of some defendants. Before prosecuting a child as a criminal in an integrated court, a legislature must address issues of substance and procedure. Substantive justice requires a rationale to sentence younger offenders differently, and more leniently, than older defendants, a formal recognition of youthfulness as a mitigating factor in sentencing. Procedural justice requires providing youths with full procedural parity with adult defendants and additional safeguards to account for the disadvantages of youth in the justice system. Taken in combination, these substantive and procedural modifications can avoid the "worst of both worlds," provide youths with protections functionally equivalent to those accorded adults, and do justice in sentencing.

Politically popular "sound-bites"—"old enough to do the crime, old enough to do the time" or "adult crime, adult time"—do not analyze adequately the complexities of a youth sentencing policy. My proposal to abolish the juvenile court constitutes neither an unqualified endorsement of punishment nor a primitive throw-back to earlier centuries' views of young people as miniature adults. Rather, it honestly acknowledges that juvenile courts currently engage in criminal social control, asserts that younger offenders in a criminal justice system deserve less severe consequences for their misdeeds than do more mature offenders simply because they are young, and addresses many problems created by trying to maintain binary, dichotomous, and contradictory criminal justice systems based on an arbitrary age classification of a youth as a child or as an adult. . . .

Summary and Conclusions: Let's Be Honest About Youth Crime Control

Law reforms that tinker with the boundaries of childhood or modify judicial procedures do not appear to reduce appreciably offenders' probabilities of recidivism or increase public safety. Even far-reaching justice system changes can have only a marginal impact on social problems as complex as crime and violence. Rather, a proposal to abolish the juvenile court and to try all young offenders in an integrated justice system makes no utilitarian claims, but represents a commitment to honesty about state coercion. States bring young offenders who commit crimes to juvenile court for social control and to punish them. Juvenile courts' rehabilitative claims fly in the face of their penal reality, undermine their legitimacy, and impair their ability to function as judicial agencies. Because punishment is an unpleasant topic, juvenile courts attempt to evade those disagreeable qualities by obscuring their reality with rehabilitative euphemisms, psycho-babble, and judicial "double-speak" like "sometimes punishment is treatment."

The shortcomings of the "rehabilitative" juvenile court run far deeper than inadequate resources and rudimentary and unproven treatment techniques. Rather, the flaw lies in the very idea that the juvenile court can combine successfully criminal social control and social welfare in one system. Similarly, a separate "criminal" juvenile court cannot succeed or long survive because it lacks a coherent rationale to distinguish it from a "real" criminal court. A scaled-down separate criminal court for youths simply represents a temporary way-station on the road to substantive and procedural convergence with the criminal court. Only an integrated criminal justice that formally recognizes adolescence as a developmental continuum may effectively address many of the problems created by our . . . conceptions of youth and social control.

Enhanced procedural protections, a "youth discount" of sentences, and age-segregated dispositional facilities recognize and respond to the "real" developmental differences between young people and adult offenders in the justice system. Because these policy proposals require state legislators courageous enough to adopt them, several thoughtful commentators question whether elected public officials in a "get tough" political climate would make explicit the leniency implicit in the contemporary juvenile court. While the public unknowingly may tolerate nominal sanctions administered to young offenders in low visibility juvenile proceedings, politicians may balk at openly acknowledging a policy of moderation. Many elected officials prefer to demagogue about crime and posture politically to "crack down" on youth crime rather than to responsibly educate the public about the realistic limits of the justice system to control it. Some would rather fan the flames of fear for political advantage despite overwhelming evidence that escalating rates of imprisonment represent a failed policy that ultimately leads only to fiscal and moral bankruptcy.

I propose to abolish the juvenile court with trepidation. On the one hand, combining enhanced procedural safeguards with a "youth discount" in an integrated criminal court can provide young offenders with greater protections and justice than they currently receive in the juvenile system, and more proportional and humane consequences than judges presently inflict on them in the criminal justice system. Integration may foster a more consistent crime control response than the present dual systems permit to violent and chronic young offenders at various stages of the developmental and criminal career continuum. On the other hand, politicians may ignore the significance of youthfulness as a mitigating factor and use these proposals to escalate the punishment of young people. Although abolition of the juvenile court, enhanced procedural protections, and a "youth discount" constitute essential components of a youth sentencing policy package, nothing can prevent legislators from selectively choosing only those elements that serve their "get tough" agenda, even though doing so unravels the threads that make coherent a proposal for an integrated court.

In either event, the ensuing debate about a youth sentencing policy would require them to consider whether to focus primarily on the fact that young offenders are young or offenders. A public policy debate about when the child is a criminal and the criminal is a child forces a long overdue and critical reassessment of the entire social construction of "childhood." To what extent do adolescents really differ from adults? To what extent do differences in competency and judgment result from physical or psychological developmental processes, or from social arrangements and institutions that systematically disable young people? If politicians ultimately insist upon treating young people primarily as offenders and the equals of adults, can they simultaneously maintain without contradiction other age-graded legal distinctions such as denial of the right to vote or to exercise self-determination?

The idea of the juvenile court is fundamentally flawed because it attempts to combine criminal social control and social welfare goals. My proposal to abolish the juvenile court does not entail an abandonment of its welfare ideal. Rather, uncoupling policies of social welfare from penal social control enables us to expand a societal commitment to the welfare of all children regardless of their criminality. If we frame child welfare policy reforms in terms of child welfare rather than crime control, then we may expand the possibilities for positive intervention for all young people. For example, a public health approach to youth crime that identified the social, environmental, community structural, and ecological correlates of youth violence, such as poverty, the proliferation of handguns, and the commercialization of violence, would suggest wholly different intervention strategies than simply incarcerating minority youths. Youth violence occurs as part of a social ecological structure; high rates of violent youth crime arise in areas of concentrated poverty, high teenage pregnancy, and AFDC dependency. Such social indicators could identify census tracts or even zip-codes for community organizing, economic development, and preventive and remedial intervention.

Three aspects of youth crime and violence suggest future social welfare policy directions regardless of their immediate impact on recidivism. First, it is imperative to provide a hopeful future for all young people. As a result of structural and economic changes since the 1980s, the ability of families to raise children, to prepare them for the transition to adulthood, and to provide them with a more promising future has declined. Many social indicators of the status of young people—poverty, homelessness, violent victimization, and crime—are negative and some of those adverse trends are accelerating. Without realistic hope for their future, young people fall into despair, nihilism, and violence. Second, the disproportionate over-representation of minority youths in the juvenile justice system makes imperative the pursuit of racial and social justice. A generation ago, the Kerner Commission warned that the United States was "moving toward two societies, one black, one white—separate and unequal." The Kerner Commission predicted that to continue present policies was "to make permanent the division of our country into two societies; one, largely Negro and poor, located in the central cities; the other, predominantly white and affluent, located in the suburbs." Today we reap the bitter harvest of racial segregation, concentrated poverty, urban social disintegration, and youth violence sown by social policies and public neglect a generation ago. Third, youth violence has become increasingly lethal as the proliferation of handguns transforms adolescent altercations into homicidal encounters. Only public policies that reduce and reverse the proliferation of guns in the youth population will stem the carnage.

While politicians may be unwilling to invest scarce social resources in young "criminals," particularly those of other colors or cultures, a demographic shift and an aging population give all of us a stake in young people and encourage us to invest in their human capital for their and our own future well-being and to maintain an inter-generational compact. Social welfare and legal policies to provide all young people with a hopeful future, to reduce racial and social inequality, and to reduce access to and use of firearms require a public and political commitment to the welfare of children that extends far beyond the resources or competencies of any juvenile justice system.

NO 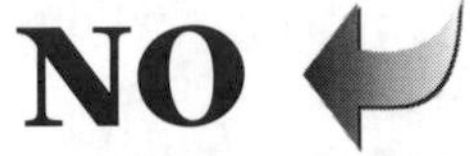

Thomas F. Geraghty

Justice for Children: How Do We Get There?

Introduction

This article is the response of a lawyer who represents children charged with crimes in juvenile court to those who call for the abolition of the juvenile court and for placing increased criminal responsibility upon delinquent youth. I argue that the juvenile court and the juvenile justice system (including community-based support programs for children and families) should be retained after being reinvigorated with both financial and human resources. These investments will allow the juvenile courts to perform credibly—even when dealing with the relatively few "serious" or "violent" offenders who now pass through our juvenile justice system.

I make this argument because I see daily the tragic impact of the criminalization of the juvenile court and referral of my clients to criminal court and believe that this trend does not serve victims or society at-large. The acts of a very few children and their access to guns drive the campaign for "get tough" measures which include increased transfer of youth to criminal court and, tragically, the marginalization of juvenile courts. In the course of representing the increasingly young children who find themselves in jeopardy of becoming defendants in criminal court, I learn about their experiences and about what has brought them to this tragic point. I do not claim that this perspective is unique or that it should be the only perspective considered in this debate. But it is an important perspective that has heretofore carried relatively little weight.

My perspective is informed by practice in the Juvenile Court of Cook County, and so admittedly some of the lessons I have learned and the conclusions I draw may be parochial. I leave it to the readers with knowledge of other juvenile court systems to judge whether my conclusions resonate with theirs. . . .

A Case

In an effort to make my arguments and my perspective more concrete, let me describe a composite of the increasingly typical case seen in the clinical pro-

From *Journal of Criminal Law & Criminology*, vol. 88, issue 1, Fall 1997.

gram at the Northwestern University School of Law and the Juvenile Court of Cook County.

The Crime

The neighborhood is gang-controlled. The gang's major source of income comes from the sale of drugs. The gang has a hierarchy. The bottom rung is occupied by the ten to twelve-year-olds, including my client, who do the bidding of older members of the gang. My client's biological family consists of his mother and several siblings. An older gang member, age twenty-one, engages my client to sell drugs. An occupant of a large apartment building, outside of which drugs are being sold, calls the police to report the drug dealing. The drug trade is temporarily disrupted. The older gang member tells one of his younger "employees" to burn the building down. Late one evening, a fire starts in the building. An elderly woman dies of smoke inhalation. Other occupants of the building are injured as they attempt to flee the burning building. The person who complained about the gang's drug selling says that she thinks she sees my client coming out of her building just before the fire started.

My Client

My client is thirteen-years-old. He is charged with murder of the elderly woman who died in the fire. The State wants to try him as an adult. He is the smallest person I have ever represented. When he sits up straight at counsel table in juvenile court, his chin rests on the surface of the table. His I.Q. is 54. He reads at a third grade level. His record contains eight prior "station adjustments" and three referrals to juvenile court—all occurring within the last eighteen months. At the time of this incident he was on probation for criminal damage to property. He seems to have little comprehension of what is going on around him in court. When he was placed on probation six months ago, the juvenile court judge who sentenced him ordered the Department of Children and Family Services (DCFS) to find him a residential placement. He was sent home to await placement. No placement was found. The DCFS worker was looking for a placement when my client was arrested for the murder. The only assistance or guidance he received during the four months he spent at home waiting for placement were two counseling sessions.

The client's narrative of his family history and of his alleged involvement in the crime is difficult to obtain and to organize. He lacks the ability to recount these "stories" spontaneously and accurately. Much work needs to be done by his legal team to gather information from him and from the members of his family. Social workers, psychologists, and psychiatrists are enlisted to help develop a family history and to identify educational deficits and emotional and psychiatric needs.

The work of the lawyer, social worker, psychologist, and psychiatrist team reveals that our client is heavily gang-involved, primarily as a result of the gang allegiance of his older brother. Our client is failing in school. He attends school infrequently. His mother is a single parent who is unemployed.

She is challenged by the task of nurturing and supporting her two sons and three daughters, all under age seventeen.

The Courtroom

The courtroom is in the Juvenile Court of Cook County, a building which contains not only the sixteen delinquency courts, but also the sixteen neglect and abuse courts as well. In addition, the building houses the Cook County Juvenile Temporary Detention Center, where children in custody pending trial are held. While waiting trial in the Detention Center, they attend school, some for the first sustained period in their lives. They are also well fed. There are no adults facing criminal charges housed with the children in the Temporary Juvenile Detention Center. The Detention Center is, however, overcrowded with almost a third more children there than it is licensed to accommodate.

In the courtroom during the hearing are my client, my colleagues and law students on the defense team, the judge, the prosecutor, the probation officer, and the victim's family. With the victim's family is a witness advocate from the prosecutor's office. The victim's family occupies the first row of seats. My client's family sits behind the victim's family. My client sits between his lawyers at counsel table.

If you were to approach counsel table from the rear as you enter the courtroom, you would be struck by the comparison in size between his two lawyers, whose bodies are both below and above the table, and my client, who, except for his head, is below the table. My client doodles on a legal pad while the testimony is presented. He is not listening. He nudges his lawyers when he has drawn something of which he is particularly proud.

The Evidence

A police officer testifies that my client admitted to him that he acted as a "lookout" while other youngsters went into the building. The police officer cannot recall if my client said anything that supports the prosecution's contention that my client played a part in the scheme to set the fire. The judge rules that the state has made a showing that a grand jury would probably indict. The state presents a probation officer and a psychiatrist who describe the child's history and mental status. Neither the probation officer nor the psychiatrist recommend transfer to criminal court. We present a psychologist who has diagnosed our client as having a conduct disorder with adolescent onset, the significance of which, our witness contends, is that my client is a good candidate for treatment interventions.

All of the witnesses agree that my client will probably be rehabilitated within the seven years that he would be required to spend in the Juvenile Division of the Department of Corrections if he were to be convicted of murder in the juvenile court. We call the DCFS worker responsible for finding a placement for our client. He testifies that indeed no treatment or services were provided. Closing arguments are given.

My colleagues and I leave the courtroom convinced that our client has understood little about the nature and purpose of the proceedings that he has just witnessed. He understands even less about the momentous decision that the juvenile court judge is about to make about his future. His lack of comprehension persists despite our repeated efforts to explain to him the significance of the transfer hearing.

Why begin this article with an example from the real world of community, courts, and practice? Because the example places in perspective the dilemmas involved in charting the course of the future of justice for children. Without taking into account such examples, we are unlikely to fashion solutions which respond to realities. What is the level of the moral responsibility of my client? To what extent should we take into account factors such as the capacity of his family to nurture him, his subservience to older gang members, and his low intellectual functioning? Can the juvenile justice system "rehabilitate" my client so that, assuming he is now "dangerous," he will no longer be so when released? What kind of justice system holds the most promise for supporting my client's development as an adolescent while at the same time protecting society?

The Problems

As a practitioner in juvenile court, and as one who follows the public perception of juvenile courts in the media, I know that the future of juvenile courts is in jeopardy now just as it was only a few years after it was created, and just as it has been throughout its history. Reasons for the uncertainties regarding the future of juvenile courts are the same as those which gave our ancestors pause shortly after the court was founded: (1) lack of consensus about the definition and viability of the juvenile court's mission; (2) concerns about the capabilities of those working within the juvenile justice system to produce results; (3) under-funding and/or inefficient use of funds by juvenile courts and associated agencies; and (4) lack of confidence in the effectiveness of interventions designed to turn children away from delinquent conduct. These concerns have paralyzed juvenile courts. This paralysis has taken the form of demoralization, adherence to old models out of defensiveness, and consequent failure to articulate new visions. Moreover, although there are positive responses to each of the four criticisms of the juvenile system set forth above, those answers have not received the same degree of attention that the criticisms have received. A positive, rather than a defensive, approach to reinvigorating juvenile courts may hold the key.

Mission

The controversial aspect of the juvenile court's mission in today's political and social context is the extent to which juvenile courts should attempt to adjudicate and dispose of cases involving youth who commit serious crimes. What kind of juvenile crime and what kinds of children can juvenile courts effectively manage? A narrow vision of a juvenile court's role is that it exists to address the problems of non-serious offenders; indeed, this was probably the objective of the original juvenile court. The narrow vision, need not of course be narrow. By focusing on relatively less serious offenders, the court may be able to offer more services to youth at risk to prevent them from becoming serious offenders.

A more expansive vision would have juvenile courts adjudicating, prescribing interventions, and/or incarcerating both non-serious and serious juvenile offenders. Some argue that the juvenile court will not survive if it takes on the challenge and the "heat" of attempting to deal with older children who commit serious crimes. This is so because there is a widely held public perception that in these cases there is great risk that "treatment" will not work and because the punitive sanctions available to juvenile courts are simply not severe enough to satisfy societal norms of punishment. Given the risk that juvenile courts will "fail" when dealing with the "serious" or "violent" offender, it would be better, some juvenile court preservationists argue, not to subject juvenile courts to this risk of public condemnation.

Both the less expansive vision and the most expansive vision fail to take into account a number of creative solutions that permit both rehabilitation and lengthy incarceration if treatment fails or is impossible. These solutions would permit us to retain the "best of both worlds" by maintaining incentives for rehabilitation, yet ensuring as best as possible the protection of the public. The experience of those states which have experimented with various combinations of juvenile and adult sanctions and programs should be evaluated.

People

A mission statement is important. But from this practitioner's perspective, people are the key. It is the work and decision-making of the people who interact with children who determine the quality of fact finding, the thorough exploration of dispositional alternatives, and the performance of treatment and correctional agencies. This will be true in any system that we design, although good people can be burdened to such an extent that even the most highly motivated throw up their hands or become demoralized. Unless the juvenile courts can identify and train good people and support their work in ways which provide them with incentives to continue, juvenile justice systems will not realize their potential.

I am not a personnel specialist. I have not studied the hiring, promotion, and termination practices of juvenile courts. I have not studied organizational behavior. But I have been going to the Juvenile Court of Cook County once or twice a week for the last twenty-eight years. Based on this experience, I concede it would be difficult to remain a highly motivated full-time employee in that system, given the crushing caseloads. I have been able to continue to maintain my enthusiasm for the representation of children in juvenile court in part because I am not there every day.

Under more favorable circumstances, the potential for attracting good people to juvenile court is limitless because the mission of juvenile courts promises the ability to intervene meaningfully in the lives of troubled children. Those of us who teach law students know that they clamor for the opportunity to work with young clients and for careers in juvenile court. Many would sacrifice prestigious law firm jobs and high salaries for this opportunity. I am sure that the same holds true for young social workers, psychologists, and psychiatrists. Why then do juvenile courts consistently fail to take advantage of the talents of people who would like to devote their lives to serving children?

The answer is simple. The work of the lawyers and judges in our juvenile court and in most large urban courts is simply unmanageable. It is impossible to do one's job thoroughly. The numbers simply do not permit sufficient attention to individual cases. Moreover, there are few dispositional alternatives which adequately meet the needs of the children who come before the court. This is demoralizing to those who care about their work. As a consequence, positions are hard to fill with highly skilled people; many highly motivated people leave out of frustration.

Funding

Our juvenile court judges are paid reasonable salaries. So are our public defenders, public guardians, and state's attorneys. This is not to say that they do not deserve more. There is great demand for these jobs as there is for the positions of probation officer, deputy sheriff, and court clerk. Cook County has recently devoted substantial funds for renovation and new building at our juvenile court complex. However, the fact remains that the Circuit Court of Cook County would not tolerate the levels of caseload per judge in its "complex case" civil division as seen in the Cook County Juvenile Court. No private law office would saddle its lawyers with 400–500 cases each as is common in our Cook County Public Defender's office. The choices seem clear: reduce intake through utilization of effective screening protocols and community-based diversion programs, or increase the number of personnel required competently to address the needs of the children and families who appear in juvenile court.

Does lack of funding drive the difficulty in obtaining social and treatment services for my clients? In some cases yes, in some cases no. Often, the reasons for the "unavailability" of services are lack of knowledge about their availability and the difficulty of securing funding for them. Indeed, the tasks of knowing about available services and how to fund them are important but neglected sub-specialties which should be better developed within juvenile courts. In addition, our juvenile court has no power to order state or private agencies to fund services or placements. It can only commit children to state agencies (the Department of Children and Family Services or the Department of Corrections). The agency then has the discretion to decide how to place and treat the child; the juvenile court has no authority to see to it that the agency performs its assignment. Moreover, once a child is committed to a state agency, lack of funding may constrain the agency's decision to provide needed services.

Effectiveness of Interventions

The old saying that "nothing works" has been pretty well discredited. Those of us who represent children in juvenile court, the vast majority of whom are poor, know that an individual or a program that forges a relationship with a child has a good chance of succeeding. Indeed, families with financial resources who have access to effective services often experience successful treatment outcomes. The problem for most poor children is finding the appropriate program and figuring out how to pay for it. In Illinois, unfortunately, few such programs for poor children exist. This means that failure of juvenile court intervention is caused not by programs that do not work, but by the unavailability of or failure to identify programs that do work. A multitude of programs designed to reduce recidivism among young offenders have been shown to be successful. Moreover, new approaches to interventions designed to change the behaviors of children charged with crimes, such as the "balanced and restorative justice" model are receiving substantial attention from legislators and juvenile court personnel.

Recent initiatives to improve juvenile courts hold promise that we can develop a juvenile justice system that will effectively and humanely balance the needs of children and the protection of the public. Initiatives such as these spark new excitement, commitment, and sense of professionalism among all who work in juvenile courts and hold the potential to attract needed talent to this vital institution.

Response to the Problems: The Practitioner's Perspective

I recognize that the ideas of those who practice in juvenile court are not the only perspectives to be valued in this debate; input from a variety of perspectives is essential to determining the best possible way to address the problems of delinquent youth and protection of the public. The future of juvenile courts uniquely depends on a multitude of interests and influences. Judges, lawyers, social workers, psychologists, court administrators, child welfare agencies, state departments of child welfare and corrections all have considerable influence in the debate. Perhaps most important are the state legislators who are responsible for writing juvenile justice legislation and thus have the ultimate power to shape the future of juvenile courts. There has been little discussion about how constructive dialogues can be initiated between those who study juvenile court, those who work in them, and the legislators who shape and implement juvenile justice policy. For our juvenile justice system to succeed, there must be a constructive collaboration between practitioners, scholars, court administrators, and legislators. . . .

There are additional questions to ask in deciding the future of justice for children. Perhaps the most important questions are: (1) what kind of system of justice for children is most likely to be flexible and child-centered while at the same time taking into account the needs and interests of the public? and (2) what kind of system of justice for children will continue to motivate our society to continue to search, with flexibility in light of experience, for new answers to the question of how best to adjudicate and treat young people accused of crimes?

Areas of Agreement: Abolitionists and Preservationists Concur

Identification of areas of consensus regarding a debated issue sometimes has the effect of demonstrating that the "disputants" agree on more issues than they debate. Refining the debate to the actual disputed points focuses the discussion and makes it more productive. In the debate over the future of justice for children, there are three points that are not in controversy: (1) children are fundamentally different in their cognitive and moral decision-making capabilities than adults; (2) the juvenile justice system has failed to satisfy expectations for providing procedural protection and successful interventions; and (3) the juvenile justice system cannot survive solely by relying upon the historical justifications for its founding. The point that is in controversy is Professor Feld's conclusion that juvenile courts should be abolished as a consequence of points 1 and 2. However, a close examination of the points of agreement, I argue, makes abolition of the juvenile court unnecessary and undesirable.

The developmental and "moral decision-making" differences between children and adults support the proposition that we should distinguish between the sanctions we impose upon children and those we impose upon adults. The fact that juvenile courts have failed to live up to expectations requires that we reconceptualize and re-tool the court rather than abolish it. The lack of procedural protections which are of concern to Professor Feld can be solved by providing child-sensitive jury trials in juvenile court.

Children Are Fundamentally Different Than Adults

The reality that children are fundamentally different than adults in their ability to make moral judgments and more amenable to treatment than adults has always been at the heart of the juvenile court movement. These differences are not disputed by any of the authors in this Symposium. Indeed, the developmental differences between children and adults are acknowledged and underscored by many authors and by psychologists and psychiatrists.

Neither Professor Feld nor Professor Morse dispute these basic propositions about the relative capacity of children and adults to make reasoned judgments. Of course, the extent of the "fundamental difference" between children and adults depends on the age, sophistication, and personality development of the child at issue. A "just" system, therefore, would be a system which combines fair adjudication, punishment in proportion to the child's responsibility, and dispositions that recognize rehabilitation, consistent with a "responsibility" message, and the need to protect the public. Professors Feld and Morse would not dissent from this proposition either. A "just" system, especially one that addresses the problems of young people, must be flexible but consistent in its response to individual children, to the nature of the societal problems presented to it, and to the evolving lessons of child and adolescent development. Morse's position that children should have imposed on them more responsibility for their actions and Feld's argument that more consistency can be achieved in the adult court setting with a "youth discount" mitigating the harshness of adult sentences, are not incompatible with these propositions.

The Juvenile Justice System Has Failed to Satisfy Expectations

Another fact that is not disputed is that juvenile courts and their associated agencies have historically fallen short. Juvenile courts have failed to adequately protect the procedural rights of the children who appear in juvenile court. Associated agencies have failed to provide sufficient state-of-the-art interventions. The first set of criticisms is justified: juvenile courts (and, indeed, criminal courts) have failed to adhere to the highest ideals of due process. The second set of criticisms, while justified, should not compel the conclusion that juvenile courts be abolished. Juvenile courts should not shoulder the blame for inadequate or unsuccessful interventions on behalf of children.

Failure to Adhere to Due Process

Although the parens patriae and rehabilitative ideals of the court have long enjoyed considerable appeal, the implementation of those ideals has been problematic. The parens patriae philosophy led to the abuses of judicial and administrative power that Gault sought to curtail. The Supreme Court's decision in Gault did not eradicate those abuses. Lack of resources and power allocated to defense counsel for children, as well as continuing reluctance on the part of judges to fully implement due process protections, leave many children in our juvenile courts in the pre-Gault "worst of both worlds." . . .

Failure to Solve the Problem of Crime Committed by Children

Many of the critics of juvenile courts argue that the jurisdiction of juvenile courts should be limited and that juvenile courts should be abolished because they have not been effective in preventing crime committed by children. However, the role of a court is not to curb crime. The role of a court is to find facts fairly and to impose sentences which take into account a myriad of factors, including the seriousness of the offense, the culpability of the child, the defendant's potential for rehabilitation, and protection of the public.

The unfairness to children and to the concept of the juvenile court (admittedly a lesser consideration) of expecting that juvenile courts can, by themselves, curb crime is underscored by the fact that many of our largest juvenile courts have always been under funded and understaffed. An example of this phenomenon is, again, the juvenile Court of Cook County, where judges in the delinquency division of the court have 1,500–2,000 cases on their calendars. Public defenders' caseloads can be as high as 400 cases at any one time. The three to four state's attorneys assigned to each of these courtrooms are responsible for prosecuting all of the cases assigned to the judge. Under these circumstances, we cannot expect any court to meet expectations. However, transferring the problems of this over-loaded system to the adult criminal courts (which are themselves stretched beyond capacity) cannot be the answer. . . .

No Agreement: Professor Feld's Proposal to Abolish The Juvenile Court

I make two arguments which support retaining and strengthening juvenile courts rather than abolishing them. The first is that criminal courts will never adapt themselves to the distinct challenges of doing justice to children. The second argument is that procedural protections (including the right to jury trial) could be provided in "re-tooled" juvenile courts without destroying the distinctive mission of juvenile courts. First, I turn to the reasons for not relying upon criminal courts to process all criminal cases involving children.

The Operation of Criminal Courts, Especially Those in Urban Areas, Falls Short

Criminal courts in large urban areas are overburdened. There are too many cases, too few lawyers representing too many defendants, and too few resources to support probation and correctional services. Indeed, many argue that our criminal justice system (courts and correctional systems) are in a state of crisis, despite the best intentions of the many and dedicated lawyers, judges, and correctional workers who populate the system. Overburdened courts and correctional agencies are simply not prepared to absorb the number and character of the cases which, if juvenile courts were abolished, would flood criminal systems. This would be true even if all juvenile court resources were shifted to criminal courts, because the crisis within our criminal courts will likely not permit sufficient focus on resources to be directed to the problems of children.

Children Will Be Second Class Citizens in Criminal Court

We know that given the history of the separate juvenile court, and the history of child welfare systems generally, that children would be second class citizens in a unified criminal court. We know this from the history of juvenile courts themselves: juvenile courts have always been the neglected stepchildren of court systems. This is because the children in juvenile court have no social or economic power. The status of the special needs of children within a criminal court system would be even lower.

In a unified system, there would be no hope that a sophisticated children's court, with judges, defenders, and prosecutors who specialize in the adjudication and disposition of offenses committed by children, would develop. There is substantial evidence that these specialties will develop in the near future in separate juvenile courts. Although this argument would be more powerful if juvenile courts had performed better and had even more promise, we should not make matters worse for children and for society by subjecting children to a criminal justice system that has no incentives to take their special needs into account.

In juvenile courts, children's advocates "lobby" for better court administration, better judges, and better services. Some of this lobbying is performed by lawyers in the context of the representation of individual clients. Good probation and social service providers lobby for better resources with which to serve the children for whom they are responsible. The potential for improvement of court and social services through collaboration between legal and social service providers is enormous.

Needless to say, this "lobbying" on behalf of the interests of children is not always as effective as it could be. However, children tried in criminal court would have less effective special voices advocating for their interests, thus making their plight worse than it is now. The very existence of juvenile courts keeps alive a special focus on the causes, prevention, and cures for delinquent behavior. The interests of children and the special focus on causes, prevention, and cures in a unified criminal system would necessarily become subsidiary to the goal of the new unified criminal court—that goal being the efficient trial of cases and sentencing of all defendants.

Children Will Be Subjected to the Influence of Adults Charged with Crimes Tried in Criminal Court

One goal of maintaining separate juvenile court systems is the separation of children from adult criminal defendants. There are common sense reasons for this. Children should be protected from older and stronger adults who might assault and injure them. Children are easily pressured into criminal behavior by adults. One answer to this objection to abolition of juvenile courts is that a unified juvenile/criminal justice system could function without mixing children with adults. Separate detention facilities could be maintained. Within criminal court systems, separate courtrooms and divisions could be established to handle cases involving children. Will such attempts at physical separation be successful? Although strict age guidelines could be used for purposes of placement in detention, will it be desirable even to have older and younger people charged with crimes mixing together in the hallways and courtrooms of criminal courts?

How will the new court that Professor Feld envisions determine which children should remain separated from adult criminal defendants? Will age be the determining factor? Will judges be required to determine the degree of the child's sophistication before requiring separation from adults? The opportunities for domination and influence of the younger by the older multiply in a criminal court system responsible for trying both children and adults. . . .

The existence of separate juvenile courts is a powerful and enduring symbol of the fact that children are in most cases less morally responsible for commission of crime than adults. Without a separate court this basic difference will be lost on our justice system. Moreover, the impact of our juvenile and criminal justice systems are felt disproportionately by African-American and Hispanic youth and by children with low socio-economic status. Thus the population most in need of social services will be deprived of them. Youth most at risk will receive even less attention than they receive now.

Jury Trials Conducted in Criminal Courts Will Be Incomprehensible and Intimidating to Children

Under Professor Feld's proposal, jury trials would be guaranteed to juveniles as a consequence of being tried in criminal court. Will the availability of a jury trial in a criminal court benefit juvenile defendants? This is a subject about which there is much disagreement. Before reaching that question, however, it should be noted that whether juveniles are afforded jury trials or not need not depend on whether they are tried in adult or in juvenile court. Juvenile courts could continue to function as separate entities and provide jury trials; there is no inconsistency between the goals of a rehabilitation, balanced punishment, and the availability of jury trials.

There is no reason that legislators must choose between a purely punitive, adversarial system and one whose only priority is rehabilitation. It is possible to combine all elements of a desirable justice system into one court that would provide all due process protections available to adults, including jury trials, as well as specialized and flexible rehabilitative and correctional dispositions. We can address Professor Feld's concerns about the arbitrariness of juvenile court judges by making jury trials more available in juvenile court and by placing the most highly qualified public defenders, prosecutors, and judges in juvenile court.

Providing jury trials to children in juvenile court need not transform juvenile courts into adult criminal courts. First, the exercise of the right would probably be infrequent. Second, juvenile courts could adopt practices and procedures that would adapt jury trials to the capacities and needs of children, something that would probably not happen in adult criminal courts. . . .

The Legal Culture of Criminal Courts Will Damage Children

The adult criminal court's law practice culture would also do great damage to children, where the culture of law practice is characterized by combativeness. Prosecutors in adult court are likely to bring to the courtroom a harder edge to jury trials in adult court than in jury trials in juvenile court because prosecutors in adult court are judged by their superiors on their success in obtaining convictions. The phenomenon of a "harder edge" includes a greater degree of aggressiveness, of inflexibility, and retributivist motivation. Those of us who practice in adult court know that as adversarial as some juvenile proceedings are, the degree of adversariness in criminal court often far exceeds the contentiousness found in juvenile court. In juvenile courts, it is at least more likely that prosecutors are committed to the mission of protecting the public and fashioning balanced dispositions which serve the best interests of children. Moreover, judges in juvenile courts may be more vigilant in protecting juveniles from the retributionist leanings of prosecutors.

The behavior of the lawyers who represent children in criminal court will also be more contentious. The very environment of the criminal courtroom will generate and make necessary this attitude on the part of lawyers who represent children. If the prosecutor in the adult court views the child as an adult, the defense lawyer must respond in kind. This means submitting to the unfortunate reality that a jury trial involving a child defendant is no different than one involving an adult defendant. . . .

Plea Bargaining in Adult Court Will Be Unfair to Children

Many of the children I represent in criminal court do not understand the consequences of the decision to go to trial or to accept a negotiated plea bargain. This is particularly true when children are asked to make the choice between pleading guilty and accepting a lengthy prison sentence, and going to trial. They have little ability to gauge the probability of a conviction and cannot comprehend the impact of a short or lengthy sentence upon their lives.

Sentences in Adult Court Will Be Too Harsh and the Focus on the Development of Youth-Oriented Correctional Systems Will Be Abandoned

Children will face harsher penalties in adult court than in juvenile court. The solution of a "youth discount" may impose some flexibility and rationality upon sentencing decisions. However, in light of the complaints about the inflexibility of the federal sentencing guidelines, and other mandatory sentencing schemes, we should think long and hard before imposing a similarly rigid system upon children who arguably could benefit from well-informed flexibility in sentencing. The perceived, and some times real, need to provide long-term incarceration for the small minority of children who must be institutionalized could be satisfied by the "blended sentencing" schemes. Under these provisions, children receive both a juvenile and an adult sentence in juvenile court. Based after their responsiveness to programming within the juvenile system, they are evaluated to determine whether they will be released after their juvenile sentence or whether they should serve out an adult sentence. This decision is made based upon the experience with the child of the juvenile correctional system over a lengthy period of time. It is thus a better informed decision regarding prognosis for treatment and protection of the public than the automatic and ill-informed decision that is made in the context of adult protection initiated by an automatic transfer. . . .

Adult Court Judges, Prosecutors, and Defenders Will Not Be Child Specialists

Other objections to trying children in adult court may be even more substantial. Personnel in adult court—judges, prosecutors, defense lawyers, probation officers, custodial workers—are unlikely to receive the training necessary to sensitize them to the special needs of children. There is no reason to think that in a criminal system more resources would be devoted to juvenile than to adult probation services. There is every reason to believe that just the opposite will occur. In many jurisdictions, probation officers assigned to juvenile cases have lighter caseloads and are more highly motivated to secure rehabilitative services than their counterparts in adult court. Again, it is unlikely that in a criminal court setting specialized and effective approaches to developing and supporting the competencies of children and families will develop. Indeed, quite the opposite may occur. Placing children in adult court will make them indistinguishable from adults and may lead to the stifling of initiatives and learning.

How Can We Reinvigorate Juvenile Courts?

Legislators will make decisions about the future of juvenile justice. Legislators are free to construct systems for providing justice for children which contain the best of the ideas from scholars such as Morse, Feld, Scott and Grisso and from other experts, including judges, lawyers, social workers, doctors, and correctional officials. However, recent trends suggest that legislators rely more on public opinion than information as their guide. There is also substantial evidence that legislators use "get tough" messages to win re-election. In fact, recent juvenile justice legislation has been enacted in Illinois in response to particularly notorious cases, instead of on the actual data regarding crime trends and the newest learning about successful interactions. Unfortunately, there is little that lawyers who represent children can do to influence this unfortunate political process. It should be noted, however, that Professor Feld's involvement in Minnesota's juvenile justice reform provides a model for positive interactions between the world of academics and the world of politics.

Putting the political process aside and turning to the merits, what would be the nature of a constructive compromise? How can we satisfy the need for more appropriate sentencing, recognition of consequences, the need for more procedural protection, and the need to develop and to utilize new ways of supporting and rehabilitating children? The answer, and admittedly a very general one, is that juvenile courts must preserve individualized decision-making with respect to the culpability and developmental needs of children, while insisting on appropriate imposition of responsibility. Post-disposition, we must develop ways of moving away from institutionalized "treatment" of children to community-based programs designed to support children and families and to build self-esteem and competencies.

The juvenile court must be transformed in a way that permits and indeed requires children to be treated as our autonomous and individual children, and which provides for the public safety. This requires changes in the ways that juvenile courts adjudicate and dispose of cases. It requires a reorganization of services for children so that the interests of children—not those of institutions or agencies—prevail.

We Must Learn from History the Problems That Have Brought the Juvenile Court to Its Weakened and Diminished Authority, and These Problems Must Be Recognized and Addressed

Any attempt to bring together those who argue that the juvenile court should be abolished and those who believe that it should be invigorated and preserved must address the concerns of those who seek the juvenile court's abolition. For example, Professor Feld argues that the juvenile court is still the "worst of both worlds;" it punishes without procedural protections, and it offers no treatment in exchange for forfeiture of rights.

Many juvenile courts, perhaps most, are subject to this criticism. But is the answer to this criticism to abolish the court? Professor Feld's proposal has a rational basis, especially in light of the fact that the juvenile court still hasn't got it right after almost 100 years of existence. The proposal is flawed, however, because it fails to take into account ideas which could make an essentially good idea—a highly functioning special court for children—a reality.

There Has Never Been a Dedicated, Concerted Effort to Create and Support Excellent Juvenile Courts

The historical evidence demonstrates that even from the beginning, we have failed both to create and to sustain excellent juvenile courts. Only one judge presided over the first juvenile court. That judge had few resources; there was a well-founded worry even then that paying probation officers with government funds would result in a patronage-driven system. Indeed it is remarkable how soon after the founding of the juvenile court the same shortcomings that concern us today surfaced. The one judge assigned to the court had too many cases, so a mechanism for "screening" cases was established. Judge Mack, the second presiding judge of the juvenile court, was transferred from the juvenile court because he became angered at the practice of congregate care institutions of releasing, without notice to him, children he had committed. In response to that practice, he placed more children on probation so that he could personally supervise them. He was transferred to criminal court as a result of the political outcry that resulted. He was the first juvenile court judge to express frustration with child care agencies. The tactic that he employed to address the problem—less reliance on institutionalization—earned him the equivalent of the modern day label "soft on crime." . . .

In Many Juvenile Courts the Quality of Adjudication Is Poor

There is not enough attention paid to accurate fact-finding during adjudicatory hearings The adjudicatory phase of a delinquency proceeding is not taken seriously enough; there is not enough attention paid to accurate fact-finding. There are a number of reasons for this. Children are discouraged by the judge, by the prosecutors and by defense lawyers from taking their cases to trial. The ethic in juvenile courts is still that confession (or admission) is good for the soul, although it is difficult to know whether the best interests of the children or heavy caseloads lie at the heart of the juvenile court's failure to be careful about the facts. High caseloads pressure children, prosecutors, defense lawyers and judges to gloss over relevant facts, to ignore possible defenses, and to avoid the kind of attention to detail that makes for accurate determinations of fact.

There is too much reliance on plea bargaining in juvenile courts There is too much reliance on plea bargaining without adequate consultation with the client and without adequate supervision by judges. When a child is told to choose between going to trial and risking incarceration, versus pleading guilty to a lesser charge in return for probation, the deal is almost impossible to resist. Unless handled properly, a child's response to such an offer after plea bargaining may not be voluntary. . . .

Plea bargaining also fosters cynicism. The child who is not guilty and who pleads to something that he did not do under the threat of a harsher penalty will not leave court impressed with the integrity of the system. The child who is offered a better deal than he should be offered feels that he has beaten the system. We should worry about these same phenomena when evaluating plea bargaining in the context of our adult criminal justice system. However, the deficits of plea bargaining seem even more pronounced when we involve children in it unless we are especially sensitive to how the bargaining is conducted and how the child is brought into the process.

The quality of judging, lawyering, and social work in juvenile courts must be improved The most pervasive cause of the low quality of juvenile court personnel is that many of the people who work in juvenile court do not want to be there. Advocates for children, be they prosecutors or defense lawyers, repeatedly have their efforts undermined by inefficient, ill-informed, or downright hostile judges. Judges who want to make a difference find themselves hamstrung by lawyers and child welfare personnel who are not as knowledgeable or as committed as they should be. . . .

Solving the Problems of Juvenile Courts: Establishing Realistic Expectations, Meeting Realistic Expectations

Establishing Realistic Expectations

The juvenile court is in jeopardy not because it has failed, but because it has been unable, in a relatively short period of time, to respond to new realities of children. However, the expectation that a court should have immediate solutions to increased violence among youth is simply wrong-headed. We do not expect courts to solve social problems. We do expect courts to be fair, efficient, and just.

Meeting Realistic Expectations

What should juvenile courts be expected to accomplish in order to satisfy those who are skeptical about their continuing utility?

Juvenile Courts Should Provide Fair, Impartial, and Informed Adjudications and Dispositions of Cases

First, juvenile courts should have as their hallmark the fair, impartial, and informed adjudication and disposition of cases. This means that juvenile court judges must hold the state to the requirement of proof beyond a reasonable doubt, that excessive plea bargaining in order to deal with case backlogs should be eliminated, and that judges and lawyers in juvenile court be specially trained to recognize the educational, social, and treatment needs of children and families in crisis. It is no longer enough, and it probably never was enough, that judges have a sincere desire to help children. Thus, judges must be generalists in the sense that they know how a case should be tried and specialists in their knowledge of juvenile law and procedure, child development, and treatment strategies.

Lawyers in Juvenile Courts Must Be Both Generalists and Specialists

We also need generalists and specialists in the corps of lawyers who prosecute and defend juvenile delinquency cases; generalists in the sense that they have a broad range of lawyering skills and specialists in dealing with children, families, and treatment providers. That corps of highly qualified generalists and specialists has never existed in juvenile court; it is as though we have been trying to run a children's hospital without a staff of pediatricians. For the most part, those who prosecute and defend juvenile cases do so only for a short period of time and move on. Juvenile court is a training ground for them, nothing more. Juvenile courts cannot possibly succeed without a level of professionalism and experience that we would require for any important endeavor. We have never been serious about organizing, funding, and staffing juvenile courts.

Treatment and Rehabilitation Services Must Function Properly

Moving beyond the court, probation services, residential programs, and correctional programs must function properly if the juvenile court is to succeed. In most jurisdictions, these services are far from state-of-the-art. The failures of these institutions undermine the court's work and its public image. The failures of treatment/rehabilitation services rarely come back to haunt those who are providing the services. They often come back to haunt the juvenile court judge who took the risk of sending a child for treatment rather than long-term incarceration and incapacitation. No treatment/correctional system can guarantee success. However, increased focus on improving the quality of interventions will make juvenile courts viable.

An effective strategy for preserving and strengthening juvenile courts can only be built upon investing in the people who serve children in juvenile courts and in public and private child service organizations. The best interests of children and the protection of the public will ultimately not be achieved by resting decision-making regarding the future of juvenile justice on the wholesale reorganization of existing systems or upon rethinking the question of the extent to which children should be held to be as responsible as adults.

The key question is how to deliver legal and social services to children fairly, efficiently, and effectively. This is, indeed a "systems" problem. Systems problems are relatively easy to solve. Just change the system. But the more important problem is how to motivate the people who work within the system to turn out the best possible product. This problem will exist if children are treated as fully responsible adults, it will exist if the juvenile court is abolished, and it will exist if we seek to save the juvenile court by understanding more deeply the delinquent behaviors of children and adolescents.

Conclusion

This article began with a case study describing the interaction between a young person charged with serious crimes, his lawyers, and the juvenile court. The case study was meant to set the stage for the discussion that followed about the realities of juvenile crime statistics and the capabilities and role of juvenile courts. Since writing the introduction to this article, an even more distressing crime was allegedly committed by an even younger child in Chicago. The newest case involves a twelve-year-old who allegedly shot and killed two teenagers, allegedly in an effort to prove his worthiness to older gang members. Interestingly, the reaction of the press to this incident focused on causes and prevention rather than amending legislation to make it possible to try this child as an adult. The Chicago Sun-Times referred to this incident as "Everyone's Problem." The Chicago Tribune described in detail the social and educational history of the troubled child charged with the crime. Again, rather than calling for this child to be tried as an adult, at this writing, public opinion seems to be calling for an effort to understand what produced this tragedy and how to prevent such tragedies from occurring in the future.

Perhaps the reason for the measured and constructive reaction to this latest awful event is the extreme youth of the child involved and the uncontested fact that he acted seeking approval from or following the instructions of older gang members. Perhaps the reaction is the result of the fact that the reporters who covered the story did much the same kind of investigation that good lawyers would do on behalf of this child: they went into the community, and interviewed family and friends of the child and of the victims, interviewed the child's school teachers and neighbors. What came out of this investigation was the story of a child's life. It turned out to be a story of a broken home, a child lost to gang culture despite the efforts of his family and school teachers, and access to a snub-nosed .38 caliber gun. The story of this child's life, like the story of the young man whose progress through the juvenile court began this article, is the product of all if its parts. Unless we focus our efforts on understanding these stories, in a setting supportive of understanding, we are unlikely to provide justice for children.

POSTSCRIPT

Should the United States Abolish the Juvenile Court Systems?

The juvenile courts have generated substantial controversy in the U.S. legal system. Opponents of these courts have argued that they have failed to provide children with due process safeguards. In addition, they do not provide effective treatment. Juvenile court advocates often contend that these courts lack sufficient resources to do an effective job. Proper funding and additional qualified personnel would help juvenile courts to fulfill their therapeutic mission.

The U.S. Supreme Court has noted these problems. In *McKeiver v. Pennsylvania*, 403 U.S. 528 (1971), it stated:

> Too often the juvenile court judge falls far short of that stalwart, protective and communicating figure the system envisaged. The judge community's unwillingness to provide people and facilities and to be concerned, the insufficiency of time devoted, the scarcity of professional help, the inadequacy of dispositional alternatives, and our general lack of knowledge all contribute to dissatisfaction with the experiment. [Footnotes omitted.]

In light of these problems, what is the solution? Is it likely that state governments will dramatically increase funding for crowded juvenile courts at a time of fiscal austerity? That is doubtful. However, think back to our discussion of Gerald Gault's case in the Introduction to this issue. The 15-year-old boy, who was not even given an opportunity to even question the witness against him, was effectively sentenced to a six-year term of imprisonment in a juvenile detention facility based on flimsy evidence. Moreover, his alleged offense was making a lewd telephone call, a misdemeanor under the laws of most states. How many of the people reading this discussion have done similar childish things in the past? Can we as a civilized nation tolerate this type of arbitrary treatment of children in our juvenile courts? Wasn't it essential for the Supreme Court to impose an intermediate standard of due process protections on juvenile court proceedings?

So where should we go with the juvenile courts? Professor Feld argues that juvenile courts have become deficient criminal courts in which children receive neither therapeutic treatment nor sufficient due process safeguards. Thus, he argues that we should abolish juvenile courts and formally recognize youthfulness as a mitigating factor at the sentencing stage of a normal criminal proceeding with full due process safeguards.

Attorney Thomas F. Geraghty contends that we should retain the juvenile courts after investing more substantial resources in the juvenile justice system. This would enhance the performance of the juvenile courts and allow them to deal effectively with the relatively few "serious" or "violent" offenders who pass through the juvenile justice system.

Both of these authors have made compelling arguments. Which position do you feel has the most merit? For additional information on these issues, see Emily Buss, "The Missed Opportunity in Gault," *The University of Chicago Law Review* (vol. 70, no. 1, 2003); Ellen Marrus, "Effective Assistance of Counsel in the Wonderland of 'Kiddie Court'—Why the Queen of Hearts Trumps Strickland," *Criminal Law Bulletin* (vol. 39, no. 4, 2003); Barry C. Feld, "The Politics of Race and Juvenile Justice: The 'Due Process Revolution' and the Conservative Reaction," *Justice Quarterly* (vol. 20, no. 4, 2003); Jeffrey A. Butts, and Daniel P. Mears, "Reviving Juvenile Justice in a Get-Tough Era," *Youth and Society* (vol. 33, no. 2, 2001); Alison G. Turoff, "Throwing Away the Key on Society's Youngest Sex Offenders," *Journal of Criminal Law & Criminology* (vol. 91, no. 4, 2001); Paige Harrison, James R. Maupin, and F. Larry Mays, "Teen Court: An Examination of Processes and Outcomes," *Crime and Delinquency* (vol. 7, no. 2, 2001); Robert E. Shepard, Jr., "Speedy Trials for Juveniles," *Criminal Justice* (vol. 14, no. 4, 2000); Steven H. Rosenbaum, "Civil Rights Issues in Juvenile Detention and Correctional Systems," *Corrections Today* (vol. 61, no. 6, 1999); Wanda Mohr, Richard J. Gelles, and Ira M. Schwartz, "Shackled in the Land of Liberty: No Rights for Children," *Annals of the American Academy of Political and Social Science* (vol. 564, no. 37, 1999); John Johnson Kerbs, "(Un)equal Justice: Juvenile Court Abolition and African Americans," *Annals of the American Academy of Political and Social Science* (vol. 564, no. 109, 1999); Barry Krisberg, "Reforming Juvenile Justice," *The American Prospect* (vol. 16, no. 9, 2005); Alvin W. Cohn, "Planning for the Future of Juvenile Justice," *Federal Probation* (vol. 68, no. 3, 2004); and Thomas F. Geraghty, "Juvenile Justice and Strategies to Control Youth Violence: Is There a Conflict?" *Journal of Criminal Law & Criminology* (vol. 94, no. 2, 2004).

ISSUE 11

Should Cameras Be Allowed Inside U.S. Courtrooms?

YES: Steven Brill, from "Courtroom Cameras," *Notre Dame Law Review* (May 1997)

NO: Anonymous, from "Judicial Conference Nixes Camera in Courtrooms," *Defense Counsel Journal* (September 6, 2000)

ISSUE SUMMARY

YES: Steven Brill, the founder of the Courtroom Television Network, asserts that the public lacks confidence in the U.S. legal system because they have not been exposed to the real workings of the system. Brill believes that cameras in the courtrooms may remedy this problem and restore the public's faith in the court system.

NO: U.S. Court of Appeals Chief Judge Edward R. Becker contends that camera coverage can do irreparable harm to a citizen's right to a fair trial and can create privacy concerns and courtroom security problems.

Do you recall the O.J. Simpson murder trial? Considered by many to be a riveting courtroom drama, it received extremely high television ratings. The cast included flamboyant attorneys F. Lee Bailey and Johnnie Cochran. Judge Lance Ito was accused by some commentators of "conducting a courtroom circus." One state court judge commented at the conclusion of the trial: "The judge lost control of his courtroom."

After seeing what happened in the O.J. Simpson case, do cameras belong in a courtroom? Will having a camera in the courtroom turn a sensational criminal trial into a legal circus, with judges, lawyers, and witnesses playing to the audience? Does the Sixth Amendment right to a public trial include the right of a defendant to have the trial broadcast over television networks? Does the U.S. Constitution grant members of the media a First Amendment right to attend trials at all?

To answer the last question, in *Richmond Newspapers, Inc. v. Virginia,* 448 U.S. 555 (1980), the U.S. Supreme Courts held that "a trial courtroom is a public place where the people generally—and representatives of the media—have a right to be present and where their presence historically has been thought to enhance the integrity and quality of what takes place." The Court continued: "Absent an overriding interest articulated in findings, the trial of a criminal case must be open to the public." The Court has never stated, however, that the media has a right to broadcast, record, or televise a trial.

The court rules of many states permit a trial judge to allow "the taking of photographs, the broadcasting, televising, and recording of court proceedings." Thus, whether to permit media coverage within a courtroom is a matter within the sole discretion of a trial judge. However, this does not answer the question of whether judges should allow trials to be televised.

Many judges do not like the idea of allowing television cameras to broadcast sensational trials. Some judges believe that permitting a trial to be televised detracts from courtroom decorum and runs the risk of turning the proceedings into a media circus. Other judges, however, feel that allowing trials to be televised may help the public to develop a more realistic sense of how the courts operate and how the U.S. justice system actually works. These disparate views mirror those of the authors of the works in this section.

Steven Brill, the founder of the Courtroom Television Network (CTN), argues that the public lacks confidence in the U.S. legal system because people have not been exposed to the real working of the justice system. Not surprisingly, Brill believes that cameras in the courtrooms are "the best thing imaginable for those worried about the public's confidence in lawyers and the legal system."

Former U.S. Court of Appeals (3rd Cir.) Chief Judge Edward E. Becker does not share Steven Brill's enthusiasm for televising trials, however. Judge Becker states:

> [I] believe that the intimidating effect of cameras on the litigants, witnesses and jurors has a profoundly negative impact on the trial process. Moreover, in civil cases cameras can intimidate civil defendants who, regardless of the merits of their case, might prefer to settle rather than risk damaging accusations in a televised trial. Cameras can also create security concerns in the federal courts. Finally, cameras can create privacy concerns for countless numbers of persons, many of whom are not even parties to the case, but about whom very personal information may be revealed at trial. . . .

What is your opinion about allowing television cameras in U.S. courtrooms? Would allowing trials to be televised be an effective way to teach the American public about the U.S. justice system? Or, would it detract from the privacy rights of participants in the trial and perhaps even compromise a defendant's right to a fair trial? Is there an effective way to balance the public's right to information with litigants' rights to privacy and the impartial administration of justice?

Steven Brill

Courtroom Cameras

Thank you for inviting me to address this illustrious group. I'm delighted to be here.

But I'm intimidated, too. And not simply because of who you are. But also because of who I am.

You see, lately I've been thinking about my dual life as a member of the legal community and as a journalist. And so I've come to the conclusion that I belong to not one, but two of the most reviled professions on this planet.

We all know how much people say they don't like lawyers and distrust the legal system. But journalists and the media—they're even worse. For when it comes to arrogance, when it comes to unaccountability, when it comes to making a buck in the name of supposedly higher values—such as the public's right to know—we journalists make lawyers look good.

Indeed, however much we want to criticize lawyers for not enforcing their code of professional responsibility, at least lawyers have a code. Journalists don't, which is something I've been writing and talking about lately, but which is a subject I guess I should save for another day.

So let's talk about lawyers—and judges—and the legal system.

I want to talk tonight about what I see is a huge gap between the reality of the law and the legal system and the public perception of it. And I say that not as an apologist for everything in the legal world. I do believe that there's lots that can still be fixed in our system, especially in areas like judicial elections and lawyer discipline.

But I also think—and this is what I'm really here to talk about—that some judges, and lawyers, by insisting on secrecy, and being defensive about the faults in the system that need fixing, and being insecure about how the pubic will understand and appreciate their legal system if they can see it, have created the crisis in confidence that they now face and don't deserve.

Let me put it a bit differently. I believe in public exposure for the courts and the legal system because I think it's right and it's consistent with all of our democratic values. But I also believe in it because I think it's the best thing for the legal system and for preserving confidence in it.

You see, I have a theory about judges. Like lawyers, I think they undersell themselves. And I think they so believe in the inability of lay people to appreciate what they do, that they are reluctant when it comes to public exposure.

With that in mind, let me tell you two recent stories. Last week, our newspaper in Washington, *Legal Times,* invited one of Washington's top federal appellate judges in for an off the record luncheon. I'd tell you his name, but he insisted that the lunch—in which he did not in any way discuss pending matters but really talked about the court and his own life and his approach to legal issues—be strictly off the record. In any event, following the lunch, I asked our editor there how it had gone. His reaction on a one to ten scale of enthusiasm (and this is a cynical, tough editor) was about an eleven. The judge was a really terrific guy, he said. All of the staff loved him. He was so, so impressive. Someone who really cares about doing the right thing. What a great public servant, my editor concluded. If only he was more visible. If only . . . . Story number two: about a year ago, I had the same kind of encounter with another judge who is probably one of the more misunderstood and misperceived figures in legal public life. If only more people could see him in action, I thought. If only . . . . You see, at the risk of sounding obsequious, I have to tell you that while our publications have proudly pioneered writing about the bad apples in the judiciary, we've also relished writing about the good judges and great judges. And at Court TV we've delighted in showing judges—my guess is probably 550 out of the 555 we've shown on Court TV—who come to work on time, make tough decisions fairly and generally outshine their counterparts in the executive and legislative branches.

Yet, as I've said, most lawyers and judges believe the bad press clips the profession gets, or at least do nothing to try to counter that bad, unfair image.

Indeed, instead of letting the world know what they really do—instead of, for example, wanting the public to see for themselves the best legal system the world has ever created—lots of lawyers and judges prefer to keep cameras out of courts, which, of course results in leaving it to Hollywood and tabloid writers and pundits to tell the American people and the world what the world's greatest legal system is all about.

And so it frustrates me to see that those in the courts and in the legal profession generally—those who are celebrated for their ability to articulate and persuade, and simultaneously vilified for their power—find today that their agenda and image are being set by knee jerk editorial page writers; by Hollywood and by anyone else with an apocryphal and usually sensational story.

And the blame doesn't really lie with the public, which is seduced by these stories. The blame lies with those who let fiction thrive in a vacuum while they complain amongst themselves that the lay public just doesn't understand. If the profession wants the public to learn the truth about the system, I think we have no alternative but to stop discussing it amongst ourselves and begin to open discussions with the people whom we serve.

It's the same with journalists, by the way. We have endless meetings and seminars wringing our hands over the public's loss of confidence in the press and the public's flight to entertainment—but we never deal with how the public really sees us, which is as a self-righteous, unaccountable elite who bury corrections of our stories (in the rare instance that we admit them) on page ninety-six and refuse to speak out about the ethics of covering sleaze stories instead of important stories.

I can remember when we first implemented the corrections policy that we now use at all of our papers and at Court TV: the correction had to be candid, clear and prominent. When we started doing it, several of our reporters complained that if we bared our souls that way we would be embarrassed when we screwed up and that people would ultimately have less confidence in all of our reporting. I replied that if we showed that we were willing to admit mistakes, people would end up having more confidence in us. I also said that if we were embarrassed for screwing up, it might make us focus more on the screw-ups.

Now, I have to tell you that that conversation sounds hauntingly like a lot of conversations I've had with judges in the aftermath of the Simpson case. Cameras were bad, some judges said, because they embarrassed the judiciary and gave the public less confidence in judges. You should have no trouble figuring out how I have replied to that.

I should also add that in this room I am speaking in some substantial part to a converted choir. Many of you have led the way in opening the legal systems in your state to public scrutiny and to cameras.

In many ways, as I think of the future of our state supreme courts I think that we stand at a crossroads. We have the technology to relay the wonderful arguments themselves—the spirited and articulate give and take of ideas, values, philosophies and consequences—directly to the citizens with no intrusion whatsoever into the courtroom. And I cannot urge you strongly enough to encourage its use in your own courtrooms. I think it is not only available to you, I think it is part of your mission, indeed part of your raison d'etre to share what you do with your citizens.

I would hesitate to speak so confidently and directly to you were it not for the support these same ideas are finding among you. Right now, forty-seven states allow camera coverage of appeals. True there are restrictions and attitudes which make it more difficult in some states than others. But, in just the few years since I launched Court TV, I see more and more of your colleagues welcoming cameras. In Washington state I'm told the supreme court of Chief Justice Barbara Durham routinely televises almost all of its arguments. In Ohio, Chief Justice Thomas Moyer, has said that—quote—"if we are truly sincere about our efforts and desire to make the public more aware about the work and role of our courts, cameras must be part of the process."

Indeed, Chief Justice Moyer has argued that he thinks we should have "regional Court TV's"—an idea, by the way that I am developing right now. And this year, Chief Justice Birch of Tennessee and Chief Justice Shepard of Indiana each broke new ground in televising court proceedings in their states.

To anyone who has listened to many of my fellow journalists, these advances would come as a surprise. After all, since the Simpson case ended over a year ago, the media has regularly reported that there is a backlash against cameras. That the Simpson case spelled the demise of gavel-to-gavel coverage. But the truth is that judges have had mixed responses to that watershed trial and I am confident that the backlash, such as it is, has already passed.

Because, if you ask real people what was wrong with the O.J. Simpson case they will not say that what was wrong with it is that they got to see it!

Instead, the televising of the Simpson case and the hostile reaction to it of many judges—especially those sitting in southern California—raise a different, larger point. Which is that for fear of the one bad case that looks bad and demands reform, many in the legal community seemed prepared right after that case, though less so now, to throw out the best thing imaginable for those worried about the public's confidence in lawyers and the legal system—and that's cameras in the courts.

Obviously, I think that response is wrong. Was there heightened scrutiny in that case—in and out of the courtroom? Absolutely.

Was some of it uncomfortable and disheartening? Again, absolutely.

But, did it result in an improved awareness of how the system works in one place versus others—such as the fact that, according to the *Los Angeles Times*, the courthouse in which Simpson was tried has only a 32% conviction rate in homicide trials—lower than all the surrounding courthouses and much, much lower than the nationwide 80% plus conviction rate? Absolutely!

I would be astonished if any of you seriously thought that the public or the courts would be better off if such truths were never discovered, or, if you thought that showing people how well the system usually works was not important.

You see, I did start Court TV to "expose" the legal system. But not quite the way you might think. For I really believed that if all Americans could see real law instead of *L.A. Law* or Clint Eastwood movies or apocryphal and usually false accounts of litigation gone haywire, and if they could see real lawyers in public defenders' offices and prosecutors' offices and in small and large firms doing the work of everyday justice, they would sometimes see something to be angry about, but more often see a dignified, fair—indeed inspiring—proceeding that is a model for the world.

And I was right. A study done by the independent Times Mirror Center for The People and The Press has found that a significant plurality of Americans who have watched trials on Court TV have come away having much more respect for, and confidence in, their legal system. And I think those numbers would be even higher among those viewers on Court TV who watch On Appeal, our show dedicated exclusively to covering appellate proceedings, where judges press lawyers to articulate the consequences and philosophical and legal underpinnings of their clients' positions.

So despite my intention—and the proven result of 550 Court TV trials and appeals later of having made good on that intention—of showing people a system they would usually be proud of, I found myself after the Simpson case defending Court TV from those who thought, to be blunt, that because one of those 550 trials made the system look bad to lots of people, the whole idea of allowing lots of Americans to see a trial should be abandoned.

I did not doubt the sincerity and good intentions of those on the side of removing the camera. Indeed, I shared their frustration that the Simpson case left Americans with such a distorted impression of our legal system. And I shared their frustration that some of the media that benefited from the pool camera that we operated in that trial exploited it in a way that no one with a press card should be proud of. I just happened to think that the answer to the distorted impression left by one aberrant trial was not to make it so that the public would now not see any other trials or appeals. Put differently, and more bluntly, the answer to the public image presented by one court's performance was not to make sure that no other courts are allowed to present a different, more representative image.

And the courtroom camera sets the record straight in other ways as well. I am willing to bet that almost every one of you has participated in or presided over an important trial or appeal and been frustrated at the evening news account's spectacularly shallow (if not downright inaccurate) coverage. I'd bet you've had the experience of reading the next morning's paper and thinking, "Gee, I thought that reporter and I were in the same courtroom; but it sure doesn't seem like it."

Courtroom cameras always show the truth. And that simple fact sets them above any other form of journalism or court-sponsored public information in existence.

Which is why right after the Simpson case I took to the speaking circuit whenever I could and argued harder than ever for more, not less, public exposure to our legal system.

And which is why I am delighted to report that a year and a half after the verdict, the pendulum seems now to have swung back the other way. And not in the state courts alone. I am delighted that the Second and Ninth Circuits recently opened up their Courts of Appeal to cameras, delighted that several cases we litigated in the Southern and Eastern Districts of New York have opened federal civil trials to cameras if the district courts, district by district, are willing to allow it.

And I am delighted that the judicial task force set up after Governor Wilson recommended (on the day of the Simpson verdict) that cameras be removed from California courts voted unanimously to keep cameras.

You see, I think that the answer to the possibility that on occasion the lawyers in the Simpson case played to the camera is to make sure that the judge does not allow them to, just as the judges in the thirty-three other cases that Court TV televised from start to finish during the Simpson trial made sure that that did not happen. And having observed the thoughtful manner in which he completed the California judiciary's inquiry into this issue, I think Chief Justice Ronald George might even agree with me.

With all of that in mind, I want to talk about a particular aspect of debate that was re-ignited after the Simpson verdict.

As that renewed debate in California proceeded, I noticed that opponents of cameras—and even some supporters of cameras—talked about the constitutional mandate that trials be public as a pesky requirement that is to be tolerated—not an essential component of our trials that is to be maximized.

Indeed, while I think there is a unique and powerful educational value to televising the appellate courts, I want to talk a bit more about public trials—because I happen to think they're crucial to restoring confidence in the system.

The opponents like to say that if, as in the Simpson case, there were about twenty seats for reporters and ten for the rest of the public, that was enough for the trial to meet the requirement of being public. Indeed, they like to argue that because a few people can come down to a courthouse to watch one of the many uncelebrated cases that Court TV televises every day that this is enough, that there is no reason for a camera to be there.

Well, with that in mind, I think we may need a history lesson. And that lesson is simple: the framers of the Constitution didn't require public trials because they wanted to throw a symbolic bone to the public or to the press, but because they thought public trials were part of the essence of what a trial was in colonial America and in the mother country before that.

Trials were not supposed to be merely unsecret; they were intended to be very public. Indeed they were meant to be as public as possible.

For example, here's a description written in 1807 of the probable cause hearing for Aaron Burr in Virginia:

> At ten o'clock, MARSHALL, Chief Justice, took his seat on the bench, in the court room, which was densely filled with citizens . . . . On the suggestion of counsel that it would be impossible to accommodate the spectators in the court room, the chief justice adjourned to the hall of the house of delegates.

Or, as Justice Holmes wrote in 1884, "it is desirable that the trial . . . take place under the public eye . . . that every citizen should be able to satisfy himself with his own eyes as to the mode in which a public duty is performed."

Chief Justice Burger, who was no great admirer of the press, understood that when he wrote in the landmark Richmond Newspapers case in 1980 that the constitutional right to a public trial belongs not only to defendants but to the public. "The historical evidence demonstrates conclusively," the Chief Justice wrote, "that at the time when our organic laws were adopted, criminal trials both here and in England had long been presumptively open. This is no quirk of history," he added, "rather, it has long been recognized as an indispensable attribute of an Anglo-American trial."

Burger went on to quote Jeremy Bentham, who had written, "without publicity,"—note he said publicity, not a few people watching the trial from the audience of a tiny courtroom—"all other checks are insufficient: in comparison of publicity, all other checks are of small account."

Bentham had written from an historical context in which public trials were so vital to the essence of the trial itself that in the sixteenth century all the townspeople were actually required to attend trials. Later, that rule had been eased but only insofar as all people were encouraged to attend. And anyone who chose to do so usually could because the audience galleries were huge, theater-like set-ups which is exactly the way American courtrooms of the 1700s and 1800s were built.

And, I should add, there was no illusion then that some trials when made so public would not become spectator events in their own right. For these trials, as with some trials that Court TV has televised, often became what Professor Lawrence Friedman, in his 1993 book *Crime and Punishment* in American History called "high drama," and a "great spectator sport."

Nonetheless, trials were made as public as possible. There were often attempts made to quiet the audiences' cheers and jeers, but no attempt made to limit this essential ingredient of Anglo-American justice.

Chief Justice Burger endorsed exactly that notion of not compromising the public nature of a trial even in the face of audience misconduct or exploitation of the event. In the Richmond case he quoted a colonial historian as follows:

> Indeed, when in the mid-1600's the Virginia Assembly felt that the respect due the courts was "by the clamorous unmannerlynes of the people lost, and order, gravity and decoram which should manifest the authority of a court in the court it selfe neglected," the response was not to restrict the openness of the trials to the public, but instead to prescribe rules for the conduct of those attending them.

Burger went on to quote the Journals of the Continental Congress as extolling the necessity of a trial "'in open Court, before as many people as chuse to attend . . . .'"

As many people as choose to attend.

Compare this notion—Bentham's, the founding fathers', and Chief Justice Burger's—with that of some California opponents of cameras in the courts who surfaced after the Simpson verdict.

In the Simpson aftermath, Governor Pete Wilson's counsel, pressing the governor's new post O.J. Simpson position that cameras should now be banned from criminal trials, compared the nine month trial in New York in 1995 of those charged with a terrorist conspiracy to blow up various New York landmarks and the Holland Tunnel to that of Mr. Simpson. Because the federal New York bombing conspiracy trial, he noted, had not been televised, it had not been highly publicized and in fact had "slipped from the public consciousness." His words.

That, the governor's counsel said, was a good thing.

To the post O.J. opponents of cameras in the courts, a trial that "slips from the public consciousness" is a good trial. Thus, the second Menendez brothers trial was presumably a better one than the first. Even though without cameras and with far fewer witnesses, it grinded on to a verdict almost exactly as long as the endless first trial (eighty-seven days versus eighty-six days, putting the lie to the notion that cameras prolong trials). And the Oklahoma City bombing trial will presumably be fine if it doesn't attract too much attention. And a key federal civil rights trial or a Microsoft antitrust case, or a political corruption trial will be just right if the lawyers and the judge are left to sort it all out on their own.

Would the founding fathers have thought that was a good thing? Wouldn't it have been better for Court TV and CNN and others to have televised that New York bombing conspiracy trial—which involved basic issues of national security juxtaposed against defense charges of entrapment and official misconduct—instead of having it "slip from the public consciousness?"

Was that the founding fathers' original intent?

Is that the standard John Marshall had in mind when he moved the Aaron Burr trial to a huge auditorium? Was he worried about the lawyers playing to the crowd, or did he understand that controlling those lawyers was part of his job?

Did he confuse the notion of the dignity of the proceedings with the idea of keeping the proceedings out of the view of the masses? No way. Because he understood that the best justice is very public justice. Not justice that "slips from the public consciousness."

Indeed, I submit to you that the problem we have today with public confidence in our legal system is that the real workings of the system have slipped from public consciousness and been replaced by mystery and by myth.

"As many people as chuse to attend." That's a far cry from the tiny courtrooms that have lately become the norm in America, usually because of tight budgets, tight space, crowded dockets, our national evolution from town-square-based villages to urban-suburban metroplexes, and, I submit, a straying from this hallowed tradition of public trials.

Since when are de facto non-public trials good?

Sure it may mean that some trials replace soap operas and freak-of-the-day talk shows as daily entertainment fare. But, assuming any of us can define entertainment, let alone constitutionally distinguish it as something less worthy than news, is that trade-off of soap opera fiction and talk show sleaze for non-fiction justice bad, let alone something the founding fathers—who regularly saw trials captivate the throngs in the huge town square courthouses—would have wanted the government to define and prohibit? No way. They understood that the dignity of the courts came from the courtroom, itself, and from the values on display there, and that those values would be invigorated, not undercut, by having the so-called "masses" there to watch.

It is true that Chief Justice Burger and his brethren were not talking about cameras when they opened the Court. But he was talking about the press as a surrogate for the people who could not attend public trials. And he was ruling fifteen years after the Billie Sol Estes case, the Supreme Court case that is thought to be the ruling that says that there is not a constitutional right to cameras in the courts. But that case involved the wires and lights and general circus atmosphere surrounding a trial that had been televised; and the ruling had to do with all of those physical intrusions imposed by the electronic media—intrusions that today's technology has eliminated. Indeed, Justice Clark in his plurality opinion in Estes explicitly noted that "when the advances in these [television] arts permit reporting . . . by television without [its] present hazards to a fair trial we will have another case."

So let me close by presenting in its simplest terms that new case Justice Clark envisioned. Suppose Jeremy Bentham or the founding fathers or Chief Justice Marshall were in this audience and suppose I presented them with the following proposition: courtrooms today are not nearly as accessible as they were in the 1700s. And the community's interest in many trials these days extends far beyond a town or city's borders. However, we can use technology to make up for that. We can make trials totally public to millions of Americans without any physical intrusion and with no chance of noise or other disruption from this huge audience. True, some trials will be seen by some as entertainment, just the way they were in the old days when there were hoots and cheers from huge audience galleries and vendors sold souvenirs outside the courthouse. But now the audience will be at home and quiet and able to see and hear everything without disrupting or otherwise affecting the proceedings or distracting or intimidating the jury.

Would the founding fathers—the people who wanted as many people as possible to see the government at work when it decides whether to deprive someone of his or her liberty—have liked that idea? Or would they have said, no, sometimes the system will look bad, and we don't want that.

Or, no, we can't trust the public to understand what they are seeing.

Or, no, such a huge but silent audience will impair the dignity of the proceedings.

Or, no, we really would prefer that trials "slip from the public consciousness."

I think we all know the answer. I think we all know that public trials should be celebrated. For they are an idea, and an ideal, that is basic to the kind of justice that our forefathers cherished and that we should cherish.

I also hope that you can see that not only is a public process the right process, but it's also the process that can restore faith in our legal system and in our lawyers.

I want to close by quoting two judges who I believe are moving forward to realize the educational responsibilities of the courts. One is your colleague, Chief Justice Adolpho Birch of Tennessee, who said a couple of weeks ago that after experimenting for a year his state was ready to adopt a more liberal camera access law because "the court is committed to keeping the public informed about the judicial system. One method for doing that is to allow cameras in courtrooms."

The other is federal District Judge Jack Weinstein who in October allowed cameras into a trial in the Eastern District of New York for the first time in history. As he wrote: "in our democracy, the knowledgeable tend to be more robustly engaged in public issues. Information received by direct observation is often more useful than that strained through the media." So, as a journalist and as a citizen, I want to thank those of you—perhaps most of you—who have willingly opened your supreme courts to the public through cameras. To those who have been reluctant, I urge you to discuss it candidly with your colleagues here today.

Finally, I want to ask all of you to consider the overwhelmingly positive experience America has had in recent years of televised trials. Please—speak to trial court judges you know and respect who have actually had cameras in their courtrooms. The rare media side show, you will find, is vastly outweighed by the serious coverage possible only with a camera.

My point is simple. Our courts are among the most inspiring institutions of our democracy. And yet, despite the efforts of many people in this room, they remain in most states and certainly in the federal sphere the least visible and least understood. It was never meant to be that way. We should be proud, not afraid—in fact, we should be aggressively proud—to have them be seen.

NO 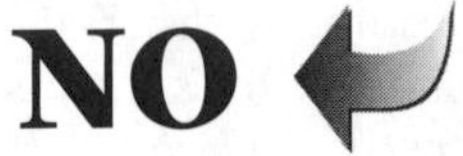

Anonymous

Judicial Conference Nixes Cameras in Courtroom

A bill in the U.S. Senate to allow cameras in federal courtrooms under certain conditions could "seriously jeopardize" the rights of citizens to a fair trial, the U.S. Judicial Conference has stated to a Senate subcommittee. Chief Judge Edward E. Becker of the Third Circuit testified before the Senate Judiciary Subcommittee on Administrative Oversight and the Courts on September 6 on behalf of the conference.

The bill, S. 721, sponsored by Sen. Charles E. Grassley of Iowa, would authorize the presiding judge of a district court or a court of appeals to permit the photographing, electronic recording, broadcasting or televising of court proceedings, and it authorizes the Judicial Conference to promulgate advisory guidelines. It directs that district courts inform witnesses other than a party of their right to have their faces and voices disguised or otherwise obscured.

Following are excerpts from the testimony of Judge Becker, a member of the Executive Committee of the Judicial Conference, outlining the conference's position:

Statement of Chief Judge Becker

The Judicial Conference strongly opposes S. 721, a bill that would "allow media coverage of court proceedings."

The federal judiciary has examined the issue of whether cameras should be permuted in the federal courts for more than six decades, both through case law and Judicial Conference consideration. The Judicial Conference in its role as the policymaking body for the federal judiciary has consistently expressed the view that camera coverage can do irreparable harm to a citizen's right to a fair and impartial trial. We believe that the intimidating effect of cameras on litigants, witnesses and jurors has a profoundly negative impact on the trial process. Moreover, in civil cases cameras can intimidate civil defendants who, regardless of the merits of their case, might prefer to settle rather than risk damaging accusations in a televised trial. Cameras can also create security concerns in the federal courts. Finally, cameras can create privacy concerns for countless numbers of persons, many of whom are not even

From *Defense Counsel Journal*, vol. 67, issue 4, October 2000, pp. 429-435.

parties to the case, but about whom very personal information may be revealed at trial. . . .

The federal courts have shown strong leadership in the continuing effort to modernize the litigation process. This has been particularly true of the federal judiciary's willingness to embrace new technologies, such as electronic case filing and access, videoconferencing, and electronic evidence presentation systems. The federal courts have also established community outreach programs in which several thousand students and teachers nationwide have come to federal courthouses to learn about court proceedings. Our opposition to this legislation, therefore, is not, as some may suggest, borne of a desire to stem technology or access to the courts. We oppose the broadcasting of federal court proceedings because it is contrary to the interests of justice, which it is our most solemn duty to uphold. . . .

The current policy, as published in the Guide to Judiciary Policies and Procedures, states:

> A judge may authorize broadcasting, televising, recording, or taking photographs in the courtroom and in adjacent areas during investigative, naturalization, or other ceremonial proceedings. A judge may authorize such activities in the courtroom or adjacent areas during other proceedings, or recesses between such proceedings, only: (a) for the presentation of evidence; (b) for the perpetuation of the record of the proceedings; (c) for security purposes; (d) for other purposes of judicial administration; or (e) in accordance with pilot programs approved by the Judicial Conference of the United States.

Presently, only two of the 13 appellate courts, the Second and Ninth Circuits, have decided to permit camera coverage in appellate proceedings. This decision was made by the judges of each court. As for cameras in district courts, most circuit councils have either adopted resolutions prohibiting cameras in the district courts or acknowledged that the district courts in that circuit already have such a prohibition.

Finally, it may be helpful to describe the state rules regarding cameras in the courtroom. While it is true that most states permit some use of cameras in their courts, such access by the media is not unlimited. The majority of states have imposed restrictions on the use of cameras in the court or have banned cameras altogether in certain proceedings.

Although it is somewhat difficult to obtain current information, it appears that approximately 20 states that permit cameras have restrictions of some kind written into their authorizing statutes, such as prohibiting coverage of certain proceedings or witnesses, and/or requiring the consent of the parties, victims of sex offenses, and witnesses. Eleven states do not allow coverage of criminal trials. In eight states, cameras are allowed only in appellate courts. Mississippi, South Dakota, and the District of Columbia prohibit cameras altogether. Utah allows only still photography at civil trials, and Nebraska allows only audio coverage in civil trials. In fact, only 16 states provide the presiding judge with the type of broad discretion over the use of cameras contained in this legislation.

It is clear from the widely varying approaches to the use of cameras that the state courts are far from being of one mind in the approach to, or on the propriety and extent of, the use of cameras in the courtroom.

Specific Concerns

A. Negative Impact

The conference maintains that camera coverage would indeed have a notably adverse impact on court proceedings. This includes the impact the camera and its attendant audience would have on the attorneys, jurors, witnesses and judges. We believe, for example, that a witness telling facts to a jury will often act differently when he or she knows that thousands of people are watching and listening to the story. This change in a witness's demeanor could have a profound impact on a jury's ability to accurately assess the veracity of that witness.

Media coverage could exacerbate any number of human emotions in a witness from bravado and over dramatization, to self-consciousness and under reaction. In fact, even according to the 1994 Federal Judicial Center study, 64 percent of the participating judges reported that, at least to some extent, cameras make witnesses more nervous. In addition, 46 percent of the judges believed that, at least to some extent, cameras make witnesses less willing to appear in court, and 41 percent found that, at least to some extent, cameras distract witnesses . . . .

B. Right to Fair Trial

The primary goal of this legislation is to allow radio and television coverage of federal court cases. While there are several provisions aimed at limiting coverage (i.e., allowing judges the discretion to allow or decline media coverage, authorizing the Judicial Conference to develop advisory guidelines regarding media coverage, and requiring courts to disguise the face and voice of a witness upon his or her request), the conference is convinced that camera coverage could, in certain cases, so indelibly affect the dynamics of the trial process that it would impair citizens' ability to receive a fair trial.

For example, Section l(a) and (b) of the bill would allow the presiding judge of an appellate or district court to decide whether to allow cameras in a particular proceeding before that court. If this legislation were to be enacted, we are confident that all federal judges would use extreme care and judgment in making this determination. Nonetheless, federal judges are not clairvoyants. Even the most straightforward or "run of the mill" cases have unforeseen developments. Obviously a judge never knows how a lawyer will proceed or how a witness or party will testify. And these events can have a tremendous impact on the trial participants.

Currently, courts have recourse to instruct the jury to disregard certain testimony or, in extreme situations, to declare a mistrial if the trial process is irreparably harmed. If camera coverage is allowed, however, there is no opportunity to later rescind remarks heard by the larger television audience. This concern is of such importance to the conference that it opposes legislation that would give a judge discretion to evaluate in advance whether television cameras should be permitted in particular cases.

We also are concerned about the provision that would require courts to disguise the face and voice of a witness upon his or her request. Anyone who has been in court knows how defensive witnesses can be. Frequently they have a right to be. Witnesses are summoned into court to be examined in public. Sometimes they are embarrassed or even humiliated. Providing them the choice of whether to testify in the open or blur their image and voice would be cold comfort given the fact that their name and their testimony will be broadcast to the community. It would not be in the interest of the administration of justice to unnecessarily increase the already existing pressures on witnesses . . . .

C. Trial Tactic

Cameras provide a very strong temptation for both attorneys and witnesses to try their cases in the court of public opinion rather than in a court of law. Allowing camera coverage would almost certainly become a potent negotiating tactic in pretrial settlement negotiations. For example, in a high-stakes case involving millions of dollars, the simple threat that the president of a defendant corporation could be forced to testify and be cross examined, for the edification of the general public, might well be a real disincentive to the corporation's exercising its right to a public trial.

D. Security Concerns

Although the bill includes language allowing witnesses who testify to be disguised, the bill does not address security concerns or make similar provision regarding other participants in judicial proceedings. The presence of cameras in the courtroom is likely to heighten the level and the potential of threats to judges. The number of threats against judges has escalated over the years, and widespread media exposure could exacerbate the problem. Additionally, all witnesses, jurors and United States Marshals Service personnel may be put at risk because they would no longer have a low public profile.

Also, national and international camera coverage of trials in federal courthouses, would place these buildings, and all in them, at greater risk from terrorists, who tend to choose targets for destruction that will give their "messages" the widest exposure. Such threats would require increased personnel and funding to adequately protect participants in court proceedings.

E. Privacy Concerns

There is a rising tide of concern among Americans regarding privacy rights and the Internet. Numerous bills have been introduced in both the Congress and state legislatures to protect the rights of individual citizens from the indiscriminate dissemination of personal information that once was, to use a phrase coined by the Supreme Court, hidden by "practical obscurity" [United States Department of Justice v. Reporters Committee for the Freedom of the

Press, 489 U.S. 749, 764 (1989)], but now is available to anyone at any time because of the advances of technology. The judiciary is studying this issue carefully with respect to court records, and Congress has before it a bipartisan proposal to create a Privacy Study Commission to look at a number of issues, including public records.

Broadcasting of trials presents many of the same concerns about privacy as does the indiscriminate dissemination of information on the Internet that was once only available at the courthouse. Witnesses and counsel frequently discuss very sensitive information during the course of a trial. Often this information relates to individuals who are not even parties to the case, but about whom personal information may be revealed.

Also, in many criminal and civil trials, which the media would most likely be interested in televising, much of the evidence introduced may be of an extremely private nature, revealing family relationships and personal facts, including medical and financial information. This type of information provided in open court is already available to the public through the media. Televising these matters sensationalizes these details for no apparent good reason . . . .

F. Complexities of Camera Coverage

Media coverage of a trial would have a significant impact on that trial process. There are major policy implications as well as many technical rules issues to be considered, none of which are addressed in the proposed legislation. For example, televising a trial makes certain court orders, such as those sequestering witnesses, more difficult to enforce. In a typical criminal trial, most witnesses are sequestered at some point. In addition, many related technical issues would have to be addressed, including advance notice to the media and trial participants, limitations on coverage and camera control, coverage of the jury box, and sound and light criteria.

Finally, S. 721 includes no funding authorization for implementation of its mandates. Regardless of whether funding is authorized, there is no guarantee that needed funds would be appropriated. The costs associated with allowing cameras, however, could be significant . . . .

G. No Constitutional Right

Some have asserted that there is a constitutional "right" to bring cameras into the courtroom and that the First Amendment requires that court proceedings be open in this manner to the news media. The Judicial Conference responds to such assertions by stating that today, as in the past, federal court proceedings are open to the public; however, nothing in the First Amendment requires televised trials.

The seminal case on this issue is Estes v. Texas, 381 U.S. 532 (1965). In Estes, the Supreme Court directly faced the question whether a defendant was deprived of his right under the Fourteenth Amendment to due process by the televising and broadcasting of his trial. The Court held that such broadcasting in that case violated the defendant's right to due process of law. At the same time, a majority of the Court's members addressed the media's right to telecast as relevant to determining whether due process required excluding cameras from the courtroom. Justice Clark's plurality opinion and Justice Harlan's concurrence indicated that the First Amendment did not extend the right to the news media to televise from the courtroom.

Similarly, Chief Justice Warren's concurrence, joined by Justices Douglas and Goldberg, stated:

> [n]or does the exclusion of television cameras from the courtroom in any way impinge upon the freedoms of speech and the press. . . . So long as the television industry, like the other communications media, is free to send representatives to trials and to report on those trials to its viewers, there is no abridgement of the freedom of press. [Estes, 381 U.S. at 584-85 (Warren, C.J., concurring)]

In the case of Westmoreland v. Columbia Broadcasting System Inc., 752 F.2d 16 (2d Cir. 1984), the Second Circuit was called upon to consider whether a cable news network had a right to televise a federal civil trial and whether the public had a right to view that trial. In that case, both parties had consented to the presence of television cameras in the courtroom under the close supervision of a willing court, but a facially applicable court rule prohibited the presence of such cameras.

The Second Circuit denied the attempt to televise that trial, saying that no case has held that the public has a right to televised trials. As stated by the court, "[t]here is a long leap . . . between a public right under the First Amendment to attend trials and a public right under the First Amendment to see a given trial televised. It is a leap that is not supported by history." Westmoreland, 752 F.2d at 23.

Similarly, in United States v. Edwards, 785 F.2d 1293 (5th Cir. 1986), the court discussed whether the First Amendment encompasses a night to cameras in the courtroom, stating: "No case suggests that this right of access includes a right to televise, record, or otherwise broadcast trials. To the contrary, the Supreme Court has indicated that the First Amendment does not guarantee a positive right to televise or broadcast criminal trials." Edwards, 785 F.2d at 1295. The court went on to explain that while television coverage may not always be constitutionally prohibited, that is a far cry from suggesting that television coverage is ever constitutionally mandated.

These cases forcefully make the point that, while all trials are public, there is no constitutional night of media to broadcast federal district court or appellate court proceedings.

H. Teachings of FJC Study

Proponents of S. 721 have indicated that the legislation is justified in part by the [1994] Federal Judicial Center study. The Judicial Conference based, in part, its opposition to cameras in the courtroom on the same study. Given this apparent inconsistency, it may be useful to highlight several important findings and limitations of the study.

The recommendations included in the FJC report, which were proposed by the research project staff, were reviewed within the FJC but not by its board.

First, the study only pertained to civil cases. This legislation, if enacted, would allow camera coverage in both civil and criminal cases. The number of criminal cases in the federal courts continues to rise. One could expect that most of the media requests for coverage would be in sensational criminal cases, where the problems for witnesses, including victims of crimes, and jurors are most acute.

Second, the study's conclusions ignore a large amount of significant negative statistical data. For example, the study reports on attorney ratings of electronic media effects in proceedings in which they were involved.

Among these negative statistics were the following:

- 32 percent of the attorneys who responded felt that, at least to some extent, the cameras distract witnesses;
- 40 percent felt that, at least to some extent, the cameras make witnesses more nervous than they otherwise would be;
- 19 percent believed that, at least to some extent, the cameras distract jurors;
- 21 percent believed that, at least to some extent, the cameras cause attorneys to be more theatrical in their presentations;
- 27 percent believed that, at least to some extent, the cameras have the effect of distracting the attorneys; and
- 21 percent believed that, at least to some extent, the cameras disrupt the courtroom proceedings.

When trial judges were asked these same questions, the percentages of negative responses were even higher:

- 46 percent believed that, at least to some extent, the cameras make witnesses less willing to appear in court;
- 41 percent found that, at least to some extent, the cameras distract witnesses;
- 64 percent reported that, at least to some extent, the cameras make witnesses more nervous than they otherwise would be;
- 17 percent responded that, at least to some extent, cameras prompt people who see the coverage to try to influence juror friends;
- 64 percent found that, at least to some extent, the cameras cause attorneys to be more theatrical in their presentations;
- 9 percent reported that, at least to some extent, the cameras cause judges to avoid unpopular decisions or positions; and
- 17 percent found that, at least to some extent, cameras disrupt courtroom proceedings.

These negative statistical responses from judges and attorneys involved in the pilot project dominated the Judicial Conference debate and were highly influential in the conference's conclusion that the intimidating effect of cameras on witnesses and jurors was cause for alarm. . . .

For the appellate courts, an even larger percentage of judges who participated in the study related negative responses:

- 47 percent of the appellate judges who responded found that, at least to some extent, the cameras cause attorneys to be more theatrical in their presentations;
- 56 percent found that, at least to some extent, the cameras cause attorneys to change the emphasis or content of their oral arguments;
- 34 percent reported that, at least to some extent, cameras cause judges to change the emphasis or content of their questions at oral arguments; and
- 26 percent reported that, at least to some extent, the cameras disrupt courtroom proceedings.

While the conference did allow each United States court of appeals to determine whether to permit the use of cameras in that circuit, these high negative responses give us a very real indication as to why only two out of 13 courts of appeals have allowed their proceedings to be televised. The two courts that do allow camera coverage are the Second and Ninth Circuits, which voluntarily participated in the pilot project.

Carefully read, the FJC study does not reach the firm conclusions for which it is repeatedly cited. The negative responses described above undermine such a reading. When considering legislation affecting cameras in the courtroom with such permanent and long-range implications for the judicial process, the negative responses should be fully considered. Certainly that is what the conference focused on. In reality, the recommendations of the study reflect a balancing exercise which may seem proper to social scientists but which is unacceptable to judges who cannot compromise the interests of the litigants, jurors and witnesses, even for some amorphous public good . . . .

The Judicial Conference supports that goal but does not agree that cameras in courtrooms will significantly further it.

Ghost of Simpson

When almost anyone in this country thinks of cameras in the courtroom today, they inevitably think of the Simpson case. I sincerely doubt anyone believes that the presence of cameras in that courtroom did not have an impact on the conduct of the attorneys, witnesses, jurors and judges almost universally to the detriment of the trial process. Admittedly, few cases are Simpson-like cases, but the inherent effects of the presence of cameras in the courtroom are, in some respects, the same, whether or not it is a high-publicity case. Furthermore, there is a legitimate concern that if the federal courts were to allow camera coverage of cases that are not sensational, it would become increasingly difficult to limit coverage in the high-profile and high-publicity cases where such limitation, almost all would agree, would be warranted.

This is not a debate about whether judges would be discomfited with camera coverage. Nor is it a debate about whether the federal courts are afraid of public scrutiny. They are not. Open hearings are a hallmark of the federal judiciary. It is also not about increasing the educational opportunities for the public to learn about the federal courts or the litigation process. The judiciary strongly endorses educational outreach, which could better be achieved through increased and targeted community outreach programs.

Rather, this is a decision about how individual Americans—whether they are plaintiffs, defendants, witnesses or jurors—are treated by the federal judicial process. It is the fundamental duty of the federal judiciary to ensure that every citizen receives his or her constitutionally guaranteed right to a fair trial. . . . As the Supreme Court stated in Estes, "[w]e have always held that the atmosphere essential to the preservation of a fair trial—the most fundamental of all freedoms—must be maintained at all costs." 381 U.S. at 540. . . .

POSTSCRIPT

Should Cameras Be Allowed Inside U.S. Courtrooms?

In the case discussed in the Introduction to this issue, *Richmond Newspapers, Inc. v. Virginia,* the Supreme Court stated: "Absent an overriding public interest . . . articulated in findings, the trial of a criminal case must be open to the public." In your opinion, what might constitute an "overriding public interest" that would justify closing a criminal case to the public? Would a case involving a serious sex offense against a child victim, constitute an overriding public interest that would justify closing the case?

Clearly, there are some moments in sensitive cases such as those involving a child victim, where he or she is likely to give graphic and potentially embarrassing testimony, which should be closed to the public. At such times, the court rules in most jurisdictions give trial judges the discretion to close the criminal trial for the duration of the salacious testimony. In considering whether to close the proceedings, however, the trial judge must balance the First Amendment rights of the public and the media to attend the proceedings, with the privacy interests of the victim. Moreover, the judge must consider the defendant's Sixth Amendment right to a public trial. This can be a challenging balancing act.

Imagine yourself in the place of a state court trial judge in a highly sensational case involving a celebrity defendant and a six-year-old victim of sexual abuse. A media frenzy surrounds the case, and you are concerned both with the psychological welfare of the victim and the right of the defendant to receive a fair trial. The prosecutor moves to close the trial to the public and the media during the victim's testimony. Assume further that the court rules in your jurisdiction give you the sole authority to decide whether to close the proceedings during the child's testimony. How would you rule? If you would rule to close the proceedings, would you order the case closed to the media and the public for the duration of the trial or just for the child's testimony? You would be much more likely to be able to withstand a constitutional challenge by the defendant on appeal if you were to close it solely for the child's testimony.

Did the articles in this section lead you to form a conclusion about whether cameras should be allowed in the courtroom? Were you persuaded by Mr. Brill or Judge Becker? These are interesting issues. Perhaps the most reasonable solution is the one that has been adopted in most states: assume that trials must be open to the press and the public unless there is an important reason to close the proceeding, and leave the ultimate decision to the trial judge.

For additional perspectives on the issues considered in this section, see Richard P. Matsch, "Television in the Courtroom: Mightier than the Pen?" *Michigan Law Review* (vol. 97, no. 6, 1999); Howard Rosenberg, "Let TV Go to the Circus," *Broadcasting & Cable* (vol. 135, no. 10, 2005) Edward J. Klaris, "Justice Can't Be Done in Secret," *The Nation* (vol. 274, no. 22, 2002); Eddie Florek, Rebecca Daugherty, and Kirsten B. Mitchell, "Camera Controversy in Courtrooms Continues," *News Media and the Law* (vol. 29, no. 1, 2005); Leonard Post, "The Jury Room as Reality TV Venue," *National Law Journal* (vol. 26, no. 22, 2004); Nadya Labi, "Cameras? Jury's Still Out," *Time* (vol. 160, no. 24, 2002); David Richert, "Cameras in the Court," *Judicature* (vol. 85, no. 5, 2002); Francis T. Murphy, "Televised Criminal Trials May Deny Defendant a Fair Trial," *Journal–New York State Bar Association* (vol. 72, no. 3, 2000); Linda Deutsch, "Backlash from Simpson Case Curbs Access in Courts," *New York Beacon* (vol. 6, no. 23, 1999); "Cameras in Court: Television on Trial," *The Economist* (vol. 349, no. 8099, 1998); and Kenneth C. Killebrew, Jr., "TV or not TV: Television, Justice, and the Courts," *Journalism and Mass Communication Quarterly* (vol. 75, no. 3, 1998).

ISSUE 12

Do "Three Strikes" Sentencing Laws Help to Reduce Serious Crime?

YES: John R. Schafer, from "The Deterrent Effect of Three Strikes Laws," *FBI Law Enforcement Bulletin* (April 1999)

NO: Michael Vitiello, from "Three Strikes Laws," *Human Rights* (Spring 2002)

ISSUE SUMMARY

YES: FBI Special Agent John R. Schafer argues that strictly enforced three strikes laws are an effective crime control policy and may break the cycle of crime for youthful offenders.

NO: Attorney Michael Vitiello asserts that three strikes laws have not delivered on their promises to reduce serious crime. Moreover, the costs of such laws appear to outweigh their benefits.

In the late 1700s, Cesare Beccaria and the early classicists asserted that people are motivated by hedonism, the pursuit of pleasure and avoidance of pain. The classicists believed as well that human beings have free will and possess the capacity for rational thought. Consequently, a cornerstone of their penal philosophy was to make punishments for crimes slightly more severe than the pleasure to be derived from the criminal acts. Beccaria believed that such policies would deter criminal behavior.

Moreover, Beccaria, Jeremy Bentham, and other reformers of the time believed in the use of imprisonment as a form of punishment. In fact, Bentham proposed building prisons in the middle of European cities, so that the sight of prisoners suffering would deter others from committing crimes.

During the mid-1800s, as more people began to embrace the scientific method, the classical model in criminology gave way to a more scientific approach to studying crime and criminals—the positive school. Early members of the positive school, including Cesare Lombroso, traced the origins of criminal behavior to biological factors. In fact, Lombroso asserted that some individuals were "born criminals" who had a biological predisposition to commit crimes. Moreover, based on the theories of Charles Darwin, Lombroso and many others believed that some criminals were "atavistic" throwbacks to an earlier stage in our evolutionary past. According to the early positivists, additional ostensible causes of crime included epilepsy, the contours of the skull, moral insanity, virtually any type of mental illness, alcoholism, and moral degeneracy. The biological paradigm in criminology was paramount for many years.

In the early 1920s and 1930s, however, the biological perspective in criminology began to yield to theories that stressed the social origins of crime. The sociological positivists emphasized the social causes of criminal behavior such as poverty, social disorganization, gang membership, broken homes, lack of community, and immigration patterns. These theories of crime held sway until the early 1970s.

During the early 1970s, a more conservative climate swept the United States. Part of that movement was a return to the classical approach to crime control. Repackaged as rational choice theory by prominent scholars such as Professor James Q. Wilson, it emphasized stringent punishment as a deterrent to criminal behavior. To paraphrase Professor Wilson: "Wicked people exist, set them apart." The ultimate solution to rising crime rates was to make punishment sufficiently severe to deter criminals from committing antisocial acts. This idea has been termed the logical general deterrence model of punishment.

Three strikes laws, which began to appear in the early 1990s, are a logical extension of rational choice theory. They provide generally that upon conviction of a third felony offense, an offender will be sentenced to life in prison. The ultimate question, however, is whether they have any appreciable effect on crime rates.

F.B.I. Special Agent John R. Schafer argues that strictly enforced three strikes laws are an effective crime control policy that may break the cycle of crime for youthful offenders. Attorney Michael Vitiello argues, however, that three strikes laws have not delivered on their promises to reduce serious crime. Moreover, he believes that the costs of such laws appear to outweigh their benefits.

So, who is correct? Are three strikes laws an effective way to deter repeat offenders from committing additional crimes? Or, are three strikes sentencing laws effectively turning our prisons into expensive retirement homes for an aging inmate population? These are compelling questions with significant implications for social policy formulation in the United States.

John R. Schafer

The Deterrent Effect of Three Strikes Law

Since their inception, societies have attempted to control their members in one form or another. The particular behaviors that become the focus of that control can vary from one culture to another; however, the mechanisms that regulate the behavior remain constant. Essentially, punishment or the threat of punishment for social noncompliance represents the mechanism that deters individuals from engaging in deviant activity. The penalty for unwanted behavior can take the form of legal prosecution, social sanctions, or a combination of both. Researchers have labeled this phenomenon perceptual deterrence.

The concept of deterrence can be divided into two categories: general deterrence and specific deterrence. General deterrence occurs when potential offenders see the consequences of other people's actions and decide not to engage in the same behavior. Specific deterrence is triggered when offenders realize the consequences of their own past behavior and decide not to commit the same acts.

Building on the deterrence principle, three strikes laws often are seen as the answer to crime problems in America. Such laws attempt to reduce crime either by incarcerating habitual offenders or deterring potential offenders from committing future crimes. By 1997, 24 states, as well as the federal government, had enacted some form of mandatory sentencing. Although all of these laws are referred to as three strikes laws, the provisions and enforcement of each vary greatly from state to state.

In California, for example, offenders accrue strikes when they get convicted of serious or violent felonies, and offenders with two strikes receive a third strike when they get convicted of any subsequent felony, violent or nonviolent. As of December 1996, the state had prosecuted over 26,000 offenders for their second or third strikes.

But questions remain: Will the advent of three strikes laws deter crime, and, more important, will offenders become more likely to kill victims, witnesses, and police officers to avoid a life sentence? These questions represent important concerns as the cost of implementing mandatory sentencing laws may well include human lives in addition to monetary resources.

From *FBI Law Enforcement Bulletin,* vol. 68, issue 4, April 1999, pp. 6-10. Notes omitted.

California's Experience

The deterrent effect of three strikes laws can be measured best by examining the law's impact on crime in California, which aggressively prosecutes offenders under the provisions of the state's three strikes law. Moreover, because young adults remain responsible for the majority of the crimes, any deterrent effect of this group should significantly reduce the crime rate.

Since California enacted its three strikes law in 1994, crime has dropped 26.9 percent, which translates to 815,000 fewer crimes. While the three strikes law cannot be given sole credit for the drop in crime, in many cases it proved an essential missing piece of the crime control puzzle. Furthermore, in the year prior to the law's passage, California's population of paroled felons increased by 226 as felons from other states moved to California. In the year after the law's enactment, the number of paroled felons plunged as 1,335 moved out of California. Though not conclusive, this decrease may portend the deterrent effect of the state's three strikes law.

Critics of the three strikes law cite the fact that the overall crime rate in 1996 declined nationwide and, more germane, that crime fell in states with no mandatory sentencing laws. These critics attribute the drop to demographics and cite the unusually low number of males in their mid-teens, the crime-prone years. Researchers predict that the crime rate will increase dramatically in the near future because the number of juveniles currently in their preteens far exceeds the normal demographic expectation.

The Juvenile Factor

In truth, crime remains an activity for the young, particularly young men. In 1996, males under age 25 made up 45 percent of the individuals arrested in the United States for index offenses. This group also committed 46 percent of the violent crimes and 59 percent of property crimes. Another well-replicated study found that approximately 6 percent of all juveniles commit more than half of the crimes in the United States.

Not surprisingly, although the overall crime rate in the United States has declined, the juvenile arrest rate for the 5-year period from 1992 to 1996 increased by 21 percent, while adult arrests rose only 7 percent during the same time period. A more frightening statistic reveals that each generation of juvenile offenders has been more violent then the generation that preceded it. The data suggest that a small number of young offenders commit numerous unpunished crimes because the courts, especially the juvenile justice system, provide the offenders with countless "second chances." These offenders are not held accountable for their actions and thus are not motivated to change their criminal behavior.

In 1899, Illinois passed the first Juvenile Court Act in the United States. This act removed adolescents from the formal criminal justice system and created special programs for delinquent, dependent, and neglected children. Over the ensuing century, juvenile justice has remained cyclical. The cycle typically begins when a juvenile or group of juveniles commits an unusually heinous crime that evokes a public outcry. In turn, lawmakers pass stronger legislation for reform. After the tempest subsides, society once again retreats to a position of indifference, only to be aroused by yet another reprehensible act. This cycle is punctuated by attempts to rehabilitate juvenile offenders; however, these attempts largely have failed. No evidence exists to indicate that traditional one-on-one or group psychotherapy reduces the recidivism rate. Other variables—such as education, vocational training, social worker intervention—or any other methods tried to date have not proven effective in deterring crime.

In short, the current juvenile justice system does little to rehabilitate or deter young offenders from a life of crime. This lack of success has frustrated the public to the point where long-term incarceration appears to be the only solution. For this reason, under the provisions of some three strikes laws, an offender could enter prison as a juvenile and, after a long sentence, be paroled as a middle-aged adult. Long prison sentences incapacitate chronic offenders during their crime-prone years and allow them to reintegrate into society when they have grown less likely to commit additional crimes.

In an effort to measure the perceived deterrent effect of California's three strikes law, the author administered an 18-question survey to all of the 604 offenders housed at Challenger Memorial Youth Center (CMYC), an all-male, residential lock-down facility under the authority of the Los Angeles County Probation Department, in Lancaster, California. Five hundred and twenty-three juvenile offenders chose to complete the survey over a 3-day period in March 1997.

The Survey

The author designed the survey to measure the offenders' experiences with the consequences of their own crimes (specific deterrence), the offenders' vicarious experiences with the consequences of other people's crimes (general deterrence), and the likelihood that the offenders would kill to avoid a life sentence. Three questions measured specific deterrence, three measured general deterrence, and one measured the offenders' intent. The data was sorted according to the following variables: race, age, education, family upbringing, offspring, and gang membership.

Results

The survey found that 78 percent of the offenders surveyed understood the provisions of California's three strikes law. The questions that addressed the individual components of the law demonstrated both a specific and general deterrent effect. Specifically, 61 percent of the offenders said they would not or probably would not commit a serious or violent crime if they knew their prison sentence would be doubled; 70 percent said they would not or probably would not commit the crime if they knew they would receive life in prison, thus demonstrating a specific deterrent effect. By comparison, these percentages decreased to 32 percent and 42 percent, respectively, when offenders were asked if they thought someone else would commit a crime facing similar prison terms, illustrating a general deterrence effect.

However, when offenders viewed the law in general terms, no deterrent effect existed. That is, when the question asked if offenders thought the "three strikes law" would stop them or someone else from committing a serious or violent crime, most offenders said no. These findings suggest that when offenders are confronted with the severity of their punishment in specific, personal terms, the law has a deterrent effect, but if the law is defined in general terms, the deterrent effect wanes.

In addition, the survey found that 54 percent of the offenders indicated that they would kill or probably would kill witnesses or law enforcement officers to avoid a life sentence. This figure rose to 62 percent among offenders who claimed gang membership. These findings should serve as a warning to all law enforcement officers that when offenders, especially gang members, have two or more strikes, the likelihood of violence increases substantially.

The survey also determined that race, age, and education did not significantly impact the specific or general deterrent effect of the law. Rather, family upbringing, gang affiliation, and offspring proved the most important variables related to deterrence. The family had a positive influence on offenders, while gang affiliation produced a negative effect. Offenders raised in a home with both parents said they would be less likely to kill witnesses to avoid life in prison and more likely to be deterred by the three strikes laws. Interestingly, offenders with children were less likely to be deterred by the three strikes law than offenders without children. Conventional thinking would suggest that offenders with children of their own would lead more responsible lives in an effort to care for their children; however, this was not the case. One explanation for this finding is that individuals who do not foresee the consequences of their actions routinely engage in risky behavior and so become more likely to have children as juveniles.

An overwhelming majority of the offenders who responded to the survey believed that the three strikes law was not fair and that offenders should receive more than three chances. During the postsurvey discussions with the offenders, most believed that the number of chances afforded offenders should equal one more than the number of crimes for which they themselves had been convicted.

Recommendations

In view of the findings of this study, additional data should be gathered from offenders in California, as well as other states, to determine if the results of this study are part of a greater phenomenon or specific to the offenders surveyed. If these findings hold true, the consequences of three strikes law should be explained to offenders in specific terms, in order to maximize their deterrent effect.

In addition, as more states enact and enforce three strikes laws, the number of offenders willing to use violence to escape arrest likely will increase, as well. Accordingly, law enforcement officers should approach suspects with extra caution and, whenever possible, should run National Crime Information Center and criminal history checks prior to confronting suspects.

In many respects, the findings in this survey are not surprising. The family unit in America has deteriorated slowly over the past few decades. Many children grow up in broken homes with few, if any, role models to teach them right from wrong, much less instill them with the courage to make morally correct decisions. Indeed, gang rituals have replaced family traditions; gang violence has replaced family values. Thus, crime prevention strategies that target entire families and intervene early, combined with swift and sure punishment for lawbreakers, including aggressively enforced three strikes laws, may produce the greatest deterrent effect.

Conclusion

Many offenders who have been through the criminal justice system repeatedly have learned through experience that the punishment for their actions is not severe enough to deter them from reaping the rewards of future criminal acts. Juvenile offenders learn the same lesson at an age that may make them destined for a life of crime. Yet, the results of a survey of a group of juvenile offenders in California suggest that when young criminals face specific, long-term sanctions for repeated offenses, they may be deterred from committing future acts. Thus, strictly enforced three strikes laws may break the cycle of crime that often begins early in a youth's life.

Scholars and practitioners alike continue to debate whether criminals are products of their genes or their environments. Those who believe criminals are born advocate incarceration as a means of incapacitation, while those who think criminals are made favor rehabilitation. The continuing controversy of whether the purpose of incarceration is for rehabilitation or incapacitation will continue for some time to come. Until this debate is resolved, offenders, at least in states with three strikes legislation, will have fewer opportunities to prey on innocent victims.

NO 

Michael Vitiello

Three Strikes Law

A Real or Imagined Deterrent to Crime?

The 1990s were dominated by get-tough-on-crime measures, dramatically increasing the nation's prison population and the length of prison sentences. Those measures culminated with the enactment of "three strikes" legislation around the nation. Beginning with Washington State in 1993, by the end of the decade, the federal government and over half of all states had enacted some form of a "three strikes" law. Roughly contemporaneous with these measures, crime rates have declined nationwide. Advocates of severe incarceration policies have claimed that "three strikes" laws are responsible for that decline.

Nowhere in the nation are the stakes higher than in California. Called "the biggest penal experiment of its kind in modern American history," due to its distinctive provisions, California's "three strikes" law accounts for the vast majority of "three strikes" cases nationwide. Its sentence enhancements include not just the widely advertised twenty-five-year-to-life terms for third-strike felons, but also a doubling of the nominal sentence for many second-strike offenders. Further, its provisions include residential burglary as a possible qualifying strike. Finally, the third-strike, triggering the twenty-five-year-to-life term of imprisonment, may be any felony. As a result, California accounts for over 90 percent of all "three strikes" sentences nationwide.

"Three strikes" advocates in California point to dramatic declines in crime rates since its passage and claim victory. For example, former Attorney General Dan Lungren's office reported that "[s]ince the passage of 'Three Strikes,' . . . the violent crime rate in California has dropped 26.9 percent with a 30.8 percent drop in the six major crime categories." Secretary of State Bill Jones, who sponsored the "three strikes" legislation as an assemblyman, has suggested that three strikes is responsible for most, if not all, of that drop in crime. Justice James Ardaiz, who assisted in drafting the original bill, is even more explicit: "Crime in California has declined dramatically since 1993. The only things that are different are more police, tougher laws, and Three Strikes . . . . [W]here there are a number of explanations for a given result, the simplest explanation is usually correct. The Three Strikes Law is that explanation." Jones points to additional support for the beneficial role of

From *Human Rights*, vol. 29, no. 2, Spring 2002, pp. 3-5.

"three strikes": while crime rates declined across the nation, the decline in California significantly outstripped that in the rest of the nation. For example, over a six-month period in 1995, crime declined only 1 percent nationwide while it dropped 7 percent in California.

While commentators disagree about whether the law is theoretically justified, much of the debate focuses on empirical data. If "three strikes" accounts for the dramatic decline in crime, theoretical objections, including moral concerns about its fairness, are not likely to move legislators or the public. And as indicated above, "three strikes" supporters argue that empirical data support their position.

However, despite the claims of "three strikes" supporters, the data on which they rely do not withstand close scrutiny. More recent empirical research supports many of the claims of "three strikes" critics that the law simply cannot deliver on its promises and insofar as it may have some marginal deterrent effect, it comes at too high a cost.

Comparing California's decline in crime with the national average, as Secretary of State Jones does when he asserts that "three strikes" accounts for California exceeding the decline in crime nationwide, cuts both ways. New York, not California, showed the sharpest decline in crime during the time in question. While some of New York's policing policies have raised serious civil rights concerns, it was not one of the states that adopted a "three strikes" law during the 1990s. Hence, its decline in crime cannot be attributed to such legislation.

A number of recently published studies also raise doubts about the true effectiveness of "three strikes" laws in lowering California's crime rate. For example, within California, counties that aggressively enforce the law "had no greater declines in crime than did counties that used it far more sparingly." One study found that crime dropped by 21.3 percent in the six most lenient "three strikes" counties, compared to a 12.7 percent drop in the toughest counties.

A recently published book, *Punishment and Democracy: Three Strikes and You're Out in California*, reports the results of the most comprehensive study of "three strikes" to date. The authors' findings suggest that, prior to "three strikes," crime rates were declining already and, after "three strikes" they continued to decline at about the same rate, suggesting that whatever effect "three strikes" had, it was small at best. The book also notes that, partly because "three strikes" casts such a broad net, the offenders arrested under its provisions were no more likely to be high-rate offenders than non–"three strikes" arrestees. Nor were they more likely to commit violent offenses.

Although its proponents originally explained that "three strikes" would work because it would incapacitate high-rate offenders, the decline in the crime rate came too early to be explained on that basis—"three strikes" is a sentence enhancement provision and the enhancements do not kick in immediately, whereas the decline in the crime rate occurred immediately. As a result, "three strikes" proponents were forced to shift their explanation—the law deterred potential offenders.

The authors of *Punishment and Democracy* attempted to measure the law's deterrent effect. In certain instances, depending on which method the authors used, they did find a marginal deterrent effect. But the effect was extremely small and cannot explain the significant overall decline in the crime rate. *Punishment and Democracy* also addressed the claim of the law's proponents that a sharp decline in the crime rate followed passage of the law. Contrary to this claim, the authors found that the decline in the crime rate preceded passage of the law. Further, were "three strikes" the cause of a significant part of the decline, the rate of decline should have increased after its passage. Instead, the rate of decline remained constant, suggesting that the causes of the decline that were operating prior to the passage of the law continued to be the primary reason for the drop in crime rates.

Empirical studies suggest that California would have experienced virtually all of its decline in crime without "three strikes." At the same time, "three strikes" will have a significant cumulative effect on the size of the prison population, an expense that will grow over time. One effect will be to increase the number of older prisoners, a group that represents a low social risk because most offenders become less criminally active as they age. Not only are older prisoners not likely to commit crimes if set free, but they cost the state much more to keep incarcerated than younger, healthier offenders.

None of this comes as a surprise to many commentators who doubted the wisdom of "three strikes," certainly as it was enacted in California. But none of us who opposed "three strikes" can take much comfort in knowing that our concerns were borne out. The important policy question is how can we reform the law to avoid its excesses?

Few politicians were willing to oppose "three strikes" during its passage. And while most politicians in the past decade have feared being labeled as soft on crime, that fear was exacerbated during the legislation's passage. Aided by the kidnapping and murder of young Polly Klaas, Mike Reynolds, the father of a murder victim, pushed the bill through the legislature with remarkable resolve. He was unwilling to compromise or allow amendments to the bill (or to a virtually identical ballot initiative). His sway with the legislature was extraordinary, with most afraid that if they opposed him, he would portray them as soft on crime. Since the law's passage, passions have cooled somewhat. But one legacy of the charged political environment in which the law passed is that its amendment requires a supermajority. As a result, even those few politicians who are now willing to propose amendments face an uphill battle at best.

In theory, both the California and the U.S. Constitutions protect against the imposition of disproportionate criminal penalties. But outside of the death penalty context, that protection is more theoretical than real. During the 1970s and 1980s, the California Supreme Court was active in reviewing indeterminate sentences and developed a body of case law wherein it overturned numerous sentences as excessive in violation of California's protection against "cruel or unusual punishment." A number of trial courts relied on that case law in striking down some of the more extreme "three strikes" sentences shortly after the law became effective. Despite supreme court precedent and considerable sentiment among trial courts that some "three strikes" sentences were excessive, no California district court of appeal agreed. In light of unanimity among the district courts of appeal, the California Supreme Court has shown no inclination to revisit the question.

More recently, in a denial of certiorari, four U.S. Supreme Court justices suggested that some "three strikes" sentences might violate the Eighth Amendment's prohibition against cruel and unusual punishment. Riggs v. California, 525 U.S. 1114 (1999). Since then, the Ninth Circuit has held in three separate cases that a "three strikes" offense violates the Eighth Amendment.

Meaningful review of "three strikes" sentences might weed out many of the cases in which twenty-five-year-to-life sentences seem excessive. But two important questions remain. First, even the Ninth Circuit's decisions may be severely limited in their scope. All three cases decided thus far have involved petty theft as the third strike offense. Under California law, petty theft is a "wobbler," an offense that may be a misdemeanor or a felony. Under the circumstances of the cases before the court, the offenders' records have led to the crime being treated as a felony. Once escalated to a felony, the crime becomes the third strike. The effect of the unique features of California's sentencing laws is that what might be a misdemeanor ends up resulting in a life sentence. If the Ninth Circuit's approach turns on that feature of the law, the impact of these cases is quite limited, perhaps to as few as 300-350 cases out of over thousands of "three strikes" cases. For example, if so limited, the Ninth Circuit's approach would offer little hope for an offender whose third strike was a minor possession of narcotics or marijuana offense.

The other important question is whether the Ninth Circuit's decisions will survive U.S. Supreme Court scrutiny. Earlier this year, the Supreme Court granted California's petition for a writ of certiorari. As indicated earlier, four justices raised concerns about "three strikes" sentences, again in the context of a theft "wobbler" case. But whether a fifth justice would agree is open to serious question.

The Supreme Court has overturned a term of imprisonment as a violation of the Eighth Amendment in only one case. In Solem v. Helm, 463 U.S. 277 (1983), the Court struck down a true life sentence imposed on a habitual offender whose criminal record, although extensive, did not include any crimes of violence. The offense that triggered the life sentence was for writing a bad check, an offense described by the Court as passive and nonviolent. Although a majority of the Court refused to overrule Helm when it next considered the question, the Court did uphold a true life sentence for possession of more than 650 grams of cocaine. In addition, prior to Helm, the Court upheld a parolable life sentence in Rummel v. Estelle, 445 U.S. 263 (1980), and a sentence of forty years for possession of marijuana in Hutto v. Davis, 454 U.S. 370 (1982). Were the Court to apply that case law to "three strikes," whether it would find any given sentence a violation of the Eighth Amendment is uncertain.

"Three strikes" requires a significant minimum sentence, one that can be reduced by at most 20 percent for good time. Hence, a "three strikes" offender must serve a minimum sentence of at least twenty years. That may seem significant, and in some rough sense, disproportionate to an offender's third-strike offense (for example, possession of a small amount of drugs). But the punishment is less severe than, say, the offender in Hutto v. Davis, whose forty-year sentence was not unconstitutionally excessive. Instead, like Rummel, the offender in Rummel v. Estelle, the offender is not condemned to a true life sentence. Even if the long minimum sentence has the practical effect of a true life sentence—for example, when it is imposed on an older offender who as a practical matter will probably die in prison before serving his entire sentence—the case may not come within Solem v. Helm. While the Court struck down a sentence imposed on a habitual offender, his entire criminal record did not include a crime of violence. At least for those offenders whose earlier crimes have included crimes of violence, their earlier criminal records may be enough to take them out of Helm's narrow holding. Perhaps an older offender whose minimum sentence may be the equivalent of a life sentence and whose two strikes were residential burglaries and whose third strike is a relatively minor offense, like possession of drugs, could invoke Eighth Amendment protection. But those cases may be too few to have much of an impact on the problem created by "three strikes."

The issue bears watching. Excessive punishment raises serious moral questions. Beyond the moral question, "three strikes" opponents have mounting empirical evidence that "three strikes" cannot deliver on its overblown promises. But legislative reform, difficult under normal circumstance due to politicians' fears of being labeled soft on crime, is doubly difficult because of the supermajority requirement. We are left hoping that the courts will save us from our own excesses; whether they will is very much up for grabs.

POSTSCRIPT

Do "Three Strikes" Sentencing Laws Help to Reduce Serious Crime?

The old baseball metaphor says "three strikes, you're out." With regard to three strikes sentencing laws, should the metaphor be changed to "Three strikes, we're out?" Three strikes sentencing laws came into vogue in the early 1990s. Since then, some good empirical data have been collected, and scholars and social policymakers have begun to consider the overall effects of these laws.

The U.S. Bureau of Justice Statistics has found that in 2000, persons 45 years of age or more, who comprise approximately 33 percent of the U.S. population, accounted for less than 10 percent of the serious crime arrests. One study has projected that in 2010, U.S. prisons will house approximately 200,000 elderly inmates who will require special treatment and advanced medical care. At an average cost of $75,000 for each elderly inmate, that amounts to a price tag of approximately $15 billion annually to confine individuals who, in the aggregate, represent little threat to society. While some serious offenders such as mass murderers and psychotic killers should be confined permanently because they represent a continuing menace to society, the weight of the evidence indicates that diverting elderly inmates into less expensive community-based correctional programs may produce the greatest benefit for society.

Moreover, a recent large-scale study of the impact of three strikes sentencing laws in 188 U.S. cities with populations of 100,000 or more by Kovandzic, Sloan, and Vieratis states:

> Consistent with other studies, ours finds no credible statistical evidence that passage of three strikes laws reduces crime by deterring potential criminals or incapacitating repeat offenders. The results . . . provided no evidence of an immediate or gradual decrease in crime rates, *and homicide rates were actually positively associated with the passage of three strikes laws.* [Emphasis added.]

The conclusions of this methodologically rigorous study are simply incredible. Three strikes laws appear to have little deterrent effect. Moreover, the authors found that the passage of three strikes laws in a jurisdiction was positively related to homicide rates. This means that those jurisdictions with three strikes laws had higher homicide rates than those that did not.

So, do three strikes laws help to reduce serious crime? At this point in time, the weight of the evidence appears to indicate that they do not, although F.B.I. Special Agent John R. Schafer would almost certainly question the reliability of the data generated by studies such as the one considered above. Attorney Michael Vitiello would cite these studies as further evidence that three strikes laws do not work and are an expensive social policy failure.

After considering the arguments, what is your opinion? Do three strikes laws help to reduce serious crime, or are they another example of a failed social experiment? Fortunately, there are additional resources to help you to answer these questions. See Tomislav V. Kovandzic, John J. Sloan III, and Lynne M. Vieraltis, " 'Striking Out' as Crime Reduction Policy: The Impact of 'Three Strikes' Laws on Crime Rates in U.S. Cities," *Justice Quarterly* (vol. 21, no. 2, 2004); Alex Vitale, "3 Strikes for 3 Strikes," *Radical Society* (vol. 29, no. 2, 2002); Jonathan P. Caulkins, "How Large Should the Strike Zone Be in 'Three Strikes and You're Out' Sentencing Laws?" *Journal of Quantitative Criminology* (vol. 17, no. 3, 2001); Carl P. Schmertmann, Adansi A. Amankwaa, and Robert D. Long, "Three Strikes and You're Out: Demographic Analysis of Mandatory Prison Sentencing," *Demography* (vol. 35, no. 4, 1998); Julie C. Kunselman and Gennaro F. Vito, "Questioning Mandatory Sentencing Efficiency: A Case Study of Persistent Felony Offender Rapists in Kentucky," *American Journal of Criminal Justice* (vol. 27, no. 1, 2002); and Kathleen Auerhahn, "Selective Incapacitation, Three Strikes, and the Problem of Aging Prison Populations: Using Simulation Modeling to See the Future," *Criminology & Public Policy* (vol. 1, no. 3, 2002).

On the Internet . . .

Academy of Criminal Justice Sciences

This site is an excellent resource for a wide variety of information about the U.S. justice system. It provides links to a number of resources that consider various aspects of justice system processes, including the police, the courts, punishment, and corrections.

http://www.acjs.org/

American Correctional Association (ACA)

The ACA is the oldest and largest international correctional association in the world. ACA serves all disciplines within the corrections profession and is dedicated to excellence in every aspect of the field.

http://www.aca.org/

National Criminal Justice Reference Service (NCJRS)

This very comprehensive database provides a wealth of information about justice system processes. Topics include corrections, courts, crime prevention, crime rates, drugs, the criminal justice system, juvenile justice, law enforcement, and the victims of crime. It also provides links to NCJRS-sponsored research on virtually every aspect of the criminal justice system.

http://www.ncjrs.org/

The Sentencing Project

The Sentencing Project is a non-profit organization that promotes reduced reliance on incarceration and increased use of more effective and humane alternatives to deal with crime. It is a nationally recognized source of criminal justice policy analysis, data, and information.

http://www.sentencingproject.org/

PART 4

Punishment

Punishment is a necessary component of a justice system that serves important functions for society. According to prominent social theorists, it serves to define and reinforce the rules of proper behavior for everyone in society. Punishing those who break society's laws also enhances social solidarity and may deter others from committing similar offenses. In our justice system, punishments must comply with the mandates imposed by the U.S. Constitution and may not be "cruel and unusual," be applied in a discriminatory manner, or be disproportionate to the original offense. Punishment issues are explored in this section.

- Does Confining Sex Offenders Indefinitely in Mental Hospitals After They Have Served Their Prison Sentences Violate the Constitution?
- Should Homosexual Prison Inmates Have a Right to Share the Same Cell?
- Are Supermax (Control Unit) Prisons an Appropriate Way to Punish Hardened Criminals?
- Should Private "For Profit" Corporations Be Allowed to Run U.S. Prisons?

ISSUE 13

Does Confining Sex Offenders Indefinitely in Mental Hospitals After They Have Served Their Prison Sentences Violate the Constitution?

YES: Stephen Breyer, from Dissenting Opinion, *Kansas v. Hendricks*, U.S. Supreme Court (1997)

NO: Clarence Thomas, from Opinion, *Kansas v. Hendricks*, U.S. Supreme Court (1997)

ISSUE SUMMARY

YES: Associate Justice Stephen Breyer asserts that if a state's law attempts to inflict additional punishment on an offender after he has served a prison sentence, it will violate the federal Constitution.

NO: Associate Justice Clarence Thomas, writing for the Court, contends that post-imprisonment civil confinement laws do not violate the Constitution.

Imagine for a moment that you are a criminal who has been sentenced to a term of incarceration in a state prison and that you have almost completed your sentence. One month before you are to be released, you learn that the state alleges that you pose a continuing threat to society and will initiate a civil commitment proceeding designed to confine you indefinitely in a state mental hospital. How would you react? Would you attempt to challenge the state's authority to keep you confined beyond your original prison term? Which legal theories would you use?

One possible legal theory is that the potential commitment is a violation of the Fifth Amendment's double jeopardy clause. The Supreme Court has held that the double jeopardy protection extends not only to two trials for the same offense but also to two punishments for the same crime. Would it seem like a "slam dunk" argument that a mandatory confinement in a mental institution after someone has served their full prison sentence for the same crime violates the double jeopardy clause? Don't bet on it.

Kansas v. Hendricks, 521 U.S. 346 (1997) presented similar facts. Shortly before he was to be released from a Kansas prison to a halfway house from his sentence for taking indecent liberties with two adolescents, Hendricks was found by a jury to be a sexually violent predator. During the trial, he agreed with the state physician's diagnosis that he suffered from pedophilia. The trial judge ordered Hendricks, under the Kansas Sexually Violent Predator Act, committed to a mental institution for an indefinite period, although the continuing necessity of his confinement was subject to an annual review by the court. On appeal, the Kansas supreme court held that the commitment violated Hendricks's Fourteenth Amendment due process rights.

The Court held too that a confinement in a state mental institution after the completion of an offender's original prison sentence does not violate the Fifth Amendment's double jeopardy clause because that provision prohibits only a second *punishment* for the same offense. Stated Thomas: "The State may take measures to restrict the freedom of the dangerously mentally ill. This is a legitimate non-punitive governmental objective and has been historically so regarded."

Are you persuaded by the Court's reasoning? Justice Thomas contends that Hendricks' indefinite incarceration, after he had completed his state prison sentence for the *same offenses*, did not violate the double jeopardy clause. As a number of commentators have pointed out, the line between punishment and indefinite commitment to a mental institution may be a difficult one to identify.

Justice Stephen Breyer's dissenting opinion disagrees with the majority's holding that Hendricks's later confinement in a state mental institution did not constitute punishment. Stated Justice Breyer: "The statutory provisions before us do amount to punishment primarily because, as I have said, the legislature did not tailor the statute to fit the nonpunitive civil aim of treatment, which it concedes exists in Hendricks' case."

What is your view of this issue? Is it fundamentally fair to apply to a convict a statute passed after they had committed their offense? Moreover, does society have a right to protect itself from dangerous sexual predators by keeping them confined? The available evidence in this area suggests that many pedophiles have long careers involving numerous child-victims. Must we wait for someone like Hendricks to commit another pedophilic incident before we can incapacitate him? These difficult issues may be the real foundation of this decision. It is sometimes said that "hard cases make bad law." This may be a case where we like the results of the decision, even though the legal reasoning supporting the decision is less than completely persuasive. As a member of the U.S. Supreme Court, how would you decide this case?

Stephen Breyer

Dissenting Opinion

I agree with the majority that the Kansas Act's "definition of 'mental abnormality'" satisfies the "substantive" requirements of the Due Process Clause. Kansas, however, concedes that Hendricks' condition is treatable; yet the Act did not provide Hendricks (or others like him) with any treatment until after his release date from prison and only inadequate treatment thereafter. These, and certain other special features of the Act convince me that it was not simply an effort to commit Hendricks civilly, but rather an effort to inflict further punishment upon him. The *Ex Post Facto* Clause therefore prohibits the Act's application to Hendricks, who committed his crimes prior to its enactment.

I

I begin with the area of agreement. This Court has held that the civil commitment of a "mentally ill" and "dangerous" person does not automatically violate the Due Process Clause provided that the commitment takes place pursuant to proper procedures and evidentiary standards. The Kansas Supreme Court, however, held that the Due Process Clause forbids application of the Act to Hendricks for "substantive" reasons, *i.e.*, irrespective of the procedures or evidentiary standards used. The court reasoned that Kansas had not satisfied the "mentally ill" requirement of the Due Process Clause because Hendricks was not "mentally ill." Moreover, Kansas had not satisfied what the court believed was an additional "substantive due process" requirement, namely the provision of treatment. I shall consider each of these matters briefly.

A

In my view, the Due Process Clause permits Kansas to classify Hendricks as a mentally ill and dangerous person for civil commitment purposes. I agree with the majority that the Constitution gives States a degree of leeway in making this kind of determination. But, because I do not subscribe to all of its reasoning, I shall set forth three sets of circumstances that, taken together, convince me that Kansas has acted within the limits that the Due Process Clause substantively sets.

Dissenting Opinion, Kansas v. Hendricks, Supreme Court, 1997. Some court case citations omitted.

First, the psychiatric profession itself classifies the kind of problem from which Hendricks suffers as a serious mental disorder. But the very presence and vigor of this debate is important. The Constitution permits a State to follow one reasonable professional view, while rejecting another. The psychiatric debate, therefore, helps to inform the law by setting the bounds of what is reasonable, but it cannot here decide just how States must write their laws within those bounds.

Second, Hendricks' abnormality does not consist simply of a long course of antisocial behavior, but rather it includes a specific, serious, and highly unusual inability to control his actions. (For example, Hendricks testified that, when he gets "stressed out," he cannot "control the urge" to molest children.) The law traditionally has considered this kind of abnormality akin to insanity for purposes of confinement. Indeed, the notion of an "irresistible impulse" often has helped to shape criminal law's insanity defense and to inform the related recommendations of legal experts as they seek to translate the insights of mental health professionals into workable legal rules.

Third, Hendricks' mental abnormality also makes him dangerous. Hendricks "has been convicted of . . . a sexually violent offense," and a jury found that he "suffers from a mental abnormality . . . which makes" him "likely to engage" in similar "acts of sexual violence" in the future. The evidence at trial favored the State. Dr. Befort, for example, explained why Hendricks was likely to commit further acts of sexual violence if released. And Hendricks' own testimony about what happens when he gets "stressed out" confirmed Dr. Befort's diagnosis.

Because (1) many mental health professionals consider pedophilia a serious mental disorder; and (2) Hendricks suffers from a classic case of irresistible impulse, namely he is so afflicted with pedophilia that he cannot "control the urge" to molest children; and (3) his pedophilia presents a serious danger to those children; I believe that Kansas can classify Hendricks as "mentally ill" and "dangerous" as this Court used those terms in *Foucha*.

The Kansas Supreme Court's contrary conclusion rested primarily upon that court's view that Hendricks would not qualify for civil commitment under Kansas own state civil commitment statute. The issue before us, however, is one of constitutional interpretation. The Constitution does not require Kansas to write all of its civil commitment rules in a single statute or forbid it to write two separate statutes each covering somewhat different classes of committable individuals. Moreover, Hendricks apparently falls outside the scope of the Kansas general civil commitment statute because that statute permits confinement only of those who "lack capacity to make an informed decision concerning treatment." The statute does not tell us why it imposes this requirement. Capacity to make an informed decision about treatment is not always or obviously incompatible with severe mental illness. Neither Hendricks nor his *amici* point to a uniform body of professional opinion that says as much, and we have not found any. Consequently, the boundaries of the federal Constitution and those of Kansas' general civil commitment statute are not congruent.

B

The Kansas Supreme Court also held that the Due Process Clause requires a State to provide treatment to those whom it civilly confines (as "mentally ill" and "dangerous"). It found that Kansas did not provide Hendricks with significant treatment. And it concluded that Hendricks' confinement violated the Due Process Clause for this reason as well.

This case does not require us to consider whether the Due Process Clause *always* requires treatment—whether, for example, it would forbid civil confinement of an *untreatable* mentally ill, dangerous person. To the contrary, Kansas argues that pedophilia is an "abnormality" or "illness" that can be treated. Two groups of mental health professionals agree. Indeed, no one argues the contrary. Hence the legal question before us is whether the Clause forbids Hendricks' confinement unless Kansas provides him with treatment *that it concedes is available.*

Nor does anyone argue that Kansas somehow could have violated the Due Process Clause's *treatment* concerns had it provided Hendricks with the treatment that is potentially available (and I do not see how any such argument could succeed). Rather, the basic substantive due process treatment question is whether that Clause requires Kansas to provide treatment that it concedes is potentially available to a person whom it concedes is treatable. This same question is at the heart of my discussion of whether Hendricks' confinement violates the Constitution's *Ex Post Facto* Clause. For that reason, I shall not consider the substantive due process treatment question separately, but instead shall simply turn to the *Ex Post Facto* Clause discussion.

II

Kansas' 1994 Act violates the Federal Constitution's prohibition of "any . . . *ex post facto* Law" if it "inflicts" upon Hendricks "a greater punishment" than did the law "annexed to" his "crimes" when he "committed" those crimes in 1984. The majority agrees that the Clause "'forbids the application of any *new punitive measure* to a crime already consummated.'" But it finds the Act is not "punitive." With respect to that basic question, I disagree with the majority.

Certain resemblances between the Act's "civil commitment" and traditional criminal punishments are obvious. Like criminal imprisonment, the Act's civil commitment amounts to "secure" confinement, and "incarceration against one's will." In addition, a basic objective of the Act is incapacitation, which, as Blackstone said in describing an objective of criminal law, is to "deprive the party injuring of the power to do future mischief."

Moreover, the Act, like criminal punishment, imposes its confinement (or sanction) only upon an individual who has previously committed a criminal offense. And the Act imposes that confinement through the use of persons (county prosecutors), procedural guarantees (trial by jury, assistance of counsel, psychiatric evaluations), and standards ("beyond a reasonable doubt") traditionally associated with the criminal law.

These obvious resemblances by themselves, however, are not legally sufficient to transform what the Act calls "civil commitment" into a criminal punishment. Civil commitment of dangerous, mentally ill individuals by its very nature involves confinement and incapacitation. Yet "civil commitment," from a constitutional perspective, nonetheless remains civil. Nor does the fact that criminal behavior triggers the Act make the critical difference. The Act's insistence upon a prior crime, by screening out those whose past behavior does not concretely demonstrate the existence of a mental problem or potential future danger, may serve an important noncriminal evidentiary purpose. Neither is the presence of criminal law-type procedures determinative. Those procedures can serve an important purpose that in this context one might consider noncriminal, namely helping to prevent judgmental mistakes that would wrongly deprive a person of important liberty.

If these obvious similarities cannot by themselves prove that Kansas' "civil commitment" statute is criminal, neither can the word "civil" written into the statute, by itself prove the contrary. This Court has said that only the "clearest proof" could establish that a law the legislature called "civil," was, in reality a "punitive" measure. But the Court has also reiterated that a "civil label is not always dispositive"; it has said that in close cases the label is "'not of paramount importance'"; and it has looked behind a "civil" label fairly often.

In this circumstance, with important features of the Act pointing in opposite directions, I would place particular importance upon those features that would likely distinguish between a basically punitive and a basically nonpunitive purpose. And I note that the Court, in an earlier civil commitment case, looked primarily to the law's concern for treatment as an important distinguishing feature. I do not believe that *Allen* means that a particular law's lack of concern for treatment, by itself, is enough to make an incapacitative law punitive. But, for reasons I will point out, when a State believes that treatment does exist, and then couples that admission with a legislatively required delay of such treatment until a person is at the end of his jail term (so that further incapacitation is therefore necessary), such a legislative scheme begins to look punitive.

In *Allen*, the Court considered whether, for Fifth Amendment purposes, proceedings under an Illinois statute were civil or "criminal." The Illinois statute, rather like the Kansas statute here, authorized the confinement of persons who were sexually dangerous, who had committed at least one prior sexual assault, and who suffered from a "mental disorder." The *Allen* Court, looking behind the statute's "civil commitment" label, found the statute civil—in important part because the State had "provided for the treatment of those it commits." (also referring to facts that the State had "disavowed any interest in punishment" and that it had "established a system under which committed persons may be released after the briefest time in confinement").

In reaching this conclusion, the Court noted that the State Supreme Court had found the proceedings "'essentially civil'" because the statute's aim was to provide "'treatment, not punishment.'" It observed that the State had "a statutory obligation to provide 'care and treatment . . . designed to effect recovery'" in a "facility set aside to provide psychiatric care." And it referred to the State's purpose as one of "*treating* rather than punishing sexually dangerous persons."

The *Allen* Court's focus upon treatment, as a kind of touchstone helping to distinguish civil from punitive purposes, is not surprising, for one would expect a nonpunitive statutory scheme to confine, not simply in order to protect, but also in order to cure. That is to say, one would expect a nonpunitively motivated legislature that confines *because of* a dangerous mental abnormality to seek to help the individual himself overcome that abnormality (at least insofar as professional treatment for the abnormality exists and is potentially helpful, as Kansas, supported by some groups of mental health professionals, argues is the case here). Conversely, a statutory scheme that provides confinement that does not reasonably fit a practically available, medically oriented treatment objective, more likely reflects a primarily punitive legislative purpose.

Several important treatment-related factors—factors of a kind that led the five-member *Allen* majority to conclude that the Illinois' legislature's purpose was primarily civil, not punitive—in this case suggest precisely the opposite. First, the State Supreme Court here, unlike the state court in *Allen,* has held that treatment is not a significant objective of the Act. The Kansas court wrote that the Act's purpose is "segregation of sexually violent offenders," with "treatment" a matter that was "incidental at best." By way of contrast, in *Allen* the Illinois court had written that "'treatment, not punishment'" was "the aim of the statute."

We have generally given considerable weight to the findings of state and lower federal courts regarding the intent or purpose underlying state officials' actions, although the level of deference given to such findings varies with the circumstances, and is not always as conclusive as a state court's construction of one of its statutes. For example, *Allen*'s dissenters, as well as its majority, considered the state court's characterization of the state law's purpose an important factor in determining the constitutionality of that statute.

The record provides support for the Kansas court's conclusion. The court found that, as of the time of Hendricks' commitment, the State had not funded treatment, it had not entered into treatment contracts, and it had little, if any, qualified treatment staff. Indeed, were we to follow the majority's invitation to look beyond the record in this case, an invitation with which we disagree, it would reveal that Hendricks, according to the commitment program's own director, was receiving "essentially no treatment."

It is therefore not surprising that some of the Act's official supporters had seen in it an opportunity permanently to confine dangerous sex offenders. Others thought that effective treatment did not exist—a view, by the way, that the State of Kansas, supported by groups of informed mental health professionals, here strongly denies.

The Kansas court acknowledged the existence of "provisions of the Act for treatment" (although it called them "somewhat disingenuous"). Nor did the court deny that Kansas could later increase the amount of treatment it provided. But the Kansas Supreme Court could, and did, use the Act's language, history, and initial implementation to help it characterize the Act's primary purposes.

Second, the Kansas statute insofar as it applies to previously convicted offenders, such as Hendricks, commits, confines, and treats those offenders *after* they have served virtually their entire criminal sentence. That time-related circumstance seems deliberate. The Act explicitly defers diagnosis, evaluation, and commitment proceedings until a few weeks prior to the "anticipated release" of a previously convicted offender from prison. But why, one might ask, does the Act not commit and require treatment of sex offenders sooner, say soon after they begin to serve their sentences?

An Act that simply seeks confinement, of course, would not need to begin civil commitment proceedings sooner. Such an Act would have to begin proceedings only when an offender's prison term ends, threatening his release from the confinement that imprisonment assures. But it is difficult to see why rational legislators who seek treatment would write the Act in this way—providing treatment years after the criminal act that indicated its necessity. And it is particularly difficult to see why legislators who specifically wrote into the statute a finding that "prognosis for rehabilitating . . . in a prison setting is poor" would leave an offender in that setting for months or years before beginning treatment. This is to say, the timing provisions of the statute confirm the Kansas Supreme Court's view that treatment was not a particularly important legislative objective.

I recognize one possible counter-argument. A State, wanting both to punish Hendricks (say, for deterrence purposes) and also to treat him, might argue that it should be permitted to postpone treatment until after punishment in order to make certain that the punishment in fact occurs. But any such reasoning is out of place here. Much of the treatment that Kansas offered here (called "ward milieu" and "group therapy") can be given at the same time as, and in the same place where, Hendricks serves his punishment. The evidence adduced at the state habeas proceeding, were we to assume it properly before the Court, see *infra*, at 20-21, supports this conclusion as well. Hence, assuming arguendo that it would be otherwise permissible, Kansas need not postpone treatment in order to make certain that sex offenders serve their full terms of imprisonment, *i.e.*, to make certain that they receive the entire punishment that Kansas criminal law provides. To the contrary, the statement in the Act itself, that the Act aims to respond to special "long term" "treatment needs," suggests that treatment should begin during imprisonment. It also suggests that, were those long-term treatment needs (rather than further punishment) Kansas' primary aim, the State would require that treatment begin soon after conviction, not 10 or more years later.

Third, the statute, at least as of the time Kansas applied it to Hendricks, did not require the committing authority to consider the possibility of using less restrictive alternatives, such as postrelease supervision, halfway houses, or other methods that *amici* supporting Kansas here have mentioned. The laws of many other States require such consideration. This Court has said that a failure to consider, or to use, "alternative and less harsh methods" to achieve a nonpunitive objective can help to show that legislature's "purpose . . . was to punish." And one can draw a similar conclusion here. Legislation that seeks to help the individual offender as well as to protect the public would avoid significantly greater restriction of an individual's liberty than public safety requires. Legislation that seeks almost exclusively to incapacitate the individual through confinement, however, would not necessarily concern itself with potentially less restrictive forms of incapacitation. I would reemphasize that this is not a case in which the State claims there is no treatment potentially available. Rather, Kansas, and supporting *amici,* argue that pedophilia is treatable.

Fourth, the laws of other States confirm, through comparison, that Kansas' "civil commitment" objectives do not require the statutory features that indicate a punitive purpose. I have found 17 States with laws that seek to protect the public from mentally abnormal, sexually dangerous individuals through civil commitment or other mandatory treatment programs. Ten of those statutes, unlike the Kansas statute, begin treatment of an offender soon after he has been apprehended and charged with a serious sex offense. Only seven, like Kansas, delay "civil" commitment (and treatment) until the offender has served his criminal sentence (and this figure includes the Acts of Minnesota and New Jersey, both of which generally do not delay treatment). Of these seven, however, six (unlike Kansas) require consideration of less restrictive alternatives. Only one State other than Kansas, namely Iowa, both delays civil commitment (and consequent treatment) and does not explicitly consider less restrictive alternatives. But the law of that State applies prospectively only, thereby avoiding *ex post facto* problems. Thus the practical experience of other States, as revealed by their statutes, confirms what the Kansas Supreme Court's finding, the timing of the civil commitment proceeding, and the failure to consider less restrictive alternatives, themselves suggest, namely, that for *Ex Post Facto* Clause purposes, the purpose of the Kansas Act (as applied to previously convicted offenders) has a punitive, rather than a purely civil, purpose.

Kansas points to several cases as support for a contrary conclusion. It points to *Allen*—which is, as we have seen, a case in which the Court concluded that Illinois' "civil commitment" proceedings were not criminal. I have explained in detail, however, how the statute here differs from that in *Allen,* and why *Allen*'s reasoning leads to a different conclusion in this litigation.

Kansas also points to *Addington* v. *Texas,* where the Court held that the Constitution does not require application of criminal law's "beyond a reasonable doubt" standard in a civil commitment proceeding. Nothing I say here would change the reach or holding of *Addington* in any way. That is, a State is free to commit those who are dangerous and mentally ill in order to treat them. Nor does my decision preclude a State from deciding that a certain subset of people are mentally ill, dangerous, and untreatable, and that confinement of this subset is therefore necessary (again, assuming that all the procedural safeguards of *Addington* are in place). But when a State decides offenders can be treated and confines an offender to provide that treatment, but then refuses to provide it, the refusal to treat while a person is fully incapacitated begins to look punitive.

The majority suggests that this is the very case I say it is not, namely a case of a mentally ill person who is *untreatable.* And it quotes a long excerpt from the Kansas Supreme Court's opinion in support. That court, however, did not find that Hendricks was untreat*able*; it found that he was untreat*ed*—quite a different matter. Had the Kansas Supreme Court thought that Hendricks, or others like him, are untreatable, it could not have written the words that follow that excerpt, adopting by reference the words of another court opinion:

> "The statute forecloses the possibility that offenders will be evaluated and treated until after they have been punished. . . . Setting aside the question of whether a prison term exacerbates or minimizes the mental condition of a sex offender, it plainly delays the treatment that must constitutionally accompany commitment pursuant to the Statute. The failure of the Statute to provide for examination or treatment prior to the completion of the punishment phase strongly suggests that treatment is of secondary, rather than primary, concern."

This quotation, and the rest of the opinion, make clear that the court is finding it objectionable that the Statute, among other things, has not provided adequate treatment to one who, all parties here concede, *can* be treated. . . .

. . . We have found no evidence in the record to support the conclusion that Kansas was in fact providing the treatment that all parties agree that it could provide. Thus, even had the Kansas Supreme Court considered the majority's new evidence—which it did not—it is not likely to have changed its characterization of the Act's treatment provisions as "somewhat disingenuous."

Regardless, the Kansas Supreme court did so characterize the Act's treatment provisions and did find that treatment was "at best" an "incidental" objective. Thus, the circumstances here are different from *Allen,* where the Illinois Supreme Court explicitly found that the statute's aim was to provide treatment, not punishment. There is no evidence in the record that contradicts the finding of the Kansas court. Thus, *Allen*'s approach—its reliance on the State court—if followed here would mean the Act as applied to *Leroy Hendricks* (as opposed to others who may have received treatment or who were sentenced after the effective date of the Act), is punitive.

Finally, Kansas points to *United States* v. *Salerno,* a case in which this Court held preventive detention of a dangerous accused person pending trial constitutionally permissible. *Salerno,* however, involved the brief detention of that person, after a finding of "probable cause" that he had committed a crime that would justify further imprisonment, and only pending a speedy judicial determination of guilt or innocence. This Court, in *Foucha,* emphasized the fact that the confinement at issue in *Salerno* was "strictly limited in duration." 504 U.S. at 82. It described that "pretrial detention of arrestees" as "one of those carefully limited exceptions permitted by the Due Process Clause." And it held that *Salerno* did not authorize the indefinite detention, on grounds of dangerousness, of "insanity acquittees who are not mentally ill but who do not prove they would not be dangerous to others." Whatever *Salerno*'s "due process" implications may be, it does not focus upon, nor control, the question at issue here, the question of "punishment" for purposes of the *Ex Post Facto* Clause.

One other case warrants mention. In *Kennedy* v. *Mendoza-Martinez,* this Court listed seven factors that helped it determine whether a particular statute was primarily punitive for purposes of applying the Fifth and Sixth Amendments. Those factors include whether a sanction involves an affirmative restraint, how history has regarded it, whether it applies to behavior already a crime, the need for a finding of scienter, its relationship to a traditional aim of punishment, the presence of a nonpunitive alternative purpose, and whether it is excessive in relation to that purpose. This Court has said that these seven factors are "neither exhaustive nor dispositive," but nonetheless "helpful." *Ward,* 448 U.S. at 249. Paraphrasing them here, I believe the Act before us involves an affirmative restraint historically regarded as punishment; imposed upon behavior already a crime after a finding of scienter; which restraint, namely confinement, serves a traditional aim of punishment, does not primarily serve an alternative purpose (such as treatment) and is excessive in relation to any alternative purpose assigned.

This is to say that each of the factors the Court mentioned in *Martinez-Mendoza* on balance argues here in favor of a constitutional characterization as "punishment." It is not to say that I have found "a single 'formula' for identifying those legislative changes that have a sufficient effect on substantive crimes or punishments to fall within the constitutional prohibition." We have not previously done so, and I do not do so here. Rather, I have pointed to those features of the Act itself, in the context of this litigation, that lead me to conclude, in light of our precedent, that the added confinement the Act imposes upon Hendricks is basically punitive. This analysis, rooted in the facts surrounding Kansas' failure to treat Hendricks, cannot answer the question whether the Kansas Act, as it now stands, and in light of its current implementation, is punitive towards people other than he. And I do not attempt to do so here.

III

To find that the confinement the Act imposes upon Hendricks is "punishment" is to find a violation of the *Ex Post Facto* Clause. Kansas does not deny that the 1994 Act changed the legal consequences that attached to Hendricks earlier crimes, and in a way that significantly "disadvantaged the offender."

To find a violation of that Clause here, however, is not to hold that the Clause prevents Kansas, or other States, from enacting dangerous sexual offender statutes. A statute that operates prospectively, for example, does not offend the *Ex Post Facto* Clause. Neither does it offend the *Ex Post Facto* Clause for a State to sentence offenders to the fully authorized sentence, to seek consecutive, rather than concurrent, sentences, or to invoke recidivism statutes to lengthen imprisonment. Moreover, a statute that operates retroactively, like Kansas' statute, nonetheless does not offend the Clause *if the confinement that it imposes is not punishment*—if, that is to say, the legislature does not simply add a later criminal punishment to an earlier one.

The statutory provisions before us do amount to punishment primarily because, as I have said, the legislature did not tailor the statute to fit the non-punitive civil aim of treatment, which it concedes exists in Hendricks' case. The Clause in these circumstances does not stand as an obstacle to achieving important protections for the public's safety; rather it provides an assurance that, where so significant a restriction of an individual's basic freedoms is at issue, a State cannot cut corners. Rather, the legislature must hew to the Constitution's liberty-protecting line.

NO 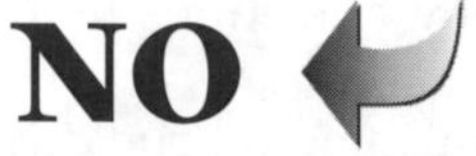

Clarence Thomas

Opinion

JUSTICE THOMAS delivered the opinion of the Court.

In 1994, Kansas enacted the Sexually Violent Predator Act, which establishes procedures for the civil commitment of persons who, due to a "mental abnormality" or a "personality disorder," are likely to engage in "predatory acts of sexual violence." The State invoked the Act for the first time to commit Leroy Hendricks, an inmate who had a long history of sexually molesting children, and who was scheduled for release from prison shortly after the Act became law. Hendricks challenged his commitment on, *inter alia,* "substantive" due process, double jeopardy, and *ex post facto* grounds. The Kansas Supreme Court invalidated the Act, holding that its pre-commitment condition of a "mental abnormality" did not satisfy what the court perceived to be the "substantive" due process requirement that involuntary civil commitment must be predicated on a finding of "mental illness." The State of Kansas petitioned for certiorari.

I

A

The Kansas Legislature enacted the Sexually Violent Predator Act (Act) in 1994 to grapple with the problem of managing repeat sexual offenders. Although Kansas already had a statute addressing the involuntary commitment of those defined as "mentally ill," the legislature determined that existing civil commitment procedures were inadequate to confront the risks presented by "sexually violent predators." In the Act's preamble, the legislature explained:

> "[A] small but extremely dangerous group of sexually violent predators exist who do not have a mental disease or defect that renders them appropriate for involuntary treatment pursuant to the [general involuntary civil commitment statute] . . . . In contrast to persons appropriate for civil commitment under the [general involuntary civil commitment statute], sexually violent predators generally have anti-social personality features which are unamenable to existing mental illness treatment modalities and those features render them likely to engage in sexually violent behavior. The legislature further finds that sexually violent predators' likelihood of engag-

Dissenting Opinion, Kansas v. Hendricks, Supreme Court, 1997. Some court case citations omitted. Notes omitted.

> ing in repeat acts of predatory sexual violence is high. The existing involuntary commitment procedure . . . is inadequate to address the risk these sexually violent predators pose to society. The legislature further finds that the prognosis for rehabilitating sexually violent predators in a prison setting is poor, the treatment needs of this population are very long term and the treatment modalities for this population are very different than the traditional treatment modalities for people appropriate for commitment under the [general involuntary civil commitment statute]."

As a result, the Legislature found it necessary to establish "a civil commitment procedure for the long-term care and treatment of the sexually violent predator." The Act defined a "sexually violent predator" as:

> "any person who has been convicted of or charged with a sexually violent offense and who suffers from a mental abnormality or personality disorder which makes the person likely to engage in the predatory acts of sexual violence."

A "mental abnormality" was defined, in turn, as a "congenital or acquired condition affecting the emotional or volitional capacity which predisposes the person to commit sexually violent offenses in a degree constituting such person a menace to the health and safety of others."

As originally structured, the Act's civil commitment procedures pertained to: (1) a presently confined person who, like Hendricks, "has been convicted of a sexually violent offense" and is scheduled for release; (2) a person who has been "charged with a sexually violent offense" but has been found incompetent to stand trial; (3) a person who has been found "not guilty by reason of insanity of a sexually violent offense"; and (4) a person found "not guilty" of a sexually violent offense because of a mental disease or defect.

The initial version of the Act, as applied to a currently confined person such as Hendricks, was designed to initiate a specific series of procedures. The custodial agency was required to notify the local prosecutor 60 days before the anticipated release of a person who might have met the Act's criteria. The prosecutor was then obligated, within 45 days, to decide whether to file a petition in state court seeking the person's involuntary commitment. If such a petition were filed, the court was to determine whether "probable cause" existed to support a finding that the person was a "sexually violent predator" and thus eligible for civil commitment. Upon such a determination, transfer of the individual to a secure facility for professional evaluation would occur. After that evaluation, a trial would be held to determine beyond a reasonable doubt whether the individual was a sexually violent predator. If that determination were made, the person would then be transferred to the custody of the Secretary of Social and Rehabilitation Services (Secretary) for "control, care and treatment until such time as the person's mental abnormality or personality disorder has so changed that the person is safe to be at large."

In addition to placing the burden of proof upon the State, the Act afforded the individual a number of other procedural safeguards. In the case of an indigent person, the State was required to provide, at public expense, the assistance of counsel and an examination by mental health care professionals. The individual also received the right to present and cross-examine witnesses, and the opportunity to review documentary evidence presented by the State.

Once an individual was confined, the Act required that "the involuntary detention or commitment . . . shall conform to constitutional requirements for care and treatment." Confined persons were afforded three different avenues of review: First, the committing court was obligated to conduct an annual review to determine whether continued detention was warranted. Second, the Secretary was permitted, at any time, to decide that the confined individual's condition had so changed that release was appropriate, and could then authorize the person to petition for release. Finally, even without the Secretary's permission, the confined person could at any time file a release petition. If the court found that the State could no longer satisfy its burden under the initial commitment standard, the individual would be freed from confinement.

B

In 1984, Hendricks was convicted of taking "indecent liberties" with two 13-year-old boys. After serving nearly 10 years of his sentence, he was slated for release to a halfway house. Shortly before his scheduled release, however, the State filed a petition in state court seeking Hendricks' civil confinement as a sexually violent predator. On August 19, 1994, Hendricks appeared before the court with counsel and moved to dismiss the petition on the grounds that the Act violated various federal constitutional provisions. Although the court reserved ruling on the Act's constitutionality, it concluded that there was probable cause to support a finding that Hendricks was a sexually violent predator, and therefore ordered that he be evaluated at the Larned State Security Hospital.

Hendricks subsequently requested a jury trial to determine whether he qualified as a sexually violent predator. During that trial, Hendricks' own testimony revealed a chilling history of repeated child sexual molestation and abuse, beginning in 1955 when he exposed his genitals to two young girls. At that time, he pleaded guilty to indecent exposure. Then, in 1957, he was convicted of lewdness involving a young girl and received a brief jail sentence. In 1960, he molested two young boys while he worked for a carnival. After serving two years in prison for that offense, he was paroled, only to be rearrested for molesting a 7-year-old girl. Attempts were made to treat him for his sexual deviance, and in 1965 he was considered "safe to be at large," and was discharged from a state psychiatric hospital

Shortly thereafter, however, Hendricks sexually assaulted another young boy and girl—he performed oral sex on the 8-year-old girl and fondled the 11-year-old boy. He was again imprisoned in 1967, but refused to participate in a sex offender treatment program, and thus remained incarcerated until his parole in 1972. Diagnosed as a pedophile, Hendricks entered into, but then abandoned, a treatment program. He testified that despite having received professional help for his pedophilia, he continued to harbor sexual desires for children. Indeed, soon after his 1972 parole, Hendricks began to abuse his own stepdaughter and stepson. He forced the children to engage in sexual activity with him over a period of approximately four years. Then, as noted above, Hendricks was convicted of "taking indecent liberties" with two adolescent boys after he attempted to fondle them. As a result of that conviction, he was once again imprisoned, and was serving that sentence when he reached his conditional release date in September 1994.

Hendricks admitted that he had repeatedly abused children whenever he was not confined. He explained that when he "gets stressed out," he "can't control the urge" to molest children. Although Hendricks recognized that his behavior harms children, and he hoped he would not sexually molest children again, he stated that the only sure way he could keep from sexually abusing children in the future was "to die." Hendricks readily agreed with the state physician's diagnosis that he suffers from pedophilia and that he is not cured of the condition; indeed, he told the physician that "treatment is bull–. The jury unanimously found beyond a reasonable doubt that Hendricks was a sexually violent predator. The trial court subsequently determined, as a matter of state law, that pedophilia qualifies as a "mental abnormality" as defined by the Act, and thus ordered Hendricks committed to the Secretary's custody.

Hendricks appealed, claiming, among other things, that application of the Act to him violated the Federal Constitution's Due Process, Double Jeopardy, and *ExPost Facto* Clauses. The Kansas Supreme Court accepted Hendricks' due process claim. The court declared that in order to commit a person involuntarily in a civil proceeding, a State is required by "substantive" due process to prove by clear and convincing evidence that the person is both (1) mentally ill, and (2) a danger to himself or to others. The court then determined that the Act's definition of "mental abnormality" did not satisfy what it perceived to be this Court's "mental illness" requirement in the civil commitment context. As a result, the court held that "the Act violates Hendricks' substantive due process rights."

The majority did not address Hendricks' *ex post facto* or double jeopardy claims. The dissent, however, considered each of Hendricks' constitutional arguments and rejected them.

II

A

Kansas argues that the Act's definition of "mental abnormality" satisfies "substantive" due process requirements. We agree. Although freedom from physical restraint "has always been at the core of the liberty protected by the Due Process Clause from arbitrary governmental action," that liberty interest is not absolute. The Court has recognized that an individual's constitutionally protected interest in avoiding physical restraint may be overridden even in the civil context:

> "The liberty secured by the Constitution of the United States to every person within its jurisdiction does not import an absolute right in each per-

son to be, at all times and in all circumstances, wholly free from restraint. There are manifold restraints to which every person is necessarily subject for the common good. On any other basis organized society could not exist with safety to its members."

Accordingly, States have in certain narrow circumstances provided for the forcible civil detainment of people who are unable to control their behavior and who thereby pose a danger to the public health and safety. We have consistently upheld such involuntary commitment statutes provided the confinement takes place pursuant to proper procedures and evidentiary standards. It thus cannot be said that the involuntary civil confinement of a limited subclass of dangerous persons is contrary to our understanding of ordered liberty.

The challenged Act unambiguously requires a finding of dangerousness either to one's self or to others as a prerequisite to involuntary confinement. Commitment proceedings can be initiated only when a person "has been convicted of or charged with a sexually violent offense," and "suffers from a mental abnormality or personality disorder which makes the person likely to engage in the predatory acts of sexual violence." The statute thus requires proof of more than a mere predisposition to violence; rather, it requires evidence of past sexually violent behavior and a present mental condition that creates a likelihood of such conduct in the future if the person is not incapacitated. As we have recognized, "previous instances of violent behavior are an important indicator of future violent tendencies." A finding of dangerousness, standing alone, is ordinarily not a sufficient ground upon which to justify indefinite involuntary commitment. We have sustained civil commitment statutes when they have coupled proof of dangerousness with the proof of some additional factor, such as a "mental illness" or "mental abnormality." These added statutory requirements serve to limit involuntary civil confinement to those who suffer from a volitional impairment rendering them dangerous beyond their control. The Kansas Act is plainly of a kind with these other civil commitment statutes: It requires a finding of future dangerousness, and then links that finding to the existence of a "mental abnormality" or "personality disorder" that makes it difficult, if not impossible, for the person to control his dangerous behavior. The precommitment requirement of a "mental abnormality" or "personality disorder" is consistent with the requirements of these other statutes that we have upheld in that it narrows the class of persons eligible for confinement to those who are unable to control their dangerousness.

Hendricks nonetheless argues that our earlier cases dictate a finding of "mental illness" as a prerequisite for civil commitment. He then asserts that a "mental abnormality" is *not* equivalent to a "mental illness" because it is a term coined by the Kansas Legislature, rather than by the psychiatric community. Contrary to Hendricks' assertion, the term "mental illness" is devoid of any talismanic significance. Not only do "psychiatrists disagree widely and frequently on what constitutes mental illness," but the Court itself has used a variety of expressions to describe the mental condition of those properly subject to civil confinement.

To the extent that the civil commitment statutes we have considered set forth criteria relating to an individual's inability to control his dangerousness, the Kansas Act sets forth comparable criteria and Hendricks' condition doubtless satisfies those criteria. The mental health professionals who evaluated Hendricks diagnosed him as suffering from pedophilia, a condition the psychiatric profession itself classifies as a serious mental disorder. Hendricks even conceded that, when he becomes "stressed out," he cannot "control the urge" to molest children. This admitted lack of volitional control, coupled with a prediction of future dangerousness, adequately distinguishes Hendricks from other dangerous persons who are perhaps more properly dealt with exclusively through criminal proceedings. Hendricks' diagnosis as a pedophile, which qualifies as a "mental abnormality" under the Act, thus plainly suffices for due process purposes.

B

We granted Hendricks' cross-petition to determine whether the Act violates the Constitution's double jeopardy prohibition or its ban on *ex post facto* lawmaking. The thrust of Hendricks' argument is that the Act establishes criminal proceedings; hence confinement under it necessarily constitutes punishment. He contends that where, as here, newly enacted "punishment" is predicated upon past conduct for which he has already been convicted and forced to serve a prison sentence, the Constitution's Double Jeopardy and *Ex Post Facto* Clauses are violated. We are unpersuaded by Hendricks' argument that Kansas has established criminal proceedings.

The categorization of a particular proceeding as civil or criminal "is first of all a question of statutory construction." We must initially ascertain whether the legislature meant the statute to establish "civil" proceedings. If so, we ordinarily defer to the legislature's stated intent. Here, Kansas' objective to create a civil proceeding is evidenced by its placement of the Sexually Violent Predator Act within the Kansas probate code, instead of the criminal code, as well as its description of the Act as creating a "*civil commitment procedure.*" Nothing on the face of the statute suggests that the legislature sought to create anything other than a civil commitment scheme designed to protect the public from harm.

Although we recognize that a "civil label is not always dispositive," we will reject the legislature's manifest intent only where a party challenging the statute provides "the clearest proof" that "the statutory scheme [is] so punitive either in purpose or effect as to negate [the State's] intention" to deem it "civil." In those limited circumstances, we will consider the statute to have established criminal proceedings for constitutional purposes. Hendricks, however, has failed to satisfy this heavy burden.

As a threshold matter, commitment under the Act does not implicate either of the two primary objectives of criminal punishment: retribution or deterrence. The Act's purpose is not retributive because it does not affix culpability for prior criminal conduct. Instead, such conduct is used solely for evidentiary purposes, either to demonstrate that a "mental abnormality" exists or to support a finding of future dangerousness. We have previously concluded that an Illinois statute was nonpunitive even though it was triggered by the commission of a sexual assault, explaining that evidence of the prior criminal conduct was "received not to punish past misdeeds, but primarily to show the accused's mental condition and to predict future behavior." In addition, the Kansas Act does not make a criminal conviction a prerequisite for commitment—persons absolved of criminal responsibility may nonetheless be subject to confinement under the Act. An absence of the necessary criminal responsibility suggests that the State is not seeking retribution for a past misdeed. Thus, the fact that the Act may be "tied to criminal activity" is "insufficient to render the statute punitive."

Moreover, unlike a criminal statute, no finding of scienter is required to commit an individual who is found to be a sexually violent predator; instead, the commitment determination is made based on a "mental abnormality" or "personality disorder" rather than on one's criminal intent. The existence of a scienter requirement is customarily an important element in distinguishing criminal from civil statutes. The absence of such a requirement here is evidence that confinement under the statute is not intended to be retributive.

Nor can it be said that the legislature intended the Act to function as a deterrent. Those persons committed under the Act are, by definition, suffering from a "mental abnormality" or a "personality disorder" that prevents them from exercising adequate control over their behavior. Such persons are therefore unlikely to be deterred by the threat of confinement. And the conditions surrounding that confinement do not suggest a punitive purpose on the State's part. The State has represented that an individual confined under the Act is not subject to the more restrictive conditions placed on state prisoners, but instead experiences essentially the same conditions as any involuntarily committed patient in the state mental institution. Because none of the parties argues that people institutionalized under the Kansas general civil commitment statute are subject to punitive conditions, even though they may be involuntarily confined, it is difficult to conclude that persons confined under this Act are being "punished."

Although the civil commitment scheme at issue here does involve an affirmative restraint, "the mere fact that a person is detained does not inexorably lead to the conclusion that the government has imposed punishment." The State may take measures to restrict the freedom of the dangerously mentally ill. This is a legitimate non-punitive governmental objective and has been historically so regarded. The Court has, in fact, cited the confinement of "mentally unstable individuals who present a danger to the public" as one classic example of nonpunitive detention. If detention for the purpose of protecting the community from harm *necessarily* constituted punishment, then all involuntary civil commitments would have to be considered punishment. But we have never so held.

Hendricks focuses on his confinement's potentially indefinite duration as evidence of the State's punitive intent. That focus, however, is misplaced.

Far from any punitive objective, the confinement's duration is instead linked to the stated purposes of the commitment, namely, to hold the person until his mental abnormality no longer causes him to be a threat to others. If, at any time, the confined person is adjudged "safe to be at large," he is statutorily entitled to immediate release.

Furthermore, commitment under the Act is only *potentially* indefinite. The maximum amount of time an individual can be incapacitated pursuant to a single judicial proceeding is one year. If Kansas seeks to continue the detention beyond that year, a court must once again determine beyond a reasonable doubt that the detainee satisfies the same standards as required for the initial confinement. This requirement again demonstrates that Kansas does not intend an individual committed pursuant to the Act to remain confined any longer than he suffers from a mental abnormality rendering him unable to control his dangerousness.

Hendricks next contends that the State's use of procedural safeguards traditionally found in criminal trials makes the proceedings here criminal rather than civil. In *Allen*, we confronted a similar argument. There, the petitioner "placed great reliance on the fact that proceedings under the Act are accompanied by procedural safeguards usually found in criminal trials" to argue that the proceedings were civil in name only. We rejected that argument, however, explaining that the State's decision "to provide some of the safeguards applicable in criminal trials cannot itself turn these proceedings into criminal prosecutions." The numerous procedural and evidentiary protections afforded here demonstrate that the Kansas Legislature has taken great care to confine only a narrow class of particularly dangerous individuals, and then only after meeting the strictest procedural standards. That Kansas chose to afford such procedural protections does not transform a civil commitment proceeding into a criminal prosecution.

Finally, Hendricks argues that the Act is necessarily punitive because it fails to offer any legitimate "treatment." Without such treatment, Hendricks asserts, confinement under the Act amounts to little more than disguised punishment. Hendricks' argument assumes that treatment for his condition is available, but that the State has failed (or refused) to provide it. The Kansas Supreme Court, however, apparently rejected this assumption, explaining:

> "It is clear that the overriding concern of the legislature is to continue the segregation of sexually violent offenders from the public. Treatment with the goal of reintegrating them into society is incidental, at best. The record reflects that treatment for sexually violent predators is all but nonexistent. The legislature concedes that sexually violent predators are not amenable to treatment under [the existing Kansas involuntary commitment statute]. If there is nothing to treat under [that statute], then there is no mental illness. In that light, the provisions of the Act for treatment appear somewhat disingenuous."

It is possible to read this passage as a determination that Hendricks' condition was *untreatable* under the existing Kansas civil commitment statute, and thus the Act's sole purpose was incapacitation. Absent a treatable mental illness, the Kansas court concluded, Hendricks could not be detained against his will.

Accepting the Kansas court's apparent determination that treatment is not possible for this category of individuals does not obligate us to adopt its legal conclusions. We have already observed that, under the appropriate circumstances and when accompanied by proper procedures, incapacitation may be a legitimate end of the civil law. Accordingly, the Kansas court's determination that the Act's "overriding concern" was the continued "segregation of sexually violent offenders" is consistent with our conclusion that the Act establishes civil proceedings, especially when that concern is coupled with the State's ancillary goal of providing treatment to those offenders, if such is possible. While we have upheld state civil commitment statutes that aim both to incapacitate and to treat, see *Allen, supra*, we have never held that the Constitution prevents a State from civilly detaining those for whom no treatment is available, but who nevertheless pose a danger to others. A State could hardly be seen as furthering a "punitive" purpose by involuntarily confining persons afflicted with an untreatable, highly contagious disease. Similarly, it would be of little value to require treatment as a precondition for civil confinement of the dangerously insane when no acceptable treatment existed. To conclude otherwise would obligate a State to release certain confined individuals who were both mentally ill and dangerous simply because they could not be successfully treated for their afflictions. . . .

Although the treatment program initially offered Hendricks may have seemed somewhat meager, it must be remembered that he was the first person committed under the Act. That the State did not have all of its treatment procedures in place is thus not surprising. What is significant, however, is that Hendricks was placed under the supervision of the Kansas Department of Health and Social and Rehabilitative Services, housed in a unit segregated from the general prison population and operated not by employees of the Department of Corrections, but by other trained individuals. And, before this Court, Kansas declared "absolutely" that persons committed under the Act are now receiving in the neighborhood of "31.5 hours of treatment per week."

Where the State has "disavowed any punitive intent"; limited confinement to a small segment of particularly dangerous individuals; provided strict procedural safeguards; directed that confined persons be segregated from the general prison population and afforded the same status as others who have been civilly committed; recommended treatment if such is possible; and permitted immediate release upon a showing that the individual is no longer dangerous or mentally impaired, we cannot say that it acted with punitive intent. We therefore hold that the Act does not establish criminal proceedings and that involuntary confinement pursuant to the Act is not punitive. Our conclusion that the Act is nonpunitive thus removes an essential prerequisite for both Hendricks' double jeopardy and *ex post facto* claims.

1

The Double Jeopardy Clause provides: "Nor shall any person be subject for the same offence to be twice put in jeopardy of life or limb." Although generally understood to preclude a second prosecution for the same offense, the Court has also interpreted this prohibition to prevent the State from "punishing twice, or attempting a second time to punish criminally, for the same offense." Hendricks argues that, as applied to him, the Act violates double jeopardy principles because his confinement under the Act, imposed after a conviction and a term of incarceration, amounted to both a second prosecution and a second punishment for the same offense. We disagree.

Because we have determined that the Kansas Act is civil in nature, initiation of its commitment proceedings does not constitute a second prosecution. Moreover, as commitment under the Act is not tantamount to "punishment," Hendricks' involuntary detention does not violate the Double Jeopardy Clause, even though that confinement may follow a prison term. Indeed, in *Baxstrom* v. *Herold,* we expressly recognized that civil commitment could follow the expiration of a prison term without offending double jeopardy principles. We reasoned that "there is no conceivable basis for distinguishing the commitment of a person who is nearing the end of a penal term from all other civil commitments." If an individual otherwise meets the requirements for involuntary civil commitment, the State is under no obligation to release that individual simply because the detention would follow a period of incarceration. . . .

2

Hendricks' *ex post facto* claim is similarly flawed. The *Ex Post Facto* Clause, which "'forbids the application of any new punitive measure to a crime already consummated,'" has been interpreted to pertain exclusively to penal statutes. As we have previously determined, the Act does not impose punishment; thus, its application does not raise *ex post facto* concerns. Moreover, the Act clearly does not have retroactive effect. Rather, the Act permits involuntary confinement based upon a determination that the person *currently* both suffers from a "mental abnormality" or "personality disorder" and is likely to pose a future danger to the public. To the extent that past behavior is taken into account, it is used, as noted above, solely for evidentiary purposes. Because the Act does not criminalize conduct legal before its enactment, nor deprive Hendricks of any defense that was available to him at the time of his crimes, the Act does not violate the *Ex Post Facto* Clause.

III

We hold that the Kansas Sexually Violent Predator Act comports with due process requirements and neither runs afoul of double jeopardy principles nor constitutes an exercise in impermissible *ex post facto* lawmaking. Accordingly, the judgment of the Kansas Supreme Court is reversed.

POSTSCRIPT

Does Confining Sex Offenders Indefinitely in Mental Hospitals After They Have Served Their Prison Sentences Violate the Constitution?

The readings in this section were excerpts from the U.S. Supreme Court's decision in *Kansas v. Hendricks*. If you were a member of the Court, would you have joined the majority opinion, or would you have joined Justice Breyer's dissent? Do you agree with Justice Breyer's assertion that the Kansas Sexually Violent Predator Act is an unconstitutional ex post facto law as applied in this case?

Moreover, are you convinced by Justice Thomas' contention that committing someone to confinement in a state mental institution after they have completed their prison sentence does not constitute *punishment*? Rather, according to the Court, confining someone in this manner is therapeutic *treatment*. Therefore, the Fifth Amendment's double jeopardy clause does not bar the additional confinement. Is the distinction that the Court has drawn between punishment and treatment a matter of form triumphing over substance? Is this a case where you agree with the result—dangerous pedophiles should not be allowed to prey on our children, but disagree with how the court reached their conclusion?

Please recall the debate presented in Issue 3 about whether to castrate serious sex offenders. What if a state were to pass a law providing that after receiving a complete psychiatric exam, a certified pedophile about to be released from prison could have the choice of undergoing physical castration in lieu of an indefinite commitment to a mental institution? What constitutional issues would you raise as the attorney for the sex offender faced with this difficult choice?

Another interesting issue concerns the sex offender's Sixth Amendment right to counsel. Suppose that as an attorney you were appointed by a court to represent someone like Leroy Hendricks in a proceeding to determine whether he would be indefinitely confined to a mental hospital following the completion of his sentence. Would you accept the case? The Rules of Professional Responsibility that govern the conduct of attorneys provide that if you accept the case, you must defend the offender's interest to the best of your ability. The Rules provide as well that if you cannot do so, you must refuse to take the case. What would you do?

The issue considered in this section is a challenging one. Fortunately there are additional resources that add substantially to the discussion of these matters. See American Psychiatric Association, *Dangerous Sex Offenders: A Task Force Report of the American Psychiatric Association* (American Psychiatric Press, 1999); Lisa L. Sample and Timothy M. Bray, "Are Sex Offenders Dangerous?" *Criminology & Public Policy* (vol. 3, no. 1, 2003); Holly A. Miller, Amy E. Amenta, and Mary Alice Conroy, "Sexually Violent Predator Evaluations: Empirical Evidence, Strategies for Professionals, and Research Directions," *Law & Human Behavior* (vol. 29, no. 1, 2005); Leam A. Craig, Kevin D. Browne, Ian Stringer, and Anthony Beech, "Limitations in Actuarial Rist Assessment of Sexual Offenders: A Methodological Note," *The British Journal of Forensic Practice* (vol. 6, no. 1, 2004); Wanda D. Beyer Kendall and Monit Cheung, "Sexually Violent Predators and Civil Commitment Laws," *Journal of Child Sexual Abuse* (vol. 13, no. 2, 2004).

Additional resources include Ron Langevin, Suzanne Cumoe, Paul Federoff, and Renee Bennett, et al., "Lifetime Sex Offender Recidivism: A 25-Year Follow-Up Study," *Canadian Journal of Criminology and Criminal Justice* (vol. 46, no. 5, 2004); Kyron Huigens, "Dignity and Desert in Punishment Theory," *Harvard Journal of Law and Public Policy* (vol. 27, no. 1, 2003); Patricia E. Erickson, "The Legal Standard of Volitional Impairment: An Analysis of Substantive Due Process and the United States Supreme Court's Decision in Kansas v. Hendricks," *Journal of Criminal Justice* (vol. 30, no. 1, 2002); and Eric S. Janus, "Sex Predator Commitment Laws: Constitutional but Unwise," *Psychiatric Annals* (vol. 30, no. 6, 2000).

ISSUE 14

Should Homosexual Prison Inmates Have a Right to Share the Same Cell?

YES: Jeffrey P. Brinkman, from "*Veney v. Wyche:* Not in My Cell—The Constitutionality of Segregating Prisoners Based on Their Sexual Orientation," *Law & Sexuality* (2003)

NO: Karen J. Williams, from Opinion, *Veney v. Wyche*, Fourth Circuit U.S. Court of Appeals (2002)

ISSUE SUMMARY

YES: Attorney Jeffrey P. Brinkman argues that giving prison officials the discretion to segregate homosexual prisoners has helped to justify the isolation that homosexuals feel not only in prisons, but also in society as a whole.

NO: Judge Karen J. Williams, writing the majority opinion for the U.S. Court of Appeals in *Veney v. Wyche*, asserts that safety and security are legitimate penological interests that justify a prison policy of not allowing homosexual males to live in double-occupancy cells.

Imagine for a moment what it must be like to be confined in a prison. The atmosphere of tension, stress, and anxiety would be more than many people could handle. It will probably come as no surprise to you that prisons have high rates of suicide, violent assault, sexual assault, murder, and mental illness. It is difficult for most people to conceive of the pressures that must exist within these environments.

One of the ways that inmates adapt to life in prison is to form their own social system, with its own culture, goals, and values. One of the values of the inmate social system involves the acceptance of some forms of homosexual behavior. According to some prison experts, because inmates are denied the opportunity for normal heterosexual relationships, a large number of inmates will engage in homosexual behavior at some time during their confinement. Most of the individuals who engage in this behavior are not committed homosexuals and return to a heterosexual lifestyle upon release.

Some inmates are confirmed homosexuals, however, who may have embraced a gay lifestyle even before coming to prison. A number of commentators have suggested that these individuals face a greater danger of being the victims of violent assault in prison. *Veney v. Wyche*, a decision by the Fourth Circuit U.S. Court of Appeals, involves inmates who have adopted a homosexual lifestyle in prison and wish to share cells with other inmates. Should they have a constitutional right to do so?

The U.S. Supreme Court has held that prison inmates retain a number of constitutional rights, such as the right to worship, receive mail, have access to the courts and to their attorneys, and the right not to be exposed to cruel and unusual punishment. Prison inmates do not, however, retain those constitutional rights "that are inconsistent with their status as prisoners."

The Supreme Court has held as well that prison administrators have great authority and discretion to decide how to perform their duties. In fact, it has held consistently that "the need to maintain order and institutional security" justifies numerous restrictions on inmates' constitutional rights. For example, prison inmates do not have a right to privacy in their cells. Thus, prison authorities may conduct unannounced cell searches at any time. They may also screen all inmate mail for contraband and regulate prisoner associations. For example, prison authorities may prevent the formation of a prisoner's labor union. Thus, prison officials have great discretion to regulate most aspects of an inmate's life.

Do you believe that prison authorities should be given the discretion to pass a regulation preventing homosexual inmates from living in a double-occupancy cell while at the same time allowing heterosexual inmates to do so? If such a regulation can be shown by the authorities to be related to the need to maintain institutional order or security, it is likely to be upheld by the courts. How would an attorney for the state argue that such a regulation is necessary to maintain institutional order and security? The Fourth Circuit's opinion in *Veney v. Wyche* gives us an indication.

Judge Karen J. Williams, writing for the majority, asserts that safety and security are legitimate penological interests that justify a prison policy of not allowing homosexual inmates to live in double-occupancy cells. Attorney Jeffrey P. Brinkman disagrees with the court's conclusion, however. He argues that giving prison officials the discretion to segregate homosexual prisoners has helped to justify the isolation that homosexuals feel not only in prisons, but also in society as a whole.

Do you believe it is necessary to segregate homosexual inmates in a prison setting? Should the courts give substantial deference to the decisions of prison administrators? If so, why should they accord this deference? These are important questions that the authors of the articles in this section will answer very differently.

Jeffrey P. Brinkman

Veney v. Wyche: Not in My Cell—The Constitutionality of Segregating Prisoners Based on Their Sexual Orientation

I. Introduction

Daniel L. Veney, a prisoner at Virginia's Riverside Regional Jail (Riverside) brought an action against the jail and named as defendants Lieutenant T.V. Wyche and Superintendent Darnley R. Hodge, claiming that they violated his rights under the Equal Protection Clause of the United States Constitution by treating him differently based on his sexual orientation and gender. Veney had been incarcerated at Riverside since 2000 and alleged that he was repeatedly denied the right to move into a double occupancy cell based on his sexual orientation. In December 2000, Veney filed a grievance with Riverside, but the institution found no evidence of discrimination. Subsequently, he filed a pro se complaint in the United States District Court for the Eastern District of Virginia alleging a violation of equal protection. The district court found that Veney failed to state a claim sufficient to grant relief and dismissed his complaint.

Veney appealed the dismissal of his suit, claiming that he was being treated differently from similarly situated heterosexual male and homosexual female inmates without a legitimate penological justification. The United States Court of Appeals for the Fourth Circuit held that legitimate penological interests justified both the segregation of homosexual male inmates and any disparate impact based on gender that may have arisen from that penological interest; the court also found that the absence of ready alternatives was further evidence of the reasonableness of Riverside's segregation system.

II. Background

This case illustrates the implications of an equal protection claim arising within the context of the prison system. While Section 1 of the Fourteenth Amendment guarantees equal protection under the law, claims that it has been violated within the prison arena face an additional obstacle, given courts' deference to security interests and concerns inherent in prison officials' decisions. Prisoners often find that their equal protection claims will be dismissed because courts will apply special deference, similar to a rational basis standard of review, to decisions made and systems established by prison officials. . . .

Determining which level of scrutiny to utilize when reviewing an equal protection violation is dependent upon the classification of the harmed individual or group. In Craig v. Boren, male plaintiffs challenged the constitutionality of an Oklahoma statute that allowed females over the age of eighteen and males over the age of twenty-one to buy 3.2% beer. The court found that evidence linking increased driving under the influence by males to the 3.2% beer was unconvincing and insufficient to justify implementing a gender division within the law. The law could not survive intermediate scrutiny because classification by gender, while serving the important governmental objective in reducing arrests for driving under the influence, was not substantially related to achieving that goal. Craig established that any law discriminating based on sex would have to survive intermediate scrutiny.

Determining the standard of review employed for equal protection claims brought by homosexuals is more problematic. In Romer v. Evans, the Court invalidated Colorado's Amendment 2 under rational basis review. Amendment 2 denied homosexuals any special legal protection against discrimination adopted at either the local or state levels of government. The Court found the statute unconstitutional because it failed to serve any important governmental interest: the motivation behind the statute to be one of irrational fear and prejudice. Furthermore, the Court found the sheer breadth of Amendment 2 to be too extensive; by virtue of Amendment 2, Colorado could deny any type of protection afforded to homosexuals. Romer illustrated that animosity and fear as legislative motivations will not survive the most deferential standard of review: the rational basis standard. While a victory for homosexuals in Colorado, Romer failed to guarantee the label of a suspect class to homosexuals, thus denying them any heightened scrutiny for equal protection claims.

Despite these established levels of scrutiny as applied to equal protection claims, courts have approached these cases differently when they arise in the prison context. In essence, courts have given deference to decisions made by prison officials in an effort to maintain safe and secure facilities.

The leading case for equal protection claims made by prisoners is Turner v. Safley. The plaintiffs in Turner brought a class action against the Missouri Department of Corrections, challenging regulations that limited correspondence between inmates and the inability of an inmate to enter into marriage as violations of both their First Amendment rights and guarantee of equal protection under the Fourteenth Amendment. The Court found that the rule limiting correspondence was rationally related to the important governmental interest of preventing escapes and uprisings, but found the limitations on an inmate's right to marry to be unduly burdensome and, thus, a violation of the prisoners' fundamental right to marry.

In an effort to establish a test to evaluate the reasonableness of a prison regulation, the Court created a four factor test. The first factor resembles the rational basis standard of review: there must be a rational nexus between the "prison regulation and the legitimate governmental interest put forward to justify it." Second, a court should consider whether alternative methods exist for a prisoner to practice the challenged right. A third relevant factor is the impact that accommodation of such a right could be expected to have on all other interested parties. The Court in Turner held that if such accommodation would have a significant effect on other inmates and prison officials, courts should then give deference to decisions made by prison officials. The final consideration is whether readily available alternatives exist to the challenged regulation. If there are obvious alternatives, then the regulation should not be viewed as reasonable. The Court, however, cautioned that this should not be viewed as a "least restrictive alternative" standard. By emphasizing this point, the Court appears to have reaffirmed the necessary deference owed to the decisions of prison officials.

III. The Court's Decision

In the noted case, the Fourth Circuit relied heavily on the factors set forth in Turner and held that the segregation of homosexual male inmates was based upon legitimate penological concerns, and that any disparate impact based on gender as a result of such segregation was rationally related to concerns over homophobic violence and the spread of sexually transmitted diseases, including HIV. Furthermore, the court ruled that the absence of ready alternatives to Veney's asserted interest in living in a double occupancy cell was further evidence of the reasonableness of Riverside's segregation plan. In reaching this conclusion, the court proceeded through a three-step analysis: (1) determining the initial sufficiency of Veney's claim; (2) deciding the level of scrutiny to apply to Veney's equal protection claim; and (3) applying the Turner factors to the challenged prison regulation.

Under the Prison Litigation Reform Act of 1996, the United States District Court for the Eastern District of Virginia was required to review Veney's complaint for any identifiable claims. Because the district court dismissed the complaint based on a failure to state a claim, the Fourth Circuit was required to review the dismissal de novo. The court acknowledged that when a civil rights complaint is at issue, the complaint should receive heightened attention unless it is fairly certain that no legal theory will support relief sought under the facts asserted. Applying Morrison v. Garraghty, the court found that the plaintiff was required to demonstrate that he was similarly situated to other inmates at Riverside, and that the segregation was intentional discrimination because of his homosexuality. The court diminished this hurdle for Veney and assumed that he was similarly situated to the other inmates at Riverside and that Riverside's denial of his request for a double occupancy cell was because he is a homosexual male.

Because Veney satisfied the initial requirements of his claim, the court turned to the question of which standard of review to apply. Veney asserted that the discrimination by Riverside in their housing policy was based on both his sexual orientation and gender. Gender discrimination merits intermediate scrutiny, therefore Riverside's housing policy would have to be substantially related to an important governmental interest. Veney's claim of sexual orientation discrimination, however, was subject only to rational basis review. For Veney to succeed with this component of his equal protection claim, he needed to show that no rational connection between the prison's housing policy and any governmental interest existed.

The plaintiff's status as a prisoner, however, added a new, yet critical, element to the standard of review issue. The court found that prisons should be accorded additional discretion in their decisions in order to maintain necessary penological interests. In order to evaluate whether Riverside's segregation of homosexual male inmates was rationally related to any legitimate penological interests, the court utilized the Turner factors.

The first Turner factor the court considered was the rational connection between Riverside's segregation of homosexual males and any legitimate penological interests. The court found that such a connection existed, and noted several legitimate penological interests justifying the housing policy and supporting the accordance of deference to the prison officials. The court agreed with Riverside and found that housing homosexuals together would lead to increased sexual activity, which would jeopardize prison security. A further implication was the increased possibility of HIV transmission and other sexually transmitted diseases, which would likely result in greater cost to prisons that are required to treat medical conditions.

While the implications of sexual activity constituted a legitimate penological concern, the court also found other arguments by the prison to be persuasive. Riverside argued that housing heterosexuals with homosexual males could lead to tension, and possibly violence. The court found that anti-homosexual feelings and violence are prevalent in our society and that such evidence should influence the constitutionality of laws and regulations. Riverside used evidence of hate crime statutes that have been passed in nearly half of the states to support their contention that violence against homosexuals is not only a fact within our society, but also warrants the segregation of homosexual males in prisons. To further its position, Riverside also presented statistics that reflected the probability that known homosexuals are more likely to be sexually assaulted in prison. The court agreed with these two lines of argument, and held that the fear of anti-homosexual violence is a legitimate penological concern.

The plaintiff also alleged that he was the victim of gender discrimination because the prison only relegated homosexual males to single occupancy cells. To justify this disparate impact, Riverside presented evidence that male inmates are more likely than female inmates to have homophobic attitudes, thus placing homosexual male inmates in a more vulnerable position for violence and other attacks. The court, believing it more likely that homosexual male inmates would be victims of violence, found that legitimate concerns over prisoner safety and security outweighed the resulting disparate impact in the housing policy.

The court was more cursory in its assessment of the remaining two Turner factors. When it weighed the impact the accommodation of Veney's asserted right to be housed in a double occupancy cell would have on other parties, the court found that the effect would be significant. The court hypothesized that prison officials would have to invest additional time monitoring the placement of prisoners so as not to house a homosexual inmate together with a possibly violent, homophobic cellmate. It also found that guards would assume a greater burden in their responsibilities if they were forced to monitor possible conflicts between heterosexual and homosexual male inmates. The court held that administrative challenges and security concerns outweighed accommodating Veney's asserted right to live in a double occupancy cell.

The third Turner factor considered in this case is the "absence of ready alternatives as evidence of the reasonableness" of Riverside's regulation. The court found that allowing Veney to reside with another inmate would create the exact situation that the prison was attempting to prevent: conflicts and possible bias-motivated violence. Therefore, the absence of ready alternatives in this case demonstrated to the court the reasonableness of the Riverside regulation.

IV. Analysis

In order to justify Riverside's housing policy on the grounds of protecting homosexual male inmates, the court apparently ignored several important questions and utilized broad assumptions regarding not only the homosexual lifestyle, but also prison culture. While the court in the noted case correctly applied the Turner factors to this equal protection claim arising out of the prison context, it failed to closely examine other alternatives to the regulation, and in turn may have helped promote long-established stereotypes regarding homosexuals.

Allowing special deference to prison officials does have a rational basis, especially given the various social dynamics among inmates, including race, sexual orientation, and age. Prison officials are the appropriate parties to regulate these situations given their proximity to the day-to-day routines and nuances of the system. While deference to prisons such as Riverside may be necessary, the court in the noted case may have been too hasty in finding Riverside's housing policy appropriate.

Riverside asserted that segregating homosexual males would prevent transmission of diseases, sexual orientation-motivated violence, increased sexual activity, and further security concerns. The court and Riverside assumed that housing two homosexual inmates in the same cell would result in not only a sexual relationship, but also in a future conflict. This type of assumption seems to promulgate the stereotype that homosexuals are hypersexual. The court offered no support for the myth that a homosexual male inmate will have sex with every other homosexual male inmate.

While preventing the transmission of diseases is a laudable goal, the segregation of homosexual male inmates may not be the most effective method of achieving such a result. Prison subculture often involves many sexual relationships, not exclusive to identifiable homosexual individuals. Inmates who would label themselves as heterosexual will, at times, participate in sexual activities with another inmate of the same sex, or, unfortunately, be an aggressor or victim in a prison sexual assault. Therefore, the fear of sexually transmitted diseases is present for many, not just those inmates who label themselves as homosexuals. As a result of the reality of prison life, Riverside's segregation of male homosexual inmates may not be the best method for stopping the spread of disease within the prison.

Protecting inmates from violence should be a goal for all prisons. Homosexual inmates, as evidenced by statistical data, appear to be more likely victims of attacks within prison. While placing a homosexual inmate in a cell with a known violent, homophobic inmate is no doubt dangerous, segregating all homosexual inmates seems to be an extreme solution. Prisons such as Riverside could take additional time and effort to research the backgrounds of inmates before making housing assignments. If an inmate is known to be homophobic, he should not be placed in a cell with a known homosexual. This extra research would likely place few new burdens on prison officials who are responsible for placing prisoners in cells. The extreme position of segregating all homosexual males at Riverside might have the emotional effect of making those particular inmates feel isolated and on a different social level than their fellow inmates.

A further problem with Riverside's segregation policy that is ignored by the court is determining which inmates are homosexual. The court does not discuss how the prison makes these determinations. If Riverside questions prisoners about their sexual orientation upon entry into prison, it would stand to reason that some inmates would lie or deny any homosexual tendencies. If this is true, then Riverside's policy does little to prevent the transmission of disease for these "undercover" homosexual inmates who may be having sex with their cellmates. If a determination of homosexuality is based on observed behavior, then Riverside's policy faces additional problems: not all male prisoners who engage in sex with fellow inmates would label themselves as homosexuals. Defining sexual orientation within Riverside, or any other prison, presents too many problems that do not justify segregating homosexual male inmates.

The court, while giving appropriate and probably necessary deference to prison officials, failed to examine the inherent problems and unanswered questions underlying Riverside's policy of segregating homosexual male inmates. While Turner anticipated that prisons would not be subject to a less restrictive alternative standard, allowing prisons to take radical measures such as segregating homosexual prisoners without constitutional criticism by courts seems outside the bounds of the Supreme Court's holding. By not giving due attention to these issues, the Veney court has helped justify the isolation that homosexuals feel not only in prisons, but also in our society as a whole.

NO 

Karen J. Williams

Opinion

WILLIAMS, Circuit Judge:

Daniel L. Veney, an inmate incarcerated at Riverside Regional Jail in Hopewell, Virginia, filed the present action under 42 U.S.C.A. § 1983, alleging that defendants Lieutenant T. V. Wyche and Superintendent Darnley R. Hodge violated his rights under the Equal Protection Clause of the United States Constitution by treating him differently from other inmates because of his gender and sexual preference. Specifically, Veney claims that defendants denied his requests to move from his single-occupancy cell into a double-occupancy cell because he is a homosexual male. The district court, after screening Veney's complaint, dismissed the complaint for failure to state a claim upon which relief may be granted. Because we agree with the district court that even if all of Veney's allegations were true, he would not be entitled to relief, we affirm.

I.

Veney has been incarcerated at Riverside since January 23, 2000. With the exception of two days, he has been held in a single-occupancy cell. On December 17, 2000, after several requests to switch into a double-occupancy cell were denied, Veney filed a grievance with Riverside alleging that prison officials, by not allowing him to switch cells with other inmates, were discriminating against him because he is a homosexual male. On December 22, 2000, Captain L. White ruled that Veney was not being discriminated against. Veney unsuccessfully appealed White's decision under the Riverside grievance procedure. On March 7, 2001, Veney filed a pro se complaint in the United States District Court for the Eastern District of Virginia under 42 U.S.C.A. § 1983, alleging that prison officials had violated his constitutional right to equal protection of the law.

In his complaint, Veney claims that he is being treated differently from similarly situated heterosexual males and homosexual females, both of whom, asserts Veney, are housed in double-occupancy cells at Riverside. The district court, as required under the Prison Litigation Reform Act of 1996 (PLRA), reviewed Veney's complaint to identify any cognizable claims. After careful consideration of Veney's pleadings, the district court determined that his com-

Opinion of the Fourth Circuit U.S. Court of Appeals, Veney v. Wyche, 2002. Court case citations and notes omitted.

plaint failed to state a claim upon which relief may be granted and dismissed the action. On appeal, Veney challenges the district court's dismissal of his equal protection claim, asserting that his complaint alleges specific facts showing that correctional officials treated him differently from similarly situated inmates without a legitimate penological reason for doing so.

II.

Under § 1915A, the provision at issue in this case, the district court is required to review any "complaint in a civil action in which a prisoner seeks redress from a governmental entity or officer or employee of a governmental entity . . . [and] identify cognizable claims or dismiss the complaint, or any portion of the complaint, if the complaint . . . fails to state a claim upon which relief may be granted . . . ." We review dismissals for failure to state a claim de novo.

A complaint should not be dismissed for failure to state a claim upon which relief may be granted unless "after accepting all well-pleaded allegations in the plaintiff's complaint as true and drawing all reasonable factual inferences from those facts in the plaintiff's favor, it appears certain that the plaintiff cannot prove any set of facts in support of his claim entitling him to relief." Moreover, when such a dismissal involves a civil rights complaint, "we must be especially solicitous of the wrongs alleged" and "must not dismiss the complaint unless it appears to a certainty that the plaintiff would not be entitled to relief under any legal theory which might plausibly be suggested by the facts alleged." We are not required, however, "to accept as true allegations that are merely conclusory, unwarranted deductions of fact, or unreasonable inferences." Nor must we "accept as true allegations that contradict matters properly subject to judicial notice or by exhibit." These principles guide our de novo review of the district court's dismissal of Veney's complaint.

III.

The Equal Protection Clause of the Fourteenth Amendment provides that "no State shall . . . deny to any person within its jurisdiction the equal protection of the laws." U.S. Const. amend. XIV, § 1. The equal protection requirement "does not take from the States all power of classification," but "keeps governmental decision-makers from treating differently persons who are in all relevant respects alike." To succeed on an equal protection claim, Veney "must first demonstrate that he has been treated differently from others with whom he is similarly situated and that the unequal treatment was the result of intentional or purposeful discrimination." If he makes this showing, "the court proceeds to determine whether the disparity in treatment can be justified under the requisite level of scrutiny." To state an equal protection claim, Veney must plead sufficient facts to satisfy each requirement, which we discuss in turn.

A.

Veney claims that he is not allowed to occupy a double-occupancy cell because he is a homosexual male. He asserts that both heterosexual males and homosexual females at Riverside are housed in double-occupancy cells, while his requests to move from his single-occupancy cell have been consistently denied. Veney further alleges that requests to move into a double-occupancy cell made by "seemingly heterosexual" males were granted. For purposes of this appeal, we must accept Veney's allegations as true and draw all inferences in his favor. We therefore assume that Veney is not allowed to move into a double-occupancy cell because he is a homosexual male. We also assume, without deciding, that in all relevant respects, Veney is similarly situated to the other inmates at Riverside. Veney's complaint therefore sufficiently alleges that Riverside is intentionally discriminating against him by treating him differently from similarly situated heterosexual males and homosexual females.

B.

Having determined that Veney's complaint alleges disparate treatment based upon intentional discrimination, we turn to our second inquiry of whether Veney has alleged facts that, if found to be true, would demonstrate that the disparate treatment lacks justification under the requisite level of scrutiny. Ordinarily, when a state regulation or policy is challenged under the Equal Protection Clause, unless it involves a fundamental right or a suspect class, it is presumed to be valid and will be sustained "if there is a rational relationship between the disparity of treatment and some legitimate governmental purpose." Veney's case does not involve a fundamental right. . . . Rather, he claims that he has been discriminated against on the basis of sexual preference and gender. Outside the prison context, the former is subject to rational basis review. When equal protection challenges arise in a prison context, however, courts must adjust the level of scrutiny to ensure that prison officials are afforded the necessary discretion to operate their facilities in a safe and secure manner. In a prison context, therefore, we must determine whether the disparate treatment is "reasonably related to [any] legitimate penological interests." We apply this deferential standard "even when the alleged infringed constitutional right would otherwise warrant higher scrutiny;" however, this more deferential review does not make us ignorant to the concerns that justify application of a heightened standard outside of the prison context. Accordingly, to state a claim upon which relief may be granted, Veney must allege facts sufficient to overcome the presumption of reasonableness applied to prison policies.

As we noted in *Morrison*, to evaluate the reasonableness of Riverside's policy, we apply the factors set forth in *Turner v. Safley,* 482 U.S. 78, 89-90 (1987). Three of the four factors are relevant to Veney's equal protection claim. "First, there must be a 'valid, rational connection' between the prison regulation and the legitimate governmental interest put forward to justify it." Second, a court must consider "the impact accommodation of the asserted consitutional right will have on guards and other inmates, and on the allocation of prison resources generally." Third, "the absence of ready alternatives is evidence of the reasonableness of a prison regulation."

1.

Veney argues that "there is no legitimate penological interest for the segregation of homosexual, male inmates." We disagree. Prison safety and security are legitimate penological interests that we must consider. Thus, applying the *Turner* factors, we must first determine whether there is a valid, rational connection between safety and security and housing homosexual males in single-occupancy cells. In conducting this inquiry, we note that decisions relating to the accommodation of inmates, such as cell assignments, are the type of day-to-day judgments that rest firmly in the discretion of prison officials. Second-guessing such judgments "would seriously hamper [the prison officials'] ability to anticipate security problems and to adopt innovative solutions to the intractable problems of prison administration."

With this deference in mind, we recognize that there are many valid reasons that support the prison officials' conclusion that homosexuals should not be assigned to double-occupancy cells. For example, housing homosexuals with other homosexuals could lead to sexual activity between cellmates, which, as counsel for Appellees pointed out at oral argument, would jeopardize prison security. Sexual activity between cellmates also raises concerns about the transmission of diseases, such as HIV. Similarly, housing homosexuals with heterosexuals might cause friction between cellmates that potentially could lead to violence. In light of examples of anti-homosexual violence in our society, we cannot ignore the fact that homosexuals are subject to bias-motivated attacks from heterosexuals. Outside of the prison environment, concerns of bias-motivated attacks on homosexuals have prompted almost half of the states to protect homosexuals with hate crime statutes. Studies also have shown that inmates known to be homosexuals are at a greater risk of being sexually attacked in prison. Thus, in the prison environment, where inmates live in close quarters and their movements are restricted, prison officials reasonably may conclude that more proactive measures are required to protect homosexuals from bias-motivated attacks. Not allowing heterosexuals to share cells with homosexuals is a rational means of preventing violence between the groups. Moreover, not allowing homosexuals to share cells with other homosexuals is a rational means of preventing sexual activity and the spread of sexually transmitted diseases. The authorities at Riverside are, therefore, not constitutionally precluded from limiting homosexuals to single-occupancy cells.

This does not end our inquiry, however, because Veney alleges that Riverside discriminates against him not only because he is a homosexual, but also because he is a male. We must, therefore, consider whether the gender-based dimension of the alleged discrimination is rationally connected to safety and security concerns in the prison, while again keeping in mind the deferential standard applicable to decisions regarding day-to-day prison management.

At Riverside, females and males are housed separately, and each gender faces unique safety and security concerns of various degrees. Indeed, it is a well-documented reality that institutions for females generally are much less violent than those for males. Moreover, studies show that male inmates are more likely than female inmates to have homophobic attitudes. Insofar as homophobic attitudes lead to bias-motivated attacks, and males are more likely to have such attitudes than are females, prison officials would be justified in concluding that male inmates present a greater threat than female inmates of initiating such attacks. In formulating and executing decisions relating to cell assignments, we must allow prison authorities the discretion to take into account the particular safety and security concerns facing male inmates, even though such considerations result in disparate treatment based upon gender. Accordingly, because the safety and security concerns that arise from housing homosexuals in double-occupancy cells are more significant with respect to males than they are with respect to females, we conclude that the complained of gender-related disparate treatment in the housing of homosexuals is rationally calibrated to address legitimate penological concerns.

2.

The second *Turner* factor we must consider is the impact of accommodating the asserted constitutional right. Accommodating homosexual males in double-occupancy cells would require prison officials to devote more time to making cell assignments because they would have to ensure that homosexuals were not housed with other homosexuals or with violent homophobic inmates. Furthermore, the sexual tension caused by such a living arrangement would place a greater burden on guards who would have to prevent and control disturbances between homosexual and heterosexual cellmates.

3.

The third *Turner* factor informs us that "the absence of ready alternatives is evidence of the reasonableness of a prison regulation." Because part of the friction that Riverside aims to prevent results from homosexual males and heterosexual males living together, there is no ready alternative to the prison's policy of not letting members of these two groups live in the same cell. We conclude, therefore, that the prison policy of not letting homosexual males live in double-occupancy cells is reasonably justified by a legitimate penological interest. Because Veney has not alleged facts that, if proven true, would demonstrate that the alleged prison policy at issue is not reasonably related to legitimate penological interests, his complaint fails to state a claim upon which relief may be granted.

IV.

Because the disparate treatment alleged by Veney is justified by legitimate penological interests, he would not be entitled to relief even if all of his allegations were true. Accordingly, we affirm the district court's dismissal under § 1915A.

AFFIRMED

POSTSCRIPT

Should Homosexual Prison Inmates Have a Right to Share the Same Cell?

Intimate relationships are an important part of our normal lives. This principle applies with equal force to heterosexuals and homosexuals. The U.S. Supreme Court recognized this recently in *Lawrence v. Texas*, 539 U.S. 558 (2003), when it held unconstitutional a Texas law making it a crime for two persons of the same sex to engage in deviate sexual intercourse. Justice Anthony Kennedy, writing for the Court, stated:

> [This case involves] two adults who, with full and mutual consent from each other, engaged in sexual practices common to a homosexual lifestyle. The petitioners are entitled to respect for their private lives. The State cannot demean their existence or control their destiny by making their private sexual conduct a crime. Their right to liberty under the Due Process Clause gives them the full right to engage in their conduct without intervention of the government.

It is noteworthy that in *Lawrence v. Texas* the defendant was arrested for having had sexual relations in the privacy of his own home. The Supreme Court has held that prison inmates have no comparable right to privacy in their prison cells. The Court stated that recognizing such a right would be inconsistent with their status as prisoners.

In light of these precedents, should homosexual prison inmates have a right to share the same cell? A number of arguments can be made to support this proposition. First, why make incarceration any more painful than necessary? If cellmates can have a mutually supportive and intimate relationship, why is it necessary to deny them this opportunity? Second, homosexual inmates are frequently the victims of assault by other homophobic inmates. Permitting homosexual inmates to share a cell may enhance their personal safety. Attorney Jeffrey P. Brinkman also points out that just because a homosexual inmate shares a cell with another inmate, does not mean that they will have sex with each other.

On the other side, prison administrators may well have legitimate reasons for denying homosexual inmates the right to share a cell. For example, as Judge Williams states, housing homosexual inmates in the same cell may lead to sexual activity between cellmates and raise concerns about disease transmission. Moreover, if a homosexual inmate is placed in a cell with another homophobic inmate, there is substantial potential for a violent conflict.

Do you agree with Attorney Brinkman or Judge Williams? Can you identify a middle ground between these positions? Should courts defer to the decisions of prison authorities in these matters? These are interesting questions. Fortunately, there are a number of resources that may shed additional light on these questions. See Samantha Banbury, "Coercive Sexual Behaviour in British Prisons as Reported by Adult Ex-Prisoners," *The Howard Journal of Criminal Justice* (vol. 43, no. 2, 2004); L.F. Alarid, "Prison Sex: Practice and Policy," *Crime, Law and Social Change* (vol. 41, no. 3, 2004); Holly M. Hamer, "Relationships Between Incarcerated Women: Moving Beyond Stereotypes," *Journal of Psychosocial Nursing & Mental Health Services* (vol. 42, no. 1, 2004); Kate Dolan, David Lowe, and James Shearer, "Evaluation of Condom Distribution Program in New South Wales Prisons, Australia," *The Journal of Law, Medicine & Ethics* (vol. 32, no. 1, 2004); Donald L. Braithwaite and Kimberly R.J. Arriola, "Male Prisoners and HIV Prevention: A Call for Action Ignored," *American Journal of Public Health* (vol. 93, no. 5, 2003); J. Green, J. Strang, J. Heterton, and C. Whiteley, et al., "Same-sex Sexual Activity of Male Prisoners in England and Wales," *International Journal of STD & AIDS* (vol. 14, no. 4, 2003); Mary Anne Case, "Of 'This' and 'That' in *Lawrence v. Texas*," *Supreme Court Review* (2003); Christopher P. Krebs and Melanie Simmons, "Intraprison HIV Transmission: An Assessment of Whether It Occurs, How It Occurs, and Who Is at Risk," *AIDS Education and Prevention* (vol. 14, no. 5, 2002); and Dale Carpenter, "The Unknown Past of *Lawrence v. Texas*," *Michigan Law Review* (vol. 102, no. 7, 2004).

ISSUE 15

Are Supermax (Control Unit) Prisons an Appropriate Way to Punish Hardened Criminals?

YES: Gregory L. Hershberger, from "To the Max," *Corrections Today* (February 1998)

NO: Rodney J. Henningsen, W. Wesley Johnson, and Terry Wells, from "Supermax Prisons: Panacea or Desperation?" *Corrections Management Quarterly* (Spring 1999)

ISSUE SUMMARY

YES: Federal Bureau of Prisons Regional Director Gregory L. Hershberger contends that the challenges posed by hardened prison inmates support confining all of its dangerous offenders in one supermax prison facility. This approach may increase the safety of staff and inmates at other locations in the system and allow them to operate in a more effective manner.

NO: Rodney J. Henningsen, W. Wesley Johnson, and Terry Wells argue, however, that supermax prisons are symbolic of the desperation Americans face in trying to reduce crime using traditional formal social control methods. Moreover, as the cost of incarceration continues to increase, public officials may be forced to consider a more balanced approach to crime control.

Supermaximum security prisons often house the worst criminals in our nation's prison systems. Strict regulations and policies in these prisons regulate virtually every aspect of an inmate's life. It is not uncommon to discover that inmates in supermaximum prisons spend 23 hours of every day locked in a small cell. Their communications with other inmates are highly restricted, and reading materials and other "privileges" must be earned by the inmates through good behavior. It should not be surprising then that the regimentation and sensory deprivation used in these facilities appears to produce a substantially higher rate of mental illness among inmates.

As corrections scholar Hans Toch has observed, such penal techniques are nothing new. Prison conditions resembling those in supermax prisons have been adopted on several different occasions in the past but were abandoned because they produced high rates of mental illness among inmates. Sasha Abramsky states that supermax prisons have become the high-tech equivalent of the nineteenth-century snake pit.

In general, U.S. courts have accorded great deference to prison authorities' decisions regarding the conditions of confinement in our prison systems. This approach to corrections law, which the courts followed carefully until the 1960s, has been termed the "hands-off" doctrine. It assumed that because correctional administrators were the "experts," courts should defer to their judgment.

You may recall a now classic movie starring Paul Newman and George Kennedy titled "Cool Hand Luke," which illustrated just how bad the conditions were in some 1950s-era correctional facilities. Due in large part to the inhumane conditions existing in some prison systems, the courts gradually started to scrutinize the decisions of correctional administrators. In fact, during the 1960s, the conditions of confinement in several state prison systems were held to violate the Eighth Amendment's prohibition on cruel and unusual punishment, and significant correctional reforms were instituted.

The decade of the 1970s witnessed an increasing conservatism in the United States. At least partially in response to rising crime rates and the widely held belief that prison rehabilitation programs were ineffective, some scholars and politicians began to advocate a "get tough" approach to crime control. The justice system policies that resulted from this approach included mandatory sentencing laws and a correctional philosophy that emphasized incapacitation and punishment, rather than rehabilitation. The development of supermax prison facilities in the 1980s were the logical extension of this new philosophy.

In the Introduction to this volume, we considered the doctrine of social utility. Basically, this concept asserts that the guiding principle for all social policies should be the well-being of the majority of people. Does the use of supermaximum prison facilities satisfy this principle? Are they an appropriate way to punish hardened criminals? The authors of the articles in this section would answer these questions in very different ways.

Federal Bureau of Prisons regional director Gregory L. Hershberger contends that the challenges posed by hardened prison inmates support confining the worst offenders in a supermaximum prison facility. This approach may increase the safety of staff and inmates at other locations in the system and allow it to operate in a more effective manner. Professors Rodney J. Henningsen, W. Wesley Johnson, and Terry Wells would take issue with Director Hershberger's view of supermax prisons.

Do you agree initially with Director Hershberger, or with Professors Henningsen, Johnson, and Wells? Do you believe that supermax prisons are an effective and justified approach to punishing hardened criminals, or are they inconsistent with human value and dignity? These are intriguing questions that will have a highly significant impact on corrections policy in the new millennium.

Gregory L. Hershberger

To the Max

Over the past decade, correctional systems around the nation have activated several high security prisons, which are popularly known as "supermax" institutions. These facilities are designed to hold the most violent, disruptive or escape-prone offenders. By isolating the "worst of the worst," these facilities increase the safety of staff, other inmates and the general public. They also allow inmates in other institutions to live in a more normalized prison environment, with greater freedom of movement and access to educational, vocational and other correctional programs.

In some correctional systems, offenders may be sent to supermax facilities as direct commitments from the courts, but most inmates are sent to them because of their behavior in prison. Among the roughly 400 inmates in the Federal Bureau of Prisons' (BOP) most secure facility, the U.S. Penitentiary Administrative Maximum (ADX) in Florence, Colo., approximately 20 percent are there for the murder or attempted murder of a fellow inmate, 18 percent for assaulting another inmate with a weapon, 16 percent for serious assault on a staff member, 10 percent for a serious escape attempt and 5 percent for rioting. Other reasons for placement in this facility include attempted murder of a staff member, taking a staff member hostage, leading a work or food strike, introducing narcotics into an institution and having a leadership role in a prison gang. Only about 3 percent of the inmates were sent there directly from court. About 6 percent are state boarders, inmates who were involved in the murder of state correctional staff, or inmates who are too disruptive or dangerous for state officials to house safely.

Dispersion vs. Consolidation

For years, correctional administrators have used various strategies for handling especially dangerous inmates and minimizing the disruption they cause to the rest of the system. Historically, they have used two basic models—dispersion and consolidation.

The dispersion model scatters offenders with unusually dangerous histories or disruptive behavioral patterns throughout the correctional system, thus avoiding a concentration of such offenders in any one location. Staff in each institution share the burden and dangers of supervising and controlling

From *Corrections Today*, vol. 60, issue 1, February 1998, pp. 54-57.

these inmates. In smaller prison systems, the aggressive conduct of these inmates often results in their placement in long-term segregation or detention status. In larger systems, administrators transfer inmates from one institution to another, if only to disrupt their alliances and give staff relief from the stress of dealing with them. In the past, entire institutions often were managed in a more rigid, highly controlled manner in order to reduce the threat posed by this relatively small number of inmates.

Among the benefits of the dispersion model is the fact that no single institution is required to deal with a large number of problem inmates. In addition, some prison administrators believe that it is easier to manage small groups of inmates of this caliber. Finally, it was once thought that a number of institutions holding a few such individuals each would require the allocation of fewer security-related resources overall.

In contrast, the consolidation model involves placing all highly dangerous inmates at one location and controlling them through reliance on heightened security procedures. The potential drawback of adopting a consolidation model is that the institution holding this group is necessarily subjected to a dramatically different routine and will, in all likelihood, require additional staff and expensive security modifications.

Alcatraz was the prototypical consolidation-model institution at the federal level. From 1934 to 1963, it operated as the prime federal prison resource, housing many of the more notorious or dangerous offenders in the federal system. Alcatraz was closed in 1963—not because of flaws in the consolidation model, but because the island prison was very expensive to operate and maintain, and because there was a shift in correctional philosophy during the so-called "medical model" or rehabilitation era.

When the BOP closed Alcatraz, it decided to disperse its hard-core offenders throughout the various federal prisons, rather than move them as a group to another single location. During most of the 1960s and the early 1970s, the BOP managed its most dangerous offenders by using the dispersion model. However, in the late '70s, the BOP began moving toward the consolidation model once again, concentrating its most troublesome inmates at the U.S. Penitentiary in Marion, Ill.

Consolidation Pros and Cons

Focusing extra security resources on a single location is thought by many corrections practitioners to be far more efficient and effective. Under the consolidation model, staff training for managing this more homogeneous group is simplified, and operational procedures are much more refined. But more important, staff and inmates in other institutions throughout the prison system see their safety enhanced, and rigid controls lessened, once the most dangerous individuals are removed to a single, more highly controlled location.

The BOP recognized that the consolidation strategy for reducing violence in its mainline institutions had its risks. While the benefits in terms of overall system safety and order clearly were worthwhile, the dimensions of those risks soon became evident. In 1979, a series of serious assaults, inmate murders and the attempted murders of two staff in Marion's dining room demonstrated the volatility and potential danger of the new population mixture. A special task force, convened to deal with the increasing violence at Marion, recommended that the institution be converted to a tightly controlled, unitized operation that would permit the continued consolidation of the most violent, assaultive and disruptive inmates at one institution and would better protect staff and inmates from violence. However, implementation of that recommendation was deferred, and Marion's daily routines continued to resemble those of a traditional institution.

By 1980, Marion's operation began to show clear signs of the underlying stresses of using this quasi-normal system to deal with such aggressive offenders. Assaults on inmates and staff continued; there were major incidents in the administrative detention unit; and inmates staged three major work stoppages, the last of which lasted for four months. The BOP decided to remove industrial operations from Marion altogether, and convert the institution into the more highly structured operation envisioned several years earlier. This was done by expanding the restricted movement and program procedures which were initiated during the strike.

Management Challenges

Prison administrators recognize better than most the difficulty of operating a minimum privilege, maximum control facility. As a result, even though numerous serious incidents underscored the difficult and dangerous nature of the inmate group at Marion, various attempts were made to return the institution to some semblance of normalcy throughout 1982 and most of 1983. Unfortunately, each step toward normalization was met by additional assaults and other serious incidents, generating increased concern for the safety of staff and inmates. In October 1983, two staff members who were working in the most secure area of Marion were murdered in separate incidents on the same day, and two other staff were seriously injured. Just days later, an inmate was murdered and several staff were assaulted during a group disturbance. These events culminated in the final realization that the type of inmates confined at Marion could not be managed in the same manner as typical penitentiary inmates. Thus, the decision was made to convert the institution into a long-term, highly controlled operation—a "supermax" facility.

While this management program seemed to control the inmate population, the BOP found that Marion's design and layout was not particularly well-suited for its mission. For example, because education, recreation, health services and other vital program areas were centrally located, inmates often had to be moved from one location to another. For security reasons, each move had to be escorted. Consequently, the high volume of inmate movement consumed an enormous number of staff hours and significantly threatened staff safety. Accordingly, in the mid-'80s, BOP administrators began thinking about a new high-security facility, one that was designed specifically for high-security operations and that took advantage of the many advances in inmate management and correctional technology that occurred between 1960 and 1980.

After years of careful planning, the BOP opened ADX Florence—one of the most sophisticated supermax prisons in the nation. Since its activation in 1994, ADX Florence has been extremely effective in housing the federal prison system's most dangerous offenders in a safe, secure and humane manner.

ADX Operations

Supermax facilities have been incorrectly characterized as "lockdown" institutions. This is misleading. Lockdowns are relatively short periods of time when all inmates in an institution are confined to their cells because of an institutional emergency, or for some other overriding reason such as a facilitywide shakedown. During a lockdown, all but the most basic services are suspended. True supermax facilities operate quite differently. A supermax facility is not simply a segregation unit in a maximum security penitentiary. It is a full institution, with unique security elements and programmatic features.

The main purpose of a supermax facility is to control the inmates' behavior until they demonstrate that they can be moved back to a traditional, open-population penitentiary. As they demonstrate increasingly responsible behavior, ADX inmates move incrementally from more to less restrictive housing units. Each successive unit allows more privileges and more interaction with staff and other inmates.

Administrative maximum security operations differ from typical penitentiary operations in several ways. Inmates are handcuffed whenever they come in contact with staff; this prevents violent offenders from assaulting staff and other inmates, and eliminates the possibility that escape-prone inmates will attempt to take a hostage or access an area of the institution that will facilitate an escape. Inmates eat and recreate individually, or in small, carefully screened and supervised groups; this differs from procedures in a typical prison, where inmates have largely unrestrained contact with each other and staff throughout the day. Inmates are confined in their cells for larger portions of the day; in a typical prison, an inmate would have 12 to 16 hours of out-of-cell time, while an inmate in an administrative maximum security institution would be much more restricted.

Programs in an administrative maximum security setting rely primarily upon individual inmate-based delivery systems (self-study courses, closed circuit television, staff visits to the housing unit) as opposed to having inmates go in groups to a central program area. Visiting in such an institution is generally noncontact, in contrast to the contact visiting that is permitted in most institutions. Staff/inmate ratios are higher, to provide increased supervision and capability for searching inmates, cells and other areas of the institution in order to prevent assaults and disruptive incidents.

Unique Confinement Conditions

While conditions of confinement for inmates in an administrative maximum security setting are highly restrictive relative to the general population of most typical penitentiaries, these facilities are an improvement on conditions in a typical detention or segregation unit at a regular penitentiary, because they provide increased movement, more contact with staff and more opportunities to participate in programs. Institutions such as ADX Florence are intended to control disruptive and dangerous behavior, yet also permit a reasonable amount of access to necessary programs and offer inmates the means to progress to a more typical penitentiary setting.

Rather than being housed in traditional lockdown conditions, inmates at ADX Florence, for example, are offered a range of programs and services. Most are delivered at the inmate's cell or in the individual unit, eliminating the danger and expense associated with frequent escorted moves. Inmates do start their time at Florence under relatively close controls; they spend the majority of their time in their cells or in the cellhouse. On- and off-unit recreation, visiting, medical care, in-cell television, religious activities, education and other self-improvement programs are available from the day of arrival at Florence. The federal courts have consistently found that the BOP's administrative maximum operations are consistent with constitutional requirements related to conditions of confinement.

ADX inmates are offered an opportunity to demonstrate nondangerous behavior through compliance with institutional rules. As they do, they progress through a graduated system of housing units, with each unit providing increased freedom and work opportunities, all contingent on the inmate avoiding misconduct. Proper conduct in this program results in eventual transfer to other, less controlled institutions.

The ADX program is based on the assumption that every inmate will be given the opportunity to demonstrate that he or she doesn't need to be at the ADX. Most progress through the program in a little more than three years (42 months, on average) and then are returned to open population prisons. Once in regular penitentiaries, more than 80 percent of former administrative maximum inmates behave well enough that a return to the program is unnecessary.

Conclusion

The essential challenge of operating a supermax facility is to properly balance staff and inmate safety needs against important constitutional and correctional management principles that govern prison life. It is critical to remember that with this type of offender, good treatment starts with vital safety considerations—for both staff and inmates.

The challenges posed by these inmates are very real, as are the dangers they present to staff, other inmates and the public. If a prison system confines all of its dangerous offenders in one institution, it can increase the safety of staff and inmates at other locations in the system and operate these facilities in a more open, normalized fashion. Highly refined security procedures and appropriate programming within the supermax facility allow for safe and secure operations while providing even the most dangerous offenders with reasonable opportunities to demonstrate pro-social behavior and earn their way back into an open population institution.

NO

Rodney J. Henningsen, W. Wesley Johnson, and Terry Wells

Supermax Prisons: Panacea or Desperation?

FOR OVER A century Americans have sought to find the silver bullet to solve its crime problems. Fads and experiments in corrections have included public humiliation, singleceiling, silent systems, 12-step recovery programs, boot camps, electronic surveillance, and now, supermax. Supermax prisons have evolved out of America's love-hate relationship with crime and punishment. A supermax prison has been defined as:

> A free-standing facility, or distinct unit within a facility, that provides for the management and secure control of inmates who have been officially designated as exhibiting violent or seriously disruptive behavior while incarcerated. Such inmates have been determined to be a threat to safety and security in traditional high-security facilities, and their behavior can be controlled by separation, restricted movement, and limited access to staff and other inmates.

At least in theory, this type of prison unit can and should be distinguished from administrative segregation (ad-seg). While most every prison has administrative segregation cells used for holding prisoners in short-term disciplinary or protective custody, supermax units are designed to house prisoners for a much longer period of time. Proponents of supermax prisons contend that they warehouse the worst of the worst, the most violent prisoners who threaten the security of guards and other prisoners while undermining the moral fabric of American society.

While the American public has increasingly turned to government for solutions to its social problems in the last 30 years, its perceptions of the criminal justice system have remained jaundiced. Over 75 percent of respondents in a recent national survey reported only "some" or "very little" confidence in state prison systems. Similarly, over 80 percent of people surveyed each year since 1980 have indicated that the courts are too soft on crime.

The American judiciary has responded to public concerns that they are soft on crime and cries for vengeance by placing more people under correctional supervision than ever before. To accommodate the increases in new

From *Corrections Management Quarterly*, vol. 3, issue 2, Spring 1999, pp. 53-59. References omitted.

prison admissions and increases in time served by prisoners, some 168 state and 45 federal prisons have been built since 1990. Today, there are a total of approximately 1,500 state and federal prisons. Between 1990 and 1995, the number of prison beds increased by 41 percent. Despite this tremendous fiscal investment, there are both state and federal prisons that operate in excess of their design capacity, state prisons by 3 percent and federal prisons by 24 percent.

While there are more prisons and prisoners than ever before, there is sustained interest in making prisons even "tougher." This interest may be based on the notion, not strongly supported in the criminological research on recidivism that prisons deter. Another reason may be simply that victims of crime, and those that see themselves as potential victims, want prisoners to suffer. While harm is a critical component of punishment, its generic application to prison life creates unique challenges for correctional officers, staff, and correctional executives.

Political Popularity of Supermax Prisons

Getting tough on crime has become an increasingly popular campaign platform among elected officials, and support of supermax institutions is a politically popular position in many areas across the country. The American judiciary has also supported the need for supermax prison environments. In Bruscino v Carlson, federal prisoners at Marion, Illinois, sought compensation for the attacks on them by correctional officers during the October 1983 shakedown and relief from the ongoing conditions created by the subsequent lockdown. A 1985 U.S. Magistrate's Report approved by the U.S. District Court for Southern Illinois in 1987 indicated that 50 prisoners who testified to beatings and other brutalities were not credible witnesses, and that only the single prisoner who testified that there were no beatings was believable. When the prisoners appealed the decision, the ruling of the Fifth Circuit Court of Appeals described conditions at Marion as "ghastly," "sordid and horrible," and "depressing in extreme," but the court maintained that they were necessary for security reasons and did not violate prisoners' constitutional rights.

The New Controversial Control Models

Today, control units go by many different names. They have been referred to as adjustment centers, security housing units, maximum control complexes, administrative maximum (Ad-Max), special housing units, violence control units, special management units, intensive management units, management control units, or "supermax" prisons. These new units are designed to subdue any and all resistance to order. A survey by the Federal Bureau of Prisons conducted in 1990 found that 36 states operated some form of supermax security prison or unit within a prison. At that time, another six states were planning to build supermax prisons. By 1993, 25 states had specialized control units and control unit prisons were in operation in every part of the country.

The new model for high-security prisons is the security housing unit (SITU) at Pelican Bay Prison in California. Pelican Bay opened in December

1989. Prisoners in such units are kept in solitary confinement in relatively small cells between 22 and 23 hours a day. There is no congregate dining or congregate exercise, and there are no work opportunities or congregate religious services. Prisoners are denied standard vocational, educational, and recreational activities.

The conditions are officially justified not as punishment for prisoners, but as an administrative measure. Prisoners are placed in control units as a result of an administrative decision. Because such moves are a result of an administrative decision, prisoners' ability to challenge such changes in imprisonment is severely limited. Today, throughout the country, conditions in "new" supermax prisons closely resemble those set forth at Pelican Bay.

Since their inception, supermax prison units have had their opponents. Typically, opponents have focused upon conditions that allegedly are illegal or inhumane. In some reports, prison guards have testified to shackling prisoners to their beds and spraying them with high-pressure fire hoses. Other criticisms have centered on issues surrounding arbitrary placement/assignment to control unit the long-term psychological effects from years of isolation from both prison and outside communities while being housed in solitary or small group isolation (celled 22.5 hours/day) denial of access to educational, religious, or work programs physical torture, such as forced cell extractions, four-point restraint and hog-tying, caging, beating after restraint, back-room beatings, and staged fights for officer entertainment. . . .

Arbitrary Placement

Prisoners are placed in high-security units for administrative and/or disciplinary reasons. Such decisions are based on results during (re-) classification hearings. Critics have called the hearings a kangaroo court claiming prisoners are being denied due process. What is called misbehavior is (arbitrarily) decided by the guard on duty and has been known to include refusing to make beds or complaining about clogged and overflowing toilets.

Violations of Human Rights and Abuses

There are many claims of human rights violations and abuses in control units, including denial of medical care to injured and/or sick prisoners (including diabetics and epileptics), extremely cold cells during winter months and extremely hot cells during summer months, arbitrary beatings, psychological abuse of mentally unstable prisoners, illegal censorship of mail, extended isolation and indoor confinement, denial of access to educational programs, and administrative rather than judicial decisions about punishment for misbehaved prisoners.

Ability to Reduce Violence in Prisons and Society

Prison officials claim that Marion, Pelican Bay, and the other supermax-type control units reduce violence in the rest of the prison system. All the evidence points to the opposite being true. The creation of control units and increased use of administrative segregation have not reduced the level of violence within general prison populations. In fact, assaults on prison staff nationwide rose from 175 in 1991 to 906 to 1993. The number of inmate assaults on prison employees reached 14,000 in 1995. That was up 32 percent from 1990. The number of assaults per 1,000 employees remained stable at 15. It may also be that the potential of supermax prisons to reduce overall prison violence has yet to be realized. As more disruptive inmates are placed in supermax prison cells, assaults in prisons may decline.

While supermax prisons provide correctional executives with another weapon to facilitate order in prison, most supermax prisoners are released back into the general prison population or into society. Conditions in control units produce feelings of resentment and rage and exacerbate mental deterioration. It is anticipated that control unit prisoners who re-enter the general prison population or society will have even greater difficulty coping with social situations than in the past.

The Texas Experience

Overcrowding and the control of violence are critical issues in correctional management, especially in states like Texas where the federal government, in Ruiz v Texas, declared the entire department of corrections unconstitutional. As a result of the Ruiz decision, the federal government actively monitored virtually every facet of the Texas Department of Corrections–Institutional Division for over 20 years. In attempts to shed federal control over Texas prisons, relieve massive prison overcrowding, and avoid future lawsuits, an unprecedented number of new prisons were built in a relatively short period of time. In August 1993, the Texas Department of Criminal Justice, one of the largest correctional systems in the world, operated 54 inmate facilities. By August 1998, the number of correctional facilities in Texas doubled, housing prisoners in 107 correctional facilities.

According to David Stanley, of the Executive Services, Texas Department of Criminal Justice-Institutional Division, Texas prisons will soon be at maximum capacity again. In August 1997, Texas's men's prisons were at 98 percent of their capacity, while women's prisons approached 85 percent of their design capacity. Currently, there are about 126,000 men and 10,000 women incarcerated in Texas prisons. Estimates are that maximum design capacity for housing male inmates will be reached in little more than a year. If current inmate population trends continue, many institutions across the country will be operating above design capacity. These factors, combined with the fact that more violent offenders are now entering prisons at an earlier age for longer periods of time than just a decade ago, affect correctional administrators' ability to maintain order and protect their own staff from assaults.

In attempts to keep the lid on a more volatile prison population, Texas has been one of the first states to make a commitment to new prison construction and new state-of-the-art high-security, supermax correctional facilities. This commitment has required an investment of substantial tax revenues. The new high-security prisons, according to a spokesman for the Texas Department of Criminal Justice–Institutional Division, Larry Fitzgerald, are being built and designed with efficiency and economy in mind. The estimated cost of the some 1,300 beds (double-celled) in the new control units will be a mere $19,000 compared to the current national average of $79,770 per maximum-security bed. Costs are being reduced by using inmate labor for nonsecurity tasks, such as masonry, painting, and welding.

Currently, one high-security unit has been completed near Huntsville, Texas and construction on two other similar units has already begun. Officials estimated that inmate labor saved Texas taxpayers over 2 million dollars in the construction of the new control unit near Huntsville, Texas. Currently, high-security inmates are housed in single-cells.

On August 4, 1997, inmates began arriving at the new $25 million high-security unit of the Texas prison system. The high-security unit is located on the grounds of the Estelle Unit near Huntsville. Similar to high-security units in other states, Texas inmates who are placed in the new high-security unit are put there for one of three reasons: (1) they have tried to escape; (2) they pose a physical threat to staff or inmates; or (3) they are members of disruptive groups, such as an organized gang. Approximately 50 percent to 60 percent of the current residents have been officially classified as belonging to a particular gang.

The Gilbane Corporation, with the help of inmates, began construction on the 65,780 square foot facility in October 1995. Outside, two motion detector fences surround the prison. The exterior of the new unit, although secured by electronic surveillance of the outer fence and certain portions of the building and a patrol vehicle, ironically gives less of the appearance of a traditional fortress prison in that there is no guard tower. Some have likened its appearance to that of a modern high school gym.

Despite its relative benign external appearance, its overall design seeks to provide an alternative for the most recalcitrant inmates. Although two beds per cell are still found in accordance with the original plan, a change from the original purpose of the facility now calls for one inmate per cell. While it would be possible to house 1,300 inmates, the current plan is to house only 650 inmates.

The building has a central corridor with two-story wings on the east and west sides. The east wings contain 63 cells with two beds per cell. The east side recreation yard is 22,451 square feet with 42 individual yards. The west wings have 67 cells with two beds per cell. The west side recreation yard is 24,857 square feet and contains 40 individual yards.

The concern for security prompted the design to establish 8 × 10-foot cells. Unlike the traditional cell with barred doors, all doors on this unit consist of a solid sheet of steel. A slot in the door allows officers to pass items to inmates. An inmate can contact an officer by using an intercom system in his cell. The unit's supporters champion these new doors, convinced that officers will no longer need to fear being assaulted by inmates or their waste products as they walk the unit.

The computerized high-tech design is used to monitor staff as well as inmates. All of the projected 246 employees are required to go through extensive security checks upon entering the building. They are required to place their right hands into a palm print recognition station and then enter their four-digit code. Their name and time of entrance into the unit are recorded and stored digitally.

Once access is authorized, a steel door is opened and shut electronically. The computer keeps a log of all times the door was opened and closed. This feature serves as a source of information for administrators to monitor employee traffic and as an additional source of information when prisoners file allegations of abuse or neglect. All incoming on-duty officers then proceed to a central room near the facility's entrance where monitors with split screens transmit views from the many cameras providing surveillance everywhere both inside and outside the unit.

The central control room, which contains several split-screen monitors, is the hub for internal surveillance. Smaller versions of these computerized nerve centers are found in all prison wings and in the hallways. The setup makes it possible for one officer to monitor each wing.

Operational Conditions in the Texas High Security Unit

Most of the conditions found in other control units are also found in the new unit in Texas as well. As in other such units the main objective is to minimize/eliminate an inmates' contact with staff and other prisoners. Such isolation is routine and can be up to 24 hours a day. The inmates in the new Texas control unit will spend most of their time alone in cells. Virtually all their activities both day and night take place in their cells. They eat, shower, and use the restroom in their own cells. The ability to shower the entire unit within a few hours is a major cost- and time-savings procedure, especially compared to showering individual ad-seg inmates under double and sometimes triple custody.

Each cell contains a steel toilet, sink, and showerhead. These are all bolted into the wall. Inmates have the opportunity to shower daily; at other times showers are turned off. Water for the sink and toilet is made available at all times. However, like other "amenities," they can be shut off by the central control system should the cell occupant try to flood his cell block. Inmates receive daily meals in their cells. The food is prepared within the unit by inmates from another institution and is delivered to the inmates by officers.

The high-security unit has no day rooms or television sets other than computer monitors. It does have a visitation room, however, where inmates and their visitors are separated by a thick, impact-resistant glass wall. A steel stool bolted to the floor and a two-way telephone are the only items in the room. No physical contact is possible between inmates and visitors. Likewise, inmates approved for legally prescribed visits may visit other inmates under similar conditions. Such visits are generally conducted in holding cells. Here a wall with a small window, crisscrossed by bars for communication, separates the two inmates who are seated on either side of the wall on a single steel stool bolted to the floor.

Inmates, depending on their level of classification, receive from one hour, three days a week to one hour, seven days a week outdoor recreation time. Oftentimes the only real reprieve from their nearly total isolation takes place at these times. During this time, inmates are moved to individual "cages" where they are separated physically from other inmates by (only) fences. There they are able to see and talk to other inmates. The 18′ × 20′ enclosed recreation yards include a basketball court, a chin-up bar, and a hard wall on which inmates can play handball. Each "cage" is secured by a floor-to-ceiling 35-foot-high mesh steel fence. If other inmates are nearby, they can converse.

While out-of-cell programming is available to supermax inmates in 13 states, in Texas, the intense physical limitations are compounded by the absence of educational, training, or recreational programs. Thus far, supermax imprisonment in Texas has not attempted to include formal rehabilitation programs as part of its daily routine.

Consequences of Total Control

As a result, control unit inmates live in a psychologically assaultive environment that destabilizes personal and social identities. While the same can be said of the prison system as a whole, in control units mind control is a primary weapon, implemented through architectural design and a day-to-day regimen that produces isolation, inwardness, and self-containment. Within this severely limited space, inmates are under constant scrutiny and observation. In the unit, cameras and listening devices ensure constant surveillance and control of not only the inmate but also every movement of the staff.

The rural location of control units increases (or supplements) isolation and makes contact with family and community difficult for many. The difficulty for inmates in maintaining contacts with the outside world is exacerbated by the unit's isolation from major urban centers. This alienation heightens inmate frustration, deprivation, and despair. Over long periods of time, the inevitable result is the creation of dysfunctional individuals who are completely self-involved, socially neutered, unable to participate in organized social activities, and unprepared for eventual reintegration into either the general prison population, or life on the outside. Those inmates who resist less, demand less, and see each other as fierce competitors for the few privileges allowed will fare best in the system. Programs that normally exist in other prisons to rehabilitate are deemed frivolous here.

Discussion

The present system of mass incarceration accompanied by the specter of more and more control units can only be maintained with at least the tacit approval of society as whole. In times of relative economic prosperity, America has had the luxury of focusing its resources on crime reduction. As the new millennium approaches, crime and its control has become a major industry. Despite the lack of valid scientific evidence that massive imprisonment reduces crime, billions of dollars have been spent to build new prisons and satisfy the American public's growing desire for vengeance. While there is some scientific evidence that there is a (weak) negative correlation between imprisonment and crime rates, the vast majority of studies indicate that imprisonment is not causally related to the variability in crime. Critics of current imprisonment trends have argued that imprisoning large numbers of people in order to stop crime has been a spectacular and massively expensive failure. Even prison officials sometimes admit to the reality of the situation.

Supermax prisons, perhaps our most costly prison experiment ever, have been promoted as the new panacea for correctional management problems, a form of deterrence that is guaranteed to work. On the other hand, supermax prisons are symbolic of the desperation Americans face in trying to take out crime using traditional formal control methods. The efficacy of such approaches is generally limited by their reactive nature. As the cost of incarceration continues to increase, public officials may be forced to consider a more balanced approach incorporating a more holistic view of crime control; one which focuses more on community and restoration and less on imprisonment. The challenge of the future lies in the creation of a society and a criminal justice system that is able to thwart violence with less violent means.

What we need, in all seriousness, is a better class of inmates. Such change will take time and substantial resources. As we approach the next century, we have the luxury of a relatively strong economy. While many planners have their eye on the future of the global market, failure to learn from our mistakes of the past and strategically invest in proactive crime control strategies in local communities, will eventually limit our ability to compete with other countries and life in America will become, in the words of Hobbes, even more "short, brutish, and nasty."

POSTSCRIPT

Are Supermax (Control Unit) Prisons an Appropriate Way to Punish Hardened Criminals?

The use of supermaximum security prisons is a controversial practice in the U.S. justice system. On one hand, Director Hershberger's perspective on this issue is a compelling one: It may make sense to confine the "worst of the worst" inmates in one supermax facility where every facet of their lives can be regulated and we can minimize the dangers they pose to the prison staff and other inmates. On the other side, however, is the issue that if supermaximum security prisons are simply another "quick fix" for America's crime problems, we are likely to be sorely disappointed in these costly corrections experiments.

Moreover, control unit prison facilities are nothing new. As Hans Toch has observed, correctional policy makers have used the types of control techniques employed in supermax prisons at different times in the past. For example, the "Pennsylvania" system of prison discipline was developed in the late 1700s at the Walnut Street Jail in Philadelphia. The basic assumption of this system, based on the ideas of prison reformers including Benjamin Franklin and Benjamin Rush, was that prisoners should be placed in solitary confinement and not permitted to work. The assumption was that they would reflect on their crimes and become reformed. Eventually, the system's administrators realized that the prisoners had to be given activities such as work to occupy their time. Without meaningful activity, many inmates experience various forms of mental illness. Based on your knowledge of the history of our justice system, do you find it ironic that, as in the case of supermax prisons, we appear to be forever destined to repeat the past?

Another interesting aspect of the supermax prison debate is the role of the courts in assessing the conditions of confinement in these total institutions. As noted in the Introduction to this issue, since the late 1970s, U.S. courts have been highly deferential to the decisions of correctional administrators regarding the appropriate conditions of confinement in our nation's prisons. However, when a U.S. District Court considered the conditions in the Pelican Bay State Prison, a supermaximum facility operated by the State of California, it found some of the conditions there to be constitutionally intolerable. In *Madrid v. Gomez,* 889 F. Supp. 1146 (1995), inmates confined at the Pelican Bay State Prison filed a class action lawsuit challenging a broad range of conditions and practices that impacted almost every facet of their prison life. The inmates sought to have the conditions of confinement at Pelican Bay declared to be a violation of their civil rights and the U.S. Constitution. One portion of this huge lawsuit asserted that prison authorities had engaged in a pattern of using excessive force against the inmates. On this issue, the Court concluded:

> [T]he Court is compelled to conclude that the Eighth Amendment's restraint on using excessive force has been repeatedly violated at Pelican Bay, leading to a conspicuous pattern of excessive force. In many instances, there was either no justification for the use of force, or alternately, the use of force was appropriate, but the amount of force applied was so strikingly disproportionate to the circumstances that it was imposed, more likely than not for the very purpose of causing harm, rather than in a good faith effort to restore or maintain order.

Inmates in this case were not so successful with a number of their other claims, however. But, *Madrid v. Gomez* does appear to indicate that there is some reason to believe that the federal courts will intervene in state supermax conditions cases where there is significant reason to believe that prison authorities are not acting in good faith.

Fortunately, there are additional resources that discuss the issues considered in this section. See Lorna A. Rhodes, *Total Confinement: Madness and Reason in the Maximum Security Prison* (University of California Press, 2004); Michael Tonry, ed., *The Future of Imprisonment* (Oxford University Press, 2004); Harry L. Allen and Clifford E. Simonsen, *Corrections in America: An Introduction*, 8th ed. (Prentice Hall, 1998); Lorna A. Rhodes, "Changing the Subject: Conversation in Supermax," *Cultural Anthropology* (vol. 20, no. 3, 2005); "United States: Hell on Earth; The Delights of Supermax Prisons," *The Economist* (April 2, 2005); Jesenia Pizarro and Vanja M. K. Stenius, "Supermax Prisons: Their Rise, Current Practices, and Effect on Inmates," *The Prison Journal* (vol. 84, no. 2, 2004); Mikel-Meredith Weidman, "The Culture of Judicial Deference and the Problem of Supermax Prisons," *UCLA Law Review* (vol. 51, no. 5, 2004); Chad S. Briggs, Jody L. Sundt, and Thomas C. Castellano, "The Effect of Supermaximum Security Prisons on Aggregate Levels of Institutional Violence," *Criminology* (vol. 41, no. 4, 2003); Hans Toch, "The Contemporary Relevance of Early Experiments with Supermax Reform," *The Prison Journal* (vol. 83, no. 2, 2003); Craig Haney, "Mental Health Issues in Long-Term Solitary and 'Supermax' Confinement," *Crime & Delinquency* (vol. 49, no. 1, 2003); Sasha Abramsky, "Return of the Madhouse," *The American Prospect* (vol. 13, no. 3, 2002); and Hans Toch, "The Future of Supermax Confinement," *The Prison Journal* (vol. 81, no. 3, 2001).

ISSUE 16

Should Private "For Profit" Corporations Be Allowed to Run U.S. Prisons?

YES: Wayne H. Calabrese, from "Low Cost, High Quality, Good Fit: Why Not Privatization?" in Gary W. Bowman, Simon Hakim, and Paul Seidenstat, eds., *Privatizing Correctional Institutions* (Transaction Publishers, 1993)

NO: Jeff Sinden, from "The Problem of Prison Privatization: The U.S. Experience," in Andrew Cole, Allison Campbell, and Rodney Newfeld, eds., *Capitalist Punishment: Prison Privatization & Human Rights* (Clarity Press, 2003)

ISSUE SUMMARY

YES: Wayne H. Calabrese, vice president of the Wackenhut Corporation, argues that the privatization of U.S. prisons saves money and provides quality services.

NO: Jeff Sinden, managing editor of *Human Rights Tribune*, contends that the private prison industry has failed to achieve substantial cost savings and that there have been systemic human rights abuses in for-profit correctional institutions.

Should private corporations be allowed to profit from the punishment of prison inmates? Is there something morally wrong with allowing a corporation's stockholders to make a profit from human misery? These are difficult questions that will become increasingly relevant as governmental administrators try to squeeze limited financial resources from tight state budgets.

Private prisons are not a new development. As Jeff Sinden observes, privately run jails operated in England centuries ago. Moreover, in the United States, early prisons in California and Texas were privately owned. The operation of U.S. prisons became a governmental responsibility during the twentieth century as a direct result of the squalid conditions existing in the privately owned penal facilities.

The contemporary privatization movement in American corrections has focused on providing a number of different types of services: inmate health care, psychological services, food services, educational programs, maintenance, as well as traditional confinement and security. It is also noteworthy that many college students may have something in common with some of our nation's prison inmates: Sodexho Marriott Services provides food services for a number of state correctional systems as well as many colleges and universities.

On a theoretical level, an offender is sentenced to prison for committing an act that has somehow harmed society. Most persons would have little trouble with the proposition that society has a right to punish the person and that the government, as society's representative, should administer the appropriate sanctions. Privatization of correctional facilities, however, appears to be somewhat inconsistent with this basic proposition.

The Introduction to this edition discussed the contemporary state of American corrections. According to recent studies, the United States has the highest imprisonment rates in the entire world. The total number of people housed in American prisons has reached 2.1 million and is continuing to grow at an alarming rate. This has occurred at a time when the crime rate in this country is actually falling! A large number of these individuals are confined to prisons for nonviolent offenses, such as possession of illegal drugs, and the cost to house them is staggering—perhaps as much as $15 billion for drug offenders alone.

Given the amount of money involved, is it surprising that private industry would become interested in providing correctional services? Is it an accident that conservative politicians, who receive campaign contributions from the private corrections corporations, would develop ever more draconian laws that will result in the incarceration of increasing numbers of non-violent offenders? These are interesting questions that the authors of the articles in this section would be likely to answer in a very different way.

Wayne H. Calabrese, of the Wackenhut Corporation, asserts that in a time of dwindling public sector budgets, privatizing corrections services has one great advantage over governmental programs: highly significant cost savings. He believes that money is saved because "no one has yet developed a better pencil sharpener than free market competition."

Jeff Sinden, in contrast, maintains that the promised cost savings have not materialized. He cites a 2001 U.S. Department of Justice study concluding that "rather than the projected 20% savings, the average saving from privatization was only about one percent, and most of that was achieved through lower labor costs."

What are the arguments on both sides of the private prison debate? Do you believe that saving money is a good enough reason to privatize U.S. prisons? Moreover, does the move toward the privatization of our correctional institutions distract us from addressing more fundamental questions about the morality of our contemporary penal system? As you read the articles in this section, try to develop a sense of whether privatization is likely to become the dominant model for U.S. corrections in the twenty-first century.

Wayne H. Calabrese

Low Cost, High Quality, Good Fit: Why Not Privatization?

As the privatization of corrections has taken root and grown, initial questions of propriety—"Should this be done?"—have given way to secondary questions of efficacy—"Does this work?" Perhaps inevitably in a time of dwindling public sector budgets and rising public service demands, those who seek a definitive answer to the question of privatization's value look to cost comparisons between public and private corrections. While the evidence thus far clearly establishes the economic advantages of privatized corrections, a careful analysis of the reasons for such advantages reveals a number of complex and subtle factors which contribute to cost savings. . . .

Of course, the inquiry into the relative worth of privatized corrections does not end with a chart of purported cost savings. Indeed, those who are critical of privatized corrections often cite reluctantly admitted cost savings as direct evidence of failed service delivery. To these critics, a dollar saved is a service shorted. The record indicates otherwise. The quality of services delivered by privatized corrections has, in the main, been equal or superior to the quality of correctional services delivered by the public sector. The second part of this chapter explores the ways public sector administrators can ensure adherence to quality standards by private providers of correctional services.

Finally, the third part of this chapter addresses a proper role for privatization in our criminal justice system, a role which can complement existing prison systems without unduly threatening the continued central role of public sector corrections departments.

Cost Comparisons

Add to the list of life's great imponderables the question of how much we are paying for our prisons. Political and religious discourse appear deliberate and calm compared to the sparks raised by those who grind their axes on the stone of public/private corrections cost comparisons. The pitfalls are legion: aging public facilities compared to newly designed and constructed private facilities; security level, average length of stay, and offense category of compared incarcerated populations; required offender programming for public vs. private providers and degree of adherence to required standards; indirect and hidden public sector costs; to name only a few. . . .

Nevertheless, cost comparisons have been made that clearly indicate that privatization of correctional facilities leads to significant cost savings. In an article first published in the September/October 1989 issue of *NIJ Reports,* Charles Logan and Bill W. McGriff (1989) exhaustively examined the cost savings that Hamilton County, Tennessee realized through the privatization of its 350-bed Hamilton County Penal Farm. The authors state,

> Hamilton County found that contracting out prison management generated annual savings of at least 4 to 8 percent—and more likely in the range of 5 to 15 percent—compared to the estimated cost of direct county management. (Logan and McGriff 1989, 2)

In a report of the University of Florida at Gainesville, Center for Studies in Criminology and Law, Charles W. Thomas (1990) examined available data on forty-five privately managed correctional facilities. Of the ten facilities readily capable of cost comparison with a public counterpart, all ten evidenced cost savings ranging from 10.71 percent to 52.23 percent. . . .

Construction Costs

While design-build and construction management models of new construction have made some inroads into public sector construction, the traditional three-party "pyramid" format, with the government/owner independently contracting with an architect-engineer firm to design the facility and with a general contractor to construct the facility, still prevails in most jurisdictions. The reasons for this continuing adherence to the traditional format include statutory/regulatory impediments or prohibitions, lack of public sector expertise or experience with relatively newer models, comfort with established methods, and so on.

The traditional public sector approach to constructing a new correctional facility has within its seemingly elegant three-sided design a built-in paradigm for cost overruns and missed schedules. First, the design phase must generally be completed before the construction begins. This lineal format adds months and consequential costs to the construction process. Second, the general contractor is generally selected through competitive bidding which requires an award to the "lowest and best bid." While the low bidder is not always selected, experienced contractors know that the "bottom line" receives significantly more scrutiny than the experience and credit-worthiness of the subcontractors contributing to the total. Accordingly, subcontractors are frequently selected for the wrong reason—low cost—without regard to the level of experience or expertise they may bring to the project.

Third, the contractor may intentionally underbid the project, relying upon anticipated change-orders to regain the temporarily lost profit margin. No construction contract yet devised can eliminate all "gray areas." The traditional public sector construction model requires the architect-engineer firm to approve and certify all change orders and then pays the architect-engineer firm a percentage of the cost of any such changes. This feature alone virtually guarantees cost overruns. . . .

This system has many advantages. First, the design and construction processes are begun in coordinated tandem, saving months in the construction timetable. These time savings result in substantial cost savings based upon reduced project capitalized interest. Second, the general contractor is selected, as in turn are his subcontractors, based upon demonstrated expertise, experience and reliability. The experienced private provider is therefore confident that the general contractor's bottom line is not a bottomless well. A bond of trust in this essential relationship can develop due, in part, to the contractor's desire to become part of the private provider's established team for future projects. . . .

Inasmuch as the project is delivered to the public sector client on a "turnkey" basis, the need for public sector participation in the day-to-day construction process is greatly reduced. Construction is monitored, rather than managed by the client. Only projects completed in accordance with project specifications and standards are accepted and paid for; incentive enough to generally guarantee completion of private design-build projects on time and within budget.

Operational Costs

Many of those who readily accept and agree with the premise that private providers can construct the same correctional facility in less time and at lower cost than the public sector, nevertheless have difficulty accepting the premise that the same private provider can manage and operate the facility at less cost with equivalent quality of service. Again, an examination of the factors contributing to operating costs reveals an almost inevitable cost advantage in privatizing corrections without any sacrifice of service quality.

Operational costs may be understood as consisting of three main categories: direct, indirect, and hidden. Direct costs, in turn, include costs associated with labor, supplies and services. Labor costs are comprised of wages and benefits. Private providers can, and generally will, pay wages equivalent to their public sector counterparts. Contrary to what some critics suggest, non-competitive wages result in disproportionately higher costs due to unacceptable levels of employee attrition. This results in increased employee training costs and other losses generally attributable to organizational upheaval.

The provision of employee benefits does, in fact, differ substantially between the public sector and the private provider. Public sector benefits include a retirement benefit known as a defined benefit plan which essentially guarantees the covered employee a specified benefit level upon retirement. This is generally expressed as a percentage of highest earnings formula. Private providers tend to either eliminate direct employer contribution retirement benefits, or if provided, the benefit is of the type known as a defined contribution plan. The defined contribution plan guarantees a level of contribution to a tax-deferred employee retirement account. . . .

The savings resulting from this single benefit are enormous. Public employee retirement contributions currently hover between 20 percent to 25 percent of the employee's wages in most public sector systems. Privatization offers the public sector client the flexibility to eliminate or modify the cost of such benefits without demonstrably affecting the quality of provided service.

Private providers also save money with respect to the procurement of facility supplies. Bulk purchasing through established national accounts, together with less bureaucratic purchasing systems, reduce costs through competitive pricing and reduced administrative overhead. The procurement of facility services such as medical, food, program instructors, counselors, and so on also benefit from competitive private sector pricing and lower administrative overhead. In short, the direct costs of operating a facility will almost always be lower for the private provider than the public sector, for reasons inherent in the respective systems of each. To recognize this advantage of the private provider is not to indict the public sector employee as less capable or motivated; rather, it is a recognition that public sector protections and systemic redundancies are purchased at a cost and eliminated or modified at a savings. . . .

No discussion of private/public cost comparisons would be complete without mention of the "hidden costs" of public sector corrections. These hidden costs are endemic to the public sector system. Private providers are sometimes criticized for operating on a for-profit basis, almost as though profitability is incompatible with the public good. The private providers have shareholder investors; the public sector has taxpayer investors. Both sets of investors expect a reasonable return on their investments. It is the means by which these expectations are measured that distinguish the private and public sectors from one another. The private sector marketplace regulates cost efficiency and quality of service by rewarding success and punishing failure. The public sector is not subject to the same rigors of the marketplace, and therefore is insulated in its "investor accountability." Public "profits" are seldom, if ever, returned to the investor. Budgets are exceeded and expanded, service quality suffers, and the hidden costs skyrocket until, as now, new and creative private market solutions are demanded by taxpayer investors in search of accountability. . . .

Resource Allocation

. . . [Public] sector corrections departments often perceive privatization as a threat or potential embarrassment. Yet, properly viewed, privatization can be presented as an integral part of a comprehensive correctional system with potential benefits to taxpayers and public sector departments alike.

Nearly every level of government responsible for incarcerating arrested or sentenced individuals is experiencing dramatic overcrowding and underfunding. Incarceration rates in the United States are at an all time high and continue to spiral upward in response to social pressures to remove offenders from our streets, neighborhoods and communities. From Willie Horton presidential politics to worried local elected officials scanning the morning headlines for news of heinous crimes committed by felons released after serving as little as one-fifth of their sentence, prisons and prison costs remain the number one domestic issue facing America today.

There are hardened criminals in our society who require hard time behind bars. Maximum security prison beds are expensive to build and costly to operate. Too often, however, these maximum security beds are home to medium and minimum security inmates, inmates who require neither the level of security nor the allocation of cost attendant to the level of security built into the design of their cells.

Rather than spend scarce tax dollars on the construction and operation of more maximum security prisons, the public sector should, whenever possible, reallocate its resources to the construction and operation of lower security diversionary or pre-release detention facilities designed to concentrate on the specific security, programmatic, and rehabilitative needs of the intended incarcerated population.

When viewed as a continuum, the correctional system offers many opportunities for maximizing limited public resources. First-time offenders, nonviolent offenders, parole violators, sentenced offenders within one or two years of release, geriatric offenders, offenders suffering from mental illness, and so on, all represent "niche" populations capable of being incarcerated in facilities that cost less to build, and operate than the maximum security prisons in which they are currently housed. Privatization is perfectly suited to meet the needs of such populations. Private providers can design, finance, build and operate efficient facilities dedicated to the specific correctional needs of a specified population group. Based upon consistent average-lengths-of-stay, type of offense, security level, and so on, appropriate programmatic and rehabilitative services can be tailored to meet the needs of the incarcerated population.

By removing and allocating minimum/medium security inmates from maximum security beds, at least two important goals are met. First, the number of available maximum security beds within a system is increased at a lower cost than through the construction of new high security prisons; and second, targeted offender populations can be dealt with in a manner consistent with their level of security and classification, hopefully with better rehabilitative results. Public sector corrections officials should therefore regard privatized corrections as less threatening to their continued core function as keeper of our most hardened cases.

This is not to say that private providers cannot effectively manage and operate maximum security facilities. Obviously, nothing in the nature of maximum security prisons, in and of itself, mitigates against the use of private providers. The suggestion to concentrate on the privatization of the many "niche" offender populations is merely a recognition of deeply felt institutional resistance and acknowledgment of a cost-effective, less threatening, direction for embracing privatization as a meaningful part of a larger whole.

Conclusion

While advocates and opponents continue to make their closing arguments with respect to the advantages and disadvantages of privatized corrections, the jury has returned its verdict: privatization saves money, provides quality services and fulfills a need. Money is saved because no one has yet developed a better pencil sharpener than free market competition. Quality services can be ensured through careful attention to sound drafting of competitive procurement solicitations and resulting operating contracts. When properly utilized, privatization can become a cost-effective tool for fashioning specific correctional solutions within the context of the larger correctional system continuum.

References

Logan, Charles H. and Bill McGriff. (1989) *Comparing Costs of Public and Private Prisons: A Case Study.* NU Reports (September/October).

Thomas, Charles W. (1990) *Private Corrections Adult Secure Facility Census.* Correction Studies in Criminology and Law. Gainesville, Florida: University of Florida, May.

NO 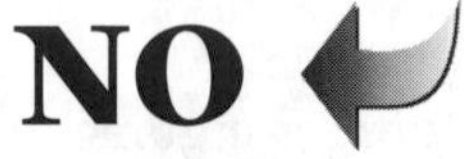

Jeff Sinden

The Problem of Prison Privatization: The U.S. Experience

The past two decades have witnessed a disturbing trend in the American criminal justice system. From immigration detention centers and work farms to county jails and state prisons, private corporations have entered the incarceration 'business' en masse. In fact, there are currently more than 100,000 people incarcerated in private prisons in the United States.[1] Privatization of the criminal justice system has been driven largely by the currently dominant ethos of a neoliberal agenda in which a wide variety of traditionally public goods have been transferred to the supposedly more efficient and less corrupt private sector. However, correctional services are fundamentally different from other goods, such as garbage collection, which have been transferred into private hands. Providing correctional services is a vastly complex and difficult task. Institutions are charged with the task not only of protecting society but also caring for the physical, psychological and emotional needs of inmates so that they may one day successfully return to the community. Unfortunately, private corrections firms have failed miserably in the task they were so eager to take on, as systematic human rights abuses have become the rule and not the exception.

Various forms of private sector involvement in the corrections industry exist in the United States, some more problematic than others. The most common and least controversial involves the private delivery of goods and services in publicly run prisons. According to a report by the US Bureau of Justice Assistance, during the past twenty years, "the practice of state and local correctional agencies contracting with private entities for medical, mental health, educational, food services, maintenance, and administrative office security functions has risen sharply."[2] For example, Sodexho Marriott Services provides food services for public correctional institutions (and college and university campuses) across North America.[3] Generally, this practice is not incompatible with a healthy respect for prisoners' rights.

. . . [H]owever, many aspects of privatization have been much more problematic. For example, the private delivery of medical services in correctional institutions, both public and private, has caused significant problems as every dollar of a fixed annual stipend not spent on health services for prisoners benefits the company's bottom line, encouraging an unacceptable incentive to skimp on critical care.[4] In fact, a 1998 independent prison health care audit found that "more than twenty inmates died as a result of negligence, indifference, under-staffing, inadequate training or overzealous cost-cutting."[5]

The use of prisoner labor by the private sector to produce goods and services has also been controversial. There has been a long tradition of exploiting prison labor in the United States and throughout the world by governments and corporations alike.[6] For example, during the 19th century, inmates at the Kingston, Ontario penitentiary in Canada "were either leased out to farmers, or their work was contracted to provide industry with cheap Iabor."[7] While this practice was largely abolished during the early twentieth century, it has returned as of late. In 1986, former US Supreme Court Justice Warren Burger called for prisons in the United States to be transformed into "factories with fences" in order to reduce the costs of incarceration.[8] Prison administrators have taken his advice to heart as many states have allowed corporations to purchase convict labor at cut-rate prices. For example, in California, prisoners who make clothing for export make between 35 cents and $1 an hour.[9] Similarly, in Ohio, prisoners are paid approximately 50 cents an hour for data entry work.[10]

The most controversial form of private sector involvement in correctional services is the management and operation of entire correctional facilities by for-profit corporations. In some cases, private firms have taken over the operation of public facilities; in others, corporations have constructed and then managed entire sites. This type of involvement has fostered situations in which a myriad of human rights abuses have occurred.

In many cases, the corporation's desire for cost-effectiveness has led to simple corner-cutting, which in turn fosters abuses. For example, low pay and a subsequently high turnover rate has led to a grossly underqualified and inexperienced staff at many institutions.[11] Far too often, this has resulted in the flagrant abuse of prisoners. In 1997, a videotape surfaced in the media that showed guards at a private facility in Texas shooting unresisting prisoners with stun guns and kicking them to the ground. One of the guards involved had recently been fired from a government-run prison for similar conduct.[12]

Rehabilitation costs have also been systematically slashed by the prison firms. In many of the institutions, opportunities for meaningful education, exercise and rehabilitation are virtually non-existent. For example, in 1995 a private jail in Texas was investigated for diverting $700,000 intended for drug treatment when it was found that inmates with dependency problems were receiving absolutely no treatment.[13] This type of flagrant neglect amounts to abuse and almost certain recidivism as job training and education programs, drug and alcohol rehabilitation services, as well as social and psychological counseling, are absolutely critical if the transition back into society is to be successful.

Neoliberalism, Increased Criminalization and the Drive to Privatize

Privately operated prisons are not a new phenomenon in the United States or in the Western world. In fact, privately run jails were in operation centuries ago in medieval England.[14] In the US, the seventeenth and eighteenth centuries witnessed the private ownership and operation of prisons in several states.[15] During this period, the Texas state penitentiary was leased out to a private business, which in turn subleased inmate labor to farms and industry. Similarly, the California state penitentiary at San Quentin was constructed and operated by private business.[16] "Conditions were so horrid" in these facilities, states John Dilulio "that some inmates were driven to suicide while others maimed themselves to get out of work or as a pathetic form of protest."[17]

Partly as a result of poor conditions and systematic abuse, the ownership and operation of private correctional facilities were transferred to the state in the early 20th century and thereafter "the operations and administrative functions in correctional facilitates were delegated to governmental agencies, authorized by statute, staffed by government employees, and funded solely by the government."[18] During the ensuing period, there was virtually no private sector involvement in correctional services. This changed rapidly in the 1980s.

The 1980s saw the return of neo-liberal, market-driven policies championed by President Reagan in the United States and Prime Minister Thatcher in the United Kingdom. In 1980, Ronald Reagan roared into the White House, riding a wave of popular anti-government sentiment and Cold War fear. His promise to get the government "off the backs" of the American people was welcomed by many in the US who were tired of the deep economic recession and growing public debt. Reagan's neoliberal mantra included deregulation, free trade, a hostility towards taxes and the labor unions and an almost maniacal desire for defense spending.[19] However, the central value of Reagan's doctrine and of neoliberalism itself is the notion of free-market competition. . . .

The American criminal justice system was seen as ripe for privatization by Reagan's supporters largely as a result of the rapid and steady increase in the cost of correctional services over the previous several years. According to the US General Accounting Office (GAO), total prison operating costs (for both federal and state) grew from about US $3.1 billion in 1980 to more than $17 billion in 1994, an increase of nearly 550 percent based on inflation-adjusted dollars.[20]

These increasing costs were a direct result of a similar rise in the prison population as the past twenty years has seen an explosion in the number of individuals incarcerated in America. The number of prisoners–with 2 million currently behind bars–has increased three fold since 1980.[21] This scale of imprisonment is unmatched throughout the world (with the possible exception of Russia); in 1998, the US incarcerated 690 residents per 100,000, compared with 123 per 100,000 in Canada and 60 per 100,000 in Sweden.[22]

How can this huge increase in the prison population be explained? Rising crime and arrests are clearly not the cause. Douglas McDonald documents that "the annual number of arrests nationwide rose only slightly during this period"[23] The increase is due mainly to sentencing policies. According to a 1996 report by the US GAO, "inmate population growth in recent years can be traced in large part to major legislation intended to get tough on criminals, particularly drug offenders. Examples of this new "get tough" policy include mandatory minimum sentences and repeat offender provisions."[24]

The War on Drugs, Mandatory Minimums, and Three Strikes Legislation

In the early 1980s, President Reagan began a concerted 'war on drugs', which he and First Lady Nancy Reagan pursued with enthusiasm throughout their tenure in the White House. Anyone involved with the drug trade—producers, traffickers, dealers and users—was to be identified, criminalized and harshly punished. To this end, Reagan significantly increased the budget of law enforcement agencies, doubling the FBI's funding and increasing the resources of the Drug Enforcement Administration.[25] Additionally, he oversaw the creation of new institutions such as the Organized Crime Drug Enforcement Task Force (OCDETF), whose mandate is to coordinate the efforts of the multitude of agencies that fight the war on drugs.[26] Federal legislators also embraced the drug war, enacting comprehensive laws to deal with convicted offenders.

In 1984 the US Congress enacted both the Comprehensive Crime Control Act and the Sentencing Reform Act. These laws eliminated federal parole and established mandatory minimums for many drug-related offences.[27] Mandatory minimum sentences impose a strict lower limit on the number of years an individual convicted of a particular crime must serve in prison. Regardless of their assessment of the appropriateness of the punishment, judges must sentence convicted defendants to the minimum prison term. . . .

The war on drugs continues unabated to this day. According to the Office of National Drug Control Policy, the US federal government will spend over $19.2 billion on the war on drugs in 2001.[28] This massive amount of funds is not without result. It is estimated that more than 1.5 million people were arrested for drug-related charges in 2001 alone.[29]

The war on drugs and its cohort, mandatory minimum sentencing, are together part of a broader trend which, during the past two decades, has seen politicians across the US clamoring to 'get tough on crime'. One of the most dramatic illustrations of this has been the so-called 'Three Strikes' legislation, first passed by the state of California in 1994. Under this law, individuals convicted of a third felony offense are automatically sentenced to twenty-five years to life in prison. Since 1994, half of the states in the US have enacted similar laws.[30]

While the three strikes law was ostensibly designed to isolate and punish the most serious, habitual offenders, far too often this has not been the case as "an ever increasing number of 'three strikes' prosecutions are for crimes as menial as petty theft of a can of beer or a few packs of batteries."[31] For example, one California man is currently serving a sentence of 25 years to life after being convicted of stealing a pair of sneakers (he was previously convicted twice for theft).[32] In 2000, another man's appeal of a three strikes sentence for the theft of $20 worth of instant coffee was denied.[33] . . .

The 'war on drugs', featuring mandatory minimums and other 'tough on crime' legislation such as the three strikes law, has been largely responsible for the explosive scale of incarceration in the US since the 1980s. The public corrections system was overwhelmed by the huge influx of inmates during this period. The system, it was argued, simply could not accommodate the sheer number of prisoners as prisons were consistently overflowing. This overcrowded system, coupled with ballooning costs and the rise of neo-liberalism, set the stage for private sector involvement in American corrections in the early 1980s. The market was quick to react, and a number of firms emerged to fill the newly found niche. These corporations promised to provide the same level of correctional services for substantially less money—predicting savings to be between 5 and 15 percent.[34]

It was argued that privately operated facilities could perform more efficiently than their public counterparts for several reasons. Firstly, public agencies are believed to have few incentives to reduce costs. In fact, many public administration experts argue that public bureaucracies have a natural tendency to seek to increase their own budgets.[35] Conversely, in the private sector, competition in the marketplace and the possibility of loss and bankruptcy require managers to minimize costs. According to privatization advocates, pressure from shareholders to provide dividends will lead to more cost-effective operations.[36]

Another major advantage of the private sector often cited by prison privatization advocates is the speed and efficiency with which the market can finance and construct new prison facilities. The rapidly increasing prison population has necessitated the construction of countless new facilities throughout the US. In fact, the annual cost of building new penitentiaries in the past decade has been approximately $7 billion per year.[37] While state governments have generally taken five to six years to construct each new facility, private companies claimed to be able to do the same job in half the time.[38]

The Re-emergence of Private Prisons in the US

Privately owned and operated prisons first re-emerged in the US in the early 1980s in response to an acute overcrowding problem in Immigration and Naturalization Service (INS) facilities in Texas and California. State governments transferred some of their detainees to institutions run by Behavioral Systems Southwest (BSS), a for-profit firm, for a daily fee of $2 per prisoner plus costs.[39] While the lifespan of BSS was relatively short, the practice of detaining undocumented people in private institutions quickly became commonplace. By 1986, 25 percent of all INS detention facilities were operated by private firms.[40]

State governments soon followed suit. By 1989 private correctional firms were operating approximately two dozen major facilitates, including three medium or maximum adult correctional institutions.[41] Today there are approximately 102 private facilities, holding more than 100,000 prisoners across the US.[42] Texas currently has the most facilities (43), followed by California (24), Florida (10), and Colorado (9).[43] In 1999, a corporate plan to take control of the entire Tennessee prison system was narrowly averted, as anti-privatization advocates succeeded in having the enacting legislation quashed in the state legislature.[44]

A few major players have emerged in the private prison industry, the oldest and largest of which is the Tennessee-based Corrections Corporation of America (CCA) established by the same entrepreneurs as was the Kentucky Fried Chicken fast-food chain. CCA currently controls approximately half of the private prison beds in the United States and has operations in the United Kingdom and until recently Australia.[45] The next largest prison corporation, controlling about a quarter of the private prison beds in the US, is Wackenhut Corrections, a subsidiary of the well-established Wackenhut private security service.[46] In addition to CCA and Wackenhut, there are about a dozen other for-profit prison firms currently operating in the US.[47]

Most private institutions are located in small towns in the southern and western United States. Politicians offer tax breaks and low, non-union wages in order to attract investment and jobs to their often poverty-stricken jurisdictions. A prison can literally 'make' a small town, providing hundreds of jobs and millions of tax dollars.[48] In order to fill the facilities, prisoners are often shipped in from out of state. Private prisons in Arizona, for example, have been stocked with Native Americans from as far away as Alaska.[49]

The private corrections industry quickly became a favorite on Wall Street. From an initial public offering price of $8 per share in 1995, the price of CCA stocks quadrupled in less than a year and hit highs of more than $100 in 1998 as investors rushed to secure their place in the booming industry.[50] Similarly, Wackenhut investors were treated to skyrocketing share prices in the mid 1990's.[51] While both have come down from their dizzying heights (CCA shares are currently at approximately $13 while Wackenhut's are at about $16), they are still seen by experts as secure investments[52] with excellent fundamentals: a recent report by the US Department of Justice estimates that annual total revenues for the industry are approximately $1 billion.[53]

Legal and Human Rights Issues

The emergence of the private prison industry in the US has fostered a tense legal debate. Many have questioned whether it is legal for federal and state governments to source out correctional services. One of the major features of the modern nation state is its monopoly on the legitimate use of violence and coercion in society. Only the state can detain, arrest and punish criminals. Many argue that "to continue to be legitimate and morally significant, the authority to govern those behind bars, to deprive citizens of their liberty, to coerce (and even kill) them, must remain in the hands of government authorities."[54] The American Bar Association has pointed out that "incarceration is an inherent function of the government and that the government should not abdicate this responsibility by turning over prison operations to private industry.[55] However, most legal scholars have suggested that private prisons are in fact legal in the US, unless specifically prohibited within a jurisdiction: "the question of whether a state can delegate the task of imprisonment has been raised occasionally, but thus far no authoritative court ruling or constitutional provision has been cited to prevent such delegation."[56] . . .

Conclusion

An exploding prison population in the US and the rising costs accompanying it, coupled with a neoliberal reliance on the market for the provision of traditionally public goods and services, provided an impetus for prison privatization in the early 1980s. State and federal legislatures were lured by the promise of substantial savings made by for-profit jailers. Interestingly, the cost savings that were promised by the industry have not materialized. In 1996, the US GAO "could not conclude whether privatization saved money."[57] Similarly, a 2001 study commissioned by the US Department of Justice concluded that "rather than the projected 20 percent savings, the average saving from privatization was only about 1 percent, and most of that was achieved though lower labor costs."[58]

The private prison industry has clearly not achieved the substantial cost savings that were billed as a major feature in the drive to privatize. Nevertheless, free-market advocates may be inclined to argue that the services provided by private facilities are more efficient and of a higher quality than that provided by government-run operations. However, as subsequent chapters will clearly show, human rights abuses in for-profit correctional institutions have been systemic.

Endnotes

1. J. Austin and G. Coventry, *Emerging Issues on Privatized Prisons* (2001): x.
2. *Id.,* 2.
3. <www.sodexhousa.com/>.
4. W. Allen and K. Bell, "Death, Neglect and the Bottom Line: Push to Cut Costs Poses Risks," St. *Louis Post-Dispatch,* 27 September 1998.
5. *Id.*
6. D. Shicor, *Punishment for Profit: Private Prisons/Public Concerns* (1995): 31.
7. J. Gandy and L. Hurl, "Private sector involvement in prison industries" (1987): 186.
8. P. Wright, "Slaves of the State," Prison Legal News, May 1994.
9. *Id.*
10. D. Cahill, "The Global Economy Behind Ohio Prison Walls," *Prison Legal News,* March 1995 / April 1996.
11. J. Greene, "Prison Privatization: Recent Developments in the United States," Presented at the International Conference on Penal Abolition, 12 May 2000.
12. S. Smalley, "For-profit prisons offer privatization lessons," *National Journal,* 3 May 1999.
13. K. Silverstein, "America's Private Gulag," *Prison Legal News,* June 1997.
14. R. Pugh, *Imprisonment in Medieval England* (1968).
15. J. Dilulio, "The duty to govern" (1990): 158.
16. J. Austin and G. Coventry, *Emerging* Issues *on Privatized Prisons, supra* note 1 at 10.
17. J. Dilulio, "The duty to govern," *supra* note 15 at 159.
18. J. Austin and G. Coventry, *Emerging Issues on Privatized Prisons, supra* note 1 at 11.
19. J. Karaagac, *Between promise and policy* (2000).
20. *Id.,* 1.
21. "US Jails Two Millionth Inmate," *Manchester Guardian Weekly,* 17 February 2000: 1.

22. R. Walmsley, *World Prison Population List* (2000).
23. D. McDonald, ed., *Private Prisons and the Public Interest* (1990): 5.
24. United States General Accounting Office, "Private and public prisons — studies comparing operational costs and / or quality of service," (1996).
25. C. Parenti (1999): 17.
26. *Id.*
27. *Id.*, 50.
28. Office of National Drug Control Policy <www.whitehousedrugpolicy.gov>.
29. Federal Bureau of Investigation, Uniform Crime Reports <www.fbi.gov/ucr/99cius.htm>.
30. Sentencing Project, *supra* note 31.
31. *Id.*
32. *Id.*
33. *Id.*
34. J. Austin and G. Coventry, *Emerging Issues on Privatized Prisons, supra* note 1 at 22.
35. Public choice theorists argue that the self-interest of public bureaucrats leads them to maximize their bureau's budget because larger budgets are a source of power, prestige and higher salaries. Please see Iain McLean, *Public Choice: An Introduction* (Oxford: Basil Blackwell, 1987).
36. C. Thomas, *Corrections in America* (1987).
37. C. Parenti, *supra* note 27 at 213.
38. J. Austin and G. Coventry, *Emerging Issues on Privatized Prisons, supra* note at 15.
39. A. Press, "The Good, the Bad and the Ugly" (1990): 25.
40. *Id.*, 25.
41. D. McDonald, *Private Prisons and the Public Interest, supra* note 25 at 1.
42. J. Austin and G. Coventry, *Emerging Issues on Privatized Prisons, supra* note 1.
43. *Id.*, ix.
44. A. Press, "The Good, the Bad and the Ugly," *supra* note 46 at 28.
45. C. Parenti, *supra* note 27 at 218.
46. *Id.*
47. *Id.*
48. *Id.*, 212.
49. *Id.*
50. S. Smalley, "For-profit prisons offer privatization lessons; *supra* note 12.
51. *Id.*
52. C. Parenti, *supra* note 27 at 219.
53. J. Austin and G. Coventry, *Emerging Issues on Privatized Prisons, supra* note 1 at ix.
54. J. Dilulio, The duty to govern," *supra* note 15 at 159.
55. D. Shicor, *Punishment for Profit, supra* note 6 at 52.
56. A. Press, "The Good, the Bad and the Ugly," *supra* note 46 at 25.
57. J. Austin and G. Coventry, *Emerging Issues on Privatized Prisons, supra* note 1 at iii.
58. *Id.*

POSTSCRIPT

Should Private "For Profit" Corporations Be Allowed to Run U.S. Prisons?

The Introduction to this edition discussed George Santayana's often-repeated observation that those who fail to learn from history are doomed to repeat it. It is interesting to consider whether this principle applies compellingly to the contemporary privatization movement in U.S. corrections.

Privatized correctional institutions are nothing new. As Jeff Sinden observes, privately owned jails operated in England centuries ago. In the United States, early prisons in California and Texas were privately owned. Corrections emerged as a governmental responsibility as a direct consequence of the problems with these privately owned facilities.

Privately held corporations have one basic responsibility: to generate a profit for their investors. Suppose you were the director of a privately owned prison or jail that houses 2,000 detainees per year. Your contract with the corporation provides that you are to receive an annual performance bonus based on the profit generated at your facility. Assume further that it costs $12 per day to feed each inmate. If you could reduce the cost to $10 per day, your institution would save $1,460,000 in the following year. Would you be tempted to do so to improve the facility's bottom line and the prospects for your annual bonus? The same principle would apply to reducing the costs of medical care, clothing, security, education, drug and alcohol treatment, and job training.

The point is that the philosophy of correctional privatization may be fundamentally incompatible with what the ultimate goal of "corrections" should be: rehabilitating a person and enabling him or her to return to the community as a productive member of society. Privatizing corrections may distract us as well from attempting to find more effective alternatives to confinement for non-violent offenders. In addition, if private industry has invested huge sums of money in corrections facilities, is it likely that unscrupulous politicians, who have been known to benefit from corporate campaign contributions, will simply continue to pass draconian measures that will generate more unwilling "clients?"

There are many additional resources that will shed additional light on the issues presented in this section. See Martha Minow, "Public and Private Partnerships: Accounting for the New Religion," *Harvard Law Review* (March 2003); Gerald G. Gaes, "Prison Privatization in Florida: Promise, Premise, and Performance," *Criminology & Public Policy* (February 2005); William D. Bales, Laura E. Beddard, Susan T. Quinn, David Ensley, and Glen P. Holley, "Recidivism of Public and Private State Prison Inmates in Florida," *Criminology & Public Policy* (February 2005); Colin Fenwick, "Private Use of Prisoners' Labor:

Paradoxes of International Human Rights Law," *Human Rights Quarterly* (February 2005); Sasha Abramsky, "Incarceration, Inc.," *The Nation* (July 19–26, 2004); Mark Wilson, "Capitalist Punishment: Prison Privatization & Human Rights," *Prison Legal News* (June 2004); Sean Nicholson-Crotty, "The Politics of Privatization: Contracting Out for Corrections Management in the United States," *Policy Studies Journal* (February 2004); Patricia Lefevere, "Mixing Prisons and the Profit Motive," *National Catholic Reporter* (September 5, 2003); Gilbert Geis, Alan Mobeley, and David Shichor, "Private Prisons, Criminological Research, and Conflict of Interest: A Case Study," *Crime and Delinquency* (vol. 45, no. 3, 1999); L. Lanza-Kaduce, K.F. Parker, and C.W. Thomas, "Comparative Recidivism Analysis of Releasees from Private and Public Prisons," *Crime and Delinquency* (vol. 45, no. 1, 1999); and Charles H. Logan, "Well Kept: Comparing Quality of Confinement in Private and Public Prisons," *Journal of Criminal Law and Criminology* (vol. 83, no. 3, 1992).

Additional resources that provide competing viewpoints on these issues include Gary W. Bowman, Simon Hakim, and Paul Seidenstat, eds., *Privatizing Correctional Institutions* (Transaction Publishers, 1993); Andrew Coyle, Allison Campbell, and Rodney Neufeld, eds., *Capitalist Punishment: Prison Privatization & Human Rights* (Clarity Press, 2003); and C. W. Thomas, M.A. Frank, and S.L. Martin, *Privatization of American Corrections: A Selected Bibliography* (University of Florida Center for Studies in Criminology and Law, 1994).

On the Internet . . .

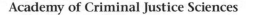

Academy of Criminal Justice Sciences

This site is an excellent resource for a wide variety of information about the U.S. justice system. It provides links to a number of resources that consider various aspects of justice system processes, including the police, the courts, punishment, and corrections.

http://www.acjs.org/

American Civil Liberties Unions (ACLU)

The ACLU is an organization dedicated to protecting Americans' constitutional freedoms.

http://www.aclu.org/

American Correctional Association (ACA)

The ACA is the oldest and largest international correctional association in the world. ACA serves all disciplines within the corrections profession and is dedicated to excellence in every aspect of the field.

http://www.aca.org/

National Criminal Justice Reference Service (NCJRS)

This very comprehensive database provides a wealth of information about justice system processes. Topics include corrections, courts, crime prevention, crime rates, drugs, the criminal justice system, juvenile justice, law enforcement, and the victims of crime. It also provides links to NCJRS-sponsored research on virtually every aspect of the criminal justice system.

http://www.ncjrs.org/

PART 5

Social Justice Issues

Newer students sometimes have a tendency to view the study of law in "black and white" terms. A number of justice system issues, however, do not lend themselves to such an easy resolution. Often, these issues have a more philosophical tone and concern matters that may have complex implications for criminal justice system policies. For example, do our current laws discriminate against members of traditionally disadvantaged groups? Or, are racial and gender stereotypes ever an effective way to develop justice system policies? The issues considered in this section have a direct impact on perceptions of the legitimacy of the U.S. justice system.

- Is the Death Penalty an Unacceptable Punishment for Juveniles?
- Should Law Enforcement Agencies Use Affirmative Action Programs to Increase the Number of Minority Police Officers?
- Are Female Police Officers as Effective as Male Officers?
- Do Crack Cocaine Laws Discriminate Against African-Americans and Other Minority Groups?

ISSUE 17

Is the Death Penalty an Unacceptable Punishment for Juveniles?

YES: Anthony Kennedy, from Opinion, *Roper v. Simmons,* U.S. Supreme Court (2005)

NO: Antonin Scalia, from Dissenting Opinion, *Roper v. Simmons,* U.S. Supreme Court (2005)

ISSUE SUMMARY

YES: Associate Justice Anthony Kennedy, writing for the Court, asserts that the death penalty is an unacceptable punishment for juveniles who commit murder because it constitutes cruel and unusual punishment in violation of the Eighth and Fourteenth Amendments.

NO: Associate Justice Antonin Scalia, dissenting in the same case, argues that there is no clear social consensus that would favor abolishing the death penalty in these cases and that in doing so the Court's majority is usurping the powers of state legislatures.

Perhaps the single most controversial issue concerning U.S. justice system policy is the use of the death penalty. A significant percentage of Americans appear to support capital punishment. A 2005 ABC News/Washington Post Poll showed that approximately 65 percent of adults surveyed nationwide favor the death penalty, while 29 percent oppose it, and 6 percent remain unsure. But, as pollsters know, how they ask the death penalty question has a great deal to do with the responses they receive. A 2005 CBS News Poll asked: "What do you think should be the penalty for persons convicted of murder: the death penalty, life in prison with no chance of parole, or a long prison sentence with a chance of parole?" Thirty-nine percent of the respondents selected the death penalty, 39 percent chose life in prison with no chance of parole, 6 percent indicated a long prison sentence with a chance of parole, and 3 percent were unsure.

What these polls show is that while death penalty proponents are quick to point to polls showing that a majority of Americans support capital punishment, the reality is that many people are somewhat ambivalent about it. When penal alternatives to capital punishment are offered, support for the death penalty is much more equivocal.

But, how do Americans feel about executing juvenile offenders? A significant majority clearly do not support it. A 2001 University of Chicago study found that while 62 percent of those surveyed supported the death penalty, only 34 percent supported it for juvenile offenders. A 2002 Gallup Poll showed similar results: While 72 percent of Americans supported the death penalty, only 26 percent supported it for juvenile offenders.

What are the arguments on both sides of the juvenile death penalty debate? One argument favoring the juvenile death penalty is that if the offender is old enough to commit a heinous crime, he or she is old enough to pay the consequences. Another related argument is based on the doctrine of "just deserts"—the offender should receive the death penalty because the act that he or she committed deserves to be punished by death. Likewise, by virtue of committing a violent murder, the juvenile offender has demonstrated that he or she is "unfit" to live and that society is justified in applying the punishment of death.

On the other side, juvenile death penalty opponents note that children have less cognitive capacity than adults. That is why our legal system assumes that children who commit crimes are less responsible for their offenses than mature adults. Accordingly, scientific research appears to indicate that the portions of the human brain that control thinking and impulsiveness are not developed until a person reaches his or her early twenties. Moreover, a strong case can be made that executing offenders for crimes committed as juveniles is simply barbaric and, according to Justice Kennedy's majority opinion in *Roper v. Simmons,* places the United States in the same category with the Democratic Republic of Congo, Iran, Nigeria, Pakistan, Saudi Arabia, and Yemen as the only countries that execute juvenile offenders.

So, should the death penalty be an unacceptable punishment for juvenile offenders? The Supreme Court justices who authored the majority and dissenting opinions in *Roper v. Simmons* have very different views of this controversy. Justice Anthony Kennedy, writing for the Court, asserted that persons should not be eligible for the death penalty if they committed their crimes as juveniles. Justice Antonin Scalia, however, believed that decisions about whether to execute juveniles should be left to state legislatures.

Based on what you know about the death penalty, should society be permitted to execute persons who committed murder as juveniles? Or, is this a barbaric practice that is inconsistent with American values and ideals? Is there a less drastic alternative method of punishing juvenile murderers? These are compelling questions.

Anthony Kennedy

Opinion

Justice Kennedy delivered the opinion of the Court.

This case requires us to address, for the second time in a decade and a half, whether it is permissible under the Eighth and Fourteenth Amendments to the Constitution of the United States to execute a juvenile offender who was older than 15 but younger than 18 when he committed a capital crime. In *Stanford* v. *Kentucky*, 492 U.S. 361, 106 L. Ed. 2d 306, 109 S. Ct. 2969 (1989), a divided Court rejected the proposition that the Constitution bars capital punishment for juvenile offenders in this age group. We reconsider the question. . . .

I

The Eighth Amendment provides: "Excessive bail shall not be required, nor excessive fines imposed, nor cruel and unusual punishments inflicted." The provision is applicable to the States through the Fourteenth Amendment. As the Court explained in *Atkins*, the Eighth Amendment guarantees individuals the right not to be subjected to excessive sanctions. The right flows from the basic "'precept of justice that punishment for crime should be graduated and proportioned to [the] offense.'" By protecting even those convicted of heinous crimes, the Eighth Amendment reaffirms the duty of the government to respect the dignity of all persons.

The prohibition against "cruel and unusual punishments," like other expansive language in the Constitution, must be interpreted according to its text, by considering history, tradition, and precedent, and with due regard for its purpose and function in the constitutional design. To implement this framework we have established the propriety and affirmed the necessity of referring to "the evolving standards of decency that mark the progress of a maturing society" to determine which punishments are so disproportionate as to be cruel and unusual.

In *Thompson* v. *Oklahoma*, a plurality of the Court determined that our standards of decency do not permit the execution of any offender under the age of 16 at the time of the crime. The plurality opinion explained that no death penalty State that had given express consideration to a minimum age for the death penalty had set the age lower than 16. The plurality also observed that "[t]he conclusion that it would offend civilized standards of

Majority Opinion, Roper v. Simmons, 543 U.S. 177 (2005). Court case citations omitted.

decency to execute a person who was less than 16 years old at the time of his or her offense is consistent with the views that have been expressed by respected professional organizations, by other nations that share our Anglo-American heritage, and by the leading members of the Western European community." The opinion further noted that juries imposed the death penalty on offenders under 16 with exceeding rarity; the last execution of an offender for a crime committed under the age of 16 had been carried out in 1948, 40 years prior.

Bringing its independent judgment to bear on the permissibility of the death penalty for a 15-year-old offender, the *Thompson* plurality stressed that "[t]he reasons why juveniles are not trusted with the privileges and responsibilities of an adult also explain why their irresponsible conduct is not as morally reprehensible as that of an adult." According to the plurality, the lesser culpability of offenders under 16 made the death penalty inappropriate as a form of retribution, while the low likelihood that offenders under 16 engaged in "the kind of cost-benefit analysis that attaches any weight to the possibility of execution" made the death penalty ineffective as a means of deterrence. With Justice O'Connor concurring in the judgment on narrower grounds, the Court set aside the death sentence that had been imposed on the 15-year-old offender.

The next year, in *Stanford* v. *Kentucky*, the Court, over a dissenting opinion joined by four Justices, referred to contemporary standards of decency in this country and concluded the Eighth and Fourteenth Amendments did not proscribe the execution of juvenile offenders over 15 but under 18. The Court noted that 22 of the 37 death penalty States permitted the death penalty for 16-year-old offenders, and, among these 37 States, 25 permitted it for 17-year-old offenders. These numbers, in the Court's view, indicated there was no national consensus "sufficient to label a particular punishment cruel and unusual." A plurality of the Court also "emphatically reject[ed]" the suggestion that the Court should bring its own judgment to bear on the acceptability of the juvenile death penalty.

The same day the Court decided *Stanford*, it held that the Eighth Amendment did not mandate a categorical exemption from the death penalty for the mentally retarded. In reaching this conclusion it stressed that only two States had enacted laws banning the imposition of the death penalty on a mentally retarded person convicted of a capital offense. According to the Court, "the two state statutes prohibiting execution of the mentally retarded, even when added to the 14 States that have rejected capital punishment completely, [did] not provide sufficient evidence at present of a national consensus."

Three Terms ago the subject was reconsidered in *Atkins*. We held that standards of decency have evolved since *Penry* and now demonstrate that the execution of the mentally retarded is cruel and unusual punishment. The Court noted objective indicia of society's standards, as expressed in legislative enactments and state practice with respect to executions of the mentally retarded. When *Atkins* was decided only a minority of States permitted the practice, and even in those States it was rare. On the basis of these indicia the Court determined that executing mentally retarded offenders "has become truly unusual, and it is fair to say that a national consensus has developed against it." . . .

Just as the *Atkins* Court reconsidered the issue decided in *Penry*, we now reconsider the issue decided in *Stanford*. The beginning point is a review of objective indicia of consensus, as expressed in particular by the enactments of legislatures that have addressed the question. This data gives us essential instruction. We then must determine, in the exercise of our own independent judgment, whether the death penalty is a disproportionate punishment for juveniles.

II

A

The evidence of national consensus against the death penalty for juveniles is similar, and in some respects parallel, to the evidence *Atkins* held sufficient to demonstrate a national consensus against the death penalty for the mentally retarded. When *Atkins* was decided, 30 States prohibited the death penalty for the mentally retarded. This number comprised 12 that had abandoned the death penalty altogether, and 18 that maintained it but excluded the mentally retarded from its reach. By a similar calculation in this case, 30 States prohibit the juvenile death penalty, comprising 12 that have rejected the death penalty altogether and 18 that maintain it but, by express provision or judicial interpretation, exclude juveniles from its reach. *Atkins* emphasized that even in the 20 States without formal prohibition, the practice of executing the mentally retarded was infrequent. Since *Penry*, only five States had executed offenders known to have an IQ under 70. In the present case, too, even in the 20 States without a formal prohibition on executing juveniles, the practice is infrequent. Since *Stanford*, six States have executed prisoners for crimes committed as juveniles. In the past 10 years, only three have done so: Oklahoma, Texas, and Virginia. In December 2003 the Governor of Kentucky decided to spare the life of Kevin Stanford, and commuted his sentence to one of life imprisonment without parole, with the declaration that "'[w]e ought not be executing people who, legally, were children.'" By this act the Governor ensured Kentucky would not add itself to the list of States that have executed juveniles within the last 10 years even by the execution of the very defendant whose death sentence the Court had upheld in *Stanford* v *Kentucky*.

There is, to be sure, at least one difference between the evidence of consensus in *Atkins* and in this case. Impressive in *Atkins* was the rate of abolition of the death penalty for the mentally retarded. Sixteen States that permitted the execution of the mentally retarded at the time of *Penry* had prohibited the practice by the time we heard *Atkins*. By contrast, the rate of change in reducing the incidence of the juvenile death penalty, or in taking specific steps to abolish it, has been slower. Five States that allowed the juvenile death penalty at the time of *Stanford* have abandoned it in the intervening 15 years—four through legislative enactments and one through judicial decision.

Though less dramatic than the change from *Penry* to *Atkins* ("telling," to borrow the word *Atkins* used to describe this difference, we still consider the change from *Stanford* to this case to be significant. As noted in *Atkins*, with respect to the States that had abandoned the death penalty for the mentally retarded since *Penry*, "[i]t is not so much the number of these States that is significant, but the consistency of the direction of change." In particular we found it significant that, in the wake of *Penry*, no State that had already prohibited the execution of the mentally retarded had passed legislation to reinstate the penalty. The number of States that have abandoned capital punishment for juvenile offenders since *Stanford* is smaller than the number of States that abandoned capital punishment for the mentally retarded after *Penry;* yet we think the same consistency of direction of change has been demonstrated. Since *Stanford*, no State that previously prohibited capital punishment for juveniles has reinstated it. This fact, coupled with the trend toward abolition of the juvenile death penalty, carries special force in light of the general popularity of anticrime legislation, and in light of the particular trend in recent years toward cracking down on juvenile crime in other respects. Any difference between this case and *Atkins* with respect to the pace of abolition is thus counterbalanced by the consistent direction of the change. . . .

As in *Atkins*, the objective indicia of consensus in this case—the rejection of the juvenile death penalty in the majority of States; the infrequency of its use even where it remains on the books; and the consistency in the trend toward abolition of the practice—provide sufficient evidence that today our society views juveniles, in the words *Atkins* used respecting the mentally retarded, as "categorically less culpable than the average criminal."

B

A majority of States have rejected the imposition of the death penalty on juvenile offenders under 18, and we now hold this is required by the Eighth Amendment.

Because the death penalty is the most severe punishment, the Eighth Amendment applies to it with special force. Capital punishment must be limited to those offenders who commit "a narrow category of the most serious crimes" and whose extreme culpability makes them "the most deserving of execution." This principle is implemented throughout the capital sentencing process. States must give narrow and precise definition to the aggravating factors that can result in a capital sentence. In any capital case a defendant has wide latitude to raise as a mitigating factor "any aspect of [his or her] character or record and any of the circumstances of the offense that the defendant proffers as a basis for a sentence less than death." There are a number of crimes that beyond question are severe in absolute terms, yet the death penalty may not be imposed for their commission. The death penalty may not be imposed on certain classes of offenders, such as juveniles under 16, the insane, and the mentally retarded, no matter how heinous the crime. These rules vindicate the underlying principle that the death penalty is reserved for a narrow category of crimes and offenders.

Three general differences between juveniles under 18 and adults demonstrate that juvenile offenders cannot with reliability be classified among the worst offenders. First, as any parent knows and as the scientific and sociological studies respondent and his *amici* cite tend to confirm, "[a] lack of maturity and an underdeveloped sense of responsibility are found in youth more often than in adults and are more understandable among the young. These qualities often result in impetuous and ill-considered actions and decisions." It has been noted that "adolescents are overrepresented statistically in virtually every category of reckless behavior." In recognition of the comparative immaturity and irresponsibility of juveniles, almost every State prohibits those under 18 years of age from voting, serving on juries, or marrying without parental consent.

The second area of difference is that juveniles are more vulnerable or susceptible to negative influences and outside pressures, including peer pressure. ("[Y]outh is more than a chronological fact. It is a time and condition of life when a person may be most susceptible to influence and to psychological damage"). This is explained in part by the prevailing circumstance that juveniles have less control, or less experience with control, over their own environment.

The third broad difference is that the character of a juvenile is not as well formed as that of an adult. The personality traits of juveniles are more transitory, less fixed.

These differences render suspect any conclusion that a juvenile falls among the worst offenders. The susceptibility of juveniles to immature and irresponsible behavior means "their irresponsible conduct is not as morally reprehensible as that of an adult." Their own vulnerability and comparative lack of control over their immediate surroundings mean juveniles have a greater claim than adults to be forgiven for failing to escape negative influences in their whole environment. The reality that juveniles still struggle to define their identity means it is less supportable to conclude that even a heinous crime committed by a juvenile is evidence of irretrievably depraved character. From a moral standpoint it would be misguided to equate the failings of a minor with those of an adult, for a greater possibility exists that a minor's character deficiencies will be reformed. Indeed, "[t]he relevance of youth as a mitigating factor derives from the fact that the signature qualities of youth are transient; as individuals mature, the impetuousness and recklessness that may dominate in younger years can subside."

Once the diminished culpability of juveniles is recognized, it is evident that the penological justifications for the death penalty apply to them with lesser force than to adults. We have held there are two distinct social purposes served by the death penalty: "'retribution and deterrence of capital crimes by prospective offenders.'" As for retribution, we remarked in *Atkins* that "[i]f the culpability of the average murderer is insufficient to justify the most extreme sanction available to the State, the lesser culpability of the mentally retarded offender surely does not merit that form of retribution." The same conclusions follow from the lesser culpability of the juvenile offender. Whether viewed as an attempt to express the community's moral outrage or as an attempt to right the balance for the wrong to the victim, the case for retribution is not as strong with a minor as with an adult. Retribution is not proportional if the law's most severe penalty is imposed on one whose culpability or blameworthiness is diminished, to a substantial degree, by reason of youth and immaturity.

As for deterrence, it is unclear whether the death penalty has a significant or even measurable deterrent effect on juveniles, as counsel for the petitioner acknowledged at oral argument. In general we leave to legislatures the assessment of the efficacy of various criminal penalty schemes. Here, however, the absence of evidence of deterrent effect is of special concern because the same characteristics that render juveniles less culpable than adults suggest as well that juveniles will be less susceptible to deterrence. In particular, as the plurality observed in *Thompson*, "[t]he likelihood that the teenage offender has made the kind of cost-benefit analysis that attaches any weight to the possibility of execution is so remote as to be virtually nonexistent." To the extent the juvenile death penalty might have residual deterrent effect, it is worth noting that the punishment of life imprisonment without the possibility of parole is itself a severe sanction, in particular for a young person.

In concluding that neither retribution nor deterrence provides adequate justification for imposing the death penalty on juvenile offenders, we cannot deny or overlook the brutal crimes too many juvenile offenders have committed. Certainly it can be argued, although we by no means concede the point, that a rare case might arise in which a juvenile offender has sufficient psychological maturity, and at the same time demonstrates sufficient depravity, to merit a sentence of death. Indeed, this possibility is the linchpin of one contention pressed by petitioner and his *amici*. They assert that even assuming the truth of the observations we have made about juveniles' diminished culpability in general, jurors nonetheless should be allowed to consider mitigating arguments related to youth on a case-by-case basis, and in some cases to impose the death penalty if justified. A central feature of death penalty sentencing is a particular assessment of the circumstances of the crime and the characteristics of the offender. The system is designed to consider both aggravating and mitigating circumstances, including youth, in every case. Given this Court's own insistence on individualized consideration, petitioner maintains that it is both arbitrary and unnecessary to adopt a categorical rule barring imposition of the death penalty on any offender under 18 years of age.

We disagree. The differences between juvenile and adult offenders are too marked and well understood to risk allowing a youthful person to receive the death penalty despite insufficient culpability. An unacceptable likelihood exists that the brutality or cold-blooded nature of any particular crime would overpower mitigating arguments based on youth as a matter of course, even where the juvenile offender's objective immaturity, vulnerability, and lack of true depravity should require a sentence less severe than death. In some cases a defendant's youth may even be counted against him. In this very case, as we noted above, the prosecutor argued Simmons' youth was aggravating rather than mitigating. While this sort of overreaching could be corrected by a particular rule to ensure that the mitigating force of youth is not overlooked, that would not address our larger concerns.

It is difficult even for expert psychologists to differentiate between the juvenile offender whose crime reflects unfortunate yet transient immaturity, and the rare juvenile offender whose crime reflects irreparable corruption. As we understand it, this difficulty underlies the rule forbidding psychiatrists from diagnosing any patient under 18 as having antisocial personality disorder, a disorder also referred to as psychopathy or sociopathy, and which is characterized by callousness, cynicism, and contempt for the feelings, rights, and suffering of others. If trained psychiatrists with the advantage of clinical testing and observation refrain, despite diagnostic expertise, from assessing any juvenile under 18 as having antisocial personality disorder, we conclude that States should refrain from asking jurors to issue a far graver condemnation—that a juvenile offender merits the death penalty. When a juvenile offender commits a heinous crime, the State can exact forfeiture of some of the most basic liberties, but the State cannot extinguish his life and his potential to attain a mature understanding of his own humanity.

Drawing the line at 18 years of age is subject, of course, to the objections always raised against categorical rules. The qualities that distinguish juveniles from adults do not disappear when an individual turns 18. By the same token, some under 18 have already attained a level of maturity some adults will never reach. For the reasons we have discussed, however, a line must be drawn. The plurality opinion in *Thompson* drew the line at 16. In the intervening years the *Thompson* plurality's conclusion that offenders under 16 may not be executed has not been challenged. The logic of *Thompson* extends to those who are under 18. The age of 18 is the point where society draws the line for many purposes between childhood and adulthood. It is, we conclude, the age at which the line for death eligibility ought to rest. . . .

III

Our determination that the death penalty is disproportionate punishment for offenders under 18 finds confirmation in the stark reality that the United States is the only country in the world that continues to give official sanction to the juvenile death penalty. This reality does not become controlling, for the task of interpreting the Eighth Amendment remains our responsibility. Yet at least from the time of the Court's decision in *Trop*, the Court has referred to the laws of other countries and to international authorities as instructive for its interpretation of the Eighth Amendment's prohibition of "cruel and unusual punishments." . . .

As respondent and a number of *amici* emphasize, Article 37 of the United Nations Convention on the Rights of the Child, which every country in the world has ratified save for the United States and Somalia, contains an express prohibition on capital punishment for crimes committed by juveniles under 18. No ratifying country has entered a reservation to the provision prohibiting the execution of juvenile offenders. Parallel prohibitions are contained in other significant international covenants.

Respondent and his *amici* have submitted, and petitioner does not contest, that only seven countries other than the United States have executed juvenile offenders since 1990: Iran, Pakistan, Saudi Arabia, Yemen, Nigeria, the Democratic Republic of Congo, and China. Since then each of these countries has either abolished capital punishment for juveniles or made public disavowal of the practice. Brief for Respondent 49-50. In sum, it is fair to say that the United States now stands alone in a world that has turned its face against the juvenile death penalty.

Though the international covenants prohibiting the juvenile death penalty are of more recent date, it is instructive to note that the United Kingdom abolished the juvenile death penalty before these covenants came into being. The United Kingdom's experience bears particular relevance here in light of the historic ties between our countries and in light of the Eighth Amendment's own origins. The Amendment was modeled on a parallel provision in the English Declaration of Rights of 1689, which provided: "[E]xcessive Bail ought not to be required nor excessive Fines imposed; nor cruel and unusual Punishments inflicted." As of now, the United Kingdom has abolished the death penalty in its entirety; but, decades before it took this step, it recognized the disproportionate nature of the juvenile death penalty; and it abolished that penalty as a separate matter.

It is proper that we acknowledge the overwhelming weight of international opinion against the juvenile death penalty, resting in large part on the understanding that the instability and emotional imbalance of young people may often be a factor in the crime. The opinion of the world community, while not controlling our outcome, does provide respected and significant confirmation for our own conclusions.

Over time, from one generation to the next, the Constitution has come to earn the high respect and even, as Madison dared to hope, the veneration of the American people. The document sets forth, and rests upon, innovative principles original to the American experience, such as federalism; a proven balance in political mechanisms through separation of powers; specific guarantees for the accused in criminal cases; and broad provisions to secure individual freedom and preserve human dignity. These doctrines and guarantees are central to the American experience and remain essential to our present-day self-definition and national identity. Not the least of the reasons we honor the Constitution, then, is because we know it to be our own. It does not lessen our fidelity to the Constitution or our pride in its origins to acknowledge that the express affirmation of certain fundamental rights by other nations and peoples simply underscores the centrality of those same rights within our own heritage of freedom. . . .

NO 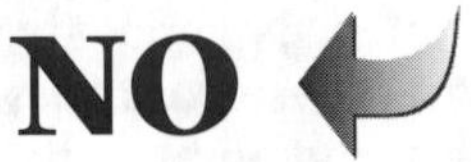

Antonin Scalia

Dissenting Opinion

Justice Scalia, with whom The Chief Justice and Justice Thomas join, dissenting.

In urging approval of a constitution that gave life-tenured judges the power to nullify laws enacted by the people's representatives, Alexander Hamilton assured the citizens of New York that there was little risk in this, since "[t]he judiciary . . . ha[s] neither FORCE nor WILL but merely judgment." But Hamilton had in mind a traditional judiciary, "bound down by strict rules and precedents which serve to define and point out their duty in every particular case that comes before them." Bound down, indeed. What a mockery today's opinion makes of Hamilton's expectation, announcing the Court's conclusion that the meaning of our Constitution has changed over the past 15 years—not, mind you, that this Court's decision 15 years ago was *wrong*, but that the Constitution *has changed*. The Court reaches this implausible result by purporting to advert, not to the original meaning of the Eighth Amendment, but to "the evolving standards of decency," of our national society. It then finds, on the flimsiest of grounds, that a national consensus which could not be perceived in our people's laws barely 15 years ago now solidly exists. Worse still, the Court says in so many words that what our people's laws say about the issue does not, in the last analysis, matter: "[I]n the end our own judgment will be brought to bear on the question of the acceptability of the death penalty under the Eighth Amendment." The Court thus proclaims itself sole arbiter of our Nation's moral standards—and in the course of discharging that awesome responsibility purports to take guidance from the views of foreign courts and legislatures. Because I do not believe that the meaning of our Eighth Amendment, any more than the meaning of other provisions of our Constitution, should be determined by the subjective views of five Members of this Court and like-minded foreigners, I dissent.

I

In determining that capital punishment of offenders who committed murder before age 18 is "cruel and unusual" under the Eighth Amendment, the Court first considers, in accordance with our modern (though in my view mistaken)

Minority Opinion, Roper v. Simmons, 543 U.S. 177 (2005). Court case citations and note omitted.

jurisprudence, whether there is a "national consensus, " that laws allowing such executions contravene our modern "standards of decency." We have held that this determination should be based on "objective indicia that reflect the public attitude toward a given sanction"—namely, "statutes passed by society's elected representatives." As in *Atkins* v. *Virginia,* the Court dutifully recites this test and claims halfheartedly that a national consensus has emerged since our decision in *Stanford,* because 18 States—or 47% of States that permit capital punishment—now have legislation prohibiting the execution of offenders under 18, and because all of four States have adopted such legislation since *Stanford.*

Words have no meaning if the views of less than 50% of death penalty States can constitute a national consensus. Our previous cases have required overwhelming opposition to a challenged practice, generally over a long period of time. In *Coker* v. *Georgia,* a plurality concluded the Eighth Amendment prohibited capital punishment for rape of an adult woman where only one jurisdiction authorized such punishment. The plurality also observed that "[a]t no time in the last 50 years ha[d] a majority of States authorized death as a punishment for rape." In *Ford* v. *Wainwright,* we held execution of the insane unconstitutional, tracing the roots of this prohibition to the common law and noting that "no State in the union permits the execution of the insane." In *Enmund* v. *Florida,* we invalidated capital punishment imposed for participation in a robbery in which an accomplice committed murder, because 78% of all death penalty States prohibited this punishment. Even there we expressed some hesitation, because the legislative judgment was "neither 'wholly unanimous among state legislatures,' . . . nor as compelling as the legislative judgments considered in *Coker.*" By contrast, agreement among 42% of death penalty States in *Stanford,* which the Court appears to believe was correctly decided at the time, was insufficient to show a national consensus.

In an attempt to keep afloat its implausible assertion of national consensus, the Court throws overboard a proposition well established in our Eighth Amendment jurisprudence. "It should be observed," the Court says, "that the *Stanford* Court should have considered those States that had abandoned the death penalty altogether as part of the consensus against the juvenile death penalty . . . ; a State's decision to bar the death penalty altogether of necessity demonstrates a judgment that the death penalty is inappropriate for all offenders, including juveniles." The insinuation that the Court's new method of counting contradicts only "the *Stanford* Court" is misleading. *None* of our cases dealing with an alleged constitutional limitation upon the death penalty has counted, as States supporting a consensus in favor of that limitation, States that have eliminated the death penalty entirely. And with good reason. Consulting States that bar the death penalty concerning the necessity of making an exception to the penalty for offenders under 18 is rather like including old-order Amishmen in a consumer-preference poll on the electric car. Of *course* they don't like it, but that sheds no light whatever on the point at issue. That 12 States favor *no* executions says something about consensus against the death penalty, but nothing—absolutely nothing—about consensus that offenders under 18 deserve special immunity from such a penalty. In repealing the death penalty, those 12 States considered *none* of the factors that the Court puts forth as determinative of the issue before us today—lower culpability of the young, inherent recklessness, lack of capacity for considered judgment, etc. What might be relevant, perhaps, is how many of those States permit 16- and 17-year-old offenders to be treated as adults with respect to noncapital offenses. (They all do; indeed, some even *require* that juveniles as young as 14 be tried as adults if they are charged with murder.) The attempt by the Court to turn its remarkable minority consensus into a faux majority by counting Amishmen is an act of nomological desperation.

Recognizing that its national-consensus argument was weak compared with our earlier cases, the *Atkins* Court found additional support in the fact that 16 States had prohibited execution of mentally retarded individuals since *Penry* v. *Lynaugh.* Indeed, the *Atkins* Court distinguished *Stanford* on that very ground, explaining that "[a]lthough we decided *Stanford* on the same day as *Penry,* apparently *only two* state legislatures have raised the threshold age for imposition of the death penalty." Now, the Court says a legislative change in four States is "significant" enough to trigger a constitutional prohibition. It is amazing to think that this subtle shift in numbers can take the issue entirely off the table for legislative debate.

I also doubt whether many of the legislators who voted to change the laws in those four States would have done so if they had known their decision would (by the pronouncement of this Court) be rendered irreversible. After all, legislative support for capital punishment, in any form, has surged and ebbed throughout our Nation's history. As Justice O'Connor has explained:

> "The history of the death penalty instructs that there is danger in inferring a settled societal consensus from statistics like those relied on in this case. In 1846, Michigan became the first State to abolish the death penalty . . . . In succeeding decades, other American States continued the trend towards abolition . . . . Later, and particularly after World War II, there ensued a steady and dramatic decline in executions . . . . In the 1950's and 1960's, more States abolished or radically restricted capital punishment, and executions ceased completely for several years beginning in 1968. . . .
>
> "In 1972, when this Court heard arguments on the constitutionality of the death penalty, such statistics might have suggested that the practice had become a relic, implicitly rejected by a new societal consensus. . . . We now know that any inference of a societal consensus rejecting the death penalty would have been mistaken. But had this Court then declared the existence of such a consensus, and outlawed capital punishment, legislatures would very likely not have been able to revive it. The mistaken premise of the decision would have been frozen into constitutional law, making it difficult to refute and even more difficult to reject."

Relying on such narrow margins is especially inappropriate in light of the fact that a number of legislatures and voters have expressly affirmed their support for capital punishment of 16- and 17-year-old offenders since *Stanford.* Though the Court is correct that no State has lowered its death penalty age, both the Missouri and Virginia Legislatures—which, at the time of *Stan-*

ford, had no minimum age requirement—expressly established 16 as the minimum. The people of Arizona and Florida have done the same by ballot initiative. Thus, even States that have not executed an under-18 offender in recent years unquestionably favor the possibility of capital punishment in some circumstances.

The Court's reliance on the infrequency of executions, for under-18 murderers, credits an argument that this Court considered and explicitly rejected in *Stanford.* That infrequency is explained, we accurately said, both by "the undisputed fact that a far smaller percentage of capital crimes are committed by persons under 18 than over 18," and by the fact that juries are required at sentencing to consider the offender's youth as a mitigating factor. Thus, "it is not only possible, but overwhelmingly probable, that the very considerations which induce [respondent] and [his] supporters to believe that death should *never* be imposed on offenders under 18 cause prosecutors and juries to believe that it should *rarely* be imposed."

It is, furthermore, unclear that executions of the relevant age group have decreased since we decided *Stanford.* Between 1990 and 2003, 123 of 3,599 death sentences, or 3.4%, were given to individuals who committed crimes before reaching age 18. By contrast, only 2.1% of those sentenced to death between 1982 and 1988 committed the crimes when they were under 18. As for actual executions of under-18 offenders, they constituted 2.4% of the total executions since 1973. In *Stanford,* we noted that only 2% of the executions between 1642 and 1986 were of under-18 offenders and found that that lower number did not demonstrate a national consensus against the penalty. Thus, the numbers of under-18 offenders subjected to the death penalty, though low compared with adults, have either held steady or slightly increased since *Stanford.* These statistics in no way support the action the Court takes today.

II

Of course, the real force driving today's decision is not the actions of four state legislatures, but the Court's "own judgment" that murderers younger than 18 can never be as morally culpable as older counterparts. The Court claims that this usurpation of the role of moral arbiter is simply a "retur[n] to the rul[e] established in decisions predating *Stanford.*" That supposed rule—which is reflected solely in dicta and never once in a *holding* that purports to supplant the consensus of the American people with the Justices' views—was repudiated in *Stanford* for the very good reason that it has no foundation in law or logic. If the Eighth Amendment set forth an ordinary rule of law, it would indeed be the role of this Court to say what the law is. But the Court having pronounced that the Eighth Amendment is an ever-changing reflection of "the evolving standards of decency" of our society, it makes no sense for the Justices then to *prescribe* those standards rather than discern them from the practices of our people. On the evolving-standards hypothesis, the only legitimate function of this Court is to identify a moral consensus of the American people. By what conceivable warrant can nine lawyers presume to be the authoritative conscience of the Nation?

The reason for insistence on legislative primacy is obvious and fundamental: "'[I]n a democratic society legislatures, not courts, are constituted to respond to the will and consequently the moral values of the people.'" For a similar reason we have, in our determination of society's moral standards, consulted the practices of sentencing juries: Juries "'maintain a link between contemporary community values and the penal system'" that this Court cannot claim for itself.

Today's opinion provides a perfect example of why judges are ill equipped to make the type of legislative judgments the Court insists on making here. To support its opinion that States should be prohibited from imposing the death penalty on anyone who committed murder before age 18, the Court looks to scientific and sociological studies, picking and choosing those that support its position. It never explains why those particular studies are methodologically sound; none was ever entered into evidence or tested in an adversarial proceeding. As The Chief Justice has explained:

> "[M]ethodological and other errors can affect the reliability and validity of estimates about the opinions and attitudes of a population derived from various sampling techniques. Everything from variations in the survey methodology, such as the choice of the target population, the sampling design used, the questions asked, and the statistical analyses used to interpret the data can skew the results."

In other words, all the Court has done today, to borrow from another context, is to look over the heads of the crowd and pick out its friends.

We need not look far to find studies contradicting the Court's conclusions. As petitioner points out, the American Psychological Association (APA), which claims in this case that scientific evidence shows persons under 18 lack the ability to take moral responsibility for their decisions, has previously taken precisely the opposite position before this very Court. In its brief in *Hodgson* v. *Minnesota,* the APA found a "rich body of research" showing that juveniles are mature enough to decide whether to obtain an abortion without parental involvement. The APA brief, citing psychology treatises and studies too numerous to list here, asserted: "[B]y middle adolescence (age 14-15) young people develop abilities similar to adults in reasoning about moral dilemmas, understanding social rules and laws, [and] reasoning about interpersonal relationships and interpersonal problems." Given the nuances of scientific methodology and conflicting views, courts—which can only consider the limited evidence on the record before them—are ill equipped to determine which view of science is the right one. Legislatures "are better qualified to weigh and 'evaluate the results of statistical studies in terms of their own local conditions and with a flexibility of approach that is not available to the courts.'"

Even putting aside questions of methodology, the studies cited by the Court offer scant support for a categorical prohibition of the death penalty for murderers under 18. At most, these studies conclude that, *on average,* or *in most cases*, persons under 18 are unable to take moral responsibility for their actions. Not one of the cited studies opines that all individuals under 18 are unable to appreciate the nature of their crimes.

Moreover, the cited studies describe only adolescents who engage in risky or antisocial behavior, as many young people do. Murder, however, is more than just risky or antisocial behavior. It is entirely consistent to believe that young people often act impetuously and lack judgment, but, at the same time, to believe that those who commit premeditated murder are—at least sometimes—just as culpable as adults. Christopher Simmons, who was only seven months shy of his 18th birthday when he murdered Shirley Crook, described to his friends *beforehand*—"[i]n chilling, callous terms," as the Court puts it—the murder he planned to commit. He then broke into the home of an innocent woman, bound her with duct tape and electrical wire, and threw her off a bridge alive and conscious. In their *amici* brief, the States of Alabama, Delaware, Oklahoma, Texas, Utah, and Virginia offer additional examples of murders committed by individuals under 18 that involve truly monstrous acts. In Alabama, two 17-year-olds, one 16-year-old, and one 19-year-old picked up a female hitchhiker, threw bottles at her, and kicked and stomped her for approximately 30 minutes until she died. They then sexually assaulted her lifeless body and, when they were finished, threw her body off a cliff. They later returned to the crime scene to mutilate her corpse. Other examples in the brief are equally shocking. Though these cases are assuredly the exception rather than the rule, the studies the Court cites in no way justify a constitutional imperative that prevents legislatures and juries from treating exceptional cases in an exceptional way—by determining that some murders are not just the acts of happy-go-lucky teenagers, but heinous crimes deserving of death.

That "almost every State prohibits those under 18 years of age from voting, serving on juries, or marrying without parental consent," is patently irrelevant—and is yet another resurrection of an argument that this Court gave a decent burial in *Stanford*. (What kind of Equal Justice under Law is it that—without so much as a "Sorry about that"—gives as the basis for sparing one person from execution arguments *explicitly rejected* in refusing to spare another?) As we explained in *Stanford*, it is "absurd to think that one must be mature enough to drive carefully, to drink responsibly, or to vote intelligently, in order to be mature enough to understand that murdering another human being is profoundly wrong, and to conform one's conduct to that most minimal of all civilized standards." Serving on a jury or entering into marriage also involve decisions far more sophisticated than the simple decision not to take another's life.

Moreover, the age statutes the Court lists "set the appropriate ages for the operation of a system that makes its determinations in gross, and that does not conduct individualized maturity tests." The criminal justice system, by contrast, provides for individualized consideration of each defendant. In capital cases, this Court requires the sentencer to make an individualized determination, which includes weighing aggravating factors and mitigating factors, such as youth. In other contexts where individualized consideration is provided, we have recognized that at least some minors will be mature enough to make difficult decisions that involve moral considerations. For instance, we have struck down abortion statutes that do not allow minors deemed mature by courts to bypass parental notification provisions. It is hard to see why this context should be any different. Whether to obtain an abortion is surely a much more complex decision for a young person than whether to kill an innocent person in cold blood.

The Court concludes, however, that juries cannot be trusted with the delicate task of weighing a defendant's youth along with the other mitigating and aggravating factors of his crime. This startling conclusion undermines the very foundations of our capital sentencing system, which entrusts juries with "mak[ing] the difficult and uniquely human judgments that defy codification and that 'buil[d] discretion, equity, and flexibility into a legal system.'" The Court says, that juries will be unable to appreciate the significance of a defendant's youth when faced with details of a brutal crime. This assertion is based on no evidence; to the contrary, the Court itself acknowledges that the execution of under-18 offenders is "infrequent" even in the States "without a formal prohibition on executing juveniles," suggesting that juries take seriously their responsibility to weigh youth as a mitigating factor.

Nor does the Court suggest a stopping point for its reasoning. If juries cannot make appropriate determinations in cases involving murderers under 18, in what other kinds of cases will the Court find jurors deficient? We have already held that no jury may consider whether a mentally deficient defendant can receive the death penalty, irrespective of his crime. Why not take other mitigating factors, such as considerations of childhood abuse or poverty, away from juries as well? Surely jurors "overpower[ed]" by "the brutality or cold-blooded nature" of a crime, could not adequately weigh these mitigating factors either.

The Court's contention that the goals of retribution and deterrence are not served by executing murderers under 18 is also transparently false. The argument that "[r]etribution is not proportional if the law's most severe penalty is imposed on one whose culpability or blameworthiness is diminished," is simply an extension of the earlier, false generalization that youth *always* defeats culpability. The Court claims that "juveniles will be less susceptible to deterrence," because "'[t]he likelihood that the teenage offender has made the kind of cost-benefit analysis that attaches any weight to the possibility of execution is so remote as to be virtually nonexistent.'" The Court unsurprisingly finds no support for this astounding proposition, save its own case law. The facts of this very case show the proposition to be false. Before committing the crime, Simmons encouraged his friends to join him by assuring them that they could "get away with it" because they were minors. This fact may have influenced the jury's decision to impose capital punishment despite Simmons' age. Because the Court refuses to entertain the possibility that its own unsubstantiated generalization about juveniles could be wrong, it ignores this evidence entirely.

III

Though the views of our own citizens are essentially irrelevant to the Court's decision today, the views of other countries and the so-called international community take center stage.

The Court begins by noting that "Article 37 of the United Nations Convention on the Rights of the Child, which every country in the world has ratified *save for the United States* and Somalia, contains an express prohibition on capital punishment for crimes committed by juveniles under 18." . . .

Unless the Court has added to its arsenal the power to join and ratify treaties on behalf of the United States, I cannot see how this evidence favors, rather than refutes, its position. That the Senate and the President—those actors our Constitution empowers to enter into treaties, see Art. II, § 2—have declined to join and ratify treaties prohibiting execution of under-18 offenders can only suggest that *our country* has either not reached a national consensus on the question, or has reached a consensus contrary to what the Court announces. That the reservation to the ICCPR was made in 1992 does not suggest otherwise, since the reservation still remains in place today. It is also worth noting that, in addition to barring the execution of under-18 offenders, the United Nations Convention on the Rights of the Child prohibits punishing them with life in prison without the possibility of release. If we are truly going to get in line with the international community, then the Court's reassurance that the death penalty is really not needed, since "the punishment of life imprisonment without the possibility of parole is itself a severe sanction," gives little comfort.

It is interesting that whereas the Court is not content to accept what the States of our Federal Union *say*, but insists on inquiring into what they *do* (specifically, whether they in fact *apply* the juvenile death penalty that their laws allow), the Court is quite willing to believe that every foreign nation—of whatever tyrannical political makeup and with however subservient or incompetent a court system—in fact *adheres* to a rule of no death penalty for offenders under 18. Nor does the Court inquire into how many of the countries that have the death penalty, but have forsworn (on paper at least) imposing that penalty on offenders under 18, have what no State of this country can constitutionally have: a *mandatory* death penalty for certain crimes, with no possibility of mitigation by the sentencing authority, for youth or any other reason. I suspect it is most of them. To forbid the death penalty for juveniles under such a system may be a good idea, but it says nothing about our system, in which the sentencing authority, typically a jury, always can, and almost always does, withhold the death penalty from an under-18 offender except, after considering all the circumstances, in the rare cases where it is warranted. The foreign authorities, in other words, do not even speak to the issue before us here.

More fundamentally, however, the basic premise of the Court's argument—that American law should conform to the laws of the rest of the world—ought to be rejected out of hand. In fact the Court itself does not believe it. In many significant respects the laws of most other countries differ from our law—including not only such explicit provisions of our Constitution as the right to jury trial and grand jury indictment, but even many interpretations of the Constitution prescribed by this Court itself. . . .

The Court has been oblivious to the views of other countries when deciding how to interpret our Constitution's requirement that "Congress shall make no law respecting an establishment of religion. . . ." Most other countries—including those committed to religious neutrality—do not insist on the degree of separation between church and state that this Court requires. . . .

And let us not forget the Court's abortion jurisprudence, which makes us one of only six countries that allow abortion on demand until the point of viability. . . .

The Court's special reliance on the laws of the United Kingdom is perhaps the most indefensible part of its opinion. It is of course true that we share a common history with the United Kingdom, and that we often consult English sources when asked to discern the meaning of a constitutional text written against the backdrop of 18th-century English law and legal thought. If we applied that approach today, our task would be an easy one. . . . It is beyond comprehension why we should look, for that purpose, to a country that has developed, in the centuries since the Revolutionary War—and with increasing speed since the United Kingdom's recent submission to the jurisprudence of European courts dominated by continental jurists—a legal, political, and social culture quite different from our own. If we took the Court's directive seriously, we would also consider relaxing our double jeopardy prohibition, since the British Law Commission recently published a report that would significantly extend the rights of the prosecution to appeal cases where an acquittal was the result of a judge's ruling that was legally incorrect. . . .

The Court should either profess its willingness to reconsider all these matters in light of the views of foreigners, or else it should cease putting forth foreigners' views as part of the *reasoned basis* of its decisions. To invoke alien law when it agrees with one's own thinking, and ignore it otherwise, is not reasoned decisionmaking, but sophistry.

The Court responds that "[i]t does not lessen our fidelity to the Constitution or our pride in its origins to acknowledge that the express affirmation of certain fundamental rights by other nations and peoples simply underscores the centrality of those same rights within our own heritage of freedom." To begin with, I do not believe that approval by "other nations and peoples" should buttress our commitment to American principles any more than (what should logically follow) disapproval by "other nations and peoples" should weaken that commitment. More importantly, however, the Court's statement flatly misdescribes what is going on here. Foreign sources are cited today, *not* to underscore our "fidelity" to the Constitution, our "pride in its origins," and "our own [American] heritage." To the contrary, they are cited *to set aside* the centuries-old American practice—a practice still engaged in by a large majority of the relevant States—of letting a jury of 12 citizens decide whether, in the particular case, youth should be the basis for withholding the death penalty. What these foreign sources "affirm," rather than repudiate, is the Justices' own notion of how the world ought to be, and their diktat that it shall be so henceforth in America. The Court's parting attempt to downplay the significance of its extensive discussion of foreign law is unconvincing. "Acknowledgment" of foreign approval has no place in the legal opinion of this Court *unless it is part of the basis for the Court's judgment*—which is surely what it parades as today.

IV

To add insult to injury, the Court affirms the Missouri Supreme Court without even admonishing that court for its flagrant disregard of our precedent in *Stanford.* Until today, we have always held that "it is this Court's prerogative alone to overrule one of its precedents." That has been true even where "'changes in judicial doctrine' ha[ve] significantly undermined" our prior holding, and even where our prior holding "appears to rest on reasons rejected in some other line of decisions." Today, however, the Court silently approves a state-court decision that blatantly rejected controlling precedent.

One must admit that the Missouri Supreme Court's action, and this Court's indulgent reaction, are, in a way, understandable. In a system based upon constitutional and statutory text democratically adopted, the concept of "law" ordinarily signifies that particular words have a fixed meaning. Such law does not change, and this Court's pronouncement of it therefore remains authoritative until (confessing our prior error) we overrule. The Court has purported to make of the Eighth Amendment, however, a mirror of the passing and changing sentiment of American society regarding penology. The lower courts can look into that mirror as well as we can; and what we saw 15 years ago bears no necessary relationship to what they see today. Since they are not looking at the same text, but at a different scene, why should our earlier decision control their judgment?

However sound philosophically, this is no way to run a legal system. We must disregard the new reality that, to the extent our Eighth Amendment decisions constitute something more than a show of hands on the current Justices' current personal views about penology, they purport to be nothing more than a snapshot of American public opinion at a particular point in time (with the timeframes now shortened to a mere 15 years). We must treat these decisions just as though they represented *real* law, *real* prescriptions democratically adopted by the American people, as conclusively (rather than sequentially) construed by this Court. Allowing lower courts to reinterpret the Eighth Amendment whenever they decide enough time has passed for a new snapshot leaves this Court's decisions without any force—especially since the "evolution" of our Eighth Amendment is no longer determined by objective criteria. To allow lower courts to behave as we do, "updating" the Eighth Amendment as needed, destroys stability and makes our case law an unreliable basis for the designing of laws by citizens and their representatives, and for action by public officials. The result will be to crown arbitrariness with chaos.

POSTSCRIPT

Is the Death Penalty an Unacceptable Punishment for Juveniles?

The opinion poll results we examined in the Introduction to this issue provided some very interesting information. First, support for the death penalty when the alternative of sentencing someone to a life term in prison without the possibility of parole was provided was equivocal—as many Americans supported the imprisonment option as favored the death penalty. Second, only a small number of Americans support using the death penalty for criminals who committed their crimes as juveniles. This would seem to support Justice Kennedy's position that the "evolving standards of decency that mark the progress of a maturing society," would counsel against imposition of the death penalty for juveniles.

Moreover, the United States was the only Western nation that still permitted individuals to be executed for the crimes they committed as juveniles. Although this factor did not appear to be the sole motivation for the Court's decision in *Roper v. Simmons*, that fact did seem to influence some of the justices. Justice Kennedy noted this fact:

> Article 37 of the United Nations Convention on the Rights of the Child, which every country in the world has ratified save for the United States and Somalia, contains an express prohibition on capital punishment for crimes committed by juveniles under 18. . . . [O]nly seven countries other than the United States have executed juvenile offenders since 1990: Iran, Pakistan, Saudi Arabia, Yemen, Nigeria, the Democratic Republic of Congo, and China. Since then each of these countries has either abolished capital punishment for juveniles or made public disavowal of the practice.

Do you think that the justice system policies of other nations should influence penal practices in the United States? If the United States is out of step with the world community, should we not search consciences to determine if we have made a serious mistake?

Another significant issue surrounding the use of capital punishment that has become prominent in recent years is the fact that our justice system has made mistakes in the past. A 2002 study conducted by Columbia Law School Professor James Liebman concluded that "aggressive death sentencing is a magnet for serious error." Liebman's study, which tried to answer the question of why so many mistakes happen in death penalty cases, found that 68 percent of all death verdicts reviewed from 1973 to 1995 were reversed by courts. Of these reversals, 82 percent resulted in less severe sentences, and 9 percent of these individuals were found not guilty. Moreover, Liebman observes that since the death penalty was reinstituted in the United States in 1973, 99 death row inmates have been found innocent and released.

These data indicate that our justice system makes mistakes. If a convicted offender is sentenced to prison and it later becomes clear that he or she did not commit the crime, society can release the individual and provide appropriate compensation. If we have executed the accused, however, there is no way to rectify the mistake. The finality of the death penalty thus makes it unlike any other type of sentence in our justice system. This fact may make this punishment even more questionable in cases involving juvenile offenders.

There are many additional resources that shed light on the issues considered in this section. See Mary Ann Mason, "The U.S. and the International Children's Rights Crusade: Leader or Laggard," *Journal of Social History* (vol. 38, no. 4, 2005); Robert H. Bork, "Travesty Time, Again," *National Review* (vol. 57, no. 5, 2005); Kenneth Anderson, "Foreign Law and the U.S. Constitution," *Policy Review* (vol. 131, 2005); Jeffrey Fagan and Valerie West, "The Decline of the Juvenile Death Penalty: Scientific Evidence of Evolving Norms," *Journal of Criminal Law & Criminology* (vol. 95, no. 2, 2005); James Liebman, Andrew Gelman, Alexander Kiss, and Valerie West, "A Broken System: The Persistent Pattern of Reversals of Death Penalty Cases," *Journal of Empirical Legal Studies* (vol. 1, no. 209, 2004); James D. Unnever and Francis Cullen, "Executing the Innocent and Support for Capital Punishment: Implications for Public Policy," *Criminology & Public Policy* (vol. 4, no. 1, 2005); Lucy C. Ferguson, "The Implications of Developmental Cognitive Research on 'Evolving Standards of Decency' and the Imposition of the Death Penalty on Juveniles," *American University Law Review* (vol. 54, no. 2, 2004); Donna M. Bishop, "Injustice and Irrationality in Contemporary Youth Policy," *Criminology & Public Policy* (vol. 3, no. 4, 2004); Scott Vollum, Dennis R. Longmire, and Jacqueline Buffinton-Vollum, "Confidence in the Death Penalty and Support for Its Use: Exploring the Value-Expressive Dimension of Death Penalty Attitudes," *Justice Quarterly* (vol. 21, no. 3, 2004); and Michael E. Antonio, Benjamin D. Fleury-Steiner, Valerie P. Hans, and William J. Bowers, "Capital Jurors as the Litmus Test of Community Conscience for the Juvenile Death Penalty," *Judicature* (vol. 87, no. 6, 2004).

ISSUE 18

Should Law Enforcement Agencies Use Affirmative Action Programs to Increase the Number of Minority Police Officers?

YES: Brad Bennett, from "Beyond Affirmative Action, Police Response to a Changing Society," *Journal of California Law Enforcement* (vol. 33, no. 2, 1999)

NO: Jan Golab and Erica Walter, from "How Racial P.C. Corrupted the LAPD," *The American Enterprise* (June 2005)

ISSUE SUMMARY

YES: Dr. Brad Bennett, chief of police and fire for South Lake Tahoe, California, asserts that although there has been a recent backlash against affirmative action programs, the acceptance of diversity is essential to modern police organizations.

NO: Authors Jan Golab and Erica Walter argue that the Los Angeles Police Department (LAPD) was once regarded as the world's best police department due to its stringent screening of police recruits; however, in an effort to appease racial activists and meet federal court decrees, strict screening and testing measures were dismantled. Golab and Walter believe that this has resulted in the wholesale corruption of this once fine police department.

Affirmative action programs are a contentious matter. Proponents of affirmative action assert that these programs have resulted in more equal opportunities and greater racial diversity in the United States. Opponents of these programs believe that U.S. laws should be colorblind and that you cannot redress the wrongs caused by racism by using social programs that discriminate. Moreover, opponents of affirmative action programs contend that the Fourteenth Amendment to the U.S. Constitution means exactly what it says: "No State shall make or enforce any law which shall . . . deny to any person the equal protection of the laws."

In general, the U.S. Supreme Court has held that laws passed by legislatures that grant a benefit based on race receive "strict scrutiny" and are presumed to be invalid. To survive this standard, a state would have to show a "compelling" interest supporting its law, and virtually no other way to accomplish its objective. For example, suppose state X passed a law that limited enrollment in its state universities to "Caucasians." State X contends that the purpose for the law is to preserve scarce state resources and conserve limited space in its university system. A reviewing court will consider first if there is a "compelling state interest" present in the case. Assume for the sake of argument that saving state resources and conserving limited space in the state university system are "compelling" interests. The reviewing court would next consider whether there were better, "race neutral" ways to accomplish these objectives. One that quickly comes to mind is a policy of raising admissions standards for everyone. Because there is a more race-neutral solution to the state's problem, its law will fail strict scrutiny and will be held unconstitutional by the reviewing court.

In recent cases, the U.S. Supreme Court appears to have taken a somewhat ambivalent approach to the issue of affirmative action programs. In *Grutter v. Bollinger*, 539 U.S. 306 (2003), the Supreme Court upheld an affirmative action program at the University of Michigan law school by a 5-4 vote. The Court held that the Michigan program did not violate the Equal Protection Clause or the Civil Rights Act of 1964 because it used a multifactor system, which required an individualized assessment of each applicant to make an admissions decision. Justice Sandra Day O'Connor also stated that in 25 years, "the use of racial preferences" will no longer be necessary.

In a companion case, *Gratz v. Bollinger*, 539 U.S. 244 (2003), the Court struck down the University of Michigan's affirmative action program for undergraduate admissions in the College of Literature, Science, and the Arts. That program had automatically awarded 20 points on a 100-point admissions scale to every underrepresented minority applicant. The Court concluded that this type of program, in effect, used a racial quota that violated the Equal Protection Clause and Title VI of the Civil Rights Act of 1964.

Dr. Brad Bennett, chief of police and fire for South Lake Tahoe, California, asserts that although there has been a recent backlash against affirmative action programs, the acceptance of diversity is essential to modern police organizations. Authors Jan Golab and Erica Walter assert, however, that the Los Angeles Police Department (LAPD) was once regarded as the world's best police department due to its stringent screening of police recruits; in an effort to appease racial activists and meet federal court decrees, strict screening and testing measures were dismantled. Golab and Walter believe that this has resulted in the wholesale corruption of this once fine police department.

What do you think about the use of affirmative action programs in law enforcement agencies? Do such programs improve an agency's service to the community by enhancing the racial diversity of the workforce? Or, does the adoption of affirmative action programs result in a less-qualified workforce that is more prone to corruption? The writers of the articles in this section have very different perspectives on these issues.

Brad Bennett

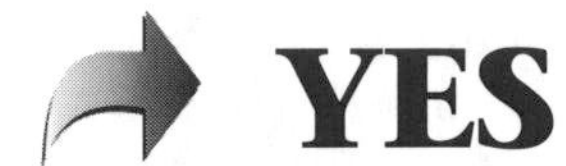

Beyond Affirmative Action, Police Response to a Changing Society

Affirmative Action, particularly when bound to preferential hiring, quotas and set-asides, is losing its thrust in the United States. The American people have become more vocal and aggressive in their opposition to Affirmative Action. Through popular opinion, as expressed in the Proposition 209 vote in California outlawing preferential hiring practices and judicial influence as expressed in recent court decisions, Affirmative Action as a policy is declining in popularity.

Have civil rights legislation and employment discrimination litigation reduced discrimination and opened doors for minorities and women? The answer would appear to be a resounding yes. Most people would agree that both Equal Employment Opportunity, designed to protect individual rights, and Affirmative Action, oriented toward the value of social equity, have had a positive impact in providing opportunity for qualified minorities and women. It does seem clear that the kinds of discrimination that came before the courts in the 1970s has decreased and the value of social equity has challenged organizations to demonstrate that personnel practices once assumed to be job related were in fact job related, a benefit to all employees, regardless of race or gender. Yet most Americans are opposed to preferential employment rules in general because they are perceived as a form of discrimination themselves.

While there has been a backlash against Affirmative Action, the acceptance of diversity should continue to be an important part of the value structure of all Americans. Despite the move away from preferential treatment, the diversification of society and the work force will continue to profoundly impact organizations, particularly police organizations.

From Affirmative Action to Work Force Diversity

The population of the United States continues to grow diverse. The work force is made up increasingly of people of color, women and immigrants. To be responsive to the changing demographics, both in their communities and in their potential work forces, police administrators need to change their organizations. This change can best occur by incorporating a philosophy of "work force diversity." Workforce diversity describes the range of employee charac-

From *Journal of California Law Enforcement*, vol. 33, issue 2, 1999, pp. 10-15. References omitted.

teristics that are increasingly present in the work force of the United States. Continued social and political changes are now leading to the welcoming of diversity as a desirable political and social condition in many forward-thinking organizations. These organizations recognize the advantage of work force diversity. It is probably best to view Affirmative Action simply as a political stage that America needed to go through on its way to accepting increasing cultural and therefore work force diversity.

Work force diversity differs from Affirmative Action in many ways. Affirmative Action programs tend to be viewed negatively by police managers and officers because they are often based on a negative premise (What changes must we make to demonstrate a good-faith effort to achieve a representative work force and thereby avoid sanctions by Affirmative Action compliance agencies or the courts?). In contrast, successful work force diversification programs are generally viewed as positive by police managers and officers because they are based on a different question (What changes can we make in our organization's mission, culture, policies and programs in order to become more effective and responsive to our communities?). This changes the organizational condition from being tolerant of Affirmative Action to embracing and seeking out work force diversity.

Strategies to Diversify the Work Force

Many police organizations have launched a variety of diversity programs to prepare for a changing and diverse society. Numerous attempts at diversification have been superficial and few have been successful. Some police departments have made serious commitments to workplace diversification and have been very successful in diversifying their organizations in a positive manner that makes them more responsive to their communities. The following is an examination of three police agencies of varying sizes that have embraced work force diversity.

San Jose Police Department

Matching the composition of the department with the diverse composition of the city has been the goal of the San Jose Police Department for many years. In recent years the impetus has been on being proactive rather than reactive to recruiting and promoting officers from diverse ethnic backgrounds.

When this philosophy was first developed it met with some resistance. The police officers' association was concerned about the potential lowering of employment standards, an apprehension with quotas, and a general fear of change. The leadership of the department worked with the police association to gain acceptance to the change in philosophy and practice that was occurring in the community and the benefits of changing the department to be more responsive to the community. Task forces, made up of a cross section of officers and ranks, were set up internally to provide an arena for communication. The administration met with community members to work closely and openly in being responsive to the community. The administration then met with the task forces to discuss concerns related to the changing hiring practices.

Within the department, culturally diverse officers were establishing associations to represent their needs and interests. The police leadership's response was to value these alliances and to work closely with them in meeting common goals.

The San Jose Police Department has developed a wide variety of policies and programs to insure the continued emphasis on their philosophy of "reflecting the community." Work force diversity is an intrinsic part of the department's culture and is emphasized in their recruiting, retention and promotion policies. While there were initial fears that employment standards would be lowered to meet the goals of a diversified work force, no evidence shows this occurred. San Jose is one of the few local level police agencies that requires two years of college for its police officer candidates, a requirement since the 1960s. Employment criteria that were changed generally reflected antiquated or illegal standards for particular hiring practices.

The personnel and recruiting unit of the department is staffed by officers from diverse ethnic backgrounds. Reflecting the community is a high priority for this unit in recruiting efforts. Persons identified as potential candidates are provided assistance and training in overcoming obstacles, cultural or otherwise, in preparing for departmental testing procedures.

The various ethnic associations within the department are also involved in the recruiting of culturally diverse officers. These associations offer a variety of support, including mentor programs, for ethnic officers during the early phases of their careers. These mentor programs are encouraged and supported by the leadership of the department. The ethnic associations are very involved with the community and provide role models for youth in the various communities.

The department has also developed a program that can potentially involve all officers in the recruiting of culturally diverse work force. This program rewards officers who recruit culturally diverse candidates with paid leave of up to 40 hours if their recruits successfully become police officers. This program reinforces the "reflect the community" philosophy of the department.

The department encourages the valuing of diversity among recruits and regular officers through a program that gives incentives to officers who speak any of eight certified foreign languages. Applicants with certifiable ability in these languages are brought to the top of an eligibility list to be considered for hiring. Regular officers certified in speaking any of these languages receive incentive pay.

Promotional procedures have been developed throughout the department that recognize the value of a diverse work force. Major strides have been made in the promotion of officers from a wide variety of culturally diverse backgrounds. The department also continually reviews the makeup of special units to insure that the units are representative of the community and the department.

Garden Grove Police Department

The Garden Grove Police Department has developed a variety of policies and programs in an effort to become more representative and responsive to their

changing and diverse community. The department obtained grants that allowed them to hire community service officers (nonsworn) to work in the department's Community Relations Unit. These positions were specifically aimed at opening up communications with various Asian populations within the city.

More recently the police and the city personnel departments have broadened their efforts and have become more proactive in recruiting culturally diverse employees. A City Cultural Cohesiveness committee works with city personnel and the police department and makes recommendations related to recruiting efforts. The use of culturally diverse officers is being expanded in recruiting efforts as well, by having those officers attend job fairs, community gatherings and festivals, and meetings that are related to diversity and recruitment. Persons who are fluent in foreign languages are also utilized in these recruitment efforts.

As an aid to recruitment, the police department encourages assistance from community organizations and civic leaders. On a regular basis, the personnel sergeant and Personnel Services staff meet with various community domains to discuss recruiting efforts. The validity and utility of the selection process are regularly monitored to assure there is no unfair adverse impact on culturally diverse applicants.

Culturally diverse individuals are also being recruited as police reserves, cadets and explorers. These positions provide a pool from which many of the department's full-time police officer needs are met. The police department makes efforts to assure that, wherever possible, qualified employees of both sexes and various ethnic and racial backgrounds are included in the selection process. The Police Department, in conjunction with the Personnel Department, identifies the qualified employees and assures that appropriate training is given before assignment to any part of the selection process.

Promotion of culturally diverse officers is also receiving added attention. Career skill and staff development programs, although open to all workers, are aimed at culturally diverse employees of the Police Department and the city. Officers from culturally diverse backgrounds have also been placed in specialty assignments that recognize, value and use the diverse skills of these individuals.

Long Beach Police Department

The Long Beach Police Department has taken several different approaches to recruiting and incorporating citizens of diverse ethnic cultures into the police department. Recruiting efforts have been aimed at a personnel philosophy of reflecting the community. Fraternal police officer groups within the department, representing a diverse cross section of community and department members, aid in recruiting for a diverse work force. These groups work within the ethnic communities in their city, particularly with the young, in mentoring programs that establish ties to the various diverse communities.

Community leaders also assist in recruiting efforts by helping train people within their cultural groups so they can qualify for positions within the

Police Department and in local city government. Recognizing the value to the department, hiring practices include the ability to consider the value of ethnicity and diverse language skills in the selection processes. During the promotion process, the police chief is allowed to consider many qualifying factors, including diversity.

During recruit officer basic training, a team approach is stressed. Officers are placed in teams and the success of the team is emphasized. This builds a recognition of the importance of team work and additionally aids officers whose diverse cultures may cause them some difficulties in training. After training, all recruits receive mentoring to aid them through the probationary period.

Advantages of Work Force Diversity

Most police departments are moving toward some form of community policing in an effort to be more responsive to the needs of their communities and to involve the members in community problem solving efforts. An important consideration in community policing is the recognition that it must be responsive to specific needs of citizens in particular areas. Whatever strategy a police organization develops to become more responsive to its changing and diverse community, it must become an interactive and integrated organization. The police can interact with its community and acquire information through a variety of methods including police-citizen interaction, citizen surveys, community advisory groups and from neighborhood leaders.

Responsiveness includes the need for the internal makeup of the organization to be representative of all members of the community. Sincere efforts must be made to insure the opportunity for the representation of diverse community members throughout the organization. Using information developed externally and internally, police departments can develop thorough strategic plans that are responsive and meet the specific needs of all community members. Work force diversity is a fundamental and positive component to being genuinely responsive to a community.

To be effective in the community a police organization should reflect the community it serves. As our nation becomes more diverse, police departments need to reflect their communities' demographics to function effectively and safety. A representative department is best for its community and an equally valid argument can be made that a police department with a work force diversity philosophy is a safer department for its members. A diverse police department is usually perceived as a fairer police department and one that reflects the shared values of its community.

Police agencies similar to those discussed who embrace work force diversity are the ones who will be ready to face the challenges of a changing and diverse society. Their strategies will reflect a concern for community problems and a social responsibility that goes beyond affirmative action; even beyond traditional law enforcement approaches. They will recognize the need for police to broaden their efforts beyond just responding to crime, to recognition that crime prevention is a community matter.

NO 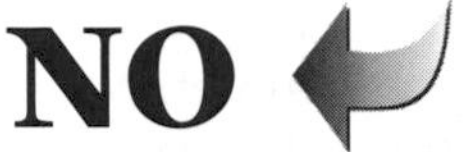

Jan Golab and Erica Walter

How Racial P.C. Corrupted the LAPD

The LAPD was once known as "the world's greatest police department"—due largely to its stringent character screening. Back in the era of Sergeant Joe Friday, LAPD candidates were checked out as thoroughly as homicide suspects. Even a casual relationship with any known criminal excluded a candidate from being considered as a police officer.

All that is now history. In a bid to appease racial activists and meet federal decrees, strict screening and testing measures were dismantled. New black and Hispanic officer candidates were hustled into the ranks at any cost. What former deputy chief Steve Downing called "a quagmire of quota systems" was set up, and "standards were lowered and merit took a back seat to the new political imperatives."

It was back in 1981 that the LAPD first entered into a federal consent decree that instituted quotas for female and minority hiring. To meet these demands, the standards for physical capability, intellectual capacity, and personal character were lowered. The result was that many incapable or mediocre recruits—even significant numbers with criminal links or gang associations—were accepted into the department.

L.A. is not the only city that damaged its police force in a headlong rush for "diversity." During the 1990s, Washington, D.C. had to fire or indict 250 cops after a similar lowering of standards, and New Orleans indicted more than 100 crooked or inept cops who had been hired—it was later found—due to "political pressures." Miami had a similar scandal after scores of cops hastily recruited in response to race riots and an immigration surge got involved in robbing cocaine dealers and reselling their drugs. "We didn't get the quality of officers we should have," acknowledged department spokesman Dave Magnusson.

A scholarly study published in April 2000 in the professional journal *Economic Inquiry* found that aggressive "affirmative action" hiring raised crime rates in many parts of the U.S. In careful statistical analysis of 1987–1993 U.S. Department of Justice data from hundreds of cities, economist John Lott (then of the Yale School of Law, now a resident scholar at the American Enterprise Institute) found that quotas requiring more black and minority police officers clearly increase crime rates. When affirmative action rules take over, he reports, the standards on physical strength tests, mental aptitude tests, and

From *American Enterprise*, vol. 16, issue 4, June 2005, pp. 18-25.

other forms of screening are lowered. The result is a reduced quality of officers—both minority and non-minority recruits end up being less impressive.

Politicians refuse to admit that dropping standards can create problems, but other L.A. authorities are blunt about it. Los Angeles's police academy, training experts say, can no longer reliably be used as "a de-selector" (to use the P.C.-speak). "I had mediocre trainees, some just plain incompetent. They were giving us trash. I finally transferred out because I didn't want to go out in the field with these kids anymore," explained retired LAPD training officer Jim Peasha. When he got a bad minority recruit, Peasha couldn't drum him or her out, no matter what. "I had some fantastic minority recruits. One black kid was the best I ever had. But I also had one guy who I knew was on drugs and I couldn't get him out. He wound up getting caught working as a guard at a rock [cocaine] house. An off-duty cop!"

Rot Protected by Race

On March 16, 1997, black off-duty LAPD officer Kevin Gaines was shot and killed in a "road rage" dispute. Gaines, angry and out of control, had pulled a gun on motorist Frank Lyga and threatened to "cap his ass." Lyga, it turned out, was an undercover LAPD narcotics detective. He drew his 9 mm pistol and shot Gaines through the heart. Only later did he learn that Gaines was also LAPD. The incident made international headlines: "Cop Kills Cop."

Russell Poole, who had a reputation as one of the LAPD's best homicide detectives, was assigned to investigate the shooting. He discovered that Kevin Gaines drove an expensive Mercedes Benz, wore $5,000 suits, $1,000 Versace shirts, and lived his off-duty life in the fast lane of L.A. and Las Vegas nightclubs, a lifestyle he obviously didn't maintain on his $55,000-per-year policeman's salary. Gaines had many credit cards with expenses like the $952 he had dropped just the month before for lunch at Monty's Steakhouse in Westwood, a favorite hangout for black gangster rappers. And at the time of his death, Gaines was living with the ex-wife of gangster rap music mogul Suge Knight—whose own criminal history included eight felony convictions.

It turned out that Gaines, like a significant number of other LAPD officers, was working on the side to provide "security" for Death Row Records, Knight's notorious hoodlum rap music business that was deeply enmeshed in drugs and gang violence. The FBI had been following Gaines, who they suspected was moving drugs and money around L.A. for Death Row. Gaines was shameless. The vanity plates on his Mercedes read "ITS OK IA"—a brash taunt to the department's Internal Affairs department.

While investigating Gaines, Poole was led to another flashy black cop named David Mack. Mack had grown up in a gang-infested Compton neighborhood before being hired by the LAPD. His nearly inseparable friend was fellow police officer Rafael Perez. Like Gaines, Mack and Perez lived large—nightclubs, girls, expensive cars and clothes.

In December 1997, David Mack was arrested for the armed robbery of a Bank of America branch in which he got away with $772,000. He was convicted and sentenced to 17 years in prison. Meanwhile, Perez's comings and goings—and his astounding number of short cellular phone calls—convinced investigators he was dealing drugs. Following a six-month investigation, he was arrested for stealing eight pounds of cocaine from LAPD evidence lockers. Perez cut a deal for a 12-year prison sentence and talked.

The discovery of these dirty cops became known as the Rampart Scandal, the worst in LAPD history. Perez's confession exposed a group of police officers who engaged in theft, drug dealing, perjury, improper shootings, evidence tampering, false arrests, witness intimidation, and beatings. They cribbed up in bachelor pad apartments for sex parties with hookers. These men were as out of control as the gangs they were supposed to police—in too many cases they were from the gangs they were supposed to police.

More than 30 officers were suspended or fired in the Rampart probe. Hundreds of criminal convictions tainted by links to Rampart cops were overturned. Although it did not receive much attention in the mainstream media, an embarrassing truth was exposed: Many L.A. cops had been corrupted by black gangsters (just as many New York cops were corrupted in another era by the Italian mob). "Rampart wasn't about cops who became gangsters," explained former LAPD deputy chief Downing. "It was about gangsters who became cops."

How did city officials react to this painful lesson? By paying $70 million in settlements. By doing nothing about the P.C. race rules that opened the floodgates. And by agreeing to a consent decree that turned control of the LAPD over to the Feds. The consent decree drained crucial resources from crime fighting, nearly 350 department supervisors were permanently assigned to reporting on the decree, and tens of thousands of hours were spent by other officers on its mandates.

This was salt in the wounds of a department already hogtied by paperwork. After the Rodney King riots, the Christopher Commission (chaired by Bill Clinton's future secretary of State) demanded that the LAPD investigate every single civilian complaint against any officer, no matter how frivolous. This required three or four supervisors at each division to spend full time on complaint duty. Department investigators often ended up devoting more days to interviewing witnesses about bogus complaints, and meeting RC mandates on domestic violence cases, than to investigating crimes. Motivated by the media-fueled presumption that brutality and racism were "endemic" in the LAPD, Bill Clinton's Justice Department also demanded detailed racial data to see if cops were "racially profiling." Not surprisingly, serious felonies rose dramatically during this period in Los Angeles.

Ignoring Root Causes

Police Chief Bernard Parks fired more than 100 police officers at about this time, citing a wide range of infractions including unapproved off-duty work as security guards at gangster rap functions. Many believe he was quietly trying to purge the department of cops who had gang associations. But officially, the city of Los Angeles never faced up to how it had gotten into this dreadful mess.

One indication is the $250,000 payment to the family of gangster-cop Kevin Gaines that city fathers quietly agreed to in 1999. Race-baiting attorney Johnny Cochran had sued the city for $100 million, accusing Frank Lyga of being an out-of-control white racist officer. The backroom deal, brokered by city attorney James Hahn (now L.A.'s mayor), and approved by Chief Parks (who ran for mayor in 2005), was deliberately shielded from the public and the L.A. City Council.

Lyga's shooting of Gaines had been found justifiable by three board panels. The Police Commission ruled that he acted in self-defense. Yet the city paid off Johnny Cochran to bury the evidence that his client was part of a cancerous knot of minority cops hurriedly introduced into the force without adequate screening, and left there even after evidence accumulated that they were not law-abiding citizens themselves. The city hung Detective Lyga out to dry.

Poole believes that had natural leads been followed, the Rampart miscreants and other incompetent or corrupt officers could have been exposed at least a year before Rafael Perez spilled his guts. Poole had alerted Chief Parks—an African American brought in to generate racial amity after the Rodney King riots—that Rampart Division was out of control, but he was told to limit his investigations. Poole was so distraught, he resigned. "I left because the department literally wanted me to lie and keep things from the D.A.'s office. They knew the seriousness of what was going on, but they did not want to pursue it aggressively. They just wanted to let it go." It was all too embarrassing to liberal pieties.

After Rampart blew up, hundreds of experts eventually produced three major reports on the scandal. Each concluded that department standards had been lowered. "But not a single one dealt with the core problem," says Steve Downing. "Where did all these crooked cops come from? How did they ever get hired in the first place? That's the question nobody will address." Because it is politically incorrect.

The core problem behind L.A.'s Rampart, and similar corruption and competence scandals in other police departments, was that politicians insisted on forcing racial minorities into police ranks no matter what. Even now, years after the sour fruits of such efforts have been exposed, elected officials refuse to state out loud the obvious: Institutionalized practice of reverse racial discrimination "allowed persons of poor character to be hired," as Downing summarizes.

At one time in the late 1990s, as many as 25 black police officers in the Los Angeles Police Department were believed to have direct ties to the criminal gangs they were supposed to be stamping out. The problem extended to other police departments in the area as well, including Hawthorne, Inglewood, Compton, and the L.A. County sheriffs. "This is not an LAPD problem," stated one top LAPD official during the Rampart scandal. "This is a black problem."

The local and national press were no braver than the politicians at facing this issue. Despite a supertanker of ink spilled on Rampart stories, no reporters or editors had the stomach to address its causes. Only a few radio hosts broached the truth voiced by virtually every L.A. cop. "The corruption of affirmative action," states Steve Downing, "has been treated as if it never occurred."

The Racial No-fly Zone

For the past 25 years, Los Angeles has been like Russia under Krushchev: Everybody knows the truth, but nobody dares to speak it. Much as Pravda ignored Moscow meat and bread shortages, the *Los Angeles Times* has adamantly refused to report on the damage caused by racial demogoguery and quotas. No one dares challenge the party line lest he be punished. "Don't ask me to go there," a city official once told me. "I have a family, a mortgage, a car, and a dog, and I have to work in this city."

Late last year, the *Times* finally ran a four-part exposé on Martin Luther King Hospital in south Los Angeles. A team of reporters spent a year examining the scandalous number of unexplained deaths and administrative peculiarities that led to the closure of the hospital's trauma center and the loss of its national accreditation. One of the conclusions of the series was that the hospital, which may be forced to close completely, had avoided normal scrutiny for the past 30 years due to racial politics. "Why Supervisors Let Deadly Problems Slide," read one headline. "Fearful of provoking black protests, they shied away from imposing tough remedies on inept administrators," read the subhead.

For three decades, nobody would speak the truth about MLK Hospital. The *Times* celebrated with champagne when its series won a Pulitzer in April—but the paper could have prevented the tragedy by writing two decades earlier. Everybody knew MLK was substandard, that's why folks in South Central dubbed it "Killer King." Alternative publications wrote about it, but the *Times* and network TV wouldn't touch it. Their refusal to hold incompetent blacks accountable allowed the disaster to compound.

Politically correct reporting on the LAPD has had even more tragic consequences. The media have not only failed to acknowledge the corruption of affirmative action, they have leapt at every opportunity to brand the LAPD as racist, undercutting many dedicated officers, and deeply corroding the force's ability to battle crime.

The tragedy that took place this February 6 is the latest example. A little before 4 a.m., two officers in an LAPD patrol car saw a Toyota Camry run a red light. When they tried to pull the car over, the driver took off. After a high speed chase lasting several minutes, the car left the road and slid to a halt. Disregarding commands to leave the vehicle, the driver then backed up directly at officer Steve Garcia as he exited the squad car's passenger door. In fear for his life, Garcia shot several times as the Toyota smashed into his cruiser.

The car was found to be stolen. The driver—who died from gunshot wounds—turned out to be a black 13-year-old named Devin Brown. Neighbors reported that the teenager had become involved with the local Van Ness Bloods gang, and police stated that he had been at a gang gathering prior to this incident. The media described Brown as unarmed, ignoring how lethal a car can be when used as a weapon.

A mob of politicians and race activists, including inflammatory Congresswoman Maxine Waters, immediately condemned the act as yet another example of LAPD racism. Crowds gathered at the scene chanting "No Justice, No Peace," and waving placards that read "LAPD = KKK" and "Kill The Pigs."

"Children tend to be mischievous," one woman complained at a subsequent protest, "but they shouldn't have to die. . . . Children do stuff like that all the time." To which an L.A. police officer writing in *National Review Online* answered, "Children? Mischievous? Devin Brown, God rest his soul, was not out toilet-papering the gym teacher's house. He committed at least three felonies, crimes which might have resulted in the death of a police officer, his own passenger, or some innocent bystander." This same officer later noted that more than 20 U.S. police officers have been killed over the last five years by suspects deliberately running them over with cars.

Before the investigation into this event even got serious, Mayor James Hahn convinced the L.A. Police Commission to change regulations. A new policy now prohibits officers from firing into moving vehicles. In one more little way, the police have been hamstrung by the racialized fallout of a sad criminal incident.

A Presumption of Prejudice

Ever since the Watts riots of 1964, the media have pandered to the presumption of prejudice in the LAPD. Black Los Angeleno Eulia Love was shot and killed in 1979 by two cops. One of the officers was black, one Hispanic-Native American, yet they were both vilified as racists. Today, whenever the L.A. media refer to this incident they invariably report that Ms. Love was killed over a $20 gas bill. They always fail to mention that she attacked the gasman with a shovel, or that the hysterical, mentally deranged, foaming at the mouth Ms. Love threw a knife at the officers who responded to his complaint. Race had nothing to do with the tragic demise of Eulia Love, yet thanks to years of politically correct commentary, most Los Angelenos now believe it to be an historic fact that she was a victim of a "racist shooting."

Another notorious case involved Clarence Chance and Benny Powell, two black men who spent 17 years in prison for killing a black L.A. County sheriff. They were freed in 1992—shortly after a spasm of post-Rodney King guilt swept liberal Los Angeles—because it was alleged they had been "framed by the LAPD." The L.A. City Council awarded them $7 million, and the media turned them into international folk heroes, second only to Rodney King himself as symbols of racial injustice in America.

The truth is that Chance and Powell were released due to an expedient and highly symbolic decision by L.A. officials. With Daryl Gates, Mark Fuhrman, and the rest of the LAPD on the roasting spit, nobody dared question claims of an LAPD racist frame-up. It didn't seem to matter that the murder victim was black, or that the eyewitness who identified Chance and Powell was black, or that 17 years later she stuck to her ID.

Upon his release, Benny Powell, now a millionaire, was feted on TV talk shows. He also embarked on a rampage of drugs, rape, beatings, car chases, and shootings. One shootout landed him in the hospital—between two paid speaking engagements. After a brutal day-long cocaine-fueled motel rape of a UCLA student (in which he employed an ax handle as his raping tool), he was finally arrested for good when a witness saw Powell in a field chasing a nude woman with her hands tied behind her as Powell beat her with a stick.

Nobody in the media ever interviewed the UCLA coed except me. I remember her thousand-mile stare, a life ruined, as she explained why she had agreed to go on a road trip with Benny Powell. "I thought he was found innocent," she stated, having read all about Benny Powell in the *Los Angeles Times*, including what a sad victim and genuine hero he was. Her innocence combined with politically correct lies nearly cost her her life.

The Nazi Cops Myth

The O. J. Simpson verdict just two years later, which ended with the judgment that O. J. had been framed, was built on the assumption that LAPD detective Mark Fuhrman was a racist. When I wrote a story for *Los Angeles* magazine on Fuhrman's former partners, none of them, including blacks and Hispanics, believed he was racist. One black female cop who had only praise for Fuhrman begged me not to quote her because, she explained, "it would ruin my career and my life." The Oscar Joel Bryant Association, the LAPD's black officers group, would blackball her. Her kids would come home from school crying that she was an Aunt Thomasina.

In another feature I wrote for the same magazine, about L. A. cops who retired to Idaho, I brushed up against the virulent anti-cop bias of many reporters, which helped form the mindset of the O. J. jurors. So many L.A. cops retire near Coeur d'Alene, Idaho, that they have an annual retired-LAPD barbecue there. Police officers move there for affordable housing, and because it is a hunter's and fisherman's paradise. But that's not what the public was told Mark Fuhrman wanted up there.

The week after Fuhrman moved to Sandpoint, Idaho, the founder of the white supremacist group Aryan Nations, Richard Butler, was quoted from nearby Hayden Lake by every national TV network, wire service, and newspaper. In each interview (a swastika visible over his shoulder), Butler claimed that cops who came to Idaho were racists. The media never questioned the assertion.

I was the only reporter who bothered to fly up to Butler's Hayden Lake "compound" (five small clapboard shacks in the middle of the woods) and ask him about his assertions.

Q: "Mr. Butler, do you know Mark Fuhrman?"

A: "Well, no."

Q: "Have you ever talked to Mark Fuhrman?"

A: "Uh, well, no."

Q: "Has Mark Fuhrman ever visited you?"

A: "No."

Q: "Is Mark Fuhrman a member of your organization?"

A: "No."

Q: "Are any cops members of your organization?"

A: "No."

Richard Butler turned out to be a pathetic, doddering old man. His "followers"—as many as two at any given time—were marginal characters more worthy of pity than fear.

But just before my trip to Idaho, the Sunday *New York Times Magazine* had run a cover story with a two-page photo of a Hayden Lake cross-burning. Millions of people saw that picture. What they didn't know was that only five people witnessed the event in person: Richard Butler with his German Shepherd, two of Butler's followers, and the *Times* photographer and his assistant—for whose benefit the cross had been set aflame in the first place. Mike Feiler, managing editor of the *Coeur d'Alene Press*, described to me the reporters who had swarmed the area after Fuhrman's arrival: "Every one of them has come in here with marching orders, not to get the truth, but to get the story of white supremacist cops in north Idaho."

The Aryan Nations is a powerless group listened to by nobody. But the *Times* newspapers of Los Angeles and New York influence millions of people every day. And they rarely pass up an opportunity to lambaste "the racist LAPD" and drive a wedge into the heart of my city.

When Diversity Trumps Truth and Justice

Three decades of deplorable coverage of Los Angeles policing—from Rodney King to O. J. to Rampart and now Devin Brown—have left all Americans with a horrific legacy. Today, cops all across the United States battle a foe as destructive as crime itself: the presumption of common prejudice. "You only stopped me because I'm black."

This view has been fanned by a media elite which has made "diversity" its virtual religion. Since the late 1980s, newspapers have mandated diversity management seminars, held multicultural weekend retreats, and hired diversity consultants to remake their newsrooms and reporting guidelines. Editors' salaries are often based on the number of minorities they hire and promote. There are editorial guidelines for racial and ethnic balance in sourcing. Minorities are encouraged to complain about any perceived slights to their particular group, and to challenge the assumptions of "the white male hegemony." At one point the *Los Angeles Times* put a hiring freeze on white males, and issued highly tendentious style guides to its writers, along with lists of forbidden "insensitive" terms.

Minority journalists regularly circulate petitions demanding that un-P.C. colleagues be chastised or fired. They demand meetings with management to discuss editorial transgressions. The chill that this racial mau-mauing exerts on frank reporting is profound. When someone in the newsroom cries "racism," "sexism," or "homophobia," everyone backs away. Even the most dedicated reporters eventually give up and stop following leads on stories they know will never see print, and could even lead to persecution.

Hence, most of the elite media's sins are now sins of omission—the stories never told. Propaganda, as Orwell said, is in what gets left out. This syndrome extends far beyond reporting on crime and policing. To demonstrate "moral neutrality," terrorists are no longer identified as terrorists at many publications; AIDS is misrepresented as a primarily heterosexual disease in the West in order to show sensitivity to gays; troubling realities that plague our urban underclass, like illegitimacy, welfare dependency, and criminal behavior, are ignored. These evasions cause problems to be mis- and undiagnosed, and lead to millions of misspent dollars and unnecessary deaths.

But the literal life-and-death risks of political correctness are nowhere more visible than in policing. Blind eyes have been turned to the grave risks created by quota hiring, lowered standards, the fomenting of racialized suspicions in the citizenry, P.C. policies toward aliens and immigrants, draconian restraint of officers in the field, the explosion of complaints and lawsuits that shake down officers with claims of harassment and excessive force.

Meanwhile, police-attackers like Sara Jane Olson are often lionized. In 2001, Olson finally pled guilty to her role in placing a bomb under an LAPD squad car in 1975. But the '60s radical had turned "respectable" Minnesota housewife during her years on the run, and generated sympathy from the left-wing aristocracy as deep as the outrage she inspired from police officers. She became one more focal point for the political forces that have long embraced violent outlaws like the Black Panthers and various criminals and gang members when they become locked in conflicts with law enforcement.

These Sara Janes in policy-making positions, activist organizations, law offices, and newsrooms have wreaked more havoc on civic peace and safe streets than any bomb placed under a squad car. Radicals no longer call for people to "Kill the Pigs," they now bring down whole police departments with procedural coups. They turned "motorist Rodney King" (a violent, intoxicated, out-of-control, fleeing felon) into an international symbol of racial injustice, and the 1992 L.A. riots into a political "uprising." They have assassinated the character of scores of officers, and painted the whole department as racist. They have pandered to the paranoia that "O. J. was framed by the LAPD," and turned the indispensable tool of "criminal profiling" into the unacceptable horror of "racial profiling." They shut down the LAPD's Intelligence Division, making it (among other things) impossible for the city to identify foreign terrorists. They have fostered a view of police officers as bullies and oppressors not to be cooperated with. Collectively, the Sara Janes have made it nearly impossible for the LAPD to suppress gangs, control drugs, arrest criminals, or keep the peace. The result is that many neighborhoods (though not the wealthy ones the Sara Janes live in) are run by hoodlums, and thousands of innocents live in fear.

The Victims of Political Correctness

Los Angeles County averages 1,000 murders every year, two thirds of them carried out by gangs. Most of the victims never make the papers (though every charge of "racial profiling" by an ACLU attorney gets headlines). After the Rampart scandal, L.A.'s anti-gang units were disbanded, leaving the gang-directed narcotics trade virtually unpoliced. During the year that followed, crime increased 10 percent, and the murder rate rose 25 percent, while arrests dropped 25 percent. The best cops fled to jobs at more supportive departments and communities.

By 2001, the LAPD was 884 officers short of full strength. Half the cops on the street suddenly had less than five years experience. The remaining veterans continued to leave in droves; at some divisions, 40 percent of the officers were applying for jobs at other departments. The attrition rate was double the hiring rate. Special units were disbanded or cannibalized just to keep officers on the street.

"We have money to hire officers but we can't get them," explained Dennis Zine of the Los Angeles Police Protective League in 2001. Good candidates "won't go to a police department in turmoil. And the message in the recent verdicts is that Los Angelenos are going to believe the gangbangers. There's a 'hang the cops at the airport' mentality." Zine was so appalled by the city's failed leadership that he ran for city council, and won. "The city leaders were culpable for allowing the LAPD to get into a situation where officers were afraid to do their jobs. And they cost the taxpayers millions. They settled every lawsuit. They rolled over and accepted a consent decree. They wouldn't fight for the department."

Local newspapers suggested officers were leaving because they had suddenly found more convenient schedules, fatter benefits, or better retirement packages at other departments. But the real issues driving cops away, wholly ignored by the media, were racial suspicions, absurd constraints, and the hostile complaint system imposed upon the LAPD by politically correct "reformers."

Any citizen complaint, no matter how petty, was required to be fully investigated, a process that could take as long as a year, stalling promotions, raises, or transfers, and blackening an officer's name. For a while, the LAPD was investigating ten times the number of complaints as most departments. Nearly one third of all LAPD man-hours were spent investigating each other. And the gangbangers knew this. By filing a complaint, they could "jam up" a cop—while simultaneously taking another officer off the streets to investigate the complaint.

In response, the LAPD resorted to a "3-12" work schedule. This allows cops to work three 12-hour shifts while taking the rest of the week off. The mass exodus of officers stopped, but no one asked why "the nation's best police department" needed to give its employees four days off every week (one third of them now hold a second job during that time) to make them stay.

This coincided with the arrival of Bill Bratton as L.A.'s new police chief in 2002. The renowned former Boston and New York City chief knew he had to take emergency measures to stanch the bleeding at the department, and he has. By most accounts, Bratton has pulled the department back from the precipice with a combination of good leadership, smart personnel choices, a return to reasonable discretion in the complaint process (reformers be damned), along with some tireless handholding with the black community.

The result has been an 18 percent decline in violent crime from the recent peaks. Bratton has won the respect of citizens and officers alike, achieving an 85 percent vote of confidence among the police rank and file. But the LAPD still has 215 fewer officers than when Bratton arrived. A ballot initiative that would have provided funding for an additional 1,260 officers failed to pass last November—in part due to the anti-police attitudes long fomented among Los Angelenos. "The LAPD is struggling to hold off an inferno of criminal activity," Bratton has said of his undermanned force. "As soon as the department puts out one fire by mustering its scarce resources to respond to a flashpoint of violent crime, the violence jumps to a new location."

Despite Bratton's admirable improvements, the LAPD remains on a knife's edge, one politicized incident away from disaster. How will the media and local citizens react to the next "racial incident"? Has anyone learned anything from the disaster of the last decades?

POSTSCRIPT

Should Law Enforcement Agencies Use Affirmative Action Programs to Increase the Number of Minority Police Officers?

Few issues raise more controversy in modern law enforcement agencies than the use of affirmative action programs. On one hand, many people believe that police agencies should reflect the demographic composition of the cities they serve. Moreover, the residents of many of our nation's cities are minority group members who may come from a very different cultural background than middle-class white police officers. Affirmative action programs may help to insure that there are police officers who understand the cultural backgrounds of a city's minority residents.

In contrast, opponents of affirmative action programs believe that the U.S. Constitution is clear: The government may not deny the equal protection of the laws. Governmental policies that give preferential treatment to one racial group over another violate the Fourteenth Amendment.

U.S. courts have appeared to be ambivalent about the issue of affirmative action. As the Introduction to this issue noted, the Supreme Court has sanctioned some limited affirmative action programs. However, it has hesitated to allow governmental agencies to significantly expand the reach of preferential employment policies. For example, in *Firefighters Local Union No. 1784 v. Stotts*, 467 U.S. 561 (1984), an affirmative action program developed by the City of Memphis came into conflict with the union's seniority system over the issue of employee layoffs. The principal issue was whether minority workers hired under the affirmative action plan had priority over white employees who had more seniority. The Supreme Court held that because the minority workers did not demonstrate that they themselves had been the victims of discrimination by the City, the seniority plan had priority.

Do you believe that the Supreme Court made the right decision in this case? Should the minority firefighters have had the burden to prove that they were personally discriminated against in order to prevail? This would have been a very difficult burden to carry.

What about the issue of employee competence? After reading the articles in this issue, do you believe that when governmental agencies adopt affirmative action plans the quality of employees who are hired declines? Suppose that a governmental agency uses a testing program to hire employees. As part of an affirmative action program, do you believe it is proper to maintain a lower threshold score to increase the number of minority employees? If not, would the following circumstances change your opinion? Suppose you learned that a governmental agency, such as a city police department, had a long history of discriminating against minority candidates. As a consequence, the department is comprised of less than 2 percent minority group members in a city with a 24 percent minority population. Should the department adopt an affirmative action program in these circumstances?

These are very difficult questions that provoke strong opinions on both sides of the issue. There are many resources for additional information on these topics. See William T. Bielby, "Minimizing Workplace Gender and Racial Bias," *Contemporary Sociology* (vol. 29, no. 1, 2000); Kenneth A. Kovach, David A. Kravitz, and Allen A. Hughes, "Affirmative Action: How Can We Be So Lost When We Don't Even Know Where We Are Going?" *Labor Law Journal* (vol. 55, no. 1, 2004); Nicholas P. Lovrich, Jr. and Brent S. Steel, "Affirmative Action and Productivity in Law Enforcement Agencies," *Review of Public Personnel Administration* (vol. 4, no. 1, 1983); Anthony R. Pratkanis and Marlene E. Turner, "The Proactive Removal of Discriminatory Barriers: Affirmative Action as Effective Help," *The Journal of Social Issues* (vol. 52, no. 4, 1996); Ronald J. Burke and Aslaug Mikkelsen, "Gender Issues in Policing: Do They Matter?" *Women in Management* (vol. 20, no. 1/2, 2005); Dennis A. Deslippe, "Do Whites Have Rights? White Detroit Policemen and 'Reverse Discrimination' Protests in the 1970s," *Journal of American History* (vol. 91, no. 3, 2004); John R. Lott, Jr., "Does a Helping Hand Put Others at Risk? Affirmative Action, Police Departments, and Crime," *Economic Inquiry* (vol. 38, no. 2, 2000); and Mary Dodge and Mark Pogrebin, "African-American Policewomen: An Exploration of Professional Relationships," *Policing* (vol. 24, no. 4, 2001).

ISSUE 19

Are Female Police Officers as Effective as Male Officers?

YES: Jeanne McDowell, from "Are Women Better Cops?" *Time* (February 17, 1992)

NO: Erica Walter, from "Cops and Gender P.C.," *The American Enterprise* (June 2005)

ISSUE SUMMARY

YES: Author Jeanne McDowell contends that in some important ways, including a cool, calm, and communicative demeanor, female police officers may be more effective than their male counterparts in defusing violent situations.

NO: Writer Erica Walter asserts that law enforcement organizations must respect the reality that male and female officers are not interchangeable. Moreover, female officers' limited ability to handle violent encounters with citizens may endanger both the police and the public.

The last issue considered the use of affirmative action programs in law enforcement agencies. Issue 19 considers a related issue: Are female police officers are as effective as male officers?

Prior to the 1970s, there were few female police officers in the United States. Over the years, however, our nation's law enforcement administrators began to recognize that women could function effectively as police officers. Initially, the role of women in law enforcement organizations was restricted stereotypically—they were generally assigned to juvenile bureaus and to conduct rape investigations, duties that were regarded as "more appropriate" for women. Eventually, police administrators began to realize that women could work effectively in a wide variety of law enforcement roles. The question remains, however, whether they are as effective as male officers.

What is your opinion? Do you have any preconceived notions about women who serve in this traditionally male-dominated occupation? Are they somehow "less feminine" than "normal" women? Do women handle the exercise of authority differently than men? These are only some of the questions and obstacles that women in the law enforcement profession have had to face. It is clear that many misconceptions may exist in the public mind based on erroneous information and popular stereotypes. But, what conclusion can we draw about women in policing based on the available objective data?

The evidence suggests that women are very effective police officers. Most of the empirical studies conducted to date have concluded that there is little difference between the performance of male and female officers. According to Professor Samuel Walker, however, women are still seriously underrepresented in many of our nation's police forces. In 1986, women comprised approximately 40 percent of the U.S. labor force, yet only about 8.8 percent of all sworn officers in cities with populations of 50,000 or more people are women. Moreover, women are underrepresented in law enforcement managerial positions.

As in the case of minority group members, affirmative action programs have been used by female police officers to help facilitate their entry into administrative positions and roles involving more traditional law enforcement functions, such as routine patrol. In effect, women have been forced to use gender discrimination lawsuits to "pry open the door" to this traditionally male-dominated profession.

So, what do you think? Are women officers as effective as male officers? Should there be some jobs in law enforcement that are handled exclusively by males (and conversely, some jobs that should be handled exclusively by females)? The authors of the articles in this section would answer this question in very different ways.

Author Jeanne McDowell contends that in some important ways, including a cool, calm, and communicative demeanor, female police officers may be more effective than their male counterparts in defusing violent situations.

Author Erica Walter would disagree with McDowell. Walter asserts that law enforcement organizations must respect the reality that male and female officers are not interchangeable. Moreover, female officers' limited ability to handle violent encounters with citizens may endanger both the police and the public.

Do you agree with Jeanne McDowell or Erica Walter? Do you believe that female police officers are as effective as their male counterparts? These are compelling questions that will shape the character of modern law enforcement in the twenty-first century.

Jeanne McDowell

Are Women Better Cops?

Among the residents, merchants and criminals of Venice, Calif., officer Kelly Shea is as well known as the neighborhood gang leaders. The blond mane neatly tied back, slender figure and pink lipstick violate the stereotype of guardian of law and order; but Shea, 32, has managed to win the respect of street thugs who usually answer more readily to the slam of a cop's billy club. She speaks softly, raising her voice only as needed. While her record of arrests during her 10 years on patrol is comparable to those of the men in her division, she has been involved in only two street fights, a small number by any cop's standard. Faced with hulking, 6-ft. 2-in. suspects, she admits that her physical strength cannot match theirs. "Coming across aggressively doesn't work with gang members," says Shea. "If that first encounter is direct, knowledgeable and made with authority, they respond. It takes a few more words, but it works."

Hers is a far cry from the in-your-face style that has been the hallmark of mostly male police forces for years. But while women constitute only 9% of the nation's 523,262 police officers, they are bringing a distinctly different, and valuable, set of skills to the streets and the station house that may change the way the police are perceived in the community. Only on television is police work largely about high-speed heroics and gunfights in alleys. Experts estimate that 90% of an officer's day involves talking to citizens, doing paperwork and handling public relations. Many cops retire after sterling careers never having drawn their gun.

As the job description expands beyond crime fighting into community service, the growing presence of women may help burnish the tarnished image of police officers, improve community relations and foster a more flexible, and less violent, approach to keeping the peace. "Policing today requires considerable intelligence, communication, compassion and diplomacy," says Houston police chief Elizabeth Watson, the only female in the nation to head a major metropolitan force. "Women tend to rely more on intellectual than physical prowess. From that standpoint, policing is a natural match for them."

Such traits take on new value in police departments that have come under fire for the brutal treatment of suspects in their custody. The videotaped beating of motorist Rodney King by four Los Angeles cops last year threw a spotlight on the use of excessive force by police. The number of reports continues to remain high across the country after the furor that followed that attack. Female officers have been conspicuously absent from these charges: the independent Christopher commission, which investigated the L.A.P.D. in the aftermath of the King beating, found that the 120 officers with the most use-of-force reports were all men. Civilian complaints against women are also consistently lower. In San Francisco, for example female officers account for only 5% of complaints although they make up 10% of the 1,839-person force. "And when you see a reference to a female," says Eileen Luna, former chief investigator for the San Francisco citizen review board, "it's often the positive effect she has had in taking control in a different way from male officers."

Though much of the evidence is anecdotal, experts in policing say the verbal skills many women officers possess often have a calming effect that defuses potentially explosive situations. "As a rule, they tend to be much more likely to go in and talk rather than try to get control in a way that makes everyone defensive," says Joanne Belknap, an associate professor of criminal justice at the University of Cincinnati. Women cops, she has found, perceive themselves as peacekeepers and negotiators. "We're like pacifiers in these situations," says Lieut. Helen DeWitte, a 21-year veteran of the Chicago force who was the first woman in the department to be shot in the line of duty. Having women partners for 14 years taught San Francisco sergeant Tim Foley to use a softer touch with suspects, instead of always opening with a shove. "It's non-threatening and disarming," he says, "and in the long run, it is easier than struggling."

Such a measured style is especially effective in handling rape and domestic-violence calls, in which the victims are usually women. In 1985 a study of police officers' treatment of spousal-abuse cases by two University of Detroit professors concluded that female officers show more empathy and commitment to resolving these conflicts. While generalizations invite unfair stereotyping, male officers often tend not to take these calls as seriously, despite improved training and arrest policies in almost half of all states. "Men tend to come on with a stronger approach to quiet a recalcitrant male suspect," notes Baltimore County police chief Cornelius Behan, whose 1,580-member force includes 143 women. "It gets his macho up, and he wants to take on the cop."

Despite the research, the notion of "female" and "male" policing styles remains a controversial one. Individual temperament is more important than gender in the way cops perform, argues Edwin Delattre, author of *Character and* Cops*: Ethics in Policing*. Other experts contend that aggressiveness among officers is more a measure of a department's philosophy and the tone set by its top managers. "When cops are trained to think of themselves as fighters in a war against crime, they come to view the public as the enemy," observes James Fyfe, a criminal-justice professor at The American University.

Some female officers have qualms as well about highlighting gender-based differences in police work, especially women who have struggled for years to achieve equity in mostly male departments. The women fear that emphasizing their "people skills" will reinforce the charge that they don't have the heft or toughness to handle a crisis on the street. But while women generally lack upper-body strength, studies consistently show that in situations in which force is needed, they perform as effectively as their male counterparts by using alternatives, such as karate, twist locks or a baton instead of their fists.

Yet the harassment that persists in many precinct houses tempts female cops to try to blend in and be one of the boys. All too often that means enduring the lewd jokes transmitted over police-car radios and the sexist remarks in the halls. In most places it means wearing an uncomfortable uniform designed for a man, including bulletproof vests that have not been adapted to women's figures. The atmosphere is made worse because about 3% of supervisors over the rank of sergeant are women, in part owing to lack of seniority. Milwaukee police officer Kay Hanna remembers being reprimanded for going to the bathroom while on duty. Chicago Lieut. DeWitte found condoms and nude centerfolds in her mailbox when she started working patrol.

Women cops who have fought discrimination in court have fared well. Los Angeles officer Fanchon Blake settled a memorable lawsuit in 1980 that opened up the ranks above sergeant to women. Last May, New York City detective Kathleen Burke won a settlement of $85,000 and a public promotion to detective first-grade. In her suit she had alleged that her supervisor's demeaning comments about her performance and his unwillingness to give her more responsible assignments impeded her professional progress. He denied the charges. But many women still fear that complaining about such treatment carries its own risks. Beverly Harvard, deputy chief of administrative services in Atlanta, says a female officer would have to wonder "whether she would get a quick response to a call for backup later on."

Resistance toward women cops stems in part from the fact that they are still relative newcomers to the beat. In the years after 1910, when a Los Angeles social worker named Alice Stebbins Wells became the country's first full-fledged female police officer, women served mostly as radio dispatchers, matrons, and social workers for juveniles and female prison inmates. Not until 1968 did Indianapolis become the first force in the country to assign a woman to full-time field patrol. Since then, the numbers of women in policing have risen steadily, thanks largely to changes in federal antidiscrimination laws. Madison, Wis., boasts a 25% female force, the highest percentage of any department in the country.

Because female cops are still relatively few in number, a woman answering a police call often evokes a mixed response. Reno officer Judy Holloday recalls arriving at the scene of a crime and being asked, "Where's the real cop?" Detective Burke, who stands 5 ft. 2 in. and has weighed 100 lbs. for most of her 23 years on the force, says she made 2,000 felony arrests and was never handicapped by a lack of physical strength. Burke recalls subduing a 6-ft. 4-in., 240-lb. robbery suspect who was wildly ranting about Jesus Christ. She pulled out her rosary beads and told him God had sent her to make the arrest. "You use whatever you got," she says. When it looks as though a cop may be overpowered, the appropriate response for any officer–male or female–is to call for backup. "It's foolish for a cop of either sex to start dukin' it out," says Susan Martin, author of *On the Move: The Status of Women in Policing.*

A growing emphasis on other skills, especially communication, comes from a movement in many police departments away from traditional law enforcement into a community-oriented role. In major cities such as New York, Houston and Kansas City, the mark of a good officer is no longer simply responding to distress calls but working in partnership with citizens and local merchants to head off crime and improve the quality of life in neighborhoods. In Madison, which has been transformed from a traditional, call-driven department into a community-oriented operation in the past 20 years, police chief David Couper says female officers have helped usher in a "kinder, gentler organization." Says Couper: "Police cooperation and a willingness to report domestic abuse and sexual assaults are all up. If a person is arrested, there is more of a feeling that he will be treated right instead of getting beat up in the elevator."

In Los Angeles the city council is expected to pass a resolution next month that will lead to a 43% female force by the year 2000, up from 13.4 % now. "We have so much to gain by achieving gender balance, we'd be nuts not to do it," says councilman Zev Yaroslavsky. Ideally, the solution in all cities and towns is a healthy mix of male and female officers that reflects the constituency they serve and the changing demands of the job.

NO 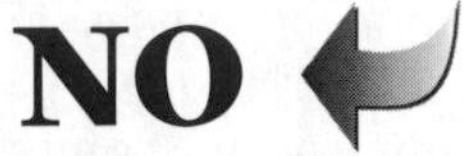

Erica Walter

Cops and Gender

An Atlanta courthouse was recently the scene of slaughter as a six-foot-one former linebacker awaiting trial for rape took the gun from his lone guard, a five-foot, 50-something grandmother. After murdering a judge, a court reporter, and a deputy, Brian Nichols allegedly killed a fourth person before kidnapping Ashley Smith at two o'clock in the morning, taking her back to her apartment, and tying the young woman up in her bathtub.

The story ended with a twist: The murderous chaos the first woman allowed to erupt was ended by the second woman, as Ashley Smith in just a few hours managed to gain the man's trust, and then to change his course from violence to peace. The gunman let Smith go and surrendered to the police around noon.

Almost no press stories dared say much about the politically incorrect aspect of this bloodbath: that a 210-pound man charged with a violent crime, who only a week before had been found with metal shanks hidden in his socks, should not have been guarded by a petite grandmother who had been forced to take remedial firearms training the year before. This and other similar stories confirm that, whether anyone cares to admit it, sex differences remain a powerful fact of life—and when ignored in fields like policing can have deadly repercussions.

Take the Rodney King arrest. When an intoxicated King zoomed past California Highway Patrol officer Melanie Singer, she started a high-speed pursuit. By the time he stopped, several LAPD cops had joined the chase and watched as Singer, not a physically prepossessing woman, approached the large, bizarrely acting King with her gun drawn. This dangerous tack was too much for the LAPD cops, who pulled rank, told Singer to "stand back," and took over the arrest. The most experienced officers on the scene became upset when Singer approached King with her gun drawn. They envisioned bad consequences—either an unarmed suspect needlessly shot (as would apparently happen a few months later in a Washington, D.C. case) or (as we just saw in Atlanta) a large criminal taking a small female cop's gun and inflicting mayhem. Or, one other LAPD cop worried, the criminal may lunge at the woman and cause the less experienced officers at the scene to shoot them both in a desperate attempt to save her.

From *American Enterprise*, vol. 16, issue 4, June 2005, pp. 18-25.

The Rodney King arrest involves many other issues besides female cops, but in Official Negligence, his definitive history of the case, *Washington Post* reporter Lou Cannon makes clear that the LAPD veterans were legitimately disturbed at Melanie Singer's actions. King's reaction to the fact that it was a female cop barking orders at him was part of the problem. He was disrespectful and sexual: "He grabbed his butt with both hands and began to shake and gyrate his fanny in a sexually suggestive fashion," Stacey Koon of the LAPD stated. The chain of events that followed led to the 1992 Los Angeles riots that raged for six days, leaving 34 people dead, 1,032 injured, and millions of dollars of property stolen and destroyed.

A smaller but also traumatic incident that occurred in Washington, D.C. a couple of months after King's arrest was perhaps a more representative example of the same problem. In the Mount Pleasant neighborhood, whose population includes many poor Latino immigrants, two Hispanic men were drunk and disorderly, according to the initial police report. As they were being arrested by two female police officers, Girsel Del Valle and her rookie partner Angela Jewell, a third man, Daniel Enrique Gomez, became disorderly. As the officers tried to subdue Gomez, a fourth man began to assault the cops, who by now numbered three women and one man. Gomez was not fully handcuffed; he pulled out a knife and thrust it at Jewell. Drawing her revolver while backing away, she ordered him to drop the knife. He lunged at her, and she shot him.

That is not, however, the way other Latinos who were watching the arrest saw things, and they became angry because they thought the shooting unjustified. Some said that they saw no knife and that the man who was shot had both hands behind his back, although they admitted he was walking toward Jewell and using foul language. Within hours, riots broke out in Mount Pleasant and adjoining neighborhoods and continued through the next two nights, resulting in hundreds of thousands of dollars in damage to cars and businesses.

At trial, the police dropped any claim that Gomez had lunged at Jewell with the knife, and the "fourth man" disappeared from the story. Given these discrepancies and the fierce anger of nearby observers, one may suspect that Gomez, who was drunk and probably using foul language, while approaching Jewell, managed both to offend and frighten her, which led to her shooting him, perhaps unnecessarily.

The Dangers of Pretending Sex Doesn't Matter

A veteran detective, who asked to remain anonymous, reports having seen similar problems again and again. He points out that very few men measuring five to five-and-a-half feet tall, 100 to 130 pounds, are hired, yet most female officers fit that description and are in danger of being overpowered by big thugs. (A few years ago, the LAPD, in reaction to pressure from feminist groups, even dropped its requirement that officers be at least five feet tall.) "Most bad guys fall into two categories," reports the detective. "Either they show no respect to female cops because they know they can take them, or they fear female cops because they know the women know they can be taken and will shoot quickly."

He also observes that typical men who become cops "have already been exposed to the fist fights, pushing matches, and other physical contact of the job. They also read other men better—the physical stances, clenching of fists, rolling up on the balls of the feet to get ready to fight." Most male cops, but few female ones, have also played contact sports and had some exposure to firearms. They've bloodied and been bloodied by others. He says male cops, in his experience, are also more likely to enjoy gun practice and physical exercise, and more likely to be experienced and competent at the aggressive high-speed driving sometimes required of officers. Conversely, most of the women couldn't carry a wounded officer to safety, though he adds, "Some would try. It isn't a case of bravery or sacrifice. It's a matter of strength."

None of this means we should denigrate the risks and sacrifices made by women police, or that all male cops are excellent. Another complicating factor in the Rodney King case was a male officer who wasn't in good physical shape, hadn't mastered his baton, and didn't keep his composure once the fight broke out. That only further illustrates the importance of strength, size, weapons proficiency, and mental toughness.

One study of public safety officers found that the women had only half to two thirds the upper body strength, and half to four fifths the lower body strength of male counterparts. Presumably this explains the finding by AEI economist John Lott, drawing on U.S. Department of Justice statistics, that increasing the number of female officers in a police force by 1 percentage point appears to increase assaults on police by 15 to 19 percent.

Women can be amazingly courageous. Ashley Smith's taming of the Atlanta shooter proves that. At one point the murderer told Smith to follow him in her car while he drove a stolen truck. She could have escaped then, but didn't because she feared if she did, he would kill more people.

But when the murderer put his guns down in her apartment, Smith didn't grab them and try to overpower him, tough-guy style. Instead of using the classic masculine virtues, she used the classic feminine ones. She listened to him, cooked him breakfast, opened up her heart and persuaded him to open up his. She encouraged him by telling him she had faith in his ability to make amends for the wrongs he'd committed, and she urged him to improve his life. The hope Smith held out for him was not that some judge would let him off, but that once he was in prison he could share the Christian faith he and Smith had in common, with other inmates. It was Smith's "gentle" virtues-and perhaps that they were displayed by a woman—that made this violent man willing to drop his guard and act right.

These same virtues are why women are often excellent police officers outside of the aspects of the job that involve violence and physical confrontation. As policing expert and former TAE editor Eli Lehrer points out:

> Policing is fundamentally a helping profession, and the non-violent parts of the job involve talking with people and human relations—things that women are generally better at than men. For some crimes, like domestic

> violence, women are better at dealing with it in almost all cases. Women also do a better job building cases based on detailed evidence, like solving car break-ins. Male cops are perpetrators in 95 percent of police bribery cases. They're not as good at report writing (the key to getting bad guys locked up). Good departments, therefore, need both male and female officers.

The key, then, is for police forces to respect the reality that male and female officers are not interchangeable. The real-world results of pretending are ugly. They can be seen on the Atlanta videotape showing Brian Nichols smashing a grandmother's head on the courthouse floor, sending her to the hospital in critical condition before he sends four more victims to the morgue.

Our refusal to acknowledge differences between men and women, and the ways those differences affect our social interactions, can be called many things. Just don't call it progress for women.

POSTSCRIPT

Are Female Police Officers as Effective as Male Officers?

Lawsuits are sometimes a good thing for society. Think about the civil rights movement in the United States during the 1950s and 1960s. Would we as a society have started to confront segregation and racism without people who were willing to challenge traditional racial stereotypes?

More recently, our society has begun to challenge traditional gender stereotypes. Title VII of the Civil Rights Act of 1964 prohibits employment discrimination based on a number of factors, including gender. In 1977, the U.S. Supreme Court considered a Title VII challenge to the Alabama Department of Corrections' height and weight requirements for prison guards who worked in "contact positions" with inmates in their maximum security prisons. The regulations provided that guards had to be at least five feet, two inches tall and had to weigh at least 120 pounds. A female applicant for one of the positions challenged these regulations, alleging that they discriminated against women.

The Supreme Court held that due to the deplorable conditions existing in that prison system:

> A woman's relative ability to maintain order in a male, maximum-security, unclassified penitentiary of the type Alabama now runs could be directly reduced by her womanhood. There is a basis in fact for expecting that sex offenders who have criminally assaulted women in the past would be moved to do so again if access to women were established within the prison. There would also be a real risk that other inmates, deprived of a normal heterosexual environment, would assault women guards because they were women. In a prison system where violence is the order of the day, where inmate access to guards is facilitated by dormitory living arrangements, where every institution is understaffed, and where a substantial portion of the inmate population is composed of sex offenders mixed at random with other prisoners, there are few visible deterrents to inmate assaults on women custodians.

The Court held, therefore, that *in the circumstances of this case* the height and weight regulations did not violate Title VII. Although the Supreme Court has not considered the issue, some lower courts have held that similar height and weight restrictions for law enforcement officers will violate Title VII.

It seems fairly safe to assume that on average, males are larger physically than females. Do you think that the relative sizes of men and women influence their ability to serve effectively as law enforcement officers? In general, the available research suggests that physical size makes little difference in the ability of people to be effective law enforcement officers.

Additional resources to supplement this discussion include Kenneth J. Peak, *Policing America: Methods, Issues, Challenges* (Prentice Hall, 1993); Samuel Walker, *The Police in America: An Introduction* (McGraw Hill, 1992); Louis A. Radelet and David L. Carter, *The Police and the Community*, 5th ed. (Macmillian, 1994); and Roger G. Dunham and Geoffrey P. Alpert, *Critical Issues in Policing: Contemporary Readings*, 2d ed. (Waveland Press, 1993). Please see Ronald J. Burke and Aslaug Mikkelsen, "Gender Issues in Policing: Do They Matter?" *Women in Management* (vol. 20, no. ½, 2005); Deborah Prussel and Kimberly A. Lonsway, "Recruiting Women Police Officers," *Law & Order* (vol. 49, no. 7, 2001); and Mary Dodge and Mark Pogrebin, "African-American Policewomen: An Exploration of Professional Relationships," *Policing* (vol. 24, no. 4, 2001).

ISSUE 20

Do Crack Cocaine Laws Discriminate Against African-Americans and Other Minority Groups?

YES: Michael Coyle, from "Race and Class Penalties in Crack Cocaine Sentencing," *The Sentencing Project* (2002)

NO: Randall Kennedy, from "The State, Criminal Law, and Racial Discrimination: A Comment," *Harvard Law Review* (April 1994)

ISSUE SUMMARY

YES: Michael Coyle, a research associate with The Sentencing Project, asserts that crack cocaine sentencing policy is unconscionable in light of its impact on minority group members. Moreover, crack cocaine laws punish poor people more severely because they obtain the more affordable form of the drug, while wealthier people, who are more likely to use powdered cocaine, are punished less stringently.

NO: Harvard Law School Professor Randall Kennedy contends, however, that racial disparities in crack cocaine sentencing are not a mark of discrimination by white legislatures against blacks as much as a sensible response to the desires of all law-abiding people for protection against criminals.

Laws against crack cocaine are very strict indeed. For example, in the State of Florida, simple possession of any amount of crack is a felony that can get you up to 5 years in prison. If you possess crack with intent to sell, you can get up to 15 years. One of the problems is that in the federal system and in some states, possession of crack is punished differently than possession of traditional powder cocaine, even though the products are identical chemically. Moreover, the federal sentencing guidelines, which govern criminal sentencing in the federal courts, are based on the idea that crack is 50 times more addictive than powdered cocaine. In addition, crack is the only drug that provides a mandatory prison sentence for first-offense possession. The essential question for purposes of this issue is why?

Michael Coyle, research associate for The Sentencing Project, states:

> The failure of Congress to amend the sentencing disparities between crack cocaine and powder cocaine reflects a culture-wide set of misconception about crack—who uses it, who sells it, and what the consequences of its trade, such as violence, have been. Many have submitted that the disparities illustrate something much more disturbing, namely, a deeply embedded racist and classist undertone to our society's political, legal and law enforcement structure.

Coyle maintains as well that because crack cocaine is cheaper, minorities and poor people are more likely to use it than the powder alternative. This has also resulted in the prosecution and imprisonment of low-level crack users and street-dealers, rather than high-level cocaine traffickers.

Professor Randall Kennedy, of the Harvard Law School, disagrees. He believes that U.S. courts should defer to legislative judgments about our nation's drug laws, including the penalties for crack cocaine. Kennedy observes that U.S. courts have uniformly rejected challenges under the Federal Equal Protection Clause because of the absence of sufficient proof of a discriminatory purpose. Because no one has been able to identify such a racially discriminatory purpose, Kennedy believes that legislatures should be left to develop appropriate penalties for crimes, including crack cocaine offenses.

So, who do you think is right? Do you agree with Michael Coyle that crack cocaine laws specifically target African-Americans and the poor? If so, should they be held unconstitutional? Or, is your position more consistent with Professor Kennedy's view that these issues should be left to the discretion of state and federal legislatures? Moreover, what are your views on the use of social science data by courts to infer discrimination? For example, in *United States v. Clary,* the Court considered data indicating that 55 African-Americans had been prosecuted for crack cocaine offenses for every white defendant. It stated that this disparate racial impact was "so great as to shock the conscience of the court." Does this type of disparity "shock your conscience?" Or, as Professor Kennedy suggests, should defendants be required to demonstrate some actual "discriminatory intent" by the legislature before they can prevail against these laws in court? Is this a realistic standard, or simply a defense of the status quo and our nation's draconian drug laws? These are interesting questions.

Michael Coyle

Race and Class Penalties in Crack Cocaine Sentencing

Overview

After a decade of contentious debate regarding the federal sentencing disparities between crack cocaine and powder cocaine, a number of significant initiatives to reform current policy have recently emerged. These include legislation introduced in Congress and a series of hearings resulting in recommendations by the United States Sentencing Commission.

This . . . paper provides the background to these initiatives by surveying the differences between crack cocaine and powder cocaine as currently held by medical and other professionals. It also reviews the development of federal legislation that has created greater criminal penalties for crack than powder, and assesses recent developments in the effort to resolve these sentencing disparities.

Crack cocaine became prevalent in the mid-1980s and received massive media attention due in part to its exponential growth in the drug market. The explosive popularity of crack cocaine was associated with its cheap price, which for the first time made cocaine available to a wider economic class. In the wake of widespread media attention, crack was portrayed as a violence inducing, highly addictive drug that created a plague of social problems, especially in inner city communities.

With the media spotlight focusing on crack, Congress quickly passed federal sentencing legislation in both 1986 and 1988. This included mandatory sentencing laws based on the premise that crack cocaine was 50 times more addictive than powder cocaine. For good measure, Congress doubled that number and came up with a sentencing policy based on the weight of the drug an individual was convicted of selling. Thus, federal sentences for crack were constructed to relate to sentences for powder cocaine in a 100:1 quantity ratio. The result is that while a conviction for the sale of 500 grams of powder cocaine triggers a 5-year mandatory sentence, only 5 grams of crack cocaine are required to trigger the same 5-year mandatory sentence. Similarly, while sale of 5,000 grams of powder leads to a 10-year sentence, only 50 grams of crack trigger the same 10-year sentence. These laws remain in effect today.

The Difference between Crack Cocaine and Powder Cocaine

Powder cocaine is made from coca paste, which is derived from the leaves of the coca plant. Crack cocaine is simply made by taking powder cocaine and cooking it with baking soda and water until it forms a hard rocky substance. These "rocks" are then broken into pieces and sold in small quantities.

Initially, crack cocaine was widely viewed as a social menace that was categorically different from powder cocaine in its physiological and psychotropic effects. However, these assumptions were more reflective of the prevalent panic and fear that arose out of the explosive growth of the crack market than conclusions of scientific investigation. While federal law has constructed a penalty structure that reflects these assumptions, only 14 states have adopted laws that distinguish between powder cocaine and crack cocaine in their penalty schemes, and only one (Iowa) utilizes the 100:1 quantity ratio of the federal system.

Over time, numerous studies have shown that the physiological and psychotropic effects of crack and powder are the same, and they are now widely acknowledged as pharmacologically identical. For example, a 1996 study published in the *Journal of the American Medical Association* finds analogous effects on the body for both crack cocaine and powder cocaine. Similarly, Charles Schuster, former Director of the National Institute on Drug Abuse and Professor of Psychiatry and Behavioral Sciences, found that once cocaine is absorbed into the bloodstream and reaches the brain, its effects on brain chemistry are identical regardless of whether it is crack or powder.

Violence and the Myth of the "Crack Baby"

While politicians in the capital debated policy, crack cocaine, like all illicit drugs, found its niche on the street. When crack hit the drug market in the 1980s it arrived as a technological innovation that made the "pleasures" of cocaine available to people who could not previously afford it in the expensive powder form. As Alfred Blumstein, of Carnegie Mellon University points out, crack cocaine, as an innovation, initially produced vigorous competition in the drug market. As with all illegal markets, crack distribution rights and boundaries were apportioned amongst competitors with the use of violence. In time the dust has settled, the markets have matured, and the associated violence has significantly decreased.

Initially, the high violence associated with the maturation process of the crack market fostered a perception that the ingestion of crack instigated violent behavior in the individual user. However, studies have since shown otherwise. Charles Schuster, who argues that prolonged use of high doses of crack or powder can produce a form of paranoid toxic psychosis in which aggressive acts are more likely, also qualifies that he "know(s) of no evidence, however, that this is more likely to occur after the use of crack as opposed to powder cocaine."

In its May 2002 recommendations to Congress, the United States Sentencing Commission (the Commission) stated that the current penalties on crack are based on beliefs about the association of crack offenses with violence that have been shown to be inaccurate. The Commission concluded that the violence associated with crack is primarily related to the drug trade and not to the effects of the drug itself, and further, that both powder and crack cocaine cause distribution-related violence. In a study of thousands of federally prosecuted cocaine cases, the Commission reports that, for FY 2000, weapon involvement for powder cocaine offenses was 25.4% and for crack cocaine offenses, 35.2%. The frequency with which weapons are actually used is much lower. For powder offenders the use rate is 1.2% and for crack offenders it is 2.3%, not a difference, the Commission argues, that justifies a 100:1 quantity disparity. The Commission also argues that the solution is not to encapsulate offenders in lengthy mandatory sentences that assume all crack offenders are violent. Rather, the commissioners suggest federal law should begin by assuming crack offenders are nonviolent and then apply new guidelines for increased punishment for violent offenses.

Crack cocaine was also initially widely viewed as a menace that was ravaging not only inner city adults but also innocent babies. The notion of the "crack baby" became common and was associated with the weak, shivering and inconsolable newborn (most often African American) infant, experiencing immediate and long-term effects of withdrawal from crack. Over time these descriptions have been interpreted in the medical field as the result of hysteria and not fact. Deborah Frank, a professor of Pediatrics at Boston University describes the "crack baby" as "a grotesque media stereotype (and) not a scientific diagnosis." She also finds that in pregnant crack users the effects on the fetus are no different than for those who are pregnant and in poverty, or those using tobacco or alcohol, or those having poor prenatal care or poor nutrition. Finally, from her studies she concludes there is no evidence of increased risk of birth defects for women using crack during pregnancy, and that newborns of crack-addicted mothers have no withdrawal symptoms. The crack baby, it turns out, was a ghost.

Drug Quantities and Crack Cocaine Penalties

The federal sentencing laws Congress passed in 1986 and 1988 were designed in part with the purpose of hindering the crack cocaine drug trade. The intent of Congress was to impose a minimum ten-year prison sentence on a major trafficker (e.g. a manufacturer or head of organization distributing large drug quantities) and a minimum five-year sentence on a serious trafficker (e.g. a manager of a substantial drug-trade business). As such, the laws were constructed to respond to the quantity of drugs involved in the offense.

However, the weight numbers attached to the sentences via the Anti-Drug Abuse Act of 1986 fail to capture the different roles associated with the crack trade. As research from the Commission has shown, the 5 grams of crack set by Congress as the trigger for a five-year mandatory sentence is not a quantity associated with mid-level, much less serious, traffickers (see Table 1). The median crack cocaine street level dealer (comprising two-thirds of federal crack defendants) charged in federal court was arrested holding 52 grams of the substance, enough to trigger a 10-year mandatory sentence. For powder cocaine, the medidan street level dealer is charged with holding 340 grams of drugs, not enough even to trigger the 5-year sentence.

Table 1

Median Street Level Dealer Drug Quantitites and Mandatory Minimums

Drug	Median Drug Weight	Applicable Mandatory Minimum
Crack Cocaine	52 grams	10 years
Powder Cocaine	340 grams	none

The results of these erroneous calculations have been dual. First, they have resulted in extremely severe prison terms for low-level crack offenders, who form two out of every three crack offenders. Second, with mandatory minimum sentences focusing solely on quantities, offenders with different levels of culpability are often lumped together. As the Commission's May 2002 report to Congress stipulates, "Contrary to the intent of Congress, the five and ten year minimum penalties most often apply to low level crack cocaine traffickers, rather than to serious or major traffickers."

Some experts believe crack is more likely to be abused because of its brief high and low price. Charles Schuster argues that while research illustrates smoked crack and intravenous powder offer the same high, and that while the 100:1 ratio is indefensible, a ratio of disparity should be kept. The reason for this, he contends, is that crack cocaine has adverse public health and social consequences that are potentially greater than those for powder because of the ease with which crack can be smoked repeatedly. This ease, he argues, makes crack appealing to many who would not put needles into their bodies. Thus, "although individual risk may not vary between smoked crack and injected powder the numbers (of people) at risk of becoming addicted to crack may be significantly greater." Consequently, his recommendation is a 3:1 ratio.

Critics of the sentencing disparities between crack and powder have drawn other arguments. For example, Los Angeles federal Judge Terry Hatter argues that contrary to what is in place currently, penalties for powder should be higher than crack since the latter cannot be made without the former. Professor Blumstein makes the same argument for a different reason. He believes that powder sentences should be higher than crack sentences because (a) powder trafficking has more offenders above the street level than crack trafficking (in federal powder offenses only 29% are street-level, whereas in federal crack offenses 66% are street-level), and (b) while only 37% of powder offenses are limited to neighborhood or city areas, 75% of crack offenses are limited to the same areas.

The disparity between the two cocaines goes beyond the 100:1 quantity ratio. Crack is also the only drug that carries a mandatory prison sentence for first offense possession. For example, a person convicted in federal court of possession of 5 grams of crack automatically receives a five-year prison term while a person convicted of possessing 5 grams of powder will probably receive a probation sentence. In fact, the maximum sentence for simple possession of any other drug, be it powder cocaine or heroin, is 1 year in prison.

For most, the 100:1 sentencing ratio between crack and powder appears inexplicably extreme. Even many intimately involved with enforcing crack penalties find current federal law overly punitive and assert it inappropriately targets a drug population that consists primarily of addicts who possess or sell crack to support their own habit.

Evolution of the Sentencing Disparity between Crack Cocaine and Powder Cocaine

In 1984 Congress created the United States Sentencing Commission to develop federal sentencing guidelines that would, among other goals, reduce unwarranted sentencing disparity. In 1994, as part of the Omnibus Violent Crime Control and Law Enforcement Act, the Commission was directed to study the differing penalties for powder and crack. After a yearlong study the Commission recommended to Congress a revision of the crack/powder 100:1 sentencing disparity, finding it to be unjustified by the small differences between the two forms of cocaine. The Commission advised equalizing (1:1) the quantity ratio that would trigger the mandatory sentences. The Commission also counseled that the federal sentencing guidelines should provide criteria other than drug type to determine sentence lengths, so that, for example, offenders engaging in violence would receive longer sentences than offenders who do not. Congress rejected the recommendations and refused to change the law, which marked the first time it did so in the Commission's history.

Two years later, in April 1997, the Commission once more recommended that the disparity between crack and powder cocaine be reduced, again by weight, this time providing Congress a range of 2:1 to 15:1 to choose from. The new recommendation was based on both raising the quantity of crack and lowering the quantity of powder required to trigger mandatory minimum sentences. Congress, however, again did not act on the recommendation. By the end of the year the Clinton Administration, which throughout the "tough on crime" political climate of the 1990s had supported Congress' rejections of the Commission's recommendations, signaled some agreement with the Commission's call for reform. Though not until the last year of his second term, President Clinton did endorse a 10:1 ratio to be arrived at by raising crack weight minimums and lowering powder ones. Congress, however, made no revisions.

In 2001–02 there has been a new thrust to reconsider crack cocaine policies. As evinced in its 2002 *Report to Congress*, which again calls for reducing sentencing disparities, the Commission conducted extensive studies and held three public hearings at which it received testimony from the medical and scientific communities, federal and local law enforcement officials, criminal justice practitioners, academics, and civil rights organizations. In addition, the last year has seen the Drug Sentencing Reform Act of 2001 proposal, which in a like manner seeks to transform current crack cocaine federal sentencing policy. The bill, which has not yet been heard on the floor, was introduced by Senator Jeff Sessions (R-AL) and co-sponsored by Senator Orrin Hatch (R-UT), two leading conservative members of the Senate. The fate of this bill, along with that of the Commission's 2002 recommendations (see below), is yet to be determined.

In its May 2002 *Report to Congress*, the Commission unveiled a study of thousands of federally prosecuted cocaine cases sentenced between 1995 and 2000, expert testimony gathered from a series of public hearings and a survey of U.S. district and appellate judges. In the report the Commission unanimously affirmed that while a greater punishment for crack vs. powder is warranted, the disparity of 100:1 ratio is not appropriate. Specifically, the report recommends Congress:

- Increase crack weight minimums:
  - For the five-year mandatory sentence from 5 to 25 grams (a 20:1 ratio)
  - For the ten-year mandatory sentence from 50 to 250 grams (a 20:1 ratio)
- Repeal the mandatory minimum for simple possession of crack cocaine
- Direct the Commission to provide enhancements for a drug crime that involves a dangerous firearm, violence resulting in bodily injury, distribution to protected individuals/locations, repeat offenders, and importation of drugs by offenders who do not perform a mitigating role in the offense
- Maintain the powder trigger at present levels of 500 and 5,000 grams

The Commission argues that if adopted, the recommendations would narrow the difference between average sentences for crack and powder from 44 months to 12 months, and that the average crack sentence would change from 118 to 95 months and for powder from 74 to 83 months.

Race and Class in Crack Cocaine and Powder Cocaine Law and Enforcement

The failure of Congress to amend the sentencing disparities between crack cocaine and powder cocaine reflects a culture-wide set of misconceptions about crack—who uses it, who sells it, and what the consequences of its trade, such as violence, have been. Many have submitted that the disparities illustrate something much more disturbing, namely, a deeply embedded racist and classist undertone to our society's political, legal and law enforcement structure.

In its February 2002 testimony before the U.S. Sentencing Commission, the Leadership Conference on Civil Rights reports that despite similar drug use rates between minorities and whites, minorities are disproportionately subject to the penalties for both types of cocaine. Congress has not lacked this information, as the Commission has been reporting it for over a decade. Research on patterns of drug purchase and use demonstrates that overall drug users report their main drug providers are sellers of the same racial or ethnic background as they are. Yet, as the Commission's data shows, in the year 2000, of all federal crack defendants, 84% were black.

Most criminal justice analysts argue that racial disparities in arrest and imprisonment relate to demographics. Crack is usually sold in small quantities in open-air markets. Powder is more expensive and is usually sold in larger quantities behind closed doors in locations that are inherently private. In urban areas the "fronts" of crack use and sales are large metropolitan centers which gather the greater emphasis of law enforcement. Since minorities and lower income persons are most likely to inhabit these areas, they are therefore at greater risk of arrest for crack cocaine possession than are white and higher income powder offenders. The latter inhabit working class and upper-class neighborhoods where drug sales are more likely to occur indoors instead of the street sales of the urban neighborhoods that receive disproportionate (greater) attention from law enforcement. Though it is true that open-air drug sales are easier to observe than indoor drug sales, the current allocation of law enforcement resources results in a policing structure that is race and class imbalanced. Coupled with the harshly unequal penalties between the two cocaine drugs, the result can only be described as a race and class oriented drug policy. Understandably, such law enforcement has been called evidence of racial profiling.

Since the two forms of cocaine are pharmacologically indistinguishable, by dictating harsher sentences for possession of crack than for possession of powder, the law is more severely punishing the poor, who obtain the affordable form of cocaine (crack), than the affluent, who obtain the more expensive form of the same drug (powder). Were alcohol illegal, this would be the equivalent of imposing a higher punishment for the sale of a cheap jug of wine than for an expensive French wine.

The 100:1 quantity ratio in the federal system has been legally challenged as unconstitutional on the grounds that it denies equal protection or due process, and because the penalties constitute cruel and unusual punishment. However, courts have generally not responded positively to such a claim, not least because a "discriminatory intent" on behalf of lawmakers' cannot be proven. Human Rights Watch, on the other hand, has not hesitated to describe federal crack sentencing policy as "an indefensible sentencing differential (that is) unconscionable in light of its racial impact."

Reforming the Crack Cocaine and Powder Cocaine Sentencing Disparity

In his 2002 testimony to the Commission, Deputy Attorney General Larry D. Thompson, the second-ranking official in the Department of Justice, argued that the current federal policy and guidelines for sentencing crack cocaine offenses are appropriate. Thompson claims that the high rate of persons of color affected by crack in inner city neighborhoods translates into a responsibility to protect minorities from drug sellers in their communities, and that hence stricter sentences for crack are not only justified but necessary. Ethan Nadelmann, executive director of the Drug Policy Alliance, a New York group that promotes alternatives to the war on drugs, says the government claims to be protecting minority communities but its harsher enforcement of crack has never worked out that way. As Charles J. Hynes, the District Attorney for Kings County in New York, sums up, "the simple fact is that although both populations have similar rates of drug abuse, minority drug defendants are serving substantially longer prison sentences than non-minority defendants."

While others, such as the International Association of Chiefs of Police, have joined the Department of Justice's call for lowering powder cocaine weight minimums that trigger the mandatory sentences, none note how such an act will, again, mostly affect low-level defendants. The wisdom of such a move that would fill even more cells with low-level offenders serving long mandatory sentences at enormous public expense is questionable. As Federal Bureau of Prisons Director Kathy Hawk Sawyer has testified to Congress "70-some percent of our female populations are low-level, nonviolent offenders. The fact that they even have to come into prison is a question mark for me. I think it has been an unintended consequence of the sentencing guidelines and the mandatory minimums."

The American Civil Liberties Union has argued that lowering powder minimums under the current racially uneven enforcement patterns would have the effect of increasing the number of minorities in prison. Indeed, as the Commission's 2000 report shows, even though the black proportion (30.3%) of powder cases is much lower than that for crack, most of the white defendants are ethnically Hispanic (50.6%)–which means the total minority proportion of powder cases is 81%. Assuming law enforcement practices in the drug market remained the same, it would be the case that instead of decreasing disparities for African American and Hispanic communities, decreasing the amount of powder required to trigger minimum sentences would actually increase disparities.

The ACLU further claims congressional resistance to reform is based on ignorance and fueled by media hysteria, and accuses Congress of tying the hands of judges by forcing them to impose unfair and extraordinary harsh mandatory minimum sentences on low-level crack offenders. Senator Leahy also argues that to increase powder penalties to counteract imbalances created by levels set for crack when no sector of law enforcement has made the proposal that current cocaine law is not sufficient makes little sense.

Another argument has come from former White House Special Counsel and Professor of Law, George Mason University, William G. Otis. At a May 2002 hearing of the Subcommittee on Crime and Drugs of the Senate Judiciary Committee Professor Otis claimed that though the sentencing disparity should be addressed, this should not be done by increasing the minimum crack weights. His argument is that such a change will send the wrong message, namely that it is now less dangerous to consume or deal crack. Professor Otis claimed a sentencing system should not be engineered with one eye to race and also argues that race disparities can work the other way: for example, blacks constitute only 1% of defendants sentenced for methamphetamine offenses.

In conclusion, the current 100:1 sentencing ratio communicates to minorities and the poor a message of inherit inequity in both the law and the courts. This message breeds discontent and creates cynicism about law enforcement, and is becoming a social fact of great consequence. As Wade Henderson of the Leadership Conference on Civil Rights argues, "The drug war will continue to lack credibility in minority communities until these sentencing laws are changed." The Commission's 2002 report to Congress argues that even the perception of racial disparity is problematic because it fosters disrespect for and lack of confidence in the criminal justice system among the very groups Congress intended would benefit from the heightened penalties for crack cocaine offenses. The consequences are visible. As Charles J. Hynes, District Attorney for New York's Kings County disclosed in his testimony to a hearing of the Judiciary Committee, in selecting jurists he and his prosecutorial colleagues are faced with the "fact (that) minorities believe overall that law is unfair towards minorities."

Conclusion

In its May 2002 report to Congress the Commission reported that for FY 2000 a street-level dealer of crack on average received a sentence of 103.5 months—almost nine years. In comparison the mean maximum state prison sentence for all violent offenses is 100 months. While dramatic hyperbole has defined much of the history of crack cocaine and its prosecution, increasingly a sober and impartial assessment of drug sentencing is being called for.

The call for a new assessment of sentencing has come from diverse voices, and a plethora of useful ideas in need of immediate implementation have surfaced. The Leadership Conference on Civil Rights has asked Congress to review the interaction of mandatory minimum drug sentencing laws and the tactics and priorities of federal law enforcement agencies. The National Council of La Raza and the Mexican American Legal Defense and Education Fund have recommended turning the tide of drug use by investing in alternatives to punishment for first time, non-violent, low-level drug offenders. In his Drug Sentencing Reform Act of 2001 Senator Sessions has suggested a pilot program to remove federal nonviolent elderly offenders (65 and over) from prisons into home detention. Perhaps most interestingly, Alfred Blumstein asked the U.S. Sentencing Commission to urge Congress to sunset its mandatory minimum sentencing drug laws to enable the Commission to emerge with a careful, rational and deliberative structure. Professor Blumstein's idea responds to most legislators' fear of appearing "soft on crime" and the consequent difficulty they would have in voting for a repeal of any drug or crime law. With sunsetting, such laws would have to be reconsidered after some period of time, and the ineffective ones left to quietly disappear in the absence of a strong reason to extend them.

Lastly, Congress would do well to consider District Attorney Charles J. Hynes' model of the Drug Treatment Alternative to Prison program (DTAP). This program takes chronic drug offenders who sell drugs to support their habit, a revolving door population in prisons, and subjects them to a 15 to 24 month rigorous, intensive residential drug treatment. The recidivism rate of its graduates at the end of their first post-treatment year is half the rate of eligible defendants who did not participate and were sentenced to state prison. Hynes contends that the program is saving the state of New York almost two million dollars a year. As he says, "it makes no sense to warehouse nonviolent drug abusers in prison . . . only to have them return to a life of crime and drugs when they are released to the community." Indeed, few changes would have as great an impact on the drug war as legislative revisions aimed at mandating treatment alternatives for a drug population that consists primarily of addicts who possess or sell drugs to support their habit.

Drug policy is a critical aspect of today's criminal justice system as it constitutes a major feeder into the mostly African American and Latino prison/jail population of nearly two million people. What is at issue in considering the legislation of crack cocaine sentencing is proportionate punishment that will be free of racial, ethnic or class discrimination. As one Senator put it, the principles that guided the first acts of Congress on crack cocaine were at best uninformed. It remains to be seen whether Congress or the Bush Administration will accept more modest recommendations that will eliminate the race and class penalty of the drug war. Public opinion will ultimately be critical to influencing public policy on this often-emotional issue.

NO  **Randall Kennedy**

The State, Criminal Law, and Racial Discrimination: A Comment

Crime is widely perceived as a major blight that decreases happiness, productivity, and security in the United States. Defining crimes and protecting people from criminality are central tasks that we assign to the state. Like many social ills, crime afflicts African-Americans with a special vengeance. African-Americans are considerably more likely than whites to be raped, robbed, assaulted, and murdered. Many of those who seek to champion the interests of African-Americans, however, wrongly retard efforts to control criminality. They charge that the state, at least in its role as administrator of criminal justice, is now (as it has been historically) an instrument of racist oppression. In all too many instances, these allegations are overblown and counterproductive; they exaggerate the extent of racial prejudice in the criminal justice system and detract attention from other problems of law enforcement that warrant more consideration. What such critiques ignore or minimize is that the main problem confronting black communities in the United States is not excessive policing and invidious punishment but rather a failure of the state to provide black communities with the equal *protection* of the laws. Although this failure often stems from a pervasive and racist devaluation of black victims of crime, ironically, a substantial contributing cause is a misguided antagonism toward efforts to preserve public safety.

...[In this article] I discuss *State v. Russell,* a Minnesota Supreme Court case that invalidated a state law that punished possession of crack cocaine more harshly than possession of powdered cocaine. The court invalidated the differential punishment largely on the grounds that it constituted an illicit racial discrimination—most persons convicted of possessing powdered cocaine were white, and most convicted of possessing crack were black. After noting that the reasoning of *Russell* reflects a widespread misperception that is gaining influence, I explain why *Russell* was wrongly decided. I argue that, as a constitutional matter, the state was justified in penalizing possession of crack cocaine more harshly than possession of powdered cocaine notwithstanding the racial demographics that emerged from the operation of this sentencing scheme. I also argue that the court was simplistic in its approach to deciphering the meaning of racial disparities arising from even-handed enforcement of race neutral laws. I maintain that the court failed to take into account properly the benefit presumably bestowed upon the citizenry—including, of course, law-abiding black citizens—by the challenged sentencing scheme. I also maintain that the court was insufficiently attentive to the difference between a law that burdens a racial minority community as a whole as distinct from a law that burdens a mere subset of that community. . . .

I. Critiques of the Criminal Justice System Critiqued

Conventional racial critiques of the state maintain that the criminal justice system is infected with a pervasive, systemic racial bias. This bias, the argument goes, subjects African-Americans (particularly men) to unfair targeting at every level of contact that individuals have with officials charged with protecting the public safety: surveillance, stops, arrests, prosecutions, and sentencing. These critics (depending on age) allude to bitter memories of the Scottsboro Boys or Rodney King, and portray the police as colonial forces of occupation and prisons as centers of racist oppression.

These sentiments have been expressed in a variety of media, including the literature of legal academia. For example, Professor Dorothy Roberts writes that the white power structure "constructs crime in terms of race and race in terms of crime," and thereby creates a "racial *ideology* of crime that sustains continued white domination of blacks in the guise of crime control." John A. Powell and Eileen Hershenov assert that the most prominent initiative in American law enforcement—the so-called "war on drugs"—could "more aptly be called a war on the minority populations." Similarly, Professor Gary Peller contends that:

> [R]acial power is often most dramatically exercised, and most easily recognized, in the enforcement of criminal laws. . . . No fancy theoretical conceptualization is necessary to explain how race figures in police brutality, in prosecutorial decisions, in jury selection, in conviction rates, and in the incarceration and capital sentencing of people of color in America.

Fueled by the conviction that invidious racial discrimination pervades definitions of criminality and the administration of law enforcement, these beliefs give rise to a distinctive stance characterized by hostility toward the agencies of crime control, sympathetic identification with defendants and convicts, and a commitment to policies aimed at narrowly constraining the powers of law enforcement authorities. . . . But, of course, there has been substantial change in the terrain of race relations, and today, some of the policies most heatedly criticized by certain sectors of black communities are supported and enforced by other African-Americans within these same communities. These facts call for a reconsideration of old . . . images that guide intuitions about the meaning of racial disparities in arrests, prosecutions, and sentencing. Although the administration of criminal justice has, at times, been used as an instrument of racial oppression, the principal problem facing African-Americans in the context of criminal justice today is not over-enforcement but under-enforcement of the laws. The most lethal danger facing African-Americans in their day-to-day lives is not white, racist officials of the state, but private, violent criminals (typically black) who attack those most vulnerable to them without regard to racial identity.

Acknowledgment of these realities gives rise to attitudes that differ greatly from the attitudes of those who view the criminal justice system with fear and loathing. These attitudes include a perception of criminal law enforcement as a public good, a sympathetic identification with the actual and potential victims of crime, and a commitment to policies that offer greater physical security to minority communities, even if that means ceding greater powers to law enforcement agencies and thus concomitantly narrowing the formal liberties that individuals currently enjoy.

Unfortunately, efforts to address the danger crime poses to minority communities are confused and hobbled by a reflexive, self-defeating resort to charges of racism when a policy, racially neutral on its face, gives rise to racial disparities when applied. Such overheated allegations of racism obscure analysis of a wide range of problems in the criminal justice system. Consider, for instance, the stifling of intelligent debate over drug policy by the rhetoric of paranoia. On the one hand, some condemn as "genocide" the punitive "war on drugs" because a disproportionate number of those subjected to arrest, prosecution, and incarceration for drug use are black. At the same time, others, including Representative Charles Rangel and Director of the Office of National Drug Control Policy Lee Brown, condemn proposals for decriminalizing drug use on the grounds that such policies would amount to genocide because racial minorities would constitute a disproportionate number of those allowed to pursue their drug habits without deterrent intervention by the state. No one in either of these camps has come forward with credible evidence to suggest that American drug policy is truly genocidal—that is, *deliberately* designed to eradicate a people. Yet the rhetoric of racial genocide clearly influences the public debate about this aspect of criminal law enforcement policy.

II. *State v. Russell*

Overheated and under-analyzed claims of racial discrimination also affect judicial attitudes and, hence, decisionmaking. Consider, for example, *State v. Russell.* In *Russell,* five African-American men were prosecuted for possessing crack cocaine and were sentenced under a statute that penalized possession of crack cocaine more harshly than it penalized the possession of similar amounts of powdered cocaine. Possession of three grams of crack cocaine carried a penalty of twenty years in prison, while possession of an equal amount of powdered cocaine carried a maximum penalty of only five years in prison. Russell and his co-defendants argued that no rational basis justified the difference in punishment. Moreover, they argued that this difference was racially discriminatory because it adversely affected, with insufficient justification, black cocaine users relative to their white counterparts. They based this argument on the fact that greater numbers of African-Americans use crack over powder. Statistics referred to by the Supreme Court indicated that in Minnesota in 1988, 96.6% of all persons charged with possession of crack cocaine were black, while 79.6% of all persons charged with possession of powdered cocaine were white.

The trial court invalidated Minnesota's sentencing scheme, and the Minnesota Supreme Court affirmed. The court's reason for invalidating the sentencing scheme was that, under the state constitution, no rational basis supported the differential punishment. Although the court might have reached the same conclusion in the absence of the racial disparities noted above, the court's belief that the sentencing statute created a racial injustice clearly played a major, if not decisive, role in its reasoning. "While we are ordinarily loathe to intrude or even inquire into the legislative process on matters of criminal punishment," Justice Rosalie E. Wahl noted in the principal opinion announcing *Russell,* "the correlation between race and the use of [crack] or powder and the gross disparity in resulting punishment cries out for closer scrutiny of the challenged laws." . . .

The State justified its heavier punishment of crack possession on three grounds. First, crack and powder have different sociologies of use and distribution; dealing can be inferred from the possession of smaller amounts of crack. Second, crack has a more potent physiological impact. Third, more violence is associated with the distribution and use of crack.

The Minnesota Supreme Court rejected these justifications and concluded that they failed to offer even a rational basis for punishing possession of crack cocaine more harshly than possession of powdered cocaine. The court dismissed testimony about the amounts of drugs that signaled dealing as opposed to mere possession as "purely anecdotal." The court also noted that, although crack and powdered cocaine are typically ingested through different methods—crack by smoking, powder by sniffing—if powder is dissolved in water and injected intravenously, the effect on the body is similar to the effect of smoking crack. From these two propositions, the court concluded that the state's distinction for purposes of punishment was based on different methods of ingestion rather than on an inherent difference between the two forms of the drug. As Justice Wahl put the matter: "Disparate treatment of crack and powdered cocaine users is not justified on the basis of crack's greater dangerousness when there is evidence that powdered cocaine could readily produce the effects purported to justify a harsher penalty for possession of crack." Finally, the court rejected the testimony associating greater violence with crack as opposed to powdered cocaine because it was "not only anecdotal, but pale[d] in light of official observation that if there is more violence associated with crack use, 'that difference could be caused more by factors such as gang warfare and certain group behaviors than by the pharmacological effects of crack.'" . . .

In pursuing this course, the *Russell* court ignored the realities that have made the invention of crack a watershed in the history of illicit drugs. Although the court asserted that nothing substantial differentiates crack cocaine from powdered cocaine, the record before it indicated otherwise. Students of the drug trade note with awe the technological and marketing "advances" that distinguish crack and that have enabled it to transform the illicit drug industry. Mark A. R. Kleiman observes:

> In 1978, cocaine was something between a curiosity and a menace. . . . By 1988, cocaine had become the drug problem par excellence, with a retail market nearly equal to those for heroin and marijuana combined. . . . How did a minor drug become so major, a seemingly benign drug so horrible? In a word, crack happened.

The court's hostility to the Minnesota sentencing statute stemmed from its perception that, in Justice Wahl's words, the law "appears to impose a substantially disproportionate burden" on blacks, "the very class of persons whose history [of oppression] inspired the principles of equal protection." There are two related difficulties with this statement: one has to do with what constitutes a "burden," and the second has to do with what makes a law or policy racially discriminatory.

First, Justice Wahl's portrayal of Minnesota's sentencing statute as a "burden" to blacks as a class is simplistic. Assuming that one believes in criminalizing the distribution of crack cocaine, punishing this conduct is a public good. It is a "burden" on those who are convicted of engaging in this conduct. But it is presumably a benefit for the great mass of law-abiding people. Professor Kate Stith articulates this point with clarity. Commenting on *Russell,* she keenly observes:

> While it appears true that the enhanced penalties for crack cocaine more often fall upon black defendants, the legislature's action might also have been viewed as a laudatory attempt to provide enhanced protection to those communities—largely black, according to the court's own statistics—who are ravaged by abuse of this potent drug. . . . [I]f dealers in crack cocaine have their liberty significantly restricted, this will afford greater liberties to the majority of citizens who are the potential victims of drug dealing and associated violent behaviors. *This is the logic of the criminal law,* and it is distressing that a majority of the Minnesota Supreme Court recognized only half of this logic—the denial of liberty to lawbreakers.

When discussing racial issues and the administration of criminal justice, some commentators think immediately and, all too often, *solely* about invidious criminal prosecution of people of color. There is reason for that. Throughout American history, officials have wielded the criminal law as a weapon with which to intimidate blacks and other people of color. But the flip side of racially invidious over-enforcement of the criminal law is often minimized. Racially invidious under-enforcement purposefully denies African-American victims of violence the things that all persons legitimately expect from the state: civil order and, in the event that crimes are committed, best efforts to apprehend and punish offenders. For most of the nation's history, blacks were denied this public good. The history of antiblack lynching and the failure of the states and the federal government to combat it effectively offers only the most notorious example. In many contexts, in comparison to the treatment accorded to whites, blacks have been denied quite literally the equal *protection* of the law.

Many have observed that, all too frequently, politicians, newspaper editors, and police officials express concern about crime only if they perceive that it inflicts injury upon whites. The more crime affects whites, the more likely officials are to respond. The less whites are harmed, the less likely officials are to respond. This critique suggests a very different approach to the crack cocaine-powdered cocaine distinction from that taken by the Minnesota Supreme Court. It suggests that we ought to commend rather than condemn the legislature's distinction between crack and powdered cocaine. If it is true that blacks as a class are disproportionately *victimized* by the conduct punished by the statute at issue, then it follows that blacks as a class may be *helped* by measures reasonably thought to discourage such conduct.

To get at the second difficulty with the *Russell* court's perception of the punishment at issue—its conception of the sentencing statute as an instance of "racial" discrimination—one must focus on the punishment's relationship to those on whom it *does* place a burden, namely, persons convicted of possessing a certain amount of crack cocaine. The Minnesota Supreme Court condemned the statute as imposing an unjustifiable racially discriminatory burden. But what is "racial" about the punishment? Justice Wahl writes as though the punishment falls upon blacks as a class. But to the extent that the heavier punishment for possession of crack falls upon blacks, it falls not upon blacks as a class but rather upon a subset of the black population—those in violation of the law who are apprehended. . . .

III. Equal Protection and Discriminatory Purpose

What should be the significance of purpose in determining whether official action amounts to unconstitutional racial discrimination? Under federal constitutional doctrine, a finding of racially discriminatory purpose is essential to a holding that the state has violated the Equal Protection Clause. . . .

To prevail, a person challenging a state action need not prove the action rests solely or even primarily upon a racially discriminatory purpose. Except for narrowly limited circumstances, proof that a discriminatory purpose has merely been among the motivating factors will suffice to invalidate the challenged state action. Still later, the Court stipulated that "[discriminatory purpose] implies that the decisionmaker . . . selected or reaffirmed a particular course of action at least in part 'because of,' not merely 'in spite of,' its adverse effects upon an identifiable group." The Court recognizes that racial disparities can be evidence of discriminatory purpose and that, in some cases, disparities can be so stark as to raise by themselves a presumption of discriminatory purpose.

Courts have uniformly rejected challenges under the Federal Equal Protection Clause to differential punishment for possession of crack cocaine as opposed to powdered cocaine because of an absence of sufficient proof of discriminatory purpose. This is so even though these challenges have been directed against a federal sentencing statute under which the difference in punishment for use of crack cocaine as opposed to powdered cocaine is far more extreme than in *Russell.* For purposes of sentencing under federal law, one gram of crack cocaine is equivalent to one hundred grams of powdered cocaine. To some, including an increasing number of judges and legal scholars, this record shows that the Supreme Court is wrong in requiring that discriminatory purpose be shown to establish an equal protection violation. . . .

It is true . . . that the requirement of a finding of discriminatory purpose prevents the judiciary, on the basis of the Equal Protection Clause alone, from addressing many layers of deprivation, deposited by ages of racist oppression. But federal constitutional doctrine is only one aspect of a larger network of laws that is shaped by other authoritative political bodies in the society, most notably legislatures. Those who feel that they need more power or solicitude than that to which they are entitled under the constitutional minimum should take their case to legislatures, which should instruct courts and other agencies on the extent to which society's resources should be spent redressing inequalities caused by historical injustices. Some might object that this prescription condemns blacks to the realm of majoritarian electoral politics, in which they will be perpetual losers. But over the past quarter century, when "condemned" to the electoral arena, blacks—or, more accurately, certain sectors of the black population deemed to be acting on behalf of the whole—have succeeded in obtaining through legislation political goods that the federal judiciary had declined to give them through federal constitutional litigation. For example, the Supreme Court has declined, as a matter of constitutional law, to obligate state and federal governments to take affirmative measures to aid blacks as a class in terms of employment and electoral politics. Congress, however, has enacted statutes to address some of the asserted inequities left unaddressed by the Court's interpretation of the Equal Protection Clause.

IV. Conclusion

Given the complexity of "the black community," conflicting desires among its various sectors, differential effects upon these sectors by facially race neutral laws, and hence, the difficulty of confidently identifying *racial* subordination in the absence of discriminatory purpose, the federal constitutional standard for determining what counts as impermissible state action is attractively prudent. In contrast to the approach typified by *Russell,* it does not force legislatures to erase what appear to be "racial" disparities either by leveling down (for example, lowering to the powdered cocaine standard the punishment for possessors of crack) or leveling up (for example, raising to the crack cocaine standard the punishment for possessors of powder). To be sure, appearances are important. Indeed, the strength of that concern, measured against competing considerations, might well counsel in favor of pursuing one policy over another. The conclusion reached here is simply that, in the absence of findings of discriminatory purpose (or some such other violation of constitutional norms) legislatures are more fitting fora than courts for such calculations.

Finally, to return to the point of departure—the intersection of state crime control policy and racial politics—it is worth noting that, to an increasing extent, across the political spectrum and within black communities, priority of sympathetic identification is flowing to victims as opposed to perpetrators of crime. Sometimes people with these sentiments become inhibited when they confront the paradox that increasing the extent and severity of state crime control policy to protect law-abiding blacks will result in higher rates of incarceration and heavier punishments for black perpetrators, as most of those who commit crimes against blacks are themselves black. Perhaps, however, they will come to accept that disparities like those in *Russell* may be the mark, not of a white-dominated state apparatus "discriminating" against blacks, but instead, of a state apparatus responding sensibly to the desires of law-abiding people—including the great mass of black communities—or protection against criminals preying upon them. This response may be wrong. Perhaps lowering the punishment for possession of crack would be a better policy. Perhaps decriminalizing the use of cocaine and other illicit drugs would be a better policy. But being wrong is different from being racist, and the difference is one that matters greatly.

POSTSCRIPT

Do Crack Cocaine Laws Discriminate Against African-Americans and Other Minority Groups?

U.S. crack cocaine laws are a controversial matter. On one hand, many judges, attorneys, and scholars believe that such laws discriminate against African-Americans and the poor. Others believe, however, that even if statistical trends can be shown that appear to indicate that these laws discriminate, these laws should be upheld unless it can be proven that there was an actual intent by the legislatures to discriminate against minorities.

In general, U.S. courts have sided with the latter view. For example, in *U.S. v. Harding*, 971 F. 2d 410 (1992), the U.S. Court of Appeals for the Ninth Circuit considered an equal protection challenge to the federal sentencing guidelines for crack cocaine. The Court stated:

> The distinction between crack and powder cocaine is neither arbitrary nor irrational. . . . [T]he penalties embodied in this statute legitimately further the important government interest of eliminating controlled substance distribution and abuse. Crack presents a much larger problem than powder cocaine, both in the number of users and the drug's effects on the individual. If the extent of the problem posed by the sale of crack and the need for more severe penalties than for powder cocaine are not clearly evident, these issues are at least highly debatable. This is enough to prevent invalidation of the statutory classification. [Citations omitted.]

A review of the case law in this area reveals that the Ninth Circuit's position regarding the federal sentencing provisions for crack cocaine has been embraced widely by other courts. Thus, defendants attempting to challenge the validity of the crack cocaine sentencing laws under the Constitution's Equal Protection Clause will face an uphill battle.

But, simply because our nation's crack cocaine laws have been upheld by the courts, does that make them right? In the Introduction to this book, we considered the doctrine of social utility, which asserts that the guiding principle for social policies should be whether they constitute the greatest good for society. Do you believe that our crack cocaine laws and drug policies constitute the greatest good for most people?

Moreover, how should we regard the statistical evidence about the effects of crack cocaine laws on minority group members? It is highly unlikely that African-American defendants in crack cases will ever be able to show that members of the U.S. Congress or a group of state legislators sat down and decided to develop a crack cocaine sentencing policy to "get African-Americans." However, if it can be shown that as in the *Clary* case, prosecutors charge 55 African-Americans for crack cocaine offenses to every one white person, doesn't that say something? Does it not suggest a systematic bias in the way these cases are processed? U.S. courts have decided it does not. Do you agree?

Fortunately, there are numerous resources to shed additional light on the issues considered in this section. See Alisa Smith, *Law, Social Science, and the Criminal Courts* (Carolina Academic Press, 2004); Kendall Thomas, "Racial Justice: Moral or Political?" *National Black Law Journal* (vol. 17, no. 2, 2003); Roy L. Austin and Mark D. Allen, "Racial Disparity in Arrest Rates as an Explanation of Racial Disparity in Commitment to Pennsylvania's Prisons," *The Journal of Research in Crime and Delinquency* (vol. 37, no. 2, 2000); Paul J. Hofer, Kevin R. Blackwell, and R. Barry Ruback, "The Effect of the Federal Sentencing Guidelines on Inter-Judge Sentencing Disparity," *Journal of Criminal Law & Criminology* (vol. 90, no. 1, 1999); Jerome H. Skolnick, "The Color Line of Punishment," *Michigan Law Review* (vol. 96, no. 6, 1998); William A. Galston and David T. Wasserman, "Color-Blind Justice," *The Wilson Quarterly* (vol. 21, no. 2, 1997); Paul Butler, "Racially Based Jury Nullification: Black Power in the Criminal Justice System," *The Yale Law Journal* (vol. 105, no. 3, 1995); David A. Sklansky, "Cocaine, Race, and Equal Protection," *Stanford Law Review* (vol. 47, no. 6, 1995); Susan R. Klein and Jordan M. Steiker, "The Search for Equality in Criminal Sentencing," *Supreme Court Review* (2002, p. 223); Roger Clegg, "The Bad Law of 'Disparate Impact,'" *Public Interest* (vol. 138, 2000); and Rudolph Alexander, Jr., and Jacquelyn Gyamerah, "Differential Punishing of African Americans and Whites Who Possess Drugs: A Just Policy or Continuation of the Past?" *Journal of Black Studies* (vol. 28, no. 1, 1997).

Contributors to This Volume

EDITOR

THOMAS J. HICKEY is a professor of criminology at the University of Tampa. He received his bachelor's degree from Providence College, masters and Ph.D. degrees from Sam Houston State University, and a law degree from the University of Oregon, School of Law. His areas of expertise include criminology and law, and he is the author of numerous books and articles, including *Taking Sides: Clashing Views in Crime and Criminology,* 7th ed. (McGraw-Hill, 2006), *Criminal Procedure* (McGraw-Hill, 1998, 2001) and *Stand: Legal Issues* (Coursewise, 1999). Professor Hickey may be reached by e-mail at `thickey@ut.edu`.

STAFF

Larry Loeppke	Managing Editor
Jill Peter	Senior Developmental Editor
Nichole Altman	Developmental Editor
Beth Kundert	Production Manager
Jane Mohr	Project Manager
Tara McDermott	Design Coordinator
Bonnie Coakley	Editorial Assistant
Lori Church	Permissions
Julie J. Keck	Senior Marketing Manager
Mary S. Klein	Marketing Communications Specialist
Alice M. Link	Marketing Coordinator
Tracie A. Kammerude	Senior Marketing Assistant

AUTHORS

AKHIL REED AMAR is the Southmayd Professor of Law at Yale Law School where he teaches constitutional law, criminal procedure, federal jurisdiction, and American legal history. He is a prolific author who has published numerous books and academic articles, including *Processes of Constitutional Decisionmaking: Cases and Materials* (ed., with Paul Breas, Sanford Levinson, and J.M. Balkin).

EDWARD R. BECKER formerly served for a number of years as chief judge of the U.S. Court of Appeals for the Third Circuit. He presently serves as a senior judge. Judge Becker was active in the work of the judicial conference of the United States as a member of the probation, criminal law, long range planning, and executive committees. He graduated from the University of Pennsylvania with a B.A. in 1954 and received his law degree from the Yale Law School.

BRAD BENNETT is the former chief of police and fire for the city of South Lake Tahoe, California. He has many years of law enforcement experience and is a graduate of the FBI National Academy. He also holds a doctorate in public administration from the University of Southern California.

STEPHEN BREYER is an associate justice of the U.S. Supreme Court. Justice Breyer received his bachelor's degree in philosophy from Stanford University, a B.A. from Magdalen College of the University of Oxford as a Marshall Scholar, and a law degree from Harvard Law School. He served as a law clerk to U.S. Supreme Court Justice Arthur Goldberg and as an assistant special prosecutor of the Watergate Special Prosecution Force. He was also a professor at Harvard Law School for 27 years. He has served on the U.S. Supreme Court since 1994.

STEVEN BRILL is a graduate of Yale University and the Yale Law School. He is the founder of *The American Lawyer* magazine, Court TV, and *Brill's Content*. Brill serves presently as a columnist for *Newsweek* and as an NBC analyst on post–9/11 issues. He is the author of the best-selling work *The Teamsters*.

PAUL G. CASSELL is a U.S. District Court judge. A graduate of Stanford Law School who was appointed to the federal bench in 2002, Judge Cassell had previously served as a law clerk to then-judge Antonin Scalia of the U.S. Court of Appeals for the D.C. Circuit and later as a law clerk to former U.S. Supreme Court Chief Justice Warren E. Burger. He served formerly as associate deputy, U.S. Department of Justice Office of the Deputy Attorney General and serves presently as a professor at the University of Utah, College of Law.

ALAN M. DERSHOWITZ is the Felix Frankfurter Professor of Law at the Harvard Law School. He attended Brooklyn College and Yale Law School and is an internationally recognized expert in constitutional law, civil liberties, and criminal law. Professor Dershowitz is also a prolific author. His recent works include *Shouting Fire: Civil Liberties in a Turbulent Age* (2002) and *Why Terrorism Works* (2002).

BARRY C. FELD is the Centennial Professor of Law at the University of Minnesota Law School. He has written five books and more than 30 articles on juvenile justice and serious offenders, procedural issues, and juvenile sentencing policies.

THOMAS F. GERAGHTY is a professor of law at the Northwestern University School of Law and director of the University's Bluhm Legal Clinic. Professor Geraghty maintains an active law practice focusing on criminal and juvenile defense, death penalty appeals, and child-centered projects dealing with the representation of children and juvenile court reform. He received his bachelor's degree at Harvard University and law degree from Northwestern University.

JAN GOLAB is the author of *The Dark Side of the Force: A True Story of Corruption and Murder in the L.A.P.D.* Golab is also a former editor with *Los Angeles Magazine* and *Playboy.*

DOUGLAS D. GUIDORIZZI is a practicing attorney. He received his B.A. from the American University, Washington, D.C., in 1994, and his law degree from Emory University School of Law in 1998.

PAUL HARRIS teaches "guerrilla law" at New College's public interest law school in San Francisco. He was co-founder of the S.F. Community Law Collective, and was selected as one of the best criminal trial lawyers in America. He is a former president of the National Lawyers Guild. His Web site can be found at `http://www. guerrillalaw.com.`

RODNEY J. HENNINGSEN is a retired professor from the College of Criminal Justice at Sam Houston State University. He received his Ph.D. from the University of Nebraska at Lincoln. He has taught and published in the areas of criminology, juvenile delinquency, and corrections.

GREGORY L. HERSHBERGER is a former regional director for the north central region of the Federal Bureau of Prisons. He is a former warden of ADX Florence, as well as other BOP institutions.

YALE KAMISAR is the Clarence Darrow Distinguished University Professor of Law Emeritus at the University of Michigan School of Law. He is an internationally recognized authority of constitutional law and criminal procedure. A graduate of New York University and Columbia Law School, he has written extensively on criminal law, the administration of criminal justice, and the "politics of crime."

ANTHONY KENNEDY is an associate justice of the U.S. Supreme Court. He received his B.A. in political science from Stanford University, a second B.A. from the London School of Economics, and his law degree from Harvard University. He served as a judge on the U.S. Court of Appeals for the Ninth Circuit for 13 years and was confirmed as a U.S. Supreme Court Justice in 1988.

RANDALL KENNEDY is the Michael R. Klein Professor of Law at Harvard Law School. He received his B.A. from Princeton University and law degree from Yale Law School. Professor Kennedy's areas of academic interest include civil rights and liberties, civil rights legislation, and the U.S.

Supreme Court. His recent publications include *Interracial Intimacies: Sex, Marriage, Identity and Adoption* (2003) and *Race, Crime, and the Law* (1997).

MARGARET H. MARSHALL is the chief justice of the Supreme Judicial Court of Massachusetts. A native of South Africa, she graduated from Witwatersrand University in Johannesburg, received a master's degree from Harvard University, and her law degree from Yale Law School. Before her appointment to the court, she served as vice president and general counsel of Harvard University. Chief Justice Marshall is the second woman to serve on the Supreme Judicial Court in its more than 300-year history, and the first woman to serve as chief justice.

ELISA MASSIMINO is Washington director of Human Rights First. She is the organization's chief advocacy strategist, an expert on a range of international human rights issues and a national authority on U.S. compliance with human rights law. She holds philosophy degrees from Trinity University (B.A., 1982) and Johns Hopkins (M.A., 1984), and a J.D. from the University of Michigan School of Law. She has taught international human rights law at the University of Virginia School of Law and teaches refugee and asylum law at George Washington University School of Law.

JEANNE MCDOWELL is a writer for *Time.*

ANDREW A. MOHER received his B.A. from the University of Michigan (2002) and his J.D. from the Thomas Jefferson School of Law (2005). He is now a practicing attorney.

JEFF PALMER received his bachelor's degree from West Point in 1994 and his law degree from the University of Texas School of Law. He previously served as the executive editor of volume 27 of the *American Journal of Criminal Law.*

JEFFREY REIMAN is the William Fraser McDowell Professor of Philosophy at American University in Washington, D.C. He received his Ph.D. in philosophy from the Pennsylvania State University in 1968. He is a member of the Phi Beta Kappa and the author of numerous books and articles, including *In Defense of Political Philosophy, The Death Penalty: For and Against* (with Louis P. Pojman), and *Abortion and the Way We Value Human Life,* as well as more than 50 articles in philosophy and criminal justice publications.

ANTONIN SCALIA has served as an associate justice of the U.S. Supreme Court since 1986. He received his A.B. from Georgetown University in 1957 and graduated from the Harvard Law School in 1960. Prior to his appointment to the Court, he had served as a law professor at the University of Virginia, and general counsel for the U.S. Office of Telecommunications Policy, under President Richard M. Nixon.

JOHN R. SCHAFER is a special agent assigned to the FBI's Lancaster, California, resident office. He also serves as a member of the FBI's National Security Division's Behavioral Analysis Program.

STEPHEN J. SCHULHOFER is the Robert B. McKay Professor of Law at the New York University School of Law. He teaches criminal procedure, criminal law, and indigent legal defense. Schulhofer is a graduate of Princeton University and Harvard Law School. He is a prolific writer whose recent works include *Rethinking the Patriot Act: Keeping American Safe and Free* (2005), and *The War on Our Freedoms: Civil Liberties in an Age of Terrorism* (2003).

JEFF SINDEN, managing editor of the *Human Rights Tribune*, is a staunch opponent of prison privatization and was formerly a research associate at Human Rights Internet.

MARTHA B. SOSMAN is an associate justice of the Massachusetts Supreme Judicial Court. Justice Sosman received her degrees from Middlebury College and the University of Michigan Law School. She served formerly as an assistant United States attorney and as chief of the civil division of the United States Attorney's Office in Boston. She was appointed to the Supreme Judicial Court in 2000.

LANCE K. STELL received his M.A. and Ph.D. from the University of Michigan. He is currently the Charles A. Dana Professor and Director of Medical Humanities in the department of philosophy at Davidson College. He holds a faculty appointment in the department of internal medicine at Carolinas Medical Center, a teaching hospital in Charlotte. Dr. Stell also serves as a consultant to hospitals and professional medical associations.

CLARENCE THOMAS is an associate justice of the U.S. Supreme Court. He was appointed to the Court in 1991. He received his bachelor's degree from College of the Holy Cross, where he co-founded the Black Student Union. He received his law degree from the Yale Law School in 1974.

KARI A. VANDERZYL is a graduate of the Northern Illinois University School of Law and is a licensed attorney in the State of Illinois.

MICHAEL VITIELLO is a professor of law at the University of the Pacific McGeorge School of Law. His scholarship focuses on constitutional and criminal law, and his numerous articles have appeared in law journals at schools such as the University of San Francisco, Ohio State, the University of California, Hastings, and the University of California, Berkeley. He is also a member of the American Law Institute (ALI).

ERICA WALTER is a writer living in Alexandria, Virginia.

KAREN J. WILLIAMS is a judge of the U.S. Court of Appeals for the Fourth Circuit. She received her B.A. from Columbia College in 1972, and her J.D. from the University of South Carolina Law Center in 1980. She was previously employed as an attorney in private law practice in Orangeburg, South Carolina.

JAMES Q. WILSON is the Ronald Reagan Professor of Public Policy at Pepperdine University and a professor emeritus at UCLA. He received his Ph.D. in 1959 from the University of Chicago. He is the former chairman of the White House Task Force on Crime, of the National Advisory Commission on Drug Abuse Prevention, of the Attorney General's Task Force on Violent Crime, and the president's Foreign Intelligence Advisory Board. He is the author of numerous books and articles including *Thinking About Crime, Crime and Human Nature* (with Richard Herrnstein), and *The Moral Sense.*

LAWRENCE WRIGHT is a graduate of Tulane University and the American University in Cairo, where he taught English and received an M.A. in applied linguistics in 1969. He has worked for *Texas Monthly* and *Rolling Stone.* He has written several books and is currently writing a history of al-Queda for Knopf, which is scheduled to be published in Fall 2006. Wright is co-author of *The Seige,* which starred Denzel Washington, Bruce Willis, and Annette Benning. He has won the New York University Olive Branch Award for international reporting as well as the Overseas Press Club's Ed Cunningham Award for best magazine reporting.

FRANKLIN E. ZIMRING is the William G. Simon Professor of Law at the University of California School of Law (Berkeley). He is the author of many books on topics including deterrence, adolescence, capital punishment, and drug control policies. His recent books include *Contradictions of American Capital Punishment* (2003) and *American Youth Violence* (1998). He is also an international authority on the issue of the effects of gun control on rates of violence in society.

Index